# ADVANCED IP ROUTING IN CISCO NETWORKS

**McGraw-Hill Cisco Technical Expert Titles**

ARS    *Troubleshooting Cisco Internetworks*    0-07-047235-1
Fisher    *Configuring Cisco Routers for ISDN*    0-07-022073-5
Gai    *Internetworking IPv6 with Cisco Routers*    0-07-022836-1
Lewis    *Cisco TCP/IP Professional Reference*    0-07-041140-1
Parkhurst    *Cisco Router OSPF Design and Implementation*    0-07-048626-3
Sackett    *Cisco Router Handbook*    0-07-058097-9
Slattery/Burton    *Advanced IP Routing in Cisco Networks*    0-07-058144-4

To order or receive additional information on these or any other McGraw-Hill titles, in the United States please call 1-800-722-4726, or visit us at www.computing.mcgraw-hill.com. In other countries, contact your McGraw-Hill representative.

# Advanced IP Routing in Cisco Networks

Terry Slattery
William Burton

**McGraw-Hill**

New York   San Francisco   Washington, D.C.   Auckland   Bogotá
Caracas   Lisbon   London   Madrid   Mexico City   Milan   Montreal
New Delhi   San Juan   Singapore   Sydney   Tokyo   Toronto

**McGraw-Hill**

*A Division of The McGraw-Hill Companies*

Copyright © 1999 by The McGraw-Hill Companies, Inc. All rights reserved.
Printed in the United States of America. Except as permitted under the United
States Copyright Act of 1976, no part of this publication may be reproduced or
distributed in any form or by any means, or stored in a data base or retrieval
system, without the prior written permission of the publisher.

1 2 3 4 5 6 7 8 9 0   AGM/AGM   9 0 3 2 1 0 9 8

ISBN   0-07-058144-4

*The sponsoring editor for this book was Steven Elliot, and the production supervisor was
Clare Stanley. It was set in Vendome by **TIPS** Technical Publishing.*

*Printed and bound by Quebecor/Martinsburg.*

McGraw-Hill books are available at special quantity discounts to use as premi-
ums and sales promotions, or for use in corporate training programs. For more
information, please write to the Director of Special Sales, McGraw-Hill, 11 West
19th Street, New York, NY 10011. Or contact your local bookstore.

 This book is printed on recycled, acid-free paper containing a minimum
of 50% recycled, de-inked fiber.

# CONTENTS

# Contents

# FOREWORD

Cisco routers perform a broad range of functions as they inhabit homes, small/medium businesses, and the enterprise and service provider backbones. The current Cisco IOS command summary is over 2 inches (5cm) thick, with over 2,400 commands, most of which have many options. Every Cisco router requires some number of "config" commands to make it work. Interestingly, this may also lead to many combinations of "config" commands resulting in the same job being performed. Configurations based on a thorough understanding of the Cisco IOS will perform the same tasks with higher performance and reliability.

Individuals who manage and configure Cisco routers are always looking for examples of the "right" configuration to use in their specific environment. Cisco's configuration guides and training courses provide just this type of information. They may not, however, satisfy the router manager who is looking for advanced information and an explanation to go along with it. The next step is usually to resort to posting to known newsgroups, mailing friendly router wizards, and asking Cisco instructors to find the right answers.

If you have ever found yourself in this position, really wanting an in depth explanation to go along with the solution, then this book is for you. *Advanced IP Routing in Cisco Networks* walks the reader through IP and routing from the basic configuration, Static, Classful, Classless, Interior and Exterior routing, to various Internet connectivity options. Each chapter includes fully documented configuration examples for Cisco routers. Use the book as a ready reference, or read from cover to cover for an in depth understanding of how Cisco routers work. As someone who interacts with Cisco technology and those trying to learn about it on a daily basis, I cannot recommend this book highly enough.

*Anthony Wolfenden*
*Senior Manager*
*Delivery Services*
*World Wide Training*
*Cisco Systems*

# ACKNOWLEDGMENTS

Like any large task, writing and publishing a book is accomplished with the support of a team of people. First, I want to thank Peggy, my wife, for her support and willingness to put our personal life on hold while I wrote this book. She is a true friend and wonderful companion in life.

Without Bill Burton's assistance, this book would not have happened. It was a lot of fun to share ideas, do the work, and talk about what we discovered. Thanks, Bill!

I would like to dedicate this book to the team at Chesapeake Computer Consultants, Inc. The Chesapeake team consists of the best Cisco experts in the country and a group of people who make sure that all Cisco classes we do are the best in the world. The talent and the dedication of this group of people is beyond words. Thank you, Chesapeake, for creating an environment in which everyone is learning, growing, and taking on new challenges.

This book would not have happened without association with the many, many students who have graced the classrooms of the Cisco classes taught by Chesapeake. It is your questions, particularly the ones that caused us to go research some topic, that have inspired us to write this book.

Appreciation is also due to MentorLabs for access to their amazing vLAB system so I could do the development of the lab examples from anywhere.

*Terry Slattery, CCIE #1026*

I want to thank Terry Slattery for the opportunity to participate in writing this book. Writing this book is the achievement of one of my long-term goals and is the culmination of the knowledge acquired during the last six years working with Cisco routers. The number of people involved in this process makes it too difficult to name everyone, and includes instructors, friends, and students.

My thanks to the folks at MentorLabs for providing the equipment used in generating the examples in this book. The ability to configure and test configurations across the Internet was invaluable with my travel schedule.

To my family, and all my friends who supported me in this venture, my heartfelt thanks for your support.

*William E. Burton, CCIE #1119*

We would both like to acknowledge the efforts of Bob Kern at TIPS Technical Publishing, Inc., for working with us to produce the completed book in a very short time. Adam Newton contributed many helpful suggestions during the proofreading steps, and Manny Rosa spent many hours working with the publishing software to produce a nice looking book. The folks at McGraw-Hill, our editor, Steve Elliot, and his assistant, Alice Tung, were immensely helpful and supportive during the writing process.

Thanks, folks! We couldn't have done it without your help.

*Terry and Bill*

# INTRODUCTION

Thank you for selecting *Advanced IP Routing in Cisco Networks*. We've incorporated years of hands-on experience and training knowledge into its pages with the hope that you will find it useful in learning how to apply Cisco routers in your networks. This book is unique in that it incorporates numerous network examples and the corresponding Cisco configurations. We discuss the relevant parts of the configurations so that you understand what is happening. The full configurations are listed so that you have the complete configuration upon which the example is based.

One of our goals with this book is to provide a guide that you can use to learn how TCP/IP operates at a detailed level and how to configure it on Cisco routers. By reading and understanding the concepts and examples presented, you will be better prepared to run today's large and complex IP networks or to tackle the Cisco Certified Internetwork Expert (CCIE) program. (Check Cisco's or Chesapeake's Web page at www.cisco.com or www.ccci.com for further information on the CCIE program.)

We also wanted to produce a practical reference guide that can help you with the daily operation of IP-based networks. TCP/IP is now the protocol of choice, primarily due to the explosion of the Internet and the World Wide Web. But there are several TCP/IP routing protocols, and a reference guide is needed that shows you which ones are best for specific functions and how to configure them in real-world situations.

Regardless of whether you're a consultant or a network administrator in a small company, we want you to find this book useful enough to you in your daily work that you'll keep a copy handy. We welcome your feedback at www.ccci.com on how to improve upon it in future editions.

## What to Expect

In writing an advanced book like this, we had to decide what base knowledge you should have and set the level of material appropriately. We didn't want to create a basic Cisco router configuration guide, since Chris Lewis has already done that in his book, *Cisco TCP/IP Routing Professional Reference* (Lewis 1998). The real question was whether we should cover how IP works. After discussing it for a while, we decided that—based on the questions we receive in our classes—a chapter on the basics of how TCP/IP works would provide a consistent foundation upon which we could build. References to other sources will help you fill any gaps about TCP/IP that remain.

This book isn't about TCP/IP applications. If you want to learn more about TFTP, SMTP, SNMP, and the other protocols that use TCP/IP, we refer you to Paul Simoneau's book *Hands-On TCP/IP* (1997). His book is also a good basic reference on the operation of TCP/IP itself.

If you have a solid background in TCP/IP, then you may skip Chapter 1, "TCP/IP Overview." Even though this is basic knowledge, we included this chapter after finding that many people in our classes did not understand the basics of how the protocols operate. In this section, we describe how TCP/IP operates and how port numbers are used to multiplex and demultiplex data streams. An analogy to the way the post office works is used to relate to how TCP/IP works in the real world around us.

Chapter 2, "How Routing Works," describes the process by which routers determine the best path that a given packet should follow on its path to its destination. How the network mask is determined and used is described. Finally, we explain in great detail one of the concepts that challenges many network administrators: variable length subnet masking.

Once you understand how routers route, Chapter 3 introduces you to static routes. These are routes that you enter manually into the router. There are places to use such routes, and we explain those places. There are also places where they shouldn't be used, and we highlight them as well.

In the original Internet, all routing was done based on the class of the IP address (class A, B, C, or D). In Chapter 4, you will be introduced to the older IP routing protocols, RIP and IGRP, both of which operate in classful networks.

Then, in Chapter 5, we describe classless addressing and routing. This is the mechanism upon which today's Internet routing is based. By using classless routing, we are able to more efficiently utilize the existing IP addressing space, which was being exhausted at a very high rate. Classless addressing is used in IPv6, so understanding it will prepare you for the transition to the next generation of IP.

With classless routing as a background, you'll learn about several classless routing protocols. These protocols choose the best route by searching the routing table for the route that is the best match to the destination address. These include the RIPv2, OSPF, and Cisco's proprietary EIGRP.

In many companies, more than one routing protocol is used, so some means is needed to allow the exchange of routes between the different routing protocols. This is often where things become interesting and many problems arise. In Chapter 6, you will see how to integrate multiple protocols in ways that work and will avoid routing loops.

It has been interesting to watch the Internet grow over the last 18 years. Many companies would say "We're never going to connect to the Internet. It's too dangerous!" Then the World Wide Web was created, and a real business case was created for joining the Internet. In the next chapters, we'll cover various technologies needed to support Internet connections.

Before companies wanted to join the Internet, they often picked any IP address they wanted for internal use. Once the decision was made to join the Internet, these companies were faced with either renumbering hundreds or thousands of IP devices or installing a Network Address Translation gateway at their connection to the Internet. In Chapter 7, you'll learn how to use Cisco routers to perform this function, should you need it. You'll also learn about private addresses, which are reserved for companies that wish to separate their internal addressing from Internet addressing because of security, because of address portability between service providers, or because they'll never join the Internet.

There are several ways to connect to the Internet. The most simple way doesn't involve running a routing protocol. Instead, static routes are used to simplify the connection and to avoid the overhead of running a routing protocol on links to an Internet Service Provider. Chapter 8 discusses how to use static routes when connecting to one or more service providers.

Some companies have complex networks and Internet connections that require the use of exterior protocols. In Chapter 9, you'll learn about the Border Gateway Protocol, which is the Internet standard protocol used by service providers and large companies.

Finally, in Chapter 10, we'll cover some specifics on troubleshooting. You'll see how to use **TTCP**, **ping**, and **trace** to effectively troubleshoot TCP/IP problems. Each of the prior chapters will contain some troubleshooting tips for the topic being discussed, but sometimes you need additional information to determine where the problem lies. These tools, correctly applied, often can help you determine what to examine more closely and what you can ignore when troubleshooting complex internetwork problems.

# The Quality Challenge

In producing this book, we are very concerned about "getting it right." A number of networking books out there seem to have been written in haste and didn't get some of the very basics right. To this end, we offer you a challenge similar to one offered by Donald Knuth in his *Computing Systems* series of books.

If you find an error in the book, and you're the first one to find and report it to us, we will send you one U. S. dollar. A list of identified errors and a report form can be found on the Chesapeake Web page at www.ccci.com/books. We will evaluate your submission and determine whether the error you have reported is valid. Errors include Cisco configuration errors (relative to the IOS release shown in the example), typographical errors, grammatical errors, and in general, anything that is wrong. We will be the final judge of what constitutes an error, but we take the duty seriously because we want to produce a high-quality book.

# Tools

Chesapeake has been creating Java-based tools to help internetworking staff with networks. The Java Run-time Environment and the tools that we have developed are available from Chesapeake's Web site (www.ccci.com). We discuss some of the tools and how to use them to troubleshoot your networks. Chesapeake continues to develop new tools, so check out our Web site often to find out what is currently available, or contact Chesapeake to subscribe to our periodic publication, *The Network Monitor*.

# Hands-On Labs

Configuring Cisco routers is primarily a hands-on function. To really learn something, you have to practice it yourself and experiment with alternative implementations. If you are studying for your CCIE, it is important that you work through the labs and exercises. We've found that, while a lot of networking technology is obvious, being able to turn an exercise into a working configuration is often more time-consuming than first perceived.

Each chapter contains several hands-on lab exercises. The labs are based on a small "pod" of three routers. Two pods are used for those labs that require a more complex topology. Figure I-1 shows the two-pod "work group." Each serial connection is made using a "back-to-back" cable in which one end is the DCE (data communications equipment) device and the other end is the DTE (data terminal equipment) device. (DCE equipment is typically the clocking source for serial communications links.) The Serial 1 interface on each router is the DCE connection, which requires the addition of the **clock rate** configuration command. This is an important part of the configurations that we will be showing in our examples.

You may build your own router pod, or you can access one or more pods at MentorLabs' Virtual Lab (vLab℠) Web site for a nominal charge. From the Internet, you have access to the consoles of multiple routers with which you can experiment. There is no restriction on the router configurations you can use, and there is a configuration storage area where you can store your configurations for future sessions. Additional lab exercises will be added to our Web site in the future. For more information, visit the MentorLabs site at www.mentorlabs.com.

We have identified each router with a city name to make it easy to refer to them from the text. When issuing commands within the routers, we will use IP addresses instead of hostnames. The majority of Cisco configuration is done with IP addresses and, while hostnames might help make some of the **ping** and **trace** output easier to read, we've found that incorrect hostname tables are often a cause of network problems. If you prefer to use hostnames, please feel free to add the necessary host table to your router configurations; just watch out for address changes that invalidate your host table.

The IP addresses used on the pods will change throughout the book. This is intentional. Seldom do network problems occur on the same

**Figure I-1**

Two-pod work group

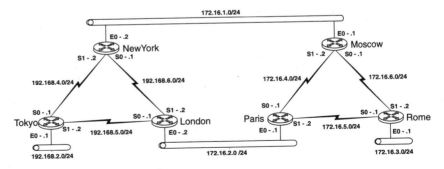

place in your network all the time. You should be used to seeing different IP addresses for each network problem. It is good practice for the real world or for the CCIE exam, where being able to quickly look at a network and determine its topology and addressing is very important.

When we use addresses, we will use them from the "private" range of addresses as defined in RFC1918 (Rekhter et al. 1996):

```
10.0.0.0-10.255.255.255 (10/8 prefix)
172.16.0.0-172.31.255.255 (172.16/12 prefix)
192.168.0.0-192.168.255.255 (192.168/16 prefix)
```

These addresses should never appear in the Internet, as they are reserved for private use by sites. By using these addresses (even in situations in this book where one normally would use an assigned address), we prevent someone from accidentally causing problems with another site's routing. (And don't even think of submitting a bug report on the use of these addresses in our examples! :-)

# Examples

This book is filled with examples of various configurations. We've seen incomplete examples and had questions about some important element that was missing. Often, more questions are raised than are answered. To remedy this, our detailed configuration and output examples have line numbers and an explanation detailing which statements are important, as shown in Figure I-2.

The routers we used for the examples in this book are all running IOS release 11.3, which is documented by Cisco at www.cisco.com (Cisco 1998b). Many of the examples and labs can be performed on older releases, but you may encounter differences in the example output if

**Figure I-2** Prototype example

```
Prototype Example
1) NewYork#sh cont s 1
2) HD unit 1, idb = 0xDAA44, driver structure at 0xDEBE0
3) buffer size 1524  HD unit 1, V.35 DCE cable
4) cpb = 0x63, eda = 0x2940, cda = 0x2800
5) RX ring with 16 entries at 0x632800

Line 3 shows that the cable connected to Serial 1 provides a DCE interface.  A clock rate
command will be needed to define the frequency of the clock supplied to the DTE device
connected to this interface.
```

you are using routers with a different IOS release. Please check this before contacting us about any differences you find.

Router configurations contain a lot of duplicate information (i.e., host tables, vty configuration, passwords, etc.). A series of examples may have an initial block of this information so that you have a full picture, while other examples have the nonrelevant information removed.

The real configuration examples will have all the details that are necessary for you to duplicate our implementation as part of your learning process. We encourage you to perform your own experiments by attempting to implement our examples and experiment with them. Any interfaces that are not shown will be administratively shutdown and are unimportant to the example.

# CCIE Preparation

The Cisco Certified Internetwork Expert certification is one of the most challenging professional tests a networking person encounters today. In each chapter, you will find a section dedicated to things that you should know to be successful in the tests. There will be additional lab exercises to implement or things to learn. If you spend the time to work through all the examples and labs, then you will be much better prepared to pass the written and hands-on tests.

Please be advised that the CCIE portions of this book are not taken from the CCIE test and that Cisco has not authorized any part of these sections. The material we are presenting covers the basics that anyone studying for the CCIE exam should know and should be prepared to implement. There will undoubtedly be things on the tests that are not covered here. But if you work through the examples and labs, you will be much better prepared.

# Conventions

Example configurations are presented in numerous figures and within the text. To make them easier to read, they are typeset in a `fixed-width font`, as you would see on a computer terminal. Command input is printed in **bold**. Configuration examples and some command output displays have line numbers so that it is easy to refer to the output.

The line numbers will not appear in the configurations or output produced by Cisco routers.

At those points where a combination of keys must be pressed, the keys will appear within angle brackets. This means that you should press all the keys simultaneously. For example, <CTRL-Z> means that you would hold down the Ctrl key while simultaneously pressing the Z key. A more complex example is <CTRL-SHIFT-6>, in which you should hold down both the Ctrl and Shift keys while you press the 6 key.

# Thank You!

Finally, we would like to thank you again for selecting this book. We hope that you find it useful and educational.

*Terry Slattery, CCIE #1026*
*Bill Burton, CCIE #1119*

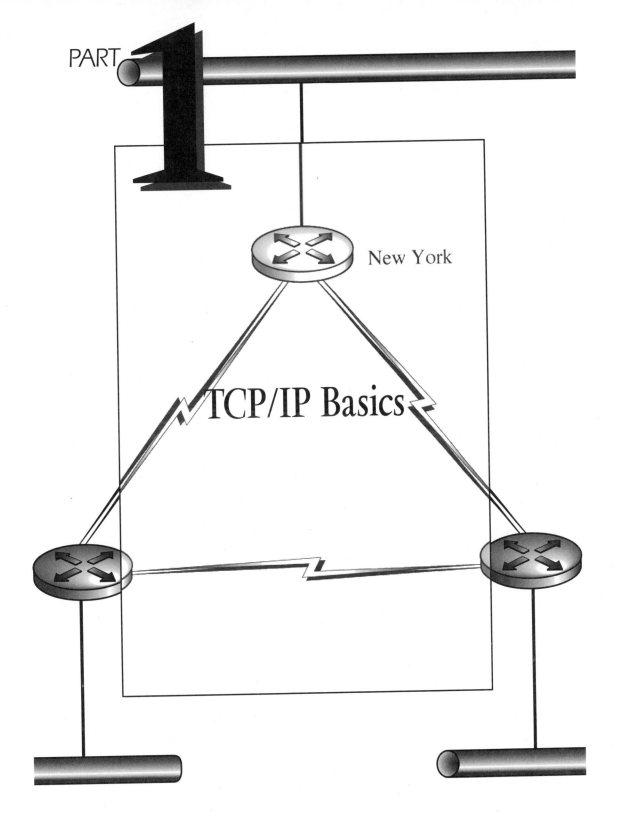

## PART 1

TCP/IP Basics

New York

# CHAPTER 1

# TCP/IP Overview

TCP/IP is an abbreviation for Transmission Control Protocol/Internet Protocol, two of the protocols used in the Internet today. The TCP/IP protocol suite is actually a collection of protocols, of which TCP and IP are the two best known. Other protocols are the User Datagram Protocol (UDP), the Internet Control Message Protocol (ICMP), and the Address Resolution Protocol (ARP). The whole suite of protocols is often referred to as TCP/IP.

So you think you already know all about TCP/IP! Are you able to explain the multiplexing that occurs at each layer of the protocol stack? Do you know the maximum window size used in most TCP implementations and how this affects the throughput of long delay paths (or of very high bandwidth pipes)?

In this chapter, we will review the important points of each of the protocols in the TCP/IP suite. If you wish to learn more about the TCP/IP protocols themselves or the operation of the applications that use TCP/IP, we recommend the more detailed coverage available in Stallings (1997), Stevens (1994), Comer (1995), or Simoneau (1997).

# The OSI Model

Every networking book seems to start out with an almost obligatory description of the OSI model, shown in Figure 1-1. This isn't because everyone likes to talk about it. Describing it gives us a common terminology and frame of reference that we can use in our discussions. Really good troubleshooting people also use it to help them troubleshoot network problems. For example, finding out that your data-link layer is working allows you to focus on problems at a higher level.

It is also important to have the correct networking model to follow when learning the technology. It gives you a framework into which you can add new concepts. You know where they fit in the overall scheme of things, similar to knowing how tires and a transmission fit into the overall design and operation of an automobile.

However, the OSI model is just that: a model. It isn't a recipe that should necessarily be followed down to each teaspoon of ingredient. As a model, it gives us a framework within which we can construct, discuss, and compare network protocols.

The OSI model was developed by the International Standards Organization (ISO). OSI stands for Open Systems Interconnect. It started out as a model, which we'll describe here, but also resulted in a protocol suite by the same name. This protocol never made it into widespread use, but its development has substantially increased our understanding of network protocols and how to best develop them.

**Figure 1-1**
The OSI model

| | |
|---|---|
| 7 | **Application** |
| 6 | **Presentation** |
| 5 | **Session** |
| 4 | **Transport** |
| 3 | **Network** |
| 2 | **Data-link** |
| 1 | **Physical** |

**Figure 1-2**
The postal analogy

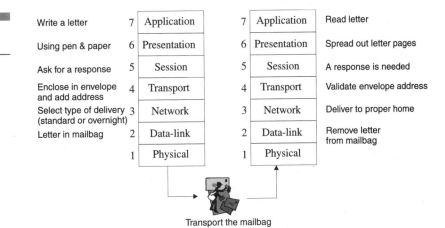

| | | | | | | |
|---|---|---|---|---|---|---|
| Write a letter | 7 | Application | | 7 | Application | Read letter |
| Using pen & paper | 6 | Presentation | | 6 | Presentation | Spread out letter pages |
| Ask for a response | 5 | Session | | 5 | Session | A response is needed |
| Enclose in envelope and add address | 4 | Transport | | 4 | Transport | Validate envelope address |
| Select type of delivery (standard or overnight) | 3 | Network | | 3 | Network | Deliver to proper home |
| Letter in mailbag | 2 | Data-link | | 2 | Data-link | Remove letter from mailbag |
| | 1 | Physical | | 1 | Physical | |

Transport the mailbag

The reason for developing the model and protocol was to have an international standard that everyone could expect to interoperate and use to communicate between network-attached devices. It turns out that the development of the OSI protocol suite took so long that companies started using TCP/IP. As more companies adopted TCP/IP, the need for the OSI protocol faded. We've finally reached the point where the objectives of OSI have been achieved by TCP/IP.

## The Post Office Analogy

By dividing the complex task of designing and building a network protocol into layers, also called a *protocol stack*, we can more easily accomplish our task. Figure 1-2 shows the seven-layer OSI model and how it relates to the postal system.

With that in mind, let's examine the OSI model as it compares to the postal system. (The comparison is surprisingly valid!)

FYI: We call the layers of a network protocol a *protocol stack*, because the layers stack on top of one another. The operation at each layer of the stack relies on the services provided by the layer below it. For example, the transport layer relies on the best-effort delivery of the network layer. The network layer relies on the data-link layer to gain access to the network medium and to package the data into *frames* that conform to the data-link layer's specifications (i.e., Ethernet framing, or TokenRing framing, or FDDI framing, depending on the media being used).

## Application Layer

The application layer is the interface between the application (e.g., Telnet, FTP, etc.) and the network protocol stack. This defines the program calls that must be done by an application to transfer data over the network.

In the postal analogy, the application might be to hold a conversation with a pen pal. The interface is selecting a pen and paper or a pencil and paper or a typewriter and paper or a computer and word processor to generate data (Figure 1-3). All data we generate at this layer is passed to the presentation layer.

## Presentation Layer

The presentation layer performs any needed data conversions when communicating with remote systems. All network protocols perform a data conversion into "network standard format." For Telnet and FTP, there are defined formats used on the network, and every system must convert its internal data representation into the network standard format. Computers that use EBCDIC character encoding must convert their data to the ASCII character set. Data encryption or compression may occur at this layer.

If you were writing a letter and wanted to keep the contents confidential, you might convert the data you wish to send into an encrypted form. A simple way to do this is to rotate the letters of the alphabet by 13 letters. The letter A becomes the letter N; the letter B becomes the letter O; C becomes P, and so on (Figure 1-4). This transformation is called Rot-13, because the letters of the alphabet are rotated by 13 characters. The transformed data is passed to the session layer.

**Figure 1-3**
Application layer—
writing a letter

Bill,
Why did the
packet cross
the router?

Terry

**Figure 1-4**
Presentation layer—
data transformation

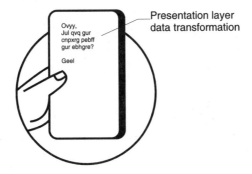

Presentation layer
data transformation

Ovyy,
Jul qvq gur
cnpxrg pebff
gur ebhgre?

Geel

Session Layer
The session layer maintains a conversation with the remote system. For a network application like Telnet, this involves determining the user's terminal type so that screen editors work correctly. It also may require negotiating per-character or line-at-a-time data transfer of the user's input.

Comparing to the postal system, we find that you needed to introduce yourself to your pen pal and decide what language will be used in the letters and whether you will alternate letters or just send one when you have something to say. The session header indicates that this letter is the entire message or that you need a response by a specific time (Figure 1-5). The data is then passed to the transport layer.

Transport Layer
The transport layer provides the method by which a computer program running in one system can communicate with a program running in another system. Most protocol stacks provide two transport mechanisms.

One transport is a reliable delivery protocol which retransmits lost or damaged data, relieving the program from this function. The other is purely a datagram service, which has less overhead but does not guarantee reliability. Programmers decide which type of protocol (reliable data stream or unreliable datagram) best fits the needs of the program being developed.

One of the primary factors the programmer must consider is whether the communications is data stream oriented (like a file transfer utility) or transaction oriented (like a database query). Another factor is built-in reliability. For reliable protocols, if a delivery failure occurs, the transport layer performs the retransmission. For datagram protocols, the

**Figure 1-5**
Session layer—
organizing the
conversation

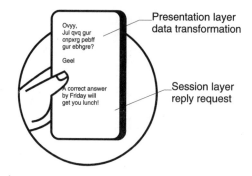

program itself must retransmit lost or damaged data. We'll learn more about the differences between these two types of transport protocols when we examine TCP and UDP later in this chapter.

At the transport layer, the data is encapsulated within the delivery envelope and the logical name of the destination is used to look up the destination address. For the postal analogy, this would include checking for the address of the pen pal and adding a sequence number to the letter. Your pen pal would then know the sequence of letters and be able either to assemble them in the correct order if they were delivered out of order or to request a retransmission if one was lost. At this layer, we see the data, including the session control information, being *encapsulated* within a transport medium—the envelope in our example (Figure 1-6). The transport layer passes its data to the network layer.

**Figure 1-6**
Transport layer—
logical addressing
and reliability

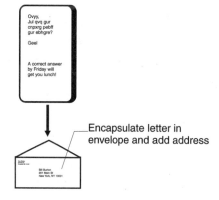

FYI: *Encapsulation* is the process of placing the data within a *capsule*, or small container. You can think of the envelope (or TCP packet) as a container that is used to transport the data across the network. The capsule has the source and destination addresses on the outside, to allow the network layer to determine the best method for forwarding the letter (or packet) to the correct destination.

Conversely, the process of extracting data from a capsule is called *decapsulation*. In the networking world, we most often see *encapsulation* and *decapsulation* occurring at the transport, network, and data-link layers. Each of these layers (capsules) has its own header which describes its contents.

Network Layer

The network layer attempts to deliver the data to the destination. At this layer, only a "best-effort" attempt at delivery is made. The destination address is examined and the best path to the destination is determined. Knowing the best path allows the network layer to determine which data-link layer to use to move the data to the next hop along this path. It then divides the data into sections that are large enough to fit the transport mechanism used to reach the next hop. The network addresses used in TCP/IP are independent of the physical network technology used to connect the systems, an important feature that is required for routers to work.

In the postal world, we have a choice of different delivery mechanisms, analogous to different network technologies. We could use a fax, the postal system, Federal Express, or any other means to transfer the letter. Making this decision—determining the outgoing path to get to the destination—is the first step of the routing process. In this case, we have written a letter that fits into a single envelope, and there are no priority delivery restraints, so the post office delivery was selected (Figure 1-7). The envelope is passed to the data-link layer.

Data-link Layer

The data-link layer is concerned only with delivering the envelope to the next hop in the path to the destination. In the networking world, we are concerned about media access (fair access to the media so that no single station monopolizes the transmission media). We also are concerned about formatting the data to allow it to be properly carried by the media. Most network media have their own addressing, which is different for

**Figure 1-7**

Network layer—path
determination

each type of media. Using higher-level addresses at the network layer creates an independence from the data-link layer addressing, making it simple to build a network of multiple types of WAN and LAN technology.

For our postal analogy, this would involve getting the envelope to the mail carrier. This could be via a mailbox. Here, the envelope must conform to certain specifications (size, weight, etc.), and the postage must be sufficient for the delivery to proceed. The carrier places (encapsulates) the envelope in a mailbag for delivery via the physical layer (Figure 1-8). Note that the mailbag itself has an address assigned, just like the data-link address on a network segment.

Physical Layer

The final layer in the OSI model is the physical layer. This layer converts the bits into electrical signals in a wire or photons of light in fiber-optic systems.

In the postal world, the letter is not converted to another representation for transmission unless we are transmitting the letter via fax. Instead, the letter is contained within the mailbag and is transported by

**Figure 1-8**

Physical layer—
preparing for delivery
by the physical
medium

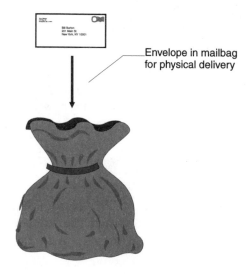

Envelope in mailbag
for physical delivery

**Figure 1-9**
Physical layer—
delivering the data

the mail carrier. Often, the mailbag is taken to the post office, much like your network data goes via an Ethernet from your workstation to a router. After sorting the letters at the post office, the letter is delivered to its destination by another mail carrier (Figure 1-9).

## Routing in the Post Office

A letter arriving in the post office is much like a packet arriving in a router. Each must be routed to the correct destination. Figure 1-10 shows the processing that happens as the letter is transported through the postal system.

The first step is that the envelope is extracted from the physical and data-link layers (the mailbag). Then, the post office examines the destination address on the envelope. In examining the address, only the most significant part of the address (the first three digits of the zip code) is examined. This determines the next hop on the route to the destination.

For example, a letter from Annapolis, MD, going to Baltimore, MD, is created and picked up by the local mail carrier (step 1). It is transported to the Annapolis post office. Here, the letter is extracted (or decapsulated) from the mailbag and the destination address examined (step 2). Since the letter is directed to Baltimore, the next hop would be to the Baltimore post office. The letter would be enclosed in a mailbag that is to go to the Baltimore post office via delivery truck (step 3). In Baltimore, the letter is decapsulated from the truck and mailbag. The letter's envelope is examined and the path to the destination determined (step 4). The next hop is via another mail carrier. This time the destination is to a street address, so the next-hop encapsulation is a mail carrier bag (step 5).

**Figure 1-10**
Post office routing

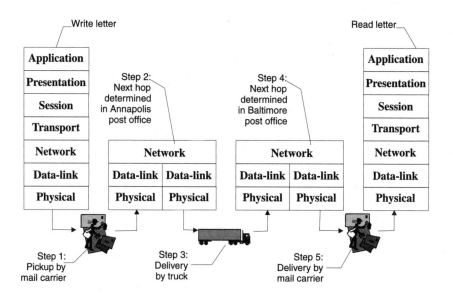

When the envelope reaches the destination address, the recipient checks the destination address and sees that it has reached the destination (this is the network-layer check). The envelope is opened and assembled in the correct order, relative to the other letters received (transport layer). The session, presentation, and application layers all perform their transformations on the data, with the result being a readable letter and a continuation of the conversation between the two pen pals.

Within each post office, the physical and data-link layers are unique to each physical transport mechanism while the network layer is common.

## Encapsulation & Decapsulation

To really understand networking, you must understand the concept of encapsulation and decapsulation. Let's take a look at how our letter may be encapsulated and decapsulated during a pen pal conversation. Looking back at Figures 1-3 through 1-9, you can see the headers being added to the data as it is processed at each layer.

Terry writes a letter to Bill. The letter is created at the application layer. There is no network encapsulation at this layer (Figure 1-3).

However, we are conducting a "secret" pen pal conversation, so we wish to encrypt the letter's contents and include a header that identifies the type of encryption used (Rot-13). This conversion happens at the presentation layer (Figure 1-4).

The encryption packet, including the encryption type and encrypted data, is encapsulated within a session packet (Figure 1-5). The session packet header tells the recipient to answer the question.

At the transport layer, a logical address header (the name of the recipient) is added to the packet (Figure 1-6). Here, we also see the addition of a sequence number to allow the recipient to organize a series of letters in the correct sequence.

The network layer adds full address, converting the recipient's name into an address that the network layer can use, see Figure 1-7. This address is written on the envelope and the data encapsulated inside.

Figure 1-8 shows that the data-link layer encapsulates the envelope within the mailbag (the delivery media). The mailbag has the address of the next-hop destination written on it.

Finally, the mailbag containing the letter is carried by the physical media (the mail carrier in Figure 1-9 and the truck in Figure 1-10) to the next hop.

Upon Bill's receipt of the letter, he would reverse the encapsulation process to view the original text. First, he would verify that he is the recipient by validating the destination address. He then would open the envelope (decapsulate the network layer). His session-layer processing would see that he needs to answer the letter. The encrypted data would require his presentation layer to perform a decryption of the data. Finally, he would read the question (application layer).

Network protocols perform the same kind of transformations and encapsulations that this example has shown. We will see later in this chapter how TCP/IP performs these functions.

## Advantages of the OSI Model

The OSI model allows us to divide the networking problem into pieces that can be more easily solved. Besides this advantage, it also allows us to more easily make substitutions of one solution for another at any point in the stack. For example, TCP/IP started out by using Ethernet as its first LAN technology. Then TokenRing was introduced, then 16Mbit TokenRing, then FDDI, and now Fast Ethernet and ATM. By simply replacing the functionality of the Ethernet data-link layer with the functionality of the TokenRing (or other technology) data-link layer, we are able to easily take advantage of the new technology.

Media independence in the networking field is just like the Pony Express being replaced or augmented by trains. The postal system today uses a variety of transport methods (vans, trucks, and airplanes), just as we do in our networks today (Ethernet, TokenRing, FDDI, ATM, PPP, Frame Relay).

The end result of using the OSI model is that the application thinks it is communicating directly to another application on another computer. However, it is not communicating directly; it is calling upon the services offered by the presentation layer to convert and deliver the data to the proper destination. Similarly, the presentation layer relies on the session layer to control the session and deliver its data to the presentation layer on the remote system. This "virtual" communications is used at each layer until we reach the physical layer, where the two devices are connected by some type of network medium. The physical layer is the layer at which communication ultimately occurs.

# TCP/IP Protocol Stack

## Overall Architecture

The TCP/IP protocol stack matches quite nicely with the OSI model as seen in Figure 1-11. In general, the TCP/IP-based applications incorporate the application, presentation, and session layers as part of the application itself. For example, Telnet includes presentation and session layer negotiation like terminal-type determination as part of the application itself. The FTP login sequence to establish an FTP session is part of the FTP application as well. All TCP/IP applications interface with either TCP (the Transmission Control Protocol) or UDP (the User Datagram Protocol) at the transport layer (we will describe TCP and UDP later in this chapter).

The layers at the transport layer and below all correspond directly with the OSI model. The transport layer adds the network addresses to the data via a TCP or UDP header. The network layer determines the best delivery path and selects the proper data-link layer driver to use (there may be several data-link layer drivers if the device has several network interfaces). The network layer adds its own header (encapsulating the data). The data-link layer encapsulates the network layer packet within a link-layer frame. A frame typically includes both a header and a trailer. The header includes the media-specific addresses and the trailer typically includes some sort of frame check code and possibly an end-of-frame delimiter.

FYI: The term frame originates from the use of the term in the wide area networking days before local area networks were invented. A set of control bits are used to identify the beginning and end of the data on the WAN link, much like a picture frame is used to mark the edges of a picture. The most common set of control bits consists of eight bits of the binary data pattern 0111 1110, which may be written in hexadecimal as 7E. This pattern appears at both the start and end of the frame. The transmission equipment makes sure that this pattern does not appear in the transmitted data by using bit stuffing, where a zero is inserted when the 7E pattern is detected in the data stream.

As we go up the protocol stack, we encounter packets. A packet is the network layer encapsulation and is carried within a frame at the data-link layer. Within a packet, we may find a UDP datagram, or a TCP segment, each of which carries data.

Let's examine how the encapsulation works for TCP/IP, using the example of sending a login prompt from a router to a user's workstation (the network configuration is shown in Figure 1-12). The data consists of the text **Username:**, which is encapsulated within a transport-layer segment. This segment in turn is encapsulated within a

**Figure 1-11**
TCP/IP and the OSI
model

| OSI Model | TCP/IP | Examples | | |
|---|---|---|---|---|
| Application | Application | Telnet | FTP | TFTP |
| Presentation | | | | |
| Session | | | | |
| Transport | Transport | TCP | TCP | UDP |
| Network | Network | IP | IP | IP |
| Data-link | Data-link | Ethernet, TokenRing, FDDI, etc. | | |
| Physical | Physical | Cabling, Connectors, Signaling, etc. | | |

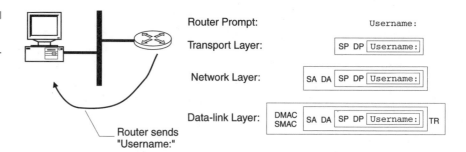

**Figure 1-12**
TCP/IP encapsulation

network-layer packet. The network-layer packet is then encapsulated within a data-link-layer frame for transmission over the selected medium. The resulting frame looks like an onion: The data is encapsulated within a segment. The segment is then encapsulated within a packet, and the packet is encapsulated within a data-link frame.

The process of encapsulation/multiplexing and decapsulation/demultiplexing is reversed when a system receives the data. As the data travels up the stack, the framing is examined, the network protocol type determined, and the framing discarded. The enclosed packet is examined to determine the transport protocol (segment or datagram). The enclosed transport protocol data is processed by one of the transport-layer processes, and the data is passed to the proper application. Each of the headers is examined for the appropriate multiplexing code at each level in the stack.

## Protocol Stack Multiplexing

There are control bytes in the segment, packet, and frame headers at each level in the TCP/IP protocol stack. These control bytes identify the source of data (when transmitting data) and identify the upper layer that should process data (when receiving data). Figure 1-13 shows the control bytes used within the TCP/IP protocol stack. When a frame is received from the physical media, the Ethernet controller passes along only those frames whose MAC address matches the MAC address on the controller card (and any broadcast or multicast addresses that the interface recognizes). The Ethernet software receives the frame and examines

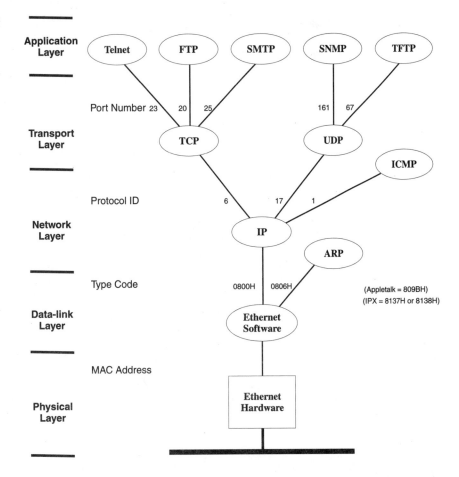

**Figure 1-13**
TCP/IP protocol
multiplexing

the type code to determine what kind of data is being carried in the frame. (A multiprotocol system may have several different protocol stacks simultaneously loaded. Figure 1-13 shows the type codes for Appletalk and IPX as well as for the IP protocols.) The type code determines which protocol stack will be given the data that was encapsulated in the frame. A code of 0800 (hexadecimal) indicates that an IP packet is encapsulated. A table of common data-link type codes appears in Table 1-1. A full list of type codes may be found in Simoneau (1997) or ISI.

**Table 1-1**

Common data-
link type codes

| Ethernet Type Code | Data Type |
|---|---|
| 0800 | Internet Protocol |
| 0806 | Address Resolution Protocol |
| 0BAD | Banyan VINES |
| 0BAE | VINES Loopback |
| 0BAF | VINES Echo |
| 6000-6009 | Digital Equipment—various protocols |
| 6010-6014 | 3Com Corporation |
| 809B | Appletalk |
| 8137-8138 | IPX (Novell) |
| 86DD | IPv6 |

Source: Data from the Ether Types list maintained at ISI.EDU (ISI). This document also includes Ether-net vendor codes, multicast address assignments, and a discussion on bit ordering on Ethernet and TokenRing networks.

The packet is then processed by IP. The IP header is examined and the destination address validated. If the destination IP address corresponds to this system, the packet's protocol ID is examined. The protocol code determines which of several possible protocols should receive the encapsulated data. A protocol code of 6 indicates TCP, while a protocol code of 17 indicates UDP. A table of IP protocol ID codes is shown in Table 1-2.

**Table 1-2**

Common
protocol IDs

| Decimal Code | Keyword | Protocol |
|---|---|---|
| 1 | ICMP | Internet Control Message Protocol |
| 6 | TCP | Transmission Control Protocol |
| 8 | EGP | Exterior Gateway Protocol |
| 17 | UDP | User Datagram Protocol |
| 41 | SIP | Simple Internet Protocol |
| 45 | IDRP | Inter-Domain Routing Protocol |
| 47 | GRE | General Routing Encapsulation |
| 54 | NHRP | NBMA Next Hop Resolution Protocol |
| 88 | IGRP | Cisco's Interior Gateway Routing Protocol |
| 89 | OSPFIGP | Open Shortest Path First Interior Gateway Protocol |

Note: A complete list of protocol codes can be found in RFC1700 (Postel 1994).

A TCP segment or UDP datagram would be examined to determine the port number, which identifies the application to receive the data. (We'll discuss port numbers in more depth in the TCP section.) For example, the port number of 23 is reserved for Telnet, and the port number of 25 is reserved for SMTP. Well-known port numbers for both TCP and UDP are shown in Table 1-3.

As you can see from the list of port numbers, many of them are listed as reserved for both TCP and UDP capabilities. In practice, you will find some applications that are implemented with only one of the two transport protocols. For example, FTP is registered for both TCP and UDP, but in practice, it uses only TCP as its transport because it relies on TCP's reliable transfer and high throughput over wide area network links. Other applications, like syslog, are registered to use only one transport.

Conversely, other applications like DNS use both TCP and UDP. These applications use the two transport protocols for different purposes at various times during the program's execution. Specifically, DNS uses UDP for normal nameserver requests and TCP for zone downloads from a primary to a secondary nameserver.

## TCP

The Transmission Control Protocol is most often used as the transport for Internet applications due to its virtual circuit (or connection-oriented) method of operation. Programs like Telnet and FTP rely on the guaranteed delivery characteristic of TCP to reliably transport their data through the network. TCP is documented in RFC793 (Postel 1981c).

In the postal analogy, TCP operates like a return receipt letter. An acknowledgment is returned to the sender when the data is delivered successfully.

### What TCP Provides

TCP is a connection-oriented protocol. It provides guaranteed, sequential data delivery between two network devices. The data segments are stored in buffers in the sending system until the receiver acknowledges their receipt. If any segment is lost, TCP automatically retransmits it. A modern TCP system will monitor the round-trip time between the sender and receiver and will reduce its transmission rate automatically when it detects packet loss that results from network congestion.

**Table 1-3**

Common well-known port numbers

| Keyword | Decimal Code | Description |
|---|---|---|
| | 0/tcp or udp | Reserved |
| tcpmux | 1/tcp or udp | TCP Port Service Multiplexer |
| echo | 7/tcp or udp | Echo (echo back to sender all received data) |
| discard | 9/tcp or udp | Discard (silently discard all received data) |
| systat | 11/tcp or udp | Active Users |
| daytime | 13/tcp or udp | Daytime |
| quotd | 17/tcp or udp | Quote of the Day |
| chargen | 19/tcp or udp | Character Generator |
| ftp-data | 20/tcp or udp | File Transfer (Default Data Port) |
| ftp | 21/tcp or udp | File Transfer (Control Port) |
| telnet | 23/tcp or udp | Telnet |
| smtp | 25/tcp or udp | Simple Mail Transfer Protocol |
| time | 37/tcp or udp | Time |
| nicname | 43/tcp or udp | Who Is |
| domain | 53/tcp or udp | Domain Name Server |
| bootps | 67/tcp or udp | Bootstrap Protocol Server |
| bootpc | 68/tcp or udp | Bootstrap Protocol Client |
| tftp | 69/tcp or udp | Trivial File Transfer Protocol |
| gopher | 70/tcp or udp | Gopher |
| finger | 79/tcp or udp | Finger |
| www-http | 80/tcp or udp | World Wide Web HTTP |
| kerberos | 88/tcp or udp | Kerberos |
| pop2 | 109/tcp or udp | Post Office Protocol version 2 |
| pop3 | 110/tcp or udp | Post Office Protocol version 3 |
| sunrpc | 111/tcp or udp | Sun Remote Procedure Call |
| nntp | 119/tcp or udp | Network News Transfer Protocol |
| ntp | 123/tcp or udp | Network Time Protocol |
| netbios-ns | 137/tcp or udp | NETBIOS Name Service |
| netbios-dgm | 138/tcp or udp | NETBIOS Datagram Service |
| netbios-ssn | 139/tcp or udp | NETBIOS Session Service |
| imap2 | 143/tcp or udp | Interim Mail Access Protocol V2 |
| snmp | 161/tcp or udp | Simple Network Management Protocol |
| bgp | 179/tcp or udp | Border Gateway Protocol |
| syslog | 514/udp | System Logger |

Note: A complete list of well-known port numbers can be found in RFC1700 (Postel 1994).

Because of the guaranteed, sequential data delivery, TCP operates like a virtual circuit connection. A virtual circuit is a connection that looks like a dedicated network segment between the sending and receiving systems. However, a TCP virtual circuit is actually implemented by sending data packets over shared network segments. It is the operation of TCP/IP that allows multiple systems to share the same network links.

When TCP segments are being sent, a change in the network (either a link change or congestion) may cause packets to arrive out of order. TCP identifies the contents of each segment and reassembles the data in the correct order at the receiving system. Once the data has been reassembled, it is passed to the application, which typically implements the upper three layers of the OSI model (the session, presentation, and application layers).

### What TCP Doesn't Provide

TCP does not provide lightweight communications. A TCP connection can be broken down into three distinct phases: the initial connection-establishment phase (the three-way handshake, described later), then the data-transfer phase, and finally the connection-close phase. Both the connection-establishment and connection-close phases require the exchange of several packets, making TCP an expensive mechanism to transfer just a few bytes of data, such as might be required by a name-server lookup.

TCP is also not a good mechanism for performing system logging type functions. With most logging functions, what is needed is a lightweight mechanism to quickly and efficiently send a message to a server to be stored and, if the message were important enough, generate an alert to the operations staff. Creating and closing a TCP connection just to transfer a one-line log message is a significant amount of overhead.

The thing that TCP doesn't do well, lightweight communications, is provided by UDP, which we will describe later.

### TCP Segment Format

TCP connections use segments to communicate between network systems. The maximum segment size is determined by TCP by discovering the maximum packet size of the outgoing interface or through negotiation with the peer system.

The TCP segment format is shown in Figure 1-14. We will cover each of the major fields in the following sections.

Port Numbers

The port numbers identify the applications (programs) in each of the two communicating network systems. When a connection is created, the source system typically asks TCP to pick an available local port number. The connection is made to a well-known port in the remote system where the server program is running.

In Figure 1-15, we see how a Telnet client uses port numbers to create a unique connection to a Telnet server. First, the Telnet client program is started and the user enters the **open** command to start a Telnet session with the remote system. In step 1, Telnet asks TCP for a local port number. Step 2 shows TCP replying with an available local port number. The Telnet client knows to use port 23 (the "well-known port" for Telnet) to connect to the Telnet server program in the remote system. So in step 3, the connection request is sent to the remote system.

The destination system receives the initial TCP session request packet, which is addressed to 172.16.1.2, port 23, and is from 172.16.1.1, port 1046. The connection request uses these four numbers, the source IP addresses, the source port number, the destination IP address, and the destination port number to uniquely identify the connection. The multiplexing in

**Figure 1-14**

TCP segment format

Bit Position

00 01 02 03 04 05 06 07 08 09 10 11 12 13 14 15 16 17 18 19 20 21 22 23 24 25 26 27 28 29 30 31

| Source Port | | Destination Port |
|---|---|---|
| Sequence Number | | |
| Acknowledgment Number | | |
| Data Offset | Reserved | U R G / A C K / P S H / R S T / S Y N / F I N | Window |
| Checksum | | Urgent Pointer |
| Options | | Padding |
| Data ... | | |

**Figure 1-15**
TCP port selection

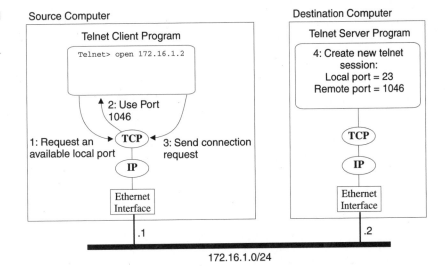

the TCP/IP protocol stack makes sure that the right application and the right user receive the correct data.

But how does this work when there is more than one Telnet user on the source system? Figure 1-16 shows a second user starting a Telnet connection to the same server. This user's Telnet client will request an available port from TCP. TCP replies that port 1093 is available. The Telnet client will then send a connection request to 172.16.1.2, port 23, from 172.16.1.1, port 1093.

Sequence Numbers & Acknowledgment Numbers
The sequence and acknowledgment numbers identify data within a TCP segment. The sequence number can start at any value (some systems start with a sequence number of 1, but many others start with a random 32-bit number). The sequence number is incremented for every byte of user data that is transmitted. The sequence numbers identify the byte at the start of the segment. The length of the segment determines the sequence of bytes being sent in a segment.

Sequence numbers serve several purposes. The first is to identify the sequence of data so that the receiver can reassemble it in the correct order before passing it along to the application. This can happen in a network where a high-speed link is brought up in parallel with a slower link. Suddenly, several data packets arrive before those already sent on the slower link.

Another use is to eliminate duplicate packets from the network. This

**Figure 1-16**
Using multiple port
numbers

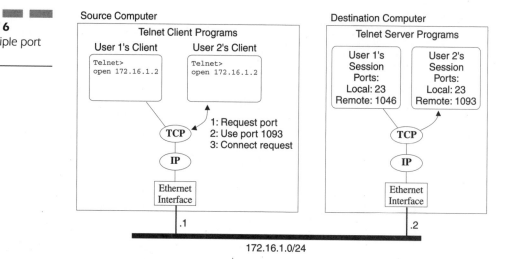

**Figure 1-16**
Using multiple port
numbers

can happen if a network device becomes congested. Several packets may be kept in the device's buffers long enough for the sending computer to think that a network failure has occurred and to retransmit the data. When the second set of data arrives, the receiver detects the duplicate sequence numbers and discards the duplicate packets.

Acknowledgment numbers are used by the receiver to tell the sender which data it has successfully received. The acknowledgment number indicates which byte the receiver is expecting next. The acknowledgment number is valid only if the ACK bit is set in the flags field, but since this bit exists in all packets, most existing implementations always set the ACK bit and have a valid number in the acknowledgment field.

We'll see how this works in the next section.

TCP Connection Establishment
The TCP connection-establishment sequence is actually a three-way handshake between the source and the destination system. The handshake allows each computer system to exchange sequence numbers and acknowledge the receipt of the sequence number from the other system.

Figures 1-17 and 1-18 show the network and router configuration of the example network. Figure 1-19 shows the three-way handshake and

**Figure 1-17**
TCP connection-
establishment
network

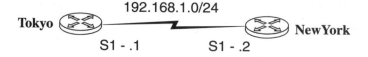

**Figure 1-18**  TCP connection-establishment router configuration

```
1 hostname NewYork
2 interface Serial1
3   ip address 192.168.1.2 255.255.255.0
4   clockrate 56000
5 end
6
7 hostname Tokyo
8 interface Serial0
9   ip address 192.168.1.1 255.255.255.0
10 end
```

the exchange of the first set of information in a Telnet session between two adjacent routers. We're monitoring the debug output on New York and establishing a Telnet connection from Tokyo to New York. Look for the port numbers, sequence numbers, and acknowledgments used in each segment.

The first segment (lines 4 and 5 in Figure 1-19) is received from Tokyo (note the I, which indicates Input). It contains the source address (192.168.1.1) and port number (11006), the destination address (192.168.1.2) and port number (23), the source system's initial sequence number (35348817), and window size (4128), which we'll discuss in the next section.

**Figure 1-19**  TCP connection-establishment output

```
1 NewYork#deb ip tcp packet
2 TCP Packet debugging is on
3 NewYork#
4 tcp0: I LISTEN 192.168.1.1:11006 192.168.1.2:23 seq 35348817
5         OPTS 4 SYN  WIN 4128
6 tcp0: O SYNRCVD 192.168.1.1:11006 192.168.1.2:23 seq 37758010
7         OPTS 4 ACK 35348818 SYN  WIN 4128
8 tcp0: I SYNRCVD 192.168.1.1:11006 192.168.1.2:23 seq 35348818
9         ACK 37758011  WIN 4128
10 tcp5: O ESTAB 192.168.1.1:11006 192.168.1.2:23 seq 37758011
11         DATA 12 ACK 35348818 PSH  WIN 4128
12 tcp5: I ESTAB 192.168.1.1:11006 192.168.1.2:23 seq 35348818
13         DATA 9 ACK 37758011 PSH  WIN 4128
14 tcp5: I ESTAB 192.168.1.1:11006 192.168.1.2:23 seq 35348827
15         ACK 37758011  WIN 4128
16 tcp5: O ESTAB 192.168.1.1:11006 192.168.1.2:23 seq 37758023
17         DATA 42 ACK 35348827 PSH  WIN 4119
```

FYI: The Cisco TCP debug output lists the IP addresses in a fixed order. The I or O flag that is the second value in each line indicates whether the packet is Input or Output, with respect to the router that is producing the debug information. This format is unlike most network analyzer software, so be careful in reading the debug output. You may need to carefully analyze the output to know which address is the source and which is the destination in the debug output.

The next segment (lines 6 and 7) is from New York back to Tokyo. (Note the O, which indicates that the packet is being Output.) New York's starting sequence number is included in this segment, the ACK bit is set, and the acknowledgment number is Tokyo's initial sequence number, incremented by one (35348818). The acknowledgment number indicates to Tokyo that New York acknowledges receipt and successful processing of Tokyo's SYN segment. Finally, in the third exchange of the three-way handshake (lines 8 and 9), New York receives an ACK from Tokyo, indicating that Tokyo has received and processed New York's SYN segment.

If all three segments are received successfully, then the connection is open and data can begin flowing. The sequence of segments starting with line 10 show an established connection and the start of the Telnet negotiation between the client and server.

TCP Sliding Window

The TCP *window* field is used to implement flow control through a mechanism called the TCP sliding window. The receiver uses the window field to tell the transmitter how much receive buffer space is available. The transmitter never transmits more than this amount of data at once, so as to not overrun the receiver's buffers. When the receiver processes some (or all) of the buffered data, it sends an acknowledgment back to the transmitter, indicating that the buffer space has increased. The transmitter uses the acknowledgment number along with the advertised window size to determine how much additional data can be sent.

This can be seen in the example transfer of Figure 1-19. During the three-way handshake, each system tells the other how much receive buffer space it has available. You can see Tokyo advertising its window of 4128 on line 5 and New York advertising its receive window of 4128 to Tokyo on line 7.

On lines 10 and 11, New York sends 12 bytes of data. Simultaneously, Tokyo sends 9 bytes of data to New York (lines 12 and 13). Lines 14 and 15 show Tokyo updating its sequence number. The 12 bytes sent by New York have not yet been accepted, so the acknowledgment number and window are not updated. New York transmits an updated acknowledgment in lines 16 and 17. Notice the reduced window size (now 4119), which indicates New York has received the data but has not yet processed it. Since these 9 bytes consume receive buffer space, the window has been reduced by 9. As the data is processed by the Telnet application, the window is increased.

The sliding window protocol used by TCP can identify lost segments and retransmit them. Due to research done by Van Jacobson, a modern TCP implementation will correctly identify an occasional lost segment and retransmit it without slowing the transfer rate. However, if the network is becoming congested, the congestion-avoidance algorithm takes over and reduces the rate at which data is sent into the network.

An excellent discussion of the operation of the TCP sliding window algorithm can be found in *TCP/IP Illustrated* (Stevens 1994).

### Checksum & Urgent Pointer

The checksum field does exactly as you would expect: It is a simple check of the contents of the segment. Even with modern data-link protocols (Ethernet and TokenRing), there are errors that can occur between the network interface and the computer system memory, making this an important data-integrity check. The algorithm is a simple 16-bit sum of the one's complement of the data. If the data is an odd number of bytes, it is padded with a single zero byte.

The urgent pointer identifies the location of urgent data in the incoming data stream. The urgent pointer is added to the sequence number of the current segment. The resulting sequence number identifies the last byte of the urgent data (see the Host Requirements RFC, RFC1122, Braden 1989). It is up to the application to determine what to do with the data up to the last byte of urgent data. For example, Telnet uses the urgent pointer to identify data that should be discarded due to the user typing the interrupt key (typically CTRL-C). Telnet can then discard the many, many bytes of data that may be in transit from the sending computer system to the user's display.

### Cisco Uses of TCP

Cisco routers use TCP for a variety of tasks. These tasks are typically to support administration of the router or for security or testing purposes. For example, all Cisco routers support the Telnet application, both as a client (where you Telnet from the router to another network device) and a server (where you Telnet into a router).

The TACACS+ protocol (an authentication, authorization, and accounting system) uses TCP to create a connection between a Cisco router or access server and the TACACS+ server. Another application is by the RCP (Remote Copy Protocol) to copy IOS images into and out of the router (because it uses TCP, it can operate over long delay and lossy paths that TFTP cannot handle). Finally, there are a whole set of small servers (echo, discard, chargen, and date) that can be enabled in Cisco equipment. These servers do exactly what they are called: echo what is sent, discard what is sent, send characters until the connection is closed, or send the date. Some of these small servers are excellent for performing network testing, as we'll see in later sections.

Cisco routers also are able to filter transit TCP traffic based on the source and/or destination port numbers and on the established state of the connection. The latter condition allows filtering connections that are in the initial three-way handshake phase. Understanding how TCP operates and its use of port numbers and the three-way handshake allows you to build effective packet filters for securing your network.

## UDP

The User Datagram Protocol is another transport layer protocol, but unlike TCP, it provides a connectionless datagram service. UDP is defined in RFC768 (Postel 1980) and is widely used for several different types of applications in IP networks. UDP is good for single-packet requests and replies (e.g., send a request for data or send update data to a server) and often is used to implement transaction-based functionality. A good example of a single-packet transaction application is the syslog function, which sends logging information to a network logging server. No reply from the server is needed by the sender. Other applications use UDP to implement simple request-reply mechanisms. A good example is the Simple Network Management Protocol (SNMP), which uses request packets to retrieve operational parameters from networked systems.

In the postal system analogy, UDP operation is similar to sending a postcard. It is lightweight and is typically used in an advisory role to inform the recipient of something or to request a specific piece of data from a server. A specific example is the postcard that your dentist sends to remind you of an upcoming appointment.

### What UDP Provides

UDP is a lightweight protocol with very little processing overhead. Because of its simplicity, it is a very good protocol for basic communications where it is not desirable to include the full features of TCP. Good examples of this are the Boot Protocol (BOOTP) and the Trivial File Transfer Protocol (TFTP). These protocols often are used by the small bootstrap operating systems in diskless workstations or network equipment to obtain initial configuration information or to retrieve an operating system from a server located elsewhere on the network.

UDP is also a very good basis for transaction processing where the client station needs to make a simple request of a server or where a server may need to service many more clients than TCP could handle (due to the overhead inherent in tracking the state of a connection). An example of a two-way transaction application is the Domain Naming System (DNS). Here, a client system uses UDP to ask a DNS server for the IP address that corresponds to the name of a device with which a user is attempting to communicate. We also see the Simple Network Management Protocol (SNMP) using UDP from a network management station to ask a network device about its current operating state.

In all these examples, the application is not adversely affected if the request or reply is damaged or discarded in the network. The application will simply repeat the request in order to get the reply that is needed.

Another good use of UDP is for logging of operational information. Many network devices have the ability to send logging information to a logging server on the network. Using UDP allows many, many network devices to all send their logging information to a single server without overloading the server with an equivalent number of connections.

### What UDP Doesn't Provide

UDP doesn't provide guaranteed delivery of its data. Each UDP datagram is carried in an IP packet and receives the same delivery guarantees any IP packet would receive. Things like network congestion can cause packets to be discarded by routers. Links that have significant errors may cause errors to appear at several different layers (the data-link layer (e.g., Ethernet), the network layer (e.g., IP), or at the transport layer (e.g., UDP). Any of these errors will cause the datagram to be discarded, resulting in loss of data. Programs that use the datagram service must provide any needed reliability themselves by resending any data that must be reliably delivered. Realistically, only a few datagrams are discarded or damaged in most networks, but the programmer must still allow for this occurrence and develop the program accordingly.

UDP datagrams also may arrive in a different order than the order in which the sending system initially transmitted them. This may happen because of a number of different scenarios, the most common of which is a change in the network that caused some UDP datagrams to be routed over a slow path while successive datagrams were routed over a faster path. In this case, the datagrams sent later over the faster path may arrive first at the destination. The program on the receiving end of the communications link must be able to handle this situation.

Datagram Format

The UDP datagram format is shown in Figure 1-20. A comparison of the UDP datagram with the TCP segment format shows that the UDP header is only eight bytes long, making it significantly smaller and simpler.

As with TCP, there are a source port and a destination port, to identify the sending and receiving applications. There is also a checksum field that is used to validate the integrity of the UDP datagram. Finally, there is a length field that holds the length of the entire UDP datagram, including the UDP header. Since this length is 16 bits, the largest size UDP datagram is 65,535 bytes ($2^{16}$-1).

Cisco Uses of UDP

Because of its simplicity, Cisco uses UDP in a variety of ways. A router that boots and finds that it doesn't have a configuration will use UDP broadcasts to find a DNS server, look up its hostname, then TFTP a copy of its configuration file from a TFTP server. This process requires that the DNS and TFTP server be local or that the network administrator has properly configured other devices on the network to forward the requests to the proper DNS and TFTP server.

Once the router is running, logging messages may be sent to a monitoring system through the use of syslog (the system logger). User login authentication can be done through the TACACS and XTACACS protocols, both of which use UDP. In January 1998, Cisco announced that it was dropping support for these protocols because they had ceased to be useful to very many customers.

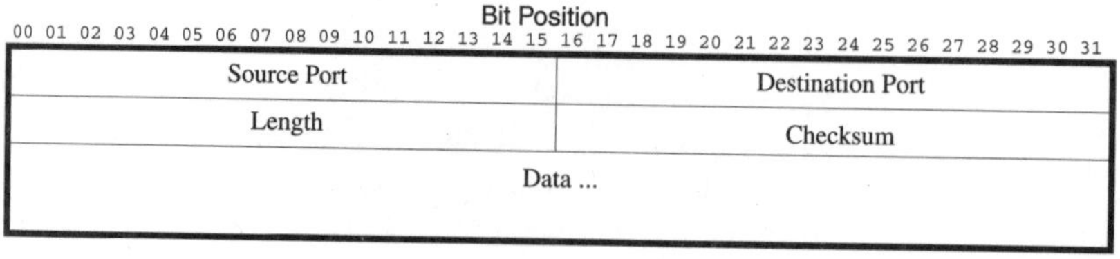

**Figure 1-20**
UDP datagram format

All Cisco equipment also implements SNMP, which uses UDP. SNMP allows network management stations to monitor, and if properly configured, manage Cisco devices on the network.

# IP

The Internet Protocol, defined in RFC791 (Postel 1981a), is the network layer protocol of the TCP/IP suite and is used to transport the TCP segments or UDP datagrams across the network. IP is where we find the use of IP addresses to identify the source and destination systems. The network layer is where routers really do their thing—examining the destination IP address, determining the best path to that destination, looking up the proper interface to use to forward the packet, and queuing the packet on the outgoing interface. Performing this set of actions quickly and efficiently is difficult.

The postal system analogy of IP is the envelope or postcard addressing and the routing functions performed by the post office.

What IP Provides

IP is simply a packet-delivery service. It is best-effort delivery only, relying on the upper-layer protocols and applications to retry the transmission if a packet is damaged or lost. Because IP examines the destination address within each packet, and dynamically determines the best path to the destination, it can easily and efficiently direct packets around network failures, as long as at least one path remains active. Reliable delivery was part of the original design specified by the U.S. Department of Defense. The need was to be able to maintain computer communications even when the network is heavily damaged. This resiliency has proven to be very useful and effective in corporate networks today, where equipment failures and cable cuts occur much too frequently.

But IP provides something that is somewhat unique: the ability to divide, or fragment, a packet into smaller pieces if it is too large for the network. However, it turns out that fragmenting a packet is costly, for both the system performing the fragmentation and the destination system, which must reassemble the fragments before handing the data to the transport layer.

An application can specify different types of service, depending on the kind of data being transported and the delivery requirements of that data. For example, a packet that is part of an audio or video data stream must reach its destination in order to be heard or viewed. If it arrives too late, it is useless. One type of service setting an application may specify is low delay. We'll see other types of service in the section on the IP packet format.

Another useful service provided by IP is to automatically discard old packets if they circulate too long in the network. This protects the network against congestive meltdown due to packets that have been caught in a routing loop and otherwise would never be properly delivered to their destination.

### What IP Doesn't Provide

IP doesn't guarantee delivery of a packet. It is simply concerned with finding the best path to the destination and forwarding the packet to the next hop along the chosen path. If a packet is damaged (perhaps due to burst errors on a WAN link) or lost (discarded because it had lived too long in the network), it is up to the upper-layer protocols or even the application to retransmit the data.

The IP checksum is used to check the IP header only. None of the data is checked. It is up to the transport-layer protocols to validate the data within the datagram or segment. While this might seem risky, it makes the processing of an IP packet very efficient. Routers shouldn't be concerned about the integrity of a packet at every hop along the path (if the network administrator is concerned about packet integrity at every hop, then a reliable delivery protocol like X.25 should be used). In practice, the delegation of data integrity checking to the transport layer is a good choice. It allows the network devices to efficiently forward packets and allows the destination system to validate the contents of the data.

### Packet Format

The format of the IP packet is shown in Figure 1-21. There is a *version* number (0100 binary for IPv4) and a *header length* field. The *type-of-service* (TOS) field allows the application to specify the type of service the packet should receive from the network.

Only one of the following characteristics may be requested:

- Low delay
- High throughput
- High reliability
- Lowest monetary cost

**Figure 1-21**
IP packet format

Bit Position

| Bit Position | | | | | | |
|---|---|---|---|---|---|---|

00 01 02 03 04 05 06 07 08 09 10 11 12 13 14 15 16 17 18 19 20 21 22 23 24 25 26 27 28 29 30 31

| Version | IHL | Type of Service | Total Length | | |
|---|---|---|---|---|---|
| Identification | | | Flags | Fragment Offset | |
| Time to Live | | Protocol | Header Checksum | | |
| Source Address | | | | | |
| Destination Address | | | | | |
| Options | | | | Padding | |
| Data ... | | | | | |

In actual practice, none of the bits in the TOS field are used today. The OSPF routing protocol specified the ability to use the TOS field for making routing decisions, but the end systems have never implemented it widely enough to make internetworking vendors implement it in the network devices. The result is that the TOS support has been dropped from the latest OSPF specification.

The *total length* field indicates the length of the entire IP packet, including all data and header. Since it is a 16-bit field, the maximum IP packet length is limited to 65,535 bytes.

The *identification* field could be thought of as a packet serial number. It is used to identify potential duplicate packets that may occur in a dynamic internetwork or that may be generated by a malfunctioning network device.

The *flags* and *fragment offset* fields are used to allow IP to subdivide a packet that is too large for the next hop's media. For example, a packet originating on a TokenRing network may have a Maximum Transmission Unit (MTU) of 4,500 bytes. If this packet must be transmitted over an Ethernet somewhere in the path from source to destination, the packet must be fragmented into multiple packets that are no larger than 1,500 bytes each (the Ethernet MTU). The flags and fragment offset fields uniquely identify each of the fragments so that the destination system can correctly reassemble the original 4,500-byte packet.

The *time-to-live* field restricts the number of hops that the packet can traverse before it must be destroyed. It is normally set to a value like 64, out of a maximum of 255, and is decremented by each router that the packet goes through. When the value reaches zero, the packet is discarded. However, when it is discarded, an ICMP *time exceeded* message is returned to the sender. Normally, a packet will be discarded in this manner only when a network routing loop has formed. The ICMP time-exceeded message informs the sending system of the network problem and allows the sender to reduce its transmission rate. This field is used by the **trace** command within the Cisco router, which we will discuss in the ICMP section of this chapter and in the Chapter 10.

IP has to be able to tell what protocol is being carried within the data portion of the packet so it can pass its data to the proper protocol processing subsystem (i.e., TCP, UDP, ICMP, etc.). The *protocol* field performs this function. For example, the protocol ID for TCP is 6 and the protocol ID for UDP is 17. Referring back to Figure 1-13, TCP/IP stack multiplexing, you can see how IP uses this field to determine which of the other protocols should process the data carried in the packet.

Each IP packet has a *header checksum* calculated on its header. The checksum protects the header contents from being damaged in transit. If the destination does not calculate the same checksum as is contained in the packet, something has changed in the header, and the packet is discarded.

Next are the source and destination IP addresses. Each address is 32 bits and is the portion of the IP header that is used when deciding the best path the packet should follow to reach its destination.

Finally, there can be a set of options in the IP packet. For example, it is possible to include an option that requires each router to include its IP address in the option field as the packet traverses each hop. Because of the limitation on the IP header length, only nine IP addresses can be stored this way, severely limiting the usefulness of this technique in today's large networks.

### IP Addressing

An IP address is a 32-bit number, which is typically written in *dotted decimal notation*, as shown in the examples of Figure 1-22. Most protocol decodes will display it in either hexadecimal or dotted decimal format. Unfortunately, we often need to work with IP addresses in binary form. We've included a binary, decimal, and hexadecimal conversion table in Appendix A to ease the task of performing these conversions.

### Classful Addressing

The IP address space traditionally has been broken into several *classes*, named class A, class B, class C, and more recently, a special class D range of addresses. Each class is designed to trade off the number of network

**Figure 1-22**
IP addressing

```
Class A      ONNN NNNN.LLLL LLLL.LLLL LLLL.LLLL LLLL
Example:     0000 1010.1100 1001.0100 0000.0000 1000
               10  .  201  .   64  .    8

Class B      10NN NNNN.NNNN NNNN.LLLL LLLL.LLLL LLLL
Example:     1000 0000.0011 1000.0010 0001.0000 0001
              128  .   56  .   33  .    1

Class C      110N NNNN.NNNN NNNN.NNNN NNNN.LLLL LLLL
Example:     1100 0010.1110 0010.0001 0011.0111 1000
              130  .  226  .   19  .  120

Class D      1110 MMMM.MMMM MMMM.MMMM MMMM.MMMM MMMM
Example:     1110 0000.0000 0000.0000 0000.0000 0101
              224  .   0  .    0  .    5
```

numbers within the class against the number of hosts within a given network number. Each class is identified by the first few bits of the 32-bit address. The next few bits identify the network number and the remaining bits are "local" and are assigned by the network administrator to identify network segments within the network and the hosts or systems on each segment. Figure 1-22 shows each class address, its binary format, and an example of each. Table 1-4 shows the ranges of addresses covered by each address class.

FYI: The term *octet* came into use to unambiguously identify an eight-bit entity. The alternative had been the word *byte*, but this didn't work well because some computers had nine-bit bytes. These machines typically used 36-bit words composed of four nine-bit bytes.

**Table 1-4**

IP classful addressing ranges

| Class | Range | Notes |
|-------|-------|-------|
| A | 0.0.0.0-127.255.255.255 | 0.0.0.0 and 127.0.0.0 are reserved |
| B | 128.0.0.0-191.255.255.255 | |
| C | 192.0.0.0-223.255.255.255 | |
| D | 224.0.0.0-239.255.255.255 | Multicast address allocation |

It is easy to recognize the class of an IP address by the range of values of the first octet. Table 1-5 shows the range of valid first-octet values for each address class.

Class A addresses have a zero in the first bit position and use the remaining bits of the first octet as the network number. A class B address has a zero in the second bit position, filling the first bit position with a one. Its network number is determined by the remaining bits in the first two octets of the address. Finally, a class C address places a zero in the third bit position, setting the first two bits to one. The remaining bits of the first three octets are used to identify the network number. In each case, the bits to the right of the network number identify the host on that network.

FYI: The class A, B, and C address ranges are easily remembered by associating them with the Jackson Five song of the 1970s, "ABC, 123," in which the lyrics say "ABC, as easy as 123." The "123" refers to the bit position in which the zero is found in each address class and the number of octets used for the network identifier.

The address classes are summarized in Figure 1-23. There are only 127 usable class A networks (network number 0.0.0.0 is reserved), but each one supports 16,777,216 addresses. The assumption is that the world only needs a few very large networks. Since 14 bits are used to identify class B networks, we can have up to 16,384 of them, each with 65,536 addresses. There are a medium number of class B networks with a medium number of hosts on each. Finally, the class C address range supports 2,097,152 networks, each with 256 addresses. The thought here is that we would need many, many small networks. The class D address range sets the fourth bit to a zero and the top three bits to one. It is used for IP multicast addressing.

**Table 1-5**

First-octet values

| Class | Value |
|---|---|
| A | 1-126 |
| B | 128-191 |
| C | 192-223 |
| D (multicast) | 224-239 |

Classful routing relies on the identification of the type of address to determine what portion of the 32-bit address should be considered the network address. For example, a class B address would have the first two bits set to 10. In this case, a network device uses the remaining six bits of the first octet, plus all eight bits of the second octet (14 bits in all), as the network address. The remaining 16 bits identify the host on the network.

Dividing an IP address into network and host components is similar to looking at a postal address as multiple components. The city and state are similar to the network identification component while the street address is similar to the identification of the host on the network. In the next chapter, we will see how these components of the network address are used to route packets to the correct destination.

Each address class consumes a portion of the overall IP address range, as shown in Figure 1-23. Because of the large size of each class A network, the total of all class A networks consumes half of the entire IP address space. As of early 1998, all class A networks had been assigned or reserved, 62 percent of class B networks had been assigned, and 36 percent of class C networks had been assigned. Classless routing, which we will discuss in Chapters 2 and 5, makes address assignment much more efficient, allowing us to use some of the addresses that have been reserved and to make much more efficient use of the addresses that are left. A new version of IP, IPv6, increases the address size to 128 bits, eliminating any addressing problems for the foreseeable future.

### Cisco Uses of IP

The operation of the Cisco router is nearly dependent on the operation of IP. Certainly, Telnet access and network management functions rely on IP for their transport. Cisco routers implement all the TCP/IP proto-

**Figure 1-23**
IP address allocation

| Address Class | A | B | C | D | Res |
|---|---|---|---|---|---|
| | 32 bits = 4,294,967,296 Addresses | | | | |
| Fraction of Total | $\frac{1}{2}$ | $\frac{1}{4}$ | $\frac{1}{8}$ | $\frac{1}{16}$ | $\frac{1}{16}$ |
| Number of Nets | 128 | 16,384 | 2,097,152 | Multicast | Reserved |
| Number of Hosts | 16,777,216 | 65,536 | 256 | | |

cols, including the possibility of enabling several "small servers," that perform TCP and UDP echo ports, discard ports, and time-of-day ports. It is difficult to effectively operate a Cisco router without IP enabled.

# Other Protocols

There are several other protocols that operate in conjunction with IP. In this section, we will discuss several of these protocols and their operation.

## Address Resolution Protocol

When delivering a packet to a destination, the router needs to determine the media-specific address that corresponds to the IP address that is contained in the IP packet. The Address Resolution Protocol is used by IP to discover the media-specific data-link address that corresponds to a given IP address.

Operation

The postal system analogy works very well to describe how ARP works. Imagine a letter or note being delivered to someone in a classroom with an instructor and 20 people. The instructor doesn't yet know the names of all the people in the class, yet wants to deliver the letter to a particular student. The letter has the student's name on it (the equivalent of the IP address.) The instructor is operating like a router. The room is a broadcast domain (the instructor can call out the person's name and everyone will hear the name being called, just like the operation of most LAN protocols).

The instructor reads the name from the envelope (the destination address). The student's name is called out: "Who is Mike?" (the ARP request). Everyone hears the request, and only Mike identifies himself as having a matching name (the address matches). Mike replies, identifying his physical location (the MAC address). The instructor can now deliver the packet to the correct physical (MAC) address.

The ARP protocol works the same way. A router has an IP packet to deliver to a system on a LAN segment. There are multiple systems on this LAN, so the router must send a broadcast asking for the MAC address of the destination system. Step 1 in Figure 1-24 shows A sending a broadcast ARP request packet ("Who is 172.16.1.209?"). Only one computer system has the matching IP address and replies in step 2 with an ARP reply ("I am 172.16.1.209 at MAC address 0008.0001.9A1D!"). Note that the ARP request is broadcast while the ARP reply is sent only to the router; it is not broadcast.

There is one difference with respect to the post office analogy we've been using. When a device must ARP for a destination, the specification requires that the IP packet that is to be sent must be discarded. We will see this in the way Cisco routers handle ping packets.

ARP information is kept in tables (called a *cache*) within the network systems (both end systems and routers). Each table entry has a timeout value associated with it. This timer removes the association of the IP address and MAC address after some number of minutes. Many end systems have a 20-minute timer, while Cisco routers have a four-hour ARP flush timer.

ARP Packet Format

All ARP packets are encapsulated directly in the LAN framing (see RFC826, Plummer 1982). The type code contained in the framing indicates that the packet is an ARP packet. The format of ARP allows for different hardware address lengths and protocol address lengths to be supported. Figure 1-25 shows the format of an IP ARP request on an Ethernet using Ethernet II framing. The destination Ethernet address is the LAN broadcast address (all bits set to 1), while the source address is set to that of the router. The frame type is set to 0x0806, which indicates that the remaining portion of the frame is an ARP request.

The *hardware type, protocol type, hardware address length*, and *protocol address length* fields are used to indicate the type and size of the hardware and protocol addresses found in the ARP request. The *operation code*

**Figure 1-24**
Address Resolution
Protocol (ARP)

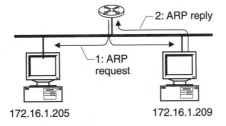

172.16.1.205          172.16.1.209

**Figure 1-25**

ARP packet format

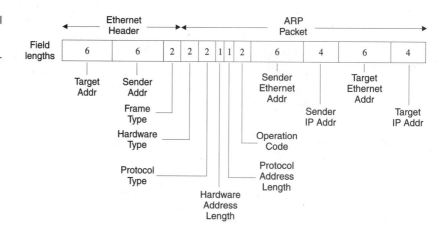

field specifies the kind of ARP packet. A value of 1 indicates ARP request, 2 is for an ARP reply, 3 indicates a reverse ARP request, and 4 is for the reverse ARP reply (reverse ARP is discussed later in this section). A full list of other protocol, hardware, and media type codes can be found in RFC1700 (Postel 1994).

The next four fields contain the sender's hardware and IP addresses and the destination's hardware and IP addresses. In the ARP request, the destination's hardware address is all zeros. In the ARP reply, all four fields are completed.

Proxy ARP

There are situations in which a network system may be configured to believe that all destinations are on the local LAN segment. In this case, a router acts on behalf of the remote system (i.e., is a proxy for the remote system).

In Figure 1-26, router A will answer any ARP request from 172.16.1.200 (system S). In this example, S is trying to reach system T at 172.16.2.14. Router A replies with its own MAC address. System S now has a MAC address to use when sending data to system T. It doesn't matter that the MAC address belongs to router A, because, when A receives the IP packet, it will forward the packet to the correct destination.

If S is configured to think that all destinations are "local," it will ARP for all destinations, even if each is on an entirely different network. As long as router A knows how to reach the destination network, it will reply to an ARP request for that network.

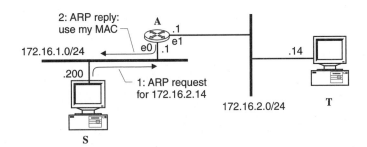

**Figure 1-26**
Proxy ARP

### Reverse ARP

The Reverse ARP process does the inverse of the ARP process. A diskless workstation, or a Cisco router with no configuration has no IP address. However, the network interface has a MAC address. The device boots and finds that it has no IP address. It then creates an ARP request with the *operation code* field set to 3, indicating a reverse ARP request. The destination MAC address on the Ethernet frame is the broadcast address, so all systems on the Ethernet will receive it. The destination IP address within the reverse ARP request is set to the IP broadcast address. The source MAC address is the address of the booting system, and the source IP address is zero.

A reverse ARP server must be configured on the LAN segment. This server must be configured with a table of known MAC addresses and the corresponding IP address. The server will send a reverse ARP reply (*operation code* 4) back to the booting system, with its IP address in the source address field.

If there is no local reverse ARP server, an alternative is to configure a helper address on a Cisco router on the LAN segment. This tells the router to forward specific packets (including reverse ARP requests) to a server at an address specified in the helper address command.

An ARP reply packet is returned to the booting system, specifying its IP address. Once the device has an IP address, it continues the boot process, which is specific to the device type.

### Use in Cisco Routers

Cisco routers implement ARP, proxy ARP, and reverse ARP. These protocols are used on all multiaccess broadcast LAN media such as Ethernet, TokenRing, and FDDI. The Cisco ARP cache timeout is four hours, which may seem like a long time but is actually reasonable in a stable network. The timeout value may be changed with the global configuration command **arp timeout** *value.*

**Figure 1-27**
ARP test network

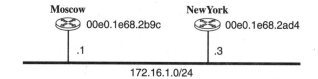

The use of ARP in a Cisco router may be viewed through use of the command **debug arp**. Figure 1-27 shows a test Ethernet connecting two Cisco routers, and Figure 1-28 shows the output of the **debug arp** command. Lines 6-9 show the output of the ARP request-and-reply sequence as NewYork pings Moscow's Ethernet interface. The end of line 9 shows the output of ping (the .!!!! sequence). The initial dot (.) indicates a timeout. The timeout is because the router dropped the first ping packet and issued an ARP request for 172.16.1.1. When the next four ping packets were transmitted, the ARP cache had been populated, and they immediately succeeded.

The contents of the ARP cache can be examined with the **show arp** command. The output, seen in Figure 1-29, shows the parameters of each cache entry: the protocol, the IP address, the age of the entry, the MAC (hardware) address, type of encapsulation, and the interface to use to reach the target system. Note that NewYork lists its own interface with no age.

Sometimes it is important to clear the ARP cache. For example, when a server needs to have its network interface card replaced (a higher-performance card is being installed, or the old card died), the replacement may be implemented before the four-hour cache timeout expires. In this

**Figure 1-28** Output of debug arp

```
1 NewYork#ping 172.16.1.1
2
3 Type escape sequence to abort.
4 Sending 5, 100-byte ICMP Echos to 172.16.1.1, timeout is 2 seconds:
5
6 IP ARP: creating incomplete entry for IP address: 172.16.1.1
7 IP ARP: sent req src 172.16.1.3 00e0.1e68.2ad4,
8                dst 172.16.1.1 0000.0000.0000 Ethernet0
9 IP ARP: rcvd rep src 172.16.1.1 00e0.1e68.2b9c, dst 172.16.1.3 Ethernet0.!!!!
10 Success rate is 80 percent (4/5), round-trip min/avg/max = 4/4/4 ms
11 NewYork#
```

**Figure 1-29** Output of show arp

```
1  NewYork#sh arp
2  Protocol  Address      Age (min)  Hardware Addr  Type  Interface
3  Internet  172.16.1.1          0   00e0.1e68.2b9c ARPA  Ethernet0
4  Internet  172.16.1.3          -   00e0.1e68.2ad4 ARPA  Ethernet0
5  Internet  172.16.1.2          3   00e0.1e68.2b11 ARPA  Ethernet0
```

case, the router may not know of the new MAC address for the server. A **clear arp** command will clear all entries in the ARP cache, forcing the router to re-ARP for the server.

## Internet Control Message Protocol

ICMP is the Control and Error Message Protocol for IP. It is used by both hosts and routers to communicate things like destinations not reachable, network congestion, redirects to better paths, packet time-to-live expiring, and many others. A full discussion of ICMP can be found in RFC 792 and in Stevens (1994).

Operation

ICMP messages are transported in IP packets and are therefore routable just like any other IP packet. Since each ICMP message is a stand-alone message, there is no flow control or acknowledgment mechanism. ICMP messages may be lost in the network due to corruption or congestion. In this case, if the error condition persists, another message will be generated. If the condition lasts long enough, the chances that one of the messages will get through is almost guaranteed. In practice, we find this to be true.

There are two major types of ICMP messages: query messages and error messages. The query messages are things like the ICMP echo request and echo reply, router advertisement, and address mask request. The majority of the message types are error messages such as destination unreachable, source quench (congestion notification), and time-to-live exceeded.

ICMP messages are never generated when the original datagram being reported upon is addressed to the broadcast or multicast address or when the source address is not a single system. Similarly, no message will be generated in response to another ICMP error message. These restrictions prevent a flood of ICMP messages due to congested networks or misconfigured systems.

Ping (Echo Request & Reply)

There are several basic useful message types. Perhaps the most useful to the network administrator is the ICMP Echo Request and Echo Reply Protocol, which has been implemented in the ping program that appears in almost all IP implementations. A ping packet is the smallest and simplest packet that can be generated and routed on an IP network, making it ideal for troubleshooting connectivity problems. The typical ping implementation will store the current time in the data field of the echo request packet. The echo request is sent to the destination, which returns it to the sender. The sender subtracts the time value contained in the packet from the received time to calculate the round-trip time.

FYI: According to Mike Muuss, ping's author, the name *ping* comes from the similarity to sonar or radar. All three transmit a short burst of energy (an ICMP request packet, a burst of sound, or a burst of radio frequency energy) and analyze the echo returned from remote objects.

The most useful error message indicates that the destination network, host, protocol, or port is unreachable or is unknown. There is one basic message type that encompasses all of these errors, through use of the message code field (shown later in this section). All of these messages indicate that some system in the path from the source to the destination could not properly process an IP packet. There are numerous reasons, ranging from no route to the destination (network or host unreachable), to the destination host not having a program waiting to process the packet when it arrived (protocol or port unreachable).

The Cisco implementation of ping has many useful features. If you enter the command **ping** without any destination address, it starts a dialog to collect information to use in the ping operation. Figure 1-30 shows the full dialog that is available. The number, size, and timeout values of the ping packets can be changed. The extended commands allow you to change the source address. Using this feature, you can specify the source IP address to be that of one of the interfaces on the router (the default is to use the IP address of the interface on which the packet will be sent).

Another extended ping option is changing the transmitted data pattern, which is useful for testing WAN circuits that are sensitive to specific

**Figure 1-30** Extended ping example

```
1 NewYork#ping
2 Protocol [ip]:
3 Target IP address: 172.16.2.2
4 Repeat count [5]:
5 Datagram size [100]:
6 Timeout in seconds [2]:
7 Extended commands [n]: y
8 Source address or interface: 192.168.4.2
9 Type of service [0]:
10 Set DF bit in IP header? [no]:
11 Validate reply data? [no]:
12 Data pattern [0xABCD]:
13 Loose, Strict, Record, Timestamp, Verbose[none]:
14 Sweep range of sizes [n]:
15 Type escape sequence to abort.
16 Sending 5, 100-byte ICMP Echos to 172.16.2.2, timeout is 2 seconds:
17 !!!!!
18) Success rate is 100 percent (5/5), round-trip min/avg/max = 36/36/40 ms
```

patterns of ones or zeros. Several of the IP options can be set, including the d*on't fragment, source route,* and r*ecord route* options. Finally, a range of packet sizes can be specified (which sweeps the range each of the times specified by the *repeat count*).

Trace (Time-to-live Exceeded & Port Unreachable)

Another ICMP message that is useful for troubleshooting is the time-to-live exceeded message. It is used by the **trace** command in the Cisco router (sometimes called *traceroute* on other systems) to report the addresses (and names) of all routers in the path from a source to a destination. Trace works by sending a UDP/IP packet from the source to the destination but sets the time-to-live (TTL) field to 1 (see Figure 1-31). The packet makes it one hop and the router there decrements the TTL, which now goes to zero. The router discards the packet because the TTL is zero and sends an ICMP time-exceeded message to the source system. The source system repeats this test three times (the number of repetitions can be modified) and reports the round-trip time for each of the three tests. The TTL field is then incremented and the test repeated (Figure 1-31 shows only one test packet at each TTL value). The process of incrementing the TTL and repeating the tests continues until the destination system is reached. The UDP packet is addressed to a high-numbered (and hopefully unused) port. When the UDP packets reach the destination, there is no process to receive and process the data, so the destination returns an ICMP *port unreachable* message to the source.

**Figure 1-31**
Trace operation

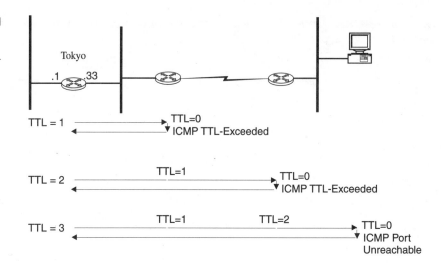

FYI: The Microsoft networking stack sends ICMP echo request packets instead of UDP packets. Theoretically, this is an acceptable mechanism since ICMP messages are carried in IP packets, and an echo request is an informational message which should be processed just like a UDP packet.

An ICMP error message should never be generated due to the failure of an ICMP error message (but may be generated due to the failure of an ICMP informational message). But we are concerned that some networking equipment may not handle a failed ICMP informational message (the echo request message) correctly, leaving the network troubleshooter with invalid or incomplete data regarding the real network problem.

When you invoke the trace command without any arguments, like ping, it interactively asks a number of questions to gather operational parameters. Figure 1-32 shows this dialog and the parameters that you can change.

Sometimes, when running trace where the target is a Cisco router, you will see an asterisk (*) instead of a round-trip time. This tells you that there was no reply received before trace timed out that probe. Cisco routers limit the number of ICMP destination unreachable packets that are generated (limiting their vulnerability to denial-of-service attacks). The * results when a Cisco router does not return an ICMP message due to a short delay between successive probe packets.

**Figure 1-32** Trace interactive dialog

```
1 Tokyo#trace
2 Protocol [ip]:
3 Target IP address: 172.18.1.2
4 Source address: 192.168.2.1
5 Numeric display [n]:
6 Timeout in seconds [3]:
7 Probe count [3]:
8 Minimum Time to Live [1]:
9 Maximum Time to Live [30]:
10 Port Number [33434]:
11 Loose, Strict, Record, Timestamp, Verbose[none]:
12 Type escape sequence to abort.
13 Tracing the route to 172.18.1.2
14
15    1 192.168.4.2 16 msec 16 msec 16 msec
16    2 172.16.1.34 40 msec *  40 msec
17 Tokyo#
```

Packet Format

The ICMP message format, shown in Figure 1-33, has only three fixed fields: *type, code,* and *checksum.* The remaining contents depend on the message type. Figure 1-33 shows the typical format for most of the messages. Refer to RFC792 (Postel 1981b) for details of each message format.

Within each ICMP message is a message type—which describes the type of the message—and a message code—which breaks down the message type into subtypes. For example, message type 3 is *destination unreachable,* which has 15 different codes that indicate why the packet was undeliverable. Some message types contain additional information. Details of the exact format of these messages may be found in RFC792 and in Stevens (1994). A full list of ICMP message types and codes may be found in Table 1-6.

The ICMP echo request and echo reply packets have a slightly different format, as shown in Figure 1-34. *Identifier* and *sequence number* fields fill the previously unused section of the ICMP message. The *identifier* field is given a unique value by each ping application so that the system can have multiple ping applications running simultaneously. This is

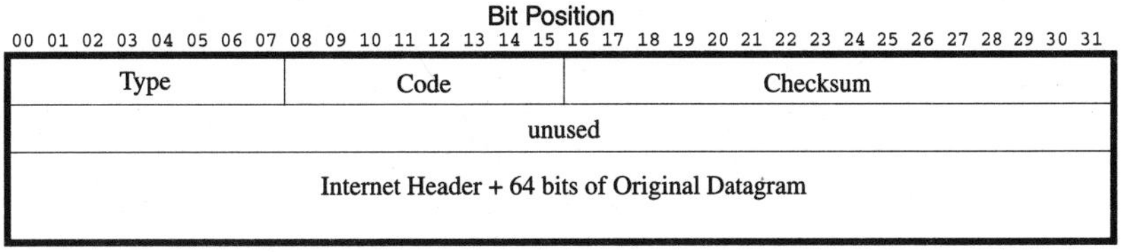

**Figure 1-33**
ICMP message
format

Bit Position
00 01 02 03 04 05 06 07 08 09 10 11 12 13 14 15 16 17 18 19 20 21 22 23 24 25 26 27 28 29 30 31

| Type | Code | Checksum |
|---|---|---|
| unused | | |
| Internet Header + 64 bits of Original Datagram | | |

analogous to the use of the port number in TCP or UDP packets. The *sequence number* field is used to uniquely identify each echo request and reply. It is used to match received replies with the corresponding request.

**Table 1-2**

Common data-link type codes

| Type | Code | Description | Informational or Error |
|------|------|-------------|------------------------|
| 1 | 0 | Echo reply | I |
| 2 | | Destination unreachable | |
| | 0 | Net unreachable | E |
| | 1 | Host unreachable | E |
| | 2 | Protocol unreachable | E |
| | 3 | Port unreachable | E |
| | 4 | Fragmentation needed and DF set | E |
| | 5 | Source route failed | E |
| | 6 | Destination network unknown | E |
| | 7 | Destination host unknown | E |
| | 8 | Source host isolated (obsolete) | E |
| | 9 | Destination network administratively prohibited | E |
| | 10 | Destination host administratively prohibited | E |
| | 11 | Network unreachable for TOS | E |
| | 12 | Host unreachable for TOS | E |
| | 13 | Communication administratively prohibited | E |
| | 14 | Host precedence violation | E |
| | 15 | Precedence cutoff in effect | E |
| 4 | 0 | Source quench | E |
| 5 | | Redirect | |
| | 0 | Redirect datagrams for the network | E |
| | 1 | Redirect datagrams for the host | E |
| | 2 | Redirect datagrams for the type of service and network | E |
| | 3 | Redirect datagrams for the type of service and host | E |
| 8 | 0 | Echo request | I |

**Table 1-2**

Continued

| Type | Code | Description | Informational or Error |
|------|------|-------------|------------------------|
| 9 | 0 | Router advertisement | I |
| 10 | 0 | Router selection | I |
| 11 | | Time exceeded | |
| | 0 | Time to live exceeded in transit | E |
| | 1 | Fragment reassembly time exceeded | E |
| 12 | | Parameter problem | |
| | 0 | Pointer indicates the error | E |
| | 1 | Missing a required option | E |
| | 2 | Bad length | E |
| 13 | 0 | Timestamp request | I |
| 14 | 0 | Timestamp reply | I |
| 15 | 0 | Information request | I |
| 16 | 0 | Information reply | I |
| 17 | 0 | Address mask request | I |
| 18 | 0 | Address mask reply | I |
| 30 | 0 | Traceroute | I |
| 31 | 0 | Datagram conversion error | E |

Source: Refer to RFC1700 (Postel 1994) for a list of ICMP types, codes, descriptions, and references.

The data field is variable in length and often contains a time stamp that is used by the sending system to determine the round-trip time. The sending system records the current time in the data field of the echo request and sends the packet. The target system does not modify the data field when the packet is received. The IP addresses are swapped, and the code field is modified to that of an echo reply packet. The echo reply packet is returned to the sender. When the echo reply is received by the sender, the current time is compared against the time recorded in the returned packet. The difference is the round-trip time. Very clever!

**Figure 1-34**
ICMP echo request/reply message format

Bit Position
00 01 02 03 04 05 06 07 08 09 10 11 12 13 14 15 16 17 18 19 20 21 22 23 24 25 26 27 28 29 30 31

| Type | Code | Checksum |
|------|------|----------|
| Identifier | | Sequence Number |
| Data... | | |

# Performance

In the mid-1980s TCP/IP performance was pretty low—about 240Kbps. A number of researchers and networking experts suggested that it could never operate at high speed. However, one researcher, Van Jacobson, didn't see where the protocol itself was limiting the throughput. So, he set out to determine if the protocol itself was the limiting factor or if existing implementations were limiting the throughput. He found that the BSD UNIX kernel performed many data copies during the processing of a single IP packet. After optimizing the operating system processing of IP, he was able to achieve 9.8Mbps performance over his laboratory Ethernet. In fact, he reported performance that was within a few percent of theoretical maximum throughput of an Ethernet.

Later research and development done by Van Jacobson, Dave Borman, and others improved TCP/IP's performance over long delay paths (multi-second round-trip times), high-bandwidth paths (45Mbps to 800Mbps), and in congested networks (congestion avoidance and slow start). In one test, Van was able to demonstrate a throughput test from his lab in California to the Interop show floor in Washington, D.C., where most of the path was over the newly completed NSF 45Mbps backbone. The test results showed more than 9Mbps throughput. Van suggested after running the test that the bandwidth of the show floor Ethernet was the likely reason the test didn't show higher throughput. Another test with Dave Borman of Cray Computers showed throughputs in excess of 800Mbps between two Cray supercomputers. Clearly, TCP/IP can move data quickly.

Jacobson's TCP improvements were only on the computer systems that were the end points of a connection. No upgrades were needed in the routers in the path between the two computer systems he used in some of his experiments. This doesn't imply that improvements to routers have not been useful. Advances in router software and hardware have allowed internetworks to support many, many people simultaneously transferring files and searching the World Wide Web.

TCP's sliding window protocol, in conjunction with some improvements in IP processing and congestion avoidance, has proven to be a very good performing internetwork protocol.

# ■ ■ ■ CCIE Tips

If you are preparing for your CCIE test or recertification, you should know how TCP/IP works, including things like port numbers, TCP windowing, the three-way handshake, and throughput issues. It is also useful to be able to use the OSI model to help you troubleshoot problems. Being able to quickly isolate a problem to a specific OSI layer and concentrating your troubleshooting at that layer will make it much easier to pass the hands-on lab test. Let's look at some specific things that you should know.

## Troubleshooting

The OSI model can be applied to many troubleshooting problems to help you isolate the source of problems. Being able to relate router diagnostic information to different layers allows you to quickly reduce the scope of a troubleshooting task. There is one particular example that has occurred to us on multiple occasions. Figure 1-35 shows a simple network topology that is not passing traffic, and Figure 1-36 shows the diagnostic steps taken to troubleshoot the problem.

Pings between Tokyo and NewYork are failing (lines 1-5). The output of **show interface** (lines 7-29) shows the interfaces to be operational (interface is up, line protocol is up). Since the line protocol is up, we know that the routers are exchanging keepalive packets, therefore, the

**Figure 1-35**
Tokyo to NewYork
network failure

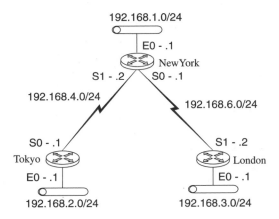

**Figure 1-36** Output of debug ip igrp

```
1  Tokyo#ping 192.168.4.2
2
3  Type escape sequence to abort.
4  Sending 5, 100-byte ICMP Echos to 192.168.4.2, timeout is 2 seconds:
5  .....
6  Success rate is 0 percent (0/5)
7  Tokyo#sh int s 0
8  Serial0 is up, line protocol is up
9    Hardware is HD64570
10    Internet address is 192.168.4.1/24
11    MTU 1500 bytes, BW 1544 Kbit, DLY 20000 usec, rely 255/255, load 1/255
12    Encapsulation HDLC, loopback not set, keepalive set (10 sec)
13    Last input 00:00:04, output 00:00:08, output hang never
14    Last clearing of "show interface" counters never
15    Input queue: 0/75/0 (size/max/drops); Total output drops: 0
16    Queueing strategy: weighted fair
17    Output queue: 0/1000/64/0 (size/max total/threshold/drops)
18       Conversations  0/1 (active/max active/threshold)
19       Reserved Conversations 0/0/64 (allocated/max allocated)
20    5 minute input rate 0 bits/sec, 0 packets/sec
21    5 minute output rate 0 bits/sec, 0 packets/sec
22       99 packets input, 6348 bytes, 0 no buffer
23       Received 95 broadcasts, 0 runts, 0 giants, 0 throttles
24       0 input errors, 0 CRC, 0 frame, 0 overrun, 0 ignored, 0 abort
25       103 packets output, 6726 bytes, 0 underruns
26       0 output errors, 0 collisions, 2 interface resets
27       0 output buffer failures, 0 output buffers swapped out
28       1 carrier transitions
29       DCD=up  DSR=up  DTR=up  RTS=up  CTS=up
30  Tokyo#
31  Tokyo#sh ip route
32  Codes: C - connected, S - static, I - IGRP, R - RIP, M - mobile, B - BGP
33         D - EIGRP, EX - EIGRP external, O - OSPF, IA - OSPF inter area
34         N1 - OSPF NSSA external type 1, N2 - OSPF NSSA external type 2
35         E1 - OSPF external type 1, E2 - OSPF external type 2, E - EGP
36         i - IS-IS, L1 - IS-IS level-1, L2 - IS-IS level-2, * - candidate default
37         U - per-user static route, o - ODR
38
39  Gateway of last resort is not set
40
41  C    192.168.4.0/24 is directly connected, Serial0
42  C    192.168.2.0/24 is directly connected, Ethernet0
43  Tokyo#debug ip igrp ev
44  IGRP event debugging is on
45  Tokyo#debug ip igrp tr
46  IGRP protocol debugging is on
47  Tokyo#
48  IGRP: sending update to 255.255.255.255 via Ethernet0 (192.168.2.1)
49        network 192.168.4.0, metric=8476
50  IGRP: Update contains 0 interior, 1 system, and 0 exterior routes.
51  IGRP: Total routes in update: 1
52  IGRP: sending update to 255.255.255.255 via Serial0 (192.168.4.1)
53        network 192.168.2.0, metric=1100
54  IGRP: Update contains 0 interior, 1 system, and 0 exterior routes.
55  IGRP: Total routes in update: 1
56  IGRP: received update from invalid source 192.168.6.1 on Serial0
57  Tokyo#
58  Tokyo#undeb all
59  All possible debugging has been turned off
```

data-link layer is operating properly. This means that there is no problem with a cabling failure or a CSU/DSU. Something must be wrong at the network layer.

The routing protocol in this case is IGRP, but there are no IGRP routes in our routing table (lines 31-42). Why are we not receiving IGRP updates? There might be some information that we could collect relative to the IGRP routing protocol failure that might point to the network-layer failure cause. It is time to use some selected debugging to gather information about the network layer operation. Using **debug ip igrp events** and **debug ip igrp transactions**, we wait for IGRP packets to be transmitted and received. Examining the debug output (line 56), we see that the address from which the packets are originating is supposed to be on the New York to London link. It seems that the serial cables from Tokyo and London were connected to the wrong ports during a recent wiring reconfiguration at New York.

The trap to avoid in this scenario is thinking that the problem lies at the data-link layer, when in fact, the data-link layer is working. Examining network layer debug output alerted us to the real problem (solvable by either address reconfiguration or by swapping cables on New York).

Similarly, the ability to ping a remote destination means that the network layer is operating correctly and that troubleshooting should focus on higher layers. But with access lists present, pings may not be forwarded, so a ping failure does not necessarily mean that the network layer is not operating properly.

## Open Jaw Routes

A very common failure in routed networks is something called *open jaw routes*. This term comes from the airline industry where a route that does not terminate at the source looks like the profile view of an open jaw (e.g. Baltimore to Dallas and then terminating in Atlanta.) In the internetworking world, this happens when a packet is correctly routed to the destination, but the return path is not available. The symptom is that there is no response from the remote system and a route exists to it.

A good way to troubleshoot this problem is with **trace**. At some point along the path, the trace will die (output a series of asterisks). In this case, a routing problem exists in at least one of the remote routers or in the destination. The next hop after the last working hop is a good place to start looking.

One caveat on open jaw routes: If a routing transition is occurring and the routers have not converged on the new routes, an open jaw route may exist until convergence is achieved. For RIP and IGRP, this may take several minutes.

## Port Numbers

Know how port numbers are used. You must know the common port numbers and how to determine which ports an application uses to allow you to properly configure access lists, where traffic filtering is needed on a per-application basis. Learn how FTP and passive FTP operate. These two versions of the File Transfer Protocol application use multiple ports in very different ways. Stevens (1994) is a good reference for review.

Can you build an access-list that allows TCP access in one direction but not in the other? This type of access-list is used to create application-level firewalls using routers. We are concentrating on routing in this book, but since one-way access-lists are often misunderstood, we'll explore this topic in more depth. For an in-depth explanation of access-lists, refer to Lewis (1998) or the Cisco documentation.

The first packet of the TCP three-way handshake is unique in the entire session. The flags field of the TCP segment will contain only the SYN flag bit set (remember, the three-way handshake is the sequence SYN, SYN+ACK, ACK). Since there is a unique packet at the start of a TCP session, we can filter on it to allow or prevent the start of a session.

The syntax of the Cisco extended access-list is as follows:

```
access-list 101 {permit|deny} tcp <src-ip> <src-wildcard-mask>
[<src-port>] <dst-ip> <dst-wildcard-mask> [<dst-port>] [<opt>
<args>] [established]
```

**Figure 1-37**
Access list network

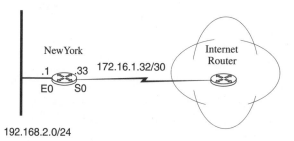

New York

.1    .33    172.16.1.32/30

E0    S0

Internet
Router

192.168.2.0/24

**Figure 1-38**  *Access list example*

```
1 hostname NewYork
2 interface Ethernet0
3  ip address 192.168.2.1 255.255.255.0
4 interface Serial0
5  ip address 172.16.1.33 255.255.255.252
6  ip access-group 101 in
7 ip route 0.0.0.0 0.0.0.0 172.16.1.34
8 access-list 101 permit tcp any 192.168.2.0 0.0.0.255 established
9 access-list 101 deny   ip any any
```

A simple packet-filtering firewall can be built that allows connections to be initiated to the "outside" and prevents connections from being initiated from outside the protected area. In Figure 1-37, we need to prevent connections from the Internet into our private network, while allowing connections initiated from within our network to still work. The router configuration that implements this filter is shown in Figure 1-38. Note the use of the **established** keyword (line 8). This allows any TCP packet from the Internet (any source address) to any host address on our protected net (192.168.1.0) to be accepted, as long as the connection was established from inside our network. All other packets inbound on this interface are denied. This access-list is applied (line 6) to all inbound traffic (that's all traffic coming in from the Internet) on Serial 0. Similar access-lists can be built to filter on specific port numbers, limiting your network's vulnerability to specific types of traffic.

# The Future of IP (IPv6)

The current TCP/IP protocol suite has been around since 1981, and while it has had a number of minor changes incorporated, it has remained nearly unchanged. It is media independent and in some cases operates over very crude media (there are stories of operation over multiple strands of barbed wire in some outlying areas of the world).

A new version of IP (not TCP) was standardized in 1995 (Deering and Hinden 1995). It is called IPv6 (IPv5 was already taken), and it simplifies the IP packet format as well as increasing the address space to 128 bits each for the source and destination addresses. This will allow TCP/IP to continue to grow to larger and larger applications. Some of the ideas being discussed are to allow each power meter in the United States to be assigned an IP address, so that they can be controlled and read remotely. Another is to address all of the cable television control boxes at each home in the United States.

Imagine extending the Internet into your home to include your stereo, microwave, coffeepot, and heating/cooling system. Such systems exist today through the use of the X-10 system of remote control devices. An IP interface to such a system is likely in the near future (if not already here). This will cause a remarkable demand for a large number of addresses—which IPv6 will support.

As we move to IPv6, the routing protocols and methods of troubleshooting will remain nearly the same. All the same tools exist (trace, ping, etc.). If you wish to learn more about IPv6, refer to Huitema (1996).

With a good understanding of the fundamentals of TCP/IP, you are prepared to tackle the issues of advanced routing.

## SUMMARY

The TCP/IP protocol suite has demonstrated its usefulness in real-world networks. The media independence and packet switching model upon which it is based provides a flexible and reliable data delivery mechanism that satisfies many of today's internetworking requirements.

The OSI model supplies us with a good conceptual model of how the components of internetworking operate together. The relationship to the operation of the post office gives us a way to relate the operation of internetworking. Conceptually, letters and packages in the post office are similar to packets in a network. Routers operate like post offices, receiving packets from one source and forwarding them to the correct destination.

We examine how data multiplexing, demultiplexing, and encapsulation are important to internetworking. As user data enters the protocol stack, each layer in the TCP/IP protocol stack performs its functions, encapsulating the user data (and any other layer information) within headers that are used for directing the data to the correct destination. Packets from multiple users or applications are multiplexed (that is, they share) the path through the TCP/IP system and onto the network.

At the destination, received packets are demultiplexed by examining the encapsulation headers and selecting the correct upper layer TCP/IP function to process the packet. As the proper upper layer TCP/IP functions are identified, the headers are stripped, decapsulating the user data. Finally, the user data are delivered to the destination application.

The protocols within the TCP/IP suite are examined, describing the functions provided by each. Each protocol specifically does not provide some functions, and these were clearly identified. The packet formats of each protocol are covered with a description of how the important fields are used. An introduction to basic IP addressing is also covered, but the addressing complexities found in today's internetworks is left for discussion in later chapters.

With the short discussion of TCP/IP, perhaps augmented by reading some of the referenced books that contain complete coverage, you should be well prepared for learning about IP routing in Cisco networks.

CHAPTER 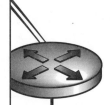 2

# How Routing Works

We've learned how TCP/IP works between two directly connected systems. But few networks are simple enough that they are comprised of only a single network segment. Most networks are built of multiple segments that are scattered throughout the organization.

This chapter will introduce you to the routing process, how network masks operate, how the route lookup is performed, and how subnetting works. As part of the discussion on how the route lookup is performed, we will describe the performance differences between the various models of Cisco routers. Our coverage of these topics will provide you a sound foundation for evaluating future routers and routing architectures as Cisco brings them to market.

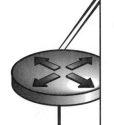

# Routers

A typical network, pictured in Figure 2-1, consists of some number of local area networks (e.g., Ethernet or TokenRing) and wide area network links (e.g., PPP over leased lines or Frame Relay), all connected by routers.

Routers may seem like very complex devices, but their basic operation is very simple. They perform two basic functions, the first of which is to direct packets toward their correct destinations. The second function is to maintain the routing tables from which the routers determine the correct paths. Let's examine how the packet forwarding process and the routing table maintenance processes work.

In Chapter 1, we discussed how the operation of TCP/IP is similar to writing a letter and sending it through the postal system. The operation of each post office is very similar to the operation of a router. The zip code is identified within the address, and the first few digits of the zip code are used to determine the best path to the destination. Eventually, the letter will be received by a post office that contains the first few digits of the zip code. Then, additional digits of the zip code will be used to select the best path from that point. This process continues, with additional digits of the zip code being used as needed to forward the letter.

Routers operate the same way. When a packet is received, the destination address is extracted from the packet. Next, the network number of the destination is found within the destination address (this is like finding the zip code within the postal address). Then the routing table is

**Figure 2-1**
Typical network

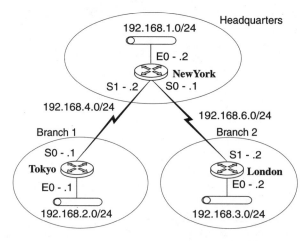

searched to find an entry that matches the network number found in the destination address. Each routing table entry contains information about which interface to use to forward the packet, as well as the address of the router that is next in the path to the destination.

In Figure 2-1, a packet from X to Z would be sent to router New York, which would determine that the packet needed to be forwarded to router London. The final step is performed by router London when it finds that host Z is connected to a network that is connected to one of its interfaces. In this case, London will use the ARP protocol to discover the MAC address of host Z and deliver the packet to its destination.

A key feature of routers that distinguishes them from bridges and switches is that they connect media types that have different data-link framing. In a typical network, there are often more than just one type of LAN and WAN technology in use, each with its own characteristics, data-link protocol, and addressing.

The second function that routers perform is to maintain routing tables. This is typically done by sharing information about the topology of the network. In the post office analogy, each post office knows about its neighbors and how to reach them. They also know, by looking at zip code routing tables, which neighboring post office is the best one to use to reach any zip code.

Routers operate in a similar manner. The information about the current topology of the network is shared among routers in an intranet. This information might consist of things like which links are operational or which links have higher capacity. The specific information shared depends on the routing protocol that is used.

In the remainder of this chapter, we'll learn how routers perform packet forwarding. We will briefly discuss the contents of the routing table in this chapter but will defer the details of individual routing protocols for later chapters.

# Finding the IP Destination Address

Just as the postal system reads the destination address from an envelope, routers read the destination address from the network-layer header of a packet. For example, locate the source IP address in the packet headers shown in Figure 2-2. It is the 32-bit number (four bytes) that starts at byte number 13 in the IP header. The destination address is next, located at bytes 17-20.

**Figure 2-2**
IP packet trace

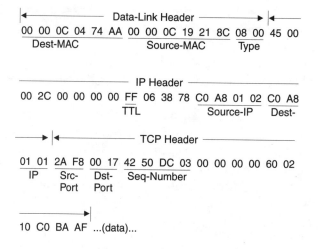

FYI: We've included the data-link, IP, and TCP headers in Figure 2-2 so you can see what a packet looks like on the wire (or as viewed by a packet-decoding tool). A few of the fields are labeled. A good exercise is to label the remainder of the fields and decode them. Some interesting ones to find are the protocol ID in the IP header, the TCP window size, the IP header length, and the total packet length.

Because all the header fields up to the address fields are fixed length, the router can quickly find the destination address: just look at bytes 17-20 of the IP packet. There you will find the hexadecimal numbers c0 a8 01 01. Using the hex-to-decimal conversion table in Appendix A, we translate each byte into its dotted decimal (also called *dotted quad*) equivalent: 192.168.1.1.

## The Network Mask

Once the router has the destination address, it must divide the destination address into two components: the network number and the ID of the host on that network. IP was designed to allow the division between the network number and the host number to be done based on the class of the address. Recall from Chapter 1 that a class A address uses one octet of network identifier, a class B uses two octets of network

**Figure 2-3**
Binary AND
operation

|  | | | | |
|---|---|---|---|---|
| 1st Bit | 0 | 0 | 1 | 1 |
| AND 2nd Bit | 0 | 1 | 0 | 1 |
| = Result | 0 | 0 | 0 | 1 |

identifier, while a class C address uses three octets of network identifier. The remaining bits of each address identify the host on those networks.

The router extracts the destination IP address from the packet, then separates the network number from the host ID, using a process called *masking*. Masking compares two binary numbers, bit position by bit position. In each bit position, when both numbers have a one, the result is a one. If the bits in either number are zero, the result is a zero. Mathematically, this is called a binary *AND* operation. A good way to remember this is that only when the two numbers are one AND one will an answer of one result. Figure 2-3 shows how this works for all combinations of zero and one. This method is applied to a set of 8-bit numbers in Figure 2-4.

There is an easy way to remember how this works. Look at the lower binary number (the mask). Where there is a one, it acts like a pipe and the upper number drops through (0 AND 1 = 0 while 1 AND 1 = 1). Where there is a zero in the mask, it acts like a stopper and nothing (a zero) is the result (0 AND 0 = 0 while 1 AND 0 = 0). This is shown in Example 4 in Figure 2-4.

But how does the router determine how many ones exist in the mask for a given address? It determines the class of the address and from that, creates the network mask, a new 32-bit number in which ones are set where the network number exists and zeros are set where the host ID exists. The network number is always on the left and the host ID is always on the right. Therefore, the network mask is really just a yardstick that is used to measure how many bits comprise the network number. Any remaining bits are set to zero, indicating that the corresponding

**Figure 2-4**
Masking

|  | Example 1 | Example 2 | Example 3 |
|---|---|---|---|
| 1st Byte | 1010 1010 | 1100 1011 | 0110 0101 |
| AND 2nd Byte | 1111 0000 | 1111 1000 | 1110 0000 |
| = Result | 1010 0000 | 1100 1000 | 0110 0000 |

Example 4

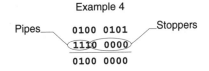

Pipes _____ 0100 0101 _____ Stoppers
1110 0000
0100 0000

**Figure 2-5**
IP Network masks

| | | | |
|---|---|---|---|
| Class A Address | 10 . 5 . 200 . 1 | | |
| Binary Format | (0)000 1010.0000 0101.1100 1000.0000 0001 | | |
| Mask | 1111 1111.0000 0000.0000 0000.0000 0000 | | |

| | | | |
|---|---|---|---|
| Class B Address | 140 . 96 . 72 . 13 | | |
| Binary Format | (10)00 1100.0110 0000.0100 1000.0000 1101 | | |
| Mask | 1111 1111.1111 1111.0000 0000.0000 0000 | | |

| | | | |
|---|---|---|---|
| Class C Address | 199 . 231 . 64 . 31 | | |
| Binary Format | (110)0 0111.1110 0111.0100 0000.0001 1111 | | |
| Mask | 1111 1111.1111 1111.1111 1111.0000 0000 | | |

portion of the destination address contains host-specific information. Figure 2-5 shows examples of network masks for several IP addresses.

The router performs the binary AND operation between the destination address and the network mask to extract the network identifier. Figure 2-6 shows the AND operation on the examples from Figure 2-5. Looking carefully at the resulting network numbers, you can see that the bits in the host ID portion of the address have been set to zero.

**Figure 2-6**
Address AND mask
operation

| | | | |
|---|---|---|---|
| Class A Address | 10 . 5 . 200 . 1 | | |
| Binary Format | 0000 1010.0000 0101.1100 1000.0000 0001 | | |
| Mask | 1111 1111.0000 0000.0000 0000.0000 0000 | | |
| **Binary AND** | | | |
| Network ID | 0000 1010.0000 0000.0000 0000.0000 0000 | | |

| | | | |
|---|---|---|---|
| Class B Address | 140 . 96 . 72 . 13 | | |
| Binary Format | 1000 1100.0110 0000.0100 1000.0000 1101 | | |
| Mask | 1111 1111.1111 1111.0000 0000.0000 0000 | | |
| **Binary AND** | | | |
| Network ID | 1000 1100.0110 0000.0000 0000.0000 0000 | | |

| | | | |
|---|---|---|---|
| Class C Address | 199 . 231 . 200 . 31 | | |
| Binary Format | 1100 0111.1110 0111.0100 0000.0001 1111 | | |
| Mask | 1111 1111.1111 1111.1111 1111.0000 0000 | | |
| **Binary AND** | | | |
| Network ID | 1100 0111.1110 0111.0100 0000.0000 0000 | | |

FYI: If you are not familiar with the binary AND operation and converting addresses from dotted decimal to binary and back, it is tempting to look at the dotted decimal addresses and try to determine the network number directly from them. This is not difficult with classful addressing, however, it will not work in many cases involving subnetting or classless addressing. We will cover both of these masking techniques in this chapter and will give you several examples that demonstrate how the dotted decimal numbers can fool even the most experienced network person. Suffice it to say that the only way to accurately determine the network number of an IP address is to do the binary AND operation we've just described. If you would like to learn more about how this process works, the Chesapeake Subnet Calculator (see Appendix B) shows the binary AND operation and the equivalent dotted decimal notation for any valid IP address.

# The Routing Process

Once the router has determined the network number, it must find which interface is the best one to use in forwarding the packet to its destination. This is accomplished by finding a matching network number from a table in the router's memory. As we'll see later, the majority of the packet-forwarding cases require multiple router hops before a packet will reach its destination.

Let's follow part of the process as a packet traverses a small network. In this case, the packet is from Tokyo and is going to the NMS workstation whose IP address is 192.168.3.3. The packet has already been sent from Tokyo to New York.

In Figure 2-7, step 1, the packet is received by New York, and its destination network number is determined. Looking in the routing table in step 2, New York finds the outgoing interface name and a next-hop address in the routing table entry. The next-hop address belongs to the next router that should receive the packet (London). Since our lab network uses a serial link, ARP is not needed, but if network 192.168.6.0 were a LAN, then New York may have to ARP for London's MAC address. If prior traffic has already forced an ARP exchange, then it is not necessary to ARP again. The packet is then delivered (step 3) to the next-hop router (London in this example).

Once the packet reaches the last router, a local delivery process is used to forward the packet to the final destination. The local delivery process

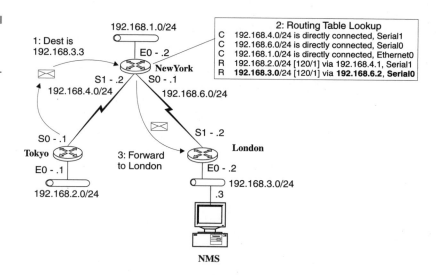

**Figure 2-7**

Routing to a remote destination

on the Ethernet uses ARP and is therefore useful to examine. In Figure 2-8, step 1, the packet addressed to the NMS workstation is received by London. In step 2, London finds that the destination host is on a network that is connected to one of its interfaces (the routing table entry is marked with a C to indicate that it is directly connected), and a local delivery must be done. An ARP request is issued (step 3) to map the IP address of the destination to its MAC address. Once the MAC address is received in the ARP reply (step 4), the packet may be forwarded directly to the destination host (step 5).

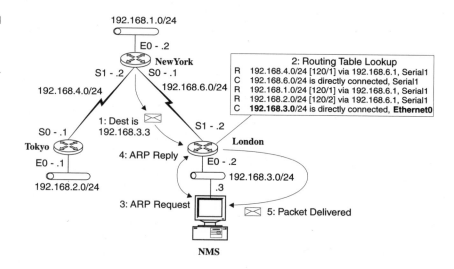

**Figure 2-8**

Routing to a local destination

# The Routing Table

The second thing routers do is maintain routing tables. These tables may be created by the network administrator (that's you!). or may be created by the exchange of routing information with other routers.

When a router is initially booted, it only knows about its directly connected interfaces. These interfaces appear as entries marked with a C in the first column (which you should have noticed in the figures in the previous section). If the routers in a network are running a routing protocol, additional routing table entries will be created as the router learns about networks connected to its neighbors. Each routing table entry will be marked with a letter to indicate the source of the routing information. Table 2-1 shows the letters that correspond to each of the common IP routing protocols.

When a packet is received, its destination address is extracted from the packet and the destination network number is determined as described earlier. The destination network number is then checked against the network number in each routing table entry. If a match is found, the packet is transmitted on the interface specified in the matching routing table entry.

| **Table 2-1** | **Letter** | **Routing Information Source** |
|---|---|---|
| Sources of routing information | C | Directly connected (an interface is connected to this network) |
| | S | Static route (manually configured by the network administrator) |
| | R | Routing Information Protocol (RIP) |
| | I | Interior Gateway Routing Protocol (Cisco's IGRP) |
| | O | Open Shortest Path First (OSPF) |
| | D | Enhanced Interior Gateway Routing Protocol (Cisco's EIGRP) |
| | B | Border Gateway Protocol (BGP) |
| | E | Exterior Gateway Protocol (EGP) |

Note: The best source for the letter designations is in the output of **show ip route**, which includes a key at the beginning of the output. Different IOS releases have support for different protocols and protocol options, so this is the best way to see which protocols are supported in your router.

```
NewYork#sh ip route
Codes: C - connected, S - static, I - IGRP, R - RIP, M - mobile, B - BGP
       D - EIGRP, EX - EIGRP external, O - OSPF, IA - OSPF inter area
       N1 - OSPF NSSA external type 1, N2 - OSPF NSSA external type 2
       E1 - OSPF external type 1, E2 - OSPF external type 2, E - EGP
       i - IS-IS, L1 - IS-IS level-1, L2 - IS-IS level-2, * - candidate default
       U - per-user static route, o - ODR

Gateway of last resort is not set

C    192.168.4.0/24 is directly connected, Serial1
C    192.168.6.0/24 is directly connected, Serial0
C    192.168.1.0/24 is directly connected, Ethernet0
R    192.168.2.0/24 [120/1] via 192.168.4.1, 00:00:11, Serial1
R    192.168.3.0/24 [120/1] via 192.168.6.2, 00:00:08, Serial0
```

Fields: 1   2   3   4   5   6   7

If the routers are configured to run a routing protocol, they will begin exchanging information about the networks to which they are connected. Through this exchange, New York will learn of the networks connected to Tokyo and London, resulting in the routing table of Figure 2-9.

The *Codes* section identifies the letters used to key the source of the routing information. The *Gateway of last resort* is empty because we have not configured a default route. Then there is a separate line for each network segment in our test lab.

There are two types of routes shown. The first are directly connected networks. They include only the network number of the segment and the interface to which the router is connected. The 192.168.1.0, 192.168.4.0, and 192.168.6.0 entries are directly connected routes.

The second type of route is one that is learned from neighboring routers via a routing protocol. The letters in Field 1 indicate the source of the routing information, as identified in the *Codes* section. Field 2 is the network number of the segment to which the route exists. Field 3 is the number of bits in the network mask. There are two numbers in Field 4: The first is the administrative distance of the information source, which we will discuss later in this chapter. The second number is the metric for the route. The metric values depend on the source of the routing information. Field 5 contains the IP address of the next-hop router, while Field 6 contains the number of seconds since this routing information was updated. Finally, Field 7 shows which interface the router will use to forward a packet toward the destination network.

Static routes (which we'll cover in depth later) have an administrative distance, next-hop IP address, and which interface to use.

Some static routes may be configured as "interface" routes, which means that they indicate only which interface to use. These routes must be on point-to-point network segments. In other words, any interface static route must be via a network link that will guarantee delivery of data to only one destination.

# Administrative Distance

Administrative distance is a way that Cisco routers use to rate the trustworthiness of routing information. Each routing protocol is assigned a default trust rating, with better protocols getting a better rating (the lower the number, the better). The range of valid values is 0-255, where zero is used for directly connected routes and 255 is used for any route from a source that cannot be trusted. The other sources of routing information fall between these values as shown in Table 2-2.

The more advanced routing protocols have lower administrative distance defaults, forcing them to be selected if there are multiple sources of routing information. For example, the network in Figure 2-10 shows segment 192.168.5.0 available via EIGRP in Tokyo and via RIP in London. New York selects the "best" source of routing information. Since EIGRP's administrative distance is 90 and RIP's administrative distance is 120, the EIGRP information is more trusted. Looking in New York's routing table, we find that EIGRP's route is preferred. A failure of the 192.168.4.0 link will result in the loss of EIGRP information from Tokyo. In this case, the RIP route via London will then be believed and will appear in the routing table.

**Table 2-2**

Administrative distance defaults

| Routing Information Source | Default Distance |
| --- | --- |
| Connected interface | 0 |
| Static route | 1 |
| Enhanced IGRP summary route | 5 |
| External BGP | 20 |
| Internal enhanced IGRP | 90 |
| IGRP | 100 |
| OSPF | 110 |
| IS-IS | 115 |
| RIP | 120 |
| EGP | 140 |
| Internal BGP | 200 |
| Unknown/untrusted | 255 |

**Figure 2-10**
Administrative
distance

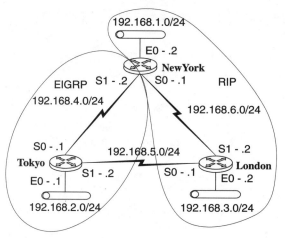

NewYork's Routing Table

```
C    192.168.4.0/24 is directly connected, Serial1
D    192.168.5.0/24 [90/2681856] via 192.168.4.1, 00:00:31, Serial1
C    192.168.6.0/24 is directly connected, Serial0
C    192.168.1.0/24 is directly connected, Ethernet0
D    192.168.2.0/24 [90/2195456] via 192.168.4.1, 00:00:31, Serial1
R    192.168.3.0/24 [120/1] via 192.168.6.2, 00:00:09, Serial0
```

FYI: A word of caution is imperative here. It is tempting to run multiple routing protocols with the idea that if one fails, the administrative distance of the other will allow it to take over. The problem is that each routing protocol has different convergence times, resulting in each protocol having a different picture of the state of the network during a transition. The result for certain topologies is that routing loops are formed until all protocols converge on the new topology. This can cause severe connectivity problems during the convergence time. Routing loops may cause links to become overloaded as routers forward packets between one another at very high speed. It is an understatement to say that this is not good.

Instead, redistribute routing protocols where it is necessary to pass routes between them. A good candidate for redistribution in Figure 2-10 is in NewYork. Checking routes in Tokyo and London shows us that neither router has a route to the Ethernet connected to the other router. This is because the routers are running different routing protocols and NewYork is not redistributing the information between the two protocols. Adding route redistribution to NewYork can propagate the RIP routes into EIGRP and vice versa. We will cover the topic of route redistribution in detail in Chapter 6.

Static routes are set by a network administrator, so they default to an administrative distance of one. You can change the default administrative distance to create floating static routes. A floating static route has its administrative distance set such that the routing protocol in use overrides the static route. But when a network failure causes loss of dynamic routing information, the static route will be used. This can be used to create backup routes, and to force a dial-on-demand link to be used as a backup. We will see how this works in the chapter on static routing.

Finally, any untrusted source of routing information should be assigned an administrative distance of 255, causing that information to be ignored by the router. This is helpful to use with routing protocols where you wish to ignore any routing information from an untrusted source.

# The Routing Table Lookup

In an operational network, routers exchange information with one another about which networks are reachable. Each router builds a table that lists all of the reachable networks. It is this table that the router checks to determine the best path to a given destination. The sample routing table shown in Figure 2-9 contains the network address, network mask, the routing metric of the path, the interface to use, and the IP address of the next router in the path to the destination (if another hop is required). We will examine Cisco routing tables in more detail in later chapters and learn other things that determine the contents of the routing tables.

Conceptually, this is a very simple operation. The router uses the network identifier that it obtained from the packet that must be forwarded. It searches the routing table for a network number that matches the one from the packet. When a match is found, the packet is forwarded to the next router in the path to the destination.

# Switching Paths in Cisco Routers

In practice, Cisco routers perform a number of high-performance speedups that make the lookup function happen very quickly. These functions have changed ºover the lifetime of the IOS. The basic lookup function (called *process switching*) relies on the router CPU to perform the lookup. The fast switching process is the next higher speed router lookup function. It uses a hashed lookup in a cache of recent destination addresses to reduce the search time. Cisco has developed a number of even faster lookup methods, some based on high-performance hardware.

The speed with which Cisco routers perform the routing table lookup depends on several factors, including the CPU type, the hardware support available, and the IOS version. In general, the faster the CPU, the better the performance is likely to be. However, some routers have a significant advantage in forwarding packets after the first packet in a flow has been routed. These routers save information about the flow and which interface and next hop will be used. When a packet is received that matches the flow, the router can quickly forward the packet.

FYI: A flow is a sequence of packets traveling from one source to one destination. The IP header is nearly the same for all packets in the flow because the source and destination IP addresses are the same. FTP is a good example of an application that generates a high volume flow from the source to the receiver. Of course, there is a flow of acknowledgments from the receiver back to the source, but with a modern TCP/IP implementation, the acknowledgements will be significantly fewer and smaller than the data-carrying packets.

When two systems are in a conversation, they exchange multiple packets in both directions. In this case, we will see two flows, one in each direction. Telnet is a good example of this. When character echo is enabled, a few characters are carried in one packet from the Telnet client to the Telnet server. The server then echoes these characters back in a return packet.

The basic mechanism that all routers have is called *process switching*. When a packet arrives, is it copied from the interface memory into the main CPU memory. The CPU extracts the IP address, determines the network number, performs the routing table lookup, and builds the MAC framing suitable for the outgoing interface around the packet. The resulting frame is copied into the output queue of the outgoing interface. The copy is done by direct memory access (DMA), which allows the copy to be done by hardware while the CPU is busy doing something else. However, the entire packet is copied from the incoming interface to the CPU memory, then back to the output interface. Therefore, it crosses

**Figure 2-11**
Switching paths

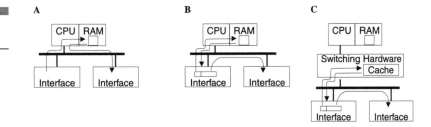

the main system bus twice. Diagram A in Figure 2-11 shows this path. Depending on the router CPU, this can yield forwarding rates of thousands of packets per second.

The next higher speed path uses fast switching. The first packet of a flow is process switched as described before. While process switching, the router loads a cache with the destination address, the interface to use, and a prebuilt MAC header appropriate for the outgoing interface. When another packet for the same destination arrives, only the necessary components of the IP header are copied into CPU memory (Figure 2-11, diagram B), reducing the amount of data being copied and saving time. The CPU checks the IP header against the cache and, if it finds a match, encapsulates the packet within the prebuilt MAC framing and queues the frame on the outgoing interface.

Four factors affect the performance improvement in the fast switching path:

- Copying only that amount of data necessary for the CPU to perform the route lookup
- Efficient lookup algorithms
- Using a prebuilt MAC header
- The outgoing interface copying the final frame from the memory where the receiving interface placed it

Avoiding each data copy from memory to memory is the key to high performance.

The other routing paths use this concept to varying degrees. In all cases, the CPU performs the routing decision on the first packet of a flow and loads a cache with the necessary forwarding information. Each high-performance forwarding mechanism then runs from the data in the cache. If a cache lookup fails, the packet falls back to being process switched.

Larger routers often contain hardware with onboard cache memory to perform high-performance forwarding. The CPU loads the cache when it determines the first packet's route. Successive packets are handled entirely by the hardware subsystem. The destination address is used to look up the forwarding information in a small, high-speed memory; the outgoing frame is built; and the new frame is queued on the outgoing interface (see Figure 2-11, diagram C).

The Cisco documentation refers to the process switching mechanism as *route determination,* while the other mechanisms are called *switching,* because they don't determine the path; they just follow directions dictated by the CPU. More recent developments include NetFlow switching, in which the first packet is process switched (including access-list checks). Successive packets in the same flow are switched using a faster mechanism (which depends on the router model and IOS release).

You can force a router to use only process switching by adding the command **no ip route-cache** to its configuration. This tells the CPU to never load any of the caches. In general, this is not advisable. We will see how the use of this command can modify the path selection process in the next section.

# Multipath Operation

Cisco routers will utilize multiple equal-cost parallel paths when such paths exist to a destination. However, the switching mechanism that is used will determine how these paths are used. The number of equal-cost parallel paths kept in the routing table depends on the IOS release. Recent versions of the IOS have increased the number of parallel paths from four to six. A path is parallel to another path if the metrics of the two paths are equal (or nearly equal for IGRP and EIGRP).

When process switching, the CPU will select the outgoing interface on a round-robin basis between all available parallel paths. The result is that load balancing happens on a per-packet basis. Sometimes this can lead to interesting path determination in highly redundant networks. Figure 2-12 shows a network (running RIP) with a redundant path between London and the 172.16.6.0 network (Moscow S0 or Rome S1). Path 1 (to Moscow's S0) is London-Paris-Moscow. Path 2 is London-Paris-Rome-Moscow (Paris can't tell from the destination address that it's actually shorter to get to Moscow via 172.16.4.2).

**Figure 2-12**
Multipath network

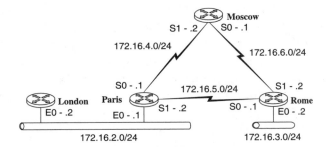

If Paris is configured with **no ip route-cache** on its serial interfaces, then it will round-robin switch packets over the available paths to the destination. This is easily seen in the **trace** command output in Figure 2-13. You can see that each probe takes a different path as Paris performs parallel path round-robin selection. Note the failure of the last probe on the second trace output (line 14). This is an example of the destination router limiting the number of ICMP destination unreachable packets being generated (as described in Chapter 1).

This sounds like wonderful news. We can build networks that perform load balancing at the packet level! But there may be a problem with this. Because we are process switching, the CPU quickly will be overloaded and performance will suffer under high loads.

A 2500 router running 11.3 has a process-switching rate of a few thousand packets per second. Two parallel paths of 10Mbps each will totally consume the CPU of this router. We will achieve better performance by using fast switching on just one of the Ethernets (14,000 pps). By

**Figure 2-13** Per-packet multipath.

```
1 London#trace 172.16.6.1
2 Type escape sequence to abort.
3 Tracing the route to 172.16.6.1
4    1 172.16.2.1 4 msec 4 msec 0 msec
5    2 172.16.5.1 20 msec
6      172.16.4.2 20 msec
7      172.16.5.1 20 msec
8
9 London#trace 172.16.6.1
10 Type escape sequence to abort.
11 Tracing the route to 172.16.6.1
12    1 172.16.2.1 4 msec 4 msec 0 msec
13    2 172.16.4.2 20 msec
14      172.16.5.1 20 msec *
```

enabling the route cache mechanism, we will have increased the performance of our network. But what about load balancing?

Reconfiguring the Paris serial interfaces to enable the use of the route cache (**ip route-cache**) changes the behavior. When Paris uses its cache, it determines which interface to use for a given destination and prebuilds the outgoing MAC header. Because the cache contains the interface and MAC header, the router performs per-destination load balancing. Since this is a more efficient switching mechanism, the router can obtain much higher packet rates. Figure 2-14 shows two **trace** tests that demonstrate the path selection.

Does this apply to all Cisco routers? Yes, it does. Even the routers with high-performance CPUs gain performance by using the fast switching path. It is best to disable fast switching only in low-speed networks where the per-packet load balancing is truly achieving increased performance.

Be careful when examining route cache behavior. Regardless of the state of the ip route-cache, packets that originate within the router (Telnet, DLSW, RSRB, or tunnel end points) will alternate between the available paths. This is because any packet originating from a process within a router is process switched, even those originating from tunnel and DLSW or RSRB configurations.

It is worth experimenting with the operation of the route-cache and how it affects packet switching. Using our lab configuration, you can experiment with enabling and disabling the route-cache on different interfaces and with different destinations. You may want to try different topologies than the one in our lab to really understand the implications of the route-cache configuration and understand when and where you should use each type of switching.

**Figure 2-14** Per-destination multipath

```
1 London#trace 172.16.6.1
2 Type escape sequence to abort.
3 Tracing the route to 172.16.6.1
4    1 172.16.2.1 4 msec 4 msec 4 msec
5    2 172.16.5.1 20 msec 20 msec 24 msec
6    3 172.16.6.1 28 msec *  28 msec
```

# Subnetting

Up to this point, we have been working with class C networks that fit our needs. In real networks, we may not have this luxury. Recall that a class B address is capable of addressing 65,534 systems. But this is much too many addresses for a single LAN segment, much less the two addresses needed for a point-to-point WAN link. Similarly, a class C network number may be allocated to a small company that has multiple network segments in two or three sites. In both cases, the organizations have a NIC address allocated that is representative of the number of hosts each needs. What we need is a way to break the single network number into many smaller segments that fit our needs.

Recall that network addresses have a NIC-assigned part and a locally administered part. To address each network segment within an organization, we need a way to subdivide the assigned network space, creating multiple subnets.

Subnetting is done by dividing the locally administered portion of the address into two parts as recommended in RFC950 (Mogul and Postel 1985). The first part identifies the subnet (a network segment) and the second part identifies the host on that subnet, as shown in Figure 2-15. The S denotes the portion of the locally administered address that is being used to identify each subnet (network segment).

This is very similar to the way phone numbers are divided. For example, the phone number 408-936-1212 is divided into three segments, just

**Figure 2-15**
Subnetting

Setting the Mask:

| | |
|---|---|
| Class B Format | `10NN NNNN.NNNN NNNN.LLLL LLLL.LLLL LLLL` |
| Divide into Subnet & Host | `10NN NNNN.NNNN NNNN.SSSS SSSS.HHHH HHHH` |
| Subnet Mask | `1111 1111.1111 1111.1111 1111.0000 0000` |

Example:

| | |
|---|---|
| Class B Address | 172 . 16 . 21 . 33 |
| Binary Format | `1010 1100.0001 0000.0001 0101.0010 0001` |
| Subnet Mask | `1111 1111.1111 1111.1111 1111.0000 0000` |
| **Binary AND** | |
| Subnet ID | `1010 1100.0001 0000.0001 0101.0000 0000` |
| | 172 . 16 . 21 . 0 |

Note that the host bits (marked H above) are removed by the AND operation (i.e., converted to zeros).

like our network address. The area code, 408, is similar to the network number portion of our address. The exchange, 936, is similar to the subnet, and 1212 is like the host address.

In Figure 2-15, the network number (172.16.0.0) is given to us by the NIC, and we cannot change it. The locally administered portion of the address is evenly divided such that the first eight bits identify each network segment (yielding 254 subnets). The last eight bits identify the hosts on each segment (addressing 254 hosts).

A subnet mask is used to identify the number of bits that identify each subnet. It is simply a measuring stick used by network devices (including routers) to mark all the bits that are used to identify a subnet. The bits in the NIC-assigned network number are included in the subnet mask. For example, in Figure 2-15, there are 16 bits of NIC-assigned address, plus eight additional bits to identify the subnets. The subnet mask (in binary) is written with ones starting at the left and extending to the right (24 bits in our example):

```
1111 1111.1111 1111.1111 1111.0000 0000 = 255.255.255.0
```

The number of subnet bits to use depends on your network's requirements. If the LANs in our network were all sized to hold fewer than 126 hosts each, then we would waste half of our address space on each subnet if we used a 24-bit mask. It would be better to use 25 bits to identify the network segments (510 subnets) and use the remaining seven bits to address the hosts on each subnet (126 hosts). The dotted decimal notation can become somewhat confusing when using nonoctet boundaries. With practice, you can become very proficient at mentally converting the dotted decimal notation into binary and back.

FYI: The Chesapeake Subnet Calculator is a useful tool to use to learn subnetting and as a design tool for new network designs. Appendix B contains more information about this useful tool.

For nine bits of subnet, we determine the subnet mask to be:

```
1111 1111.1111 1111.1111 1111.1000 0000 = 255.255.255.128
```

The routing decisions with subnetting are performed exactly the same way as with nonsubnet routing. The destination address is ANDed with the mask, and the resulting subnet number is used to find a match in the routing table.

# Subnetting Example

An example of subnetting will help clarify how it works: A small company is assigned a class C network address of 192.168.1.0, but has a requirement for five subnets, each of which must support up to 20 hosts (see Figure 2-16). We must select a subnet mask for this network.

First, find how many bits are needed to create at least five subnets. The mask for a class C network is 24 bits long:

```
255.255.255.0 = 1111 1111.1111 1111.1111 1111.0000 0000
```

There are eight locally administered bits that we can assign any way we wish.

Using the left-most bit as a subnet identifier extends the mask one bit (a total of 25 bits). This will address two subnets (0 and 1). However, the all-zeros subnet is reserved (it is the same as the assigned network number), and the all-ones subnet is reserved (for the all-subnets broadcast). There are no subnets remaining.

Extending the mask two bits (for a total of 26 bits) yields four subnets (00, 01, 10, 11). Since the all-zeros and all-ones subnets are reserved, we have two usable subnets. This isn't enough, so we extend the mask another bit to the right (for a total of 27 bits) to get eight subnets (000, 001, 010, 011, 100, 101, 110, and 111), of which six are usable. This is enough for our network.

Looking carefully at the number of bits used and the resulting number of addresses, we find that using one bit yields two addresses, using

**Figure 2-16**

Subnetting example

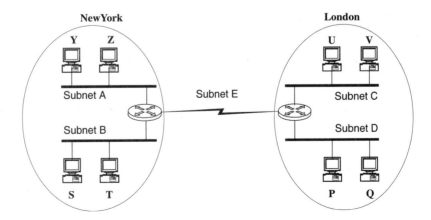

two bits yields four addresses, and three bits yields eight addresses. For every bit, the number of addresses doubles. Table 2-3 shows the progression of binary numbers and the number of binary combinations that result.

Before selecting this mask, we need to check that it will work for the number of hosts that are required on each subnet. Since three bits of subnet are used out of the eight locally administered bits, there are five remaining bits for host assignment. Table 2-3 shows that five bits can represent 32 unique addresses, of which the all-zeros address is reserved to identify the subnet itself and the all-ones address is reserved for the broadcast address. There are 30 usable addresses remaining, which more than fulfills our requirements.

Having made a valid choice of subnet mask, Figure 2-17 shows all the subnet addresses and which are usable. Note that the three subnet bits increment as you scan down the list.

**Table 2-3**

Binary progression

| Bits | Combinations |
| --- | --- |
| 0 | 0 |
| 1 | 2 |
| 2 | 4 |
| 3 | 8 |
| 4 | 16 |
| 5 | 32 |
| 6 | 64 |
| 7 | 128 |
| 8 | 256 |
| 9 | 512 |
| 10 | 1,024 |
| 11 | 2,048 |
| 12 | 4,096 |
| 13 | 8,192 |
| 14 | 16,384 |
| 15 | 32,768 |
| 16 | 65,536 |

Note: Simoneau (1997) contains tables showing the relationship between the number of subnet bits (the extension beyond the base network mask) and the number of subnets and number of hosts.

**Figure 2-17**
Subnet assignments

| Dotted Quad | Binary Format | Assignment |
|---|---|---|
| 255.255.255.224 | 1111 1111.1111 1111.1111 1111.1110 0000 | Subnet Mask |
| 192.168.1.0 | 1100 0000.1010 1000.0000 0001.0000 0000 | Reserved |
| 192.168.1.32 | 1100 0000.1010 1000.0000 0001.0010 0000 | Subnet A |
| 192.168.1.64 | 1100 0000.1010 1000.0000 0001.0100 0000 | Subnet B |
| 192.168.1.96 | 1100 0000.1010 1000.0000 0001.0110 0000 | Subnet C |
| 192.168.1.128 | 1100 0000.1010 1000.0000 0001.1000 0000 | Subnet D |
| 192.168.1.160 | 1100 0000.1010 1000.0000 0001.1010 0000 | Subnet E |
| 192.168.1.192 | 1100 0000.1010 1000.0000 0001.1100 0000 | Future |
| 192.168.1.224 | 1100 0000.1010 1000.0000 0001.1110 0000 | Reserved |

Assigned Address    Subnet Bits   Host Bits

| Address Allocation | | | | | | | | |
|---|---|---|---|---|---|---|---|---|
| 192.168.1.x | .0–.31 | .32–.63 | .64–.95 | .96–.127 | .128–.159 | .160–.191 | .192–.223 | .224–.255 |
| Subnet Assignment | Rsvd | A | B | C | D | E | F | Rsvd |

Each of the network segments is assigned a subnet number from the allocations in Figure 2-17. Then, each host on each of the subnets is assigned a host number on that subnet. It is useful to create a standard for numbering hosts, such as making the routers host number 1 or 2 on each subnet. Figure 2-18 contains the host allocations for the hosts on subnet C of Figure 2-16.

The resulting subnet design and allocation are shown in Figure 2-19.

**Figure 2-18**
Subnet C host
assignments

| Dotted Quad | Binary Format | Assignment |
|---|---|---|
| 255.255.255.224 | 1111 1111.1111 1111.1111 1111.1110 0000 | Subnet Mask |
| 192.168.1.96 | 1100 0000.1010 1000.0000 0001.0110 0000 | Subnet ID |
| 192.168.1.97 | 1100 0000.1010 1000.0000 0001.0110 0001 | NewYork E0 |
| 192.168.1.98 | 1100 0000.1010 1000.0000 0001.0110 0010 | Host U |
| 192.168.1.99 | 1100 0000.1010 1000.0000 0001.0110 0011 | Host V |
| 192.168.1.100 | 1100 0000.1010 1000.0000 0001.0110 0100 | Future |
| 192.168.1.101 | 1100 0000.1010 1000.0000 0001.0110 0101 | Future |
| . . . | . . . | . . . |
| 192.168.1.126 | 1100 0000.1010 1000.0000 0001.0111 1110 | Future |
| 192.168.1.127 | 1100 0000.1010 1000.0000 0001.0111 1111 | Broadcast |

Assigned Address    Subnet Bits   Host Bits

**Figure 2-19**
Subnet network
solution

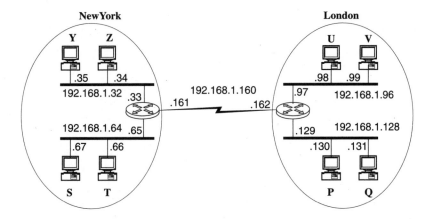

## What Mask to Use?

When matching a destination address to the routes in its routing table, a router must determine the network mask or subnet mask to use. The router determines the class of the destination address (class A, B, or C) by examining the top bits of the address. The router also knows the subnet mask used in an attached network, because the mask is configured on at least one of its interfaces.

Here is what happens. When a packet arrives, the router must decide which mask to use when checking for a match in its routing table. If the destination address is within a network about which subnetting information is known, then the appropriate subnet mask is used. However, if the destination address is within a network about which no subnetting information is known, then the network mask appropriate for the class of the address is used.

In the network shown in Figure 2-20, two packets are being received by the New York router in the small company we've been helping. The first packet is addressed to Z. Since Z's address is on a subnet that New York knows about, the subnet mask is used to strip off the host portion of the address, and the resulting subnet ID is used to perform the routing table lookup.

The second packet is addressed to K, a host somewhere in the Internet. New York doesn't have any subnetting information about K's network because the router does not have an interface connected to K's network and because the routing protocols in use do not pass the details of

**Figure 2-20**
Mask selection

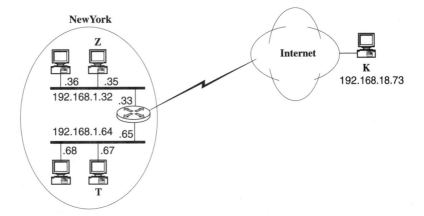

the subnetting used in K's network. Here, New York must determine the class (A, B, or C) of K's address and use its mask in the route lookup process.

The result of having only the subnet mask when the router is "local" to the destination network is that unnecessary routing detail is hidden from routers external to the "local" network. Otherwise, the size of the routing tables would be much, much larger. Today, there are roughly 40,000 routes in the Internet routing tables. Since many class B networks have hundreds of subnets, the routing tables could be hundreds of times larger. Imagine how much larger they would be if every subnet of every network were also included!

To continue our postal analogy, routing in this environment is much like the travels of a letter. When it is first sent, the post office doesn't concern itself with the detail of the street address. The post office works by looking only at the destination city and getting the letter to the city. When it arrives at the city, the post office there looks at the street address and performs more detailed routing. The routers in the Internet today work exactly the same way—minimizing detailed routing information until the packet is close to the destination.

# Variable-length Subnetting

The small company described in the previous section continues to grow and needs network connectivity to another site. But there is only one subnet left unallocated! Fewer than 25 percent of the available addresses are currently used. Figure 2-21 shows the current host allocations and

| Subnet | Name | Number of Hosts | Current or Growth |
|--------|------|-----------------|-------------------|
| A | NewYork Engineering LAN | 20 | Current |
| B | NewYork Administration LAN | 10 | Current |
| C | London Engineering LAN | 10 | Current |
| D | London Administration LAN | 5 | Current |
| E | NewYork to London WAN | 2 | Current |
|   | Tokyo LAN | 10 | Growth |
|   | NewYork to Tokyo WAN | 2 | Growth |
|   | Ontario LAN | 10 | Growth |
|   | NewYork to Ontario WAN | 2 | Growth |

**Anticipated growth from five to nine subnets. One subnet is currently unallocated.**

what is expected over the next year. The growth is from five subnets to nine, with the proposed network topology as shown in Figure 2-22. With only one subnet remaining, something different is needed.

Notice that several subnets are using only a small part of the available address space. In particular, the WAN links need only two addresses (one for the router at each end of the link), a utilization of only 7 percent of the available addresses within this subnet.

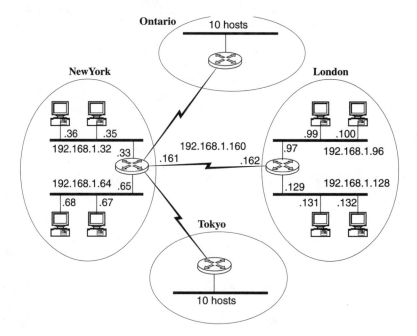

The solution is to use variable-length subnet masking (VLSM), a subnet-allocation mechanism that produces different size subnets. (See RFC1878, Pummil and Manning 1995, for a list of the sizes of each of the VLSM subnets.) There is one basic requirement for using VLSM—the routing protocol being used must support it. This includes RIPv2, OSPF, EIGRP, and BGP.

Using VLSM is simple. Subnet using a normal mask, typically the largest subnets you need. Then take one of these large subnets and subdivide it (creating subsubnets!) For the assigned class C network, we should be able to fulfill the requirements set forth earlier. The first step of creating a set of subnets is already done.

The next step is to take one of these subnets and subnet it with a longer mask. Recall that we had used a 27-bit subnet mask (a three-bit extension of a class C mask) to create our initial subnets. Let's take subnet F and subnet it to work on the WAN links, each of which can support two hosts (the routers at each end of the point-to-point links). The subnet mask must be extended to 30 bits to maximize the number of subnets and leave room for two valid host addresses (remember, four host addresses includes the subnet ID and the broadcast address, plus

**Figure 2-23**
Subnetting subnet F

| Dotted Quad | Binary Format | Assignment |
|---|---|---|
| 255.255.255.252 | 1111 1111.1111 1111.1111 1111.1111 1100 | Subnet Mask |
| 192.168.1.192 | 1100 0000.1010 1000.0000 0001.1100 0000 | NewYork to London |
| 192.168.1.196 | 1100 0000.1010 1000.0000 0001.1100 0100 | NewYork to Tokyo |
| 192.168.1.200 | 1100 0000.1010 1000.0000 0001.1100 1000 | NewYork to Ontario |
| 192.168.1.204 | 1100 0000.1010 1000.0000 0001.1100 1100 | Future |
| 192.168.1.208 | 1100 0000.1010 1000.0000 0001.1101 0000 | Future |
| 192.168.1.212 | 1100 0000.1010 1000.0000 0001.1101 0100 | Future |
| 192.168.1.216 | 1100 0000.1010 1000.0000 0001.1101 1000 | Future |
| 192.168.1.220 | 1100 0000.1010 1000.0000 0001.1101 1100 | Future |

Assigned
Address     Subnet
Bits    Host
Bits

Host Allocation in NewYork to London Subnet

| | | |
|---|---|---|
| 192.168.1.192 | 1100 0000.1010 1000.0000 0001.1100 0000 | Subnet ID |
| 192.168.1.193 | 1100 0000.1010 1000.0000 0001.1100 0101 | NewYork S0 |
| 192.168.1.194 | 1100 0000.1010 1000.0000 0001.1100 1010 | London S0 |
| 192.168.1.195 | 1100 0000.1010 1000.0000 0001.1100 1111 | Subnet Broadcast |

Host
Bits

two assignable addresses). Figure 2-23 shows the dotted decimal and binary calculations that result from extending the mask.

Note how the host field is counting up in binary for each of the four addresses. The address that has the all-zeros host field is used to identify the subnet, while the address that contains the all-ones host field is used as the broadcast. Between these two addresses lie the two valid host addresses, which we will assign to NewYork's S0 interface and London's S0 interface.

The 192.168.1.196 subsubnet is assigned to the NewYork-to-Tokyo WAN link, and the 192.168.200 subsubnet is assigned to the NewYork-to-Ontario WAN link the same way we did earlier.

With these assignments complete, subnet E (192.168.1.160) is now available for subsubnetting. Using the process of extending the subnet mask, this subnet can be divided and reallocated. Looking at the requirements stated in Figure 2-21, we see that we need several subnets with at least 10 hosts each. The smallest subnet that will work for these has four bits of host address ($2^4$=16, minus the subnet ID and the broadcast address, leaving 14 usable addresses). Extending the subnet mask one bit (to 28 bits) will yield two subnets: 192.168.1.160 and 192.168.1.176.

Looking at our network requirements, we can assign the .160 subnet to the NewYork Admin LAN and assign the .176 subnet to the London Eng LAN.

When we have converted each of these LANs to their new assignments, we will have two old subnets, the .64 and .96 subnets to use. Subsubnetting each of these to 28 bits will give us a total of four new subnets, each capable of addressing 14 hosts. By assigning the .64 subnet to the London Admin LAN, the .80 subnet to the Tokyo LAN, and the .96 subnet to the Ontario LAN, we will have accomplished our network redesign.

The following subnets are still available for future growth:

192.168.1.112/28

192.168.1.128/27

192.168.1.204/30

192.168.1.208/30

192.168.1.212/30

192.168.1.216/30

192.168.1.220/30

We're replacing the dotted decimal form of the subnet mask with the number of bits in the subnet mask. The address 192.168.1.112/28 is a different way to write 192.168.1.112 255.255.255.240. Both addresses are followed by a representation of the subnet mask—the first with the number of bits in the subnet mask and the second with the dotted decimal representation of the subnet mask.

Figure 2-24 shows the resulting network design. The principles of subnetting are applied twice: first to the assigned network number to produce a set of large subnets; second by further subnetting some of the large subnets.

In almost all networks with class B or class C assignments, there should only be two or three levels of subnetting. The large-size subnet is important to handle the LANs, while the minimum size subnet (a 30-bit mask) is needed for point-to-point WAN links. Another size subnet may be needed for medium-size LAN segments. Seldom are more than three levels of subnetting required, except in class A networks, which may require an additional level of subnetting to allow groups of large subnets to be delegated to divisions or regions.

If you have one LAN segment that is out of proportion with respect to all the other LANs, then break the LAN into two segments or assign

**Figure 2-24**
VLSM network
design

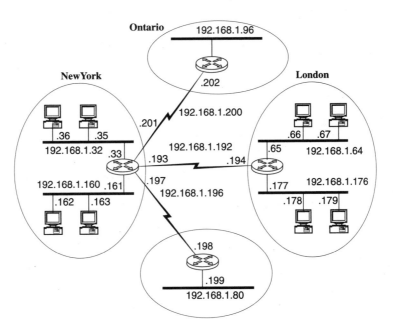

it two subnets using secondary addressing. Secondary addressing is a Cisco mechanism, and command, that allows you to assign multiple subnets to a single network segment. All routers connected to this segment *must* have the same set of secondary addresses. It is a useful technique for network segments that have outgrown the initial requirements in which using a larger subnet is not feasible.

# Classless Routing

Along with VLSM comes classless routing. Recall from earlier that the router knows only the mask of the destination by the class of the address or if the destination network is "local." With VLSM, there may be more than one mask used in a network. So the routing protocols must transport the mask along with each route (we'll talk about the protocols in later chapters).

Since the mask is propagated along with the route, there is no need to determine the class of the address and its default mask, thus the term *classless routing.* The newer routing protocols—RIPv2, OSPF, EIGRP, and BGP—propagate the mask with the route in their routing updates. More information on classless routing can be found in RFC1519 (Fuller et al. 1993) and in Chapter 5.

# CCIE tips

As a CCIE candidate, you'll need to have a solid understanding of how routing works. We've covered a complex topic in only one chapter, so you'll probably want to check out the references and other books on the topic. We've found that there is a lot of wisdom in the RFCs, and reading those RFCs that are devoted to the IP protocols and routing protocols is an easy (and inexpensive) way to learn more about them.

Obviously, you'll have to know how a router works and be able to apply that knowledge to both design and troubleshooting tasks. Knowing the typical failure modes is important (remember the discussion on open jaw routes from Chapter 1?). Can you identify the two major functions a router performs? If not, look back through this chapter. Knowing these functions is the basis for troubleshooting—can you isolate the problem to one of the two functions and make more effective use of your troubleshooting time?

You must be able to do a VLSM-based network-addressing allocation quickly and confidently. When you're in the hands-on exam and need to design a network-addressing scheme, you won't want to waste time. Reading RFC1519 on Classless Interdomain Routing (CIDR) is a useful exercise to learn more about the reasoning behind VLSM. We'll be addressing more about this topic as we work with various protocols that use it. When troubleshooting, you must be able to quickly diagnose an incorrect VLSM design where two address spaces are overlapping. Then, you need to be able to correct it. Again, practice VLSM subnet design. If necessary, draw a chart similar to the ones we used in Figures 1-23 and 2-18 to show which subnets are using a particular section of the address space.

Do you know the switching modes of Cisco routers and how to control them? This is very important for achieving the optimum performance from your network. We've seen networks that were using per-packet switching to achieve load balancing, yet were operating at reduced capacity due to the CPU limitation of this switching mechanism. You should be able to recognize the **trace** output that results from per-packet load balancing over parallel paths and be able to tune the network for optimum performance. It is also useful to learn about the new switching modes (NetFlow switching, optimum switching, etc.) and understand what these mean to router and network performance.

Is the use of administrative distance new to you? Then it's time to read up on it in the Cisco documentation. We'll also be covering it in more detail in later chapters as we customize the administrative distance on various protocols and on static routes. It is this mechanism that is sometimes used to implement dial backup between sets of routers, so it has real-world applicability.

## SUMMARY

The way routers work is very straightforward. The destination address is extracted from the received packet and the network portion of the address is determined. The routing table is searched for a matching destination network. A matching entry in the routing table contains the next-hop destination, the outgoing interface, and several other parameters related to the route. The packet is encapsulated in the framing suitable for the outgoing interface and is output by the interface.

We examined administrative distance and how it relates to the selection of the best route. Subnetting and variable-length subnet masking showed us how to subdivide large assigned network number spaces into pieces that best fit our needs. Finally, we introduced the topic of classless routing, which we will discuss further in several more chapters.

You should now have a solid understanding of how the TCP/IP suite of protocols operate at the physical, data-link, network, and transport layers. With this information as a background, we can tackle Cisco router configurations that are used in real networks.

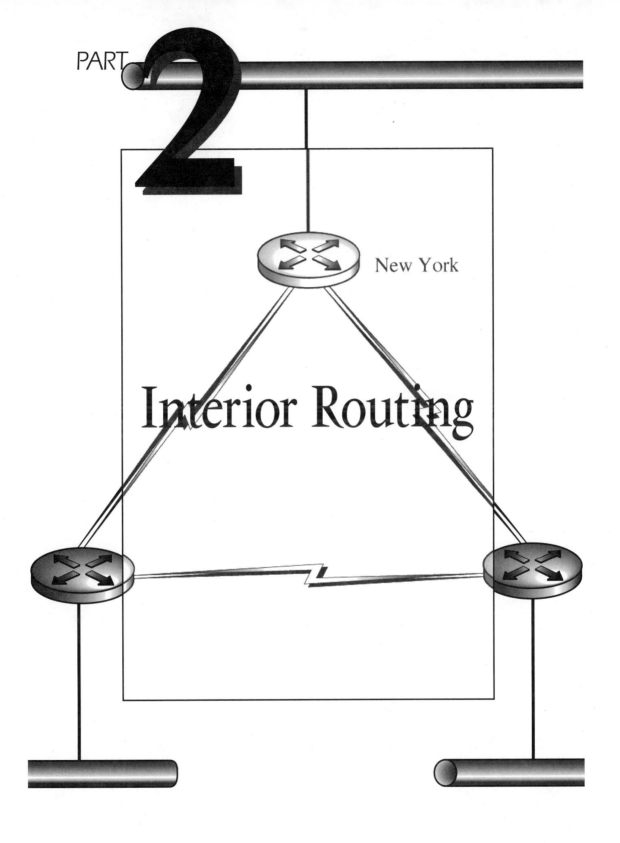

# Interior Routing

New York

# CHAPTER 3

# Static Routes

Static routes are special routes that the network administrator manually enters into the router configuration. You could build an entire network based on static routes. The problem with doing this is that when (not if!) a network failure occurs, the static route will not change without you performing the change. This isn't a good thing if the failure occurs during the middle of the night or while you are on vacation.

This is why we've all heard the chant "Don't use static routes!" However, there are many places where static routes are essential to a smoothly operating network. Careful use and placement of static routes actually may improve the performance of your network, allowing you to conserve bandwidth for important business applications. We'll cover the places where you normally would want to use static routes and where you shouldn't.

# Stub Networks

Stub networks are the ideal candidate for static routes. A stub network is like a dead-end street: There is only one link to the network. In Figure 3-1, there are two branches, each of which is a stub network. There is a LAN at each site, but there is only one link connecting them to headquarters.

There is no need to run a routing protocol over the WAN links between New York and the branches. Static routes on New York direct traffic to the LANs at the branches (we'll discuss redistribution of these static routes to other headquarters routers in this chapter and Chapter 6). Similarly, the branch routers at Tokyo and London don't need to know about all the routes in the corporate intranet. The only thing a branch router needs to know is that if the packet isn't for a network at the branch, the packet should be forwarded to New York, which has more complete routing information.

Figure 3-2 shows the static route configuration of New York and Tokyo. Lines 10 and 11 are the static routes in New York that reference the LAN at each branch. Line 19 is a default route in Tokyo (a route to network 0.0.0.0, which we will discuss in the next section) that points back to New York. London's configuration is very similar to Tokyo's, except for the hostname and the addresses assigned to the interfaces.

There is another type of static route, called the *interface static route*. It is used when you want the destination network to look as if it is attached to one of the router's interfaces. The administrative distance for an interface static route is zero, which makes it equivalent to a directly connected network route.

Figure 3-3 shows changing the static routes in New York to interface static routes. The interface static routes appear as if they were directly connected.

**Figure 3-1**

Stub network

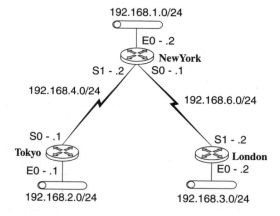

**Figure 3-2** Static route configuration

**NewYork Configuration**
```
1 hostname NewYork
2 interface Ethernet0
3  ip address 192.168.1.1 255.255.255.0
4 interface Serial0
5  ip address 192.168.6.1 255.255.255.0
6 interface Serial1
7  ip address 192.168.4.2 255.255.255.0
8  clockrate 250000
9 ip classless
10 ip route 192.168.2.0 255.255.255.0 192.168.4.1
11 ip route 192.168.3.0 255.255.255.0 192.168.6.2
12 end
```
**Tokyo Configuration**
```
13 hostname Tokyo
14 interface Ethernet0
15  ip address 192.168.2.1 255.255.255.0
16 interface Serial0
17  ip address 192.168.4.1 255.255.255.0
18 ip classless
19 ip route 0.0.0.0 0.0.0.0 192.168.4.2
20 end
```

**Figure 3-3** Interface static routes.
```
1 NewYork#conf t
2 Enter configuration commands, one per line.  End with CNTL/Z.
3 NewYork(config)#no ip route 192.168.2.0 255.255.255.0 192.168.4.1
4 NewYork(config)#no ip route 192.168.3.0 255.255.255.0 192.168.6.2
5 NewYork(config)#ip route 192.168.2.0 255.255.255.0 s 1
6 NewYork(config)#ip route 192.168.3.0 255.255.255.0 s 0
7 NewYork(config)#^Z
8 NewYork#sh ip route
9 Codes: C - connected, S - static, I - IGRP, R - RIP, M - mobile, B - BGP
10        D - EIGRP, EX - EIGRP external, O - OSPF, IA - OSPF inter area
11        N1 - OSPF NSSA external type 1, N2 - OSPF NSSA external type 2
12        E1 - OSPF external type 1, E2 - OSPF external type 2, E - EGP
13        i - IS-IS, L1 - IS-IS level-1, L2 - IS-IS level-2, * - candidate default
14        U - per-user static route, o - ODR
15
16 Gateway of last resort is not set
17
18 C    192.168.4.0/24 is directly connected, Serial1
19 C    192.168.6.0/24 is directly connected, Serial0
20 C    192.168.1.0/24 is directly connected, Ethernet0
21 S    192.168.2.0/24 is directly connected, Serial1
22 S    192.168.3.0/24 is directly connected, Serial0
```

# Default Route

Simply stated, a default route is one that is used when no matching routing table entry is found. It appears in the routing table as a route to network 0.0.0.0, and you know it is set when the output of **sho ip route** contains an entry similar to the following entry at the top of the routing table:

```
Gateway of last resort is 192.168.4.1 to network 0.0.0.0
```

Any packet whose destination address is not matched by any specific routing table entry will take the path to the gateway of last resort. The gateway of last resort should be a router that has more complete routing information and can forward the packet to its destination. If there is no default route and the packet's destination address is not found in the routing table, then the packet is dropped and an ICMP Destination or Network Unreachable is returned to the source IP address.

FYI: The term gateway originated in the early 1980s, when the world of networking equipment consisted of bridges and gateways. Bridges connect media that use the same (or nearly the same) data-link protocols, such as Ethernet to Ethernet. Gateway is the older term for a router and originated because it was the gateway through which one was able to send packets to a network that used different media and incompatible data-link protocols. In the late 1980s, the term router was coined to reflect the function of routing packets to the proper destination. Today, the term gateway refers to a networking component that converts a higher-level protocol into a different higher-level protocol. An example of this is a mail gateway that converts the OSI X.400 mail protocol into the Internet's RFC822 protocol format. The older use of the term exists in a variety of places, including older RFCs, networking texts, and software. A review of RFC1009 (Braden and Postel 1987) clearly defines the terms router and gateway.

We'll see in later chapters how default routes can be propagated throughout an intranet via an interior routing protocol such as RIP, IGRP, OSPF, or EIGRP.

# When It Is Used

As we've seen, default routes are very useful in stub networks. It is a way to eliminate the use of a routing protocol to stub networks where there is no other reason to run a routing protocol. Eliminating the use of a routing protocol saves WAN link bandwidth, router CPU processing, and router memory. In a large network containing hundreds of routes, a dynamic routing protocol may consume a significant amount of link bandwidth. Using the default route can mean using a link sized for the amount of user traffic instead of a link of much higher bandwidth. The monetary savings in using properly sized link bandwidths can be significant.

There isn't much difference in the amount of work needed to configure a stub network using a dynamic routing protocol and a configuration using static and default routes. A dynamic routing protocol will require the listing of the network number to enable the protocol on the networks to which the router is attached. Similarly, the default and static routes require entering similar network numbers. Since a manual configuration of some part of the routing system is needed in each case, why not use the one that results in less link traffic and better performance? In both cases, the configuration and design justification need to be documented so that other members of the networking team know why one of the methods was chosen over the other and what to change if the network numbers on either end are changed.

# How to Configure It

Configuring the default route requires only one statement:

```
R2(config)#ip route 0.0.0.0 0.0.0.0 192.168.4.2
```

The routing table will now include a static route to network 0.0.0.0 using a subnet mask of 0.0.0.0. The subnet mask is zero, because none of the bits in the IP address are used to identify the network number. Remember, it is the route to use (i.e., to match) when there is no specific route.

FYI: The entry for a default route looks strange in that both the network number and the mask are zero. Let's see how this works within the router.

For a packet destined for 192.168.5.2, the router is going to look through its routing table to try to find a route that matches the network portion of this address. Since it is a class C network number, the mask that will be used is 255.255.255.0. There is no match in the routing table, so the router finally checks the last entry, the default route.

This route has a mask (set by the static route command) of 0.0.0.0. Recall that the router uses the mask to determine how many destination IP address bits are network number and how many bits are "local" (i.e., subnet and host). A one is used in the mask for every bit to be used for network number, and a zero is used for the "local" portion of the address. Since the mask here is all zeros, the entire destination address is considered "local."

The binary AND operation of the destination address turns all the bits of the destination address into zeros. The comparison is then made against the network number of this static route, which is 0.0.0.0. A match occurs and the router uses the information in this routing table entry to forward the packet.

When the default route is properly configured, the router will have two important routing table entries. The first one appears before the routing table (Figure 3-4, line 9), where the gateway of last resort (another name for the default gateway) is reported. Looking at the routing table, we find the static route to the default network on line 13.

**Figure 3-4** Default routing table entry

```
1 Tokyo#sh ip route
2 Codes: C - connected, S - static, I - IGRP, R - RIP, M - mobile, B - BGP
3        D - EIGRP, EX - EIGRP external, O - OSPF, IA - OSPF inter area
4        N1 - OSPF NSSA external type 1, N2 - OSPF NSSA external type 2
5        E1 - OSPF external type 1, E2 - OSPF external type 2, E - EGP
6        i - IS-IS, L1 - IS-IS level-1, L2 - IS-IS level-2, * - candidate default
7        U - per-user static route, o - ODR
8
9 Gateway of last resort is 192.168.4.2 to network 0.0.0.0
10
11 C    192.168.4.0/24 is directly connected, Serial0
12 C    192.168.2.0/24 is directly connected, Ethernet0
13 S*   0.0.0.0/0 [1/0] via 192.168.4.2
```

## Lab Exercise

Configure each router in the pod with IP addresses. Make New York the headquarters router and Tokyo and London the branch routers. See Figure 3-5 for the network diagram. Either use the network addresses from the figure or select your own network numbers and assign IP addresses to each interface shown. Shut down the other interfaces on each router.

Using ping from New York, make sure you have connectivity to the serial interfaces on Tokyo and London. Try to ping their Ethernet interfaces. What happens? Issue the exec command **debug ip packet** and retry the ping. What do you see?

Add a static route to New York for Tokyo's Ethernet via Tokyo's serial interface IP address. Try to ping the Tokyo's Ethernet IP address. Does ping now work? What is the debug output? On Tokyo, issue the exec command **debug ip packet** and rerun the ping test. What is reported? What kind of route is this?

On Tokyo, add a default route to New York and rerun the ping test. What does debug report? Does the ping work? Add the static route to New York and default route to London and test a ping from New York to London's Ethernet.

Check that Tokyo and London can ping New York's Ethernet interface. Look at the routing tables of each router to see the static and default routes.

Try the same experiment with interface static routes on New York. Check the routing table. Does the ping test work? Use debug to see what the router is doing while the ping is running.

Can Tokyo ping London's interfaces and vice versa? If not, adjust your static and default routes in all three routers until they can.

**Figure 3-5**

Static and default route exercise network

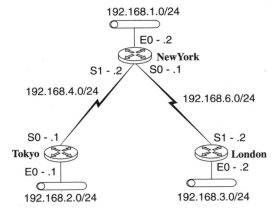

# Floating Static Routes

In mission-critical networks (is anyone running a network that isn't mission critical these days?), it is often important to have redundancy. This can be obtained with static and default routes, too. The tool to use is administrative distance. With the configuration we just finished, let's bring up the redundant serial link between Tokyo and London, as shown in Figure 3-6 (assume that it could be an on-demand link). Conceptually, the floating static route "attracts" traffic to itself but only if the primary path has failed. As long as a better route exists, the floating static route remains in the background, ready to take over if the primary path fails.

Figure 3-7 shows the configurations we used on the test network to implement this. There are several important things to learn in this configuration. NewYork has two routes to Tokyo's Ethernet. The first is via the direct link (line 11), and the second is a floating static route via London (line 12). The second route will be used only if the primary information disappears (most likely because the link went down).

Tokyo has two default routes: one via the direct link to NewYork (line 25) and a floating default route via London (line 26). Finally, London has a default route to NewYork (line 38), demonstrating that the target of a default route may itself have a default route. Line 39 of London's configuration has a floating static route to Tokyo's Ethernet.

Configuration of floating static routes is most often seen in conjunction with an interior routing protocol. In our test network, we would likely be running a dynamic routing protocol in NewYork and London,

**Figure 3-6**

Floating static route network

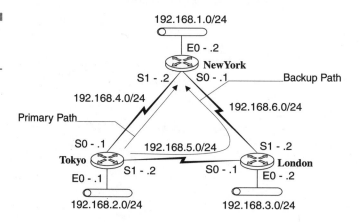

**Figure 3-7** Implementing floating static routes

**NewYork Configuration**
```
1 hostname NewYork
2 no ip domain-lookup
3 interface Ethernet0
4  ip address 192.168.1.1 255.255.255.0
5 interface Serial0
6  ip address 192.168.6.1 255.255.255.0
7 interface Serial1
8  ip address 192.168.4.2 255.255.255.0
9  clockrate 56000
10 ip classless
11 ip route 192.168.2.0 255.255.255.0 192.168.4.1
12 ip route 192.168.2.0 255.255.255.0 192.168.6.2 250
13 ip route 192.168.3.0 255.255.255.0 192.168.6.2
14 end
```
**Tokyo Configuration**
```
15 hostname Tokyo
16 no ip domain-lookup
17 interface Ethernet0
18  ip address 192.168.2.1 255.255.255.0
19 interface Serial0
20  ip address 192.168.4.1 255.255.255.0
21 interface Serial1
22  ip address 192.168.5.2 255.255.255.0
23 clockrate 56000
24 ip classless
25 ip route 0.0.0.0 0.0.0.0 192.168.4.2
26 ip route 0.0.0.0 0.0.0.0 192.168.5.1 250
27 end
```
**London Configuration**
```
28 hostname London
29 no ip domain-lookup
30 interface Ethernet0
31  ip address 192.168.3.1 255.255.255.0
32 interface Serial0
33  ip address 192.168.5.1 255.255.255.0
34 interface Serial1
35  ip address 192.168.6.2 255.255.255.0
36  clockrate 56000
37 ip classless
38 ip route 0.0.0.0 0.0.0.0 192.168.6.1
39 ip route 192.168.2.0 255.255.255.0 192.168.5.2 250
40 end
```

with the floating static routes used to force the backup link to be used if a network failure occurs on the primary path between NewYork and Tokyo. In this scenario, the Tokyo-to-London link is normally down. London and NewYork both use the primary path (NewYork to Tokyo) to reach Tokyo's Ethernet. If a failure occurs on the NewYork-to-Tokyo path, Tokyo becomes unreachable. The backup link is brought up between Tokyo and London, and traffic then takes this backup path.

Floating static routes are even simpler if the primary and secondary paths are on the same routers (New York and Tokyo in this case). An example of this might be an ISDN backup link that is brought up if the primary link fails. The neat thing about floating static routes is that they can be implemented on different routers (i.e., a different router can be the backup path), as we see in using London to establish the backup path.

## Lab Exercise

You can experiment with floating static routes by starting with the configurations from Figure 3-7. Try shutting down the primary path between New York and Tokyo. Enable **debug ip packet** on all three routers and perform ping tests between New York and Tokyo with different combinations of up or down state of the links between New York and Tokyo and between Tokyo and London. Be sure to check the contents of the routing tables after shutting down the New York-to-Tokyo link.

Use **trace** to verify the path that the packets are taking. What happens to the routing tables when the New York-to-Tokyo link is shut down? What happens to the routing tables when the Tokyo-to-London link is shut down?

## Default Network

Cisco routers have another command, **ip default-network**, that works along with the default route. This command tells the router to propagate the default route to other routers via IGRP or EIGRP. This allows other routers in the IGRP and EIGRP networks to learn the default route without manual configuration. The network specified in this command must be one that is being propagated via the routing protocol. Warning: if you forget to include the default-network target network in your routing updates, it will never be propagated via the routing protocol to other routers, and you'll never see it selected as the default route in them.

The syntax of the command suggests that it could be used instead of setting a default route as we did earlier. However, that's not the case. The default-network command causes IGRP and EIGRP to advertise the default route to neighboring routers.

Other routing protocols, like RIP and OSPF, use different mechanisms to propagate the default route. We'll cover how each protocol propagates default routes in later chapters.

## Lab Exercise

Let's see how static routes and default network work in the lab. The scenario is that an existing company has two sites connected via a 56K link. Each site has one Ethernet. The two sites are running IGRP between them, which is overkill for the two sites, but they are the test sites for an extensive company-wide rollout. You work for the local ISP and must help them with their router configuration modifications. The link to your ISP is 56K, and you've recommended that they not run a routing protocol over the link.

The network is shown in Figure 3-8. NewYork and Tokyo are the two company routers. The starting configurations for all three routers are shown in Figure 3-9. We'll test the configuration by pinging from NewYork and Tokyo to ISP's E0, which is an external network number. If you'd like to make this a challenge lab, stop reading now and configure the routers on your own.

The first step is to install the starting configuration (from Figure 3-9) in each router. Verify the routing tables to make sure that Tokyo and NewYork show their connected networks and IGRP routes to the Ethernets.

**Figure 3-8**
Default route lab

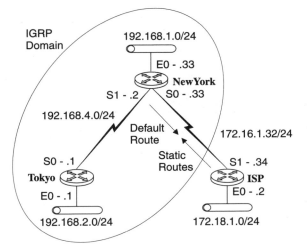

**Figure 3-9** Initial default route lab configurations

```
NewYork Configuration
1 hostname NewYork
2 no ip domain-lookup
3 interface Ethernet0
4  ip address 192.168.1.33 255.255.255.240
5 interface Serial0
6  ip address 172.16.1.33 255.255.255.252
7 interface Serial1
8  ip address 192.168.1.66 255.255.255.240
9  clockrate 56000
10 router igrp 1
11  network 192.168.1.0
12 end
Tokyo Configuration
13 hostname Tokyo
14 no ip domain-lookup
15 interface Ethernet0
16  ip address 192.168.1.97 255.255.255.240
17 interface Serial0
18  ip address 192.168.1.65 255.255.255.240
19 router igrp 1
20  network 192.168.1.0
21 end
ISP Configuration
22 hostname ISP
23 no ip domain-lookup
24 interface Ethernet0
25  ip address 172.18.1.2 255.255.255.0
26 interface Serial1
27  ip address 172.16.1.34 255.255.255.252
28  clockrate 56000
29 end
```

Next, let's establish connectivity between NewYork and ISP. Add a default route in NewYork with ISP's S1 interface as its target.

```
NewYork(config)#ip route 0.0.0.0 0.0.0.0 172.16.1.34
```

Check the routing table (**show ip route**) to verify that the gateway of last resort is set. Use the command **debug ip packet** to enable debugging on NewYork and ISP and try a ping from NewYork to ISP's E0. What do you see? To perform a better test, ping using NewYork's E0 interface address as the source address (Figure 3-10).

This requires that the packet get to ISP and that ISP knows how to get back to NewYork's internal address. What does the ping output show you?

**Figure 3-10** NewYork-to-ISP ping output

```
1 NewYork#ping
2 Protocol [ip]:
3 Target IP address: 172.18.1.2
4 Repeat count [5]:
5 Datagram size [100]:
6 Timeout in seconds [2]:
7 Extended commands [n]: y
8 Source address or interface: 192.168.1.33
9 Type of service [0]:
10 Set DF bit in IP header? [no]:
11 Validate reply data? [no]:
12 Data pattern [0xABCD]:
13 Loose, Strict, Record, Timestamp, Verbose[none]:
14 Sweep range of sizes [n]:
15 Type escape sequence to abort.
16 Sending 5, 100-byte ICMP Echos to 172.18.1.2, timeout is 2 seconds:
17
18 IP: s=192.168.1.33 (local), d=172.18.1.2 (Serial0), len 100, sending.
19 IP: s=192.168.1.33 (local), d=172.18.1.2 (Serial0), len 100, sending.
20 IP: s=192.168.1.33 (local), d=172.18.1.2 (Serial0), len 100, sending.
21 IP: s=192.168.1.33 (local), d=172.18.1.2 (Serial0), len 100, sending.
22 IP: s=192.168.1.33 (local), d=172.18.1.2 (Serial0), len 100, sending.
23 Success rate is 0 percent (0/5)
24 NewYork#
```

On line 3, we set the IP address of ISP's Ethernet interface. Using the extended ping function, on line 8 we specify the address of NewYork's Ethernet interface. Lines 18-22 show the debug output of the packet being sent, so we know that the packet is not failing within NewYork. However, the period at the end of each of these lines indicates that the echo reply packet was not received. Since NewYork has a correct route to ISP, the problem must be in ISP's configuration. As an experiment, turn on **debug ip packet** in ISP and repeat the ping test. How is its output different? What does it tell you? Use the command **show ip route** in ISP to see if it has a route back to NewYork.

Next, in ISP, add a static route to the network in our small company (192.168.1.0). This should allow NewYork to ping ISP and get a reply, even when using the E0 interface address as the source address:

```
ISP(config)#ip route 192.168.1.0 255.255.255.0 172.16.1.33
```

Now it is time to try the ping from Tokyo to ISP. What do you see? Is there a route in Tokyo to ISP's E0? Why not? Should there be one? Use **debug ip igrp transactions** and examine the debug output (you'll have to wait for updates to be generated, which are up to 90 seconds for IGRP).

Hmm, more work is needed. How about the **default-network** command? Add that to NewYork (telling it to identify 172.16.0.0 as the default network.

```
NewYork(config)#ip default-network 172.16.0.0
```

How does that change the routing updates? Does Tokyo now have a gateway of last resort set?

Checking the documentation, we find that the network specified in the **default-network** command must exist in the routing table, and Tokyo doesn't have it there. Add network 172.16.0.0 to NewYork's IGRP configuration. Don't forget to add the **passive interface s 0** command to IGRP to prevent it from consuming valuable link bandwidth on the NewYork-to-ISP link (ISP isn't running IGRP, so any updates would be wasting bandwidth).

```
NewYork(config)#router igrp 1
NewYork(config-router)#network 172.16.0.0
NewYork(config-router)#passive-interface s 0
```

Now go back and check Tokyo's routing table. Check the operation with ping. Make sure you also do a test ping with Tokyo's E0 address as a source address. Since IGRP has a 90-second update timer, you may have to wait for several minutes for the proper routing information to appear in Tokyo's routing table. This configuration adds only one route to your internal routing protocol, yet allows all the routers within the IGRP domain to route packets to any destination.

The final configuration for all three routers appears in Figure 3-11. Note that the only routers that had any configuration change were NewYork and ISP. In these routers, NewYork has four additional commands and ISP has one additional command. No changes were needed in Tokyo, showing that the routers at the border to the network are the only ones that need to have configuration changes.

For additional experience, remove the default route from NewYork and see what happens.

**Figure 3-11** Final ISP routing configurations

```
NewYork Configuration
1 hostname NewYork
2 no ip domain-lookup
3 interface Ethernet0
4  ip address 192.168.1.33 255.255.255.240
5 interface Serial0
6  ip address 172.16.1.33 255.255.255.252
7 interface Serial1
8  ip address 192.168.1.66 255.255.255.240
9  clockrate 56000
10 router igrp 1
11  passive-interface Serial0
12  network 192.168.1.0
13  network 172.16.0.0
14 ip default-network 172.16.0.0
15 ip route 0.0.0.0 0.0.0.0 172.16.1.34
16 end
Tokyo Configuration
17 hostname Tokyo
18 no ip domain-lookup
19 interface Ethernet0
20  ip address 192.168.1.97 255.255.255.240
21 interface Serial0
22  ip address 192.168.1.65 255.255.255.240
23 router igrp 1
24  network 192.168.1.0
25 end
ISP Configuration
26 hostname ISP
27 no ip domain-lookup
28 interface Ethernet0
29  ip address 172.18.1.2 255.255.255.0
30 interface Serial1
31  ip address 172.16.1.34 255.255.255.252
32  clockrate 56000
33 ip route 192.168.1.0 255.255.255.0 172.16.1.33
34 end
```

There are many other experiments you can do with this configuration. Check out distribution of the default route when you configure NewYork's default route as an interface route:

```
ip route 0.0.0.0 0.0.0.0 int s 0
```

Is there any change when 172.16.0.0 is omitted from the IGRP configuration in this scenario? What happens when you use another routing protocol?

# Multiple Default Routes

Regardless of the protocol, if more than one router is advertising a default network, then the metric and administrative distance from the neighboring routers to the advertising routers are used to determine which route is the best default. An example of this configuration is shown in Figure 3-12, in which NewYork and London are both connected to an ISP and are both advertising a default route (the use of Ethernets for these connections is irrelevant). Tokyo will receive routing updates from both NewYork and London, but with different metrics (assuming that either the OSPF, IGRP, or EIGRP routing protocol is being used; RIP uses hop count, which results in equal-cost routes via either NewYork or London).

IGRP's configuration for all three routers in this scenario is shown in Figure 3-13. The ISP "owns" the links connecting NewYork to ISP-NewYork and London to ISP-London. Configuration lines 16 and 47 are the default route in NewYork and London. Lines 15 and 46 are the **default-network** command in each. Both routers include the ISP's network in their routing protocol configuration and use the passive interface command (which we'll cover later) to eliminate the broadcast of IGRP routing information over the ISP links.

Tokyo's configuration includes only IGRP, through which it learns the default route. Since the link from Tokyo to NewYork is of higher bandwidth, IGRP will give it a better (lower) metric, as seen in Figure 3-14. Tokyo will use this route in its routing table and keep the path via London as a backup.

**Figure 3-12**
Best default route

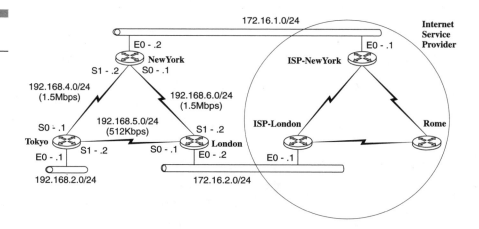

**Figure 3-13** IGRP multiple default route configuration

**NewYork Configuration**
```
1 hostname NewYork
2 interface Ethernet0
3  ip address 172.16.1.2 255.255.255.0
4  interface Serial0
5  ip address 192.168.6.1 255.255.255.0
6 interface Serial1
7  ip address 192.168.4.2 255.255.255.0
8  clockrate 1300000
9 router igrp 1
10  passive-interface Ethernet0
11  network 192.168.4.0
12  network 192.168.6.0
13  network 172.16.0.0
14 ip classless
15 ip default-network 172.16.0.0
16 ip route 0.0.0.0 0.0.0.0 172.16.1.1
17 end
```
**Tokyo Configuration**
```
18 hostname Tokyo
19 interface Ethernet0
20  ip address 192.168.2.1 255.255.255.0
21 interface Serial0
22  ip address 192.168.4.1 255.255.255.0
23 interface Serial1
24  ip address 192.168.5.2 255.255.255.0
25 clockrate 500000
26 router igrp 1
27  network 192.168.2.0
28  network 192.168.4.0
29  network 192.168.5.0
30 ip classless
31 end
```
**London Configuration**
```
32 hostname London
33 interface Ethernet0
34  ip address 172.16.2.2 255.255.255.0
35 interface Serial0
36  ip address 192.168.5.1 255.255.255.0
37 interface Serial1
38  ip address 192.168.6.2 255.255.255.0
39 clockrate 1300000
40 router igrp 1
41  passive-interface Ethernet0
42  network 192.168.5.0
43  network 192.168.6.0
44  network 172.16.0.0
45 ip classless
46 ip default-network 172.16.0.0
47 ip route 0.0.0.0 0.0.0.0 172.16.2.1
48 end
```

**Figure 3-14** Multiple default routing tables

**NewYork routing table**

```
1  NewYork#sh ip route
2  Codes: C - connected, S - static, I - IGRP, R - RIP, M - mobile, B - BGP
3         D - EIGRP, EX - EIGRP external, O - OSPF, IA - OSPF inter area
4         N1 - OSPF NSSA external type 1, N2 - OSPF NSSA external type 2
5         E1 - OSPF external type 1, E2 - OSPF external type 2, E - EGP
6         i - IS-IS, L1 - IS-IS level-1, L2 - IS-IS level-2, * - candidate default
7         U - per-user static route, o - ODR
8
9  Gateway of last resort is 172.16.1.34 to network 0.0.0.0
10
11 I*    172.16.0.0/16 [100/8576] via 192.168.6.2, 00:00:06, Serial0
12 C     192.168.4.0/24 is directly connected, Serial1
13 C     192.168.6.0/24 is directly connected, Serial0
14       192.168.1.0/28 is subnetted, 2 subnets
15 I        192.168.1.96/28 is possibly down,
16            routing via 192.168.1.65, Serial1
17 C        192.168.1.32 is directly connected, Ethernet0
18 I     192.168.2.0/24 [100/8576] via 192.168.4.1, 00:01:16, Serial1
19 S*    0.0.0.0/0 [1/0] via 172.16.1.34
20              [1/0] via 172.16.1.1
21 NewYork#
```

**Tokyo routing table**

```
22 Tokyo#sh ip route
23 Codes: C - connected, S - static, I - IGRP, R - RIP, M - mobile, B - BGP
24         D - EIGRP, EX - EIGRP external, O - OSPF, IA - OSPF inter area
25         N1 - OSPF NSSA external type 1, N2 - OSPF NSSA external type 2
26         E1 - OSPF external type 1, E2 - OSPF external type 2, E - EGP
27         i - IS-IS, L1 - IS-IS level-1, L2 - IS-IS level-2, * - candidate default
28         U - per-user static route, o - ODR
29
30 Gateway of last resort is 192.168.4.2 to network 172.16.0.0
31
32 I*    172.16.0.0/16 [100/10576] via 192.168.4.2, 00:00:05, Serial0
33 C     192.168.4.0/24 is directly connected, Serial0
34 I     192.168.6.0/24 [100/10476] via 192.168.4.2, 00:00:05, Serial0
35       192.168.1.0/24 is variably subnetted, 2 subnets, 2 masks
36 I        192.168.1.32/28 is possibly down,
37            routing via 192.168.1.66, Serial0
38 I        192.168.1.0/24 [100/8576] via 192.168.4.2, 00:00:05, Serial0
39 C     192.168.2.0/24 is directly connected, Ethernet0
40 Tokyo#
```

**London routing table**

```
41 London#sh ip route
42 Codes: C - connected, S - static, I - IGRP, R - RIP, M - mobile, B - BGP
43         D - EIGRP, EX - EIGRP external, O - OSPF, IA - OSPF inter area
44         N1 - OSPF NSSA external type 1, N2 - OSPF NSSA external type 2
45         E1 - OSPF external type 1, E2 - OSPF external type 2, E - EGP
46         i - IS-IS, L1 - IS-IS level-1, L2 - IS-IS level-2, * - candidate default
47         U - per-user static route, o - ODR
48
49 Gateway of last resort is 172.16.2.1 to network 0.0.0.0
50
51 *     172.16.0.0/24 is subnetted, 1 subnets
52 C        172.16.2.0 is directly connected, Ethernet0
53 C     192.168.6.0/24 is directly connected, Serial1
54 S*    0.0.0.0/0 [1/0] via 172.16.2.1
55 London#
```

# Debugging

Debugging static routes is relatively simple. The output of **show ip route** is the first step. But if floating static routes are in use, you also will have to examine the router's configuration (**show running-config** is best, just in case the configuration hasn't been written to NVRAM).

Running ping and trace can give you valuable information in determining which routers have invalid routing information. If ping's output includes several U's, then it is likely that some router along the path does not know how to forward the echo request packet. The best bet is to run a trace to the same destination. A likely culprit is a router that is sourcing a default route but has no static default route itself.

Sometimes, running debug on a router and watching the packet processing is useful. However, don't do this on a busy router: the CPU requirements for debugging high volumes of traffic will not leave any time to process your commands. Many network managers (including ourselves) have done this at least once. It's quite embarrassing to have to reset a router to regain control after enabling debugging on a very busy protocol. It is better to enable debugging on just the routing protocol. A good example of this is in the CCIE Tips section of Chapter 1.

# CCIE Tips

The CCIE candidate should have a good understanding of static routes and their configuration and use in large networks. Besides handling stub networks, they are useful for tying together several large networks. In this case, just duplicate the configuration we used with the network of Figure 3-10. Each regional network connects to a backbone network that has routes back to each region. Therefore, the backbone has more complete routing information than the regions. The regions, in turn, have reduced routing tables, which reduces CPU and link utilization.

If you're configuring dial-backup between the same routers that host the primary link, you should examine the Cisco documentation for its configuration. It doesn't use routing techniques to activate the backup link, so the configuration is different than dial-on-demand. But if you need the backup link to be on a different router, you'll have to use dial-on-demand techniques and floating static routes to implement it.

As we've done here, you should be able to eliminate routing updates over links to stub networks. Make sure you know how to configure the default network and how to propagate this network to other routers within the stub area. Learn how RIP, IGRP, EIGRP, and OSPF propagate the default route and how they react to having a default route sourced from a router in their area.

## SUMMARY

The biggest problem of static routing is that it requires manual configuration when the network changes. For some network topologies, this isn't a problem, because a router's configuration must be changed in any case.

The biggest mistake we've seen in operational networks is trying to fix dynamic routing problems by adding static routes. This is the road to major network failure and network staff overload. As the number of static routes increases, the effort to handle a single network link failure becomes larger and larger.

However, static routes applied in a knowledgeable way, at good places in the network, can reduce routing problems and routing traffic overhead. For example, use static routes in stub networks, where there is only one path available. Two paths can sometimes be accommodated, but the network topology must be examined to make sure that it will operate correctly when a network link or router fails.

Another place that static routes are valuable is in building very large networks in which large regions are connected via one or two major links. The isolation characteristics of static routes can help reduce the load of routing protocols over the entire network and limit the scope of routing changes and problems. We'll discuss how to integrate static routes with dynamic routing protocols in the chapters on dynamic protocols.

CHAPTER 4

# Classful Interior Routing

You've now seen that static routes do not work well in a large routed network. Manually changing the routing tables when a network problem occurs in a large network would create a tremendous, error-prone, and very boring workload.

It makes sense to have routers inform one another when a network problem occurs and to try to route packets around the problem. The task of communicating path availability is performed by routing protocols, of which there are interior and exterior forms. The interior protocols operate within an organization, while exterior protocols typically are used to exchange routing information between large organizations.

Of the interior protocols, RIP and IGRP are called classful protocols because they rely on the class (A, B, or C) of the network address to determine the mask to use for remote networks. Their simplicity of design and operation makes them very useful.

You're probably wondering why you should study these protocols—aren't they dead? In fact, they aren't. While IGRP has been replaced by EIGRP, there is currently no replacement for RIP. Many hosts use RIP to learn about routes and local routers. We'll see where this is useful.

Now that we've established that you may encounter RIP in one of your networks, why learn the details of how it works? Here's the scenario: a network outage occurs within a RIP network and your phone starts ringing immediately ("Can't you run a stable network?"). A few minutes later, just as you're about to determine the problem, you find that the network is now working correctly. But you didn't change anything. What happened?

We'll discover what causes this in the following sections. In addition, we'll cover the strengths, weaknesses, and failure modes of each protocol, to help you design, build, and operate a smoothly running network.

## Distance-Vector Protocols

The two major classful routing protocols in use in the world today are the Routing Information Protocol (RIP) and Cisco's proprietary Interior Gateway Routing Protocol (IGRP). Both of these protocols are members of a class of protocols known as distance-vector protocols.

Distance-vector protocols (also known as Bellman-Ford protocols) are based on the mathematical work of Bellman and Ford, who proved that the protocols will converge to a known topology as long as the topology remains stable. The term distance vector comes from the fact that these protocols send periodic updates containing a vector (a mathematical term for a list) of destination networks, each of which contains a "distance" from the advertising router to the destination. Because distance-vector protocols periodically transmit their full routing table to neighbors, they can consume a significant amount of network bandwidth. A good discussion of distance-vector protocols may be found in RFC1058 (Hedrick 1988), which describes RIP and the various mechanisms used by distance-vector protocols.

# RIP

RIP is the best known of the distance-vector protocols. Originally developed by Xerox in the late 1970s as a part of the Xerox Networking Services (XNS) protocol suite, RIP is a distance-vector protocol with additional features that help reduce the occurrence of routing loops. The IP version of RIP was derived from the XNS implementation and is documented in RFC1058 (Hedrick 1988). Its simplicity and ease of configuration contributed to its adoption as the first IP dynamic routing protocol.

Many hosts listen to RIP updates to learn about local routers and routes. In highly redundant networks, where there is more than one router per LAN segment, hosts often use RIP to determine the best router to use to communicate with hosts on other network segments. Figure 4-1 shows a possible network configuration in which systems A, B, and C rely on RIP from London-1 and London-2 to determine the best path to other network segments.

## Configuration

RIP is very easy to configure. You enable RIP, then add the network numbers of all directly connected networks. Cisco's RIP will remove all subnetting or host information, leaving only the base classful address. In Figure 4-2, we use 172.16.0.0, a class B network subnetted with a 27-bit mask, and 192.168.3.0, a class C network subnetted with a 28-bit mask. It is

**Figure 4-1**
RIP used for route distribution

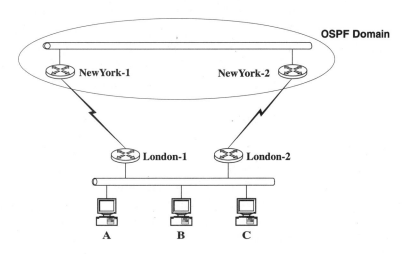

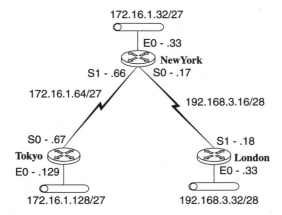

**Figure 4-2**
RIP configuration
network

172.16.1.32/27

E0 - .33

NewYork

S1 - .66        S0 - .17

172.16.1.64/27

192.168.3.16/28

S0 - .67

Tokyo

E0 - .129

S1 - .18

London

E0 - .33

172.16.1.128/27        192.168.3.32/28

not necessary to include remote networks in the RIP configuration (Figure 4-3). Each router will learn about all remote networks by listening to RIP from its neighbors.

## Lab Exercise

It is instructive to see what happens in a RIP network as routers start to exchange routing information. In the lab, configure router interfaces using the addresses shown in Figure 4-2 (try to do it without referring to the configuration in Figure 4-3). Enable RIP debugging (**debug ip rip**). Turn on RIP in NewYork. Then turn it on in London. Then add Tokyo. See what is communicated between routers as they are configured. In Tokyo, issue the configuration command **no network 172.16.0.0**, followed by **network 172.16.1.128**. Then use the exec command **show run** to examine the running configuration. What address appears in the RIP **network** subcommand? What happened to the subnet information? Use the **show ip route** command to see the routing table. Check the administrative distance and metric on each route.

## RIP Updates

There are two types of RIP packets: updates and requests. Update packets are the normal route-distribution mechanism. Request packets are used by routers to discover other RIP-speaking routers on a network. The request asks that a copy of the RIP routing table be provided back to the requester.

▬▬ ▬▬ ▬▬ ▬▬ ▬▬ ▬▬ ▬▬ ▬▬ ▬▬ ▬▬ ▬▬ ▬▬ ▬▬ ▬▬ ▬▬ ▬▬ ▬▬ ▬▬ ▬▬

**Figure 4-3** RIP configuration

**NewYork Configuration**
```
1 hostname NewYork
2 interface Ethernet0
3  ip address 172.16.1.33 255.255.255.224
4 interface Serial0
5  ip address 192.168.3.17 255.255.255.240
6 interface Serial1
7  ip address 172.16.1.66 255.255.255.224
8 clockrate 56000
9 router rip
10   network 192.168.3.0
11   network 172.16.0.0
12 end
```
**Tokyo Configuration**
```
13 hostname Tokyo
14 interface Ethernet0
15  ip address 172.16.1.129 255.255.255.224
16 interface Serial0
17  ip address 172.16.1.67 255.255.255.224
18 router rip
19   network 172.16.0.0
20 end
```
**London Configuration**
```
21 hostname London
22 interface Ethernet0
23  ip address 192.168.3.33 255.255.255.240
24 interface Serial1
25  ip address 192.168.3.18 255.255.255.240
26  clockrate 56000
27 router rip
28   network 192.168.3.0
29 end
```

**Figure 4-4**
RIP updates

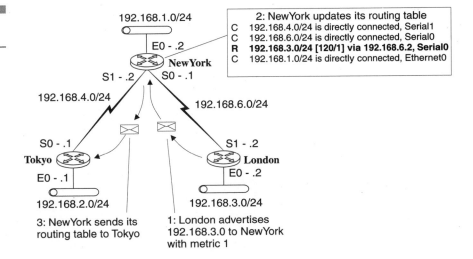

192.168.1.0/24

2: NewYork updates its routing table
C   192.168.4.0/24 is directly connected, Serial1
C   192.168.6.0/24 is directly connected, Serial0
**R   192.168.3.0/24 [120/1] via 192.168.6.2, Serial0**
C   192.168.1.0/24 is directly connected, Ethernet0

E0 - .2
**NewYork**
S1 - .2      S0 - .1

192.168.4.0/24
192.168.6.0/24

S0 - .1
**Tokyo**
E0 - .1

S1 - .2
**London**
E0 - .2

192.168.2.0/24
192.168.3.0/24

3: NewYork sends its
routing table to Tokyo

1: London advertises
192.168.3.0 to NewYork
with metric 1

A router running RIP broadcasts the contents of its routing table to its neighbors every 30 seconds using UDP datagrams on port 520. In a large network, this can result in a significant volume of overhead traffic. On the other hand, these periodic updates make it easy to troubleshoot.

The vector (list) of routes is broadcast to each of the neighboring routers as shown in Figure 4-4. Here, RIP has just been enabled on all three routers. In step 1, London advertises network 192.168.3.0 with a "distance" of one hop to NewYork. Network 192.168.6.0, connecting London to NewYork, isn't included in the advertisement, because London knows that NewYork is attached to this network. Step 2 shows NewYork's updated routing table. Step 3 shows NewYork advertising the contents of its routing table to Tokyo. Note that the locally connected networks are advertised with a distance of one hop and that London's network is advertised by NewYork with a distance of two hops.

NewYork is also sending updates to London, and Tokyo is sending updates to NewYork. Over the course of several update cycles, all routers will learn of all destination networks and their metrics.

## RIP Metrics

Distance-vector protocols transmit a "distance," or metric, with each route. For RIP, the metric is the number of hops through which the destination may be reached. Each network link is considered to be one hop. The maximum usable number of hops for RIP is 15, with 16 indicating an invalid (or infinite metric) route.

In Figure 4-5, Tokyo has a direct connection to network 192.168.2.0 (stored with a metric of zero) and advertises it with metric one. NewYork hears this advertisement and inserts this route into its routing table.

**Figure 4-5**
RIP metrics

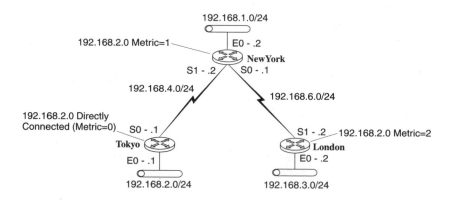

New York then advertises this same network to its neighbors with metric two (it is two hops to get to the destination network). London adds this network to its routing table.

FYI: The RIP RFC (RFC1058) specifies that a directly connected network should be stored in the routing table with a metric that corresponds to its cost (allowing for a cost other than one). RFC1058 goes on to explain that the cost of each link is added to the metric upon receipt of a routing update. Also, the metric in a received update should be stored in the routing table.

An older algorithm is documented in RFC1058, section 3.6, in which directly connected networks are stored in the routing table with a cost of zero. The cost of the outgoing link is added to the metric when a routing advertisement is constructed. The route metrics in received routing updates are stored directly in the routing table. In the network of Figure 4-5, New York receives an update from Tokyo for 192.168.2.0 with a metric of one. The output of **show ip route** shows that the stored metric for this route is one. The **debug** output from New York shows an advertisement of 192.168.2.0 with a metric of two.

In practice, both methods produce the same routing updates on the wire and will interoperate with each other. The method documented in RFC1058 increments metrics upon receipt, while the older implementation increments metrics upon transmission. Cisco routers use the older practice, as can be seen by the contents of the routing tables and debug output.

**Figure 4-6**
Count-to-infinity

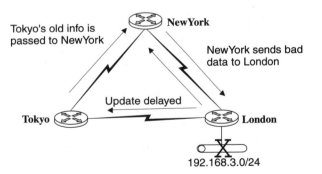

London's ethernet dies.
London sends triggered updates to New York and Tokyo.
New York receives update.
Tokyo's update is delayed by other traffic.
Tokyo sends periodic update to New York, overriding London's update.
New York sends bad data to London on its next update.
The routing information is passed around the loop until the metric reaches infinity.

# RIP Count-to-Infinity

The basic distance-vector protocols operate well in a stable network. But no network is stable forever. Routers are rebooted, links change status, and many other daily operations take place on a normal network that cause topology changes on a regular basis. In the next few sections, we'll look at the problems that occur with distance-vector protocols and mechanisms that address these problems. Note that any properly functioning distance-vector protocol has implemented all the mechanisms that prevent these problems from occurring.

The first problem is a routing loop created between neighboring routers. Figure 4-6 shows three connected routers. New York and Tokyo have a route to London's E0 (192.168.3.0). When 192.168.3.0 becomes disconnected (or shut down), London will trigger an update to both New York and Tokyo to indicate that the route is no longer valid. The updates normally happen without a problem. However, there is a timing consideration that can occur that will cause the count-to-infinity problem.

Here is the scenario: New York receives the update from London, and the route to 192.168.3.0 is marked as invalid (metric 16). Due to CPU loading and other traffic, the update to Tokyo is slightly delayed. Tokyo's normal update is then sent to New York showing 192.168.3.0 as available with metric two. New York has no ability to evaluate the overall network topology from the information in the update and doesn't know that Tokyo's route is also via London. So it updates its routing table with the information that 192.168.3.0 is reachable with metric two via Tokyo.

Tokyo now receives the correct information from London, but the (now-invalid) update has already been sent to New York. Tokyo sets its route to 192.168.3.0 to metric 16. But New York has invalid information and proceeds to pollute the network with it. On its next update cycle, New York will tell London that 192.168.3.0 is available with metric three. London accepts this information and updates its routing table with the great news! London then propagates the route with metric four to Tokyo.

Now we have invalid routing information in all the routing tables. You can see that, as the route is propagated from router to router around the circle, the metric value increments. The solution is to select some maximum value at which the route is declared invalid. For

RIP, this value is 16. The "infinite" value is selected to be high enough to be useful for most networks, yet small enough that the time needed for the routers to increment the metric to infinity is not long. This process is called *count-to-infinity*, and it breaks loops between routers when the metric reaches the metric value of infinity.

During the time when the count-to-infinity process is occurring, any packet that is sent to any address on the 192.168.3.0 network will be forwarded from router to router until the time-to-live in the IP header reaches zero. The packet is dropped, and an ICMP TTL-exceeded message is sent to the source.

## Distance-Vector Split Horizon

Another problem with distance-vector protocols involves sending routing information back to the system from which it was learned. This is like telling a joke back to someone who told it to you. They've already heard the joke and know the punch line.

We saw this in the simple example earlier, where New York heard about the route to 192.168.3.0 from Tokyo. But Tokyo initially learned the route from New York and should not send that information back to New York. This technique is called split horizon. A router that implements split horizon never sends routing information back out the interface from which the information originated. This includes a route to the network that connects two routers.

Let's see how this works. In Figure 4-7, we have a network diagram of three routers connected in series. London's E0 is disconnected. A trig-

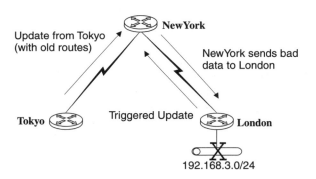

**Figure 4-7**

Split horizon

Update from Tokyo
(with old routes)

NewYork

NewYork sends bad
data to London

Tokyo

Triggered Update

London

192.168.3.0/24

gered update is generated indicating that 192.168.3.0 is no longer reachable. NewYork marks the route as unreachable in its routing table. However, Tokyo still thinks it can reach 192.168.3.0 via NewYork because no routing update has yet been generated from NewYork to Tokyo.

Tokyo's update timer triggers, and it sends an update to NewYork indicating that 192.168.3.0 is reachable with metric three. NewYork adds the new (better) route to its routing table. A count-to-infinity process is now required to clear the invalid route from the routing tables of all three routers.

Since the routing updates don't contain any information about the source of the routing information, NewYork must accept the route as valid (after all, Tokyo may have a route via another path). It is clear to us, since we have a view of the entire network that Tokyo learned of the route via NewYork and should not have advertised it back to NewYork. Split horizon prevents Tokyo from advertising any route that it learned from NewYork back to NewYork. The Cisco implementation of split horizon will not advertise any route back out the interface from which it was learned, regardless of the router that advertised it.

Consider the case where the source is a router on an Ethernet. All other routers on the Ethernet should have heard the source router's advertisement, so there is no need for any receiving router to advertise the route back to the Ethernet. A side effect of this mechanism is that it reduces the size of routing updates.

This mechanism breaks loops between adjacent routers. The Cisco version allows you to disable the split horizon mechanism with the interface subcommand **no ip split-horizon.**

## Lab Exercise

You can see this in action on our lab network. Configure the routers to use RIP with the configuration shown in Figure 4-3. Enable RIP debugging (**debug ip rip**). Watch the contents of the RIP updates. Check the routing updates from each router to see what routes it is advertising and the metrics for those routes. Disable split horizon (**no ip split-horizon**) on the serial interfaces and watch the contents of the updates change. Make sure to reenable split horizon when you are finished.

## Poison Reverse

Simple split horizon omits routing information in updates sent in the direction from which the information was learned. By advertising a route back to its source with a metric of 16 (infinity), it is possible to immediately break any loops that may occur between neighboring routers. This increases the size of routing updates but adds some additional security to the prevention of routing loops.

Cisco routers implement poison reverse with a time delay. When a route is marked invalid, it is included in the reverse updates with an infinite metric for a while after the change. When the route is flushed from the routing table, the poison reverse information is no longer advertised. This reduces the size of routing updates while providing the additional loop protection during network convergence.

## Flash Updates

Cisco routers implement a feature called flash updates. When a routing table changes, a new routing update is created and broadcast to its neighbors. Similarly, when a router starts running RIP, it broadcasts a request packet. Adjacent RIP routers must reply with a RIP update, allowing the new router to join a network without waiting for the next RIP update. The reply to a request is not broadcast—it is sent only to the requesting router, and split horizon is not performed on the routes in the reply packet.

## Lab Exercise

It is easy to see this in our lab network by using **shutdown** and **no shutdown** on an interface. With RIP running on the lab network, enable RIP debugging on NewYork and London. It is best to have a console on each router. Watch for the RIP update messages that look like the following:

```
RIP: sending v1 update to 255.255.255.255 via Serial 1 (192.168.4.2)
    network 192.168.6.0, metric 1
    network 192.168.1.0, metric 1
    network 192.168.3.0, metric 1
```

On London, enter configuration mode, specify **int e 0**, and type the command **shutdown**, but don't press the Enter key yet. Watching New York's debug output, wait until about 10 seconds after regular update, then press the Enter key on London's console. Watch the update interaction with New York on both consoles. You will have to wait several minutes for the route to age out. Look for the poison reverse route advertisement from New York back to London in its updates as we discussed in the previous section on poison reverse.

When the route to 192.168.3.0 has aged out, enter the command **no shutdown** on London. Press the Enter key on London's console a few seconds after New York's periodic update has been sent. You'll see both London and New York issue a new set of updates to propagate the new information.

In both of the previous transactions, you'll see New York issue a flash update containing the new routing information on all of its interfaces. As an additional exercise, you may wish to use more routers connected in series and watch the debug output on each router to clearly see the triggered updates and the poison reverse advertisements.

## Holddown

In distance-vector protocols, a mechanism is needed to prevent routers from believing incorrect routing information that is generated by devices that have not yet learned of a topology change. For example, the scenario we described in the count-to-infinity section has New York using incorrect information from Tokyo just after the route became invalid. With holddown, New York will not believe the new information from Tokyo. The route is "held down" in the invalid state for a period of time after it is marked invalid. This prevents a router from using any new routing information until all routers in the network have had a chance to learn about the topology change.

The holddown mechanism also prevents a flapping route from causing turmoil in a network. If a link goes down, then comes back up, goes down again, then comes back up, all in quick succession, we don't want the flapping to cause a flurry of routing information exchanges on our network. Limiting the distribution of flapping routes adds stability to the network and reduces the overhead of routing information. The cost to this is the delay from the time the route is again usable until the holddown timer expires. We'll see how the holddown timer works with the other RIP timers in the next section.

# Timers

There are several timers that work with the holddown timer to control the propagation of RIP routing information. These timers are known as the update, invalid, holddown, and flush timers. The relationships between each of these timers is shown in Figure 4-8.

The update timer is the time interval between the periodic routing updates. For RIP, this timer is 30 seconds. Cisco routers will not transmit RIP updates exactly every 30 seconds. There is a well-known phenomenon whereby network devices transmitting periodic updates will synchronize their updates with each other. This is because the CPU overhead introduced by the processing of transmitted and received updates causes the devices to eventually shift their update times until they are synchronized. Cisco modifies the update timer by some number of milliseconds on each update to prevent this.

The invalid timer is used to detect failures on network media where there is no positive indication that a neighboring device has failed or become disconnected. For RIP, this timer is set to 180 seconds. If no routing updates are received from a previously operational neighbor within this time, all routes via that neighbor are marked as invalid and will go into holddown.

The holddown timer is 180 seconds. Any route which has become unreachable will not be believed again until 180 seconds after the failure.

When a failure has occurred, another timer also is running. It is the flush timer, which for RIP is set to 240 seconds. If the route has failed and is still unavailable 240 seconds after the failure, the route will be flushed from the routing table. This is the timer that causes the route to be removed from the routing updates.

**Figure 4-8**
RIP timers

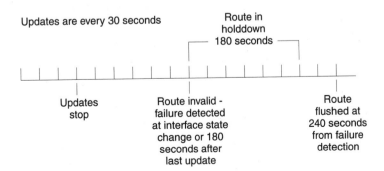

## Lab Exercise

You can see all of these timers in action on our lab network. Again, we're working with RIP starting with the lab configuration of Figure 4-3. Enable **debug ip rip** on all three routers and make sure all interfaces are enabled.

The best place to see things is to watch New York's debug output. With a stopwatch, you can time the update timers by watching for the "sending" debug output on each router. Remember, the time won't be exactly 30 seconds.

Then, on London's console, **shutdown** the E0 interface and start your stopwatch. The interface will go into the administratively shutdown state, and the routing updates will show the route with a metric of 16 (unreachable). After 240 seconds, you'll see the route flushed from London's routing table, and it will no longer be advertised. You also can see New York and Tokyo advertising the route with a poison reverse metric in the split horizon updates to London.

Issue a **no shutdown** command for London's E0 interface and watch the route become immediately available on all three routers as triggered updates propagate the information.

Now **shutdown** London's E0 interface again and restart your stopwatch. After one update cycle, you'll see that all the routers have the route marked as invalid (metric 16). At this time, bring the interface back up (**no shutdown**). Examine the debug output carefully. You'll see that London issues the triggered updates showing the route as valid (because it has a direct connection to the network, it knows that the route is valid). However, New York and Tokyo don't believe the new information. You'll see in their updates that they are still advertising the route to 192.168.3.0 with a metric of 16. This will continue until 180 seconds after the failure. At this time, they will believe the new route and advertise it with the proper metric.

**Figure 4-9**
Invalid timer network

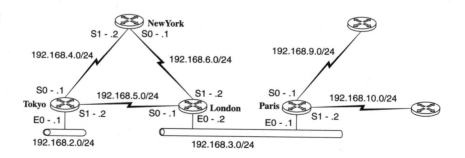

You can experiment with the invalid timer by using a configuration similar to that in Figure 4-9. Make sure Paris is configured with RIP and that the routes for its serial interfaces appear in London's routing table. Start **debug ip rip** on London. Issue a **shutdown** command on Paris E0 interface to disconnect it from the Ethernet and start your stopwatch. For a while you'll see that the routes via Paris will still be valid. Any packets that are addressed to destinations on these networks will be transmitted on the Ethernet but will not make it to Paris.

After 180 seconds, you'll see that the routes via Paris go into the invalid state. At this point, the routes will be advertised with an infinite metric, just as we saw when we shut down the serial links on London.

You can modify these timers using the router subcommand **timers basic**, but we don't recommend it. All devices that use RIP must have the same timers to operate reliably. One interesting failure is for the timers to be different on a router. This causes a route to periodically appear and disappear as the invalid timer is reached and the route goes into holddown.

## Packet Format

RIP updates are transmitted within UDP broadcasts on UDP port 520. The packet format is shown in Figure 4-10. The command and version fields are common to any RIP packet. The version of RIP that we are describing here is version 1 (we'll discuss version 2 in the classless routing protocol section).

The possible commands are shown in Table 4-1.

**Figure 4-10**
RIP packet format

Bit Position
00 01 02 03 04 05 06 07 08 09 10 11 12 13 14 15 16 17 18 19 20 21 22 23 24 25 26 27 28 29 30 31

| Command | Version | must be zero |
| Address Family Identifier | | must be zero |
| IP Address | | |
| must be zero | | |
| must be zero | | |
| Metric | | |
| . . . | | |

The portion of the datagram from Address Family Identifier
through Metric may appear up to 25 times. Additional
routes in an update must be transmitted in additional datagrams.

**Table 4-1**

RIP commands

| Command | Value | Description |
|---------|-------|-------------|
| Request | 1 | Requests all or part of the routing table of the receiving system. |
| Response | 2 | Contains all or part of the routing table of the responding system. If the routing table is larger than 25 entries, multiple response packets will be used. |

Each route is described by the next five 32-bit fields, and these five fields are repeated for each route. The address family identifier field identifies the type of address that follows. A value of 2 indicates that the next 32-bit field contains an IP address in network byte order.

FYI: Network byte order describes the order in which the bytes (or octets) of data should appear on the network. Different computer systems use different byte ordering internally. The way that these computers read bytes from memory can cause incompatible ordering of bytes on the wire. An interoperability standard was developed to address this problem. For more information on network byte order and machine representation of bytes internally, refer to IEN137 (Cohen 1980).

The IP address field contains the destination address, which may be a host address, subnet address, or network address. A system searching for the best route to use for a given destination should first search for a matching host route (a 32-bit address), then check for a matching subnet address (longer match than a network address but less than a host address), or a network address. The subnet address can be checked only if the subnet mask is known. If no mask is known for a given network, and bits are set in the host field of an address, then the router must assume that the address represents a host route.

The third and fourth 32-bit fields are not used and should be set to zero. The fifth 32-bit field is the metric of the route. Valid values are 1-15. A value of 16 indicates that the destination is unreachable (or invalid).

## Limiting RIP Updates

We've said several times that RIP uses broadcasts to transmit its updates. You can see this in the RIP debug output where the destination address of the updates is set to the IP local-wire broadcast address (255.255.255.255).

But there is a cost associated with broadcast traffic. Every computer system on multiaccess networks (e.g., Ethernet or TokenRing) will receive the broadcast. Nonrouter systems will process the received frame through the interface data-link driver, the network-layer software, and in the case of RIP, even the transport-layer software before determining that the packet should be discarded. Executing all this software and finally discarding the packet is wasteful.

Another situation is where there is no need to send an update on a given network link, primarily because the other router(s) connected to the link are not listening to RIP or where there are only host systems (and no router) on the specified network segment. Figure 4-11 shows a network in which RIP broadcasts are not needed on the Ethernet because there are no routers there (the hosts should be using proxy ARP or have their default gateway set to the router).

Using the **passive-interface** router subcommand allows us to tell the routing protocols to not transmit updates on specific interfaces (but the router listens to updates received on these interfaces). This eliminates unnecessary routing traffic on networks where routing updates are not needed.

A more advanced configuration of the network in Figure 4-11 also is possible using the **passive-interface** command. If Tokyo is servicing a stub network, it is not necessary to propagate all the backbone routes to Tokyo over the (possibly low bandwidth) serial link. We want New York to know when a failure has occurred with Tokyo's LAN, but we want to conserve network bandwidth over the serial link. The configuration appears in Figure 4-12. Tokyo uses a default route to New York, does not

**Figure 4-11**
Passive interface
network

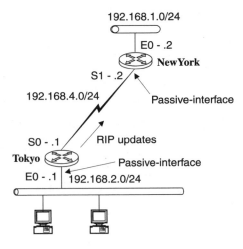

**Figure 4-12** Passive-interface configuration

**NewYork Configuration**
```
1 hostname NewYork
2 interface Ethernet0
3  ip address 192.168.1.1 255.255.255.0
4 interface Serial1
5  ip address 192.168.4.2 255.255.255.0
6  clockrate 56000
7 router rip
8  passive-interface Serial1
9  network 192.168.4.0
10  network 192.168.1.0
11 end
```
**Tokyo Configuration**
```
12 hostname Tokyo
13 interface Ethernet0
14  ip address 192.168.2.1 255.255.255.0
15 interface Serial0
16  ip address 192.168.4.1 255.255.255.0
17 router rip
18  passive-interface Ethernet0
19  network 192.168.2.0
20  network 192.168.4.0
21 ip route 0.0.0.0 0.0.0.0 192.168.4.2
22 end
```
**NewYork Debug Output**
```
23 NewYork#debug ip rip
24 RIP protocol debugging is on
25 NewYork#
26 RIP: received v1 update from 192.168.4.1 on Serial1
27      192.168.2.0 in 1 hops
28 RIP: sending v1 update to 255.255.255.255 via Ethernet0 (192.168.1.1)
29      network 192.168.4.0, metric 1
30      network 192.168.2.0, metric 2
```
**Tokyo Debug Output**
```
31 Tokyo#debug ip rip
32 RIP protocol debugging is on
33 Tokyo#
34 RIP: sending v1 update to 255.255.255.255 via Serial0 (192.168.4.1)
35      network 192.168.2.0, metric 1
```

broadcast RIP updates on its Ethernet, and NewYork does not transmit the backbone routes to Tokyo. It is useful to examine the RIP debug output to verify that this is what is happening.

NewYork's configuration is interesting. RIP is configured on the serial link to Tokyo (line 9), but that interface is specified as a passive-interface (line 8). This allows NewYork to receive Tokyo's routing update, which contains the one route to its Ethernet. But NewYork does not broadcast its (possibly large) routing table to Tokyo, conserving serial link bandwidth. Tokyo's configuration uses a default route (line 21) to force nonlocal traffic to NewYork. Ethernet 0 is set as a passive-interface to prevent RIP updates and avoid an unnecessary load on the hosts on the Ethernet.

## RIP Network Design

RIP has several constraints that need to be taken into account when designing your network routing protocol architecture. The major constraints in today's networks are because RIP is a classful routing protocol. Classful protocols do not carry the network (or subnet) mask in their routing updates. If a router running RIP does not have an interface on a subnet of a network, it cannot know what subnet mask is used on the network. In this case, the router must select a network mask to use when looking up a match in the routing table. For RIP routes to remote networks, the mask that will be used is that of the classful address.

In Figure 4-13, we have two separate network numbers, each of which is subnetted. Some subnets of each network are used on different links. Examining the routing table of Tokyo (Figure 4-14), we see that the remote network is known only by its classful address (172.16.0.0). Similarly, Rome only knows about 192.168.12.0.

It is because of the summarization to the classful network address that all RIP subnets must be contiguous. What does this mean? It means that all subnets of a given network must connect to each other. There cannot be a second network that connects two or more subnets of a network. In Figure 4-15, several subnets of a class C network are separated by a few subnets of a class B network. Looking at New York's routing table (Figure 4-16), we see two routing entries for the class C network, both with the same metric. Which subnet exists via which route? Without the specific subnet information, it is impossible to decide. Therefore, all subnets of a network must be contiguous so that any entry into a network can reach all the subnets of that network.

**Figure 4-13**
RIP summarization network

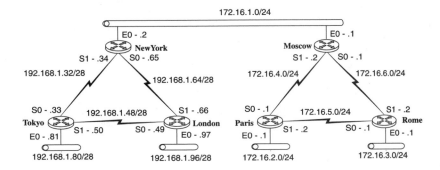

**Figure 4-14** Summarization in RIP routing tables

```
1  Tokyo#sh ip route
2  Codes: C - connected, S - static, I - IGRP, R - RIP, M - mobile, B - BGP
3         D - EIGRP, EX - EIGRP external, O - OSPF, IA - OSPF inter area
4         N1 - OSPF NSSA external type 1, N2 - OSPF NSSA external type 2
5         E1 - OSPF external type 1, E2 - OSPF external type 2, E - EGP
6         i - IS-IS, L1 - IS-IS level-1, L2 - IS-IS level-2, * - candidate default
7         U - per-user static route, o - ODR
8  Gateway of last resort is not set
9  R     172.16.0.0/16 [120/1] via 192.168.1.34, 00:00:25, Serial0
10       192.168.1.0/28 is subnetted, 5 subnets
11 R        192.168.1.96 [120/1] via 192.168.1.49, 00:00:01, Serial1
12 R        192.168.1.64 [120/1] via 192.168.1.34, 00:00:26, Serial0
13                       [120/1] via 192.168.1.49, 00:00:01, Serial1
14 C        192.168.1.80 is directly connected, Ethernet0
15 C        192.168.1.32 is directly connected, Serial0
16 C        192.168.1.48 is directly connected, Serial1
17 Tokyo#
18
19 Rome#sh ip route
20 Codes: C - connected, S - static, I - IGRP, R - RIP, M - mobile, B - BGP
21        D - EIGRP, EX - EIGRP external, O - OSPF, IA - OSPF inter area
22        N1 - OSPF NSSA external type 1, N2 - OSPF NSSA external type 2
23        E1 - OSPF external type 1, E2 - OSPF external type 2, E - EGP
24        i - IS-IS, L1 - IS-IS level-1, L2 - IS-IS level-2, * - candidate default
25        U - per-user static route, o - ODR
26 Gateway of last resort is not set
27       172.16.0.0/24 is subnetted, 6 subnets
28 R        172.16.4.0 [120/1] via 172.16.6.1, 00:00:02, Serial1
29                     [120/1] via 172.16.5.2, 00:00:00, Serial0
30 C        172.16.5.0 is directly connected, Serial0
31 C        172.16.6.0 is directly connected, Serial1
32 R        172.16.1.0 [120/1] via 172.16.6.1, 00:00:02, Serial1
33 R        172.16.2.0 [120/1] via 172.16.5.2, 00:00:00, Serial0
34 C        172.16.3.0 is directly connected, Ethernet0
35 R     192.168.1.0/24 [120/2] via 172.16.6.1, 00:00:02, Serial1
36 Rome#
```

Since our example network has equal-cost paths, let's try an experiment. Use **trace** to report the path that packets will take to get to a destination system on one of the subnets. Here, it is useful to bring up Paris on the London Ethernet and trace from NewYork to the Paris E0 inter-

**Figure 4-15**
Contiguous subnets

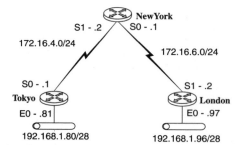

T194

**Figure 4-16** Routes to discontiguous subnets

```
1 NewYork#sh ip route
2 Codes: C - connected, S - static, I - IGRP, R - RIP, M - mobile, B - BGP
3        D - EIGRP, EX - EIGRP external, O - OSPF, IA - OSPF inter area
4        N1 - OSPF NSSA external type 1, N2 - OSPF NSSA external type 2
5        E1 - OSPF external type 1, E2 - OSPF external type 2, E - EGP
6        i - IS-IS, L1 - IS-IS level-1, L2 - IS-IS level-2, * - candidate default
7        U - per-user static route, o - ODR
8
9 Gateway of last resort is not set
10
11      172.16.0.0/24 is subnetted, 2 subnets
12 C       172.16.4.0 is directly connected, Serial1
13 C       172.16.6.0 is directly connected, Serial0
14 R    192.168.1.0/24 [120/1] via 172.16.6.2, 00:00:01, Serial0
15                     [120/1] via 172.16.4.1, 00:00:09, Serial1
16 NewYork#
```

face. A sample output is shown in Figure 4-17. Notice that every other packet is lost. This is because those packets are being sent via Tokyo. NewYork believes Tokyo can get to the London-Paris Ethernet because Tokyo is reporting that it is connected to the same base network as London and Paris. This is a case where route summarization is hiding the detailed subnet structure of 192.168.1.0 from NewYork.

**Figure 4-17** Trace into discontiguous subnets

```
1 NewYork#trace
2 Protocol [ip]:
3 Target IP address: 192.168.1.98
4 Source address: 172.16.6.1
5 Numeric display [n]:
6 Timeout in seconds [3]:
7 Probe count [3]: 6
8 Minimum Time to Live [1]:
9 Maximum Time to Live [30]:
10 Port Number [33434]:
11 Loose, Strict, Record, Timestamp, Verbose[none]:
12 Type escape sequence to abort.
13 Tracing the route to 192.168.1.98
14
15   1 172.16.6.2 20 msec
16     172.16.4.1 20 msec
17     172.16.6.2 16 msec
18     172.16.4.1 16 msec
19     172.16.6.2 16 msec
20     172.16.4.1 16 msec
21   2 192.168.1.98 24 msec
22     172.16.4.1 !H  *  !H
23     192.168.1.98 24 msec *
24 NewYork#
```

Another consideration in a subnetted network running RIP is that all subnets must be the same size. Again, this is because no subnetting information is propagated in the routing updates, so a different sized subnet may not be visible to a remote router within the routing domain. And as we saw in Chapter 2, this can result in a significant waste of addresses, especially on point-to-point serial links.

An especially important design factor is the metric used by RIP—hop-count. Since link bandwidth is not a factor, any network running RIP probably should be small and certainly should not have redundant links of different bandwidths where a slower link is used simply because it is fewer hops to the destination.

Be careful of using RIP in networks where your routing protocol needs to transport many routes. A routing table that contains 1,000 routes will require the transmission of 40 540-byte packets (512 bytes for RIP, 20 bytes for IP, 8 bytes for UDP). A full update would be 172,800 bits, or more than three seconds of transmission time every 30 seconds on a 56Kbps link. This is 10 percent of the 56K link! Imagine what happens to any interactive traffic that is queued behind one of these huge updates.

## Debugging & Show Commands

You should become familiar with the output of **show ip protocol** for all the routing protocols. RIP's important information (see Figure 4-18) includes the timers, the route filters (which we'll talk about in Chapter 6),

**Figure 4-18** Output of **show ip** protocol in a RIP network

```
1 Tokyo#sh ip proto
2 Routing Protocol is "rip"
3   Sending updates every 30 seconds, next due in 25 seconds
4   Invalid after 180 seconds, hold down 180, flushed after 240
5   Outgoing update filter list for all interfaces is not set
6   Incoming update filter list for all interfaces is not set
7   Redistributing: rip
8   Default version control: send version 1, receive any version
9     Interface      Send  Recv   Key-chain
10      Ethernet0       1    1 2
11      Serial0         1    1 2
12    Routing for Networks:
13      192.168.2.0
14      192.168.4.0
15    Routing Information Sources:
16      Gateway        Distance     Last Update
17      192.168.4.2         120     00:00:11
18    Distance: (default is 120)
```

**Figure 4-19** Output of **show ip** route

```
1 Tokyo#sh ip route
2 Codes: C - connected, S - static, I - IGRP, R - RIP, M - mobile, B - BGP
3        D - EIGRP, EX - EIGRP external, O - OSPF, IA - OSPF inter area
4        N1 - OSPF NSSA external type 1, N2 - OSPF NSSA external type 2
5        E1 - OSPF external type 1, E2 - OSPF external type 2, E - EGP
6        i - IS-IS, L1 - IS-IS level-1, L2 - IS-IS level-2, * - candidate default
7        U - per-user static route, o - ODR
8 Gateway of last resort is not set
9 C     192.168.4.0/24 is directly connected, Serial0
10 R    192.168.6.0/24 [120/1] via 192.168.4.2, 00:00:09, Serial0
11 R    192.168.1.0/24 [120/1] via 192.168.4.2, 00:00:09, Serial0
12 C    192.168.2.0/24 is directly connected, Ethernet0
13 R    192.168.3.0/24 is possibly down, routing via 192.168.4.2, Serial
```

the list of networks that RIP has been configured to handle, and the sources of RIP routing information.

The command **show ip route** displays the contents of the IP routing table. Any route that is marked with an R in the first column is a RIP-derived route. Check that all routes in your network are displayed correctly. If a particular route does not appear, check to verify that it should or should not appear in the RIP routing table (Figure 4-19).

Debugging RIP is very simple. The command **debug ip rip** enables debugging. Every 30 seconds, the router will report the transmission of RIP updates on all interfaces that have been specified to run RIP. The

**Figure 4-20** Output of **debug ip rip**

```
1 Tokyo#debug ip rip
2 RIP protocol debugging is on
3 Tokyo#
4 RIP: sending v1 update to 255.255.255.255 via Ethernet0 (192.168.2.1)
5       network 192.168.4.0, metric 1
6       network 192.168.6.0, metric 2
7       network 192.168.1.0, metric 2
8       network 192.168.3.0, metric 3
9 RIP: sending v1 update to 255.255.255.255 via Serial0 (192.168.4.1)
10       network 192.168.2.0, metric 1
11 RIP: received v1 update from 192.168.4.2 on Serial0
12       192.168.6.0 in 1 hops
13       192.168.1.0 in 1 hops
14       192.168.3.0 in 16 hops (inaccessible)
15 RIP: sending v1 update to 255.255.255.255 via Ethernet0 (192.168.2.1)
16       network 192.168.4.0, metric 1
17       network 192.168.6.0, metric 2
18       network 192.168.1.0, metric 2
19       network 192.168.3.0, metric 16
20)RIP: sending v1 update to 255.255.255.255 via Serial0 (192.168.4.1)
21       network 192.168.2.0, metric 1
22       network 192.168.3.0, metric 16
```

debug output shows the routes and metrics that are being sent in each update (Figure 4-20).

Watch out for routes that are in holddown (line 13 in Figure 4-19 and lines 19 and 22 in Figure 4-20). You will have to wait several minutes after a link goes down before it will reappear in the routing tables. This could cause you some consternation in troubleshooting a reported problem: the call comes in reporting a network connectivity problem. You quickly validate the complaint. While you're collecting information on the problem, it fixes itself. You did nothing and don't understand what happened. Think about the time delay caused by holddown. It could be that the network was in the process of converging on the new topology.

## Summary of RIP

RIP is the grandfather of routing protocols and is a good example of distance-vector protocols. It is simple and easy to configure, making it the ideal choice of small, simple networks. Unfortunately, it uses hop-count as its metric, thus limiting its usefulness in networks with varying media bandwidths. The metric size of less than 16 limits the size of the networks on which RIP can be used.

Since the routing updates do not carry subnetting information, RIP networks must have contiguous subnets. The same constraint affects address utilization since all subnets must be the same size. Depending on your network, this may not be a factor in deciding whether to use RIP.

Because of its simplicity and periodic updates, it is very easy to troubleshoot RIP networks. There are very few "knobs" to adjust with RIP, so its configuration is easy. Sometimes, it is beneficial to get a network running with a simple protocol like RIP, then transition to a more advanced routing protocol as your needs dictate.

## IGRP

IGRP was Cisco's answer to the deficiencies of RIP. IGRP is also a distance-vector protocol; however, it was designed with a metric that reflects the physical characteristics of the path, reduces the overhead by increasing the update timer, and yet is easy to configure. It has been used successfully by many companies to run global networks with hundreds or thousands of routers. A complete discussion of IGRP internals can be found in An Introduction to IGRP (Hedrick 1991).

Cisco used IGRP to its advantage in the late 1980s and early 1990s when the only thing the other router vendors had available was RIP. OSPF had not yet been standardized, and customers were demanding something that had better routing characteristics than RIP.

## Configuration

One of the advantages of IGRP is that it requires an *autonomous system number*. An autonomous system is a collection of routers being operated within a single administrative domain (i.e., they belong to one cooperating organization that configures and runs them). As with RIP, the configuration specifies only the classful network number of those networks to which the router has a direct connection. All other routes will be learned from neighboring routers. The autonomous system number must match on all neighboring routers with which you expect to exchange routing information. A received routing update that contains a different autonomous system number will be ignored.

Figure 4-21 shows a sample network topology. The router configurations are shown in Figure 4-22.

The valid range of autonomous system numbers is 1-65,535. Why is having an autonomous system number an advantage? First, it keeps a router from injecting bad routing information into the IGRP routing domain until it is properly configured.

Second, there are special cases in which it is advantageous to configure multiple IGRP routing domains and control the flow of routes between them. Imagine that, in Figure 4-23, the connection between

**Figure 4-21**
IGRP network

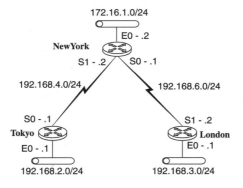

**Figure 4-22** IGRP configuration

**NewYork Configuration**
```
1 hostname NewYork
2 interface Ethernet0
3  ip address 172.16.1.2 255.255.255.0
4 interface Serial0
5  ip address 192.168.6.1 255.255.255.0
6 interface Serial1
7  ip address 192.168.4.2 255.255.255.0
8  bandwidth 56
9  clockrate 56000
10 router igrp 2
11  network 172.16.0.0
12  network 192.168.4.0
13  network 192.168.6.0
```
**Tokyo Configuration**
```
14 hostname Tokyo
15 interface Ethernet0
16  ip address 192.168.2.1 255.255.255.0
17 interface Serial0
18  ip address 192.168.4.1 255.255.255.0
19  bandwidth 56
20 router igrp 2
21  network 192.168.4.0
22  network 192.168.2.0
```
**London Configuration**
```
23 hostname London
24 interface Ethernet0
25  ip address 192.168.3.1 255.255.255.0
26 interface Serial1
27  ip address 192.168.6.2 255.255.255.0
28  bandwidth 56
29  clockrate 56000
30 router igrp 2
31  network 192.168.6.0
32  network 192.168.3.0
```

**Figure 4-23**
Multiple IGRP
domains

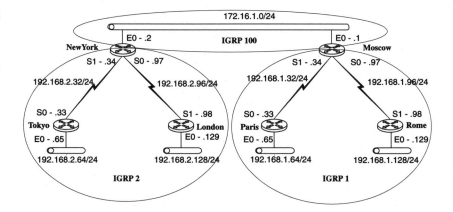

**Figure 4-24** Multiple IGRP domain configuration

**NewYork Configuration and Routes**

```
1 hostname NewYork
2 interface Ethernet0
3  ip address 172.16.1.2 255.255.255.0
4 interface Serial0
5  ip address 192.168.2.97 255.255.255.240
6 interface Serial1
7  ip address 192.168.2.34 255.255.255.240
8  bandwidth 56
9  clockrate 56000
10 router igrp 2
11  redistribute igrp 100
12  network 192.168.2.0
13  distribute-list 1 out igrp 100
14 router igrp 100
15  redistribute igrp 2
16  network 172.16.0.0
17 access-list 1 deny   192.168.2.0
18 access-list 1 permit any
19 end
20
21 NewYork#sh ip route
22 Codes: C - connected, S - static, I - IGRP, R - RIP, M - mobile, B - BGP
23        D - EIGRP, EX - EIGRP external, O - OSPF, IA - OSPF inter area
24        N1 - OSPF NSSA external type 1, N2 - OSPF NSSA external type 2
25        E1 - OSPF external type 1, E2 - OSPF external type 2, E - EGP
26        i - IS-IS, L1 - IS-IS level-1, L2 - IS-IS level-2, * - candidate default
27        U - per-user static route, o - ODR
28 Gateway of last resort is not set
29      172.16.0.0/24 is subnetted, 1 subnets
30 C       172.16.1.0 is directly connected, Ethernet0
31 I     192.168.1.0/24 [100/180671] via 172.16.1.1, 00:00:19, Ethernet0
32      192.168.2.0/28 is subnetted, 4 subnets
33 C       192.168.2.96 is directly connected, Serial0
34 I       192.168.2.64 [100/180671] via 192.168.2.33, 00:01:15, Serial1
35 C       192.168.2.32 is directly connected, Serial1
36 I       192.168.2.128 [100/8576] via 192.168.2.98, 00:00:36, Serial0
37
```

**Moscow Configuration and Routes**

```
38 hostname Moscow
39 interface Ethernet0
40  ip address 172.16.1.1 255.255.255.0
41 interface Serial0
42  ip address 192.168.1.97 255.255.255.240
43  bandwidth 56
44 interface Serial1
45  ip address 192.168.1.34 255.255.255.240
46  bandwidth 56
47  clockrate 56000
48 router igrp 100
49  redistribute igrp 1
50  network 172.16.0.0
51 router igrp 1
52  redistribute igrp 100
53  network 192.168.1.0
54  distribute-list 1 out igrp 100
55 access-list 1 deny   192.168.1.0
```

**Figure 4-24** Continued

```
56 access-list 1 permit any
57 end
58
59 Moscow#sh ip route
60 Codes: C - connected, S - static, I - IGRP, R - RIP, M - mobile, B - BGP
61        D - EIGRP, EX - EIGRP external, O - OSPF, IA - OSPF inter area
62        N1 - OSPF NSSA external type 1, N2 - OSPF NSSA external type 2
63        E1 - OSPF external type 1, E2 - OSPF external type 2, E - EGP
64        i - IS-IS, L1 - IS-IS level-1, L2 - IS-IS level-2, * - candidate default
65        U - per-user static route, o - ODR
66 Gateway of last resort is not set
67        172.16.0.0/24 is subnetted, 1 subnets
68 C        172.16.1.0 is directly connected, Ethernet0
69        192.168.1.0/28 is subnetted, 4 subnets
70 C        192.168.1.96 is directly connected, Serial0
71 I        192.168.1.64 [100/180671] via 192.168.1.33, 00:00:18, Serial1
72 C        192.168.1.32 is directly connected, Serial1
73 I        192.168.1.128 [100/180671] via 192.168.1.98, 00:00:04, Serial0
74 I     192.168.2.0/24 [100/8576] via 172.16.1.2, 00:00:11, Ethernet0
```

NewYork and Moscow is an expensive serial link and that you wanted to reduce the routing protocol overhead on this link. You also want to be able to restrict each region to access only to the backbone Ethernets and not each other. The configuration in Figure 4-24 implements this and significantly reduces the size of the routing updates over the backbone between NewYork and Moscow. Each region, including the backbone, receives a summary route to the other regions.

## Metric

IGRP uses multiple metric components in its updates (Figure 4-25). At each router, these values are incorporated into an equation that produces a single metric value against which other routes are compared (Figure 4-26). The route with the lowest metric value is the preferred path. The default values of the coefficients (K1, K2, K3, K4, and K5) in the IGRP metric equation have default values that make the bandwidth and delay factors the only ones used to calculate the metric. Experiments with using load and reliability have determined that network traffic is so bursty in nature that incorporating them causes IGRP to oscillate between multiple paths. This is not good, so our advice is to never try to adjust the IGRP metric coefficients.

**Figure 4-25**
IGRP metric components

```
IGRP Metric Components
• Bandwidth          1Kbps units; 1Kbps - 10Gbps
• Delay              10microsecond units; 10us - 168 seconds
• Load               1-255; 255 = 100% load
• Reliability        1-255; 255 = 100% reliable
• MTU                1-65535 bytes
• Hopcount           1-255; default 100 hops
```

Let's take a look at how each of the metric components is determined. First, each router advertises the metric components that it has in its routing table. For example, an attached Ethernet will have a composite metric of 1,100, which is the result of the metric calculation for a link that has a bandwidth of 10Mbps and a delay of 1000 microseconds. This is the value that is advertised to the neighboring routers. The neighbors will add the cost of the link over which the advertisement was received and enter the resulting metric values in its routing tables.

■ Bandwidth = MIN(bandwidth from update, interface bandwidth), where bandwidth = (1/bits-per-second) ˙ 1E10. This results in measuring bandwidth in 1Kbps units, with a range of 1Kbps to 10Gbps. The bandwidth parameter is known for LAN interfaces and is taken from the **bandwidth** interface subcommand on serial links. If it is not specified on serial links, it is assumed to be 1.544Mbps (T1 bandwidth).

■ Delay = delay from packet + interface delay, where delay is measured in 10-microsecond units. The range is 10 microseconds (delay = 1) to 167.772 seconds (delay = $2^{24}$-1).

■ Load = MAX(load from packet, interface load), where load is measured on a scale of 1-255, with 255 representing 100 percent load.

■ Reliability = MIN(reliability from update, interface reliability), where reliability is measured on a scale of 1-255, with 255 representing 100 percent reliable.

■ MTU = MIN(MTU from packet, interface MTU).

■ Hop count = hop count from packet + 1.

Standard values of bandwidth and delay used by Cisco for various media are shown in Table 4-2. All serial links at T1 and slower speed have default delays that are all the same. This isn't a factor in real life since the bandwidth is the critical factor in determining the final metric value. Since the router does not automatically detect the bandwidth of serial links, you'll have to set it manually using the interface subcommand

**Figure 4-26**

IGRP metric calculation equation

$$\text{Metric} = (K1 * Bandwidth) + \frac{(K2 * Bandwidth)}{(256 - Load)} + (K3 * Delay)$$

If K5 != 0, then an additional calculation is added to the Metric

$$\text{Metric} = \text{Metric} + \frac{K5}{(Reliability + K4)}$$

Defaults: K1 = K3 = 1 and K2 = K4 = K5 = 0

**bandwidth.** If you are configuring Frame Relay interfaces, use the Committed Information Rate (CIR) of the link. The default bandwidth if you don't set one is 1,544Kbps (T1 rate). It isn't a good idea to let all serial links default to this value unless all links are really T1 links. As your network changes, you'll likely install some links that are at different speeds and wind up with suboptimum routing as a result.

You've seen in the equation of Figure 4-24 that neither MTU nor hop count are used to determine the metric. The MTU is used by the router to determine whether a packet must be fragmented when traversing the route. The hop count value tells the router the number of hops (i.e., number of routers) in the path to the destination. It is used by the router to detect a routing change that may result in a routing loop. Just because the bandwidth or delay changes by some fraction doesn't mean that a network topology change occurred; it may mean that some link's characteristics changed. An increase in hop count, however, means that a topology change occurred and that the path is longer than it used to be. This is critical for determining when to place a route into holddown. The hop count component also is used to determine if a route is valid. The default maximum hops that IGRP uses is 100, but you can change this to be any value in the range of 1 to 255. There is no reason to change this value unless you have a very large network with a network diameter of greater than 100 hops.

When a route is determined to be unreachable, the delay component of the metric is set to its maximum value.

**Table 4-2**

IGRP bandwidth and delay defaults

| Media | Delay | Bandwidth | Directly Connected Metric |
|-------|-------|-----------|---------------------------|
| TokenRing (4Mbps) | 250 (2.5ms) | 2,500 | 2,750 |
| TokenRing (16Mbps) | 63 (.63ms) | 625 | 688 |
| Ethernet (10Mbps) | 100 (1ms) | 1,000 | 1,100 |
| T1 (1.544Mbps) | 2,000 (20ms) | 6,476 | 8,476 |
| 56Kbps | 2,000 (20ms) | 178,571 | 180,571 |

Source: Hedrick (1991).

## IGRP Multipath Operation

We discussed multipath operation in a previous chapter. IGRP supports up to four parallel equal-cost paths by default. In more recent IOS releases, up to six parallel paths are supported (four is still the default).

IGRP allows the use of unequal-cost paths too. There are two rules that IGRP uses to determine if a path is usable:

- The neighboring router must be closer to the destination network than this router (that is, the neighbor must have a metric lower than this router's metric for a given destination). This criteria makes sure that the neighboring router does not have a path that is "upstream" or in the "wrong direction" to get to the destination.

- The metric advertised by the neighbor must be less than the variance of the local router's metric. The variance is calculated by multiplying the variance factor (set using the **variance** router subcommand) times the local metric.

There is a side benefit from having this information available. If the primary path fails, the router has a set of alternative paths already available and can immediately converge on one of the alternate paths.

## Update, Invalid, Holddown, Flush Timers

IGRP is a distance-vector protocol and has the same set of timers as RIP. To reduce network overhead, the IGRP update timer defaults to 90 seconds. Table 4-3 shows the default values of the IGRP timers.

**Table 4-3**

Default IGRP timers

| Timer | Value (seconds) | Description |
|-------|-----------------|-------------|
| Update | 90 | Time delay between routing updates. |
| Invalid | 270 | Time from last update packet until a neighbor is marked down. Typically three times the update timer. |
| Holddown | 280 | Time that new routes are not believed after a route is marked invalid. Typically slightly longer than three times the update timer. |
| Flush | 630 | Time before a route is flushed from the routing table after it has been marked invalid. This timer must be at least the sum of the Invalid and Holddown timers. |

These timers can be modified with the command router subcommand **timers basic**. However, there is rarely a need to adjust these timers, so our recommendation is to leave them alone.

IGRP's time to converge after a network outage can be quite long. It takes 270 seconds (three missed updates) to detect a failed neighboring router on an Ethernet and another 280 seconds while it is in holddown. This is a little over nine minutes. We would certainly like to be able to have the network converge sooner than this!

A little-known feature is the ability to disable holddown on IGRP for faster convergence. This was documented by Charles Hedrick and is described in Cisco documentation (Cisco 1998a). The objective is to have IGRP switch to backup routes quickly. The router subcommand **no metric holddown** sets the holddown timer to zero, thus allowing the router to immediately use a new route when the previous route becomes invalid. But be careful, you need to have a network that has a hierarchical structure. A large network with many potential routing loops is not a good candidate for this type of configuration. A better candidate is a network with fewer than about 50 routers and few active parallel paths (a strictly hierarchical network is best). We recommend experimenting with this feature before implementing it in a production network.

## Lab Exercise

To see the IGRP timers in action, configure IGRP using the network configuration of Figure 4-3. Then, follow the steps we used in the RIP timer lab exercise to see what happens with the IGRP timers. Look for the metric to go to very large values when the delay component is set to its maximum value as a route becomes unreachable.

## Split Horizon, Poison Reverse & Flash Update

IGRP operates just like RIP when it comes to how it processes its updates. The updates are subject to the same split horizon and poison reverse rules that we saw in the RIP labs earlier in this chapter.

## Lab Exercise

For a lab experiment, go back to the RIP labs where we saw the split horizon, poison reverse, and flash updates and duplicate them using IGRP. Look for the length of time it takes IGRP to converge after a topology change.

## Packet Format

Like RIP, IGRP has two types of packets, a request and an update packet. A request packet is generated by a router on an interface when the interface is initially enabled. This allows the router to quickly learn of other IGRP speaking routers on that network segment. The request packet consists of only an IGRP header (Figure 4-27). When a request packet is received, the router must reply with an update packet.

The edition field is a serial number that is incremented whenever there is a change in the routing table. This field is currently set but is not used. Since an update may consist of multiple packets, a router cannot depend solely on the edition number in one packet to determine if it can avoid processing the packet.

The fields ninterior, nsystem, and nexterior, identify the number of interior routes (which contain subnet information), system routes (routes to other networks within the autonomous system), and exterior routers (routes to networks outside the autonomous system). An exterior route is one that originates from a route redistribution or from a static route definition. The router uses these numbers to determine which entries in the update are which type of route. The first ninterior routes are interior, the next nsystem routes are system routes, and the next nexterior routes are exterior routes.

The *checksum* uses the UDP checksum algorithm, but only checksums the IGRP packet header and routes. The checksum field is set to zero when calculating the *checksum*.

**Figure 4-27**
IGRP packet header

Bit Position

| 00 01 02 03 | 04 05 06 07 | 08 09 10 11 12 13 14 15 | 16 17 18 19 20 21 22 23 24 25 26 27 28 29 30 31 |
|---|---|---|---|
| Version | Opcode | Edition | Asystem |
| Ninterior | | | Nsystem |
| Nexterior | | | Checksum |
| routing entries ... | | | |

**Figure 4-28**
IGRP update packet
routing entry

| Bit Position | | | |
|---|---|---|---|
| 00 01 02 03 04 05 06 07 08 09 10 11 12 13 14 15 16 17 18 19 20 21 22 23 | | | 24 25 26 27 28 29 30 31 |
| Three significant octets of IP address | | | Delay... |
| ...Delay | | Bandwidth... | |
| ...Bandwidth | | MTU | Reliability |
| Load | Hopcount | (start of next entry) | |

An update packet contains a set of routing entries, each of which has the format shown in Figure 4-28. Up to 104 entries can exist in a single 1,500-byte packet (including the IP header). If more than 104 routes exist, then several update messages are sent.

The network number is not a full 32 bits. This is because if the entry is for an interior route, it is a subnet of a known network, and only the lower 24 bits are needed (we know the upper 8 bits already). Similarly, if the entry is for a system or exterior route, we don't need any of the subnetting information, and the upper 24 bits of the address is all we need (the route is to a network, so by definition, at least the lowest 8 bits will be all zero). This trick reduces the size of the routing updates.

We've already discussed the components of the composite metric and the valid values of each.

## Transport

IGRP packets are transported directly in IP packets using IP protocol number 9. Because IP is used as the transport, the routing updates can be routed. However, in normal operation, IGRP updates are sent to the broadcast address (255.255.255.255) on its configured interfaces. Since broadcasts are not forwarded, you should not see an IGRP update from a remote router.

FYI: RFC1700 lists IGRP's protocol number as 88; however, Chuck Hedrick's description of IGRP (1991) states that IGRP uses protocol number 9. An examination of the packets on the wire shows that protocol number 9 is being used.

## IGRP Network Design

Fortunately, IGRP network design is much simpler than RIP network design. This is primarily due to IGRP's use of the multivalued metric that measures network path physical characteristics.

If you want to take advantage of the **no metric holddown** command, then your network will need to have been designed with a hierarchical topology (i.e., a treelike topology). This type of topology will prevent the formation of routing loops when a link or router failure occurs. It turns out that this is also the easiest network topology to troubleshoot. If you use dial backup or dial-on-demand configurations, then you'll be able to still have redundancy and an easier time troubleshooting.

Make sure you use the bandwidth command on each serial IGRP interface. It is not a good practice to assign a bandwidth that is different than the real link capacity. As your network changes, it will likely result in suboptimum routing and confusion among the network team members.

## Debugging & Show Commands

The ease of configuration of IGRP extends to the debug and show commands. The **show ip protocol** command shows the details of any routing protocols that are enabled. The details of IGRP's configuration are shown in the sample output in Figure 4-29. Check to make sure that the autonomous system number is correct (it must match on all neighboring routers, or they will not pass routing information). Check the timers to make sure they match those of the adjacent routers. Look for routing filters that may be causing specific routes to be ignored or to be omitted from outgoing updates. Which networks are configured, and what are the sources of routing information? Make sure the neighboring routers are listed as sources of information. Have any interfaces been specified as passive interfaces (they listen to updates but don't transmit any).

The output of show ip route is particularly important for troubleshooting routed networks. Any route that is marked with an I is an IGRP route (Figure 4-30). If there is no route to an intended destination, then you have a possible routing problem (unless the router has a default route). But don't go too far just because a route exists on one router. Remember, correct routes must exist in both directions for TCP to work.

If a route that you expect to see does not appear in the routing table, then it's time to start looking for a cause. There are two IGRP debugging statements: **debug ip igrp events** and **debug ip igrp transactions**.

**Figure 4-29** Output of **show ip protocol** in an IGRP network

```
1 NewYork#sh ip proto
2 Routing Protocol is "igrp 1"
3   Sending updates every 90 seconds, next due in 50 seconds
4   Invalid after 270 seconds, hold down 280, flushed after 630
5   Outgoing update filter list for all interfaces is not set
6   Incoming update filter list for all interfaces is not set
7   Default networks flagged in outgoing updates
8   Default networks accepted from incoming updates
9   IGRP metric weight K1=1, K2=0, K3=1, K4=0, K5=0
10  IGRP maximum hopcount 100
11  IGRP maximum metric variance 1
12  Redistributing: igrp 1
13  Routing for Networks:
14    192.168.4.0
15    192.168.6.0
16    172.16.0.0
17    192.168.1.0
18  Passive Interface(s):
19    Ethernet0
20  Routing Information Sources:
21    Gateway          Distance       Last Update
22    192.168.6.2          100        00:00:10
23    192.168.4.1          100        00:00:10
24  Distance: (default is 100)
```

**Figure 4-30** Output of **show ip route**

```
1 NewYork#sh ip route
2 Codes: C - connected, S - static, I - IGRP, R - RIP, M - mobile, B - BGP
3        D - EIGRP, EX - EIGRP external, O - OSPF, IA - OSPF inter area
4        N1 - OSPF NSSA external type 1, N2 - OSPF NSSA external type 2
5        E1 - OSPF external type 1, E2 - OSPF external type 2, E - EGP
6        i - IS-IS, L1 - IS-IS level-1, L2 - IS-IS level-2, * - candidate default
7        U - per-user static route, o - ODR
8
9 Gateway of last resort is not set
10
11      172.16.0.0/24 is subnetted, 1 subnets
12 C       172.16.1.0 is directly connected, Ethernet0
13 I     192.168.1.0/24 [100/180671] via 172.16.1.1, 00:00:31, Ethernet0
14      192.168.2.0/28 is subnetted, 4 subnets
15 C       192.168.2.96 is directly connected, Serial0
16 I       192.168.2.64 [100/180671] via 192.168.2.33, 00:00:19, Serial1
17 C       192.168.2.32 is directly connected, Serial1
18 I       192.168.2.128 [100/8576] via 192.168.2.98, 00:00:04, Serial0
```

**Figure 4-31** Output of **debug ip igrp events**

```
1 Tokyo#debug ip igrp events
2 IGRP event debugging is on
3 Tokyo#
4 IGRP: received update from 192.168.4.2 on Serial0
5 IGRP: Update contains 0 interior, 2 system, and 1 exterior routes.
6 IGRP: Total routes in update: 3
```

**Figure 4-32** Output of **debug ip igrp transactions**

```
1 Tokyo#debug ip igrp trans
2 IGRP protocol debugging is on
3 Tokyo#
4 IGRP: sending update to 255.255.255.255 via Ethernet0 (192.168.2.1)
5       network 192.168.4.0, metric=8476
6       network 192.168.6.0, metric=10476
7       network 192.168.1.0, metric=8576
8       exterior 172.16.0.0, metric=10576
9 IGRP: sending update to 255.255.255.255 via Serial0 (192.168.4.1)
10       network 192.168.2.0, metric=1100
11 IGRP: received update from 192.168.4.2 on Serial0
12       network 192.168.6.0, metric 10476 (neighbor 8476)
13       network 192.168.1.0, metric 8576 (neighbor 1100)
14       exterior network 172.16.0.0, metric 10576 (neighbor 8576)
```

The first one outputs information about routing updates being received (Figure 4-31). The second one displays the contents of the routing updates in detail (Figure 4-32). In the debug output, you'll see the sources of routing updates, even if they are from the wrong network or subnet (a hint that something's amiss). In some cases, you'll have to gather debug output from several different routers in order to assemble enough data to figure out what's happening.

## Lab Exercise

Using the network diagram of Figure 4-3, configure IGRP on New York using autonomous system 1 and on Tokyo using autonomous system 2. Using the previously discussed commands, see which output shows you the information you would need to diagnose the problem.

## IGRP Summary

IGRP has been a very successful protocol. The advantage of using actual link characteristics along a path to calculate the path's metric is very useful and works well in practice. However, newer protocols that have better convergence characteristics and network utilization are replacing it in large networks. One of these protocols is EIGRP, an enhanced version of IGRP. We'll discuss this more modern routing protocol in Chapter 5.

# Routing in Classful Networks

In Chapter 2, we described the routing process, but with what we've just learned about RIP and IGRP, a review is useful. In classful routing protocols, only the route and its metric are propagated between routers. For every packet that is forwarded, each router determines the destination's network mask by one of two methods:

1. If an interface is connected to the destination network, use the network mask associated with that interface. All subnets of the subject network must be the same size.

2. Use the network mask that corresponds to the class of the destination address. Class A networks use 8 bits of mask, class B networks use 16 bits of mask, and class C networks use 24 bits of mask.

Figure 4-33 shows a network that contains a class C network and a subnetted class B network. Using method 1, a packet from Tokyo to New York's E0 interface (172.16.1.1) has a destination address that is within the class B network. Since Tokyo has an interface on this network, it examines its interface configuration and finds that a 26-bit mask is used in this network. This mask is applied to the destination address, the destination subnet is determined, the correct routing table match is found, and the packet is forwarded to New York.

Now let's look at routing in method 2. In this same network, a packet from Tokyo to London's E0 interface is addressed to the class C network. In this case, the only route Tokyo has is to the base class C network number (192.168.1.0). Tokyo doesn't have an interface on this network, so

**Figure 4-33**
Classful routing

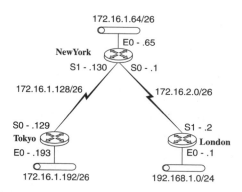

it determines the class of the address, then uses the corresponding mask (24 bits) when masking off the locally administered portion of the address and performing the routing table lookup. The lookup shows that this network is known to New York, so Tokyo forwards the packet to New York.

FYI: Using the second method, New York does not have any more information than Tokyo had. The destination network (192.168.1.0) is still remote, so New York must still use the classful mask when looking up the destination network in the routing table. New York knows only that London is the best next-hop to the destination. When London receives the packet, it determines that the packet's destination address is for itself (the E0 interface). The packet is passed to the internal TCP/IP protocol stack to be processed by one of the internal applications (ping, Telnet, etc.).

The actual routing process is the same in either method:

- Extract the destination address from the packet
- Determine the mask to use (this depends on whether the mask is known for a given network)
- Apply the mask to remove the "locally administered" bits from the destination address
- Look up the resulting network address in the routing table

The second step—determining the proper network mask to use—is the important difference.

# Route Aggregation

It is important to limit the size of the routing tables in intranets that are composed of hundreds or thousands of routers and network segments. Large routing tables affect the memory used within routers, the CPU used to process routing updates, the route lookup time, and the bandwidth used by routing updates. None of these factors are good, so reducing routing table size is a good thing to do.

Routers running classful routing protocols advertise only the classful network address to routers in other networks. For example, in Figure 4-34, there are two networks (172.16.0.0 and 192.168.3.0) connected by two links

**Figure 4-34**
Classful route
aggregation

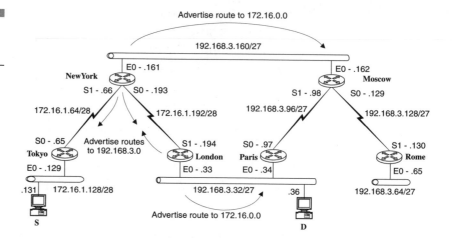

(NewYork to Moscow and London to Paris). NewYork and London will advertise 172.16.0.0 to Moscow and Paris. No subnetting information about 172.16.0.0 will be sent.

Similarly, NewYork and London will advertise only the classful address of 192.168.3.0 to Tokyo. If 172.16.0.0 has 1,000 subnets, the reduction in routing updates over the NewYork-to-Moscow and the London-to-Paris links will be significant. And Moscow, Paris, and Rome also will have greatly reduced routing tables.

There is a cost to route aggregation. It sometimes creates paths that are not optimal. A packet from host S to host D at 192.168.3.36 will take the path Tokyo, NewYork, Moscow, and Paris to D. This is a longer path than the optimum route via Tokyo, NewYork, and London to D. But the trade-off in reducing routing table size makes nonoptimum routing acceptable.

## Lab Exercise

As an exercise in routing, start with the network configuration of Figure 4-34. Assign a subnet of 172.16.0.0 to the link between Tokyo and London and bring up the link. Using either RIP or IGRP, see where the packets will be sent by using **trace** from Tokyo's E0 interface to Paris's E0 interface. Remember to check the state of the ip route-cache (see Chapter 2 for the discussion on router switching modes). Changing the use of the route cache on all the interfaces will result in different paths being used. It is important that you be able to recognize these patterns in your network.

# Discontiguous Subnets

Another very important operational constraint (briefly discussed in the RIP section) that occurs with classless routing protocols is that of discontiguous subnets. When route aggregation occurs, an internal failure that partitions an intranet may result in some loss of connectivity. Let's use the network in Figure 4-35 to see how this can happen. The link between Moscow and Paris is lost (another backhoe has broken our cable). The result is that the 192.168.3.32 subnet is separated from the remainder of 192.168.3.0 by network 172.16.0.0.

FYI: *Discontiguous* has a meaning similar to disconnected. If a network is discontiguous, it is not contiguous, or not fully connected together. In a contiguous network, all subnets of the network are adjacent to, or connected to, other subnets of the same network.

Remember from the earlier route aggregation section: The subnets of 192.168.3.0 are invisible to the routers inside 172.16.0.0. Any packet from host S to host D will take the path Tokyo, NewYork, Moscow, and Paris to D. Since the link between Moscow and Paris is down, the packet cannot be delivered. Route aggregation prevents the details of the alternate path via the NewYork-to-London link from being learned and used.

Since the destination is not reachable via Moscow, the packet is dropped and an ICMP "destination unreachable" is returned to Tokyo. The network will operate correctly only when the Moscow-to-Paris link is returned to service.

**Figure 4-35**
Discontiguous subnets

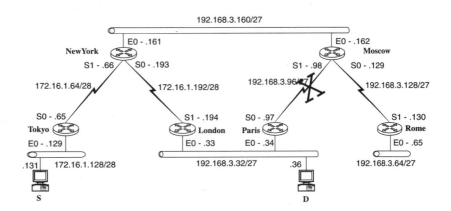

Sometimes, you must use a network topology in which discontiguous subnets occur. There are two Cisco configuration solutions that we can use to connect discontiguous subnets across another network. Both solutions do the same thing: they assign a subnet of our discontiguous network on top of the second network's links.

The first solution to discontiguous subnets is to use secondary addresses. For example, in Figure 4-33, we would assign subnet 192.168.3.160 as a secondary network on the New York-to-London link. The following configuration statements would exist in the configurations of New York and London.

New York:

```
int s 0
ip address 172.16.1.193 255.255.255.240
ip address 192.168.3.161 255.255.255.224 secondary
```

London:

```
int s 1
ip address 172.16.1.194 255.255.255.240
ip address 192.168.3.162 255.255.255.224 secondary
clock rate 56000
```

This method has existed for a long time in Cisco routers.

The second method is newer and is preferred if you are running more recent releases of the IOS. It uses subinterfaces, which are a way of assigning multiple logical interfaces to a single physical interface. Each logical interface uses the same physical interface but can have different configuration parameters. You may already be familiar with subinterfaces on Frame Relay networks, where they are used to create a separate virtual interface for each PVC. The configuration using subinterfaces for New York and London follows:

New York:

```
int s 0.1
ip address 172.16.1.193 255.255.255.240
int s 0.2
ip address 192.168.3.161 255.255.255.224
```

London:

```
int s 1
clock rate 56000
int s 1.1
ip address 172.16.1.194 255.255.255.240
```

```
int s 1.2
ip address 192.168.3.161 255.255.255.224
```

Using one of these two methods, there are now two paths that retain connectivity of the 192.168.3.32 subnet to the remainder of its network if the Moscow-to-Paris link fails.

Another approach to handling discontiguous subnets uses classless routing, which we'll cover in the next chapter. This is one of the reasons that makes classless routing more powerful and popular.

## Lab Exercise

Using the network of Figure 4-33, take down individual links and trace from Tokyo's E0 to Paris' E0 interface to see how failures affect the routing. Remember to wait for the network to converge after a topology change.

Some good examples of interfaces to change are the Moscow-to-Paris link (which we described earlier). Also try shutting down the New York-to-Moscow link. What path do the packets take? Is connectivity affected? Do the same thing with the London-to-Paris link.

Another good test is to take down the New York-to-London link and see if Tokyo can ping and trace to London's E0 interface.

## CCIE Tips

Understanding routing protocols and operation is where the CCIE candidate needs to have a very good understanding. Start with basic configuration. You should know which network numbers should be entered in the network statements of a classful routing protocol.

Know when and why you should change the routing protocol timers and whether you must have the timers match on all routers in the network or only on those routers sharing a common network link. The existence of the **timers basic** command in a router configuration should cause alarm bells to go off in your head. If a network genuinely needs the timers to be modified, understand the symptoms of mismatched timers.

If you have a flapping link, what does this do to your network? You should do some of the preceding lab exercises and expand on them.

Work with someone else who can help you simulate a flapping link (physically unplugging the hardware or shutting down the interface). Understand what effect a flapping link will have on the availability of routes that must use the link and on the routing protocol update overhead on your network.

Speaking of routing updates, you should have some idea of the size of the routing updates and how long it will take to transmit them over your slowest network link. Do you have users complaining about the network intermittently being slow, but you've never found a problem? Use a long-running ping to record the round-trip times over a long period. Does the round-trip time periodically change? Capture the results and plot them (easy to do with most spreadsheet programs). You may find an overloaded router or link using this diagnostic process.

Are the optimum paths through the network being taken? Understand the routing protocol metrics and what paths will be taken when a failure occurs within your network. Be able to use the built-in Cisco **debug**, **ping**, and **trace** commands to diagnose network connectivity and routing problems. Remember, watch out for the holddown time in these networks.

Know your network and what routes should exist at each major point in the network. In large networks, you will not be able to know all the specific routes, but you should know the major (or summary) routes that should exist. Look for strange routes due to incorrect static routes or the incorrect application of the passive interface command.

For IGRP, make sure that the AS numbers match. This is a design feature, but can cause you problems if someone gets it wrong. The network numbers also have to match the network numbers on the router's interfaces. It is very easy to type a network number incorrectly and not be able to find it for a long time.

IGRP also requires that the **bandwidth** interface subcommand configuration statement be used to tell the routing protocol the link speed. If you're running Frame Relay, then the bandwidth should be set to the Committed Information Rate (CIR) of the link.

Understand how to disable holddown in IGRP networks to improve convergence characteristics. You'll need to determine what kinds of network topologies will work well for this and which ones will not.

A network problem fixes itself a few minutes after it is reported. Think "holddown timer" first. There also may be some interaction with the ARP cache, so this isn't a firm rule. But it is good for rapid troubleshooting. When the problem is reported, quickly capture the routing tables on the affected routers.

You should be able to troubleshoot problems due to discontiguous subnets. These sometimes can be very difficult to diagnose. Particularly interesting are the remote subnets that are discontiguous and which you do not control. The network citizens at your site may be complaining to you about a problem that is outside the network that you control. Being able to find out the problem (perhaps by being able to establish that connectivity exists to another part of the remote network) and work with the remote network administrator to fix the problem is an important ability.

We've seen problems reported in networks where TCP connections are VERY slow. When this occurs, think about how TCP works. If a packet is lost, the sending system will wait a while for the acknowledgment and eventually decide to retransmit the packet. If an access list or bad route exists on one path of a dual-path network topology, then every other packet is lost. While the connection works, it is very slow. Diagnosing this network problem can be difficult because a change in one part of the network affects traffic in an (assumed) unrelated part of the network. Troubleshooting with trace or ping can help you find the problem and its location. Look for either of these tools to consistently report that every other (or every N, where N is the number of parallel paths) packet is lost. This also can happen with discontiguous subnets where some packets are going to the half of the remote network that cannot reach the destination.

# SUMMARY

We've covered how distance-vector protocols operate, using RIP and IGRP as examples. The important operational characteristics of distance-vector protocols are metrics, count-to-infinity, split horizon, poison reverse, flash updates, holddown, and timers. The router subcommand split horizon allows you to avoid the transmission of routing updates on specific interfaces.

Background information on network design for both protocols was provided. It was clear that IGRP is a much better protocol than RIP on the same network topology.

We also discussed how the network mask is selected in classful routing protocols and how that might cause discontiguous subnets as a result of route aggregation that occurs between networks that use different network numbers.

# CHAPTER 5

# Classless Routing

We've covered both static routes and classful routing protocols. Each of these routing methods uses a fixed subnet mask. The router determines the mask by the class of the address or by the mask assigned to an interface attached to a network.

Classless routing protocols, however, propagate the mask with the route in routing updates. Having both the mask and destination network address together removes the need to know the class of the address—the mask is known for each route in the routing table. The route lookup algorithm changes slightly with these new protocols, so we'll cover these changes and how they affect the router's performance.

There is a new version of the venerable RIP protocol as well as an enhanced version of IGRP (it's actually a new protocol with a similar name) and the OSPF routing protocol. In this chapter, we'll cover the operation of these new routing protocols and how to use them in today's complex networks.

# Router Operation

There are some significant differences between router operation in classful and classless environments. Classful protocols determine the mask to use, apply it to the destination address, then find a unique address in the routing table. Routers running classless protocols have to check the destination address against multiple routes, each with its own mask. It is possible that several routes will match some portion of the destination address. Instead of finding a unique match, the router must find the route that matches the largest number of bits in the destination address.

An additional change is that subnet zero is a valid subnet. By default, Cisco routers do not allow subnet zero. But with classless routing, subnet zero is allowed (you must still use the command **ip subnet-zero** to enable its use). The route to subnet zero has its own mask, which is different than the mask used for the network route. The different masks allow the router to make the correct routing decision when subnet zero is used in a network.

Let's look at a sample routing table to see how the proper route selection works. A packet addressed to 172.16.0.65 arrives in a router with the routing table shown in Figure 5-1. The destination address matches 24 bits in entry 12, 25 bits in entry 13, 25 bits in entry 15, and 26 bits in entry 16. The best (longest) match is on entry 16, which matches all the bits in this subnet's routing entry. This is the route that the router will use for forwarding the packet.

**Figure 5-1** Classless routing table

```
 1 London#sh ip route
 2 Codes: C - connected, S - static, I - IGRP, R - RIP, M - mobile, B - BGP
 3        D - EIGRP, EX - EIGRP external, O - OSPF, IA - OSPF inter area
 4        N1 - OSPF NSSA external type 1, N2 - OSPF NSSA external type 2
 5        E1 - OSPF external type 1, E2 - OSPF external type 2, E - EGP
 6        i - IS-IS, L1 - IS-IS level-1, L2 - IS-IS level-2, * - candidate default
 7        U - per-user static route, o - ODR
 8
 9 Gateway of last resort is not set
10
11       172.16.0.0/16 is variably subnetted, 5 subnets, 3 masks
12 C        172.16.0.128/26 is directly connected, Ethernet0
13 C        172.16.0.8/30 is directly connected, Serial1
14 R        172.16.4.0/24 [120/1] via 172.16.0.9, 00:00:02, Serial1
15 R        172.16.0.4/30 [120/1] via 172.16.0.9, 00:00:02, Serial1
16 R        172.16.0.64/26 [120/2] via 172.16.0.9, 00:00:02, Serial1
17 London#
```

How does the router perform all these comparisons quickly and efficiently? There are algorithms that routers use to efficiently perform these routing table lookups. The one that is typically used in classless routing table lookups is call the patricia tree algorithm (Gonnet and Baeza-Yates 1991 or Sedgewick 1988). This algorithm stores routes in a table in a way that is very efficient for finding the best route for a given destination address.

After finding the best match in the routing table, the router's operation is the same as with classful routing. The outgoing interface is identified, the packet is encapsulated within the appropriate data-link layer framing, and the new frame is transmitted by the selected interface.

# Classless Routing & Route Prefixes

As we've seen, the reason that classless routing works is that each route and its mask (also called a prefix mask or just a prefix) is propagated throughout the network. The prefix is simply the number of bits of address that comprises the nonhost portion of the address. Using this scheme, all addresses are really composed of two parts: network and host.

FYI: Remember that class A addresses had one octet of network identifier, class B addresses had two octets of network identifier, and class C addresses had three octets of network identifier. Also, the distinction of classes of address has been removed in classless routing (thus the name). Only the routing prefix determines the number of bits used for network identifier.

With the use of routing prefixes, it is now possible to assign suitable ranges of addresses to an organization based on the organization's needs. For example, if a small company needs only 50 addresses, it is possible to assign a chunk of address space with a prefix of 26 bits. An address and prefix mask that would work for this company is 172.16.1.128/26. The mask allows room for 64 addresses starting at 172.16.1.128 (172.16.1.128 through 172.16.1.191).

Similarly, a shorter mask (larger address space) than allowed in classful addressing can be used to create networks of other sizes. Let's look at a company that needs 500 addresses and expects to grow by another 200 over the next two years. If we were to look at the classful addressing space, we would assign three addresses out of the class C address range. With classless addressing, we could assign addresses out of any address range, as long as the mask allowed at least 700 addresses. To provide for this many addresses, we would need to create an address space that spans 1,024 addresses (the next smaller address space would be 512 addresses, which is too small). An example of this would be an address/mask of 192.168.4.0/22, which spans the addresses from 192.168.4.0 through 192.168.7.255.

FYI: You may see the term supernetting mentioned in networking literature. Supernetting is aggregating several classful networks together into a single address/mask, just as we have shown. It is the opposite of subnetting, in which you subdivide a classful network.

Another term you may encounter is CIDR, which is an abbreviation for Classless InterDomain Routing. CIDR addressing completely ignores the concept of classes of addresses. A CIDR route is completely described by an IP address and mask combination.

By assigning addresses using classless addressing, we are able to more efficiently use the remaining IP address space. The traditional classful way of thinking about IP addresses is now obsolete. If you are comfortable with classful addressing, it may take a while to become familiar with classless addressing. A good way to start making the transition is to stop thinking about addresses as belonging to a specific class. Instead, think of them as an address/mask combination. For example, 192.168.1.0 is a class C address but also can be identified as 192.168.1.0/24. Working with addresses and masks for a few hours will help you understand how classless mask prefixes work.

## RIP Version 2

RIP version 2 is an update to the original IP version of RIP to add features that are required in modern routing protocols. It is documented in RFC1723 (Malkin 1994). The original RIP packet format had several reserved fields, and these fields have been used in RIPv2 to provide the needed functionality. The basic protocol itself is unchanged, allowing protocol developers to quickly implement the new version.

## Differences From RIPv1

The major change in RIPv2 is to add the network mask for each route in the update. Propagating the mask with the route allows RIPv2 to be used in VLSM (Variable Length Subnet Mask) and classless routing environments. If we are using RIPv2 on all our routers, we can use the router subcommand **no auto-summary** to disable the automatic summarization that creates the problem of discontiguous subnets, as we discussed in Chapter 4. Because all subnets are visible in the adjacent network, there is no problem in determining the correct route to a given subnet.

An authentication field has been added to the packet header. Authentication helps prevent an unauthorized entity from injecting invalid or incorrect routing information into the network. Without authentication, it is possible for someone to cause all packets for a given destination to be routed via a workstation where the packets can be copied and examined. Denial-of-service attacks also can be performed by causing packets to be routed to a system that does not forward them.

Another major change is to add a next-hop address to each routing entry. A router may now specify an adjacent router as the best next hop for reaching a specific destination.

Finally, RIPv2 packets are multicast instead of broadcast, reducing the load on all systems on broadcast media (provided the systems have network interfaces that are capable of filtering on MAC address).

## Packet Format

The RIPv2 packet format is shown in Figure 5-2. You can see the similarities and the use of previously unused fields when compared to the RIP packet format in Chapter 4. The RIP header is composed of four octets containing the command, version, and unused fields.

The remainder of the packet consists of up to 25 routing entries, each 20 octets in length. Each routing entry begins with an Address Family Identifier to identify the data that is contained within the routing entry. As with RIPv1, the Address Family Identifier is set to a value of 2 when an IP route is contained in the routing entry.

The route tag field allows each route to be individually tagged with an identifier that can be used for many different filtering operations such as modifying metrics, eliminating routes from updates, selecting specific routes for redistribution, and so on. The main intent for this

**Figure 5-2**
RIPv2 packet format

Bit Position
00 01 02 03 04 05 06 07 08 09 10 11 12 13 14 15 16 17 18 19 20 21 22 23 24 25 26 27 28 29 30 31

| Command | Version | unused |
|---|---|---|
| Address Family Identifier | | Route Tag |
| IP Address | | |
| Subnet Mask | | |
| Next Hop | | |
| Metric | | |
| . . . | | |

The portion of the datagram from Address Family Identifier
through Metric may appear up to 25 times. Additional
routes in an update must be transmitted in additional datagrams.

field is to identify routes that were imported to the RIP routing domain from an external source (e.g., BGP).

If authentication is used, the first routing entry in a RIPv2 packet contains the authentication information. A RIPv2 packet that contains authentication information will start with the format shown in Figure 5-3. The address family identifier field for an authentication entry is set to 0xFFFF. The authentication type field contains a number that identifies the type of authentication to be used. An authentication type of 2 indicates that the remaining 16 bytes contain a clear-text password. Clear-text passwords are not very secure because they may be discovered by monitoring the network for RIPv2 packets. A more secure authentication mechanism using the MD5 digest format has an authentication type of 3 and is described in RFC2082 (Baker and Atkinson 1997).

When an authentication entry exists, there will be fewer routing entries in the RIP packet. Also, the MD5 digest consumes more than 16 octets that remain in a single routing entry. Refer to RFC2082 for complete details.

**Figure 5-3**
RIPv2 packet with authentication

Bit Position
00 01 02 03 04 05 06 07 08 09 10 11 12 13 14 15 16 17 18 19 20 21 22 23 24 25 26 27 28 29 30 31

| Command | Version | unused |
|---|---|---|
| 0xFFFF | | Authentication Type |
| Authentication... | | |
| ...Authentication... | | |
| ...Authentication... | | |
| ...Authentication | | |
| [up to 24 routing entries] | | |

If you operate a network in a hostile environment (such as a university), then we suggest that you seriously consider using a strong authentication mechanism for all your routing protocols.

# Configuration & Operation With RIPv1

RIPv2 configuration is similar to RIPv1 configuration. An additional command is used to specify which version of RIP is to be used. A sample configuration follows:

```
router rip
version 2
network 172.16.0.0
```

This configuration sets the default behavior for RIP. If you have a network that mixes RIPv1 and RIPv2 routers, some interfaces may need to have one version of RIP configured and other interfaces may need another version. In Figure 5-4, NewYork is using RIPv2 to Tokyo and RIPv1 to London. NewYork's configuration is shown in Figure 5-5. By default, RIP will summarize its routes to the classful boundary of each network.

In this example, Tokyo is configured with RIPv2, and London is configured to run only RIPv1. NewYork communicates the routes between the two networks by using both versions of RIP. The default version is specified as RIPv2 on line 12. But interface S0 is connected to London, which is capable only of RIPv1. Lines 6 and 7 of Figure 5-5 show RIPv1 being specified for this interface.

**Figure 5-4**
Multiple-RIP-version
network

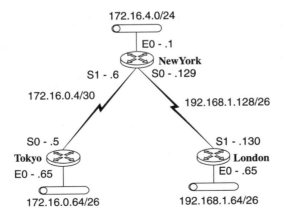

**Figure 5-5** Configuring multiple RIP versions

```
1 hostname NewYork
2 interface Ethernet0
3  ip address 172.16.4.1 255.255.255.0
4 interface Serial0
5  ip address 192.168.1.129 255.255.255.192
6  ip rip send version 1
7  ip rip receive version 1
8 interface Serial1
9  ip address 172.16.0.6 255.255.255.252
10   clockrate 56000
11 router rip
12  version 2
13  network 172.16.0.0
14  network 192.168.1.0
15 ip classless
16 end
```

**Figure 5-6** RIP clear-text authentication configurations

**NewYork RIP text authentication**
```
1 hostname NewYork
2 key chain ny-tokyo-key
3  key 1
4   key-string AnotherTest
5 interface Ethernet0
6  ip address 192.168.1.1 255.255.255.0
7 interface Serial1
8  ip address 192.168.4.2 255.255.255.0
9  ip rip authentication key-chain ny-tokyo-key
10  bandwidth 1544
11  no fair-queue
12  clockrate 1300000
13 router rip
14  version 2
15  network 192.168.1.0
16  network 192.168.4.0
17 ip classless
18 end
```

**Tokyo RIP text authentication**
```
19 hostname Tokyo
20 key chain tokyo-ny-key
21  key 1
22   key-string AnotherTest
23 interface Ethernet0
24  ip address 192.168.2.1 255.255.255.0
25 interface Serial0
26  ip address 192.168.4.1 255.255.255.0
27  ip rip authentication mode md5
28  ip rip authentication key-chain tokyo-ny-key
29  bandwidth 1544
30 router rip
31  version 2
32  network 192.168.4.0
33  network 192.168.2.0
34 ip classless
35 end
```

The previous example shows routers running two different versions of RIP over a serial link. In other scenarios, a RIPv2 router may have a LAN connection that has some routers using RIPv1 and others using RIPv2. In this case, the LAN interface should be configured with the commands **ip rip send version 1 2** and **ip rip receive version 1 2**. These commands force the router to send and receive both types of updates.

There are two types of RIP authentication possible: clear-text password and MD5 digest. As we stated earlier in this chapter, the clear-text password is useful only to prevent the accidental addition of a misconfigured router to a RIPv2 network. Better security of your routing domain requires the use of the MD5 digest. To add RIPv2 authentication to your router configuration, you must enable authentication, specify the authentication type (text or MD5), and configure the authentication key itself. Authentication is specified on a per-interface basis. Figure 5-6 shows the configurations of two routers that are using the clear-text password authentication. Lines 2-4 specify the key, and line 9 applies it to New York's Serial 0 interface. The default authentication type is clear-text, so its configuration statement does not appear in the configuration.

Figure 5-7 contains the configurations of two routers using MD5 authentication. The configuration difference between MD5 authentication and text authentication is simple. Lines 9-10 specify MD5 authentication mode and reference the proper key.

We recommend using authentication where there exists the possibility of hostile systems injecting bad routing information into your network. The key must be the same on all routers that share routing information on a single link. Different keys may be used on each interface. Since the keys are stored in clear-text form in the configuration files, it is important to protect the configurations from unauthorized access.

## Lab Exercise

Configure the lab to match Figure 5-8. Run RIPv2 on all three routers. Enable RIP debugging on New York and London to watch the operation of RIP. Look for the different versions of RIP on each router. As an added step, add RIP clear-text authentication and make sure that all routers are exchanging routing information correctly. Then change the configuration to use MD5 authentication. Again, make sure that all three routers are correctly exchanging routing information.

Shut down the link between New York and Tokyo (wait for the routes to converge or do a **clear ip route** * on each router). Try a ping from

**Figure 5-7** RIP MD5 authentication configurations

**NewYork RIP MD5 authentication**

```
1 hostname NewYork
2 key chain ny-tokyo-key
3  key 1
4   key-string AnotherTest
5 interface Ethernet0
6  ip address 192.168.1.1 255.255.255.0
7 interface Serial1
8  ip address 192.168.4.2 255.255.255.0
9  ip rip authentication mode md5
10  ip rip authentication key-chain ny-tokyo-key
11  bandwidth 1544
12  clockrate 1300000
13 router rip
14  version 2
15  network 192.168.1.0
16  network 192.168.4.0
17 ip classless
18 end
```

**Tokyo RIP MD5 authentication**

```
19 hostname Tokyo
20 key chain tokyo-ny-key
21  key 1
22   key-string AnotherTest
23 interface Ethernet0
24  ip address 192.168.2.1 255.255.255.0
25 interface Serial0
26  ip address 192.168.4.1 255.255.255.0
27  ip rip authentication mode md5
28  ip rip authentication key-chain tokyo-ny-key
29  bandwidth 1544
30 router rip
31  version 2
32  network 192.168.4.0
33  network 192.168.2.0
34 ip classless
35 end
```

**Figure 5-8**

RIP lab network

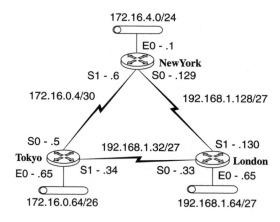

London to Tokyo's E0 interface (remember to check the state of the ip route cache). What response do you see? What is happening? Are the subnets of 172.16.0.0 contiguous? Check the routing tables. Try using **debug ip icmp** on both New York and Tokyo to see what is happening.

In New York and Tokyo, add the router subcommand **no auto-summary** and wait for the routing to converge. Check the contents of the routing updates going to London. What routes appear in London's routing table? Retry the ping test to Tokyo's E0 interface. What is the response?

Enable the link between New York and London. What changes do you see in London's routing table? Are all subnets of 172.16.0.0 visible? What routes do New York and Tokyo have?

## RIP Summary

For small networks or for small sections of a large network, RIP still makes a lot of sense. The ability to use both versions of RIP is important when transitioning a network from one version to another. RIPv2 is useful when integrating the RIP network with a classless routing environment.

# EIGRP

About the same time that OSPF development was going strong, Cisco started developing a replacement for IGRP. The original IGRP had been a good performer but lacked the convergence requirements and VLSM support that would be needed in the future. The ease of configuration of IGRP was something that OSPF lacked and was important to Cisco.

Research done by J.J. Garcia at SRI resulted in the creation of the Diffusing Update Algorithm (DUAL) (Garcia 1993 and Azumen and Garcia 1992), an alternative algorithm that was somewhat similar to a distance-vector protocol but with good convergence and operational characteristics. Cisco was able to adapt this research to create an operational protocol that uses the traditional IGRP multicomponent metric. This protocol is named Enhanced IGRP. A paper describing EIGRP's operation is available from Cisco's Web site (Cisco 1998c).

As an enhancement to DUAL and IGRP, Cisco has added the capability for EIGRP to handle routes for multiple networking protocols. A single protocol engine can collect topology information and use it to populate the routing tables for IP, Appletalk, and IPX. Having one protocol handle routing for several routing tables conserves network bandwidth, router memory, and router CPU time. When used for IP, EIGRP can share routing information with IGRP neighbors without any additional configuration, because both protocols use the same metric.

## Metric

EIGRP uses the same metric that IGRP uses—bandwidth, delay, load, reliability, and MTU (see Chapter 4 for a full discussion of the metric). The metric equation and coefficients are also the same as are used by IGRP, making bandwidth and delay the only two components that determine the final metric. As with IGRP, the lowest-value metric is the best path, and multiple paths whose metrics are within the variance of one another are allowed.

The metric coefficients must be the same on all routers running EIGRP in your network. You should not modify the metric coefficients.

## Basic Configuration

EIGRP's basic configuration is identical to IGRP's configuration. For the example network in Figure 5-9, the configurations shown in Figure 5-10 are used. In these configurations, you will see that only the networks that are directly attached to each router are listed in the network statements of EIGRP. As with IGRP, the network statement tells the router which interfaces should be running EIGRP.

**Figure 5-9**
EIGRP network

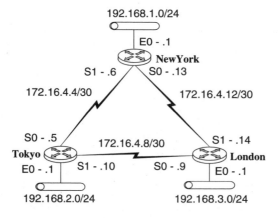

There are two EIGRP configuration items that must match in order for adjacent routers to communicate properly. The first is the EIGRP autonomous system number. The autonomous system number identifies all EIGRP routers that should share routing information because they are all administered by a single cooperating network staff. The second configuration item is that the metric equation coefficients (the K1, K2,

**Figure 5-10** EIGRP configuration

```
NewYork Configuration
1 hostname NewYork
2 key chain testlab
3  key 1
4   key-string ThisIsATest
5 key chain ny-tokyo-key
6  key 1
7   key-string AnotherTest
8 interface Ethernet0
9  ip address 192.168.1.1 255.255.255.0
10 interface Serial0
11  ip address 172.16.4.13 255.255.255.252
12  ip authentication mode eigrp 1 md5
13  ip authentication key-chain eigrp 1 testlab
14  bandwidth 1544
15 interface Serial1
16  ip address 172.16.4.6 255.255.255.252
17  ip authentication mode eigrp 1 md5
18  ip authentication key-chain eigrp 1 ny-tokyo-key
19  bandwidth 1544
20  clockrate 1300000
21 router eigrp 1
22  network 172.16.0.0
23  network 192.168.1.0
24 ip classless
25 end

Tokyo Configuation
26 hostname Tokyo
27 key chain tokyo-ny-key
28  key 1
29   key-string AnotherTest
30 key chain tokyo-london-key
31  key 1
32   key-string AnotherTest
33 interface Ethernet0
34  ip address 192.168.2.1 255.255.255.0
35 interface Serial0
36  ip address 172.16.4.5 255.255.255.252
37  ip authentication mode eigrp 1 md5
38  ip authentication key-chain eigrp 1 tokyo-ny-key
39  bandwidth 1544
40 interface Serial1
41  ip address 172.16.4.10 255.255.255.252
42  ip authentication mode eigrp 1 md5
43 ip authentication key-chain eigrp 1 tokyo-london-key
```

**Figure 5-10** Continued

```
44  clockrate 1300000
45 router eigrp 1
46  network 172.16.0.0
47  network 192.168.2.0
48 ip classless
49 end
```

**London Configuration**
```
50 hostname London
51 key chain london-ny-key
52  key 1
53   key-string ThisIsATest
54 key chain london-tokyo-key
55  key 1
56   key-string AnotherTest
57 interface Ethernet0
58  ip address 192.168.3.1 255.255.255.0
59 interface Serial0
60  ip address 172.16.4.9 255.255.255.252
61  ip authentication mode eigrp 1 md5
62  ip authentication key-chain eigrp 1 london-tokyo-key
63  bandwidth 1544
64 interface Serial1
65  ip address 172.16.4.14 255.255.255.252
66  ip authentication mode eigrp 1 md5
67  ip authentication key-chain eigrp 1 london-ny-key
68  bandwidth 1544
69  clockrate 1300000
70 router eigrp 1
71  network 172.16.0.0
72  network 192.168.3.0
73 ip classless
74 end
```

K3, K4, and K5 values that are set with the **metric weights** command) must be the same on all routers within the autonomous system.

An authentication mechanism can be used to prevent unauthorized routing information from being received by routers in the network. In Figure 5-10, lines 2-7, 12-13, and 17-18 show the authentication commands used on NewYork. The other routers are configured similarly. There may be multiple keys configured for each key chain, each with a different key chain number, key string, and optional time over which it is valid. Within a named key chain, the router will search the keys from the lowest-numbered to the highest-numbered key, using the first key that is active. A key that has no valid time specified is always valid. If you enable the keys at different times, you will need to set the time of day on the routers and configure the Network Time Protocol (NTP) to maintain the correct time so that the routers will all switch to the new keys at the same time.

Additional examples of EIGRP configuration, including route redistribution and summarization, may be found in Cisco's documentation: Integrating Enhanced IGRP Into Existing Networks (Cisco 1997). This document also includes configuration examples for AppleTalk and Novell networks.

# Operation

EIGRP uses incremental updates to limit the amount of routing traffic on the network. When a topology change occurs, the routers closest to the change will query their neighbors for an alternative route around the failure.

The neighbors propagate this query until a router is found that has a valid path around the failure. The valid information is propagated back to the routers adjacent to the failure. Since the query is propagated only as far as is needed to find an alternate path, we say that the updates diffuse across the network (thus the name of the algorithm).

EIGRP propagates the route and its mask together, making it capable of full VLSM operation. By default, routes are summarized to classful addresses at network boundaries. It is possible to propagate the subnets of a network by using the router subcommand **no auto-summary**. Using this command, you can avoid the problem of discontiguous subnets since all subnet information is propagated into the adjacent network.

EIGRP protocol transactions are sent as multicast and unicast IP packets using protocol number 88. No periodic updates are sent. Sequence numbers and acknowledgments of the transactions ensure reliable delivery of the updates, allowing EIGRP to perform incremental updates. The use of incremental updates eliminates routing protocol overhead when the network is stable.

Output rate queues on each interface are used to prevent overloading links when a network topology change causes a burst of routing protocol traffic. By default, the rate queue is set to less than 50 percent of the link bandwidth (as determined by the interface's bandwidth parameter). The rate queue percentage is adjustable through use of the command **ip bandwidth-percent eigrp *percent***.

Hello Protocol
The EIGRP hello protocol is used to establish neighbor relationships between routers and to prevent black hole routes (we discuss black hole routes in Chapter 10). Hello packets are sent every five seconds by default

on LAN media. On WAN media, the default hello packet interval is every 60 seconds, because media failures typically are detected by the CSU/DSU and reported to the router via the WAN interface cable.

But what happens if a router on an Ethernet crashes unexpectedly? It suddenly stops sending hello packets. The neighboring routers will stop using all routes through the failed router after the hold time expires. The default value for the hold time is three times the hello interval. On an Ethernet, the default hello time is five seconds, so the hold time is 15 seconds. On serial links that operate at T1 speeds and below, the default hello time is 60 seconds and the hold time is 180 seconds. Longer times on slow-speed serial links are used because the CSU/DSU will communicate link failure via a change in the link status signals (typically a change in Data Carrier Detect). The longer times also conserve link bandwidth. The default hello time on Frame Relay PVCs is 10 seconds, which sets the hold time at 30 seconds. The faster time is necessary because a PVC may fail without any other notification.

You can change the hello packet interval on all media, but the timer must be the same on all routers sharing a common network link. The selected value should be based on your network convergence and need for fast dead router detection. On point-to-point links where you have clearly verified that the link failure is reported by the CSU/DSU, you may increase the value. But beware that on some WAN media like Frame Relay or X.25, the link PVC or SVC may fail internal to the carrier's network without being detected by the CSU/DSU. The hello protocol can detect these types of failures.

Neighbor Table
The neighbor table stores the identity of each neighbor, its hold time, and the sequence number and acknowledgments used to ensure the reliable delivery of updates to and from that neighbor. The neighbor table can be viewed with the **show ip eigrp neighbor** command (Figure 5-11

**Figure 5-11** Output of show **ip eigrp neighbor**

```
1 NewYork#sh ip eigrp neighbor
2 IP-EIGRP neighbors for process 1
3 H   Address              Interface   Hold Uptime   SRTT   RTO  Q   Seq
4                                      (sec)         (ms)        Cnt  Num
5 1   172.16.4.5           Se1          12 00:21:49   28    200  0   285
6 0   172.16.4.14          Se0          12 00:22:28   20    200  0   382
7 NewYork#
```

shows the output from New York in the network of Figure 5-9). Lines 5-6 show the neighbor addresses, the interface on which the neighbor was heard, the hold time for that neighbor, the up time of the neighbor relationship, and factors that are used to implement the reliable delivery of routing information to the neighbor. A router that is constantly resetting the up-time value indicates a neighbor relationship that is constantly being restarted. The SRTT (smoothed round-trip timer) indicates the round-trip time to the neighbor (it is similar to the time reported by ping) and is used in EIGRP's reliable update mechanism.

Topology Table

The topology table is critical to the proper operation of EIGRP. In it, the router stores the metrics of each route, the metric that the neighboring router is advertising, and the identity of each neighboring router. Since the router has a copy of each neighbor's routing table (and not just information about those with the best routes), it is possible to select alternate paths quickly when network failures occur.

Routes in the topology table are used to populate the IP routing table. A route is in a passive state when the network is stable. When a failure occurs, the router must find an alternate path to any destinations which now are unreachable. The topology table is searched for a neighboring router that is a feasible successor. A feasible successor is a router that has a route to the destination and that is not part of a routing loop. We'll explain how the full rerouting process works in the next section.

The contents of the topology table can be viewed with the command **show ip eigrp topology**. Either the AS number of the EIGRP domain or the IP address of specific neighbors can be used as arguments to limit the amount of information that is displayed. Figure 5-12 shows the output of New York's topology table in the network of Figure 5-9. Lines 7-8 show a directly connected network. There is only one feasible successor, which is New York itself. Lines 13-14 show subnet 172.16.4.8, which is available via two paths: one via Tokyo and another via London.

If you were to use the command **show ip eigrp topology all-links**, you would see more paths for each subnet. The Feasibility Distance (FD) value is the metric of the current best route. Alternate routes are compared to this value to determine alternate paths. By comparing the FD for the destination subnet against the calculated metric of each of the paths, you see that only one path is valid (only one path has a metric less than FD).

**Figure 5-12** Output of show ip eigrp topology

```
1 NewYork#sh ip eigrp topology
2 IP-EIGRP Topology Table for process 1
3
4 Codes: P - Passive, A - Active, U - Update, Q - Query, R - Reply,
5        r - Reply status
6
7 P 192.168.1.0/24, 1 successors, FD is 281600
8          via Connected, Ethernet0
9 P 192.168.2.0/24, 1 successors, FD is 2195456
10         via 172.16.4.5 (2195456/281600), Serial1
11 P 192.168.3.0/24, 1 successors, FD is 2195456
12         via 172.16.4.14 (2195456/281600), Serial0
13 P 172.16.4.8/30, 2 successors, FD is 2681856
14         via 172.16.4.5 (2681856/2169856), Serial1
15         via 172.16.4.14 (2681856/2169856), Serial0
16 P 172.16.4.12/30, 1 successors, FD is 2169856
17         via Connected, Serial0
18 P 172.16.4.4/30, 1 successors, FD is 2169856
19         via Connected, Serial1
20 P 172.16.0.0/16, 1 successors, FD is 513792
21         via Summary (2169856/0), Null0
22 NewYork#
```

### The Rerouting Process

EIGRP's ability to quickly select an alternate path is demonstrated when a link failure occurs. The failure can be due to the failure of an adjacent router or because a link to a neighboring router failed. Let's see how this works.

Upon detecting a failure, the router will try to determine a feasible successor by examining its neighbor's routing information stored in its topology table. If the neighboring router has a route to the destination, and the route is not part of a routing loop (we'll see how this calculation is performed later), the feasible successor search succeeds and the route stays in the passive state. The routing table is updated to use the path via the neighbor. If the metric changed due to the selection of the feasible successor, then a routing update is sent to all neighbors.

FYI: A *feasible successor* is a router that has a loop-free alternative path to a path that just became unusable. You can think of the term feasible successor as identifying a router that is a successor to another and, because it is part of a loop-free path, it is feasible.

If no feasible successor is found by searching its topology table, the route enters the active state. In the active state, all neighbors are queried to see if one of them has a neighboring router which is a feasible successor for the failed route. Queries are propagated to other neighboring routers until a feasible successor has been determined.

A router with a feasible successor will return a reply to its neighbor. The reply is passed from router to router until it reaches the original router that detected the failure. The route is then changed to use the neighbor reporting the best metric to the destination.

If no feasible successor was detected, an empty reply packet is returned. The router detecting the failure removes the failed route from its routing table.

In either case, when the routing table is updated, an update is sent on all interfaces to tell the neighboring routers about the new route.

Now let's take a look at the details of how the route determination is performed, then see how it works in a sample network.

Finding Feasible Successors

When a network failure occurs, the routers detecting the failure immediately check their neighbor and topology tables for a feasible successor. A feasible successor is a neighboring router that has a loop-free path to the destination. A simple algorithm determines whether the neighbor's path is loop-free.

Trying to find a feasible successor requires a series of steps to be followed. First, the failed route's last-known metric is stored in a variable called FD:

```
FD = best metric of the route prior to failure
```

Then, the router searches the topology table for all neighbors whose advertised metric is less than FD. This search produces a set (or list) of routers:

```
V1 = {all neighbors with advertised metric < FD}
```

There may be zero or more routers in the set (zero because there was no neighbor with a metric better than FD). Determining the set of routers contained in V1 is the step that makes sure that the feasible successor (if one exists) has a loop-free path to the destination. If the route that the neighbor has is back through the router performing the calculation, the metric would have to be at least equal to or greater than the metric of the failed route (because the cost of the link to get to the neighbor would be included in the neighbor's metric).

Now that the router knows which neighbors have a better path than it originally had, it needs to find which neighbor is the best to use. In the next step, the router executing DUAL calculates the EIGRP metric of all routes via the neighbors that are part of the set V1. The metric includes the cost of the link between the router and its neighbors. The minimum metric of all paths via the V1 set of neighbors is found (because we want to only use the lowest cost path to the destination):

```
Dmin = MIN(all computed metrics)
```

The DUAL algorithm then finds those routers contained in V1 and through which the metric is Dmin:

```
V2 = {all neighbors in V1 AND through which the computed metric =
      Dmin}
```

As long as at least one neighbor is found in set V1, there exists a feasible successor to the failed route.

The feasibility condition calculation is performed for each destination (i.e., each network) that is affected by a topology change (i.e., a link or router failure.) The result of the feasibility condition calculation is to find alternate paths through which data may be forwarded to the destination without encountering a routing loop.

Link Failure Processing

Using the example network shown in Figure 5-13, we will examine how EIGRP operates. In this example, we will watch what happens to network connectivity for network N when the link between routers A and D fails. In this example, we'll use some simple metrics instead of the larger EIGRP metrics.

Note that each router—B, C, and D—has a topology table showing the destination network, N, and each possible route to network N. For each path, there are two metric values. The first is the metric from the router itself, and the second is the metric being advertised by the router that is the successor (the next-hop router) for that path. Finally, the table contains the successor router for the path. For example, router D has two possible routes to network N. The first is via router A. D's metric to reach N is 25, while A's metric (A is the neighbor on that path) is 15.

The second entry in D's table is via router C. D's metric via this path is 60, while C's advertised metric is 45.

Examining routers B and C shows their tables to contain information related to their paths to network N. In all cases, we have abbreviated the

**Figure 5-13**
EIGRP link failure—
initial network

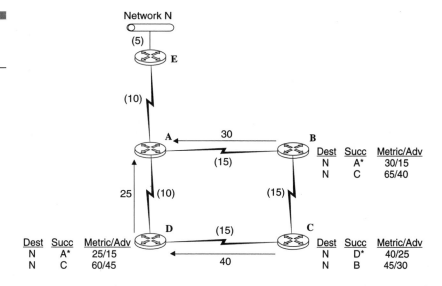

tables to show only the routes to network N. Real routers also would contain routes to all the network segments in the network.

Router B will use its minimum-cost path (30) via A. Router C will use its minimum-cost path (40) via D. Finally, router D will use its minimum-cost path (25) via router A.

Let's see, in Figure 5-14, what happens if the link between A and D fails. Router D marks that path as invalid but retains its prior metric (25)

**Figure 5-14**
EIGRP link fails

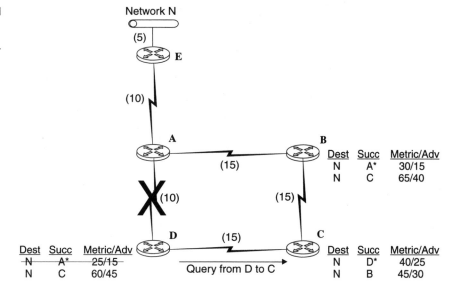

**Figure 5-15**
EIGRP neighbor finds
feasible successor
route

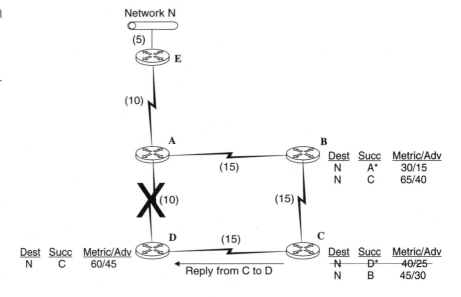

as its FD value. Router D then begins the feasibility condition analysis on topology table information it has collected from its neighbors about network N.

The feasibility condition begins by finding V1, the set of D's neighbors that have an advertised metric less than FD (25). The only other neighbor is router C, and its advertised metric is 45. This is greater than FD, so there is no feasible successor. Therefore, D places the route into the active state and sends a query to its neighbors (C is the only one in this network), asking if the neighbors have a feasible successor to network N.

In Figure 5-15, router C marks its route via D as invalid and examines its tables for network N to determine a feasible successor since the path via D has failed. Its original metric to network N was 40 via D. This is the value that C uses for its feasibility distance.

The feasibility condition starts with V1, the set of neighboring routers whose metric is less than FD (FD is 40 for C). Router B satisfies this criterion since its advertised metric is 30, as found in C's topology table.

The next requirement of the feasibility condition is that Dmin = min (all computed metrics). There is only one computed metric, which is 45 via router B (the computed metric is B's advertised metric plus the cost of the link between B and C). Therefore, Dmin = 45.

The final feasibility condition is to find the set, V2, of all routers who are members of set V1 and whose computed metric is equal to Dmin.

Router B is in V1, and its computed metric (45) is equal to Dmin (45). Router B is C's feasible successor.

C's route to network N stays in the passive state, the failed route is marked as down, and the new route is installed in the routing table. C sends a reply to D indicating that it has found a feasible successor and that its metric to network N is 45.

In Figure 5-16, D has been waiting for all its neighbors to reply to its query (the protocol waits until all neighbors reply, thus guaranteeing loop-free routing). Once it has received replies from all neighbors, it has all the neighbor information it needs to determine the best path to network N. Network N is then placed into the passive state. The successor for Network N is router C, with metric 60. Network N is added to D's routing table with metric 60 via router C, and a routing update is generated by D and sent to all its neighbors.

The topology tables show the resulting connectivity. Note that router A did not have to perform any actions, relative to network N, for the network to converge after this change. Router B did not take part in any of the actual rerouting actions either, although it had to remove the neighbor information about a path via C to network N from its topology table.

There also would have been a change in A and B and C to propagate information that the link between A and D was no longer available, but that is not related to propagating information about network N.

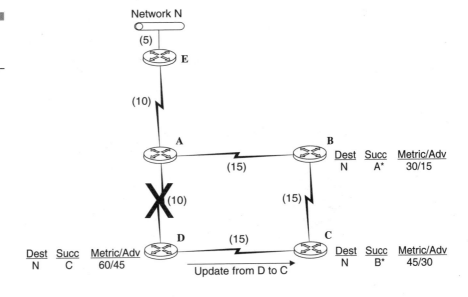

**Figure 5-16**
EIGRP update is distributed

## Lab Exercise

Configure the lab network to match the network diagram shown in Figure 5-17. When the configuration is complete, check the routing table, making sure that all subnets are visible in all routers.

Add clear-text authentication to all the routers. As you are adding authentication, check the routing tables on several routers (some that have had the authentication added and other that have not). What happens to the routing tables on these routers? How would adding authentication to an operational network have to be done?

Next, change the authentication to use MD5. MD5 authentication requires that the key be less than 15 characters to work (check release notes after 11.3 for changes to the length of the MD5 key). You may need to cycle an interface through the shutdown/no shutdown state with some versions of the IOS before authentication is checked.

When you have EIGRP routing running correctly, check the neighbor and topology tables on each router. Use each of the variations of these commands to see what information is available that might help troubleshoot any problems. In particular, try the command **show ip eigrp topology all-links** to see all the paths. Compare the FD for the destination against the calculated metric for each neighbor to see which neighbors have valid paths.

Enable neighbor logging and watch New York's output while turning off Moscow's Ethernet. Then reenable Moscow's Ethernet. What was the result? Use the command **debug ip eigrp** on Tokyo, then disable Rome's Ethernet0. How long does it take for the change to appear in Tokyo?

**Figure 5-17**
EIGRP lab exercise network

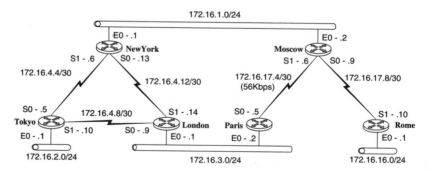

All serial links are T1 except Paris to Moscow.

## EIGRP Summary

EIGRP uses neighbor discovery (hello packets) to ensure communication of routing information and to establish the set of adjacent routers that could be queried for alternate paths in the case of a network failure.

An integral part of the algorithm is the sharing of metrics by the next-hop neighbors and storing that information in a topology database. A set of very simple calculations is used on each destination network whenever a topology change occurs that affects those destinations.

Topology changes diffuse over the network. Routers that do not need to propagate queries do not do so. Alternate-path queries are propagated only as far as needed to determine a feasible successor path.

## OSPF

The Open Shortest Path First (OSPF) routing protocol was developed in the late 1980s and early 1990s by the Internet community to fulfill the need for a modern vendor-independent protocol. At that time, RIP was the major protocol and it was beginning to run into problems as networks grew in size. Cisco's IGRP was available and had better path-selection characteristics, but it was proprietary and had long convergence times. RFC2178 (Moy 1997) is the current specification of OSPF version 2. There are several books available on OSPF, including *OSPF, Anatomy of an Internet Routing Protocol* (Moy 1998), and *Cisco Router OSPF Design and Implementation Guide* (Parkhurst 1998). Cisco's Web site has a paper describing the Cisco implementation of OSPF and the basic rules for configuring OSPF on Cisco networks (Halabi 1996). It has some useful information, but is becoming somewhat outdated as new features and functionality are added to Cisco's implementation.

OSPF developers borrowed ideas from a variety of other routing protocols, including the original ARPANET link-state protocol and the OSI protocols. Large networks running OSPF must use a hierarchical network topology, which is a better design in any case but may require a change to the topology when migrating from another protocol.

OSPF's features include VLSM, fast convergence, low network utilization, equal-cost parallel path support, the use of multicast packets, and vendor independence.

The protocol continues to undergo development to adapt to changes in networking technology. Nonbroadcast multiaccess (NBMA) networks are supported and not-so-stubby-areas (NSSAs) can be integrated into the network. We'll discuss each of these features and how to configure them.

## Operation

OSPF is a link-state protocol designed for operation within an autonomous system. Link-state protocols operate by maintaining an identical topology database within each router in the OSPF domain. This database stores the state of each network link (i.e., the state of each interface) on each router and is used to determine the shortest path to every network in the autonomous system. Routers flood the state of each network link to all neighboring routers, which update their topology database and then propagate the information to other routers. OSPF routing information exchanges are sent in IP packets using protocol ID 89.

The Dijkstra algorithm uses the information in the topological database to calculate the shortest path to each destination network, relative to the router performing the calculation. The resulting shortest paths identify the best next-hop router for each destination. The IP address and interface to use to reach the next-hop router is installed in the IP routing table. Since all routers have the same topological database, the shortest paths will be consistent even though each router is finding the shortest path from itself to each destination.

FYI: OSPF has many features, and the best way to learn is to implement them yourself. Each feature we discuss will have a network map and a set of router configurations. Our challenge to you is to examine the configurations to become familiar with the commands, then—using only the Cisco documentation and the network maps—implement the feature.

## Basic Configuration

Basic OSPF configuration in small networks is not much different than EIGRP configuration. The complexity comes from applying OSPF to large networks where area design, redundancy, on-demand links, and authentication are needed. We'll start out with a simple OSPF configuration and demonstrate the configuration of additional features as we introduce them.

The major addition in OSPF configuration, relative to the other proto-cols we've covered, is that the OSPF routing domain can be divided into smaller segments called areas. Each area is numbered, and there must always be an area zero, which is the backbone. All other areas attach to the backbone, either directly or via virtual links (which we'll discuss later). An area should contain no more than about 50-75 routers for opti-mum operation.

Let's start out with a backbone area, area zero (Figure 5-18). All routers that have an interface connected to the backbone are known as back-bone routers. Routers that have all interfaces connected to a single area are known as area routers.

With OSPF, interfaces are assigned to areas (routers are not assigned to areas). The network statements for OSPF have a wildcard mask to identi-fy specific interfaces and an area ID that assigns the area for the identi-fied interfaces. The foolproof method of assigning interfaces to areas is to list each interface with an exact-match wildcard mask. Let's look at the configuration (Figure 5-19).

Lines 11-14 show the OSPF router configuration for NewYork. There are several other ways that we could have assigned all the interfaces to area zero. One method assigns all interfaces of 172.16.0.0 and all inter-faces of 192.168.1.0 to area zero:

```
router ospf 1
network 172.16.0.0 0.0.255.255 area 0
network 192.168.1.0 0.0.0.255 area 0
```

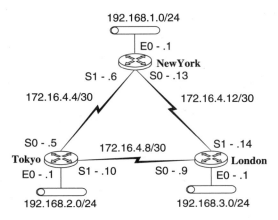

**Figure 5-18**
Single area OSPF
network

**Figure 5-19** Single area OSPF configuration

```
NewYork Configuration
1 hostname NewYork
2 interface Ethernet0
3  ip address 192.168.1.1 255.255.255.0
4 interface Serial0
5  ip address 172.16.4.13 255.255.255.252
6  ip ospf authentication-key london
7  bandwidth 1544
8 interface Serial1
9  ip address 172.16.4.6 255.255.255.252
10  ip ospf authentication-key secret-p
11  bandwidth 1544
12  clockrate 1300000
13 router ospf 1
14  network 192.168.1.1 0.0.0.0 area 0
15  network 172.16.4.13 0.0.0.0 area 0
16  network 172.16.4.6 0.0.0.0 area 0
17 area 0 authentication
18 ip classless
19 end
```

```
Tokyo Configuration
20 hostname Tokyo
21 interface Ethernet0
22  ip address 192.168.2.1 255.255.255.0
23 interface Serial0
24  ip address 172.16.4.5 255.255.255.252
25  ip ospf authentication-key secret-p
26  bandwidth 1544
27 interface Serial1
28  ip address 172.16.4.10 255.255.255.252
29  clockrate 1300000
30 router ospf 1
31  network 192.168.2.1 0.0.0.0 area 0
32  network 172.16.4.5 0.0.0.0 area 0
33  network 172.16.4.10 0.0.0.0 area 0
34 area 0 authentication
35 ip classless
36 end
```

```
London Configuration
37 hostname London
38 interface Ethernet0
39  ip address 192.168.3.1 255.255.255.0
40 interface Serial0
41  ip address 172.16.4.9 255.255.255.252
42  bandwidth 1544
43 interface Serial1
44  ip address 172.16.4.14 255.255.255.252
45  ip ospf authentication-key london
46  bandwidth 1544
47  clockrate 1300000
48 router ospf 1
49  network 172.16.4.9 0.0.0.0 area 0
50  network 172.16.4.14 0.0.0.0 area 0
51  network 192.168.3.1 0.0.0.0 area 0
52 area 0 authentication
53 ip classless
54 end
```

Another method assigns all interfaces to area zero, regardless of the interface address:

```
router ospf 1
network 0.0.0.0 255.255.255.255 area 0
```

FYI: The address and wildcard mask used in OSPF operates the same as in access-lists. The wildcard mask matches IP addresses on a bit-by-bit basis. Each bit in the mask that is a zero tells the router that the corresponding bit in the command's IP address must exactly match the same bit in the interface's address. A one in the wildcard mask tells the router that the corresponding bit position in the interface address can be either one or zero.

There are trade-offs in deciding which interface selection method to use. The method used in our configuration guarantees that each interface is properly selected and is assigned to the correct area. But more configuration statements are required. The second and third methods reduce the number of configuration statements but will cause any additional interfaces of network 172.16.0.0 or 192.168.1.0 to be added to area zero automatically. The third method also would have worked on all three routers without modification, because the interface address didn't matter; any interface address would match and be assigned to area zero.

FYI: OSPF searches the list of network statements in top-down order. An interface may match more than one statement, but the router will assign the interface to the area specified in the first statement that matches the interface address.

Authentication is an important consideration in any modern network, and like RIPv2, OSPF provides both a clear-text and an MD5 authentication mechanism. Our sample authentication is included in the configuration of Figure 5-19. Examining lines 17, 34, and 52 shows clear-text authentication is being used. The clear-text keys appear on lines 6, 10, 25, and 45. Different keys are used on the two serial links. Only eight characters (64 bits) of password are valid, even though the router will accept longer passwords.

Because the authentication appears under the routing process, you can see that only one type of authentication is possible at one time. In addition, all routers must be configured to use authentication. Once it has been enabled in the OSPF routing protocol configuration, it must be configured on all interfaces that are running OSPF, or the neighbor adjacencies (which we'll discuss later) will fail. You can see this clearly by using the command **debug ip ospf adj** while adding and changing the authentication mechanisms and keys on the lab network.

To use MD5 authentication, the configurations would look like the following, where line 6 specifies MD5 authentication, and line 3 sets the keyid and key.

```
1) interface s 0
2) ip address 172.16.4.6 255.255.255.252
3) ip ospf message-digest-key 1 md5 secret-password
4) router ospf 1
5) network 0.0.0.0 255.255.255.255 area 0
6) area 0 authentication message-digest
```

The same keyid and key must be used on all routers.

When a new key is configured on an interface, multiple copies of the same packet will be sent, each authenticated with a different key. Once the router detects that all neighbors are using the new key, it will stop using the old key. This allows you to transition to new keys without affecting network connectivity.

## Metric

The metric used in the OSPF calculations is a unitless cost. By default it is $10^8$÷bandwidth, which forces it to measure bandwidth. A 10Mbps link has a metric of 10 and a 100Mbps FDDI or fast Ethernet has a default metric of one. On serial links, you will need to specify the bandwidth of the link (or the CIR for Frame Relay links) using the bandwidth interface subcommand. Otherwise, the serial links will default to a bandwidth of 1.544Mbps, which equates to an OSPF metric of 64.

The default does not allow for link speeds higher than 100Mbps. There are two methods of assigning different costs. The first (and the method you must use for older IOS releases) is to manually configure the cost on high-speed interfaces. Most network administrators manually configure all 100Mbps links to have a metric of seven to allow for higher-speed links. A 150Mbps ATM or SONET link would be assigned

**Figure 5-20**
Shortest path
network

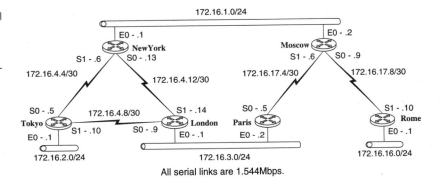

All serial links are 1.544Mbps.

metric of six, a 622Mbps ATM link would need a metric of four, and Gigabit Ethernet could be assigned a metric of three. Using this scheme, we still have room for two higher link speeds. Use the interface subcommand **ip ospf cost** to set the cost of an interface.

The second method of changing the cost used on high-speed interfaces is to use the router subcommand **ospf auto-cost reference-bandwidth** *ref-bw* to set the reference bandwidth (in Mbps) against which the interface cost is calculated. You should use a value such that the highest speed available in your network has a metric of one and the next-highest speed has a metric of less than 10, but greater than one. For example:

```
ospf auto-cost reference-bandwidth 300
```

would be appropriate for a network that contains a few gigabit network segments (cost one), more 150Mbps segments (cost two), and a lot of slower-speed segments (Ethernet cost would be 30). The cost of interfaces after adding this configuration parameter can be verified with the command **show ip ospf interface**. Make sure that all routers in the OSPF autonomous system use the same value for the reference-bandwidth, or incorrect routing will occur.

Our advice is that if you have only a few very high speed links, you should manually configure their OSPF costs instead of maintaining an additional configuration parameter on all routers in your network.

The metric is summed over all outgoing links in the path from source to destination. Only the metric on the outgoing direction is counted. One way to think of this is that the cost is for sending a packet, while receiving a packet costs nothing. Using the network of Figure 5-20 and running the OSPF algorithm on Tokyo, the shortest path tree from Tokyo to Rome's Ethernet 0 is shown in Figure 5-21. The shortest path is

**Figure 5-21**
Shortest path tree
from Tokyo to
172.16.16.0

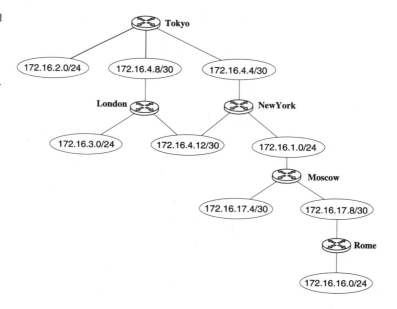

via NewYork, Moscow, and Rome, with a total path metric of 148. Note that Paris doesn't appear in the graph because it is not a destination network, and from Tokyo's perspective, Paris plays no role in reaching either 172.16.3.0 or 172.16.17.4.

## OSPF Areas

An OSPF network may be broken into areas to reduce the memory and computational load on the routers. Areas are identified by a number, and there must always be an area zero, which is the backbone area, as shown in Figure 5-22. Routers that connect more than one area are called Area Border Routers (ABRs). NewYork and Moscow are ABRs because they connect to area zero and their respective areas. These routers will have more than one area specified in the OSPF network statements and will run a copy of the OSPF algorithm for each area to which they are attached.

ABRs advertise the routes within each area to the backbone. Alternatively, the ABRs can create summary routes of each nonbackbone area and report these summaries to the backbone area. In turn, the backbone routers collect the routes (either type) and advertise them back to each area. In effect, the backbone is acting as a reflector. Routes advertised to it from an area are distributed to other areas.

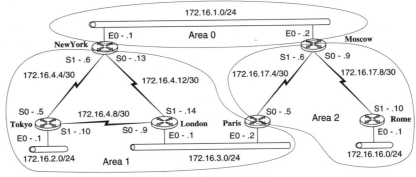

**Figure 5-22**
OSPF areas and
summary route
distribution

All serial links are 1.544Mbps.

OSPF has a hierarchy for routing packets to destinations that are intra-area (within the area) and inter-area (between areas). First, all packets for destinations within an area must stay within the area. Second, all packets for destinations in another area must pass through the backbone. Even if two areas connect to one router, if that router is not also a backbone router, the packets must be routed to a backbone router to be forwarded to the other area. The reason for the "round the world" routing is that the summary routes from all areas are originated by a backbone router. A non-backbone router that connects two areas does not distribute routes between the two areas.

The multi-area configuration of NewYork, Tokyo, London, Moscow, Paris, and Rome in the network of Figure 5-22 is shown in Figure 5-23. The important parts of each configuration are the OSPF network statements. Paris is a bit different than the other routers in that it is connected to two nonbackbone areas. Try running **trace** from Tokyo to Rome and from London to Rome. In both cases, the packets travel to NewYork, across the backbone to Moscow, then to Rome.

Notice the summarization of the serial links into a single routing entry to the backbone. This is done only on the area border routers (NewYork and Moscow). By default, OSPF will not summarize the subnets, and more memory and network bandwidth will be needed to carry the individual subnet routes in the backbone and in the other areas. The output of **show ip route** on Rome (Figure 5-24, line 15) shows the routes to the serial interface subnets being advertised as a single summary route to 172.16.4.0/24 from area one.

When designing an OSPF network, you should be careful to not have too many areas terminate in a single router. All routers connected to each area share a common set of OSPF data structures and runs a sepa-

**Figure 5-23** OSPF multiarea configuration

**NewYork Configuration**
```
1 hostname NewYork
2 interface Ethernet0
3  ip address 172.16.1.1 255.255.255.0
4 interface Serial0
5  ip address 172.16.4.13 255.255.255.252
6  ip ospf authentication-key london
7  bandwidth 1544
8 interface Serial1
9  ip address 172.16.4.6 255.255.255.252
10  ip ospf authentication-key secret-p
11  bandwidth 1544
12 clockrate 1300000
13 router ospf 1
14  network 172.16.1.1 0.0.0.0 area 0
15  network 172.16.4.13 0.0.0.0 area 1
16  network 172.16.4.6 0.0.0.0 area 1
17  area 1 range 172.16.4.0 255.255.255.0
18 ip classless
19 end
```

**Tokyo Configuration**
```
20 hostname Tokyo
21
22 interface Ethernet0
23  ip address 172.16.2.1 255.255.255.0
24 interface Serial0
25  ip address 172.16.4.5 255.255.255.252
26  ip ospf authentication-key secret-p
27  bandwidth 1544
28 interface Serial1
29  ip address 172.16.4.10 255.255.255.252
30  clockrate 1300000
31 router ospf 1
32  network 172.16.2.1 0.0.0.0 area 1
33  network 172.16.4.5 0.0.0.0 area 1
34  network 172.16.4.10 0.0.0.0 area 1
35 ip classless
36 end
```

**London Configuration**
```
37 hostname London
38 interface Ethernet0
39  ip address 172.16.3.1 255.255.255.0
40 interface Serial0
41  ip address 172.16.4.9 255.255.255.252
42  bandwidth 1544
43 interface Serial1
44  ip address 172.16.4.14 255.255.255.252
45  bandwidth 1544
46  clockrate 1300000
47 router ospf 1
48  network 172.16.4.9 0.0.0.0 area 1
49  network 172.16.4.14 0.0.0.0 area 1
50  network 172.16.3.1 0.0.0.0 area 1
51 ip classless
52 end
```

**Moscow Configuration**
```
53 hostname Moscow
54 interface Ethernet0
55  ip address 172.16.1.2 255.255.255.0
56 interface Serial0
57  ip address 172.16.17.9 255.255.255.252
58  bandwidth 1544
59 interface Serial1
60  ip address 172.16.17.6 255.255.255.252
61  bandwidth 1544
62  clockrate 1300000
63 router ospf 1
64  network 172.16.1.2 0.0.0.0 area 0
65  network 172.16.17.6 0.0.0.0 area 2
66  network 172.16.17.9 0.0.0.0 area 2
67  area 2 range 172.16.17.0 255.255.255.0
68 ip classless
69 end
```

**Paris Configuration**
```
70 hostname Paris
71 interface Ethernet0
72  ip address 172.16.3.2 255.255.255.0
73 interface Serial0
74  ip address 172.16.17.5 255.255.255.252
75  bandwidth 1544
76 interface Serial1
77  ip address 172.16.4.10 255.255.255.252
78  shutdown
79  clockrate 1300000
80 router ospf 1
81  network 172.16.3.2 0.0.0.0 area 1
82  network 172.16.17.5 0.0.0.0 area 2
83 ip classless
84 end
```

**Rome Configuration**
```
85 hostname Rome
86 interface Ethernet0
87  ip address 172.16.16.1 255.255.255.0
88 interface Serial1
89  ip address 172.16.17.10 255.255.255.252
90  clockrate 1300000
91 router ospf 1
92  network 172.16.16.1 0.0.0.0 area 2
93  network 172.16.17.10 0.0.0.0 area 2
94 ip classless
95 end
```

rate copy of the OSPF algorithm. If a single router is connected to too many areas, all the router's memory may be allocated or the CPU may become overloaded. A good rule to follow in OSPF network design is to limit the number of areas that connect to a single router to three. If you have a router with a high-speed CPU and lots of free memory, then it may be able to handle more areas.

**Figure 5-24** Output of show ip route with area summarization enabled

```
 1 Rome#sh ip route
 2 Codes: C - connected, S - static, I - IGRP, R - RIP, M - mobile, B - BGP
 3        D - EIGRP, EX - EIGRP external, O - OSPF, IA - OSPF inter area
 4        N1 - OSPF NSSA external type 1, N2 - OSPF NSSA external type 2
 5        E1 - OSPF external type 1, E2 - OSPF external type 2, E - EGP
 6        i - IS-IS, L1 - IS-IS level-1, L2 - IS-IS level-2, * - candidate default
 7        U - per-user static route, o - ODR
 8
 9 Gateway of last resort is not set
10
11        172.16.0.0/16 is variably subnetted, 7 subnets, 2 masks
12 C         172.16.17.8/30 is directly connected, Serial1
13 O         172.16.17.4/30 [110/128] via 172.16.17.9, 00:40:11, Serial1
14 C         172.16.16.0/24 is directly connected, Ethernet0
15 O IA      172.16.4.0/24 [110/138] via 172.16.17.9, 00:11:11, Serial1
16 O IA      172.16.1.0/24 [110/74] via 172.16.17.9, 00:40:11, Serial1
17 O IA      172.16.2.0/24 [110/148] via 172.16.17.9, 00:40:11, Serial1
18 O IA      172.16.3.0/24 [110/148] via 172.16.17.9, 00:40:11, Serial1
```

# Virtual Links,
# Router ID & Loopback Interfaces

The backbone area must always remain fully connected, and all areas must attach to area zero. If area zero becomes partitioned into two or more sections, some destinations will become unreachable. There are two ways to prevent area 0 partitioning. First, make sure that area 0 contains enough links to avoid partitioning in case of a single failure. Second, install virtual links through non-backbone areas as a backup path. You can think of virtual links as a way of tunneling area zero connectivity through another area. Using our test network, shown in Figure 5-25, we'll configure a virtual link to allow area zero to remain contiguous if the link between New York and Moscow were to fail.

A design decision we need to make is to decide whether to allocate IP addresses for the loopback from our network address space (which means assigning a subnet to each loopback) or to use arbitrary IP addresses outside our assigned address space. OSPF doesn't care which addresses are used. Operationally, it is useful to use addresses from our assigned address space so that routes to the interfaces appear in the routing table, and we can more easily find the router that corresponds to a given router ID. If your address space is limited, it is OK to use

**Figure 5-25**

Backup backbone
connectivity via
virtual links

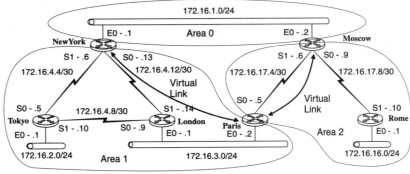

All serial links are 1.544Mbps.

arbitrary IP addresses on the loopback interfaces. You'll want to document the router ID so you can find which router corresponds to a given router ID when you are troubleshooting or configuring other virtual links.

FYI: Virtual link configurations use something called the *router ID* to identify the end points of the virtual links. By default, the OSPF router ID is the address assigned to the first loopback interface or, if there is no loopback interface, the highest-numbered IP address on the router. Up to this point, we have not used loopback interfaces. However, it makes sense to use them now. A loopback interface is an ephemeral interface—that is, it is created by identifying it to the router. All data sent to the loopback interface loops back to the router. The advantage of the loopback interface is that it is not connected to any hardware and therefore cannot be disconnected or fail (unless the entire box fails). Using the loopback interface for virtual link end points is useful because the router ID can be assigned, and you know it will always exist, and as long as the router is reachable via a physical interface, the virtual link will work.

If you've configured your loopbacks after starting OSPF, you'll have to reload the routers to force the new addresses to be used for the router ID.

The virtual links must extend area zero from New York to Paris and from Moscow to Paris. London is not included in the configuration because it is an internal area router. Only Paris has interfaces in both area one and area two. We've added loopback interfaces to each router, using subnets out of the 172.16.4.0 range for area one routers and subnets out of the 172.16.17.0 range for area two routers. In Figure 5-26, line 21, in New York's configuration and line 92 of Paris's configuration, implement the virtual link through area one. Line 76 of Moscow's configuration and line 94 of Paris's configuration implement the virtual link through area two. The state of the virtual links on Paris is shown in lines 111-127. These links cause London and Paris to become backbone routers, providing connectivity between area one and area two. A side benefit of this extension is that the two areas share two connections to area zero. Inter-area traffic now can take either the New York-to-Moscow or the London-to-Paris path.

Don't forget to apply the same area summary statements (**area *area-id* range *ip-address ip-mask***) to the router(s) that are participating in the virtual links. Otherwise, the detailed routes will be propagated over the virtual links and your summary addresses on the real backbone connections will be circumvented. Lines 91 and 93 of Paris's configuration have the same summaries that New York and Moscow are applying to routes between the areas.

With the previous network and configuration, if the Ethernet between Moscow and New York were to fail (you can test this with a **shutdown** of Moscow's Ethernet 0), the connectivity between areas will still be maintained. Running **trace** from Rome to Tokyo's Ethernet 0 shows packets going via Moscow, Paris, London, then Tokyo. Our virtual link backup for the backbone is successful!

Another use of virtual links is to connect a third area through an area connected to the backbone, as shown in Figure 5-27. You might want to do this to handle the case where an area's link to the backbone has failed. Virtual links may also be used to handle the addition of a new area prior to the addition of the network links to connect it to the backbone. In both cases, the network topology prohibits the attachment of the remote area directly to area zero.

The configurations for extending the backbone are shown in Figure 5-28. Only two routers—Paris and Rome—had to change configurations from those in Figure 5-26. Moscow is shut down. The new link between Paris and Rome is brought up and added to the OSPF routing configuration. The same area range statements are used to create summary addresses between the two areas, and the same virtual link is used to connect Paris to New York. Rome's routing table is shown in lines 31-49. Note the inter-area summary address for 172.16.4.0.

**Figure 5-26** Backbone virtual link configurations

**NewYork Configuration**
```
1  hostname NewYork
2  interface Loopback0
3   ip address 172.16.4.17 255.255.255.252
4  interface Ethernet0
5   ip address 172.16.1.1 255.255.255.0
6  interface Serial0
7   ip address 172.16.4.13 255.255.255.252
8   ip ospf authentication-key london
9   bandwidth 1544
10 interface Serial1
11  ip address 172.16.4.6 255.255.255.252
12  ip ospf authentication-key secret-p
13  bandwidth 1544
14  clockrate 1300000
15 router ospf 1
16  network 172.16.1.1 0.0.0.0 area 0
17  network 172.16.4.13 0.0.0.0 area 1
18  network 172.16.4.6 0.0.0.0 area 1
19  network 172.16.4.17 0.0.0.0 area 1
20  area 1 range 172.16.4.0 255.255.255.0
21  area 1 virtual-link 172.16.17.21
22 ip classless
23 end
```

**Tokyo Configuration**
```
24 hostname Tokyo
25 interface Loopback0
26  ip address 172.16.4.21 255.255.255.252
27 interface Ethernet0
28  ip address 172.16.2.1 255.255.255.0
29 interface Serial0
30  ip address 172.16.4.5 255.255.255.252
31  ip ospf authentication-key secret-p
32  bandwidth 1544
33 interface Serial1
34  ip address 172.16.4.10 255.255.255.252
35  clockrate 1300000
36 router ospf 1
37  network 172.16.2.1 0.0.0.0 area 1
38  network 172.16.4.5 0.0.0.0 area 1
39  network 172.16.4.10 0.0.0.0 area 1
40  network 172.16.4.21 0.0.0.0 area 1
41 ip classless
42 end
```

**London Configuration**
```
43 hostname London
44 interface Loopback0
45  ip address 172.16.4.25 255.255.255.252
46 interface Ethernet0
47  ip address 172.16.3.1 255.255.255.0
48 interface Serial0
49  ip address 172.16.4.9 255.255.255.252
50  bandwidth 1544
51 interface Serial1
```

**Figure 5-26** Continued

```
52   ip address 172.16.4.14 255.255.255.252
53   bandwidth 1544
54   clockrate 1300000
55 router ospf 1
56   network 172.16.4.9 0.0.0.0 area 1
57   network 172.16.4.14 0.0.0.0 area 1
58   network 172.16.3.1 0.0.0.0 area 1
59   network 172.16.4.25 0.0.0.0 area 1
60 ip classless
61 end
```

**Moscow Configuration**

```
62 hostname Moscow
63 interface Loopback0
64   ip address 172.16.17.17 255.255.255.252
65 interface Ethernet0
66   ip address 172.16.1.2 255.255.255.0
67 interface Serial0
68   ip address 172.16.17.9 255.255.255.252
69   bandwidth 1544
70 router ospf 1
71   network 172.16.1.2 0.0.0.0 area 0
72   network 172.16.17.6 0.0.0.0 area 2
73   network 172.16.17.9 0.0.0.0 area 2
74   network 172.16.17.17 0.0.0.0 area 2
75   area 2 range 172.16.17.0 255.255.255.0
76   area 2 virtual-link 172.16.17.21
77 ip classless
78 end
```

**Paris Configuration**

```
79 hostname Paris
80 interface Loopback0
81   ip address 172.16.17.21 255.255.255.252
82 interface Ethernet0
83   ip address 172.16.3.2 255.255.255.0
84 interface Serial0
85   ip address 172.16.17.5 255.255.255.252
86   bandwidth 1544
87 router ospf 1
88   network 172.16.3.2 0.0.0.0 area 1
89   network 172.16.17.5 0.0.0.0 area 2
90   network 172.16.17.21 0.0.0.0 area 2
91   area 1 range 172.16.4.0 255.255.255.0
92   area 1 virtual-link 172.16.4.17
93   area 2 range 172.16.17.0 255.255.255.0
94   area 2 virtual-link 172.16.17.17
95 ip classless
96 end
```

**Rome Configuration**
```
97  hostname Rome
98  interface Loopback0
99   ip address 172.16.17.25 255.255.255.252
100 interface Ethernet0
101  ip address 172.16.16.1 255.255.255.0
102 interface Serial1
103  ip address 172.16.17.10 255.255.255.252
104  clockrate 1300000
105 router ospf 1
106  network 172.16.16.1 0.0.0.0 area 2
107  network 172.16.17.10 0.0.0.0 area 2
108  network 172.16.17.25 0.0.0.0 area 2
109 ip classless
110 end
```

**Paris Virtual Link Status**
```
111 Paris#sh ip ospf virtual-links
112 Virtual Link OSPF_VL1 to router 172.16.17.17 is up
113   Run as demand circuit
114   DoNotAge LSA allowed.
115   Transit area 2, via interface Serial0, Cost of using 64
116   Transmit Delay is 1 sec, State POINT_TO_POINT,
117   Timer intervals configured, Hello 10, Dead 40, Wait 40, Retransmit 5
118     Hello due in 00:00:08
119     Adjacency State FULL (Hello suppressed)
120 Virtual Link OSPF_VL0 to router 172.16.4.17 is up
121   Run as demand circuit
122   DoNotAge LSA allowed.
123   Transit area 1, via interface Ethernet0, Cost of using 74
124   Transmit Delay is 1 sec, State POINT_TO_POINT,
125   Timer intervals configured, Hello 10, Dead 40, Wait 40, Retransmit 5
126     Hello due in 00:00:07
127     Adjacency State FULL (Hello suppressed)
128 Paris#
```

**Figure 5-27**

Extending area zero to a remote area

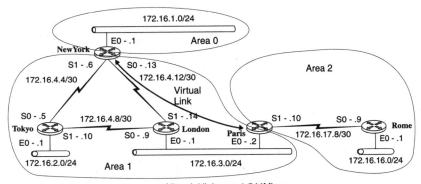

**Figure 5-28** Configurations extending area zero

**Paris Configuration**
```
1 hostname Paris
2 interface Loopback0
3  ip address 172.16.17.21 255.255.255.252
4 interface Ethernet0
5  ip address 172.16.3.2 255.255.255.0
6 interface Serial1
7  ip address 172.16.17.10 255.255.255.252
8  clockrate 1300000
9 router ospf 1
10  network 172.16.3.2 0.0.0.0 area 1
11  network 172.16.17.21 0.0.0.0 area 2
12  network 172.16.17.10 0.0.0.0 area 2
13  area 1 range 172.16.4.0 255.255.255.0
14  area 1 virtual-link 172.16.4.17
15  area 2 range 172.16.17.0 255.255.255.0
16 ip classless
17 end
```

**Rome Configuration**
```
18 hostname Rome
19 interface Loopback0
20  ip address 172.16.17.25 255.255.255.252
21 interface Ethernet0
22  ip address 172.16.16.1 255.255.255.0
23 interface Serial0
24  ip address 172.16.17.9 255.255.255.252
25 router ospf 1
26  network 172.16.16.1 0.0.0.0 area 2
27  network 172.16.17.25 0.0.0.0 area 2
28  network 172.16.17.9 0.0.0.0 area 2
29 ip classless
30 end
```

**Rome's Routing Table**
```
31 Rome#sh ip route
32 Codes: C - connected, S - static, I - IGRP, R - RIP, M - mobile, B - BGP
33        D - EIGRP, EX - EIGRP external, O - OSPF, IA - OSPF inter area
34        N1 - OSPF NSSA external type 1, N2 - OSPF NSSA external type 2
35        E1 - OSPF external type 1, E2 - OSPF external type 2, E - EGP
36        i - IS-IS, L1 - IS-IS level-1, L2 - IS-IS level-2, * - candidate default
37        U - per-user static route, o - ODR
38
39 Gateway of last resort is not set
40
41      172.16.0.0/16 is variably subnetted, 8 subnets, 3 masks
42 C       172.16.17.8/30 is directly connected, Serial0
43 C       172.16.16.0/24 is directly connected, Ethernet0
44 C       172.16.17.24/30 is directly connected, Loopback0
45 O IA    172.16.4.0/24 [110/75] via 172.16.17.10, 00:02:32, Serial0
46 O       172.16.17.21/32 [110/65] via 172.16.17.10, 00:02:32, Serial0
47 O IA    172.16.1.0/24 [110/148] via 172.16.17.10, 00:02:32, Serial0
48 O IA    172.16.2.0/24 [110/148] via 172.16.17.10, 00:02:32, Serial0
49 O IA    172.16.3.0/24 [110/74] via 172.16.17.10, 00:02:32, Serial0
```

# External Routes

Most OSPF networks today connect to other networks and need to share routing information with those networks. Sharing routing information may be done by a variety of mechanisms, including static routes, default routes, and route redistribution. Any route that originates from outside the OSPF routing domain is considered an external route.

There are two types of external routes: external type 1 and external type 2. The difference between the two is how the metric of the route is calculated. Figure 5-29 shows an example of both types of routes. External type 1 routes (abbreviated E1) use a metric that is the sum of the external metric and the internal cost of reaching the Autonomous System Border Router (ASBR). External type 2 routes (E2 routes) use a metric that is based only on the external metric, regardless of the internal cost to reach the advertising ASBR.

In Figure 5-30, lines 24-26, Tokyo has an E1 metric of 138 to 172.20.1.8 and an E2 metric of 64 to 172.20.1.12. You can even check the value of the E1 metric: The Tokyo-to-London link is 64, plus the London-to-Paris Ethernet is 10, plus the redistribution metric of 64 = 138. The configurations of Moscow, Paris, and Rome also are included in Figure 5-30. The configurations for New York, Tokyo, and London are almost unchanged from the configurations that appear in Figure 5-28. The only change is that New York's virtual link has been removed.

Examining these configurations, you'll see that redistribution is being done in both directions. A **distribute-list** is used to filter routes coming back into RIP from OSPF. This filter is very important to prevent

**Figure 5-29**
OSPF E1 and E2
routes

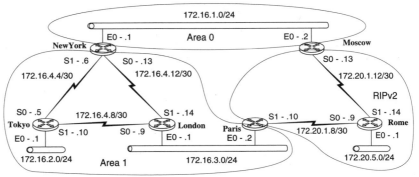

All serial links are 1.544Mbps.

■■ ■■ ■■ ■■ ■■ ■■ ■■ ■■ ■■ ■■ ■■ ■■ ■■ ■■ ■■ ■■ ■■ ■■

**Figure 5-30** Redistribution from RIP into OSPF

```
Tokyo's routing table
1 Tokyo#sh ip route
2 Codes: C - connected, S - static, I - IGRP, R - RIP, M - mobile, B - BGP
3        D - EIGRP, EX - EIGRP external, O - OSPF, IA - OSPF inter area
4        N1 - OSPF NSSA external type 1, N2 - OSPF NSSA external type 2
5        E1 - OSPF external type 1, E2 - OSPF external type 2, E - EGP
6        i - IS-IS, L1 - IS-IS level-1, L2 - IS-IS level-2, * - candidate default
7        U - per-user static route, o - ODR
8
9 Gateway of last resort is not set
10
11      172.16.0.0/16 is variably subnetted, 11 subnets, 3 masks
12 O       172.16.4.25/32 [110/65] via 172.16.4.9, 00:35:55, Serial1
13 O       172.16.4.29/32 [110/75] via 172.16.4.9, 00:35:55, Serial1
14 O       172.16.4.17/32 [110/65] via 172.16.4.6, 00:35:55, Serial0
15 C       172.16.4.20/30 is directly connected, Loopback0
16 C       172.16.4.8/30 is directly connected, Serial1
17 O       172.16.4.12/30 [110/128] via 172.16.4.9, 00:35:55, Serial1
18 O IA    172.16.17.17/32 [110/75] via 172.16.4.6, 00:21:40, Serial0
19 C       172.16.4.4/30 is directly connected, Serial0
20 O IA    172.16.1.0/24 [110/74] via 172.16.4.6, 00:21:40, Serial0
21 C       172.16.2.0/24 is directly connected, Ethernet0
22 O       172.16.3.0/24 [110/74] via 172.16.4.9, 00:35:56, Serial1
23      172.20.0.0/16 is variably subnetted, 3 subnets, 2 masks
24 O E1    172.20.1.8/30 [110/138] via 172.16.4.9, 00:12:27, Serial1
25 O E2    172.20.1.12/30 [110/64] via 172.16.4.6, 00:21:41, Serial0
26 O E2    172.20.5.0/24 [110/64] via 172.16.4.6, 00:19:40, Serial0
27 Tokyo#

Moscow Configuration
28 hostname Moscow
29 interface Loopback0
30  ip address 172.16.17.17 255.255.255.252
31 interface Ethernet0
32  ip address 172.16.1.2 255.255.255.0
33 interface Serial0
34  ip address 172.20.1.13 255.255.255.252
35  bandwidth 1544
36 router ospf 1
37  redistribute rip metric 64 subnets
38  network 172.16.1.2 0.0.0.0 area 0
39  network 172.16.17.17 0.0.0.0 area 0
40 router rip
41  version 2
42  redistribute ospf 1 metric 5
43  network 172.20.0.0
44  distribute-list 1 out ospf 1
45 ip classless
46 access-list 1 deny   172.20.0.0 0.0.255.255
47 access-list 1 permit any
48 end
```

**Paris Configuration**
```
49 hostname Paris
50 interface Loopback0
51  ip address 172.16.4.29 255.255.255.252
52 interface Ethernet0
53  ip address 172.16.3.2 255.255.255.0
54 interface Serial1
55  ip address 172.20.1.10 255.255.255.252
56  clockrate 1300000
57 router ospf 1
58  redistribute rip metric 64 metric-type 1 subnets
59  network 172.16.3.2 0.0.0.0 area 1
60  network 172.16.4.29 0.0.0.0 area 1
61 router rip
62  version 2
63  redistribute ospf 1 metric 5
64  network 172.20.0.0
65  distribute-list 1 out ospf 1
66 ip classless
67 access-list 1 deny   172.20.0.0 0.0.255.255
68 access-list 1 permit any
69 end
```

**Rome Configuration**
```
70 hostname Rome
71 interface Ethernet0
72  ip address 172.20.5.1 255.255.255.0
73 interface Serial0
74  ip address 172.20.1.9 255.255.255.252
75 interface Serial1
76  ip address 172.20.1.14 255.255.255.252
77  clockrate 1300000
78 router rip
79  version 2
80  network 172.20.0.0
81 ip classless
82 end
```

routing loops. The distribution from RIP into OSPF occurs on lines 37 and 58. Note the use of the subnets keywords to allow the distribution of the individual subnets of network 172.20.0.0. The RIP configuration is a bit more interesting because this is where the filtering is being done. Lines 40-44 and 61-65 include the distribution of OSPF routes into RIP and the reference to the **distribute-list**. The **access-list** for the filter is the same on both Moscow and Paris: Deny any address in 172.20.0.0 and permit everything else (lines 46-47 and 67-68).

If you're following along with your own experimentation on a set of routers, then see what happens when you omit the **subnets** modifier on the **redistribute** command. Also try using a **route-map** instead of the distribute-list.

# Redistributing the Default Route

While we're discussing external routes, let's see how default routes are handled in OSPF. The typical use of default routes is when a company connects to the Internet. As we discussed in Chapter 3, there is often no reason to run a dynamic routing protocol over an Internet link. But the Internet-connected router (called the Autonomous System Border Router, or ASBR) needs a way to tell the other OSPF routers that it is the best path to all external destinations.

Figure 5-31 shows a typical network topology, where Moscow is the ASBR and ISP is the name of the Internet Service Provider router. Our task is to configure Moscow with a default route (that's easy!) and configure OSPF to distribute that default route within the OSPF portion of the network.

There are only three routers that have important configuration changes to implement OSPF default routing: Moscow, Paris, and ISP (formerly known as Rome). If you are implementing this in a test lab, you can start with the configurations shown in Figure 5-28 by removing the virtual links and renumbering the appropriate interfaces. Paris has all interfaces shutdown. In the modified configurations shown in Figure 5-32, Moscow is no longer running RIP and has a default route to the ISP router added (line 14). To distribute the default route to the other OSPF routers, the router subcommand **default-information originate always** was added (line 12). We specified 64 as the advertised metric (the same as a T1 link).

Moscow's routing table is shown in Figure 5-32. Note the gateway of last resort (line 34) and the static default route (line 44). The keyword **always** on the **default-information originate** command tells OSPF to

**Figure 5-31**

OSPF default route network

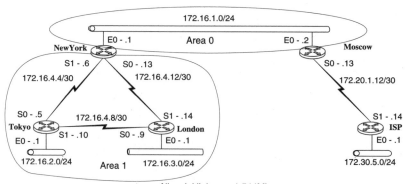

always originate a default route to other OSPF routers, even if the router containing this configuration does not actually have a default route. However, the default route may disappear for some reason, probably because the ISP link failed. Moscow would still advertise an OSPF default route but would not be able to forward the packets, creating a "black hole route" (a route that goes nowhere).

A network that has only one Internet connection may not be concerned about the disappearance of the default route. After all, there is only one way to the Internet, and if it is down, there are no alternatives. In this scenario, Moscow will return an ICMP destination unreachable message for any packets that need a default route when one does not exist. But why should we send packets all the way across the OSPF network, just to have them discarded and an ICMP message returned?

An alternative is to omit the keyword **always** from the **default-information** command. With this configuration, Moscow will originate a default route into the OSPF network only when a default route really exists. This method is also useful when there are two exit points from the OSPF network. With two exit points, if one path fails, only the router with the valid default route will be advertising the default.

Another configuration tip is to add the keyword **metric-type 1** to the **default-information** command. By adding this option, you force OSPF to use the lowest internal cost of reaching the Internet. Your packets get out of the OSPF network sooner but hopefully to a router that has more complete routing information and can make better routing decisions than your internal routers.

**Figure 5-32** OSPF default route configuration

```
Moscow's Configuration
1 hostname Moscow
2 interface Loopback0
3   ip address 172.16.17.17 255.255.255.252
4 interface Ethernet0
5   ip address 172.16.1.2 255.255.255.0
6 interface Serial0
7   ip address 172.20.1.13 255.255.255.252
8   bandwidth 1544
9 router ospf 1
10   network 172.16.1.2 0.0.0.0 area 0
11   network 172.16.17.17 0.0.0.0 area 0
12   default-information originate always metric 64
13 ip classless
14 ip route 0.0.0.0 0.0.0.0 172.20.1.14
15 end
```

**Figure 5-32** Continued

**Rome's Configuration**
```
16 hostname Rome
17 interface Ethernet0
18  ip address 172.30.5.1 255.255.255.0
19 interface Serial1
20  ip address 172.20.1.14 255.255.255.252
21  bandwidth 1544
22  clockrate 1300000
23 ip classless
24 ip route 172.16.0.0 255.255.0.0 172.20.1.13
25 end
```

**Moscow's routing table**
```
26 Moscow#sh ip route
27 Codes: C - connected, S - static, I - IGRP, R - RIP, M - mobile, B - BGP
28        D - EIGRP, EX - EIGRP external, O - OSPF, IA - OSPF inter area
29        N1 - OSPF NSSA external type 1, N2 - OSPF NSSA external type 2
30        E1 - OSPF external type 1, E2 - OSPF external type 2, E - EGP
31        i - IS-IS, L1 - IS-IS level-1, L2 - IS-IS level-2, * - candidate default
32        U - per-user static route, o - ODR
33
34 Gateway of last resort is 172.20.1.14 to network 0.0.0.0
35
36      172.16.0.0/16 is variably subnetted, 5 subnets, 2 masks
37 O IA    172.16.4.0/24 [110/11] via 172.16.1.1, 00:47:29, Ethernet0
38 C       172.16.1.0/24 is directly connected, Ethernet0
39 C       172.16.17.16/30 is directly connected, Loopback0
40 O IA    172.16.2.0/24 [110/1582] via 172.16.1.1, 00:47:29, Ethernet0
41 O IA    172.16.3.0/24 [110/1582] via 172.16.1.1, 00:47:29, Ethernet0
42      172.20.0.0/30 is subnetted, 1 subnets
43 C       172.20.1.12 is directly connected, Serial0
44 S*  0.0.0.0/0 [1/0] via 172.20.1.14
```

# Stub & Not-So-Stubby Areas

Some OSPF networks, typically those run by ISPs, contain a large number of external routes. Outside area zero, few areas need the full set of external routes. It isn't necessary, nor is it typically useful, to pass all the external routes into these areas. Instead, a default route can be distributed into the area by the ABR. An area configured in this manner is called a stub area.

There are several requirements for an area to be a stub area. First, it must depend on default routes for reaching all destinations external to the OSPF domain, even if the default route causes nonoptimum path selection. Second, the stub area must not have any virtual links configured through it. And third, it must not itself be a source of any external routes generated by an Autonomous System Border Router (ASBR).

Reducing the volume routing information reduces the load on the routers in the stub area, allowing lower-performance (therefore lower-cost) routers to be used in these areas. An example of a stub area appears in Figure 5-33.

The configurations of all routers attached to a stub area must specify the area as a stub by adding the router subcommand **area *area-id* stub.** Examining the configurations of Figure 5-34 (lines 18 and 48), we see area two is defined as a stub area in London. Also included is the output of **show ip route** on London. On line 70, the default route is now listed as an inter-area route, not an external route.

For very large OSPF networks, it is sometimes useful to limit the distribution of inter-area routes into stub areas. On an ABR, use the router subcommand **area *area-id* stub no-summary** to force an area to contain only intra-area and default routes. This configuration creates a totally stubby area, which reduces the volume of OSPF routing information within the area. The ABR also will need the **default-information originate** router subcommand to force it to originate a default route into a stub network. The default cost of the default route will be the cost of the default at the originating ABR, plus one. If you want to use an additive value other than one, it may be specified by using the command **area *area-id* default-cost *cost*.** To experiment with these commands in our test network, we performed the following configuration commands on NewYork:

```
router ospf 1
area 2 stub no-summary
default-information originate
area 2 default-cost 5
```

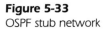

**Figure 5-33**
OSPF stub network

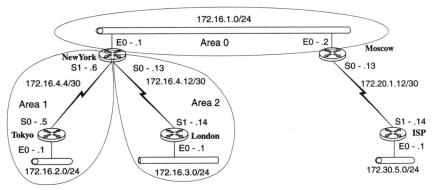

All serial links are 1.544Mbps.

**Figure 5-34** Stub network configurations

**NewYork Configuration**
```
1 hostname NewYork
2 interface Loopback0
3  ip address 172.16.4.17 255.255.255.252
4 interface Ethernet0
5  ip address 172.16.1.1 255.255.255.0
6 interface Serial0
7  ip address 172.16.4.13 255.255.255.252
8 bandwidth 1544
9 interface Serial1
10  ip address 172.16.4.6 255.255.255.252
11 bandwidth 1544
12  clockrate 1300000
13 router ospf 1
14  network 172.16.1.1 0.0.0.0 area 0
15  network 172.16.4.6 0.0.0.0 area 1
16  network 172.16.4.13 0.0.0.0 area 2
17  network 172.16.4.17 0.0.0.0 area 1
18 area 2 stub
19 ip classless
20 end
```

**Tokyo Configuration**
```
21 hostname Tokyo
22 interface Loopback0
23  ip address 172.16.4.21 255.255.255.252
24 interface Ethernet0
25  ip address 172.16.2.1 255.255.255.0
26 interface Serial0
27  ip address 172.16.4.5 255.255.255.252
28 bandwidth 1544
29 router ospf 1
30  network 172.16.2.1 0.0.0.0 area 1
31  network 172.16.4.5 0.0.0.0 area 1
32  network 172.16.4.21 0.0.0.0 area 1
33 ip classless
34 end
```

**London Configuration**
```
35 hostname London
36 interface Loopback0
37  ip address 172.16.4.25 255.255.255.252
38 interface Ethernet0
39  ip address 172.16.3.1 255.255.255.0
40 interface Serial1
41  ip address 172.16.4.14 255.255.255.252
42 bandwidth 1544
43  clockrate 1300000
44 router ospf 1
45  network 172.16.4.14 0.0.0.0 area 2
46  network 172.16.3.1 0.0.0.0 area 2
47  network 172.16.4.25 0.0.0.0 area 2
48  area 2 stub
49 ip classless
50 end
```

```
London's routing table
51 London#sh ip route
52 %SYS-5-CONFIG_I: Configured from console by consolete
53 Codes: C - connected, S - static, I - IGRP, R - RIP, M - mobile, B - BGP
54        D - EIGRP, EX - EIGRP external, O - OSPF, IA - OSPF inter area
55        N1 - OSPF NSSA external type 1, N2 - OSPF NSSA external type 2
56        E1 - OSPF external type 1, E2 - OSPF external type 2, E - EGP
57        i - IS-IS, L1 - IS-IS level-1, L2 - IS-IS level-2, * - candidate default
58        U - per-user static route, o - ODR
59
60 Gateway of last resort is 172.16.4.13 to network 0.0.0.0
61
62        172.16.0.0/16 is variably subnetted, 7 subnets, 3 masks
63 C        172.16.4.24/30 is directly connected, Loopback0
64 O IA    172.16.4.17/32 [110/65] via 172.16.4.13, 00:01:24, Serial1
65 C        172.16.4.12/30 is directly connected, Serial1
66 O IA    172.16.17.17/32 [110/75] via 172.16.4.13, 00:01:24, Serial1
67 O IA    172.16.4.4/30 [110/128] via 172.16.4.13, 00:01:24, Serial1
68 O IA    172.16.1.0/24 [110/74] via 172.16.4.13, 00:01:24, Serial1
69 C        172.16.3.0/24 is directly connected, Ethernet0
70 O*IA 0.0.0.0/0 [110/65] via 172.16.4.13, 00:01:24, Serial1
```

The routing table on London changes significantly, as seen in Figure 5-35. Compare this routing table with the one in Figure 5-34.

We suggest experimenting with these commands yourself to gain an understanding of how they are used.

**Figure 5-35** Totally stubby area routes

```
London's totally stubby routing table
1) London#sh ip route
2) Codes: C - connected, S - static, I - IGRP, R - RIP, M - mobile, B - BGP
3)        D - EIGRP, EX - EIGRP external, O - OSPF, IA - OSPF inter area
4)        N1 - OSPF NSSA external type 1, N2 - OSPF NSSA external type 2
5)        E1 - OSPF external type 1, E2 - OSPF external type 2, E - EGP
6)        i - IS-IS, L1 - IS-IS level-1, L2 - IS-IS level-2, * - candidate default
7)        U - per-user static route, o - ODR
8)
9) Gateway of last resort is 172.16.4.13 to network 0.0.0.0
10)
11)       172.16.0.0/16 is variably subnetted, 3 subnets, 2 masks
12) C       172.16.4.24/30 is directly connected, Loopback0
13) C       172.16.4.12/30 is directly connected, Serial1
14) C       172.16.3.0/24 is directly connected, Ethernet0
15) O*IA 0.0.0.0/0 [110/65] via 172.16.4.13, 00:01:42, Serial1
```

## Not-So-Stubby Areas

The initial OSPF design had a topology limitation that allowed only fully connected areas or stub areas. However, there are some areas that are somewhat like stub areas but that share routing information with an external stub network that uses another routing protocol. A typical example is a network that uses OSPF in the core but uses RIP within a stub network that is external to the OSPF domain. The external routes to the RIP networks are imported into the OSPF area in a limited fashion. Figure 5-36 shows a typical network topology. Area one is called a not-so-stubby area (NSSA), because it is a stub area that contains an ASBR that imports external routes. To learn more about the NSSA design, read a copy of RFC1587, *The OSPF NSSA Option* (Coltun and Fuller 1994).

An important characteristic of the NSSA is that external routes carried in the backbone are not propagated into the area (but intra-area routes may be propagated into and within an NSSA). In this sense, an NSSA operates much like a stub area. For example, all routers within the area must agree that the area is an NSSA. Since no other external routes are imported into area one, the area border router will need to source a default route into area one.

Let's build a network similar to that of Figure 5-36, but since we don't have any servers or workstations, we'll configure Paris with several

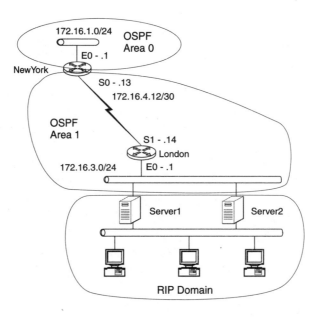

**Figure 5-36**
Example NSSA
network

loopback interfaces, each running RIP (see Figure 5-37). London will need to be configured for both OSPF and for RIP and import the RIP routes into OSPF. We'll also need to import the OSPF default route into RIP, being careful that the default route is the only route that RIP on Paris learns from London. (If you're up for a challenge, build this configuration without looking at the solution that follows.)

Figure 5-38 contains the configurations for New York, Tokyo, London, and Paris. Tokyo's configuration is standard for an OSPF internal area router. New York's configuration specifies area one as an NSSA (line 17), and we tell it to originate a default route into this area (you may want to experiment with other options to the NSSA command after getting the lab running). In the Paris configuration, we've built several loopback interfaces, each running RIP (lines 57-62 and 65-67). Enabling **debug ip rip** shows you the contents of the RIP updates. Watching the RIP debug output while you configure London is instructive.

London is where the majority of the configuration is done. In lines 42-46, we configure OSPF and specify area one as an NSSA. (What happens if you forget line 46?) Then we redistribute RIP routes into OSPF, setting the metric and metric-type and specifying that subnets should be imported.

Then, we configure RIP, shown in lines 47-51. What happens to the route in Paris if you omit the **metric 4** option to the redistribute com-

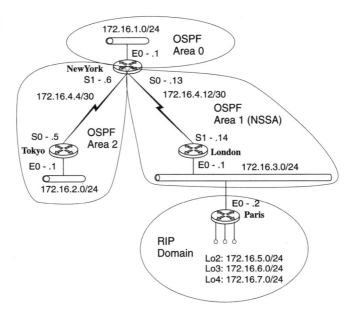

**Figure 5-37**

NSSA test network

**Figure 5-38** NSSA configuration

**NewYork Configuration**
```
1 hostname NewYork
2 interface Loopback0
3  ip address 172.16.4.9 255.255.255.252
4 interface Ethernet0
5  ip address 172.16.1.1 255.255.255.0
6 interface Serial0
7  ip address 172.16.4.13 255.255.255.252
8 bandwidth 1544
9 interface Serial1
10  ip address 172.16.4.6 255.255.255.252
11  bandwidth 1544
12  clockrate 1300000
13 router ospf 1
14  network 172.16.1.1 0.0.0.0 area 0
15  network 172.16.4.13 0.0.0.0 area 1
16  network 172.16.4.6 0.0.0.0 area 2
17  area 1 nssa default-information-originate
18 ip classless
19 end
```
**Tokyo Configuration**
```
20 hostname Tokyo
21 interface Loopback0
22  ip address 172.16.4.21 255.255.255.252
23 interface Ethernet0
24  ip address 172.16.2.1 255.255.255.0
25 interface Serial0
26  ip address 172.16.4.5 255.255.255.252
27  bandwidth 1544
28 router ospf 1
29  network 172.16.4.5 0.0.0.0 area 2
30  network 172.16.2.1 0.0.0.0 area 2
31 ip classless
32 end
```
**London Configuration**
```
33 hostname London
34 interface Loopback0
35  ip address 172.16.4.25 255.255.255.252
36 interface Ethernet0
37  ip address 172.16.3.1 255.255.255.0
38 interface Serial1
39  ip address 172.16.4.14 255.255.255.252
40  bandwidth 1544
41  clockrate 1300000
42 router ospf 1
43  redistribute rip metric 10 metric-type 1 subnets
44  network 172.16.3.1 0.0.0.0 area 1
45  network 172.16.4.14 0.0.0.0 area 1
46  area 1 nssa
47 router rip
48  redistribute ospf 1 metric 4
49  passive-interface Serial1
50  network 172.16.0.0
51  distribute-list 1 out ospf 1
52 ip classless
```

```
53 access-list 1 permit 0.0.0.0
54 access-list 1 deny   any
55 end
```
**Paris Configuration**
```
56 hostname Paris
57 interface Loopback1
58  ip address 172.16.5.1 255.255.255.0
59 interface Loopback2
60  ip address 172.16.6.1 255.255.255.0
61 interface Loopback3
62  ip address 172.16.7.1 255.255.255.0
63 interface Ethernet0
64  ip address 172.16.3.2 255.255.255.0
65 router rip
66  network 172.20.0.0
67  network 172.16.0.0
68 ip classless
69 end
```

mand? Line 51 specifies a **distribute-list** to allow only the default route (which is being advertised into area one by New York) to be distributed into RIP. The **access-list** that implements the route filter appears in lines 53-54.

The resulting routing tables of all four routers appear in Figure 5-39. The routes from the NSSA appear in New York as N1 (NSSA, type 1) routes. However, Tokyo sees these same routes as E1 routes. London has a default route to New York (lines 53 and 65), which is advertised via RIP to Paris (lines 75 and 82). Note that in the configurations, there is no explicit default route in any of the configurations.

**Figure 5-39** NSSA network routing tables

**NewYork Routes**
```
 1 NewYork#sh ip route
 2 Codes: C - connected, S - static, I - IGRP, R - RIP, M - mobile, B - BGP
 3        D - EIGRP, EX - EIGRP external, O - OSPF, IA - OSPF inter area
 4        N1 - OSPF NSSA external type 1, N2 - OSPF NSSA external type 2
 5        E1 - OSPF external type 1, E2 - OSPF external type 2, E - EGP
 6        i - IS-IS, L1 - IS-IS level-1, L2 - IS-IS level-2, * - candidate default
 7        U - per-user static route, o - ODR
 8
 9 Gateway of last resort is not set
10
11      172.16.0.0/16 is variably subnetted, 10 subnets, 2 masks
12 O N1    172.16.4.24/30 [110/74] via 172.16.4.14, 00:02:49, Serial0
13 C       172.16.4.8/30 is directly connected, Loopback0
14 C       172.16.4.12/30 is directly connected, Serial0
15 O N1    172.16.5.0/24 [110/84] via 172.16.4.14, 00:37:44, Serial0
16 O N1    172.16.6.0/24 [110/84] via 172.16.4.14, 00:37:44, Serial0
```

**Figure 5-39** Continued

```
17 O N1     172.16.7.0/24 [110/84] via 172.16.4.14, 00:37:44, Serial0
18 C        172.16.4.4/30 is directly connected, Serial1
19 C        172.16.1.0/24 is directly connected, Ethernet0
20 O        172.16.2.0/24 [110/74] via 172.16.4.5, 00:38:04, Serial1
21 O        172.16.3.0/24 [110/74] via 172.16.4.14, 00:37:44, Serial0
22 NewYork#
```

**Tokyo Routes**
```
23 Tokyo#sh ip route
24 Codes: C - connected, S - static, I - IGRP, R - RIP, M - mobile, B - BGP
25        D - EIGRP, EX - EIGRP external, O - OSPF, IA - OSPF inter area
26        N1 - OSPF NSSA external type 1, N2 - OSPF NSSA external type 2
27        E1 - OSPF external type 1, E2 - OSPF external type 2, E - EGP
28        i - IS-IS, L1 - IS-IS level-1, L2 - IS-IS level-2, * - candidate default
29        U - per-user static route, o - ODR
30
31 Gateway of last resort is not set
32
33      172.16.0.0/16 is variably subnetted, 10 subnets, 2 masks
34 O E1    172.16.4.24/30 [110/138] via 172.16.4.6, 00:03:30, Serial0
35 C       172.16.4.20/30 is directly connected, Loopback0
36 O IA    172.16.4.12/30 [110/128] via 172.16.4.6, 00:48:57, Serial0
37 O E1    172.16.5.0/24 [110/148] via 172.16.4.6, 00:38:21, Serial0
38 O E1    172.16.6.0/24 [110/148] via 172.16.4.6, 00:38:21, Serial0
39 O E1    172.16.7.0/24 [110/148] via 172.16.4.6, 00:38:21, Serial0
40 C       172.16.4.4/30 is directly connected, Serial0
41 O IA    172.16.1.0/24 [110/74] via 172.16.4.6, 00:48:57, Serial0
42 C       172.16.2.0/24 is directly connected, Ethernet0
43 O IA    172.16.3.0/24 [110/138] via 172.16.4.6, 00:38:25, Serial0
44 Tokyo#
```

**London Routes**
```
45 London#sh ip route
46 Codes: C - connected, S - static, I - IGRP, R - RIP, M - mobile, B - BGP
47        D - EIGRP, EX - EIGRP external, O - OSPF, IA - OSPF inter area
48        N1 - OSPF NSSA external type 1, N2 - OSPF NSSA external type 2
49        E1 - OSPF external type 1, E2 - OSPF external type 2, E - EGP
50        i - IS-IS, L1 - IS-IS level-1, L2 - IS-IS level-2, * - candidate default
51        U - per-user static route, o - ODR
52
53 Gateway of last resort is 172.16.4.13 to network 0.0.0.0
54
55      172.16.0.0/16 is variably subnetted, 9 subnets, 2 masks
56 C       172.16.4.24/30 is directly connected, Loopback0
57 C       172.16.4.12/30 is directly connected, Serial1
58 R       172.16.5.0/24 [120/1] via 172.16.3.2, 00:00:15, Ethernet0
59 R       172.16.6.0/24 [120/1] via 172.16.3.2, 00:00:15, Ethernet0
60 R       172.16.7.0/24 [120/1] via 172.16.3.2, 00:00:15, Ethernet0
61 O IA    172.16.4.4/30 [110/128] via 172.16.4.13, 00:37:15, Serial1
62 O IA    172.16.1.0/24 [110/74] via 172.16.4.13, 00:37:15, Serial1
63 O IA    172.16.2.0/24 [110/138] via 172.16.4.13, 00:37:15, Serial1
64 C       172.16.3.0/24 is directly connected, Ethernet0
65 O*N2 0.0.0.0/0 [110/1] via 172.16.4.13, 00:37:16, Serial1
66 London#
```

```
Paris Routes
67 Paris#sh ip route
68 Codes: C - connected, S - static, I - IGRP, R - RIP, M - mobile, B - BGP
69        D - EIGRP, EX - EIGRP external, O - OSPF, IA - OSPF inter area
70        N1 - OSPF NSSA external type 1, N2 - OSPF NSSA external type 2
71        E1 - OSPF external type 1, E2 - OSPF external type 2, E - EGP
72        i - IS-IS, L1 - IS-IS level-1, L2 - IS-IS level-2, * - candidate default
73        U - per-user static route, o - ODR
74
75 Gateway of last resort is 172.16.3.1 to network 0.0.0.0
76
77      172.16.0.0/24 is subnetted, 4 subnets
78 C       172.16.5.0 is directly connected, Loopback1
79 C       172.16.6.0 is directly connected, Loopback2
80 C       172.16.7.0 is directly connected, Loopback3
81 C       172.16.3.0 is directly connected, Ethernet0
82 R*  0.0.0.0/0 [120/4] via 172.16.3.1, 00:00:17, Ethernet0
83 Paris#
```

# Nonbroadcast Multiaccess Networks

Nonbroadcast multiaccess (NBMA) networks have been somewhat of a problem for OSPF, because they do not allow multicast distribution of link-state updates. Remember that on broadcast networks, OSPF elects a designated router (and backup DR) to form adjacencies with all neighbors and collect link-state updates, which are then multicast back to all the neighbors. There may be multiple neighbors on either Frame Relay or X.25 networks, and neither network supports multicast capability in a form that OSPF can easily use.

One way to design a network to easily support OSPF is to build a full mesh of virtual circuits (VCs) between all routers on the NBMA network. A DR election can now be performed, and everything works as you'd expect—until a network failure causes a VC to fail. Now our network is no longer a full mesh, and OSPF has problems. Our design wasn't so good after all.

Cisco and OSPF designers have provided specific mechanisms to support operation over NBMA networks. Let's take a look at how to configure OSPF on these networks.

# Subinterfaces & Point-to-point Networks

Subinterfaces are a mechanism that Cisco created to allow multiple logical interfaces to share one physical interface. It is the method recommended by Cisco, primarily because it is easier to configure, troubleshoot, and maintain. A good example of this is shown in Figure 5-40,

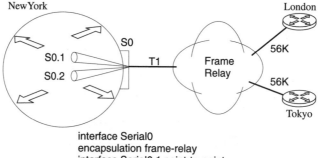

**Figure 5-40**
Subinterface model

```
interface Serial0
encapsulation frame-relay
interface Serial0.1 point-to-point
ip address 172.16.100.13 255.255.255.252
frame-relay interface-dlci 102
interface Serial0.2 point-to-point
ip address 172.16.100.6 255.255.255.252
frame-relay interface-dlci 101
```

where two Frame Relay VCs connect to a router via a single T1 circuit. Each subinterface is created when its name is entered in the router's configuration.

The subinterface names are the name of the physical interface, followed by a period and the number of the subinterface (e.g., serial 0.1). Physical interface parameters (i.e., encapsulation) are entered in the interface configuration, and parameters specific to each VC (i.e., IP address) are entered in the subinterface configuration.

Subinterfaces on serial links are often used to turn each VC into a point-to-point link, simplifying OSPF operation and making WAN networks easier to monitor, troubleshoot, and maintain. The configuration in Figure 5-40 creates two point-to-point links, one to each remote router. Each link is assigned a unique subnet.

FYI: X.25 networks are another example of NBMA networks. However, there is no inverse ARP mechanism in X.25, so we have to build our own table that maps an IP address into an X.121 address (X.121 is the official name of an X.25 address). In X.25 networks, we use the command **x25 map** to create this table.

The configuration of OSPF on a group of Frame Relay connected routers using subinterfaces is really easy. Figure 5-41 shows the network topology.

In Figure 5-42, we are configuring New York, Tokyo, and London to connect over Frame Relay. The link from New York to Tokyo uses subinterfaces on each end while the link from New York to London uses a subinterface on New York and the physical interface on London.

On New York, the encapsulation of the physical interface is set in line 8. The New York-to-Tokyo subinterface is configured in lines 9-12 and the New York-to-London subinterface is specified in lines 13-16. Each subinterface is specified as point-to-point. Next, the IP address of the subinterface is configured. Then the bandwidth of the individual subinterfaces is set to match the CIR (Committed Information Rate) of each VC (lines 11 and 15). Finally the Frame Relay DLCI of the subinterface is identified (lines 12 and 16). Then we configured OSPF for all three areas. Our OSPF configuration includes the loopback in area zero (line 21) so that if the Ethernet fails, New York will retain a connection to area zero, allowing inter-area traffic between area one and area two.

Tokyo's configuration also uses subinterfaces, so its configuration uses the same commands as with New York. The subinterface is created as a point-to-point link, the IP address set, the CIR bandwidth specified, and the DLCI identified. The OSPF configuration includes both physical interfaces in area one.

London's configuration is different because we're using the physical interface directly (no subinterface). We don't recommend this approach, because the procedure to convert to subinterfaces at some point involves moving the configuration parameters to the subinterface from the physical interface. There is no reason to not use subinterfaces right from the

**Figure 5-41**
OSPF subinterface
network

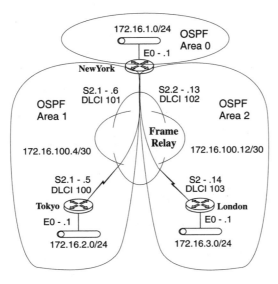

**Figure 5-42** OSPF configuration using subinterfaces

**NewYork Configuration**
```
1 hostname NewYork
2 interface Loopback0
3  ip address 172.16.4.9 255.255.255.252
4 interface Ethernet0
5  ip address 172.16.1.1 255.255.255.0
6 interface Serial2
7  no ip address
8  encapsulation frame-relay
9 interface Serial2.1 point-to-point
10  ip address 172.16.100.6 255.255.255.252
11  bandwidth 64
12  frame-relay interface-dlci 101
13 interface Serial2.2 point-to-point
14  ip address 172.16.100.13 255.255.255.252
15  bandwidth 64
16  frame-relay interface-dlci 102
17 router ospf 1
18  network 172.16.1.1 0.0.0.0 area 0
19  network 172.16.100.13 0.0.0.0 area 2
20  network 172.16.100.6 0.0.0.0 area 1
21  network 172.16.4.9 0.0.0.0 area 0
22 ip classless
23 end
```

**Tokyo Configuration**
```
24 hostname Tokyo
25 interface Loopback0
26  ip address 172.16.4.21 255.255.255.252
27 interface Ethernet0
28  ip address 172.16.2.1 255.255.255.0
29 interface Serial2
30  no ip address
31  encapsulation frame-relay
32 interface Serial2.1 point-to-point
33  ip address 172.16.100.5 255.255.255.252
34  bandwidth 64
35  frame-relay interface-dlci 100
36 router ospf 1
37  network 172.16.2.1 0.0.0.0 area 1
38  network 172.16.100.5 0.0.0.0 area 1
39 ip classless
40 end
```

**London Configuration**
```
41 hostname London
42 interface Loopback0
43  ip address 172.16.4.25 255.255.255.252
44 interface Ethernet0
45  ip address 172.16.3.1 255.255.255.0
46 interface Serial2
47  ip address 172.16.100.14 255.255.255.252
48  encapsulation frame-relay
49  ip ospf network point-to-multipoint
50  ip ospf hello-interval 10
```

```
51  bandwidth 64
52  frame-relay interface-dlci 103
53 router ospf 1
54  network 172.16.100.14 0.0.0.0 area 2
55  network 172.16.3.1 0.0.0.0 area 2
56 ip classless
57 end
```

start. And, as you'll see, the basic configuration is more complicated when the ends of the link are different interface types.

The process of building London's configuration involves troubleshooting, as we'll see. The initial configuration is just like the subinterface. A ping works over the link, but no OSPF routes appeared in the routing table. The output of **show ip ospf neighbor** showed no neighbors. Time for troubleshooting!

Using **debug ip ospf adj**, we monitor the exchange of OSPF hello packets and see the following:

```
1) OSPF: Rcv hello from  172.16.4.9  area  2  from  Serial2
   172.16.100.13
2) OSPF: Mismatched hello parameters from 172.16.100.13
3) Dead R 40 C 120,  Hello R 10 C 30 Mask R 255.255.255.252 C
   255.255.255.252
```

Line 2 tells us the problem: The hello parameters don't match. The R in line 3 shows the received parameters and the C shows the configured parameters. Sure enough, the hello update timers are different. The received parameter is 10 seconds, and the configured timer is 30 seconds. The reason is that subinterfaces need a faster hello exchange to quickly detect a failed PVC, while a physical interface relies on the modem's Data Carrier Detect (DCD) signal to indicate a link failure. The hello timer on London must match New York's subinterface hello timer. Adding line 50 fixes the problem, and the adjacency is formed.

Checking the routing table shows that OSPF routes are still not appearing, yet the output of **show ip ospf neighbor** shows New York as a neighbor:

```
1) London#sh ip ospf neigh
2)
3) Neighbor ID  Pri  State     Dead Time  Address        Interface
4) 172.16.4.9   1    FULL/BDR  00:00:30   172.16.100.13  Serial2
```

But New York's output shows a slightly different result. The key is that the State does not specify that New York is the DR:

```
1) NewYork#sh ip ospf neigh
2)
3) Neighbor ID   Pri   State    Dead Time   Address        Interface
4) 172.16.4.21   1     FULL/ -  00:00:35    172.16.100.5   Serial2.1
5) 172.16.4.25   1     FULL/ -  00:00:39    172.16.100.14  Serial2.2
```

Specifying the network type as **point-to-multipoint** on London's interface (line 49) fixes the problem, and the routers exchange link-state databases. The routing tables show the correct routes.

As we said before, this is NOT the configuration that we recommend. Both ends of an OSPF link should be the same type. Doing otherwise is to invite trouble. We would not be surprised if a future revision of the IOS caused our New York-to-London configuration to fail, due to a change in the implementation of OSPF on links that do not have the same media type at each end. We took this approach to demonstrate debugging OSPF connectivity.

# On-Demand Links

With ISDN, X.25-switched VCs, dialup connections, and ATM-switched VCs, OSPF also must deal with links that are operational only when application traffic is being carried. For these networks, Cisco has added the interface subcommand **ip ospf demand-circuit**. This feature is implemented by setting the high bit of the link-state advertisement (called the DC—Demand Circuit—bit) for a link to indicate that the link state advertisement of the link should not be aged. There is a caveat with this feature: All routers in the area must support and be configured with the demand-circuit command.

Let's look at how to configure this feature by using the New York-to-Tokyo point-to-point serial links of Figure 5-41 as if it were an on-demand circuit. Start with the configuration of Figure 5-42. Enter the command **debug ip ospf adj** on both New York and Tokyo to monitor the state of the adjacency. Then, on New York's S2.1 and Tokyo's S2.1 interface, add the interface subcommand **ip ospf demand-circuit**. Watch the debug output as the adjacencies change. Examining the routing table, you'll see that all the routes in the OSPF network are still valid. Monitoring the hello protocol on New York and Tokyo will show that hello packets are no longer being exchanged.

To make sure that OSPF is still working correctly, shutdown London's E0 interface and check Tokyo's routing table several times over the next 10 seconds. The route to 172.16.3.0 will be removed within a few seconds of the shutdown.

There are some caveats to using demand-circuits. No hello packets or link-state packets will bring up the link as long as the topology is stable. If a topology change occurs that requires a link-state advertisement to be propagated, the link will be brought up. To avoid bringing up the link due to topology changes in other areas, demand-circuits should be used only within stub or NSSA areas. Remember, both stub and NSSA areas can be configured to source only a default route from the ABR that joins to the backbone. With this configuration, only changes within the area will cause the demand-circuit to be activated.

## Hello Packets & Neighbor Adjacencies

Routers within an area establish neighbor relationships with one another, then share the contents of their topology databases. The neighbor relationship is established with the hello protocol. Hello packets are sent every 10 seconds on broadcast media (Ethernet, TokenRing, FDDI) and every 30 seconds on nonbroadcast media (X.25, Frame Relay, point-to-point links). The hello interval must be the same on all routers attached to a common network segment.

An OSPF router transmits a hello packet on each active interface. To guarantee two-way communications between routers on a single network segment, the hello packet includes a list of all routers that have been heard on the segment. Once a router is listed in the hello packets sent by a neighbor, a two-way conversation has been guaranteed, and the neighbors form an adjacency. Then the contents of the respective topological databases are exchanged and the Dijkstra algorithm is run.

The basic adjacency mechanism did not work well if there was more than a very small number of routers on a common broadcast media (Ethernet, TokenRing, etc.). If every router formed an adjacency with every other router on the LAN, then exchanged the contents of their link-state database, there would be an exponential growth in the amount of routing traffic on the LAN, not to mention the growth in processing the updates by each router.

OSPF's solution to this problem is to elect a Designated Router (DR) and a Backup Designated Router (BDR, used for redundancy) on each broadcast media segment. Every router on the segment forms an adja-

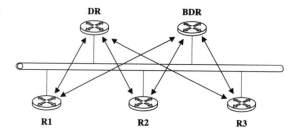

**Figure 5-43**
Designated Router
operation

cency with the DR and exchanges link-state information with the DR. The DR collects all the link-state information from all routers, then distributes the collected information back out to all routers. Using this approach reduces the amount of link-state update traffic from a volume that is roughly N x N (where N is the number of routers) to a volume that is on the order of 2 x N. Figure 5-36 shows several routers that are exchanging information with a DR on a single LAN segment.

The DR/BDR selection occurs during the initial hello packet exchange. When two routers boot simultaneously, the router with the best router priority will be selected as the DR. The router priority is a configurable parameter that is passed in the hello packets. If two routers have the same priority, the one with the highest router ID is elected as the DR. There is one problem with this scenario, however: once a router is elected as the DR, it stays the DR until some network event causes it to be disconnected from the network.

In effect, the first router that boots on a broadcast network segment will become the DR. In many networks, this is not a problem. In other networks, you don't want a minimally powered 2500 router on an important Ethernet to be the DR when you intended a 7500 to fulfill that role. The way to force the 7500 to be the DR is to set the DR priority of the 2500 to zero, which removes it from consideration in becoming the DR.

The router priority is a per-interface parameter. It is set using the interface subcommand **ip ospf priority *8-bit-number***. It is set only for multiaccess networks such as Ethernet or TokenRing.

## Troubleshooting OSPF

The hello protocol is the place to begin troubleshooting an OSPF routing problem. The neighbor adjacency must exist before OSPF can exchange routes. Start troubleshooting with the command **show ip ospf**

**neighbor.** If a neighboring router does not appear in the list of neighbors or the adjacency state is not full, then it is time to collect debugging information. The command **debug ip ospf adj** will report the hello exchanges and whether the hello parameters do not match. As we saw in the NBMA network example, if the hello parameters don't match, or if the routers don't agree on whether an area is a stub or NSSA, then the adjacency will not be formed.

Once the adjacency is formed, the routers should exchange their topology databases. At this point, a call to the TAC may be necessary to diagnose a database exchange problem, because the debug and show output is quite large and complex. In general, once the routers form their adjacencies, the database exchange occurs without a problem. There is very little delay between a router or link-state transition and the link-state flooding. You can experiment with the routing table update speed by changing the state of an interface on one router and quickly checking the routing table on another router.

## OSPF Summary

OSPF is a very good operational protocol. The convergence is extremely fast (we were able to make configuration changes and immediately checked other routers in our test network and found the changes had already been propagated).

In this section, we've covered a variety of tools that allow OSPF to scale to larger-size networks than any other protocol we've reviewed. The stub areas, default route distribution, and address summarization are some of the features that reduce the volume of OSPF routing information without sacrificing network stability and operation.

OSPF has a lot of features and requires more thought and understanding to design and operate than with any of the other protocols we've covered. There are many configuration parameters and design/implementation tips that are useful to OSPF network administrators. OSPF is definitely the power tool of the networking protocols. It is powerful, fast, and somewhat complex. Learning how to design, configure, and operate an OSPF network will assure you of a good networking job for many years to come.

## ■ ■ ■ CCIE Tips

With either version of RIP, you may have a case in which a fast router is on the same high-speed network segment as a low-speed router. When the high-speed router transmits a large routing update, it may overrun the lower-speed router's ability to handle the update. A symptom of this is that some routes appear and disappear in the slow router. If the slow router is busy with some internal task at the time an update arrives, some of the update packets may be lost, causing some of the routes to time out (remember, several consecutive updates of a given route have to be lost for this to occur).

Route redistribution is very important. Can you build a network that has a deliberate routing loop? How do you prevent routing loops between two routing protocols that are sharing routes via redistribution? When should redistribution filters be used? You should know about distribute-list and route map configurations to build routing filters. What happens to routes when a default metric value is not specified in the redistribution?

You should understand VLSM and how to design a network that incorporates multiple network masks. You'll absolutely need to know OSPF configurations and the different link-state packet types.

With many networks containing ISDN, dialup, Frame Relay, and ATM links, you must be fluent in OSPF demand-circuit connections as well as other features that reduce network loading. For example, the routing update packet delay is set with the router subcommand **output-delay** *delay*. The range of valid values is 8-50 milliseconds. Traffic shaping is also important on Frame Relay links that have a limited CIR.

You should be very familiar with the router debug commands for various protocols. Know what the debug output is telling you. For example, in our debugging scenario with New York and London over Frame Relay, we had to carefully examine the output of the **show ip ospf neighbor** command to see that the routers did not have the same status. None of the other debug or show output indicated the exact problem. If you can effectively use debug and show command output, then you'll be able to quickly repair the broken networks you encounter in the CCIE hands-on test.

The best thing you can do to obtain your CCIE is to spend some time on routers configuring various OSPF scenarios. We've covered a number of topics in this chapter that make excellent practice labs. Learn to use the OSPF debug commands to your advantage. We've found the command **debug ip ospf adj** to be extremely useful in determining why two routers are not sharing routing information. The output is not too verbose and is easily understood (unlike some of the other OSPF debug output).

There is no substitute for spending time building and troubleshooting configurations as we've been doing. Experiment with new commands and options, making sure you know how to design and build the appropriate configurations.

## SUMMARY

We've covered three important routing protocols in this chapter: RIPv2, EIGRP, and OSPF. All three support variable length subnet masking. EIGRP and OSPF can be used to build large-scale networks consisting of hundreds or thousands of routers.

Our coverage of OSPF should allow you to build configurations for a variety of situations. If you're taking our advice about studying OSPF in detail, we recommend reading the RFC (it's heavy-duty reading but worth going through) and getting a copy of John Moy's book, *OSPF, Anatomy of an Internet Routing Protocol* (1998).

# CHAPTER 6

# Integrating Multiple Routing Protocols

This chapter is dedicated to a singular topic, how to get different internal IP routing protocols to exchange the proper metric information to maintain correct IP routing tables. In order to make our examples easier to understand, we will review a few subjects:

- What is route summarization, and how do each of our IP protocols operate?

- Why do we need route maps?

- What is a routing loop, how do they happen, how do we avoid them?

- What takes place during route redistribution?

When these questions have been answered, there will be extensive complete examples demonstrating distribution between interior dynamic IP routing protocols and static routing.

# Route Summarization

Route summarization reduces the size of routing tables by allowing routes to collections of subnets or collections of networks to be identified by a single routing entry. With classful protocols, summarization occurs by default on collections of subnets, with advertised routes being those of the classful addressing boundaries (i.e., class A, B, and C network numbers). Conversely, classless routing protocols allow collections of networks to be advertised with a single routing entry. With both methods, there are some basic rules that govern when and how summarization occurs.

FYI: You also may encounter the term **address aggregation**, which means the same thing as route summarization. The alternative terminology is used to identify groups of IP class networks that are summarized into a single route that causes the multiple network class addresses to be aggregated into a single route advertisement.

With the expanding nature of the Internet and private intranets, the number of entries in the IP routing tables can make troubleshooting and managing the network an extremely difficult task. With increased routing tables, the Cisco routers require more time to process routing table lookups. Performance in the Cisco routers depends on a limited cache memory for path switching, and the greater the number of detailed destinations, the lower the percentage of different destinations that can be cached. Let's examine each of the routing protocols and how they deal with route summarization.

## RIP

RIP is a distance-vector protocol that deals with IP in a classful manner. Classful IP routing protocols summarize to an exact class A, B, or C address. RIP calculates the fastest path, or metric, to a destination network or subnet by counting each intermediate router as a hop. The fewer the number of hops, the faster the path.

Routes advertised by RIP fall into three classes—default, network, and subnet. Subnet routes are subnets of a specific class address, and the only subnet routes that are advertised are those routes that match the standard fixed subnet mask used throughout the class address. For example, if class B address 172.168.0.0 has a subnet mask of 255.255.255.0 applied, only subnets that match that specific subnet mask are sent to other RIP neighbors. Network routes are classful addresses, and only addresses that are class A, B, or C, are sent to RIP neighbors. Exterior routes can be injected into our Autonomous System from external Autonomous Systems. These exterior routes are treated as network routes and are sent to RIP neighbors as if they were part of our Autonomous System with no indication that they are external. Default routes are treated like network routes.

## RIP Version 2

The primary difference between RIP version 1 and RIP version 2 is that in version 2 the subnet routes have their associated subnet mask included in the routing update. In RIP version 1, only global subnet mask is used; in RIP version 2, variable prefix subnetworks are permitted and advertised. Example #11 later in this chapter uses RIP version 2.

## IGRP

IGRP is a distance-vector protocol that deals with IP in a classful manner. Classful IP routing protocols summarize to an exact class A, B, or C address. IGRP, by default, calculates the fastest path, or metric, to a destination using a default combination of bandwidth and delay. IGRP uses a complex formula that can include other factors such as reliability, load factor, or Maximum Tranmission Unit (data in frame). Each network or subnet segment used to reach the destination has a composite metric assigned, and IGRP adds up the delay values and the slowest link in the pathway to calculate the metric. The faster the pathway, the lower the composite metric.

Routes advertised by IGRP fall into three classes—interior, system, and exterior. Interior routes are subnets of a classful address, and the only interior routes that are advertised are those routes with the standard fixed subnet mask used throughout the classful address. For example, if class B address 172.168.0.0 has a subnet mask of 255.255.255.0 applied, only subnets that match that specific subnet mask are sent to other IGRP neighbors. System routes are classful addresses, and only addresses that are class A, B, or C are sent to IGRP neighbors. Exterior routes can be injected into our Autonomous System by setting default networks or setting up default routes. These exterior routes are treated the same as system routes and are sent to IGRP neighbors as if they were part of our Autonomous System.

## OSPF

OSPF is a link-state protocol that deals with IP in a classless manner. OSPF uses both the subnetwork and the subnet mask to calculate pathways through the IP cloud. Because the network or subnet and the subnet mask are used, all networks and subnets are maintained in the routing table. In order to process the information in the routing table, the routes within a single classful address are sorted by descending subnet prefix length. This places the more specific routes at the top of the table, and properly sends traffic to the most specific destination.

## EIGRP

EIGRP is a composite routing protocol that, by default, deals with IP in a classless manner, but automatically summarizes routes based on the classful addresses A, B, and C. Within a classful address, EIGRP uses the network or subnet in combination with the subnet mask to maintain detailed pathways within directly connected networks. Optionally, EIGRP can be configured without the default classful address summarization by manually defining a summary route to be advertised on each active interface.

# Route Maps

Route maps in the Cisco routers are one method of programming routing policy. A route map is a program within our configuration that allows us to precisely define the distribution of information during the route distribution process. In route redistribution, this process can be used to change the way IP routes are advertised between routing protocols. An example would be two class A, B, or C addresses being redistributed into RIP. One class address could be assigned a hop-count metric of three, and the other class address assigned a hop count of five. See Example #1 for a basic example of a route map and Chapter 9 for a more complex route map used with the Border Gateway Protocol.

Class maps are assigned names, and if multiple operations are required, then each operation uses a line number to place the operation in its correct sequence within the route map. If you have to make changes to the route map, adding operations are as simple as inserting the operation using a new sequence number, just like programming BASIC. Each operation consists of a match/set combination of instructions to provide a yes/no switch to distribute routing information. The two options used for each operation are permit and deny. If the deny option is used for an operation, then the match statement(s) associated with the operation select the routes to be dropped during distribution. If the permit option is used for an operation, then the match operation is used to identify the routes to be distributed, and the set operation is used to assign the metric to the routes identified in the match statement(s).

The great feature about a route map is that if changes need to be made by inserting new information, the sequence number places the new match/set operation in the correct sequence. A route map is used in Example #1 to provide different hop counts for IGRP networks being redistributed into RIP.

# Routing Loops

In route redistribution, care must be taken when injecting routes into another IP routing protocol so that proper routes are maintained. To see how multiple redistributions can create inappropriate routes, look at Example #11 later in this chapter.

When using static default routes, you must make sure that you don't create a routing loop. In Figure 6-1, a routing loop is created where traffic traveling from Host A, 10.1.0.1/16, to Host B, 10.55.0.1/16, travels through routers #1 and #2. Router #2 has an incorrect static route that directs packets destined for 10.55.0.0 to an incorrect interface, E0. Router #1 forwards IP packet A to router #2, and router #2 forwards IP packet A to router #1. This would continue until the IP packet A's time-to-live (TTL) field in the IP header decrements to zero and the packet is dropped.

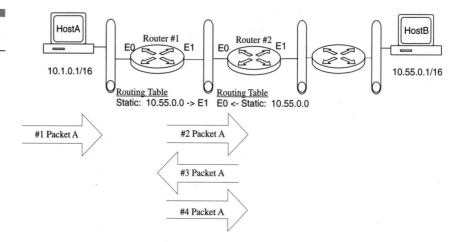

**Figure 6-1**
Simple routing loop

## Route Redistribution

There are reasons why multiple IP routing protocols are used within the same network. Legacy equipment may not be able to process the newer protocols, existing end stations may not recognize routing updates used in the balance of the network, and proprietary protocols cannot be used in a mixed vendor environment.

The process of route redistribution takes routing information from one IP routing protocol and assigns a set of metric values to the redistributed routes so they can be understood by a different IP routing protocol.

### Commands Used for Route Redistribution

There are several commands generally used during the redistribution process. The commands and their options, which are detailed in Table 6-1, will make it easier to follow the examples later in the chapter.

**Table 6-1**

Route redistribution commands

| Command | Parameters | Description |
|---------|-----------|-------------|
| **router** | *target routing protocol process* | IP routing protocol receiving redistributed information. |
| **redistribute** | *from routing protocol process* | IP routing protocol sending the redistributed information |
| | **metric** *metric* | The path cost value understood by target protocol. |
| | **metric-type** *type* | With OSPF as the *target protocol,* how do from protocol routes get advertised? |
| | | 1 = add internal to base default metric |
| | | 2 = use base as defined in default metric (default) |
| | **match** internal external 1 external 2 | With OSPF as the *from protocol,* this defines which OSPF routes get redistributed. All three are processed by default. |
| | **subnets** | With OSPF as the *target protocol,* this parameter is required to properly redistribute internal subnetworks. |
| **default-metric** | *bandwidth delay reliability load MTU* | The five values that may be used by IGRP and EIGRP to calculate metrics. |
| **default-metric** | *value* | Metric value used for RIP hop count, BGP cost, OSPF cost, EGP cost. |

# Redistribution Between Interior Protocols

The following are examples that detail the commands required to exchange information between the different routing protocols. Examples #1 through #11 are sample IP routing protocol exchanges, with #10 and #11 set up as lab exercises. These lab exercise examples provide the reader with basic configurations and show commands. The fine-tuning and tweaking commands necessary to provide clean summarized IP routing tables are missing, and your challenge is to determine which commands are needed to correct the routing tables. Each is a complex example of multiple IP routing protocols.

## Example #1—RIP & IGRP

In this example (see Figure 6-2), New York and Tokyo are using the IGRP protocol, and London is using both IGRP and RIP. If we want to be accurate during the redistribution process, then instead of using a single metric during the route redistribution process into RIP, we can provide accurate hop counts. Network 192.168.2.0 should be three hops away, networks 192.168.1.0 and 192.168.4.0 two hops away, and 192.168.6.0 one hop away. To accomplish this task, we will use a simple route map.

Tokyo is part of the IGRP 200 routing domain, and the standard routing protocol commands are shown in lines 11 through 13 in Figure 6-3.

The **show ip protocol** output in Figure 6-4 lets you see the detail of the routing processes for Tokyo.

To verify that the RIP network has been redistributed, look at line 15 for network 192.168.3.0 in the **show ip route** output in Figure 6-5.

**Figure 6-2**

Redistributing RIP and IGRP

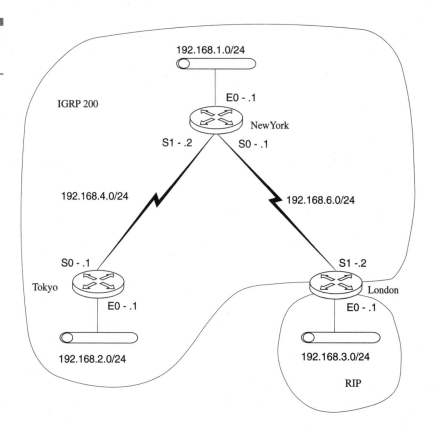

192.168.1.0/24

IGRP 200

E0 - .1

New York

S1 - .2          S0 - .1

192.168.4.0/24                    192.168.6.0/24

S0 - .1

Tokyo                                              S1 - .2

E0 - .1                                          London

E0 - .1

192.168.2.0/24                    192.168.3.0/24

RIP

**Figure 6-3**   Tokyo configuration

```
1  !
2  hostname Tokyo
3  !
4  interface Ethernet0
5   ip address 192.168.2.1 255.255.255.0
6  !
7  interface Serial0
8   ip address 192.168.4.1 255.255.255.0
9   bandwidth 56
10 !
11 router igrp 200
12   network 192.168.4.0
13   network 192.168.2.0
14 !
15 ip classless
16 !
17 line con 0
18   exec-timeout 0 0
19   length 0
20 !
21 end
```

New York is part of the IGRP 200 routing domain, and the standard routing protocol commands are shown in lines 16 through 19 in Figure 6-6.

The **show ip protocol** output in Figure 6-7 lets you see the detail of the routing processes.

To verify that the RIP network has been redistributed, look for network 192.168.3.0 in the **show ip route** output in Figure 6-8. When we move on to London to look at the redistribution process, you will note

**Figure 6-4**   Tokyo **show ip protocol** output

```
1  Tokyo#sho ip protocol
2  Routing Protocol is "igrp 200"
3    Sending updates every 90 seconds, next due in 62 seconds
4    Invalid after 270 seconds, hold down 280, flushed after 630
5    Outgoing update filter list for all interfaces is not set
6    Incoming update filter list for all interfaces is not set
7    Default networks flagged in outgoing updates
8    Default networks accepted from incoming updates
9    IGRP metric weight K1=1, K2=0, K3=1, K4=0, K5=0
10    IGRP maximum hopcount 100
11    IGRP maximum metric variance 1
12    Redistributing: igrp 200
13    Routing for Networks:
14      192.168.4.0
15      192.168.2.0
16    Routing Information Sources:
17      Gateway         Distance       Last Update
18      192.168.4.2         100        00:01:22
19    Distance: (default is 100)
```

**Figure 6-5** Tokyo **show ip route** output

```
1 Tokyo#sho ip route
2 Codes: C - connected, S - static, I - IGRP, R - RIP, M - mobile, B - BGP
3        D - EIGRP, EX - EIGRP external, O - OSPF, IA - OSPF inter area
4        N1 - OSPF NSSA external type 1, N2 - OSPF NSSA external type 2
5        E1 - OSPF external type 1, E2 - OSPF external type 2, E - EGP
6        i - IS-IS, L1 - IS-IS level-1, L2 - IS-IS level-2, * - candidate default
7        U - per-user static route, o - ODR
8
9 Gateway of last resort is not set
10
11 C    192.168.4.0/24 is directly connected, Serial0
12 I    192.168.6.0/24 [100/10476] via 192.168.4.2, 00:01:16, Serial0
13 I    192.168.1.0/24 [100/8576] via 192.168.4.2, 00:01:16, Serial0
14 C    192.168.2.0/24 is directly connected, Ethernet0
15 I    192.168.3.0/24 [100/10576] via 192.168.4.2, 00:01:16, Serial0
```

**Figure 6-6** NewYork configuration

```
1 !
2 hostname NewYork
3 !
4 interface Ethernet0
5  ip address 192.168.1.1 255.255.255.0
6 !
7 interface Serial0
8  ip address 192.168.6.1 255.255.255.0
9  bandwidth 56
10 !
11 interface Serial1
12  ip address 192.168.4.2 255.255.255.0
13  clockrate 56000
14  bandwidth 56
15 !
16 router igrp 200
17  network 192.168.1.0
18  network 192.168.4.0
19  network 192.168.6.0
20 !
21 ip classless
22 !
23 line con 0
24  exec-timeout 0 0
25  length 0
26 !
27 end
```

**Figure 6-7**  NewYork **show ip protocol** output

```
1 NewYork#sho ip protocol
2 Routing Protocol is "igrp 200"
3    Sending updates every 90 seconds, next due in 6 seconds
4    Invalid after 270 seconds, hold down 280, flushed after 630
5    Outgoing update filter list for all interfaces is not set
6    Incoming update filter list for all interfaces is not set
7    Default networks flagged in outgoing updates
8    Default networks accepted from incoming updates
9    IGRP metric weight K1=1, K2=0, K3=1, K4=0, K5=0
10   IGRP maximum hopcount 100
11   IGRP maximum metric variance 1
12   Redistributing: igrp 200
13   Routing for Networks:
14      192.168.1.0
15      192.168.4.0
16      192.168.6.0
17   Routing Information Sources:
18      Gateway         Distance      Last Update
19      192.168.6.2          100      00:01:04
20      192.168.4.1          100      00:00:14
21   Distance: (default is 100)
```

that the RIP network 192.168.3.0 is redistributed to the IGRP routing protocol with an Ethernet segment metric 10000 100 255 1 1500. Look at lines 14 and 15, and you will note that both the 192.168.2.0 and 192.168.3.0 networks have the same metric value—8,576. This is the metric value calculated using the standard IGRP metric defaults. If you look at the diagram, Figure 6-2, both networks are equidistant from New York.

London is where all the action is. Here is where we have to merge together our two routing protocols, RIP and IGRP 200. In the London configuration in Figure 6-9, line 14 identifies 192.168.3.0 as a RIP net-

**Figure 6-8**  NewYork **show ip route** output

```
1 NewYork#sho ip route
2 Codes: C - connected, S - static, I - IGRP, R - RIP, M - mobile, B - BGP
3        D - EIGRP, EX - EIGRP external, O - OSPF, IA - OSPF inter area
4        N1 - OSPF NSSA external type 1, N2 - OSPF NSSA external type 2
5        E1 - OSPF external type 1, E2 - OSPF external type 2, E - EGP
6        i - IS-IS, L1 - IS-IS level-1, L2 - IS-IS level-2, * - candidate default
7        U - per-user static route, o - ODR
8
9 Gateway of last resort is not set
10
11 C    192.168.4.0/24 is directly connected, Serial1
12 C    192.168.6.0/24 is directly connected, Serial0
13 C    192.168.1.0/24 is directly connected, Ethernet0
14 I    192.168.2.0/24 [100/8576] via 192.168.4.1, 00:00:00, Serial1
15 I    192.168.3.0/24 [100/8576] via 192.168.6.2, 00:00:49, Serial0
```

work, and all interfaces that match this network participate in the RIP routing protocol. Line 18 performs the same function for network 192.168.6.0 and the IGRP routing protocol.

Line 17 is used to redistribute RIP into IGRP with a metric that is equal to an Ethernet segment. To IGRP, network 192.168.3.0 appears as if it is an Ethernet segment.

Line 13 is used to redistribute IGRP into RIP, with the metrics to be assigned using a route map that provides a more precise method of assigning metrics to individual IP networks.

Lines 25 through 35 are our route map statements.

**Figure 6-9**  London configuration

```
1  !
2  hostname London
3  !
4  interface Ethernet0
5   ip address 192.168.3.1 255.255.255.0
6  !
7  interface Serial1
8   ip address 192.168.6.2 255.255.255.0
9   clockrate 5600
10   bandwidth 56
11  !
12 router rip
13   redistribute igrp 200 route-map igrp-to-rip
14   network 192.168.3.0
15  !
16 router igrp 200
17   redistribute rip metric 10000 100 255 1 1500
18   network 192.168.6.0
19  !
20 ip classless
21 access-list 1 permit 192.168.6.0 0.0.0.255
22 access-list 2 permit 192.168.1.0 0.0.0.255
23 access-list 2 permit 192.168.4.0 0.0.0.255
24 access-list 3 permit 192.168.2.0 0.0.0.255
25 route-map igrp-to-rip permit 10
26   match ip address 1
27   set metric 1
28  !
29 route-map igrp-to-rip permit 20
30   match ip address 2
31   set metric 2
32  !
33 route-map igrp-to-rip permit 30
34   match ip address 3
35   set metric 3
36  !
37 line con 0
38   exec-timeout 0 0
39   length 0
40  !
41 end
```

Line 25 defines the name of the route map we are going to use, igrp-to-rip, the operation type of permit, and the sequence number 10 to place the match/set combination in the correct sequence.

Line 26 defines the match operation to be the IP addresses permitted in access-list one.

Line 27 defines the set operation to use a metric of one hop for networks that match line 26.

Lines 29 through 31 define the match/set operation for the IP addresses permitted in access-list two.

Lines 33 through 35 define the match/set operation for the IP addresses permitted in access-list three.

Lines 21 through 24 are the access-lists used to identify the IP addresses permitted or denied during the match processes in our route-map.

The sample **debug** output in Figure 6-10 provides verification that our redistribution process is working properly for the IGRP routes redistributed into RIP.

Lines 4 through 8 are the output of the **debug ip rip** command and verify that our route map is working properly as each of the IGRP networks has the correct hop count.

Lines 16 and 17 are the output of the **debug ip igrp transactions** and verify that our route redistribution from RIP into IGRP is working. The metric used on line 17 is **1100**, calculated using the standard IGRP metric calculation.

The **show route-map** output in Figure 6-11, is used to verify that our route map has been constructed properly.

The **show ip protocol** output in Figure 6-12, displays both the IGRP and RIP protocol processes. Lines 12 and 25 identify the routing proto-

**Figure 6-10**  London **debug** output

```
1 London#debug ip rip
2 RIP protocol debugging is on
3 London#
4 RIP: sending v1 update to 255.255.255.255 via Ethernet0 (192.168.3.1)
5       network 192.168.4.0, metric 2
6       network 192.168.6.0, metric 1
7       network 192.168.1.0, metric 2
8       network 192.168.2.0, metric 3
9 London#debug ip igrp transactions
10 IGRP protocol debugging is on
11 London#
12 IGRP: received update from 192.168.6.1 on Serial1
13       network 192.168.4.0, metric 10476 (neighbor 8476)
14       network 192.168.1.0, metric 8576 (neighbor 1100)
15       network 192.168.2.0, metric 10576 (neighbor 8576)
16 IGRP: sending update to 255.255.255.255 via Serial1 (192.168.6.2)
17       network 192.168.3.0, metric=1100
```

**Figure 6-11** London **show route-map** output

```
1 London#sho route-map
2 route-map igrp-to-rip, permit, sequence 10
3   Match clauses:
4     ip address (access-lists): 1
5   Set clauses:
6     metric 1
7   Policy routing matches: 0 packets, 0 bytes
8 route-map igrp-to-rip, permit, sequence 20
9   Match clauses:
10     ip address (access-lists): 2
11  Set clauses:
12    metric 2
13  Policy routing matches: 0 packets, 0 bytes
14 route-map igrp-to-rip, permit, sequence 30
15  Match clauses:
16    ip address (access-lists): 3
17  Set clauses:
18    metric 3
```

**Figure 6-12** London **show ip protocol** output

```
1 London#sho ip protocol
2 Routing Protocol is "igrp 200"
3   Sending updates every 90 seconds, next due in 69 seconds
4   Invalid after 270 seconds, hold down 280, flushed after 630
5   Outgoing update filter list for all interfaces is not set
6   Incoming update filter list for all interfaces is not set
7   Default networks flagged in outgoing updates
8   Default networks accepted from incoming updates
9   IGRP metric weight K1=1, K2=0, K3=1, K4=0, K5=0
10   IGRP maximum hopcount 100
11   IGRP maximum metric variance 1
12   Redistributing: igrp 200, rip
13   Routing for Networks:
14     192.168.6.0
15   Routing Information Sources:
16     Gateway         Distance      Last Update
17     192.168.6.1          100      00:00:26
18   Distance: (default is 100)
19
20 Routing Protocol is "rip"
21   Sending updates every 30 seconds, next due in 5 seconds
22   Invalid after 180 seconds, hold down 180, flushed after 240
23   Outgoing update filter list for all interfaces is not set
24   Incoming update filter list for all interfaces is not set
25   Redistributing: igrp 200, rip
26   Default version control: send version 1, receive any version
27     Interface       Send Recv   Key-chain
28     Ethernet0         1    1 2
29   Routing for Networks:
30     192.168.3.0
31   Routing Information Sources:
32     Gateway         Distance      Last Update
33   Distance: (default is 120)
```

**Figure 6-13** London **show ip route** output

```
1 London#sho ip route
2 Codes: C - connected, S - static, I - IGRP, R - RIP, M - mobile, B - BGP
3         D - EIGRP, EX - EIGRP external, O - OSPF, IA - OSPF inter area
4         N1 - OSPF NSSA external type 1, N2 - OSPF NSSA external type 2
5         E1 - OSPF external type 1, E2 - OSPF external type 2, E - EGP
6         i - IS-IS, L1 - IS-IS level-1, L2 - IS-IS level-2, * - candidate default
7         U - per-user static route, o - ODR
8
9 Gateway of last resort is not set
10
11 I    192.168.4.0/24 [100/10476] via 192.168.6.1, 00:00:20, Serial1
12 C    192.168.6.0/24 is directly connected, Serial1
13 I    192.168.1.0/24 [100/8576] via 192.168.6.1, 00:00:21, Serial1
14 I    192.168.2.0/24 [100/10576] via 192.168.6.1, 00:00:21, Serial1
15 C    192.168.3.0/24 is directly connected, Ethernet0
```

cols being redistributed. Note that while there are lines (4, 5, 23, 24) that identify incoming and outgoing routing table filters, there are no lines that define the redistribution filters or route maps.

The **show ip route** output in Figure 6-13 correctly identifies all our network pathways.

FYI: Route map programming has several pitfalls. When matching IP addresses, we can use a specific IP address, a named access-list, or a numbered access-list. Watch out for the help process because it may lead you to enter a command similar to the following: **match ip address list 1**. In fact, this command sets a policy that will match the named access-list **list**, then the access-list number **1**. If the named access-list list is not defined when the route map process checks the access-list list, it takes the default for an undefined access-list, which is to permit any address. Look at the **debug** output in Figure 6-11 to verify the operation.

## Example #2—IP & EIGRP

This example, see Figure 6-14, is very similar to our previous example and is designed to highlight the differences between IGRP and EIGRP.

Tokyo is part of the EIGRP 200 routing domain, and the standard routing protocol commands are shown in lines 13 through 15 in Figure 6-15.

The **show ip protocol** output in Figure 6-16 lets you see the detail of the routing processes.

**Figure 6-14**
Redistributing RIP
and EIGRP

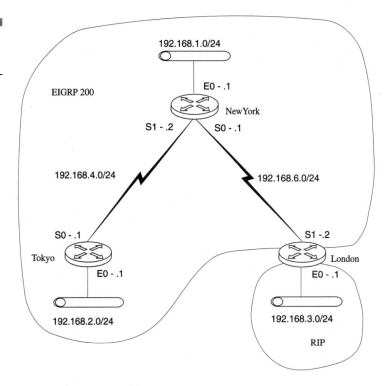

**Figure 6-15**  Tokyo configuration

```
1  !
2  hostname Tokyo
3  !
4  no ip domain-lookup
5  !
6  interface Ethernet0
7   ip address 192.168.2.1 255.255.255.0
8  !
9  interface Serial0
10   ip address 192.168.4.1 255.255.255.0
11   bandwidth 56
12 !
13 router eigrp 200
14   network 192.168.4.0
15   network 192.168.2.0
16 !
17 ip classless
18 !
19 line con 0
20   exec-timeout 0 0
21   length 0
22 !
23 end
```

**Figure 6-16** Tokyo **show ip protocol** output

```
1 Tokyo#sho ip prot
2 Routing Protocol is "eigrp 200"
3   Outgoing update filter list for all interfaces is not set
4   Incoming update filter list for all interfaces is not set
5   Default networks flagged in outgoing updates
6   Default networks accepted from incoming updates
7   EIGRP metric weight K1=1, K2=0, K3=1, K4=0, K5=0
8   EIGRP maximum hopcount 100
9   EIGRP maximum metric variance 1
10  Redistributing: eigrp 200
11  Automatic network summarization is in effect
12  Automatic address summarization:
13    192.168.4.0/24 for Ethernet0
14    192.168.2.0/24 for Serial0
15  Routing for Networks:
16    192.168.4.0
17    192.168.2.0
18  Routing Information Sources:
19    Gateway         Distance      Last Update
20    192.168.4.2           90      00:02:19
21  Distance: internal 90 external 170
```

To verify that the RIP network has been redistributed, look for network 192.168.3.0 in the **show ip route** output in Figure 6-17. With IGRP, an external route gets distributed to the balance of the Autonomous System and appears as any other IP classful address. With EIGRP, external routes are advertised as an IP classful address but show up in the routing table as an **EX** or external route to our EIGRP network environment. See line 15 in Figure 6-17.

New York is also part of our EIGRP 200 domain, and the standard IP routing commands are shown in lines 18 through 21 in Figure 6-18.

**Figure 6-17** Tokyo **show ip route** output

```
1 Tokyo#sho ip route
2 Codes: C - connected, S - static, I - IGRP, R - RIP, M - mobile, B - BGP
3        D - EIGRP, EX - EIGRP external, O - OSPF, IA - OSPF inter area
4        N1 - OSPF NSSA external type 1, N2 - OSPF NSSA external type 2
5        E1 - OSPF external type 1, E2 - OSPF external type 2, E - EGP
6        i - IS-IS, L1 - IS-IS level-1, L2 - IS-IS level-2, * - candidate default
7        U - per-user static route, o - ODR
8
9 Gateway of last resort is not set
10
11 C    192.168.4.0/24 is directly connected, Serial0
12 D    192.168.6.0/24 [90/2681856] via 192.168.4.2, 00:03:30, Serial0
13 D    192.168.1.0/24 [90/2195456] via 192.168.4.2, 00:06:05, Serial0
14 C    192.168.2.0/24 is directly connected, Ethernet0
15 D EX 192.168.3.0/24 [170/2707456] via 192.168.4.2, 00:02:14, Serial0
```

**Figure 6-18** NewYork configuration

```
1  !
2  hostname NewYork
3  !
4  no ip domain-lookup
5  !
6  interface Ethernet0
7   ip address 192.168.1.1 255.255.255.0
8  !
9  interface Serial0
10   ip address 192.168.6.1 255.255.255.0
11   bandwidth 56
12  !
13  interface Serial1
14   ip address 192.168.4.2 255.255.255.0
15   clockrate 56000
16   bandwidth 56
17  !
18  router eigrp 200
19   network 192.168.4.0
20   network 192.168.1.0
21   network 192.168.6.0
22  !
23  ip classless
24  !
25  line con 0
26   exec-timeout 0 0
27   length 0
28  !
29  end
```

The **show ip protocol** output in Figure 6-19 lets you see the detail of the routing processes.

To verify that the RIP network has been redistributed, look for network 192.168.3.0 in the **show ip route** output in Figure 6-20. With EIGRP, external routes are advertised as a class address but show up in the routing table as an **EX** or external route to our EIGRP network environment. See line 15 in Figure 6-20.

London is the router used to connect the RIP and EIGRP 200 domains. In the London configuration in Figure 6-21, line 20 identifies 192.168.3.0 as a RIP network, and all interfaces that match this network will participate in the RIP routing protocol. Line 16 performs the same function for network 192.168.6.0 and the EIGRP routing protocol.

Line 15 is used to redistribute RIP into EIGRP with a metric that is equal to an Ethernet segment. To IGRP, network 192.168.3.0 appears as if it is a single Ethernet segment.

**Figure 6-19** NewYork **show ip protocol** output

```
1 NewYork#sho ip prot
2 Routing Protocol is "eigrp 200"
3   Outgoing update filter list for all interfaces is not set
4   Incoming update filter list for all interfaces is not set
5   Default networks flagged in outgoing updates
6   Default networks accepted from incoming updates
7   EIGRP metric weight K1=1, K2=0, K3=1, K4=0, K5=0
8   EIGRP maximum hopcount 100
9   EIGRP maximum metric variance 1
10   Redistributing: eigrp 200
11   Automatic network summarization is in effect
12   Automatic address summarization:
13     192.168.4.0/24 for Ethernet0, Serial0
14     192.168.1.0/24 for Serial1, Serial0
15     192.168.6.0/24 for Ethernet0, Serial1
16   Routing for Networks:
17     192.168.4.0
18     192.168.1.0
19     192.168.6.0
20   Routing Information Sources:
21     Gateway         Distance      Last Update
22     192.168.6.2         90        00:03:46
23     192.168.4.1         90        00:03:46
24   Distance: internal 90 external 170
```

Line 19 is used to redistribute EIGRP into RIP, with the metrics assigning a fixed default of two hops.

To verify that the EIGRP routes have been correctly redistributed into the RIP process, use the **debug ip rip** command to review the updates being transmitted on the Ethernet 0 segment. Lines 5 through 8 correctly reflect our default metric of two hops as defined in London's configuration in Figure 6-22.

**Figure 6-20** NewYork **show ip route** output

```
1 NewYork#sho ip route
2 Codes: C - connected, S - static, I - IGRP, R - RIP, M - mobile, B - BGP
3        D - EIGRP, EX - EIGRP external, O - OSPF, IA - OSPF inter area
4        N1 - OSPF NSSA external type 1, N2 - OSPF NSSA external type 2
5        E1 - OSPF external type 1, E2 - OSPF external type 2, E - EGP
6        i - IS-IS, L1 - IS-IS level-1, L2 - IS-IS level-2, * - candidate default
7        U - per-user static route, o - ODR
8
9 Gateway of last resort is not set
10
11 C    192.168.4.0/24 is directly connected, Serial1
12 C    192.168.6.0/24 is directly connected, Serial0
13 C    192.168.1.0/24 is directly connected, Ethernet0
14 D    192.168.2.0/24 [90/2195456] via 192.168.4.1, 00:04:01, Serial1
15 D EX 192.168.3.0/24 [170/2195456] via 192.168.6.2, 00:03:36, Serial0
```

**Figure 6-21** London configuration

```
1  !
2  hostname London
3  !
4  no ip domain-lookup
5  !
6  interface Ethernet0
7   ip address 192.168.3.1 255.255.255.0
8  !
9  interface Serial1
10   ip address 192.168.6.2 255.255.255.0
11   clockrate 56000
12   bandwidth 56
13  !
14  router eigrp 200
15   redistribute rip metric 10000 100 255 1 1500
16   network 192.168.6.0
17  !
18  router rip
19   redistribute eigrp 200 metric 2
20   network 192.168.3.0
21  !
22  ip classless
23  !
24  line con 0
25   exec-timeout 0 0
26   length 0
27  !
28  end
```

The **show ip protocol** output in Figure 6-23 lets you see the detail of the routing processes. In the sample output, please note that there are two separate routing protocols operating to maintain the correct IP routing tables. The only indication that route redistribution is occurring is in line 7 and 25. The IP routing protocols listed on these lines are the source of the routing information used by each of the two protocols to calculate the best pathway to destination networks.

The **show ip route** output in Figure 6-24 shows a mix of routes either directly connected or EIGRP derived based on the letter codes to the left-hand side of the route entries.

**Figure 6-22** London debug output

```
1  London#debug ip rip
2  RIP protocol debugging is on
3  London#
4  RIP: sending v1 update to 255.255.255.255 via Ethernet0 (192.168.3.1)
5       network 192.168.4.0, metric 2
6       network 192.168.6.0, metric 2
7       network 192.168.1.0, metric 2
8       network 192.168.2.0, metric 2
```

**Figure 6-23** London **show ip protocol** output

```
1 London#sho ip prot
2 Routing Protocol is "rip"
3   Sending updates every 30 seconds, next due in 22 seconds
4   Invalid after 180 seconds, hold down 180, flushed after 240
5   Outgoing update filter list for all interfaces is not set
6   Incoming update filter list for all interfaces is not set
7   Redistributing: rip, eigrp 200
8   Default version control: send version 1, receive any version
9     Interface          Send  Recv   Key-chain
10     Ethernet0           1     1 2
11   Routing for Networks:
12     192.168.3.0
13   Routing Information Sources:
14     Gateway           Distance       Last Update
15   Distance: (default is 120)
16
17 Routing Protocol is "eigrp 200"
18   Outgoing update filter list for all interfaces is not set
19   Incoming update filter list for all interfaces is not set
20   Default networks flagged in outgoing updates
21   Default networks accepted from incoming updates
22   EIGRP metric weight K1=1, K2=0, K3=1, K4=0, K5=0
23   EIGRP maximum hopcount 100
24   EIGRP maximum metric variance 1
25   Redistributing: rip, eigrp 200
26   Automatic network summarization is in effect
27   Routing for Networks:
28     192.168.6.0
29   Routing Information Sources:
30     Gateway           Distance       Last Update
31     192.168.6.1          90          00:05:37
32   Distance: internal 90 external 170
```

**Figure 6-24** London **show ip route** output

```
1 London#sho ip route
2 Codes: C - connected, S - static, I - IGRP, R - RIP, M - mobile, B - BGP
3        D - EIGRP, EX - EIGRP external, O - OSPF, IA - OSPF inter area
4        N1 - OSPF NSSA external type 1, N2 - OSPF NSSA external type 2
5        E1 - OSPF external type 1, E2 - OSPF external type 2, E - EGP
6        i - IS-IS, L1 - IS-IS level-1, L2 - IS-IS level-2, * - candidate default
7        U - per-user static route, o - ODR
8
9 Gateway of last resort is not set
10
11 D    192.168.4.0/24 [90/2681856] via 192.168.6.1, 00:05:31, Serial1
12 C    192.168.6.0/24 is directly connected, Serial1
13 D    192.168.1.0/24 [90/2195456] via 192.168.6.1, 00:05:32, Serial1
14 D    192.168.2.0/24 [90/2707456] via 192.168.6.1, 00:05:32, Serial1
15 C    192.168.3.0/24 is directly connected, Ethernet0
```

# Example #3—RIP & OSPF

In this example (see Figure 6-25), we have an OSPF network that consists of a backbone area and two subareas. Each router assumes a different role in our network. Tokyo is an area 4 internal router, NewYork is an Area Border Router, and London is an Autonomous System Border Router connecting our OSPF domain with our RIP domain.

Tokyo has a basic internal routing process set up for OSPF, where all active interfaces belong to area 4. In the configuration in Figure 6-26, lines 14 and 15 tie the subnetworks used for each specific interface into OSPF area 4.

**Question #1: Can the two network commands on lines 14 and 15 be replaced with a single network command?  If so, can you construct the correct command?**

**Figure 6-25**

Redistributing RIP and OSPF

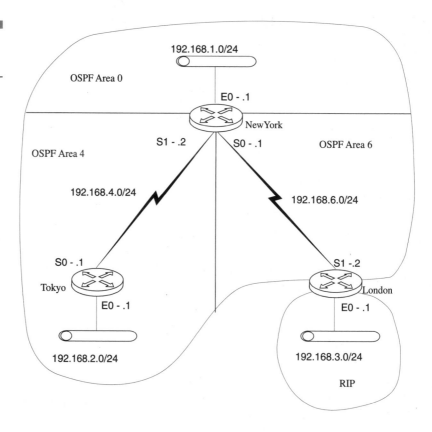

The **show ip protocol** output in Figure 6-27 lets you see the detail of the routing processes.

The **show ip route** output in Figure 6-28 shows a mix of route sources. Directly Connected (C), OSPF inter-area routes learned from the backbone (**O IA**) on lines 12 and 13, and an external network injected into our OSPF domain using the default type 2 metric (**E2**). The [**110/100**] portion of line 15 represents the Administrative Distance of 110 for OSPF and the metric of **100** for subnet 192.168.3.0/24. Look at the network topology in Figure 6-25, and compare the metric value of 100 on line 15 with the metric value of 128 for network 192.168.6.0 on line 12. The metric difference appears to place the 192.168.3.0 network closer than the 192.168.6.0 network, but further away than the 192.168.1.0 network. Remember from Chapter 5 that external type 2 routes are processed through the entire OSPF domain without changing or updating the metric assigned during redistribution. We'll check London's configuration later in this example to see if the metric of 100 is being assigned during redistribution.

NewYork is the Area Border Router in our network, connecting the backbone to the subareas. See lines 18 through 21 in Figure 6-29 for the IP routing configuration. Refer to Chapter 5 for more information on OSPF router definitions.

**Figure 6-26**   Tokyo configuration

```
Tokyo Configuration
1 !
2 hostname Tokyo
3 !
4 no ip domain-lookup
5 !
6 interface Ethernet0
7  ip address 192.168.2.1 255.255.255.0
8 !
9 interface Serial0
10  ip address 192.168.4.1 255.255.255.0
11  bandwidth 56
12 !
13 router ospf 200
14  network 192.168.4.0 0.0.0.255 area 4
15  network 192.168.2.0 0.0.0.255 area 4
16 !
17 ip classless
18 !
19 line con 0
20  exec-timeout 0 0
21  length 0
22 !
23 end
```

**Figure 6-27**   Tokyo **show ip protocol** output

```
1 Tokyo#sho ip protocol
2 Routing Protocol is "ospf 200"
3   Sending updates every 0 seconds
4   Invalid after 0 seconds, hold down 0, flushed after 0
5   Outgoing update filter list for all interfaces is not set
6   Incoming update filter list for all interfaces is not set
7   Redistributing: ospf 200
8   Routing for Networks:
9     192.168.4.0
10     192.168.2.0
11   Routing Information Sources:
12     Gateway          Distance      Last Update
13     192.168.6.2          110       00:02:25
14     192.168.6.1          110       00:02:25
15   Distance: (default is 110)
```

The **show ip protocol** output in Figure 6-30 lets you see the detail of the routing processes.

The **show ip route** command in Figure 6-31 shows a mix of routes either directly connected, OSPF inter-area derived, or external based on the letter codes to the left-hand side of the route entries.

London is again the center of attention, with the redistribution between RIP and OSPF taking place in Figure 6-32. Line 15 takes the RIP network 192.168.3.0/24 and uses the default metric of 100 during redistribution into OSPF. Because the external metric type is not specified during redistribution, the default—external type 2—is used. Look at the metric shown in the **show ip route** samples for either Tokyo or New York to verify this operation.

**Figure 6-28**   Tokyo **show ip route** output

```
1 Tokyo#sho ip route
2 Codes: C - connected, S - static, I - IGRP, R - RIP, M - mobile, B - BGP
3        D - EIGRP, EX - EIGRP external, O - OSPF, IA - OSPF inter area
4        N1 - OSPF NSSA external type 1, N2 - OSPF NSSA external type 2
5        E1 - OSPF external type 1, E2 - OSPF external type 2, E - EGP
6        i - IS-IS, L1 - IS-IS level-1, L2 - IS-IS level-2, * - candidate default
7        U - per-user static route, o - ODR
8
9 Gateway of last resort is not set
10
11 C    192.168.4.0/24 is directly connected, Serial0
12 O IA 192.168.6.0/24 [110/128] via 192.168.4.2, 00:02:20, Serial0
13 O IA 192.168.1.0/24 [110/74] via 192.168.4.2, 00:02:20, Serial0
14 C    192.168.2.0/24 is directly connected, Ethernet0
15 O E2 192.168.3.0/24 [110/100] via 192.168.4.2, 00:02:20, Serial0
```

**Figure 6-29**    NewYork configuration

```
1  !
2  hostname NewYork
3  !
4  no ip domain-lookup
5  !
6  interface Ethernet0
7   ip address 192.168.1.1 255.255.255.0
8  !
9  interface Serial0
10   ip address 192.168.6.1 255.255.255.0
11   bandwidth 56
12  !
13  interface Serial1
14   ip address 192.168.4.2 255.255.255.0
15   clockrate 56000
16   bandwidth 56
17  !
18  router ospf 200
19   network 192.168.1.0 0.0.0.255 area 0
20   network 192.168.6.0 0.0.0.255 area 6
21   network 192.168.4.0 0.0.0.255 area 4
22  !
23  ip classless
24  !
25  line con 0
26   exec-timeout 0 0
27   length 0
28  !
29  end
```

The sample **debug** commands in Figure 6-33 provide verification that our redistribution process is working properly.

Lines 5 through 8 are the output of the **debug ip rip** command and verify that our route map is working properly as each of the OSPF networks is present. Lines 11 and 12 detail the output of the external type 5

**Figure 6-30**    NewYork **show ip protocol** output

```
1  NewYork#sho ip protocol
2  Routing Protocol is "ospf 200"
3    Sending updates every 0 seconds
4    Invalid after 0 seconds, hold down 0, flushed after 0
5    Outgoing update filter list for all interfaces is not set
6    Incoming update filter list for all interfaces is not set
7    Redistributing: ospf 200
8    Routing for Networks:
9      192.168.1.0
10     192.168.6.0
11     192.168.4.0
12    Routing Information Sources:
13     Gateway          Distance      Last Update
14     192.168.6.2         110        00:03:28
15     192.168.4.1         110        00:05:39
16    Distance: (default is 110)
```

**Figure 6-31** NewYork **show ip route** output

```
1 NewYork#sho ip route
2 Codes: C - connected, S - static, I - IGRP, R - RIP, M - mobile, B - BGP
3        D - EIGRP, EX - EIGRP external, O - OSPF, IA - OSPF inter area
4        N1 - OSPF NSSA external type 1, N2 - OSPF NSSA external type 2
5        E1 - OSPF external type 1, E2 - OSPF external type 2, E - EGP
6        i - IS-IS, L1 - IS-IS level-1, L2 - IS-IS level-2, * - candidate default
7        U - per-user static route, o - ODR
8
9 Gateway of last resort is not set
10
11 C      192.168.4.0/24 is directly connected, Serial1
12 C      192.168.6.0/24 is directly connected, Serial0
13 C      192.168.1.0/24 is directly connected, Ethernet0
14 O      192.168.2.0/24 [110/74] via 192.168.4.1, 00:05:33, Serial1
15 O E2 192.168.3.0/24 [110/100] via 192.168.6.2, 00:03:22, Serial0
```

link-state announcement used to inform OSPF neighbors of the existence of the external RIP network 192.168.3.0/24. Note the metric of 100 used to advertise 192.168.3.0/24 to the balance of the OSPF routers on line 12 defaults to type 2, which will remain unchanged as it gets passed to other routers in our Autonomous System.

**Figure 6-32** London configuration

```
1 !
2 hostname London
3 !
4 no ip domain-lookup
5 !
6 interface Ethernet0
7  ip address 192.168.3.1 255.255.255.0
8 !
9 interface Serial1
10  ip address 192.168.6.2 255.255.255.0
11  clockrate 56000
12  bandwidth 56
13 !
14 router ospf 200
15  redistribute rip metric 100
16  network 192.168.6.0 0.0.0.255 area 6
17 !
18 router rip
19  redistribute ospf 200 metric 3
20  network 192.168.3.0
21 !
22 ip classless
23 !
24 line con 0
25  exec-timeout 0 0
26  length 0
27 !
28 end
```

**Figure 6-33** London **debug** output

```
1 London#debug ip rip
2 RIP protocol debugging is on
3 London#
4 RIP: sending v1 update to 255.255.255.255 via Ethernet0 (192.168.3.1)
5       network 192.168.4.0, metric 3
6       network 192.168.6.0, metric 3
7       network 192.168.1.0, metric 3
8       network 192.168.2.0, metric 3
9
10 London#debug ip ospf lsa
11 OSPF summary lsa generation debugging is on
12 OSPF: Generate external LSA 192.168.3.0, mask 255.255.255.0, type 5, age 0, metric
100, seq 0x80000001
```

The **show ip** protocol output in Figure 6-34 lets you see the detail of the routing processes. In the following sample output, please note that there are two separate routing protocols operating to maintain the correct IP routing tables. The only indication that route redistribution is occurring is in lines 7 and 23. The IP routing protocols listed on these lines are the source of the routing information used by each of the two protocols to calculate the best pathway to destination networks.

**Figure 6-34** London **show ip protocol** output

```
1 London#sho ip protocol
2 Routing Protocol is "rip"
3   Sending updates every 30 seconds, next due in 27 seconds
4   Invalid after 180 seconds, hold down 180, flushed after 240
5   Outgoing update filter list for all interfaces is not set
6   Incoming update filter list for all interfaces is not set
7   Redistributing: rip, ospf 200 (internal, external 1, external 2)
8
9   Default version control: send version 1, receive any version
10      Interface        Send  Recv   Key-chain
11      Ethernet0         1     1 2
12    Routing for Networks:
13      192.168.3.0
14    Routing Information Sources:
15      Gateway          Distance      Last Update
16    Distance: (default is 120)
17
18 Routing Protocol is "ospf 200"
19   Sending updates every 0 seconds
20   Invalid after 0 seconds, hold down 0, flushed after 0
21   Outgoing update filter list for all interfaces is not set
22   Incoming update filter list for all interfaces is not set
23   Redistributing: rip, ospf 200
24   Routing for Networks:
25      192.168.6.0
26   Routing Information Sources:
27      Gateway          Distance      Last Update
28      192.168.6.1           110      00:04:18
29   Distance: (default is 110)
```

**Figure 6-35**  London **show ip route** output

```
1 London#sho ip route
2 Codes: C - connected, S - static, I - IGRP, R - RIP, M - mobile, B - BGP
3         D - EIGRP, EX - EIGRP external, O - OSPF, IA - OSPF inter area
4         N1 - OSPF NSSA external type 1, N2 - OSPF NSSA external type 2
5         E1 - OSPF external type 1, E2 - OSPF external type 2, E - EGP
6         i - IS-IS, L1 - IS-IS level-1, L2 - IS-IS level-2, * - candidate default
7         U - per-user static route, o - ODR
8
9 Gateway of last resort is not set
10
11 O IA 192.168.4.0/24 [110/128] via 192.168.6.1, 00:04:13, Serial1
12 C    192.168.6.0/24 is directly connected, Serial1
13 O IA 192.168.1.0/24 [110/74] via 192.168.6.1, 00:04:13, Serial1
14 O IA 192.168.2.0/24 [110/138] via 192.168.6.1, 00:04:13, Serial1
15 C    192.168.3.0/24 is directly connected, Ethernet0
```

The **show ip route** command in Figure 6-35 shows a mix of routes either directly connected or EIGRP derived based on the letter codes to the left-hand side of the route entries.

## Example #4—RIP, OSPF & Static Routes

In this example, see Figure 6-36, there are two protocols involved, but instead of being directly connected, static routes are used to connect the two routing domains together. The most basic commands are used in this example, and the metrics being redistributed are left as defaults.

Tokyo has a basic internal routing process set up for OSPF, where all active interfaces belong to area 4. Configuration lines 19 and 20 in Figure 6-37 tie the subnetworks used for each specific interface into OSPF area 4.

The **show ip protocol** output in Figure 6-38 lets you see the detail of the routing processes.

The **show ip route** output in Figure 6-39 identifies the routes as connected, OSPF inter-area, or external type 2. The metric assigned to our external type 2 route on line 15 has a value of 20. This value was not specified during redistribution in New York, so we will need to investigate the New York configuration below.

Just to make sure that our route redistribution process is working properly, the **extended ping** command in Figure 6-40 was used to test the connection. The **extended ping** provides us with a variety of options to improve network testing and is initiated by entering the **ping** command at the privileged exec level without any options. If we use the standard options through line 6, the result is the same as if we

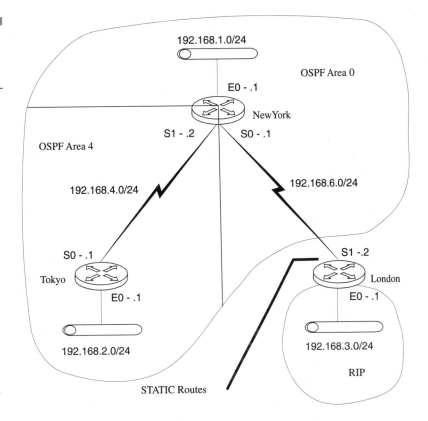

**Figure 6-36**
Redistributing RIP,
OSPF, and static
routes

192.168.1.0/24

OSPF Area 0

E0 - .1

New York

S1 - .2    S0 - .1

OSPF Area 4

192.168.4.0/24

192.168.6.0/24

S0 - .1

Tokyo

E0 - .1

S1 -.2

London

E0 - .1

192.168.2.0/24

192.168.3.0/24

RIP

STATIC Routes

typed **ping 192.168.3.1** on the command line. It is after line 7 where we specify the extended commands that the good stuff becomes available. At line 8, the command gives us the option of entering the source address to be used in the echo request packet. This IP address must be a valid IP address in use on an active router interface. If the source address used is on an interface that is not the exit interface used to reach the destination, then the packets used for pinging are sent through the IP routing table lookup process. When we get to line 13, we are asked if we wish to use several options. In this example, the option selected was **r** for Record. The **r** option records the pathway taken by the packet on its round trip to the destination. While this feature is great for short network distances, it records only up to nine connections starting with the first stop on its journey through the network. A sample of the output generated by one ping is shown in lines 20 through 24. Referring to Figure 6-36, we can trace the ping packet pathway (say that three times

**Figure 6-37**   Tokyo configuration

```
1  !
2  hostname Tokyo
3  !
4  no ip domain-lookup
5  !
6  interface Ethernet0
7   ip address 192.168.2.1 255.255.255.0
8   no ip route-cache
9   no ip mroute-cache
10 !
11 interface Serial0
12  ip address 192.168.4.1 255.255.255.0
13  no ip route-cache
14  no ip mroute-cache
15  bandwidth 125
16 !
17
18 router ospf 200
19  network 192.168.4.0 0.0.0.255 area 4
20  network 192.168.2.0 0.0.0.255 area 4
21 !
22 ip classless
23 !
24 line con 0
25  exec-timeout 0 0
26  length 0
27 !
28 end
```

quickly!) to the destination and back. The extended ping records the exit IP address of the device it leaves on the pathway to the next hop.

Finally, we have an example where something interesting happens in NewYork. NewYork is an Area Border Router between area 4 and area 0. In Figure 6-41, we have a connection via static route, line 25, to a network outside of the OSPF domain. NewYork is therefore an Autonomous System Border Router (see Chapter 5). In order to pass the route informa-

**Figure 6-38**   Tokyo **show ip protocol** output

```
1  Tokyo#sho ip prot
2  Routing Protocol is "ospf 200"
3    Sending updates every 0 seconds
4    Invalid after 0 seconds, hold down 0, flushed after 0
5    Outgoing update filter list for all interfaces is not set
6    Incoming update filter list for all interfaces is not set
7    Redistributing: ospf 200
8    Routing for Networks:
9      192.168.4.0
10     192.168.2.0
11   Routing Information Sources:
12     Gateway          Distance      Last Update
13     192.168.4.2          110       00:13:18
14   Distance: (default is 110)
```

**Figure 6-39** Tokyo **show ip route** output

```
1 Tokyo#sho ip route
2 Codes: C - connected, S - static, I - IGRP, R - RIP, M - mobile, B - BGP
3         D - EIGRP, EX - EIGRP external, O - OSPF, IA - OSPF inter area
4         N1 - OSPF NSSA external type 1, N2 - OSPF NSSA external type 2
5         E1 - OSPF external type 1, E2 - OSPF external type 2, E - EGP
6         i - IS-IS, L1 - IS-IS level-1, L2 - IS-IS level-2, * - candidate default
7         U - per-user static route, o - ODR
8
9 Gateway of last resort is not set
10
11 C    192.168.4.0/24 is directly connected, Serial0
12 O IA 192.168.6.0/24 [110/1562] via 192.168.4.2, 00:13:23, Serial0
13 O IA 192.168.1.0/24 [110/791] via 192.168.4.2, 00:13:23, Serial0
14 C    192.168.2.0/24 is directly connected, Ethernet0
15 O E2 192.168.3.0/24 [110/20] via 192.168.4.2, 00:13:23, Serial0
```

tion to the rest of our OSPF domain, the static route must be redistributed into OSPF. This is accomplished on line 19 of the configuration. We
have not defined a default metric for this redistribution, so the
192.168.3.0 route is distributed with an external type 2 metric of 20,
which is the default for directly connected or redistributed static routes.
Check out the **show ip route** output for Tokyo in Figure 6-39.

**Figure 6-40** Tokyo-to-London **ping** output

```
1 Tokyo#ping
2 Protocol [ip]:
3 Target IP address: 192.168.3.1
4 Repeat count [5]:
5 Datagram size [100]:
6 Timeout in seconds [2]:
7 Extended commands [n]: y
8 Source address or interface: 192.168.2.1
9 Type of service [0]:
10 Set DF bit in IP header? [no]:
11 Validate reply data? [no]:
12 Data pattern [0xABCD]:
13 Loose, Strict, Record, Timestamp, Verbose[none]: r
14 Number of hops [ 9 ]:
15 Loose, Strict, Record, Timestamp, Verbose[RV]:
16 Sweep range of sizes [n]:
17 Type escape sequence to abort.
18 Sending 5, 100-byte ICMP Echos to 192.168.3.1, timeout is 2 seconds:
19
20 Reply to request 0 (32 ms).  Received packet has options
21  Total option bytes= 40, padded length=40
22  Record route: 192.168.4.1 192.168.6.1 192.168.3.1 192.168.6.2
23          192.168.4.2 192.168.2.1  0.0.0.0 0.0.0.0 0.0.0.0
24  End of list
25
26 Success rate is 100 percent (5/5), round-trip min/avg/max = 32/35/36 ms
```

**Figure 6-41**   NewYork configuration

```
1 !
2 hostname NewYork
3 !
4 no ip domain-lookup
5 !
6 interface Ethernet0
7  ip address 192.168.1.1 255.255.255.0
8 !
9 interface Serial0
10  ip address 192.168.6.1 255.255.255.0
11  bandwidth 128
12 !
13 interface Serial1
14  ip address 192.168.4.2 255.255.255.0
15  bandwidth 128
16  clockrate 125000
17 !
18 router ospf 200
19  redistribute static
20  network 192.168.1.0 0.0.0.255 area 0
21  network 192.168.4.0 0.0.0.255 area 4
22  network 192.168.6.0 0.0.0.255 area 0
23 !
24 ip classless
25 ip route 192.168.3.0 255.255.255.0 192.168.6.2
26 !
27 line con 0
28  exec-timeout 0 0
29  length 0
30 !
31 end
```

**Figure 6-42**   NewYork **show ip protocol** output

```
1 NewYork#sho ip prot
2 Routing Protocol is "ospf 200"
3   Sending updates every 0 seconds
4   Invalid after 0 seconds, hold down 0, flushed after 0
5   Outgoing update filter list for all interfaces is not set
6   Incoming update filter list for all interfaces is not set
7   Redistributing: static, ospf 200
8   Routing for Networks:
9     192.168.1.0
10     192.168.4.0
11     192.168.6.0
12   Routing Information Sources:
13     Gateway         Distance      Last Update
14     192.168.4.1          110      00:17:12
15   Distance: (default is 110)
```

**Figure 6-43** NewYork **show ip route** output

```
1 NewYork#sho ip route
2 Codes: C - connected, S - static, I - IGRP, R - RIP, M - mobile, B - BGP
3        D - EIGRP, EX - EIGRP external, O - OSPF, IA - OSPF inter area
4        N1 - OSPF NSSA external type 1, N2 - OSPF NSSA external type 2
5        E1 - OSPF external type 1, E2 - OSPF external type 2, E - EGP
6        i - IS-IS, L1 - IS-IS level-1, L2 - IS-IS level-2, * - candidate default
7        U - per-user static route, o - ODR
8
9 Gateway of last resort is not set
10
11 C    192.168.4.0/24 is directly connected, Serial1
12 C    192.168.6.0/24 is directly connected, Serial0
13 C    192.168.1.0/24 is directly connected, Ethernet0
14 O    192.168.2.0/24 [110/791] via 192.168.4.1, 00:17:18, Serial1
15 S    192.168.3.0/24 [1/0] via 192.168.6.2
```

The **show ip protocol** command output in Figure 6-42 lets you see the detail of the routing processes. The only indication that route redistribution is occurring is in line 7. The IP routing protocol listed on this line is the source of the routing information used by the OSPF protocol to calculate the best pathway to destination networks.

The **show ip route** sample output in Figure 6-43 is fairly straightforward, but line 15 shows something interesting. The output for 192.168.3.0

**Figure 6-44** London configuration

```
1  !
2  hostname London
3  !
4  interface Ethernet0
5   ip address 192.168.3.1 255.255.255.0
6  !
7  interface Serial1
8   ip address 192.168.6.2 255.255.255.0
9   bandwidth 128
10  clockrate 125000
11 !
12 router rip
13  redistribute static
14  network 192.168.3.0
15 !
16 ip classless
17 ip route 192.168.1.0 255.255.255.0 192.168.6.1
18 ip route 192.168.2.0 255.255.255.0 192.168.6.1
19 !
20 line con 0
21  exec-timeout 0 0
22  length 0
23 !
24 end
```

**Figure 6-45**   London **debug** output

```
1 London#debug ip rip
2 RIP protocol debugging is on
3 London#
4 RIP: sending v1 update to 255.255.255.255 via Ethernet0 (192.168.3.1)
5     network 192.168.1.0, metric 1
6     network 192.168.2.0, metric 1
```

includes **[1/0]**, showing an Administrative Distance of one for a static route and a metric of zero.

London is still the most complex configuration in our test environment, see Figure 6-44, with redistribution taking place between RIP and the static routes to the OSPF Ethernet segments. If we are building a network for clients to access servers, then distributing route information about our WAN links serves no purpose and simply increases WAN overhead.

In the **debug ip rip** output in Figure 6-45, we send out updates for only the two Ethernet segments in our OSPF domain.

In the **show ip protocol** output in Figure 6-46, line 7 highlights the redistribution between RIP and static routes.

The **show ip route** output in Figure 6-47 details the directly connected and static routes known to London.

**Question #2: After reviewing all the information in Example #4, what would be the result of the following command: tokyo# ping 192.168.3.0?**

**Figure 6-46**   London **show ip protocol** output

```
1 London#sho ip prot
2 Routing Protocol is "rip"
3   Sending updates every 30 seconds, next due in 22 seconds
4   Invalid after 180 seconds, hold down 180, flushed after 240
5   Outgoing update filter list for all interfaces is not set
6   Incoming update filter list for all interfaces is not set
7   Redistributing: static, rip
8   Default version control: send version 1, receive any version
9     Interface        Send  Recv   Key-chain
10     Ethernet0        1      1 2
11   Routing for Networks:
12     192.168.3.0
13   Routing Information Sources:
14     Gateway         Distance     Last Update
15   Distance: (default is 120)
```

**Figure 6-47** London **show ip route** output

```
1 London#sho ip route
2 Codes: C - connected, S - static, I - IGRP, R - RIP, M - mobile, B - BGP
3        D - EIGRP, EX - EIGRP external, O - OSPF, IA - OSPF inter area
4        N1 - OSPF NSSA external type 1, N2 - OSPF NSSA external type 2
5        E1 - OSPF external type 1, E2 - OSPF external type 2, E - EGP
6        i - IS-IS, L1 - IS-IS level-1, L2 - IS-IS level-2, * - candidate default
7        U - per-user static route, o - ODR
8
9 Gateway of last resort is not set
10
11 C    192.168.6.0/24 is directly connected, Serial1
12 S    192.168.1.0/24 [1/0] via 192.168.6.1
13 S    192.168.2.0/24 [1/0] via 192.168.6.1
14 C    192.168.3.0/24 is directly connected, Ethernet0
```

# Example #5—IGRP & EIGRP, Same Autonomous Systems

In the following example Tokyo is running EIGRP 200, and both New York and London are running EIGRP 200 and IGRP 200. There is automatic route redistribution between EIGRP and IGRP if both protocols are using the same Autonomous System number. You may be surprised at the results when we take a look at the routing tables. Figure 6-48 is the network layout used in this example.

Tokyo is located in the interior of the EIGRP 200 cloud. The configuration in Figure 6-49 is straightforward, with lines 16 through 19 detailing the routing protocol and the network statements that tie all three interfaces into EIGRP 200.

Nothing new here, basic IP routing processes show up in our **show ip protocol** output in Figure 6-50.

In Figure 6-51, the **show ip route** output shows us all our networks, with our IGRP 200 networks showing up in lines 13, 14, and 17. Referring back to our network layout in Figure 6-48, 192.168.6.0 appears to be equidistant from Tokyo. The route to 192.168.6.0 on lines 13 and 14 shows two possible routes through the two serial ports. Lines 13 and 14 include **[170/46226176]**, **170** is the Administrative Distance assigned to external routes redistributed into EIGRP, and **46226176** is the metric derived during normal metric calculation, plus the automatic redistribution process between IGRP and EIGRP.

When a **ping 192.168.6.1** command is issued, we get some very

**Figure 6-48**
Redistributing IGRP
and EIGRP, same
Autonomous System

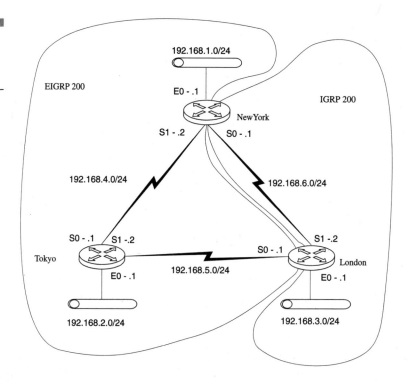

**Figure 6-49**    Tokyo configuration

```
1  !
2  hostname Tokyo
3  !
4  no ip domain-lookup
5  !
6  interface Ethernet0
7    ip address 192.168.2.1 255.255.255.0
8  !
9  interface Serial0
10   ip address 192.168.4.1 255.255.255.0
11 !
12 interface Serial1
13   ip address 192.168.5.2 255.255.255.0
14   clockrate 56000
15 !
16 router eigrp 200
17   network 192.168.2.0
18   network 192.168.4.0
19   network 192.168.5.0
20 !
21 ip classless
22 !
23 line con 0
24   exec-timeout 0 0
25   length 0
26 !
27 end
```

**Figure 6-50** Tokyo **show ip protocol** output

```
1  Tokyo#sho ip prot
2  Routing Protocol is "eigrp 200"
3    Outgoing update filter list for all interfaces is not set
4    Incoming update filter list for all interfaces is not set
5    Default networks flagged in outgoing updates
6    Default networks accepted from incoming updates
7    EIGRP metric weight K1=1, K2=0, K3=1, K4=0, K5=0
8    EIGRP maximum hopcount 100
9    EIGRP maximum metric variance 1
10   Redistributing: eigrp 200
11   Automatic network summarization is in effect
12   Automatic address summarization:
13     192.168.4.0/24 for Ethernet0, Serial1
14     192.168.2.0/24 for Serial0, Serial1
15     192.168.5.0/24 for Ethernet0, Serial0
16   Routing for Networks:
17     192.168.2.0
18     192.168.4.0
19     192.168.5.0
20   Routing Information Sources:
21     Gateway         Distance      Last Update
22     192.168.5.1           90      00:01:20
23     192.168.4.2           90      00:01:20
24   Distance: internal 90 external 170
```

strange results, see Figure 6-52. Instead of following a single pathway to reach 192.168.1, **ping** tries to reach 192.168.6.1 by going to both New York and London. IP path processing in the Cisco routers performs packet-by-packet load sharing across multiple equal pathways when the router initiates IP communications. In fact, while it shows the trace responses end after the first try, only the second attempt on line 13 actually reaches

**Figure 6-51** Tokyo **show ip route** output

```
1  Tokyo#sho ip route
2  Codes: C - connected, S - static, I - IGRP, R - RIP, M - mobile, B - BGP
3         D - EIGRP, EX - EIGRP external, O - OSPF, IA - OSPF inter area
4         N1 - OSPF NSSA external type 1, N2 - OSPF NSSA external type 2
5         E1 - OSPF external type 1, E2 - OSPF external type 2, E - EGP
6         i - IS-IS, L1 - IS-IS level-1, L2 - IS-IS level-2, * - candidate default
7         U - per-user static route, o - ODR
8
9  Gateway of last resort is not set
10
11 C    192.168.4.0/24 is directly connected, Serial0
12 C    192.168.5.0/24 is directly connected, Serial1
13 D EX 192.168.6.0/24 [170/46226176] via 192.168.4.2, 00:01:28, Serial0
14                     [170/46226176] via 192.168.5.1, 00:01:28, Serial1
15 D    192.168.1.0/24 [90/46251776] via 192.168.4.2, 00:01:28, Serial0
16 C    192.168.2.0/24 is directly connected, Ethernet0
17 D EX 192.168.3.0/24 [170/46226176] via 192.168.5.1, 00:01:28, Serial1
```

**Figure 6-52**   Tokyo-to-London **ping** output

```
1 Tokyo#ping 192.168.6.1
2
3 Type escape sequence to abort.
4 Sending 5, 100-byte ICMP Echos to 192.168.6.1, timeout is 2 seconds:
5 !!!!!
6 Success rate is 100 percent (5/5), round-trip min/avg/max = 32/40/52 ms
7 Tokyo#trace 192.168.6.1
8
9 Type escape sequence to abort.
10 Tracing the route to 192.168.6.1
11
12   1 192.168.5.1 16 msec
13     192.168.4.2 16 msec
14     192.168.5.1 16 msec
```

**Figure 6-53**   NewYork configuration

```
1 !
2 hostname NewYork
3 !
4 no ip domain-lookup
5 !
6 interface Ethernet0
7  ip address 192.168.1.1 255.255.255.0
8 !
9 interface Serial0
10  ip address 192.168.6.1 255.255.255.0
11  bandwidth 56
12 !
13 interface Serial1
14  ip address 192.168.4.2 255.255.255.0
15  clockrate 56000
16  bandwidth 56
17 !
18 router eigrp 200
19  network 192.168.1.0
20  network 192.168.4.0
21 !
22 router igrp 200
23  network 192.168.6.0
24 !
25 ip classless
26 !
27 line con 0
28 exec-timeout 0 0
29 length 0
30 !
31 end
```

the device where 192.168.1.1 exists. The other two trace steps on lines 12 and 14 end in the first step along the path, London, but do not actually reach the target of 192.168.6.1.

The New York configuration in Figure 6-53 has no special redistribution commands, but lines 18 and 22 show both IGRP and EIGRP processes with the same Autonomous System number, 200. This is the mechanism that Cisco uses to trigger automatic redistribution.

The **show ip protocol** output in Figure 6-54 has very little to indicate that redistribution is occurring: only lines 10 and 33.

**Figure 6-54** NewYork **show ip protocol** output

```
1 NewYork#sho ip protocol
2 Routing Protocol is "eigrp 200"
3   Outgoing update filter list for all interfaces is not set
4   Incoming update filter list for all interfaces is not set
5   Default networks flagged in outgoing updates
6   Default networks accepted from incoming updates
7   EIGRP metric weight K1=1, K2=0, K3=1, K4=0, K5=0
8   EIGRP maximum hopcount 100
9   EIGRP maximum metric variance 1
10  Redistributing: eigrp 200, igrp 200
11  Automatic network summarization is in effect
12  Automatic address summarization:
13    192.168.4.0/24 for Ethernet0
14    192.168.1.0/24 for Serial1
15  Routing for Networks:
16    192.168.1.0
17    192.168.4.0
18  Routing Information Sources:
19    Gateway          Distance        Last Update
20    192.168.4.1           90         00:16:13
21  Distance: internal 90 external 170
22
23 Routing Protocol is "igrp 200"
24  Sending updates every 90 seconds, next due in 54 seconds
25  Invalid after 270 seconds, hold down 280, flushed after 630
26  Outgoing update filter list for all interfaces is not set
27  Incoming update filter list for all interfaces is not set
28  Default networks flagged in outgoing updates
29  Default networks accepted from incoming updates
30  IGRP metric weight K1=1, K2=0, K3=1, K4=0, K5=0
31  IGRP maximum hopcount 100
32  IGRP maximum metric variance 1
33  Redistributing: eigrp 200, igrp 200
34  Routing for Networks:
35    192.168.6.0
36  Routing Information Sources:
37    Gateway          Distance        Last Update
38    192.168.6.2          100         00:00:17
39  Distance: (default is 100)
```

**Figure 6-55**   NewYork **show ip route** output

```
 1 NewYork#sho ip route
 2 Codes: C - connected, S - static, I - IGRP, R - RIP, M - mobile, B - BGP
 3        D - EIGRP, EX - EIGRP external, O - OSPF, IA - OSPF inter area
 4        N1 - OSPF NSSA external type 1, N2 - OSPF NSSA external type 2
 5        E1 - OSPF external type 1, E2 - OSPF external type 2, E - EGP
 6        i - IS-IS, L1 - IS-IS level-1, L2 - IS-IS level-2, * - candidate default
 7        U - per-user static route, o - ODR
 8
 9 Gateway of last resort is not set
10
11 C    192.168.4.0/24 is directly connected, Serial1
12 D    192.168.5.0/24 [90/46738176] via 192.168.4.1, 00:05:14, Serial1
13 C    192.168.6.0/24 is directly connected, Serial0
14 C    192.168.1.0/24 is directly connected, Ethernet0
15 D    192.168.2.0/24 [90/46251776] via 192.168.4.1, 00:05:14, Serial1
16 I    192.168.3.0/24 [100/180671] via 192.168.6.2, 00:00:23, Serial0
```

**Figure 6-56**   London configuration

```
 1 !
 2 hostname London
 3 !
 4 no ip domain-lookup
 5 !
 6 interface Ethernet0
 7   ip address 192.168.3.1 255.255.255.0
 8 !
 9 interface Serial0
10   ip address 192.168.5.1 255.255.255.0
11   bandwidth 56
12 !
13 interface Serial1
14 ip address 192.168.6.2 255.255.255.0
15 clockrate 56000
16 bandwidth 56
17 !
18 router eigrp 200
19   network 192.168.5.0
20 !
21 router igrp 200
22   network 192.168.6.0
23   network 192.168.3.0
24 !
25 ip classless
26 !
27 line con 0
28   exec-timeout 0 0
29   length 0
30 !
31 end
```

**Figure 6-57** London **debug** output

```
1 London#debug ip igrp events
2 IGRP event debugging is on
3 London#debug ip igrp transactions
4 IGRP protocol debugging is on
5 London#
6 IGRP: sending update to 255.255.255.255 via Serial1 (192.168.6.2)
7 IGRP: Update contains 0 interior, 5 system, and 0 exterior routes.
8 IGRP: Total routes in update: 5
9 IGRP: received update from 192.168.6.1 on Serial1
10       network 192.168.4.0, metric 182571 (neighbor 180571)
11       network 192.168.5.0, metric 184571 (neighbor 182571)
12       network 192.168.1.0, metric 180671 (neighbor 1100)
13       network 192.168.2.0, metric 182671 (neighbor 180671)
14 IGRP: Update contains 0 interior, 4 system, and 0 exterior routes.
15 IGRP: Total routes in update: 4
16 IGRP: sending update to 255.255.255.255 via Ethernet0 (192.168.3.1)
17       network 192.168.4.0, metric=182571
18       network 192.168.5.0, metric=180571
19       network 192.168.6.0, metric=180571
20       network 192.168.1.0, metric=182671
21       network 192.168.2.0, metric=180671
22 IGRP: Update contains 0 interior, 5 system, and 0 exterior routes.
23 IGRP: Total routes in update: 5
```

FYI: This has implications specifically related to TCP/IP encapsulation functions. If an external network is redistributed into EIGRP and there are two equal pathways to the destination network, it does not mean that there are going to be equal transit times for the packets following different pathways. In Example #5, the fastest pathway to our target address of 192.168.6.1 is through New York, but the fastest pathway to network 192.168.6.0 is equal through London and New York. A simple solution would be individual host routes, but that would be exactly the same individual addressing that was used in a bridged environment, which was why routers were created—to provide group addresses. Just be aware of this feature in the Cisco routers.

The **show ip route** output in Figure 6-55 shows directly connected EIGRP and IGRP routes.

London, like New York, has two routing protocols operating, IGRP, and EIGRP, but again, no special redistribution commands. See lines 18 through 23 in Figure 6-56.

To verify that the EIGRP routes are being propagated to the IGRP domain, sample **debug** output is shown in Figure 6-57. Lines 16 through

**Figure 6-58** London **show ip protocol** output

```
1 London#sho ip prot
2 Routing Protocol is "eigrp 200"
3   Outgoing update filter list for all interfaces is not set
4   Incoming update filter list for all interfaces is not set
5   Default networks flagged in outgoing updates
6   Default networks accepted from incoming updates
7   EIGRP metric weight K1=1, K2=0, K3=1, K4=0, K5=0
8   EIGRP maximum hopcount 100
9   EIGRP maximum metric variance 1
10  Redistributing: eigrp 200, igrp 200
11  Automatic network summarization is in effect
12  Routing for Networks:
13    192.168.5.0
14  Routing Information Sources:
15    Gateway         Distance      Last Update
16    192.168.5.2           90      00:11:17
17  Distance: internal 90 external 170
18
19 Routing Protocol is "igrp 200"
20  Sending updates every 90 seconds, next due in 20 seconds
21  Invalid after 270 seconds, hold down 280, flushed after 630
22  Outgoing update filter list for all interfaces is not set
23  Incoming update filter list for all interfaces is not set
24  Default networks flagged in outgoing updates
25  Default networks accepted from incoming updates
26  IGRP metric weight K1=1, K2=0, K3=1, K4=0, K5=0
27  IGRP maximum hopcount 100
28  IGRP maximum metric variance 1
29  Redistributing: eigrp 200, igrp 200
30  Routing for Networks:
31    192.168.6.0
32    192.168.3.0
33  Routing Information Sources:
34    Gateway         Distance      Last Update
35    192.168.6.1          100      00:00:47
36  Distance: (default is 100)
```

**Figure 6-59** London **show ip route** output

```
1 London#sho ip route
2 Codes: C - connected, S - static, I - IGRP, R - RIP, M - mobile, B - BGP
3        D - EIGRP, EX - EIGRP external, O - OSPF, IA - OSPF inter area
4        N1 - OSPF NSSA external type 1, N2 - OSPF NSSA external type 2
5        E1 - OSPF external type 1, E2 - OSPF external type 2, E - EGP
6        i - IS-IS, L1 - IS-IS level-1, L2 - IS-IS level-2, * - candidate default
7        U - per-user static route, o - ODR
8
9 Gateway of last resort is not set
10
11 D    192.168.4.0/24 [90/46738176] via 192.168.5.2, 00:11:21, Serial0
12 C    192.168.5.0/24 is directly connected, Serial0
13 C    192.168.6.0/24 is directly connected, Serial1
14 D    192.168.1.0/24 [90/46763776] via 192.168.5.2, 00:11:20, Serial0
15 D    192.168.2.0/24 [90/46251776] via 192.168.5.2, 00:11:22, Serial0
16 C    192.168.3.0/24 is directly connected, Ethernet0
```

21 show the IGRP transaction that announces all of our routes in the network out the Ethernet port on network 192.168.3.0.

The **show ip protocol** output in Figure 6-58 shows us the automatic route redistribution in lines 10 and 29.

All networks in the **show ip route** output in Figure 6-59 are either directly connected or derived from EIGRP.

## Example #6—IGRP & EIGRP, Different Autonomous Systems

In this example, the redistribution of routes between IGRP and EIGRP is treated differently, as there are two different Autonomous Systems involved. Figure 6-60 is the network layout for this example.

The Tokyo configuration in Figure 6-61 is plain vanilla. EIGRP 200 ties in all our interfaces.

Nothing special when we look at the routing process in the **show ip protocol** output in Figure 6-62.

Based on the network layout for this example, an examination of Tokyo's routing table using **show ip route** in Figure 6-63 should show that networks 192.168.3.0 and 192.168.6.0 are outside the EIGRP 200 domain. Lines 12 and 15 show exactly that. With EIGRP, the default redistribution metric is used as the starting point for calculating the shortest path to all external routes. As we extend these external routes, the additional metric values of the media being traversed is added to the redistributed metric. Look at the metrics assigned to our two external networks on lines 12 and 15, 192.168.6.0 is 2195456 and 192.168.3.0 is 21529600, an order-of-magnitude difference. If we look at the redistribution commands for New York, it appears that both networks being redistributed from the IGRP routing protocol should in fact have the *same* metric. However, EIGRP has detected that 192.168.6.0 is directly connected to the New York router and substituted the metric of zero, as directly connected network routes are preferred over dynamic routing protocols. There is a specific command, redistribute connected, that will produce the same results in a situation in which no other redistribution is taking place for the specified routing protocol.

To verify that redistribution is working properly, the **ping** command is executed in Figure 6-64.

The New York configuration in Figure 6-65 details the redistribution

**Figure 6-60**
Redistributing IGRP
and EIGRP, different
Autonomous Systems

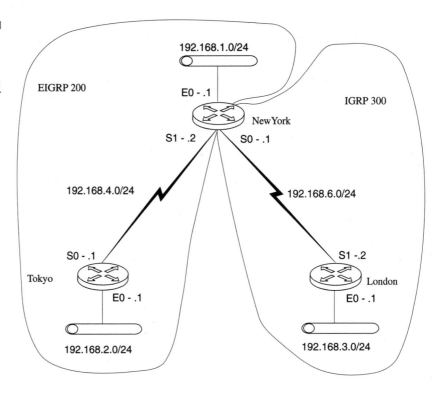

**Figure 6-61** Tokyo configuration

```
1  !
2  hostname Tokyo
3  !
4  no ip domain-lookup
5  !
6  interface Ethernet0
7    ip address 192.168.2.1 255.255.255.0
8  !
9  interface Serial0
10   ip address 192.168.4.1 255.255.255.0
11   bandwidth 125
12 !
13 router eigrp 200
14   network 192.168.2.0
15   network 192.168.4.0
16 !
17 ip classless
18 !
19 line con 0
20   exec-timeout 0 0
21   length 0
22 !
23 end
```

**Figure 6-62** Tokyo **show ip protocol** output

```
1 Tokyo#sho ip prot
2 Routing Protocol is "eigrp 200"
3   Outgoing update filter list for all interfaces is not set
4   Incoming update filter list for all interfaces is not set
5   Default networks flagged in outgoing updates
6   Default networks accepted from incoming updates
7   EIGRP metric weight K1=1, K2=0, K3=1, K4=0, K5=0
8   EIGRP maximum hopcount 100
9   EIGRP maximum metric variance 1
10   Redistributing: eigrp 200
11   Automatic network summarization is in effect
12   Automatic address summarization:
13     192.168.4.0/24 for Ethernet0
14     192.168.2.0/24 for Serial0
15   Routing for Networks:
16     192.168.2.0
17     192.168.4.0
18   Routing Information Sources:
19     Gateway          Distance      Last Update
20     192.168.4.2           90        00:05:43
21   Distance: internal 90 external 170
```

process. A generic default-metric can be defined for all protocols being redistributed as in lines 23 and 28. All redistributed routes are assigned this default-metric but can be overridden by using the metric option on the **redistribute** command.

The **show ip protocol** output in Figure 6-66 provides our redistribution confirmation on lines 11 and 35.

The **show ip route** output in Figure 6-67 identifies the three types

**Figure 6-63** Tokyo **show ip route** output

```
1 Tokyo#sho ip route
2 Codes: C - connected, S - static, I - IGRP, R - RIP, M - mobile, B - BGP
3        D - EIGRP, EX - EIGRP external, O - OSPF, IA - OSPF inter area
4        N1 - OSPF NSSA external type 1, N2 - OSPF NSSA external type 2
5        E1 - OSPF external type 1, E2 - OSPF external type 2, E - EGP
6        i - IS-IS, L1 - IS-IS level-1, L2 - IS-IS level-2, * - candidate default
7        U - per-user static route, o - ODR
8
9 Gateway of last resort is not set
10
11 C    192.168.4.0/24 is directly connected, Serial0
12 D EX 192.168.6.0/24 [170/2169856] via 192.168.4.2, 00:05:52, Serial0
13 D    192.168.1.0/24 [90/2195456] via 192.168.4.2, 00:17:36, Serial0
14 C    192.168.2.0/24 is directly connected, Ethernet0
15 D EX 192.168.3.0/24 [170/21529600] via 192.168.4.2, 00:05:51, Serial0
```

**Figure 6-64**  Tokyo-to-London **ping** output

```
1 Tokyo#ping 192.168.3.1
2
3 Type escape sequence to abort.
4 Sending 5, 100-byte ICMP Echos to 192.168.3.1, timeout is 2 seconds:
5 !!!!!
6 Success rate is 100 percent (5/5), round-trip min/avg/max = 48/48/52 ms
```

of route sources—directly connected, EIGRP, and IGRP—in lines 11 through 15.

The London configuration in Figure 6-68 is just your basic IGRP routing process for both attached networks.

Just to test out the network, we turned on IGRP debugging and

**Figure 6-65**  NewYork configuration

```
1 !
2 hostname NewYork
3 !
4 no ip domain-lookup
5 !
6 interface Ethernet0
7  ip address 192.168.1.1 255.255.255.0
8 !
9 interface Serial0
10  ip address 192.168.6.1 255.255.255.0
11  bandwidth 125
12  no fair-queue
13 !
14 interface Serial1
15  ip address 192.168.4.2 255.255.255.0
16  bandwidth 125
17  clockrate 125000
18 !
19 router eigrp 200
20  redistribute igrp 300
21  network 192.168.1.0
22  network 192.168.4.0
23  default-metric 125 1000 255 1 1500
24 !
25 router igrp 300
26  redistribute eigrp 200
27  network 192.168.6.0
28  default-metric 125 1000 255 1 1500
29 !
30 ip classless
31 !
32 line con 0
33  exec-timeout 0 0
34  length 0
35 !
36 end
```

**Figure 6-66** NewYork **show ip protocol** output

```
1 NewYork#sho ip prot
2 Routing Protocol is "eigrp 200"
3   Outgoing update filter list for all interfaces is not set
4   Incoming update filter list for all interfaces is not set
5   Default networks flagged in outgoing updates
6   Default networks accepted from incoming updates
7   EIGRP metric weight K1=1, K2=0, K3=1, K4=0, K5=0
8   EIGRP maximum hopcount 100
9   EIGRP maximum metric variance 1
10   Default redistribution metric is 125 1000 255 1 1500
11   Redistributing: eigrp 200, igrp 300
12   Automatic network summarization is in effect
13   Automatic address summarization:
14     192.168.4.0/24 for Ethernet0
15     192.168.1.0/24 for Serial1
16   Routing for Networks:
17     192.168.1.0
18     192.168.4.0
19   Routing Information Sources:
20     Gateway          Distance        Last Update
21     192.168.4.1           90         00:17:13
22   Distance: internal 90 external 170
23
24 Routing Protocol is "igrp 300"
25   Sending updates every 90 seconds, next due in 33 seconds
26   Invalid after 270 seconds, hold down 280, flushed after 630
27   Outgoing update filter list for all interfaces is not set
28   Incoming update filter list for all interfaces is not set
29   Default networks flagged in outgoing updates
30   Default networks accepted from incoming updates
31   IGRP metric weight K1=1, K2=0, K3=1, K4=0, K5=0
32   IGRP maximum hopcount 100
33   IGRP maximum metric variance 1
34   Default redistribution metric is 125 1000 255 1 1500
35   Redistributing: eigrp 200, igrp 300
36   Routing for Networks:
37     192.168.6.0
38   Routing Information Sources:
39     Gateway          Distance        Last Update
40     192.168.6.2          100         00:00:35
41   Distance: (default is 100)
```

**Figure 6-67** NewYork **show ip route** output

```
1 NewYork#sho ip route
2 Codes: C - connected, S - static, I - IGRP, R - RIP, M - mobile, B - BGP
3        D - EIGRP, EX - EIGRP external, O - OSPF, IA - OSPF inter area
4        N1 - OSPF NSSA external type 1, N2 - OSPF NSSA external type 2
5        E1 - OSPF external type 1, E2 - OSPF external type 2, E - EGP
6        i - IS-IS, L1 - IS-IS level-1, L2 - IS-IS level-2, * - candidate default
7        U - per-user static route, o - ODR
8
9 Gateway of last resort is not set
10
11 C    192.168.4.0/24 is directly connected, Serial1
12 C    192.168.6.0/24 is directly connected, Serial0
13 C    192.168.1.0/24 is directly connected, Ethernet0
14 D    192.168.2.0/24 [90/21017600] via 192.168.4.1, 00:21:39, Serial1
15 I    192.168.3.0/24 [100/82100] via 192.168.6.2, 00:00:41, Serial0
```

**Figure 6-68**  London configuration

```
1  !
2  hostname London
3  !
4  no ip domain-lookup
5  !
6  interface Ethernet0
7   ip address 192.168.3.1 255.255.255.0
8  !
9  interface Serial1
10   ip address 192.168.6.2 255.255.255.0
11   clockrate 125000
12   bandwidth 125
13  !
14  router igrp 300
15   network 192.168.3.0
16   network 192.168.6.0
17  !
18  ip classless
19  !
20  line con 0
21   exec-timeout 0 0
22   length 0
23  !
24  end
```

**Figure 6-69**  London **debug** and **ping** output

```
1  London#debug ip igrp ev
2  IGRP event debugging is on
3  London#debug ip igrp tr
4  IGRP protocol debugging is on
5  London#
6  IGRP: received update from 192.168.6.1 on Serial1
7       network 192.168.4.0, metric 84000 (neighbor 82000)
8       network 192.168.1.0, metric 8576 (neighbor 1100)
9       network 192.168.2.0, metric 84100 (neighbor 82100)
10  IGRP: Update contains 0 interior, 3 system, and 0 exterior routes.
11  IGRP: Total routes in update: 3
12  IGRP: sending update to 255.255.255.255 via Ethernet0 (192.168.3.1)
13       network 192.168.4.0, metric=84000
14       network 192.168.6.0, metric=8476
15       network 192.168.1.0, metric=8576
16       network 192.168.2.0, metric=84100
17  IGRP: Update contains 0 interior, 4 system, and 0 exterior routes.
18  IGRP: Total routes in update: 4
19  IGRP: sending update to 255.255.255.255 via Serial1 (192.168.6.2)
20       network 192.168.3.0, metric=1100
21  IGRP: Update contains 0 interior, 1 system, and 0 exterior routes.
22  IGRP: Total routes in update: 1
23  London#ping 192.168.2.1
24
25  Type escape sequence to abort.
26  Sending 5, 100-byte ICMP Echos to 192.168.2.1, timeout is 2 seconds:
27  !!!!!
28  Success rate is 100 percent (5/5), round-trip min/avg/max = 48/49/52 ms
29  London#undeb all
```

**Figure 6-70**   London **show ip protocol** output

```
1 London#sho ip prot
2 Routing Protocol is "igrp 300"
3   Sending updates every 90 seconds, next due in 62 seconds
4   Invalid after 270 seconds, hold down 280, flushed after 630
5   Outgoing update filter list for all interfaces is not set
6   Incoming update filter list for all interfaces is not set
7   Default networks flagged in outgoing updates
8   Default networks accepted from incoming updates
9   IGRP metric weight K1=1, K2=0, K3=1, K4=0, K5=0
10   IGRP maximum hopcount 100
11   IGRP maximum metric variance 1
12   Redistributing: igrp 300
13   Routing for Networks:
14     192.168.3.0
15     192.168.6.0
16   Routing Information Sources:
17     Gateway         Distance      Last Update
18     192.168.6.1          100      00:00:41
19   Distance: (default is 100)
```

pinged Tokyo to verify our redistribution process. Lines 12 through 16 in Figure 6-69 show our Ethernet 0 interface as the recipient of a complete route table. Lines 23 through 28 show our successful **ping** operation to test our Tokyo connection.

Basics again, the London **show ip protocol** in Figure 6-70 shows our basic IGRP routing process.

The **show ip route** output in Figure 6-71 correctly contains all the routes in our network, but again, an anomaly appears in our routing table. If both 192.168.4.0 and 192.168.3.0 are being redistributed into IGRP with the same default-metric, then how are they showing up with different metrics on lines 11 and 14? It is obvious that EIGRP and IGRP are closely bonded together, and while they need the default-metric command to trigger the redistribution, these two protocols also interact even if they are in different autonomous systems.

**Figure 6-71**   London **show ip route** output

```
1 London#sho ip route
2 Codes: C - connected, S - static, I - IGRP, R - RIP, M - mobile, B - BGP
3        D - EIGRP, EX - EIGRP external, O - OSPF, IA - OSPF inter area
4        N1 - OSPF NSSA external type 1, N2 - OSPF NSSA external type 2
5        E1 - OSPF external type 1, E2 - OSPF external type 2, E - EGP
6        i - IS-IS, L1 - IS-IS level-1, L2 - IS-IS level-2, * - candidate default
7        U - per-user static route, o - ODR
8
9 Gateway of last resort is not set
10
11 I    192.168.4.0/24 [100/84000] via 192.168.6.1, 00:00:43, Serial1
12 C    192.168.6.0/24 is directly connected, Serial1
13 I    192.168.1.0/24 [100/8576] via 192.168.6.1, 00:00:44, Serial1
14 I    192.168.2.0/24 [100/84100] via 192.168.6.1, 00:00:44, Serial1
15 C    192.168.3.0/24 is directly connected, Ethernet0
```

## Example #7—IGRP & OSPF

In this example, we will connect together an IGRP domain to an OSPF domain. Instead of sending all networks in the OSPF cloud to the IGRP domain, we will use the **distribute-list** command to limit the number of networks advertised. See Figure 6-72 for our network layout. End users in the IGRP 200 domain need access to servers on the LAN segments, no need to access the WAN segments.

The Tokyo configuration in Figure 6-73 shows an internal OSPF router in area 4.

The **show ip protocol** output in Figure 6-74 identifies the two networks in area 4 and our two OSPF routers that are providing updates

The **show ip route** output in Figure 6-75 shows directly connected and inter-area OSPF routes, and an external type 1 route from our IGRP domain. In OSPF, a type 1 external route adds the calculated metrics of each step from the distribution point to the base redistribution value. If

**Figure 6-72**

Redistributing IGRP and OSPF

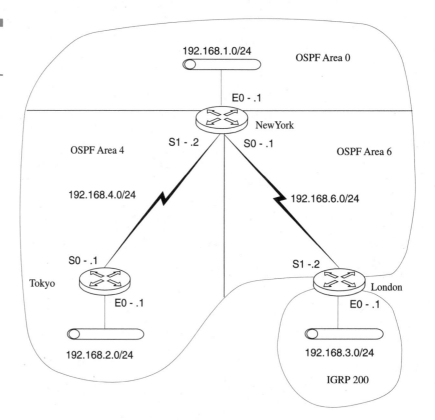

**Figure 6-73**  Tokyo configuration

```
1  !
2  hostname Tokyo
3  !
4  no ip domain-lookup
5  !
6  interface Ethernet0
7   ip address 192.168.2.1 255.255.255.0
8  !
9  interface Serial0
10  ip address 192.168.4.1 255.255.255.0
11  bandwidth 125
12 !
13 interface Serial1
14  no ip address
15  bandwidth 125
16  shutdown
17  clockrate 125000
18 !
19 router ospf 200
20  network 192.168.2.0 0.0.0.255 area 4
21  network 192.168.4.0 0.0.0.255 area 4
22 !
23 ip classless
24 !
25 line con 0
26  exec-timeout 0 0
27  length 0
28 !
29 end
```

there are multiple redistribution points, then using different redistribution values can assist you during the troubleshooting process by making route sources immediately obvious.

The **ping** output in Figure 6-76 provides proof of the end-to-end connectivity in the sample network.

The NewYork configuration in Figure 6-77 shows an OSPF Area Border Router tying together our area zero backbone and areas 4 and 6 in lines 18 through 21.

The **show ip protocol** output in Figure 6-78 identifies the networks participating in the OSPF process.

The **show ip route** output in Figure 6-79 shows the directly connected, OSPF derived, and the external type 1 from our IGRP domain. Refer to Figure 6-72 for the network layout, and then look at the routes in lines 14 and 15. According to our network layout, the two networks 192.168.2.0 and 192.168.3.0 should be equidistant from NewYork.

**Figure 6-74** Tokyo **show ip protocol** output

```
1  Tokyo#sho ip prot
2  Routing Protocol is "ospf 200"
3    Sending updates every 0 seconds
4    Invalid after 0 seconds, hold down 0, flushed after 0
5    Outgoing update filter list for all interfaces is not set
6    Incoming update filter list for all interfaces is not set
7    Redistributing: ospf 200
8    Routing for Networks:
9      192.168.2.0
10       192.168.4.0
11   Routing Information Sources:
12     Gateway           Distance      Last Update
13       192.168.6.2          110      00:01:11
14       192.168.4.2          110      00:04:55
15   Distance: (default is 110)
```

**Figure 6-75** Tokyo **show ip route** output

```
1  Tokyo#sho ip route
 2 Codes: C - connected, S - static, I - IGRP, R - RIP, M - mobile, B - BGP
 3        D - EIGRP, EX - EIGRP external, O - OSPF, IA - OSPF inter area
 4        N1 - OSPF NSSA external type 1, N2 - OSPF NSSA external type 2
 5        E1 - OSPF external type 1, E2 - OSPF external type 2, E - EGP
 6        i - IS-IS, L1 - IS-IS level-1, L2 - IS-IS level-2, * - candidate default
 7        U - per-user static route, o - ODR
 8
 9 Gateway of last resort is not set
10
11 C    192.168.4.0/24 is directly connected, Serial0
12 O IA 192.168.6.0/24 [110/1600] via 192.168.4.2, 00:05:00, Serial0
13 O IA 192.168.1.0/24 [110/810] via 192.168.4.2, 00:05:00, Serial0
14 C    192.168.2.0/24 is directly connected, Ethernet0
15 O E1 192.168.3.0/24 [110/1797] via 192.168.4.2, 00:01:16, Serial0
```

**Figure 6-76** Tokyo-to-London **ping** and **trace** output

```
1  Tokyo#ping 192.168.3.1
2
3  Type escape sequence to abort.
4  Sending 5, 100-byte ICMP Echos to 192.168.3.1, timeout is 2 seconds:
5  !!!!!
6  Success rate is 100 percent (5/5), round-trip min/avg/max = 32/35/48 ms
7  Tokyo#trace 192.168.3.1
8
9  Type escape sequence to abort.
10 Tracing the route to 192.168.3.1
11
12   1 192.168.4.2 12 msec 12 msec 12 msec
13   2 192.168.6.2 16 msec *  16 msec
```

**Figure 6-77**    NewYork configuration

```
1  !
2  hostname NewYork
3  !
4  no ip domain-lookup
5  !
6  interface Ethernet0
7    ip address 192.168.1.1 255.255.255.0
8  !
9  interface Serial0
10   ip address 192.168.6.1 255.255.255.0
11   bandwidth 125
12 !
13 interface Serial1
14   ip address 192.168.4.2 255.255.255.0
15   bandwidth 125
16   clockrate 125000
17 !
18 router ospf 200
19   network 192.168.6.0 0.0.0.255 area 6
20   network 192.168.1.0 0.0.0.255 area 0
21   network 192.168.4.0 0.0.0.255 area 4
22 !
23 ip classless
24 !
25 line con 0
26   exec-timeout 0 0
27   length 0
28 !
29 end
```

**Figure 6-78**    NewYork **show ip protocol** output

```
1  NewYork#sho ip prot
2  Routing Protocol is "ospf 200"
3    Sending updates every 0 seconds
4    Invalid after 0 seconds, hold down 0, flushed after 0
5    Outgoing update filter list for all interfaces is not set
6    Incoming update filter list for all interfaces is not set
7    Redistributing: ospf 200
8    Routing for Networks:
9      192.168.6.0
10     192.168.1.0
11     192.168.4.0
12   Routing Information Sources:
13     Gateway        Distance      Last Update
14     192.168.6.2        110       00:02:07
15     192.168.4.1        110       00:06:37
16   Distance: (default is 110)
17
```

**Figure 6-79** NewYork **show ip route** output

```
1 NewYork#sho ip route
2 Codes: C - connected, S - static, I - IGRP, R - RIP, M - mobile, B - BGP
3        D - EIGRP, EX - EIGRP external, O - OSPF, IA - OSPF inter area
4        N1 - OSPF NSSA external type 1, N2 - OSPF NSSA external type 2
5        E1 - OSPF external type 1, E2 - OSPF external type 2, E - EGP
6        i - IS-IS, L1 - IS-IS level-1, L2 - IS-IS level-2, * - candidate default
7        U - per-user static route, o - ODR
8
9 Gateway of last resort is not set
10
11 C    192.168.4.0/24 is directly connected, Serial1
12 C    192.168.6.0/24 is directly connected, Serial0
13 C    192.168.1.0/24 is directly connected, Ethernet0
14 O    192.168.2.0/24 [110/810] via 192.168.4.1, 00:06:43, Serial1
15 O E1 192.168.3.0/24 [110/997] via 192.168.6.2, 00:02:13, Serial0
```

Several interesting commands are taking place in London. The configuration in Figure 6-80 details our redistribution. In lines 14 through 16, our OSPF routing process is configured, and in lines 18 through 22, our IGRP routing process is configured.

First, let us examine OSPF. On line 15, we used the SWAG (Scientific Wild Ass Guess) method to assign a metric of 197 to represent all routes redistributed from IGRP into OSPF. This base of 197 has been assigned as a type 1 external route, so as this routing information makes its way through the OSPF network, additional metric information will be added to this base for route calculation. See line 15 in Figure 6-75, Tokyo's **show ip route** output, to see the additional metric values added to this base value.

On line 16, we identify the network and area to participate in our OSPF process.

Next, let us examine IGRP. Line 19 redistributes OSPF routes into IGRP with a metric equal to a 125kbps link.

Line 20 identifies the network 192.168.3.0, to be included in the IGRP process. An interface must belong to network 192.168.3.0 in order to participate in the IGRP process.

Line 21 identifies our Serial 1 port as a passive interface that will not be used to propagate IGRP routes.

Line 22 sets up a filter on the routing updates being redistributed from OSPF 200. **Access-list 1** on lines 25 and 26 define networks 192.168.1.0 and 192.168.2.0 as the only routes permitted into our IGRP domain.

**Figure 6-80**  London configuration

```
1  !
2  hostname London
3  !
4  no ip domain-lookup
5  !
6  interface Ethernet0
7   ip address 192.168.3.1 255.255.255.0
8  !
9  interface Serial1
10  ip address 192.168.6.2 255.255.255.0
11  bandwidth 125
12  clockrate 125000
13  !
14 router ospf 200
15  redistribute igrp 200 metric 197 metric-type 1
16  network 192.168.6.0 0.0.0.255 area 6
17  !
18 router igrp 200
19  redistribute ospf 200 metric 128 1000 255 1 1500
20  network 192.168.3.0
21  passive-interface serial 1
22  distribute-list 1 out ospf 200
23  !
24 ip classless
25 access-list 1 permit 192.168.1.0 0.0.0.255
26 access-list 1 permit 192.168.2.0 0.0.0.255
27  !
28 line con 0
29  exec-timeout 0 0
30  length 0
31  !
32 end
```

The **debug** output in Figure 6-81 shows us that only the filtered routes permitted during redistribution show up in our updates to our IGRP cloud, and there are no IGRP updates being sent out the Serial 1 interface.

The **show ip protocol** in Figure 6-82 shows both of our routing protocols, IGRP and OSPF.

Line 12 identifies the redistributed protocols, IGRP and OSPF, with all types of OSPF routes—internal, external 1, and external 2—being redistributed.

Line 13 identifies **access-list 1** as a filter on the OSPF routes being redistributed into IGRP.

Line 26 identifies the redistribution of IGRP and OSPF in the OSPF process.

**Figure 6-81**   London **debug** output

```
1 London#debug ip igrp events
2 IGRP event debugging is on
3 London#debug ip igrp transactions
4 IGRP protocol debugging is on
5 London#
6 IGRP: sending update to 255.255.255.255 via Ethernet0 (192.168.3.1)
7        network 192.168.1.0, metric=79125
8        network 192.168.2.0, metric=79125
9 IGRP: Update contains 0 interior, 2 system, and 0 exterior routes.
10 IGRP: Total routes in update: 2
```

The **show ip route** output in Figure 6-83 shows our directly connected and inter-area OSPF routes. Even though we have filtered the OSPF routes during the redistribution process, all routes are still shown in this output, as London is directly connected to the OSPF domain. Check out the **debug** output in Figure 6-81 for the filtering results.

**Figure 6-82**   London **show ip protocol** output

```
1 London#sho ip prot
2 Routing Protocol is "igrp 200"
3    Sending updates every 90 seconds, next due in 10 seconds
4    Invalid after 270 seconds, hold down 280, flushed after 630
5    Outgoing update filter list for all interfaces is not set
6    Incoming update filter list for all interfaces is not set
7    Default networks flagged in outgoing updates
8    Default networks accepted from incoming updates
9    IGRP metric weight K1=1, K2=0, K3=1, K4=0, K5=0
10    IGRP maximum hopcount 100
11    IGRP maximum metric variance 1
12    Redistributing: igrp 200, ospf 200 (internal, external 1, external 2)
13
14    Routing for Networks:
15       192.168.3.0
16    Routing Information Sources:
17       Gateway         Distance      Last Update
18    Distance: (default is 100)
19
20 Routing Protocol is "ospf 200"
21    Sending updates every 0 seconds
22    Invalid after 0 seconds, hold down 0, flushed after 0
23    Outgoing update filter list for all interfaces is not set
24    Incoming update filter list for all interfaces is not set
25    Redistributing: igrp 200, ospf 200
26    Routing for Networks:
27       192.168.6.0
28    Routing Information Sources:
29       Gateway         Distance      Last Update
30       192.168.4.2         110       00:06:52
31    Distance: (default is 110)
```

**Figure 6-83** London **show ip route** output

```
1 London#sho ip route
2 Codes: C - connected, S - static, I - IGRP, R - RIP, M - mobile, B - BGP
3        D - EIGRP, EX - EIGRP external, O - OSPF, IA - OSPF inter area
4        N1 - OSPF NSSA external type 1, N2 - OSPF NSSA external type 2
5        E1 - OSPF external type 1, E2 - OSPF external type 2, E - EGP
6        i - IS-IS, L1 - IS-IS level-1, L2 - IS-IS level-2, * - candidate default
7        U - per-user static route, o - ODR
8
9 Gateway of last resort is not set
10
11 C    192.168.6.0/24 is directly connected, Serial1
12 O IA 192.168.1.0/24 [110/810] via 192.168.6.1, 00:06:57, Serial1
13 O IA 192.168.2.0/24 [110/1610] via 192.168.6.1, 00:06:57, Serial1
14 C    192.168.3.0/24 is directly connected, Ethernet0
```

The **ping** output in Figure 6-84 verifies our connectivity to the LAN segment connected to New York.

**Question #3: What is the standard OSPF metric calculation, and what metric needs to be used in the redistribution process in London to provide more accurate IP routing?**

**Question #4: Was the passive-interface command required in the London configuration to eliminate IGRP updates going out interface Serial 1?**

**Question #5: Why are there no special route summarization commands required in our redistribution process?**

Answers to these questions may be found at the end of the chapter.

**Figure 6-84** London-to-Tokyo **ping** output

```
1 London#ping
2 Protocol [ip]:
3 Target IP address: 192.168.1.1
4 Repeat count [5]:
5 Datagram size [100]:
6 Timeout in seconds [2]:
7 Extended commands [n]: y
8 Source address or interface: 192.168.3.1
9 Type of service [0]:
10 Set DF bit in IP header? [no]:
11 Validate reply data? [no]:
12 Data pattern [0xABCD]:
13 Loose, Strict, Record, Timestamp, Verbose[none]:
14 Sweep range of sizes [n]:
15 Type escape sequence to abort.
16 Sending 5, 100-byte ICMP Echos to 192.168.1.1, timeout is 2 seconds:
17 !!!!!
18 Success rate is 100 percent (5/5), round-trip min/avg/max = 16/17/20 ms
```

## Example #8—IGRP & Static Routes

In this example, we will explore the use of the default-network command, using the network layout in Figure 6-85. Defining a default pathway to be used when no specific route exists is an excellent way to connect to an outside source of information such as the Internet, without having the extensive routing tables redistributed into our local routing protocol.

The Tokyo configuration in Figure 6-86 shows us a very generic IGRP router with no special configuration commands.

The **show ip protocol** output in Figure 6-87, shows us the standard IGRP routing process for the attached networks.

The **show ip route** output in Figure 6-88 is where we see the first indication that there is something different about the way we connect to devices outside our IGRP domain.

**Figure 6-85**
Redistributing IGRP
and static routes

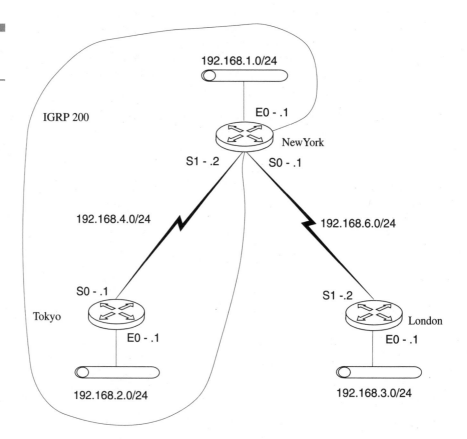

**Figure 6-86** Tokyo configuration

```
1  !
2  hostname Tokyo
3  !
4  no ip domain-lookup
5  !
6  interface Ethernet0
7   ip address 192.168.2.1 255.255.255.0
8  !
9  interface Serial0
10   ip address 192.168.4.1 255.255.255.0
11   bandwidth 125
12  !
13  router igrp 200
14   network 192.168.2.0
15   network 192.168.4.0
16  !
17  ip classless
18  !
19  line con 0
20   exec-timeout 0 0
21   length 0
22  !
23  end
```

Line 12 shows network 192.168.6.0 as an IGRP-derived route, but the **I** has an * next to it. If we look at line 6 in the legend, an * indicates that this route is a candidate default route.

Line 9 identifies the gateway (router) of last resort as 192.168.4.2, as the interim step to reach our default network of 192.168.6.0. Any destination address that does not specifically match a network found in Tokyo's

**Figure 6-87** Tokyo **show ip protocol** output

```
1  Tokyo#sho ip prot
2  Routing Protocol is "igrp 200"
3    Sending updates every 90 seconds, next due in 11 seconds
4    Invalid after 270 seconds, hold down 280, flushed after 630
5    Outgoing update filter list for all interfaces is not set
6    Incoming update filter list for all interfaces is not set
7    Default networks flagged in outgoing updates
8    Default networks accepted from incoming updates
9    IGRP metric weight K1=1, K2=0, K3=1, K4=0, K5=0
10     IGRP maximum hopcount 100
11     IGRP maximum metric variance 1
12     Redistributing: igrp 200
13     Routing for Networks:
14       192.168.2.0
15       192.168.4.0
16     Routing Information Sources:
17       Gateway          Distance      Last Update
18       192.168.4.2          100       00:01:18
19     Distance: (default is 100)
```

**Figure 6-88** Tokyo **show ip route** output

```
1 Tokyo#sho ip route
2 Codes: C - connected, S - static, I - IGRP, R - RIP, M - mobile, B - BGP
3        D - EIGRP, EX - EIGRP external, O - OSPF, IA - OSPF inter area
4        N1 - OSPF NSSA external type 1, N2 - OSPF NSSA external type 2
5        E1 - OSPF external type 1, E2 - OSPF external type 2, E - EGP
6        i - IS-IS, L1 - IS-IS level-1, L2 - IS-IS level-2, * - candidate default
7        U - per-user static route, o - ODR
8
9 Gateway of last resort is 192.168.4.2 to network 192.168.6.0
10
11 C    192.168.4.0/24 is directly connected, Serial0
12 I*   192.168.6.0/24 [100/84000] via 192.168.4.2, 00:00:00, Serial0
13 I    192.168.1.0/24 [100/82100] via 192.168.4.2, 00:00:00, Serial0
14 C    192.168.2.0/24 is directly connected, Ethernet0
```

routing table will be sent to the default gateway. Let us wait until we look at the default gateway information to figure out what happens next.

Just to make sure this works properly, the **extended ping** command output in Figure 6-89 proves we have connectivity to London.

The New York configuration in Figure 6-90 is where we further define how our **default network** gets propagated through our IGRP network.

Line 24 is the default network command itself, but by itself, this command has no effect on the IGRP routing domain. The other requirement for default-network propagation is a network statement in the routing process (see line 20).

Line 25 is a static route for network 192.168.3.0. Even though we have identified a default network and passed it on to the rest of the routers,

**Figure 6-89** Tokyo-to-London **ping** output

```
1 Tokyo#ping
2 Protocol [ip]:
3 Target IP address: 192.168.3.1
4 Repeat count [5]:
5 Datagram size [100]:
6 Timeout in seconds [2]:
7 Extended commands [n]: y
8 Source address or interface: 192.168.2.1
9 Type of service [0]:
10 Set DF bit in IP header? [no]:
11 Validate reply data? [no]:
12 Data pattern [0xABCD]:
13 Loose, Strict, Record, Timestamp, Verbose[none]:
14 Sweep range of sizes [n]:
15 Type escape sequence to abort.
16 Sending 5, 100-byte ICMP Echos to 192.168.3.1, timeout is 2 seconds:
17 !!!!!
18 Success rate is 100 percent (5/5), round-trip min/avg/max = 32/32/32 ms
```

**Figure 6-90** NewYork configuration

```
1  !
2  hostname NewYork
3  !
4  no ip domain-lookup
5  !
6  interface Ethernet0
7   ip address 192.168.1.1 255.255.255.0
8  !
9  interface Serial0
10  ip address 192.168.6.1 255.255.255.0
11  bandwidth 125
12  !
13 interface Serial1
14  ip address 192.168.4.2 255.255.255.0
15  bandwidth 125
16  clockrate 125000
17  !
18 router igrp 200
19  network 192.168.1.0
20  network 192.168.6.0
21  network 192.168.4.0
22  !
23 ip classless
24 ip default-network 192.168.6.0
25 ip route 192.168.3.0 255.255.255.0 192.168.6.2
26  !
27  !
28 line con 0
29  exec-timeout 0 0
30  length 0
31  !
32 end
```

**Figure 6-91** NewYork **debug** output

```
1  NewYork#debug ip igrp events
2  IGRP event debugging is on
3  NewYork#debug ip igrp tran
4  IGRP protocol debugging is on
5  IGRP: received update from 192.168.4.1 on Serial1
6        network 192.168.2.0, metric 82100 (neighbor 1100)
7  IGRP: Update contains 0 interior, 1 system, and 0 exterior routes.
8  IGRP: Total routes in update: 1
9  IGRP: sending update to 255.255.255.255 via Ethernet0 (192.168.1.1)
10        network 192.168.4.0, metric=82000
11        network 192.168.2.0, metric=82100
12        exterior 192.168.6.0, metric=82000
13 IGRP: Update contains 0 interior, 2 system, and 1 exterior routes.
14 IGRP: Total routes in update: 3
15 IGRP: sending update to 255.255.255.255 via Serial1 (192.168.4.2)
16        network 192.168.1.0, metric=1100
17        exterior 192.168.6.0, metric=82000
18 IGRP: Update contains 0 interior, 1 system, and 1 exterior routes.
19 IGRP: Total routes in update: 2
```

**Figure 6-92** NewYork **show ip protocol** output

```
1 NewYork#sho ip prot
2 Routing Protocol is "igrp 200"
3   Sending updates every 90 seconds, next due in 84 seconds
4   Invalid after 270 seconds, hold down 280, flushed after 630
5   Outgoing update filter list for all interfaces is not set
6   Incoming update filter list for all interfaces is not set
7   Default networks flagged in outgoing updates
8   Default networks accepted from incoming updates
9   IGRP metric weight K1=1, K2=0, K3=1, K4=0, K5=0
10   IGRP maximum hopcount 100
11   IGRP maximum metric variance 1
12   Redistributing: igrp 200
13   Routing for Networks:
14     192.168.1.0
15     192.168.6.0
16     192.168.4.0
17   Routing Information Sources:
18     Gateway          Distance      Last Update
19     192.168.4.1          100       00:00:11
20   Distance: (default is 100)
```

NewYork has no information on how to deliver unknown IP destinations. This static route identifies only one destination network that can be reached from users in the IGRP routing domain using the default gateway.

The **debug** output for IGRP in Figure 6-91 shows that our default network 192.168.6.0 is being advertised as an exterior route to the balance of the IGRP domain.

The **show ip protocol** output in Figure 6-92 shows nothing out of the ordinary, standard IGRP processing.

**Figure 6-93** NewYork **show ip route** output

```
1 NewYork#sho ip route
2 Codes: C - connected, S - static, I - IGRP, R - RIP, M - mobile, B - BGP
3        D - EIGRP, EX - EIGRP external, O - OSPF, IA - OSPF inter area
4        N1 - OSPF NSSA external type 1, N2 - OSPF NSSA external type 2
5        E1 - OSPF external type 1, E2 - OSPF external type 2, E - EGP
6        i - IS-IS, L1 - IS-IS level-1, L2 - IS-IS level-2, * - candidate default
7        U - per-user static route, o - ODR
8
9 Gateway of last resort is not set
10
11 C    192.168.4.0/24 is directly connected, Serial1
12 C*   192.168.6.0/24 is directly connected, Serial0
13 C    192.168.1.0/24 is directly connected, Ethernet0
14 I    192.168.2.0/24 [100/82100] via 192.168.4.1, 00:00:23, Serial1
15 S    192.168.3.0/24 [1/0] via 192.168.6.2
```

**Figure 6-94** London configuration

```
1  !
2  hostname London
3  !
4  no ip domain-lookup
5  !
6  interface Ethernet0
7   ip address 192.168.3.1 255.255.255.0
8  !
9  interface Serial1
10   ip address 192.168.6.2 255.255.255.0
11   bandwidth 125
12   clockrate 125000
13  !
14  ip classless
15  ip route 0.0.0.0 0.0.0.0 Serial1
16  !
17  line con 0
18   exec-timeout 0 0
19   length 0
20  !
21  end
```

The **show ip route** output in Figure 6-93, shows directly connected, IGRP derived, and a single static entry for 192.168.3.0.

This is a perfect example of a stub network configuration. The London configuration in Figure 6-94 has no routing protocol running, but has a default route defined on line 15. If traffic coming into the router has a destination address that does not match either network 192.168.3.0 or 192.168.6.0, these packets will be forwarded to the router on the other end of our serial link.

The **show ip protocol** and **show ip route** output in Figure 6-95 is a clear definition of stub network operation.

Line 1 shows us that there is no IP routing protocol running.

**Figure 6-95** London **show ip route** output

```
1  yLondon#sho ip prot
2  London#sho ip route
3  Codes: C - connected, S - static, I - IGRP, R - RIP, M - mobile, B - BGP
4         D - EIGRP, EX - EIGRP external, O - OSPF, IA - OSPF inter area
5         N1 - OSPF NSSA external type 1, N2 - OSPF NSSA external type 2
6         E1 - OSPF external type 1, E2 - OSPF external type 2, E - EGP
7         i - IS-IS, L1 - IS-IS level-1, L2 - IS-IS level-2, * - candidate default
8         U - per-user static route, o - ODR
9
10 Gateway of last resort is 0.0.0.0 to network 0.0.0.0
11
12 C    192.168.6.0/24 is directly connected, Serial1
13 C    192.168.3.0/24 is directly connected, Ethernet0
14 S*   0.0.0.0/0 is directly connected, Serial1
```

**Figure 6-96** London-to-Tokyo **ping** output

```
1 London#ping
2 Protocol [ip]:
3 Target IP address: 192.168.2.1
4 Repeat count [5]:
5 Datagram size [100]:
6 Timeout in seconds [2]:
7 Extended commands [n]: y
8 Source address or interface: 192.168.3.1
9 Type of service [0]:
10 Set DF bit in IP header? [no]:
11 Validate reply data? [no]:
12 Data pattern [0xABCD]:
13 Loose, Strict, Record, Timestamp, Verbose[none]:
14 Sweep range of sizes [n]:
15 Type escape sequence to abort.
16 Sending 5, 100-byte ICMP Echos to 192.168.2.1, timeout is 2 seconds:
17 !!!!!
18 Success rate is 100 percent (5/5), round-trip min/avg/max = 28/31/32 ms
```

Lines 12 through 14 show our two directly connected networks and the static default route to everywhere else.

Does it really work? See the **ping** output in Figure 6-96 for verification.

## Example #9—IGRP, Connected Networks & Static Routes

In this example, we will explore the use of the default-network command, using the network layout in Figure 6-97. Defining a default pathway to be used when no specific route exists is an excellent way to connect to an outside source of information such as the Internet, without having the extensive routing tables redistributed into our local routing protocol. While similar to our last example with IGRP, this EIGRP example will make use of one of the more unusual commands, **redistributed connected** in order to propagate default routes.

The Tokyo configuration in Figure 6-98 shows us a very basic EIGRP IP routing environment.

The **show ip protocol output** in Figure 6-99 shows standard options for EIGRP routing.

Notice something different in the **show ip route** output in Figure 6-100.

Network 192.168.6.0 shows up on line 12 as an external network to EIGRP, and it is a candidate default route.

**Figure 6-97**
Redistributing EIGRP
and static

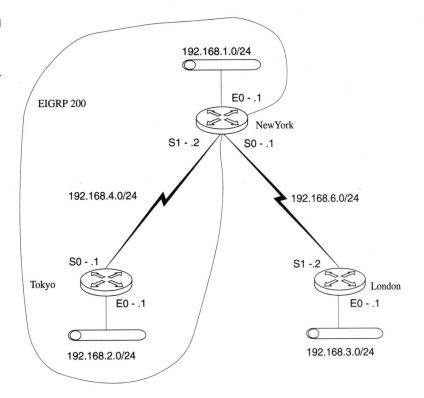

**Figure 6-98** Tokyo configuration

```
1 !
2 hostname Tokyo
3 !
4 no ip domain-lookup
5 !
6 interface Ethernet0
7  ip address 192.168.2.1 255.255.255.0
8 !
9 interface Serial0
10  ip address 192.168.4.1 255.255.255.0
11  no ip mroute-cache
12  bandwidth 125
13  no fair-queue
14 !
15 router eigrp 200
16  network 192.168.2.0
17  network 192.168.4.0
18 !
19 ip classless
20 !
21 line con 0
22  exec-timeout 0 0
23  length 0
24 !
25 end
```

**Figure 6-99** Tokyo **show ip protocol** output

```
1 Tokyo#sho ip prot
2 Routing Protocol is "eigrp 200"
3   Outgoing update filter list for all interfaces is not set
4   Incoming update filter list for all interfaces is not set
5   Default networks flagged in outgoing updates
6   Default networks accepted from incoming updates
7   EIGRP metric weight K1=1, K2=0, K3=1, K4=0, K5=0
8   EIGRP maximum hopcount 100
9   EIGRP maximum metric variance 1
10  Redistributing: eigrp 200
11  Automatic network summarization is in effect
12  Automatic address summarization:
13    192.168.4.0/24 for Ethernet0
14    192.168.2.0/24 for Serial0
15  Routing for Networks:
16    192.168.2.0
17    192.168.4.0
18  Routing Information Sources:
19    Gateway          Distance      Last Update
20    192.168.4.2            90      00:02:49
21  Distance: internal 90 external 170
```

Line 9 shows us that there has been a gateway of last resort set at 192.168.4.2 that will take us to the candidate default network of 192.168.6.0.

The **ping** output in Figure 6-101 is our verification that our router configuration is working correctly and we can reach the other side of the network.

The NewYork configuration in Figure 6-102 is where we source our default network to the rest of the EIGRP domain. Line 24 is where we define our default network 192.168.6.0. Instead of adding a network statement to our EIGRP process, we use a **redistribute connected**

**Figure 6-100** Tokyo **show ip route** output

```
1 Tokyo#sho ip route
2 Codes: C - connected, S - static, I - IGRP, R - RIP, M - mobile, B - BGP
3        D - EIGRP, EX - EIGRP external, O - OSPF, IA - OSPF inter area
4        N1 - OSPF NSSA external type 1, N2 - OSPF NSSA external type 2
5        E1 - OSPF external type 1, E2 - OSPF external type 2, E - EGP
6        i - IS-IS, L1 - IS-IS level-1, L2 - IS-IS level-2, * - candidate default
7        U - per-user static route, o - ODR
8
9 Gateway of last resort is 192.168.4.2 to network 192.168.6.0
10
11 C    192.168.4.0/24 is directly connected, Serial0
12 D*EX 192.168.6.0/24 [170/21504000] via 192.168.4.2, 00:03:10, Serial0
13 D    192.168.1.0/24 [90/21017600] via 192.168.4.2, 00:03:13, Serial0
14 C    192.168.2.0/24 is directly connected, Ethernet0
```

**Figure 6-101** Tokyo-to-London **ping** output

```
1 Tokyo#ping
2 Protocol [ip]:
3 Target IP address: 192.168.3.1
4 Repeat count [5]:
5 Datagram size [100]:
6 Timeout in seconds [2]:
7 Extended commands [n]: y
8 Source address or interface: 192.168.2.1
9 Type of service [0]:
10 Set DF bit in IP header? [no]:
11 Validate reply data? [no]:
12 Data pattern [0xABCD]:
13 Loose, Strict, Record, Timestamp, Verbose[none]:
14 Sweep range of sizes [n]:
15 Type escape sequence to abort.
16 Sending 5, 100-byte ICMP Echos to 192.168.3.1, timeout is 2 seconds:
17 !!!!!
18 Success rate is 100 percent (5/5), round-trip min/avg/max = 28/32/36 ms
```

**Figure 6-102** NewYork configuration

```
1 !
2 hostname NewYork
3 !
4 no ip domain-lookup
5 !
6 interface Ethernet0
7  ip address 192.168.1.1 255.255.255.0
8 !
9 interface Serial0
10  ip address 192.168.6.1 255.255.255.0
11  bandwidth 125
12 !
13 interface Serial1
14  ip address 192.168.4.2 255.255.255.0
15  bandwidth 125
16  clockrate 125000
17 !
18 router eigrp 200
19  redistribute connected
20  network 192.168.1.0
21  network 192.168.4.0
22 !
23 ip classless
24 ip default-network 192.168.6.0
25 ip route 192.168.3.0 255.255.255.0 192.168.6.2
26 !
27 line con 0
28  exec-timeout 0 0
29  length 0
30 !
31 end
```

**Figure 6-103** NewYork **show ip protocol** output

```
1 NewYork#sho ip prot
2 Routing Protocol is "eigrp 200"
3   Outgoing update filter list for all interfaces is not set
4   Incoming update filter list for all interfaces is not set
5   Default networks flagged in outgoing updates
6   Default networks accepted from incoming updates
7   EIGRP metric weight K1=1, K2=0, K3=1, K4=0, K5=0
8   EIGRP maximum hopcount 100
9   EIGRP maximum metric variance 1
10  Redistributing: connected, eigrp 200
11  Automatic network summarization is in effect
12  Automatic address summarization:
13    192.168.4.0/24 for Ethernet0
14    192.168.1.0/24 for Serial1
15  Routing for Networks:
16    192.168.1.0
17    192.168.4.0
18  Routing Information Sources:
19    Gateway          Distance       Last Update
20    192.168.4.1            90        00:04:29
21  Distance: internal 90 external 170
```

command. This command is especially useful when there are multiple external stub connections that you do not want included in the EIGRP process. In Example #8 with IGRP, we used a network statement to tie the default network to the routing process, and to be exact, there should been a **passive-interface serial 0** command added to the IGRP routing process. The **redistribute connected** eliminates the need for the **passive-interface** commands while it treats the connected interface addresses as if the **network** commands were used.

**Figure 6-104** NewYork **show ip route** output

```
1 NewYork#sho ip route
2 Codes: C - connected, S - static, I - IGRP, R - RIP, M - mobile, B - BGP
3        D - EIGRP, EX - EIGRP external, O - OSPF, IA - OSPF inter area
4        N1 - OSPF NSSA external type 1, N2 - OSPF NSSA external type 2
5        E1 - OSPF external type 1, E2 - OSPF external type 2, E - EGP
6        i - IS-IS, L1 - IS-IS level-1, L2 - IS-IS level-2, * - candidate default
7        U - per-user static route, o - ODR
8
9 Gateway of last resort is not set
10
11 C    192.168.4.0/24 is directly connected, Serial1
12 C*   192.168.6.0/24 is directly connected, Serial0
13 C    192.168.1.0/24 is directly connected, Ethernet0
14 D    192.168.2.0/24 [90/21017600] via 192.168.4.1, 00:05:47, Serial1
15 S    192.168.3.0/24 [1/0] via 192.168.6.2
```

**Figure 6-105** London configuration

```
1  !
2  hostname London
3  !
4  no ip domain-lookup
5  !
6  interface Ethernet0
7   ip address 192.168.3.1 255.255.255.0
8  !
9  interface Serial1
10   ip address 192.168.6.2 255.255.255.0
11   bandwidth 125
12   clockrate 125000
13  !
14  ip classless
15  ip route 0.0.0.0 0.0.0.0 Serial1
16  !
17  line con 0
18   exec-timeout 0 0
19   length 0
```

The **show ip protocol** output in Figure 6-103 is fairly standard except for line 10, where it shows that we are redistributing connected networks.

The **show ip route** output in Figure 6-104 identifies the networks as directly connected, EIGRP, or static, with line 12 identifying 192.168.6.0 as a candidate default network.

This is a an example of a stub network configuration. The London configuration in Figure 6-105 has no routing protocol running, but has a default route defined on line 15. If traffic coming into the router has a

**Figure 6-106** London **show ip route** output

```
1  London#sho ip prot
2  London#sho ip route
3  Codes: C - connected, S - static, I - IGRP, R - RIP, M - mobile, B - BGP
4         D - EIGRP, EX - EIGRP external, O - OSPF, IA - OSPF inter area
5         N1 - OSPF NSSA external type 1, N2 - OSPF NSSA external type 2
6         E1 - OSPF external type 1, E2 - OSPF external type 2, E - EGP
7         i - IS-IS, L1 - IS-IS level-1, L2 - IS-IS level-2, * - candidate default
8         U - per-user static route, o - ODR
9
10 Gateway of last resort is 0.0.0.0 to network 0.0.0.0
11
12 C    192.168.6.0/24 is directly connected, Serial1
13 C    192.168.3.0/24 is directly connected, Ethernet0
14 S*   0.0.0.0/0 is directly connected, Serial1
```

**Figure 6-107**   London-to-Tokyo **ping** output

```
1 London#ping
2 Protocol [ip]:
3 Target IP address: 192.168.2.1
4 Repeat count [5]:
5 Datagram size [100]:
6 Timeout in seconds [2]:
7 Extended commands [n]: y
8 Source address or interface: 192.168.3.1
9 Type of service [0]:
10 Set DF bit in IP header? [no]:
11 Validate reply data? [no]:
12 Data pattern [0xABCD]:
13 Loose, Strict, Record, Timestamp, Verbose[none]:
14 Sweep range of sizes [n]:
15 Type escape sequence to abort.
16 Sending 5, 100-byte ICMP Echos to 192.168.2.1, timeout is 2 seconds:
17 !!!!!
18 Success rate is 100 percent (5/5), round-trip min/avg/max = 28/31/32 ms
```

destination address that does not match either network 192.168.3.0 or 192.168.6.0, such packets will be forwarded to the router on the other end of our serial link.

The **show ip protocol** and **show ip route** output in Figure 6-106 is a clear definition of stub network operation Line 1 shows us that there is no IP routing protocol running. Lines 12 through 14 show our two directly connected networks and the static default route to everywhere else.

Does it really work? See the **ping** output in Figure 6-107 for verification.

# Example #10—EIGRP & OSPF

This example has been set up as a lab, to be solved by setting up the network and trying it out or by figuring out, which commands need to be used to clean up the router configurations. Don't worry: If you have trouble figuring out the commands, a complete set of configurations and show commands can be found at the end of the chapter.

The network layout in Figure 6-108 defines two separate routing domains with a single contact point.

**Figure 6-108**
Redistributing EIGRP
and OSPF

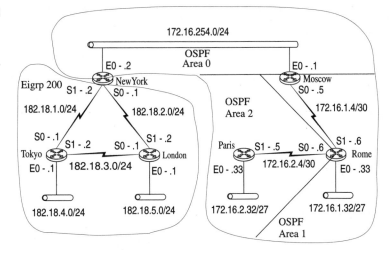

Loopback Addresses

```
NewYork   172.16.253.5/30     Area 0
Moscow    172.16.253.9/30     Area 0
Rome      172.16.1.253/30     Area 1
Paris     172.16.2.253/30     Area 2
```

The OSPF domain has a backbone area zero, a subarea 1 directly connected to the backbone, and a subarea 2 that is not directly connected to the backbone. Variable subnetwork prefixes are being used within the OSPF domain.

The EIGRP domain is connected to the OSPF backbone through the NewYork router, see Figure 6-108.

Look at the six figures, 6-109 through 6-114, for the basic configuration and show commands that are used to set up the two independent routing processes that meet in NewYork.

Specific goals for this lab are route summarization, subarea 2 connectivity, and route redistribution.

**Figure 6-109**  Tokyo configurations and **show** commands

```
Tokyo
1  !
2  hostname Tokyo
3  !
4  no ip domain-lookup
5  !
6  interface Ethernet0
7   ip address 182.18.4.1 255.255.255.0
8  !
9  interface Serial0
10   ip address 182.18.1.1 255.255.255.0
11   bandwidth 125
12  !
13  interface Serial1
14   ip address 182.18.3.2 255.255.255.0
15   bandwidth 125
16   clockrate 125000
17  !
18  interface BRI0
19   no ip address
20   shutdown
21  !
22  router eigrp 200
23   network 182.18.0.0
24  !
25  ip classless
26  !
27  line con 0
28   exec-timeout 0 0
29   length 0
30  !
31  end
32
33  Tokyo#sho ip prot
34  Routing Protocol is "eigrp 200"
35    Outgoing update filter list for all interfaces is not set
36    Incoming update filter list for all interfaces is not set
37    Default networks flagged in outgoing updates
38    Default networks accepted from incoming updates
39    EIGRP metric weight K1=1, K2=0, K3=1, K4=0, K5=0
40    EIGRP maximum hopcount 100
41    EIGRP maximum metric variance 1
42    Redistributing: eigrp 200
43    Automatic network summarization is in effect
44    Routing for Networks:
45      182.18.0.0
46    Routing Information Sources:
47      Gateway          Distance        Last Update
48      182.18.3.1          90           00:06:21
49      182.18.1.2          90           00:06:24
50    Distance: internal 90 external 170
51
52  Tokyo#sho ip route
53  Codes: C - connected, S - static, I - IGRP, R - RIP, M - mobile, B - BGP
54         D - EIGRP, EX - EIGRP external, O - OSPF, IA - OSPF inter area
55         N1 - OSPF NSSA external type 1, N2 - OSPF NSSA external type 2
```

```
56        E1 - OSPF external type 1, E2 - OSPF external type 2, E - EGP
57        i - IS-IS, L1 - IS-IS level-1, L2 - IS-IS level-2, * - candidate default
58        U - per-user static route, o - ODR
59
60 Gateway of last resort is not set
61
62      182.18.0.0/24 is subnetted, 5 subnets
63 C        182.18.4.0 is directly connected, Ethernet0
64 D        182.18.5.0 [90/21017600] via 182.18.3.1, 00:06:29, Serial1
65 C        182.18.1.0 is directly connected, Serial0
66 D        182.18.2.0 [90/21504000] via 182.18.1.2, 00:06:29, Serial0
67                    [90/21504000] via 182.18.3.1, 00:06:29, Serial1
68 C        182.18.3.0 is directly connected, Serial1
```

**Figure 6-110**   London **configurations** and **show** commands

**London**
```
1 !
2 hostname London
3 !
4 no ip domain-lookup
5 !
6 interface Ethernet0
7  ip address 182.18.5.1 255.255.255.0
8 !
9 interface Serial0
10  ip address 182.18.3.1 255.255.255.0
11  bandwidth 125
12 !
13 interface Serial1
14  ip address 182.18.2.2 255.255.255.0
15  bandwidth 125
16  clockrate 125000
17 !
18 router eigrp 200
19  network 182.18.0.0
20 !
21 ip classless
22 !
23 line con 0
24  exec-timeout 0 0
25  length 0
26 !
27 end
28
29 London#sho ip prot
30 Routing Protocol is "eigrp 200"
31   Outgoing update filter list for all interfaces is not set
32   Incoming update filter list for all interfaces is not set
33   Default networks flagged in outgoing updates
34   Default networks accepted from incoming updates
35   EIGRP metric weight K1=1, K2=0, K3=1, K4=0, K5=0
36   EIGRP maximum hopcount 100
37   EIGRP maximum metric variance 1
38   Redistributing: eigrp 200
```

**Figure 6-110** Continued

```
39   Automatic network summarization is in effect
40   Routing for Networks:
41      182.18.0.0
42   Routing Information Sources:
43      Gateway          Distance      Last Update
44      182.18.3.2             90      00:07:50
45      182.18.2.1             90      00:07:50
46   Distance: internal 90 external 170
47
48 London#sho ip route
49 Codes: C - connected, S - static, I - IGRP, R - RIP, M - mobile, B - BGP
50        D - EIGRP, EX - EIGRP external, O - OSPF, IA - OSPF inter area
51        N1 - OSPF NSSA external type 1, N2 - OSPF NSSA external type 2
52        E1 - OSPF external type 1, E2 - OSPF external type 2, E - EGP
53        i - IS-IS, L1 - IS-IS level-1, L2 - IS-IS level-2, * - candidate default
54        U - per-user static route, o - ODR
55
56 Gateway of last resort is not set
57
58      182.18.0.0/24 is subnetted, 5 subnets
59 D       182.18.4.0 [90/21017600] via 182.18.3.2, 00:08:01, Serial0
60 C       182.18.5.0 is directly connected, Ethernet0
61 D       182.18.1.0 [90/21504000] via 182.18.2.1, 00:08:01, Serial1
62                    [90/21504000] via 182.18.3.2, 00:08:01, Serial0
63 C       182.18.2.0 is directly connected, Serial1
64 C       182.18.3.0 is directly connected, Serial0
65
```

**Figure 6-111** NewYork **configurations** and **show** commands

```
NewYork
1 !
2 hostname NewYork
3 !
4 no ip domain-lookup
5 !
6 interface Loopback0
7  ip address 172.16.253.5 255.255.255.0
8 !
9 interface Ethernet0
10  ip address 172.16.254.2 255.255.255.0
11 !
12 interface Serial0
13  ip address 182.18.2.1 255.255.255.0
14  bandwidth 125
15 !
16 interface Serial1
17  ip address 182.18.1.2 255.255.255.0
18  bandwidth 125
19  clockrate 125000
20 !
21 router eigrp 200
22  network 182.18.0.0
```

```
22  network 182.18.0.0
23 !
24 router ospf 200
25  network 172.16.253.4 0.0.0.3 area 0
26  network 172.16.254.0 0.0.0.255 area 0
27 !
28 ip classless
29 !
30 line con 0
31  exec-timeout 0 0
32  length 0
33
34 !
35 end
36
37 NewYork#sho ip prot
38 Routing Protocol is "eigrp 200"
39   Outgoing update filter list for all interfaces is not set
40   Incoming update filter list for all interfaces is not set
41   Default networks flagged in outgoing updates
42   Default networks accepted from incoming updates
43   EIGRP metric weight K1=1, K2=0, K3=1, K4=0, K5=0
44   EIGRP maximum hopcount 100
45   EIGRP maximum metric variance 1
46   Redistributing: eigrp 200
47   Automatic network summarization is in effect
48   Routing for Networks:
49     182.18.0.0
50   Routing Information Sources:
51     Gateway          Distance       Last Update
52     182.18.2.2             90       00:04:47
53     182.18.1.1             90       00:04:47
54   Distance: internal 90 external 170
55
56 Routing Protocol is "ospf 200"
57   Sending updates every 0 seconds
58   Invalid after 0 seconds, hold down 0, flushed after 0
59   Outgoing update filter list for all interfaces is not set
60   Incoming update filter list for all interfaces is not set
61   Redistributing: ospf 200
62   Routing for Networks:
63     172.16.253.4/30
64     172.16.254.0/24
65   Routing Information Sources:
66     Gateway          Distance       Last Update
67     172.16.253.9          110       00:09:30
68   Distance: (default is 110)
69
70 NewYork#sho ip route
71 Codes: C - connected, S - static, I - IGRP, R - RIP, M - mobile, B - BGP
72        D - EIGRP, EX - EIGRP external, O - OSPF, IA - OSPF inter area
73        N1 - OSPF NSSA external type 1, N2 - OSPF NSSA external type 2
74        E1 - OSPF external type 1, E2 - OSPF external type 2, E - EGP
75        i - IS-IS, L1 - IS-IS level-1, L2 - IS-IS level-2, * - candidate default
76        U - per-user static route, o - ODR
77
```

**Figure 6-111** Continued

```
78 Gateway of last resort is not set
79
80      172.16.0.0/16 is variably subnetted, 6 subnets, 4 masks
81 O IA    172.16.1.253/32 [110/811] via 172.16.254.1, 00:09:44, Ethernet0
82 C       172.16.253.0/24 is directly connected, Loopback0
83 C       172.16.254.0/24 is directly connected, Ethernet0
84 O       172.16.253.9/32 [110/11] via 172.16.254.1, 00:09:44, Ethernet0
85 O IA    172.16.1.32/27 [110/820] via 172.16.254.1, 00:09:44, Ethernet0
86 O IA    172.16.1.4/30 [110/810] via 172.16.254.1, 00:09:44, Ethernet0
87     182.18.0.0/24 is subnetted, 5 subnets
88 D      182.18.4.0 [90/21017600] via 182.18.1.1, 00:05:01, Serial1
89 D      182.18.5.0 [90/21017600] via 182.18.2.2, 00:05:03, Serial0
90 C      182.18.1.0 is directly connected, Serial1
91 C      182.18.2.0 is directly connected, Serial0
92 D      182.18.3.0 [90/21504000] via 182.18.1.1, 00:05:06, Serial1
93                   [90/21504000] via 182.18.2.2, 00:05:06, Serial0
```

**Figure 6-112** Moscow **configurations** and **show** commands

```
Moscow
1 !
2 hostname Moscow
3 !
4 no ip domain-lookup
5 !
6 interface Loopback0
7  ip address 172.16.253.9 255.255.255.252
8 !
9 interface Ethernet0
10   ip address 172.16.254.1 255.255.255.0
11 !
12 interface Serial0
13   ip address 172.16.1.5 255.255.255.252
14   bandwidth 125
15 !
16 router ospf 200
17   network 172.16.254.0 0.0.0.255 area 0
18   network 172.16.253.8 0.0.0.3 area 0
19   network 172.16.1.4 0.0.0.3 area 1
20 !
21 ip classless
22 !
23 line con 0
24   exec-timeout 0 0
25   length 0
26 end
27
28 Moscow#sho ip prot
29 Routing Protocol is "ospf 200"
30   Sending updates every 0 seconds
31   Invalid after 0 seconds, hold down 0, flushed after 0
32   Outgoing update filter list for all interfaces is not set
33   Incoming update filter list for all interfaces is not set
34   Redistributing: ospf 200
35   Routing for Networks:
```

```
36      172.16.254.0/24
37      172.16.253.8/30
38      172.16.1.4/30
39   Routing Information Sources:
40     Gateway         Distance     Last Update
41     172.16.1.253       110       00:18:37
42     172.16.253.5       110       00:13:25
43   Distance: (default is 110)
44
45 Moscow#sho ip route
46 Codes: C - connected, S - static, I - IGRP, R - RIP, M - mobile, B - BGP
47        D - EIGRP, EX - EIGRP external, O - OSPF, IA - OSPF inter area
48        N1 - OSPF NSSA external type 1, N2 - OSPF NSSA external type 2
49        E1 - OSPF external type 1, E2 - OSPF external type 2, E - EGP
50        i - IS-IS, L1 - IS-IS level-1, L2 - IS-IS level-2, * - candidate default
51        U - per-user static route, o - ODR
52
53 Gateway of last resort is not set
54
55      172.16.0.0/16 is variably subnetted, 6 subnets, 4 masks
56 O       172.16.1.253/32 [110/801] via 172.16.1.6, 00:18:42, Serial0
57 C       172.16.254.0/24 is directly connected, Ethernet0
58 O       172.16.253.5/32 [110/11] via 172.16.254.2, 00:13:30, Ethernet0
59 C       172.16.253.8/30 is directly connected, Loopback0
60 O       172.16.1.32/27 [110/810] via 172.16.1.6, 00:18:42, Serial0
61 C       172.16.1.4/30 is directly connected, Serial0
62
```

---

**Figure 6-113** Rome **configurations** and **show** commands

**Rome**
```
1 !
2 hostname Rome
3 !
4 no ip domain-lookup
5 !
6 interface Loopback0
7  ip address 172.16.1.253 255.255.255.252
8 !
9 interface Ethernet0
10  ip address 172.16.1.33 255.255.255.224
11 !
12 interface Serial0
13  ip address 172.16.2.6 255.255.255.252
14  bandwidth 125
15 !
16 interface Serial1
17  ip address 172.16.1.6 255.255.255.252
18  bandwidth 125
19  clockrate 125000
20 !
```

**Figure 6-113** Continued

```
21 router ospf 200
22  network 172.16.2.4 0.0.0.3 area 2
23  network 172.16.1.4 0.0.0.3 area 1
24  network 172.16.1.252 0.0.0.3 area 1
25  network 172.16.1.32 0.0.0.31 area 1
26 !
27 ip classless
28 !
29 line con 0
30  exec-timeout 0 0
31  length 0
32 !
33 end
34
35 Rome#sho ip prot
36 Routing Protocol is "ospf 200"
37   Sending updates every 0 seconds
38   Invalid after 0 seconds, hold down 0, flushed after 0
39   Outgoing update filter list for all interfaces is not set
40   Incoming update filter list for all interfaces is not set
41   Redistributing: ospf 200
42   Routing for Networks:
43     172.16.2.4/30
44     172.16.1.4/30
45     172.16.1.252/30
46     172.16.1.32/27
47   Routing Information Sources:
48     Gateway         Distance      Last Update
49     172.16.2.253        110        00:29:52
50     172.16.253.9        110        00:19:01
51   Distance: (default is 110)
52
53 Rome#sho ip route
54 Codes: C - connected, S - static, I - IGRP, R - RIP, M - mobile, B - BGP
55        D - EIGRP, EX - EIGRP external, O - OSPF, IA - OSPF inter area
56        N1 - OSPF NSSA external type 1, N2 - OSPF NSSA external type 2
57        E1 - OSPF external type 1, E2 - OSPF external type 2, E - EGP
58        i - IS-IS, L1 - IS-IS level-1, L2 - IS-IS level-2, * - candidate default
59        U - per-user static route, o - ODR
60
61 Gateway of last resort is not set
62
63       172.16.0.0/16 is variably subnetted, 9 subnets, 4 masks
64 C        172.16.1.252/30 is directly connected, Loopback0
65 O IA     172.16.254.0/24 [110/810] via 172.16.1.5, 00:19:04, Serial1
66 O        172.16.2.253/32 [110/801] via 172.16.2.5, 00:29:56, Serial0
67 O IA     172.16.253.5/32 [110/811] via 172.16.1.5, 00:19:04, Serial1
68 O IA     172.16.253.9/32 [110/801] via 172.16.1.5, 00:24:13, Serial1
69 C        172.16.1.32/27 is directly connected, Ethernet0
70 O        172.16.2.32/27 [110/810] via 172.16.2.5, 00:29:56, Serial0
71 C        172.16.1.4/30 is directly connected, Serial1
72 C        172.16.2.4/30 is directly connected, Serial0
```

**Figure 6-114**   Paris **configurations** and **show** commands

```
Paris
1  !
2  hostname Paris
3  !
4  no ip domain-lookup
5  !
6  interface Loopback0
7   ip address 172.16.2.253 255.255.255.252
8  !
9  interface Ethernet0
10   ip address 172.16.2.33 255.255.255.224
11  !
12  interface Serial1
13   ip address 172.16.2.5 255.255.255.252
14   bandwidth 125
15   clockrate 125000
16  !
17  router ospf 200
18   network 172.16.2.252 0.0.0.3 area 2
19   network 172.16.2.4 0.0.0.3 area 2
20   network 172.16.2.32 0.0.0.31 area 2
21  !
22  ip classless
23  !
24  line con 0
25   exec-timeout 0 0
26   length 0
27  !
28  end
29
30  Paris#sho ip prot
31  Routing Protocol is "ospf 200"
32    Sending updates every 0 seconds
33    Invalid after 0 seconds, hold down 0, flushed after 0
34    Outgoing update filter list for all interfaces is not set
35    Incoming update filter list for all interfaces is not set
36    Redistributing: ospf 200
37    Routing for Networks:
38      172.16.2.252/30
39      172.16.2.4/30
40      172.16.2.32/27
41    Routing Information Sources:
42      Gateway          Distance        Last Update
43    Distance: (default is 110)
44
45  Paris#sho ip route
46  Codes: C - connected, S - static, I - IGRP, R - RIP, M - mobile, B - BGP
47         D - EIGRP, EX - EIGRP external, O - OSPF, IA - OSPF inter area
48         N1 - OSPF NSSA external type 1, N2 - OSPF NSSA external type 2
49         E1 - OSPF external type 1, E2 - OSPF external type 2, E - EGP
50         i - IS-IS, L1 - IS-IS level-1, L2 - IS-IS level-2, * - candidate default
51         U - per-user static route, o - ODR
52
53  Gateway of last resort is not set
54
55      172.16.0.0/16 is variably subnetted, 3 subnets, 2 masks
56  C      172.16.2.252/30 is directly connected, Loopback0
57  C      172.16.2.32/27 is directly connected, Ethernet0
58  C      172.16.2.4/30 is directly connected, Serial1
```

# Example #11—Complex Redistribution

The following example connects RIPv2, EIGRP, and OSPF in a very complex manner. The first set of configuration files and show commands have been partially configured for basic configuration, but problems were encountered when using the simple configurations outlined earlier. Figure 6-115 details the layout and routing domains defined.

After changes are made to three of the router configurations, the anomalies that appear in the previous configurations will be corrected.

A set of configurations, show commands, and debugging sessions, Figures 6-116 through 6-121, provide a solution to this problem and can be found at the end of this chapter.

**Figure 6-115**

RIPv2, EIGRP, and OSPF redistribution network

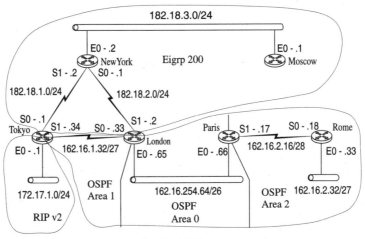

Loopback Addresses

```
Tokyo   162.16.1.193/30      Area 1
London  162.16.254.193/30    Area 0
Paris   162.16.254.197/30    Area 0
Rome    162.16.2.193/30      Area 2
```

**Figure 6-116** Tokyo configurations and **show** commands

```
Tokyo
1 !
2 hostname Tokyo
3 !
4 no ip domain-lookup
5 !
6 interface Loopback0
7  ip address 162.16.1.193 255.255.255.252
8 !
9 interface Ethernet0
10  ip address 172.17.1.1 255.255.255.0
11 !
12 interface Serial0
13  ip address 182.18.1.1 255.255.255.0
14  bandwidth 125
15 !
16 interface Serial1
17  ip address 162.16.1.34 255.255.255.224
18  bandwidth 125
19  clockrate 125000
20 !
21 router eigrp 200
22  redistribute rip metric 10000 100 255 1 1500
23  redistribute ospf 200 metric 56 2000 255 1 1500
24  passive-interface Ethernet0
25  network 182.18.0.0
26 !
27 router ospf 200
28  redistribute rip metric 100 subnets
29  redistribute eigrp 200 metric 500 subnets
30  network 162.16.1.32 0.0.0.31 area 1
31  network 162.16.1.192 0.0.0.3 area 1
32 !
33 router rip
34  version 2
35  redistribute ospf 100 metric 1
36  redistribute eigrp 200 metric 1
37  passive-interface Serial0
38  passive-interface Serial1
39  network 172.17.0.0
40 !
41 ip classless
42 !
43 line con 0
44  exec-timeout 0 0
45  length 0
46 !
47 end
48
49 Tokyo#sho ip prot
50 Routing Protocol is "rip"
51   Sending updates every 30 seconds, next due in 1 seconds
52   Invalid after 180 seconds, hold down 180, flushed after 240
53   Outgoing update filter list for all interfaces is not set
54   Incoming update filter list for all interfaces is not set
55   Redistributing: rip, ospf 100 (internal, external 1, external 2)
56
57   Redistributing: eigrp 200
58   Default version control: send version 2, receive version 2
```

**Figure 6-116** *Continued*

```
59     Interface        Send  Recv   Key-chain
60     Ethernet0         2     2
61   Routing for Networks:
62     172.17.0.0
63   Passive Interface(s):
64     Serial0
65     Serial1
66   Routing Information Sources:
67     Gateway          Distance       Last Update
68   Distance: (default is 120)
69
70 Routing Protocol is "eigrp 200"
71   Outgoing update filter list for all interfaces is not set
72   Incoming update filter list for all interfaces is not set
73   Default networks flagged in outgoing updates
74   Default networks accepted from incoming updates
75   EIGRP metric weight K1=1, K2=0, K3=1, K4=0, K5=0
76   EIGRP maximum hopcount 100
77   EIGRP maximum metric variance 1
78   Redistributing: rip, eigrp 200, ospf 200 (internal, external 1, external 2)
79
80   Automatic network summarization is in effect
81   Routing for Networks:
82     182.18.0.0
83   Passive Interface(s):
84     Ethernet0
85   Routing Information Sources:
86     Gateway          Distance       Last Update
87     182.18.1.2           90         00:16:39
88   Distance: internal 90 external 170
89
90 Routing Protocol is "ospf 200"
91   Sending updates every 0 seconds
92   Invalid after 0 seconds, hold down 0, flushed after 0
93   Outgoing update filter list for all interfaces is not set
94   Incoming update filter list for all interfaces is not set
95   Redistributing: rip, eigrp 200, ospf 200
96   Routing for Networks:
97     162.16.1.32/27
98     162.16.1.192/30
99   Routing Information Sources:
100    Gateway          Distance       Last Update
101    162.16.254.193       110        00:16:40
102  Distance: (default is 110)
103
104 Tokyo#sho ip route
105 Codes: C - connected, S - static, I - IGRP, R - RIP, M - mobile, B - BGP
106        D - EIGRP, EX - EIGRP external, O - OSPF, IA - OSPF inter area
107        N1 - OSPF NSSA external type 1, N2 - OSPF NSSA external type 2
108        E1 - OSPF external type 1, E2 - OSPF external type 2, E - EGP
109        i - IS-IS, L1 - IS-IS level-1, L2 - IS-IS level-2, * - candidate default
110        U - per-user static route, o - ODR
111
112 Gateway of last resort is not set
113
114       172.17.0.0/24 is subnetted, 1 subnets
115 C       172.17.1.0 is directly connected, Ethernet0
116       162.16.0.0/16 is variably subnetted, 10 subnets, 6 masks
117 D EX    162.16.254.64/26 [170/21529600] via 182.18.1.2, 00:16:41, Serial0
```

```
118 O IA    162.16.254.0/24 [110/801] via 162.16.1.33, 00:16:41, Serial1
119 D EX     162.16.2.193/32 [170/21529600] via 182.18.1.2, 00:17:53, Serial0
120 C        162.16.1.192/30 is directly connected, Loopback0
121 D EX     162.16.254.197/32 [170/21529600] via 182.18.1.2, 00:16:41, Serial0
122 D EX     162.16.254.192/30 [170/21529600] via 182.18.1.2, 01:17:50, Serial0
123 D EX     162.16.2.32/27 [170/21529600] via 182.18.1.2, 00:17:53, Serial0
124 C        162.16.1.32/27 is directly connected, Serial1
125 D EX     162.16.2.16/28 [170/21529600] via 182.18.1.2, 00:17:54, Serial0
126 O IA     162.16.2.0/24 [110/1610] via 162.16.1.33, 00:17:54, Serial1
127          182.18.0.0/24 is subnetted, 3 subnets
128 C        182.18.1.0 is directly connected, Serial0
129 D        182.18.2.0 [90/21504000] via 182.18.1.2, 01:17:57, Serial0
130 D        182.18.3.0 [90/21017600] via 182.18.1.2, 01:35:47, Serial0
```

**Figure 6-117**  London configurations and **show** commands

```
London
1  !
2  hostname London
3  !
4  no ip domain-lookup
5  !
6  interface Loopback0
7   ip address 162.16.254.193 255.255.255.252
8  !
9  interface Ethernet0
10   ip address 162.16.254.65 255.255.255.192
11  !
12  interface Serial0
13   ip address 162.16.1.33 255.255.255.224
14   bandwidth 125
15  !
16  interface Serial1
17   ip address 182.18.2.2 255.255.255.0
18   bandwidth 125
19   clockrate 125000
20  !
21  router eigrp 200
22   redistribute ospf 200 metric 10000 100 255 1 1500
23   network 182.18.0.0
24  !
25  router ospf 200
26   redistribute eigrp 200 metric 250 subnets
27   network 162.16.254.64 0.0.0.63 area 0
28   network 162.16.254.192 0.0.0.3 area 0
29   network 162.16.1.32 0.0.0.31 area 1
30   area 0 range 162.16.254.0 255.255.255.0
31   area 1 range 162.16.1.0 255.255.255.0
32  !
33  ip classless
34  !
35  line con 0
36   exec-timeout 0 0
37   length 0
38  !
39  end
```

**Figure 6-117** Continued

```
40
41 London#sho ip prot
42 Routing Protocol is "eigrp 200"
43   Outgoing update filter list for all interfaces is not set
44   Incoming update filter list for all interfaces is not set
45   Default networks flagged in outgoing updates
46   Default networks accepted from incoming updates
47   EIGRP metric weight K1=1, K2=0, K3=1, K4=0, K5=0
48   EIGRP maximum hopcount 100
49   EIGRP maximum metric variance 1
50   Redistributing: eigrp 200, ospf 200 (internal, external 1, external 2)
51
52   Automatic network summarization is in effect
53   Routing for Networks:
54     182.18.0.0
55   Routing Information Sources:
56     Gateway         Distance      Last Update
57     182.18.2.1           90       00:13:23
58   Distance: internal 90 external 170
59
60 Routing Protocol is "ospf 200"
61   Sending updates every 0 seconds
62   Invalid after 0 seconds, hold down 0, flushed after 0
63   Outgoing update filter list for all interfaces is not set
64   Incoming update filter list for all interfaces is not set
65   Redistributing: eigrp 200, ospf 200
66   Routing for Networks:
67     162.16.254.64/26
68     162.16.254.192/30
69     162.16.1.32/27
70   Routing Information Sources:
71     Gateway         Distance      Last Update
72     162.16.1.193         110       00:13:23
73     162.16.254.197       110       00:13:23
74   Distance: (default is 110)
75
76 London#sho ip route
77 Codes: C - connected, S - static, I - IGRP, R - RIP, M - mobile, B - BGP
78        D - EIGRP, EX - EIGRP external, O - OSPF, IA - OSPF inter area
79        N1 - OSPF NSSA external type 1, N2 - OSPF NSSA external type 2
80        E1 - OSPF external type 1, E2 - OSPF external type 2, E - EGP
81        i - IS-IS, L1 - IS-IS level-1, L2 - IS-IS level-2, * - candidate default
82        U - per-user static route, o - ODR
83
84 Gateway of last resort is not set
85
86      172.17.0.0/24 is subnetted, 1 subnets
87 O E2    172.17.1.0 [110/100] via 162.16.1.34, 00:13:15, Serial0
88      162.16.0.0/16 is variably subnetted, 11 subnets, 6 masks
89 C       162.16.254.64/26 is directly connected, Ethernet0
90 D EX    162.16.254.0/24 [170/47250176] via 182.18.2.1, 00:13:15, Serial1
91 O E2    162.16.2.193/32 [110/500] via 162.16.1.34, 00:13:15, Serial0
92 O       162.16.1.193/32 [110/801] via 162.16.1.34, 00:13:15, Serial0
93 D EX    162.16.1.192/30 [170/47250176] via 182.18.2.1, 01:12:29, Serial1
94 O       162.16.254.197/32 [110/11] via 162.16.254.66, 00:13:15, Ethernet0
95 C       162.16.254.192/30 is directly connected, Loopback0
96 O E2    162.16.2.32/27 [110/500] via 162.16.1.34, 00:13:15, Serial0
97 C       162.16.1.32/27 is directly connected, Serial0
```

```
98  O E2    162.16.2.16/28 [110/500] via 162.16.1.34, 00:13:15, Serial0
99  O IA    162.16.2.0/24 [110/810] via 162.16.254.66, 00:13:15, Ethernet0
100     182.18.0.0/24 is subnetted, 3 subnets
101 D       182.18.1.0 [90/21504000] via 182.18.2.1, 01:14:27, Serial1
102 C       182.18.2.0 is directly connected, Serial1
103 D       182.18.3.0 [90/21017600] via 182.18.2.1, 01:14:27, Serial1
```

**Figure 6-118** NewYork configurations and **show** commands

```
NewYork
1  !
2  hostname NewYork
3  !
4  no ip domain-lookup
5  !
6  interface Ethernet0
7   ip address 182.18.3.2 255.255.255.0
8  !
9  interface Serial0
10  ip address 182.18.2.1 255.255.255.0
11  bandwidth 125
12  !
13 interface Serial1
14  ip address 182.18.1.2 255.255.255.0
15  bandwidth 125
16  clockrate 125000
17  !
18 router eigrp 200
19  network 182.18.0.0
20  !
21 ip classless
22  !
23  !
24 line con 0
25  exec-timeout 0 0
26  length 0
27  !
28 end
29
30 NewYork#sho ip prot
31 Routing Protocol is "eigrp 200"
32   Outgoing update filter list for all interfaces is not set
33   Incoming update filter list for all interfaces is not set
34   Default networks flagged in outgoing updates
35   Default networks accepted from incoming updates
36   EIGRP metric weight K1=1, K2=0, K3=1, K4=0, K5=0
37   EIGRP maximum hopcount 100
38   EIGRP maximum metric variance 1
39   Redistributing: eigrp 200
40   Automatic network summarization is in effect
41   Routing for Networks:
42     182.18.0.0
43   Routing Information Sources:
44     Gateway         Distance      Last Update
45     182.18.2.2           90       00:14:23
46     182.18.1.1           90       00:14:23
47     182.18.3.1           90       00:14:23
```

**Figure 6-118** Continued

```
48   Distance: internal 90 external 170
49
50 NewYork#sho ip route
51 Codes: C - connected, S - static, I - IGRP, R - RIP, M - mobile, B - BGP
52         D - EIGRP, EX - EIGRP external, O - OSPF, IA - OSPF inter area
53         N1 - OSPF NSSA external type 1, N2 - OSPF NSSA external type 2
54         E1 - OSPF external type 1, E2 - OSPF external type 2, E - EGP
55         i - IS-IS, L1 - IS-IS level-1, L2 - IS-IS level-2, * - candidate default
56         U - per-user static route, o - ODR
57
58 Gateway of last resort is not set
59
60      172.17.0.0/24 is subnetted, 1 subnets
61 D EX    172.17.1.0 [170/21017600] via 182.18.1.1, 00:30:18, Serial1
62                    [170/21017600] via 182.18.2.2, 00:30:18, Serial0
63      162.16.0.0/16 is variably subnetted, 11 subnets, 6 masks
64 D EX    162.16.254.64/26 [170/21017600] via 182.18.2.2, 00:14:27, Serial0
65 D EX    162.16.254.0/24 [170/46738176] via 182.18.1.1, 00:14:27, Serial1
66 D EX    162.16.2.193/32 [170/21017600] via 182.18.2.2, 00:15:39, Serial0
67 D EX    162.16.1.193/32 [170/21017600] via 182.18.2.2, 01:15:36, Serial0
68 D EX    162.16.1.192/30 [170/46738176] via 182.18.1.1, 01:13:42, Serial1
69 D EX    162.16.254.197/32 [170/21017600] via 182.18.2.2, 00:14:28, Serial0
70 D EX    162.16.254.192/30 [170/21017600] via 182.18.2.2, 01:15:37, Serial0
71 D EX    162.16.2.32/27 [170/21017600] via 182.18.2.2, 00:15:40, Serial0
72 D EX    162.16.1.32/27 [170/21017600] via 182.18.2.2, 01:13:42, Serial0
73 D EX    162.16.2.16/28 [170/21017600] via 182.18.2.2, 00:15:40, Serial0
74 D EX    162.16.2.0/24 [170/21017600] via 182.18.2.2, 00:15:40, Serial0
75      182.18.0.0/24 is subnetted, 3 subnets
76 C       182.18.1.0 is directly connected, Serial1
77 C       182.18.2.0 is directly connected, Serial0
78 C       182.18.3.0 is directly connected, Ethernet0
```

**Figure 6-119** Moscow configurations and **show** commands

**Moscow**
```
1  !
2  hostname Moscow
3  !
4  no ip domain-lookup
5  !
6  interface Ethernet0
7   ip address 182.18.3.1 255.255.255.0
8  !
9  router eigrp 200
10   network 182.18.0.0
11 !
12 ip classless
13 !
14 line con 0
15   exec-timeout 0 0
```

```
16  length 0
17  !
18  end
19
20  Moscow#sho ip prot
21  Routing Protocol is "eigrp 200"
22    Outgoing update filter list for all interfaces is not set
23    Incoming update filter list for all interfaces is not set
24    Default networks flagged in outgoing updates
25    Default networks accepted from incoming updates
26    EIGRP metric weight K1=1, K2=0, K3=1, K4=0, K5=0
27    EIGRP maximum hopcount 100
28    EIGRP maximum metric variance 1
29    Redistributing: eigrp 200
30    Automatic network summarization is in effect
31    Routing for Networks:
32      182.18.0.0
33    Routing Information Sources:
34      Gateway          Distance      Last Update
35      182.18.3.2            90        00:15:50
36    Distance: internal 90 external 170
37
38  Moscow#sho ip route
39  Codes: C - connected, S - static, I - IGRP, R - RIP, M - mobile, B - BGP
40         D - EIGRP, EX - EIGRP external, O - OSPF, IA - OSPF inter area
41         N1 - OSPF NSSA external type 1, N2 - OSPF NSSA external type 2
42         E1 - OSPF external type 1, E2 - OSPF external type 2, E - EGP
43         i - IS-IS, L1 - IS-IS level-1, L2 - IS-IS level-2, * - candidate default
44         U - per-user static route, o - ODR
45
46  Gateway of last resort is not set
47
48       172.17.0.0/24 is subnetted, 1 subnets
49  D EX    172.17.1.0 [170/21043200] via 182.18.3.2, 00:31:45, Ethernet0
50       162.16.0.0/16 is variably subnetted, 11 subnets, 6 masks
51  D EX    162.16.254.64/26 [170/21043200] via 182.18.3.2, 01:17:03, Ethernet0
52  D EX    162.16.254.0/24 [170/46763776] via 182.18.3.2, 00:15:54, Ethernet0
53  D EX    162.16.2.193/32 [170/21043200] via 182.18.3.2, 00:17:06, Ethernet0
54  D EX    162.16.1.193/32 [170/21043200] via 182.18.3.2, 01:17:03, Ethernet0
55  D EX    162.16.1.192/30 [170/46763776] via 182.18.3.2, 01:15:09, Ethernet0
56  D EX    162.16.254.197/32 [170/21043200] via 182.18.3.2, 00:34:00, Ethernet0
57  D EX    162.16.254.192/30 [170/21043200] via 182.18.3.2, 01:17:04, Ethernet0
58  D EX    162.16.2.32/27 [170/21043200] via 182.18.3.2, 00:17:07, Ethernet0
59  D EX    162.16.1.32/27 [170/21043200] via 182.18.3.2, 01:17:04, Ethernet0
60  D EX    162.16.2.16/28 [170/21043200] via 182.18.3.2, 00:17:07, Ethernet0
61  D EX    162.16.2.0/24 [170/21043200] via 182.18.3.2, 00:17:07, Ethernet0
62       182.18.0.0/24 is subnetted, 3 subnets
63  D       182.18.1.0 [90/21017600] via 182.18.3.2, 01:35:02, Ethernet0
64  D       182.18.2.0 [90/21017600] via 182.18.3.2, 01:17:10, Ethernet0
65  C       182.18.3.0 is directly connected, Ethernet0
```

**Figure 6-120**    Rome configurations and **show** commands

**Rome**

```
1  !
2  hostname Rome
3  !
4  !
5  no ip domain-lookup
6  !
7  interface Loopback0
8   ip address 162.16.2.193 255.255.255.252
9  !
10 interface Ethernet0
11  ip address 162.16.2.33 255.255.255.224
12 !
13 interface Serial0
14  ip address 162.16.2.18 255.255.255.240
15  no ip mroute-cache
16  bandwidth 125
17  no fair-queue
18 !
19 interface Serial1
20  no ip address
21  bandwidth 125
22  shutdown
23  clockrate 125000
24 !
25 interface Serial2
26  no ip address
27  shutdown
28 !
29 interface Serial3
30  no ip address
31  shutdown
32 !
33 interface BRI0
34  no ip address
35  shutdown
36 !
37 router ospf 200
38  network 162.16.2.16 0.0.0.15 area 2
39  network 162.16.2.32 0.0.0.31 area 2
40  network 162.16.2.192 0.0.0.3 area 2
41 !
42 ip classless
43 !
44 !
45 line con 0
46  exec-timeout 0 0
47  length 0
48 line aux 0
49  transport input all
50 line vty 0 4
51  login
52 !
53 end
54
55 Rome#sho ip prot
```

```
56 Routing Protocol is "ospf 200"
57   Sending updates every 0 seconds
58   Invalid after 0 seconds, hold down 0, flushed after 0
59   Outgoing update filter list for all interfaces is not set
60   Incoming update filter list for all interfaces is not set
61   Redistributing: ospf 200
62   Routing for Networks:
63     162.16.2.16/28
64     162.16.2.32/27
65     162.16.2.192/30
66   Routing Information Sources:
67     Gateway          Distance      Last Update
68     162.16.1.193          110      00:11:57
69     162.16.254.197        110      00:12:12
70     162.16.254.193        110      00:15:38
71   Distance: (default is 110)
72
73 Rome#sho ip route
74 Codes: C - connected, S - static, I - IGRP, R - RIP, M - mobile, B - BGP
75        D - EIGRP, EX - EIGRP external, O - OSPF, IA - OSPF inter area
76        N1 - OSPF NSSA external type 1, N2 - OSPF NSSA external type 2
77        E1 - OSPF external type 1, E2 - OSPF external type 2, E - EGP
78        i - IS-IS, L1 - IS-IS level-1, L2 - IS-IS level-2, * - candidate default
79        U - per-user static route, o - ODR
80
81 Gateway of last resort is not set
82
83      172.17.0.0/24 is subnetted, 1 subnets
84 O E2    172.17.1.0 [110/100] via 162.16.2.17, 00:15:44, Serial0
85      162.16.0.0/16 is variably subnetted, 9 subnets, 6 masks
86 O E2    162.16.254.64/26 [110/500] via 162.16.2.17, 00:12:03, Serial0
87 O IA    162.16.254.0/24 [110/801] via 162.16.2.17, 00:13:00, Serial0
88 C       162.16.2.192/30 is directly connected, Loopback0
89 O E2    162.16.1.192/30 [110/250] via 162.16.2.17, 00:15:44, Serial0
90 O E2    162.16.254.197/32 [110/500] via 162.16.2.17, 00:12:03, Serial0
91 O E2    162.16.254.192/30 [110/500] via 162.16.2.17, 00:15:44, Serial0
92 C       162.16.2.32/27 is directly connected, Ethernet0
93 C       162.16.2.16/28 is directly connected, Serial0
94 O IA    162.16.1.0/24 [110/1610] via 162.16.2.17, 00:12:19, Serial0
95      182.18.0.0/24 is subnetted, 3 subnets
96 O E2    182.18.1.0 [110/250] via 162.16.2.17, 00:15:45, Serial0
97 O E2    182.18.2.0 [110/250] via 162.16.2.17, 00:15:45, Serial0
98 O E2    182.18.3.0 [110/250] via 162.16.2.17, 00:15:45, Serial0
```

**Figure 6-121**  Paris configurations and **show** commands

```
Paris
1 !
2 hostname Paris
3 !
4 no ip domain-lookup
5 !
6 interface Loopback0
7   ip address 162.16.254.197 255.255.255.252
8 !
9 interface Ethernet0
10  ip address 162.16.254.66 255.255.255.192
```

**Figure 6-121**  *Continued*

```
11 !
12 interface Serial1
13  ip address 162.16.2.17 255.255.255.240
14  bandwidth 125
15  clockrate 125000
16 !
17 router ospf 200
18  network 162.16.254.64 0.0.0.63 area 0
19  network 162.16.254.196 0.0.0.3 area 0
20  network 162.16.2.16 0.0.0.15 area 2
21  area 0 range 162.16.254.0 255.255.255.0
22  area 2 range 162.16.2.0 255.255.255.0
23 !
24 ip classless
25 !
26 line con 0
27  exec-timeout 0 0
28  length 0
29 !
30 end
31
32 Paris#sho ip prot
33 Routing Protocol is "ospf 200"
34   Sending updates every 0 seconds
35   Invalid after 0 seconds, hold down 0, flushed after 0
36   Outgoing update filter list for all interfaces is not set
37   Incoming update filter list for all interfaces is not set
38   Redistributing: ospf 200
39   Routing for Networks:
40     162.16.254.64/26
41     162.16.254.196/30
42     162.16.2.16/28
43   Routing Information Sources:
44     Gateway          Distance      Last Update
45     162.16.2.193          110      00:18:31
46     162.16.1.193          110      00:18:31
47     162.16.254.193        110      00:17:34
48   Distance: (default is 110)
49
50 Paris#sho ip route
51 Codes: C - connected, S - static, I - IGRP, R - RIP, M - mobile, B - BGP
52        D - EIGRP, EX - EIGRP external, O - OSPF, IA - OSPF inter area
53        N1 - OSPF NSSA external type 1, N2 - OSPF NSSA external type 2
54        E1 - OSPF external type 1, E2 - OSPF external type 2, E - EGP
55        i - IS-IS, L1 - IS-IS level-1, L2 - IS-IS level-2, * - candidate default
56        U - per-user static route, o - ODR
57
58 Gateway of last resort is not set
59
60      172.17.0.0/24 is subnetted, 1 subnets
61 O E2    172.17.1.0 [110/100] via 162.16.254.65, 00:18:41, Ethernet0
62      162.16.0.0/16 is variably subnetted, 10 subnets, 6 masks
63 C       162.16.254.64/26 is directly connected, Ethernet0
64 O E2    162.16.254.0/24 [110/250] via 162.16.254.65, 00:17:44, Ethernet0
65 O       162.16.2.193/32 [110/801] via 162.16.2.18, 00:18:41, Serial1
66 O E2    162.16.1.192/30 [110/250] via 162.16.254.65, 00:18:41, Ethernet0
```

```
67 C         162.16.254.196/30 is directly connected, Loopback0
68 O E2      162.16.254.192/30 [110/500] via 162.16.254.65, 00:18:41, Ethernet0
69 O         162.16.254.193/32 [110/11] via 162.16.254.65, 00:18:41, Ethernet0
70 O         162.16.2.32/27 [110/810] via 162.16.2.18, 00:18:42, Serial1
71 C         162.16.2.16/28 is directly connected, Serial1
72 O IA      162.16.1.0/24 [110/810] via 162.16.254.65, 00:18:00, Ethernet0
73       182.18.0.0/24 is subnetted, 3 subnets
74 O E2      182.18.1.0 [110/250] via 162.16.254.65, 00:18:42, Ethernet0
75 O E2      182.18.2.0 [110/250] via 162.16.254.65, 00:18:42, Ethernet0
76 O E2      182.18.3.0 [110/250] via 162.16.254.65, 00:18:42, Ethernet0
```

# CCIE Tips

Understanding route redistribution and route summarization is a critical skill set for CCIE candidates and in the general workplace. Most companies today are going through mergers, purchases, and network consolidation at unprecedented rates.

Test pathways to destination networks using the **ping** and **trace** commands make sure you know all the extended options available in the privileged mode.

Know your network layout and verify that there are no strange routes or duplicate routes with different netmask prefixes from different routing protocols in the **show ip route** output.

If there are two separate contact points between two IP routing protocols, a useful debugging tip is to assign different starting metrics for both protocols at each contact point to verify that the redistribution process and route calculation is working properly. Switch the metrics on both contact points, and verify again. If all indications show proper operation, then implement the appropriate metrics for full operation and verify normal operation.

When using the **default-network** command, make sure that the default network in question has been identified to the routing process with a network command or redistribution command. The **default-network** command is used to propagate gateway of last resort information to other routers in the routing protocol domain, but it does not establish an actual route to networks outside of the routing protocol domain.

For OSPF virtual links, it is important to remember that a virtual link opens up a pathway from the router to the backbone area for routing updates. Area summarization commands need to be applied to EVERY active connection between a subarea and the backbone area. See Example #10 in this chapter.

For classless routing protocols, make sure that the subnet option is used during the redistribution process into OSPF.

Route summarization is the key to making clean and compact routing tables, but make sure to clean up each protocol before the information is redistributed.

## SUMMARY

Due to the expanding nature of IP as the protocol of choice for desktop environments, it is normal to expect that interactions between routing protocols will be a part of every network in one way or another. This chapter has explained how we can use each of these routing protocols as needed, and be able to integrate these multiple routing protocols to provide optimum pathways for end-station-to-end-station traffic.

## Questions & Answers

### Question #1: Can the two network commands on lines 14 and 15 be replaced with a single command?

Yes, both class C networks could be tied into the OSPF process with the following command: network 192.168.0.0 0.0.255.255 area 4. This identifies all active interface ip addresses that start with 192.168. in the first two octets as participants in the OSPF routing process.

### Question #2: After reviewing all the information in Example #4, what would be the result of the following command: tokyo# ping 192.168.3.0?

All five **ping** attempts would time out. If you **ping** a target, the source IP address is assigned as the interface IP address used to begin the journey to the destination. If you check London's **show ip route**, there are routes to the Ethernet segments, 192.168.1.0 and 192.168.3.0, but no pathway to the 192.168.4.0 network. With the standard ping issued from Tokyo, the source address is 192.168.4.1, and after the ping reaches its destination, there is no route back to the source address.

### Question #3: What is the standard OSPF metric calculation, and what metric needs to be used in the redistribution process in London to provide more accurate IP routing?

The standard OSPF metric calculation is $10^8$/bandwidth, so an Ethernet segment would calculate out to 100,000,000/10,000,000 = 10. Remember to change all serial connections as the default bandwidth is to 1544kbps.

**Question #4: Was the passive-interface command required in the London configuration to eliminate IGRP updates going out interface Serial 1?**

No, because to participate in a routing protocol, a network statement must be present that matches the IP address on the interface. In this case, the **passive-interface** command would not needed.

**Question #5: Why are there no special route summarization commands during our redistribution process?**

IGRP is a classful routing protocol, so any routes distributed out of an IGRP cloud are summarized by default.

# Exercise Solutions

## Example #10

The six figures 6-122 through 6-127 provide one solution to clean routing tables, effective route summarization, and in OSPF, successful implementation of a virtual link.

**Figure 6-122** Tokyo configurations and **show** commands

```
Tokyo
1  !
2  hostname Tokyo
3  !
4  no ip domain-lookup
5  !
6  interface Ethernet0
7   ip address 182.18.4.1 255.255.255.0
8  !
9  interface Serial0
10  ip address 182.18.1.1 255.255.255.0
11  bandwidth 125
12 !
```

**Figure 6-122**   Continued

```
13 interface Serial1
14  ip address 182.18.3.2 255.255.255.0
15  bandwidth 125
16  clockrate 125000
17 !
18 interface BRI0
19  no ip address
20  shutdown
21 !
22 router eigrp 200
23  network 182.18.0.0
24 !
25 ip classless
26 !
27 !
28 line con 0
29  exec-timeout 0 0
30  length 0
31 !
32 end
33
34 Tokyo#sho ip prot
35 Routing Protocol is "eigrp 200"
36   Outgoing update filter list for all interfaces is not set
37   Incoming update filter list for all interfaces is not set
38   Default networks flagged in outgoing updates
39   Default networks accepted from incoming updates
40   EIGRP metric weight K1=1, K2=0, K3=1, K4=0, K5=0
41   EIGRP maximum hopcount 100
42   EIGRP maximum metric variance 1
43   Redistributing: eigrp 200
44   Automatic network summarization is in effect
45   Routing for Networks:
46     182.18.0.0
47   Routing Information Sources:
48     Gateway          Distance      Last Update
49     182.18.3.1             90      00:07:30
50     182.18.1.2             90      00:07:30
51   Distance: internal 90 external 170
52
53 Tokyo#sho ip route
54 Codes: C - connected, S - static, I - IGRP, R - RIP, M - mobile, B - BGP
55        D - EIGRP, EX - EIGRP external, O - OSPF, IA - OSPF inter area
56        N1 - OSPF NSSA external type 1, N2 - OSPF NSSA external type 2
57        E1 - OSPF external type 1, E2 - OSPF external type 2, E - EGP
58        i - IS-IS, L1 - IS-IS level-1, L2 - IS-IS level-2, * - candidate default
59        U - per-user static route, o - ODR
60
61 Gateway of last resort is not set
62
63      182.18.0.0/24 is subnetted, 5 subnets
64 C       182.18.4.0 is directly connected, Ethernet0
65 D       182.18.5.0 [90/21017600] via 182.18.3.1, 00:06:29, Serial1
66 C       182.18.1.0 is directly connected, Serial0
67 D       182.18.2.0 [90/21504000] via 182.18.1.2, 00:06:29, Serial0
68                    [90/21504000] via 182.18.3.1, 00:06:29, Serial1
69 C       182.18.3.0 is directly connected, Serial1
```

**Figure 6-123** London configurations and **show** commands

**London**
```
1  !
2  hostname London
3  !
4  no ip domain-lookup
5  !
6  interface Ethernet0
7   ip address 182.18.5.1 255.255.255.0
8  !
9  interface Serial0
10  ip address 182.18.3.1 255.255.255.0
11  bandwidth 125
12  !
13 interface Serial1
14  ip address 182.18.2.2 255.255.255.0
15  bandwidth 125
16  clockrate 125000
17 !
18 router eigrp 200
19  network 182.18.0.0
20 !
21 ip classless
22 !
23 line con 0
24  exec-timeout 0 0
25  length 0
26 !
27 end
28
29 London#sho ip prot
30 Routing Protocol is "eigrp 200"
31   Outgoing update filter list for all interfaces is not set
32   Incoming update filter list for all interfaces is not set
33   Default networks flagged in outgoing updates
34   Default networks accepted from incoming updates
35   EIGRP metric weight K1=1, K2=0, K3=1, K4=0, K5=0
36   EIGRP maximum hopcount 100
37   EIGRP maximum metric variance 1
38   Redistributing: eigrp 200
39   Automatic network summarization is in effect
40   Routing for Networks:
41     182.18.0.0
42   Routing Information Sources:
43     Gateway          Distance      Last Update
44     182.18.3.2            90        00:17:05
45     182.18.2.1            90        00:17:05
46   Distance: internal 90 external 170
47
48 London#sho ip route
49 Codes: C - connected, S - static, I - IGRP, R - RIP, M - mobile, B - BGP
50        D - EIGRP, EX - EIGRP external, O - OSPF, IA - OSPF inter area
51        N1 - OSPF NSSA external type 1, N2 - OSPF NSSA external type 2
52        E1 - OSPF external type 1, E2 - OSPF external type 2, E - EGP
53        i - IS-IS, L1 - IS-IS level-1, L2 - IS-IS level-2, * - candidate default
54        U - per-user static route, o - ODR
```

**Figure 6-123** Continued

```
55
56 Gateway of last resort is not set
57
58 D    172.16.0.0/16 [90/21248000] via 182.18.2.1, 00:17:09, Serial1
59      182.18.0.0/24 is subnetted, 5 subnets
60 D       182.18.4.0 [90/21017600] via 182.18.3.2, 00:17:10, Serial0
61 C       182.18.5.0 is directly connected, Ethernet0
62 D       182.18.1.0 [90/21504000] via 182.18.3.2, 00:17:10, Serial0
63                    [90/21504000] via 182.18.2.1, 00:17:10, Serial1
64 C       182.18.2.0 is directly connected, Serial1
65 C       182.18.3.0 is directly connected, Serial0
```

**Figure 6-124** NewYork configurations and **show** commands

**NewYork**

```
1  !
2  hostname NewYork
3  !
4  no ip domain-lookup
5  !
6  interface Loopback0
7   ip address 172.16.253.5 255.255.255.0
8  !
9  interface Ethernet0
10   ip address 172.16.254.2 255.255.255.0
11  !
12 interface Serial0
13   ip address 182.18.2.1 255.255.255.0
14   ip summary-address eigrp 200 172.16.0.0 255.255.0.0
15   bandwidth 125
16   !
17 interface Serial1
18   ip address 182.18.1.2 255.255.255.0
19   ip summary-address eigrp 200 172.16.0.0 255.255.0.0
20   bandwidth 125
21   clockrate 125000
22 !
23 router eigrp 200
24   redistribute ospf 200 metric 125000 1000 255 1 1500
25   network 182.18.0.0
26   no auto-summary
27 !
28 router ospf 200
29   summary-address 182.18.0.0 255.255.0.0
30   redistribute eigrp 200 metric 400 subnets
31   network 172.16.253.4 0.0.0.3 area 0
32   network 172.16.254.0 0.0.0.255 area 0
33   distribute-list 4 out
34 !
35 ip classless
36 access-list 4 deny    172.16.0.0
37 access-list 4 permit any
38 !
```

```
39 line con 0
40  exec-timeout 0 0
41  length 0
42 !
43 end
44
45 NewYork#sho ip prot
46 Routing Protocol is "eigrp 200"
47   Outgoing update filter list for all interfaces is not set
48   Incoming update filter list for all interfaces is not set
49   Default networks flagged in outgoing updates
50   Default networks accepted from incoming updates
51   EIGRP metric weight K1=1, K2=0, K3=1, K4=0, K5=0
52   EIGRP maximum hopcount 100
53   EIGRP maximum metric variance 1
54   Redistributing: eigrp 200
55   Automatic network summarization is in effect
56   Automatic address summarization:
57     192.168.4.0/24 for Ethernet0, Serial0
58     192.168.1.0/24 for Serial1, Serial0
59     192.168.6.0/24 for Ethernet0, Serial1
60   Routing for Networks:
61     192.168.4.0
62     192.168.1.0
63     192.168.6.0
64   Routing Information Sources:
65     Gateway         Distance      Last Update
66     192.168.6.2          90       00:03:46
67     192.168.4.1          90       00:03:46
68   Distance: internal 90 external 170
69
70 NewYork#sho ip route
71 Codes: C - connected, S - static, I - IGRP, R - RIP, M - mobile, B - BGP
72        D - EIGRP, EX - EIGRP external, O - OSPF, IA - OSPF inter area
73        N1 - OSPF NSSA external type 1, N2 - OSPF NSSA external type 2
74        E1 - OSPF external type 1, E2 - OSPF external type 2, E - EGP
75        i - IS-IS, L1 - IS-IS level-1, L2 - IS-IS level-2, * - candidate default
76        U - per-user static route, o - ODR
77
78 Gateway of last resort is not set
79
80      172.16.0.0/16 is variably subnetted, 6 subnets, 3 masks
81 C       172.16.253.0/24 is directly connected, Loopback0
82 C       172.16.254.0/24 is directly connected, Ethernet0
83 O       172.16.253.9/32 [110/11] via 172.16.254.1, 01:35:43, Ethernet0
84 D       172.16.0.0/16 is a summary, 00:06:37, Null0
85 O IA    172.16.1.0/24 [110/810] via 172.16.254.1, 01:35:43, Ethernet0
86 O IA    172.16.2.0/24 [110/1610] via 172.16.254.1, 01:35:43, Ethernet0
87      182.18.0.0/16 is variably subnetted, 6 subnets, 2 masks
88 D       182.18.4.0/24 [90/21017600] via 182.18.1.1, 00:06:39, Serial1
89 D       182.18.5.0/24 [90/21017600] via 182.18.2.2, 00:06:39, Serial0
90 O       182.18.0.0/16 is a summary, 00:05:28, Null0
91 C       182.18.1.0/24 is directly connected, Serial1
92 C       182.18.2.0/24 is directly connected, Serial0
93 D       182.18.3.0/24 [90/21504000] via 182.18.2.2, 00:06:39, Serial0
94                       [90/21504000] via 182.18.1.1, 00:06:39, Serial1
```

**Figure 6-125** Moscow configurations and **show** commands

```
Moscow
1  !
2  hostname Moscow
3  !
4  no ip domain-lookup
5  !
6  interface Loopback0
7   ip address 172.16.253.9 255.255.255.252
8  !
9  interface Ethernet0
10  ip address 172.16.254.1 255.255.255.0
11 !
12 interface Serial0
13  ip address 172.16.1.5 255.255.255.252
14  bandwidth 125
15 !
16 router ospf 200
17  network 172.16.254.0 0.0.0.255 area 0
18  network 172.16.253.8 0.0.0.3 area 0
19  network 172.16.1.4 0.0.0.3 area 1
20  area 0 range 172.16.252.0 255.255.252.0
21  area 1 range 172.16.1.0 255.255.255.0
22  area 1 virtual-link 172.16.1.253
23 !
24 ip classless
25 !
26 line con 0
27  exec-timeout 0 0
28  length 0
29 !
30 end
31
32 Moscow#sho ip prot
33 Routing Protocol is "ospf 200"
34   Sending updates every 0 seconds
35   Invalid after 0 seconds, hold down 0, flushed after 0
36   Outgoing update filter list for all interfaces is not set
37   Incoming update filter list for all interfaces is not set
38   Redistributing: ospf 200
39   Routing for Networks:
40     172.16.254.0/24
41     172.16.253.8/30
42     172.16.1.4/30
43   Routing Information Sources:
44     Gateway          Distance      Last Update
45     172.16.1.253          110      00:10:22
46     172.16.253.5          110      00:09:18
47   Distance: (default is 110)
48
49 Moscow#sho ip route
50 Codes: C - connected, S - static, I - IGRP, R - RIP, M - mobile, B - BGP
51        D - EIGRP, EX - EIGRP external, O - OSPF, IA - OSPF inter area
52        N1 - OSPF NSSA external type 1, N2 - OSPF NSSA external type 2
53        E1 - OSPF external type 1, E2 - OSPF external type 2, E - EGP
54        i - IS-IS, L1 - IS-IS level-1, L2 - IS-IS level-2, * - candidate default
```

```
55        U - per-user static route, o - ODR
56
57 Gateway of last resort is not set
58
59      172.16.0.0/16 is variably subnetted, 7 subnets, 4 masks
60 O       172.16.1.253/32 [110/801] via 172.16.1.6, 00:10:26, Serial0
61 C       172.16.254.0/24 is directly connected, Ethernet0
62 O       172.16.253.5/32 [110/11] via 172.16.254.2, 00:10:26, Ethernet0
63 C       172.16.253.8/30 is directly connected, Loopback0
64 O       172.16.1.32/27 [110/810] via 172.16.1.6, 00:10:26, Serial0
65 C       172.16.1.4/30 is directly connected, Serial0
66 O IA    172.16.2.0/24 [110/1600] via 172.16.1.6, 00:10:26, Serial0
67 O E2 182.18.0.0/16 [110/400] via 172.16.254.2, 00:10:26, Ethernet0
```

**Figure 6-126**   Rome configurations and **show** commands

**Rome**
```
1 !
2 hostname Rome
3 !
4 no ip domain-lookup
5 !
6 interface Loopback0
7  ip address 172.16.1.253 255.255.255.252
8 !
9 interface Ethernet0
10  ip address 172.16.1.33 255.255.255.224
11 !
12 interface Serial0
13  ip address 172.16.2.6 255.255.255.252
14  bandwidth 125
15 !
16 interface Serial1
17  ip address 172.16.1.6 255.255.255.252
18  bandwidth 125
19  clockrate 125000
20 !
21 router ospf 200
22  network 172.16.2.4 0.0.0.3 area 2
23  network 172.16.1.4 0.0.0.3 area 1
24  network 172.16.1.252 0.0.0.3 area 1
25  network 172.16.1.32 0.0.0.31 area 1
26  area 0 range 172.16.252.0 255.255.252.0
27  area 1 range 172.16.1.0 255.255.255.0
28  area 1 virtual-link 172.16.253.9
29  area 2 range 172.16.2.0 255.255.255.0
30 !
31 ip classless
32 !
33 line con 0
34  exec-timeout 0 0
35  length 0
36 !
37 end
38
39 Rome#sho ip prot
```

**Figure 6-126** Continued

```
40 Routing Protocol is "ospf 200"
41   Sending updates every 0 seconds
42   Invalid after 0 seconds, hold down 0, flushed after 0
43   Outgoing update filter list for all interfaces is not set
44   Incoming update filter list for all interfaces is not set
45   Redistributing: ospf 200
46   Routing for Networks:
47     172.16.2.4/30
48     172.16.1.4/30
49     172.16.1.252/30
50     172.16.1.32/27
51   Routing Information Sources:
52     Gateway          Distance      Last Update
53     172.16.2.253        110        00:01:04
54     172.16.253.5        110        00:01:05
55     172.16.253.9        110        00:01:05
56   Distance: (default is 110)
57
58 Rome#sho ip route
59 Codes: C - connected, S - static, I - IGRP, R - RIP, M - mobile, B - BGP
60        D - EIGRP, EX - EIGRP external, O - OSPF, IA - OSPF inter area
61        N1 - OSPF NSSA external type 1, N2 - OSPF NSSA external type 2
62        E1 - OSPF external type 1, E2 - OSPF external type 2, E - EGP
63        i - IS-IS, L1 - IS-IS level-1, L2 - IS-IS level-2, * - candidate default
64        U - per-user static route, o - ODR
65
66 Gateway of last resort is not set
67
68      172.16.0.0/16 is variably subnetted, 9 subnets, 4 masks
69 C       172.16.1.252/30 is directly connected, Loopback0
70 O       172.16.254.0/24 [110/810] via 172.16.1.5, 00:01:12, Serial1
71 O       172.16.2.253/32 [110/801] via 172.16.2.5, 00:01:12, Serial0
72 O       172.16.253.5/32 [110/811] via 172.16.1.5, 00:01:12, Serial1
73 O       172.16.253.9/32 [110/801] via 172.16.1.5, 00:01:12, Serial1
74 C       172.16.1.32/27 is directly connected, Ethernet0
75 O       172.16.2.32/27 [110/810] via 172.16.2.5, 00:01:12, Serial0
76 C       172.16.1.4/30 is directly connected, Serial1
77 C       172.16.2.4/30 is directly connected, Serial0
78 O E2 182.18.0.0/16 [110/400] via 172.16.1.5, 00:01:13, Serial1
```

**Figure 6-127** Paris configurations and **show** commands

```
Paris
1 !
2 hostname Paris
3 !
4 no ip domain-lookup
5 !
6 interface Loopback0
7  ip address 172.16.2.253 255.255.255.252
8 !
9 interface Ethernet0
10  ip address 172.16.2.33 255.255.255.224
11 !
```

```
12 interface Serial1
13  ip address 172.16.2.5 255.255.255.252
14  bandwidth 125
15  clockrate 125000
16 !
17 router ospf 200
18  network 172.16.2.252 0.0.0.3 area 2
19  network 172.16.2.4 0.0.0.3 area 2
20  network 172.16.2.32 0.0.0.31 area 2
21 !
22 ip classless
23 !
24 line con 0
25  exec-timeout 0 0
26  length 0
27 !
28 end
29
30 Paris#sho ip prot
31 Routing Protocol is "ospf 200"
32   Sending updates every 0 seconds
33   Invalid after 0 seconds, hold down 0, flushed after 0
34   Outgoing update filter list for all interfaces is not set
35   Incoming update filter list for all interfaces is not set
36   Redistributing: ospf 200
37   Routing for Networks:
38     172.16.2.252/30
39     172.16.2.4/30
40     172.16.2.32/27
41   Routing Information Sources:
42     Gateway          Distance       Last Update
43     172.16.1.253        110         01:43:20
44     172.16.253.5        110         00:10:03
45   Distance: (default is 110)
46
47 Paris#sho ip route
48 Codes: C - connected, S - static, I - IGRP, R - RIP, M - mobile, B - BGP
49        D - EIGRP, EX - EIGRP external, O - OSPF, IA - OSPF inter area
50        N1 - OSPF NSSA external type 1, N2 - OSPF NSSA external type 2
51        E1 - OSPF external type 1, E2 - OSPF external type 2, E - EGP
52        i - IS-IS, L1 - IS-IS level-1, L2 - IS-IS level-2, * - candidate default
53        U - per-user static route, o - ODR
54
55 Gateway of last resort is not set
56
57    172.16.0.0/16 is variably subnetted, 5 subnets, 4 masks
58 O IA    172.16.252.0/22 [110/1601] via 172.16.2.6, 00:00:09, Serial1
59 C       172.16.2.252/30 is directly connected, Loopback0
60 C       172.16.2.32/27 is directly connected, Ethernet0
61 C       172.16.2.4/30 is directly connected, Serial1
62 O IA    172.16.1.0/24 [110/801] via 172.16.2.6, 01:44:50, Serial1
63 O E2 182.18.0.0/16 [110/400] via 172.16.2.6, 01:37:25, Serial1
```

# Example #11

Take a look at the problem solutions among the six figures, 6-128 through 6-133.

**Figure 6-128** Tokyo configurations and **show** commands

```
Tokyo
1  !
2  hostname Tokyo
3  !
4  no ip domain-lookup
5  !
6  interface Loopback0
7   ip address 162.16.1.193 255.255.255.252
8  !
9  interface Ethernet0
10  ip address 172.17.1.1 255.255.255.0
11  !
12 interface Serial0
13  ip address 182.18.1.1 255.255.255.0
14  bandwidth 125
15 !
16 interface Serial1
17  ip address 162.16.1.34 255.255.255.224
18  bandwidth 125
19  clockrate 125000
20 !
21 router eigrp 200
22  redistribute rip metric 10000 100 255 1 1500
23  redistribute ospf 200 metric 56 2000 255 1 1500
24  passive-interface Ethernet0
25  network 182.18.0.0
26  distribute-list 1 out ospf 200
27  distribute-list 10 out
28 !
29 router ospf 200
30  summary-address 182.18.0.0 255.255.0.0
31  summary-address 172.17.0.0 255.255.0.0
32  redistribute rip metric 100 subnets
33  redistribute eigrp 200 metric 500 subnets
34  network 162.16.1.32 0.0.0.31 area 1
35  network 162.16.1.192 0.0.0.3 area 1
36 !
37 router rip
38  version 2
39  redistribute ospf 100 metric 1
40  redistribute eigrp 200 metric 1
41  passive-interface Serial0
42  passive-interface Serial1
43  network 172.17.0.0
```

```
44  !
45  ip classless
46  access-list 1 permit 162.16.0.0 0.0.255.255
47  access-list 10 permit 182.18.0.0 0.0.255.255
48  !
49  line con 0
50   exec-timeout 0 0
51   length 0
52  !
53  end
54
55  Tokyo#sho ip prot
56  Routing Protocol is "rip"
57    Sending updates every 30 seconds, next due in 14 seconds
58    Invalid after 180 seconds, hold down 180, flushed after 240
59    Outgoing update filter list for all interfaces is not set
60    Incoming update filter list for all interfaces is not set
61    Redistributing: rip, ospf 100 (internal, external 1, external 2)
62
63    Redistributing: eigrp 200
64    Default version control: send version 2, receive version 2
65      Interface        Send  Recv   Key-chain
66      Ethernet0         2     2
67    Routing for Networks:
68      172.17.0.0
69    Passive Interface(s):
70      Serial0
71      Serial1
72    Routing Information Sources:
73      Gateway          Distance      Last Update
74    Distance: (default is 120)
75
76  Routing Protocol is "eigrp 200"
77    Outgoing update filter list for all interfaces is 10
78      Redistributed ospf 200 filtered by 1
79    Incoming update filter list for all interfaces is not set
80    Default networks flagged in outgoing updates
81    Default networks accepted from incoming updates
82    EIGRP metric weight K1=1, K2=0, K3=1, K4=0, K5=0
83    EIGRP maximum hopcount 100
84    EIGRP maximum metric variance 1
85    Redistributing: rip, eigrp 200, ospf 200 (internal, external 1, external 2)
86
87    Automatic network summarization is in effect
88    Routing for Networks:
89      182.18.0.0
90    Passive Interface(s):
91      Ethernet0
92    Routing Information Sources:
93      Gateway          Distance      Last Update
94      182.18.1.2            90        00:04:24
95    Distance: internal 90 external 170
96
97  Routing Protocol is "ospf 200"
98    Sending updates every 0 seconds
99    Invalid after 0 seconds, hold down 0, flushed after 0
100    Outgoing update filter list for all interfaces is not set
101    Incoming update filter list for all interfaces is not set
```

**Figure 6-128** *Continued*

```
102    Redistributing: rip, eigrp 200, ospf 200
103    Address Summarization:
104    Routing for Networks:
105        162.16.1.32/27
106        162.16.1.192/30
107    Routing Information Sources:
108        Gateway          Distance      Last Update
109        (this router)        110        00:04:18
110        162.16.254.193       110        00:08:30
111    Distance: (default is 110)
112
113 Tokyo#sho ip route
114 Codes: C - connected, S - static, I - IGRP, R - RIP, M - mobile, B - BGP
115        D - EIGRP, EX - EIGRP external, O - OSPF, IA - OSPF inter area
116        N1 - OSPF NSSA external type 1, N2 - OSPF NSSA external type 2
117        E1 - OSPF external type 1, E2 - OSPF external type 2, E - EGP
118        i - IS-IS, L1 - IS-IS level-1, L2 - IS-IS level-2, * - candidate default
119        U - per-user static route, o - ODR
120
121 Gateway of last resort is not set
122
123      172.17.0.0/16 is variably subnetted, 2 subnets, 2 masks
124 C        172.17.1.0/24 is directly connected, Ethernet0
125 O        172.17.0.0/16 is a summary, 00:04:20, Null0
126      162.16.0.0/16 is variably subnetted, 5 subnets, 4 masks
127 O IA    162.16.254.0/24 [110/801] via 162.16.1.33, 01:45:16, Serial1
128 C        162.16.1.192/30 is directly connected, Loopback0
129 C        162.16.1.32/27 is directly connected, Serial1
130 O IA    162.16.2.0/24 [110/1610] via 162.16.1.33, 01:46:28, Serial1
131 D EX    162.16.0.0/16 [170/21529600] via 182.18.1.2, 00:04:27, Serial0
132      182.18.0.0/16 is variably subnetted, 4 subnets, 2 masks
133 O        182.18.0.0/16 is a summary, 00:04:20, Null0
134 C        182.18.1.0/24 is directly connected, Serial0
135 D        182.18.2.0/24 [90/21504000] via 182.18.1.2, 00:04:28, Serial0
136 D        182.18.3.0/24 [90/21017600] via 182.18.1.2, 00:04:28, Serial0
137
138 Tokyo#debug ip rip
139 RIP protocol debugging is on
140 Tokyo#undeb all
141 RIP: sending v2 update to 224.0.0.9 via Ethernet0 (172.17.1.1)
142      162.16.0.0/16 -> 0.0.0.0, metric 1, tag 0
143      182.18.0.0/16 -> 0.0.0.0, metric 1, tag 0
144 All possible debugging has been turned off
145
146 Tokyo#ping 182.18.3.1
147
148 Type escape sequence to abort.
149 Sending 5, 100-byte ICMP Echos to 182.18.3.1, timeout is 2 seconds:
150 !!!!!
151 Success rate is 100 percent (5/5), round-trip min/avg/max = 16/17/20 ms
152
153 Tokyo#trace 182.18.3.1
154
155 Type escape sequence to abort.
156 Tracing the route to 182.18.3.1
```

```
157
158    1 182.18.1.2 12 msec 8 msec 12 msec
159    2 182.18.3.1 12 msec *  8 msec
160
161 Tokyo#ping 162.16.2.33
162
163 Type escape sequence to abort.
164 Sending 5, 100-byte ICMP Echos to 162.16.2.33, timeout is 2 seconds:
165 !!!!!
166 Success rate is 100 percent (5/5), round-trip min/avg/max = 32/32/36 ms
167
168 Tokyo#trace 162.16.2.33
169
170 Type escape sequence to abort.
171 Tracing the route to 162.16.2.33
172
173    1 162.16.1.33 12 msec 8 msec 12 msec
174    2 162.16.254.66 12 msec 8 msec 8 msec
175    3 162.16.2.18 16 msec *  16 msec
```

▬▬ ▬▬ ▬▬ ▬▬ ▬▬ ▬▬ ▬▬ ▬▬ ▬▬ ▬▬ ▬▬ ▬▬ ▬▬ ▬▬ ▬▬ ▬▬ ▬▬ ▬▬

**Figure 6-129** London configurations and **show** commands

**London**

```
1 !
2 hostname London
3 !
4 no ip domain-lookup
5 !
6 interface Loopback0
7  ip address 162.16.254.193 255.255.255.252
8 !
9 interface Ethernet0
10  ip address 162.16.254.65 255.255.255.192
11 !
12 interface Serial0
13  ip address 162.16.1.33 255.255.255.224
14  bandwidth 125
15 !
16 interface Serial1
17  ip address 182.18.2.2 255.255.255.0
18  bandwidth 125
19  clockrate 125000
20 !
21 router eigrp 200
22  redistribute ospf 200 metric 10000 100 255 1 1500
23  network 182.18.0.0
24  distribute-list 1 out ospf 200
25  distribute-list 10 out
26 !
27 router ospf 200
28  summary-address 172.17.0.0 255.255.0.0
29  summary-address 182.18.0.0 255.255.0.0
30  redistribute eigrp 200 metric 250 subnets
31  network 162.16.254.64 0.0.0.63 area 0
```

**Figure 6-129** Continued

```
32  network 162.16.254.192 0.0.0.3 area 0
33  network 162.16.1.32 0.0.0.31 area 1
34  distribute-list 2 out eigrp 200
35  area 0 range 162.16.254.0 255.255.255.0
36  area 1 range 162.16.1.0 255.255.255.0
37  !
38  ip classless
39  access-list 1 permit 162.16.0.0 0.0.255.255
40  access-list 1 permit 172.17.0.0 0.0.255.255
41  access-list 2 permit 182.18.0.0 0.0.255.255
42  access-list 2 permit 172.17.0.0 0.0.255.255
43  access-list 10 permit 0.0.0.0 255.255.0.0
44  !
45  !
46  line con 0
47   exec-timeout 0 0
48   length 0
49  line aux 0
50   transport input all
51  line vty 0 4
52   login
53  !
54  end
55
56  London#sho ip prot
57  Routing Protocol is "eigrp 200"
58    Outgoing update filter list for all interfaces is 10
59      Redistributed ospf 200 filtered by 1
60    Incoming update filter list for all interfaces is not set
61    Default networks flagged in outgoing updates
62    Default networks accepted from incoming updates
63    EIGRP metric weight K1=1, K2=0, K3=1, K4=0, K5=0
64    EIGRP maximum hopcount 100
65    EIGRP maximum metric variance 1
66    Redistributing: eigrp 200, ospf 200 (internal, external 1, external 2)
67
68    Automatic network summarization is in effect
69    Routing for Networks:
70      182.18.0.0
71    Routing Information Sources:
72      Gateway          Distance      Last Update
73      182.18.2.1             90       00:12:26
74    Distance: internal 90 external 170
75
76  Routing Protocol is "ospf 200"
77    Sending updates every 0 seconds
78    Invalid after 0 seconds, hold down 0, flushed after 0
79    Outgoing update filter list for all interfaces is not set
80      Redistributed eigrp 200 filtered by 2
81    Incoming update filter list for all interfaces is not set
82    Redistributing: eigrp 200, ospf 200
83    Address Summarization:
84    Routing for Networks:
```

```
85      162.16.254.64/26
86      162.16.254.192/30
87      162.16.1.32/27
88   Routing Information Sources:
89      Gateway          Distance     Last Update
90      (this router)        110      00:12:27
91      162.16.1.193         110      00:12:27
92      162.16.254.197       110      00:26:01
93   Distance: (default is 110)
94
95 London#sho ip route
96 Codes: C - connected, S - static, I - IGRP, R - RIP, M - mobile, B - BGP
97        D - EIGRP, EX - EIGRP external, O - OSPF, IA - OSPF inter area
98        N1 - OSPF NSSA external type 1, N2 - OSPF NSSA external type 2
99        E1 - OSPF external type 1, E2 - OSPF external type 2, E - EGP
100       i - IS-IS, L1 - IS-IS level-1, L2 - IS-IS level-2, * - candidate default
101       U - per-user static route, o - ODR
102
103 Gateway of last resort is not set
104
105 O E2 172.17.0.0/16 [110/100] via 162.16.1.34, 00:12:28, Serial0
106      162.16.0.0/16 is variably subnetted, 7 subnets, 6 masks
107 C       162.16.254.64/26 is directly connected, Ethernet0
108 O       162.16.1.193/32 [110/801] via 162.16.1.34, 00:26:02, Serial0
109 O       162.16.254.197/32 [110/11] via 162.16.254.66, 00:26:02, Ethernet0
110 C       162.16.254.192/30 is directly connected, Loopback0
111 C       162.16.1.32/27 is directly connected, Serial0
112 O IA    162.16.2.0/24 [110/810] via 162.16.254.66, 00:26:02, Ethernet0
113 O       162.16.0.0/16 is a summary, 00:12:29, Null0
114      182.18.0.0/16 is variably subnetted, 4 subnets, 2 masks
115 O       182.18.0.0/16 is a summary, 00:12:29, Null0
116 D       182.18.1.0/24 [90/21504000] via 182.18.2.1, 00:13:47, Serial1
117 C       182.18.2.0/24 is directly connected, Serial1
118 D       182.18.3.0/24 [90/21017600] via 182.18.2.1, 00:13:47, Serial1
```

**Figure 6-130** NewYork configurations and **show** commands

```
NewYork
1 !
2 hostname NewYork
3 !
4 no ip domain-lookup
5 !
6 interface Ethernet0
7   ip address 182.18.3.2 255.255.255.0
8 !
9 interface Serial0
10   ip address 182.18.2.1 255.255.255.0
11   bandwidth 125
12 !
13 interface Serial1
14   ip address 182.18.1.2 255.255.255.0
15   bandwidth 125
16   clockrate 125000
```

**Figure 6-130**  NewYork configurations and **show** commands

```
17 !
18 router eigrp 200
19  network 182.18.0.0
20 !
21 ip classless
22 !
23 line con 0
24  exec-timeout 0 0
25  length 0
26 !
27 end
28
29 NewYork#sho ip prot
30 Routing Protocol is "eigrp 200"
31   Outgoing update filter list for all interfaces is not set
32   Incoming update filter list for all interfaces is not set
33   Default networks flagged in outgoing updates
34   Default networks accepted from incoming updates
35   EIGRP metric weight K1=1, K2=0, K3=1, K4=0, K5=0
36   EIGRP maximum hopcount 100
37   EIGRP maximum metric variance 1
38   Redistributing: eigrp 200
39   Automatic network summarization is in effect
40   Routing for Networks:
41     182.18.0.0
42   Routing Information Sources:
43     Gateway         Distance      Last Update
44     182.18.2.2            90      00:10:22
45     182.18.1.1            90      00:10:22
46     182.18.3.1            90      00:13:20
47   Distance: internal 90 external 170
48
49 NewYork#sho ip route
50 Codes: C - connected, S - static, I - IGRP, R - RIP, M - mobile, B - BGP
51        D - EIGRP, EX - EIGRP external, O - OSPF, IA - OSPF inter area
52        N1 - OSPF NSSA external type 1, N2 - OSPF NSSA external type 2
53        E1 - OSPF external type 1, E2 - OSPF external type 2, E - EGP
54        i - IS-IS, L1 - IS-IS level-1, L2 - IS-IS level-2, * - candidate default
55        U - per-user static route, o - ODR
56
57 Gateway of last resort is not set
58
59 D EX 172.17.0.0/16 [170/21017600] via 182.18.2.2, 00:13:26, Serial0
60 D EX 162.16.0.0/16 [170/21017600] via 182.18.2.2, 00:10:30, Serial0
61      182.18.0.0/24 is subnetted, 3 subnets
62 C       182.18.1.0 is directly connected, Serial1
63 C       182.18.2.0 is directly connected, Serial0
64 C       182.18.3.0 is directly connected, Ethernet0
```

**Figure 6-131** Moscow configurations and **show** commands

**Moscow**

```
1 !
2 hostname Moscow
3 !
4 no ip domain-lookup
5 !
6 interface Ethernet0
7  ip address 182.18.3.1 255.255.255.0
8 !
9 router eigrp 200
10  network 182.18.0.0
11 !
12 ip classless
13 !
14 line con 0
15  exec-timeout 0 0
16  length 0
17 !
18 end
19
20 Moscow#sho ip prot
21 Routing Protocol is "eigrp 200"
22   Outgoing update filter list for all interfaces is not set
23   Incoming update filter list for all interfaces is not set
24   Default networks flagged in outgoing updates
25   Default networks accepted from incoming updates
26   EIGRP metric weight K1=1, K2=0, K3=1, K4=0, K5=0
27   EIGRP maximum hopcount 100
28   EIGRP maximum metric variance 1
29   Redistributing: eigrp 200
30   Automatic network summarization is in effect
31   Routing for Networks:
32     182.18.0.0
33   Routing Information Sources:
34     Gateway          Distance       Last Update
35     182.18.3.2            90         00:14:19
36   Distance: internal 90 external 170
37
38 Moscow#sho ip route
39 Codes: C - connected, S - static, I - IGRP, R - RIP, M - mobile, B - BGP
40        D - EIGRP, EX - EIGRP external, O - OSPF, IA - OSPF inter area
41        N1 - OSPF NSSA external type 1, N2 - OSPF NSSA external type 2
42        E1 - OSPF external type 1, E2 - OSPF external type 2, E - EGP
43        i - IS-IS, L1 - IS-IS level-1, L2 - IS-IS level-2, * - candidate default
44        U - per-user static route, o - ODR
45
46 Gateway of last resort is not set
47
48 D EX 172.17.0.0/16 [170/21043200] via 182.18.3.2, 00:14:22, Ethernet0
49 D EX 162.16.0.0/16 [170/21043200] via 182.18.3.2, 00:15:39, Ethernet0
50      182.18.0.0/24 is subnetted, 3 subnets
51 D       182.18.1.0 [90/21017600] via 182.18.3.2, 03:11:22, Ethernet0
52 D       182.18.2.0 [90/21017600] via 182.18.3.2, 02:53:30, Ethernet0
53 C       182.18.3.0 is directly connected, Ethernet0
```

**Figure 6-132**   Rome configurations and **show** commands

**Rome**

```
1 !
2 hostname Rome
3 !
4 no ip domain-lookup
5 !
6 interface Loopback0
7  ip address 162.16.2.193 255.255.255.252
8 !
9 interface Ethernet0
10  ip address 162.16.2.33 255.255.255.224
11 !
12 interface Serial0
13  ip address 162.16.2.18 255.255.255.240
14  bandwidth 125
15 !
16 router ospf 200
17  network 162.16.2.16 0.0.0.15 area 2
18  network 162.16.2.32 0.0.0.31 area 2
19  network 162.16.2.192 0.0.0.3 area 2
20 !
21 ip classless
22 !
23 line con 0
24  exec-timeout 0 0
25  length 0
26 !
27 end
28
29 Rome#sho ip prot
30 Routing Protocol is "ospf 200"
31   Sending updates every 0 seconds
32   Invalid after 0 seconds, hold down 0, flushed after 0
33   Outgoing update filter list for all interfaces is not set
34   Incoming update filter list for all interfaces is not set
35   Redistributing: ospf 200
36   Routing for Networks:
37     162.16.2.16/28
38     162.16.2.32/27
39     162.16.2.192/30
40   Routing Information Sources:
41     Gateway         Distance      Last Update
42     162.16.1.193         110      00:04:57
43     162.16.254.197       110      00:28:19
44     162.16.254.193       110      00:09:13
45   Distance: (default is 110)
46
47 Rome#sho ip route
48 Codes: C - connected, S - static, I - IGRP, R - RIP, M - mobile, B - BGP
49        D - EIGRP, EX - EIGRP external, O - OSPF, IA - OSPF inter area
50        N1 - OSPF NSSA external type 1, N2 - OSPF NSSA external type 2
51        E1 - OSPF external type 1, E2 - OSPF external type 2, E - EGP
52        i - IS-IS, L1 - IS-IS level-1, L2 - IS-IS level-2, * - candidate default
53        U - per-user static route, o - ODR
54
```

**Figure 6-132** Rome configurations and **show** commands

```
55 Gateway of last resort is not set
56
57 O E2 172.17.0.0/16 [110/100] via 162.16.2.17, 00:08:15, Serial0
58      162.16.0.0/16 is variably subnetted, 6 subnets, 5 masks
59 O IA    162.16.254.0/24 [110/801] via 162.16.2.17, 00:28:30, Serial0
60 C       162.16.2.192/30 is directly connected, Loopback0
61 C       162.16.2.32/27 is directly connected, Ethernet0
62 C       162.16.2.16/28 is directly connected, Serial0
63 O E2    162.16.0.0/16 [110/500] via 162.16.2.17, 00:05:08, Serial0
64 O IA    162.16.1.0/24 [110/1610] via 162.16.2.17, 00:28:30, Serial0
65 O E2 182.18.0.0/16 [110/250] via 162.16.2.17, 00:25:44, Serial0
```

**Figure 6-133** Paris configurations and **show** commands

```
Paris
1 !
2 hostname Paris
3 !
4 no ip domain-lookup
5 !
6 interface Loopback0
7  ip address 162.16.254.197 255.255.255.252
8 !
9 interface Ethernet0
10  ip address 162.16.254.66 255.255.255.192
11 !
12 interface Serial1
13  ip address 162.16.2.17 255.255.255.240
14  bandwidth 125
15  clockrate 125000
16 !
17 router ospf 200
18  network 162.16.254.64 0.0.0.63 area 0
19  network 162.16.254.196 0.0.0.3 area 0
20  network 162.16.2.16 0.0.0.15 area 2
21  area 0 range 162.16.254.0 255.255.255.0
22  area 2 range 162.16.2.0 255.255.255.0
23 !
24 ip classless
25 !
26 line con 0
27  exec-timeout 0 0
28  length 0
29 !
30 end
31
32 Paris#sho ip prot
33 Routing Protocol is "ospf 200"
34   Sending updates every 0 seconds
35   Invalid after 0 seconds, hold down 0, flushed after 0
36   Outgoing update filter list for all interfaces is not set
37   Incoming update filter list for all interfaces is not set
38   Redistributing: ospf 200
```

**Figure 6-133** Continued

```
39    Routing for Networks:
40       162.16.254.64/26
41       162.16.254.196/30
42       162.16.2.16/28
43    Routing Information Sources:
44       Gateway          Distance      Last Update
45       162.16.2.193        110        01:50:05
46       162.16.1.193        110        00:08:13
47       162.16.254.193      110        00:12:24
48    Distance: (default is 110)
49
50 Paris#sho ip route
51 Codes: C - connected, S - static, I - IGRP, R - RIP, M - mobile, B - BGP
52        D - EIGRP, EX - EIGRP external, O - OSPF, IA - OSPF inter area
53        N1 - OSPF NSSA external type 1, N2 - OSPF NSSA external type 2
54        E1 - OSPF external type 1, E2 - OSPF external type 2, E - EGP
55        i - IS-IS, L1 - IS-IS level-1, L2 - IS-IS level-2, * - candidate default
56        U - per-user static route, o - ODR
57
58 Gateway of last resort is not set
59
60 O E2 172.17.0.0/16 [110/100] via 162.16.254.65, 00:11:21, Ethernet0
61      162.16.0.0/16 is variably subnetted, 8 subnets, 7 masks
62 C        162.16.254.64/26 is directly connected, Ethernet0
63 O        162.16.2.193/32 [110/801] via 162.16.2.18, 01:50:11, Serial1
64 C        162.16.254.196/30 is directly connected, Loopback0
65 O        162.16.254.193/32 [110/11] via 162.16.254.65, 01:50:11, Ethernet0
66 O        162.16.2.32/27 [110/810] via 162.16.2.18, 01:50:11, Serial1
67 C        162.16.2.16/28 is directly connected, Serial1
68 O E2     162.16.0.0/16 [110/500] via 162.16.254.65, 00:08:19, Ethernet0
69 O IA     162.16.1.0/24 [110/810] via 162.16.254.65, 01:49:28, Ethernet0
70 O E2 182.18.0.0/16 [110/250] via 162.16.254.65, 00:28:51, Ethernet0
```

New York

# Connecting to the Outside

# CHAPTER 7

# Network Address Translation

Network Address Translation (NAT) is an IP feature added in Cisco IOS 11.2 that provides for translating IP addresses. To make sure that this feature is available on your model 25xx router and above, be sure your IOS code contains the **s** designator.

There are several reasons to use the Network Address Translation feature:

- Private network addressing on your internal network
- Connecting to your Internet Service Provider with an unassigned but valid IP class address
- Integrating two companies that use the same private address space
- TCP load sharing among multiple hosts

Network Address Translation is defined in RFC1631, The IP Network Address Translator (NAT).

# What NAT Provides

Network Address Translation provides a method for disguising the internal nature of your private network by using an external address to represent your network addressing to the outside world.

# What NAT Does Not Provide

Network Address Translation does not provide any firewall services. While the addition of access lists to a router can improve security and bandwidth utilization, it should not be considered a firewall solution.

# Terms

Before we can configure NAT, there are some terms we need to define in order to understand the process being executed. Please refer to Figure 7-1 for definitions of terms.

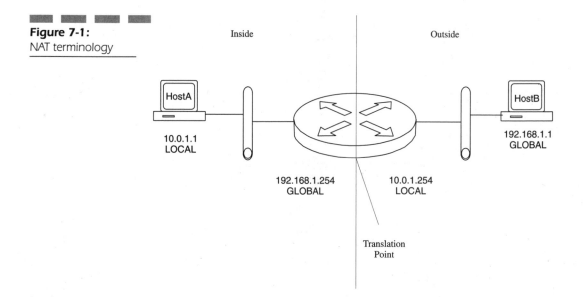

**Figure 7-1:**
NAT terminology

## Inside Local Addresses

Inside addresses are addresses used within an autonomous system. An example of an inside address would be class A address 10.0.0.0 used within your private network or a globally routable class address, not a legitimate IP address assigned by the Network Information Center (NIC) or a service provider. In Figure 7-1, Host A has been assigned an inside local address of 10.0.1.1.

## Inside Global Addresses

An inside global address is a legitimate IP address (assigned by the NIC or service provider) that represents one or more inside local IP addresses to the outside world. In Figure 7-1, 192.168.1.254 is the IP address used by Host A to communicate with the outside.

## Outside Local Addresses

An outside local address is the IP address of an outside host as it appears to the inside network. Not necessarily a legitimate address, it was allocated from address space routable on the inside. In Figure 7-1, 10.0.1.254 is the address that Host B uses for all communications on the inside of our private network.

## Outside Global Addresses

An outside global address is the IP address assigned to a host on the outside network by the host's owner. The address was allocated from globally routable address or network space. In Figure 7-1, 192.168.1.1 represents Host B to the outside address space.

## Simple Translation

Simple translation provides a one-to-one address mapping, where one inside local address requires one inside global address in order to work properly. An example would be a private inside local address using class C network 192.168.1.0 with valid class C address 200.20.45.0 as an inside global address for up to 254 simultaneous connections.

## Address Overloading

Address overloading provides the ability to use one outside address to replace multiple inside addresses by mapping conversations by port numbers as well as addresses. An example would be a private inside local address using class A network 10.0.0.0 with valid class C address 200.20.45.0 as a inside global address for more than 254 simultaneous connections. Each connection uses random inside global addresses with the original port address used by the inside local address. If we track two separate conversations from 10.1.0.1 port 1028 and 10.1.0.2 port 1042, then the inside global addresses could be 200.20.45.17 port 1028 and 200.20.45.17 port 1042. The router keeps track of these conversations. Example #2, later in this chapter, uses this address overload feature to communicate with the outside.

# Scenarios

## Private Addresses

When the Internet became the "in" technology, the rush for acquiring valid IP class addresses threatened to exhaust the networks available for distribution. Proposals for address extensions like IPng were consolidated into a new standard for IP addressing, IPv6. All standards take time to be accepted and implemented, and in the interim RFC-1918 defines the use of class A 10.0.0.0, class B addresses 172.16.0.0 through 172.31.255.255, and class C addresses 192.168.0.0 through 192.168.255.255 as internal or private network addresses for companies and organizations. To connect to the Internet, a registered class address must be used for connectivity, and Network Address Translation used to map inside private or local addresses to outside global addresses. See Example #1 for the configuration commands used to implement this feature.

If two companies use the same private addresses and they merge, this same feature can be used to connect the two organizations together. See Example #3 for the configuration commands used to implement this feature.

## Switching ISPs

With the rapid expansion in the service provider business, if one service provider is not fulfilling your needs, then you may decide to switch. Many class addresses are being distributed through service providers, and your global IP address may have to be returned to the provider. This requires that your internal addressing be completely changed to a new address space. While this address change is being planned, using Network Address Translation can give you breathing room by translating your old global addresses into the new address. See Example #2 for the configuration commands used to implement this feature.

## TCP Load Sharing

Providing services to users may require multiple servers. To make multiple servers appear as one server to your users, Network Address Translation can be used to map multiple individual host addresses to a single virtual address used by the rest of the network. See Example #4 for the configuration commands used to implement this feature.

# Configuring Address Translation

The commands in Table 7-1 are used to implement the Network Address Translation feature.

**Table 7-1**

Commands implementing Network Address Translation

| Command | G/T | Parameter | Description |
|---|---|---|---|
| ip nat pool | G | *name* | Name of the pool of addresses to be used during translation. |
| | | *start-ip* | First address in range. |
| | | *end-ip* | Last address in range. |
| | | netmask *netmask* or prefix-length *prefix-length* | Netmask in dotted decimal or prefix length in bits to be applied to the addresses. |
| | | type rotary | Optional parameter to identify real inside hosts used for TCP load distribution. |

**Table 7-1**

Continued

| Command | G/T | Parameter | Description |
|---|---|---|---|
| ip nat inside source | G | list *name* or list *number* | The named or numbered standard access-list that identifies the source addresses that are dynamically translated using addresses from the named NAT pool. |
| | | pool *name* | Name of the pool from which global addresses are assigned dynamically. |
| | | overload | Optional parameter that allows NAT to map a combination of port and a single global IP address to multiple inside addresses. |
| ip nat inside source | G | static *local-ip* | Inside local address that maps to a specific outside global address. Only one address per command. |
| | | *global-ip* | The global address statically mapped to an inside address. |
| ip nat outside source | G | list *name* or list *number* | The named or numbered standard access-list that identifies the source addresses that are dynamically translated using addresses from the named pool. |
| | | pool *name* | Name of the pool from which global addresses are assigned dynamically. |
| ip nat outside source | G | static *global-ip* | Outside global address that maps to a specific inside local address; only one address per command. |
| | | *local-ip* | The local address statically mapped to a global address. |
| ip nat inside destination | G | list *name* or list *number* | The named or numbered standard access-list that identifies the destination addresses that are dynamically translated using addresses from the named pool. |
| | | pool *name* | Name of the pool from which global addresses are assigned dynamically. |
| ip nat | I | inside | Indicates translation takes place between the inside addresses on this interface and outside addresses on designated outside interfaces. |
| | I | outside | Indicates translation takes place between the outside addresses on this interface and inside addresses on designated inside interfaces. |
| ip nat translation | G | timeout *seconds* or udp-timeout *seconds* or dns-timeout *seconds* or tcp-timeout *seconds* or finrst-timeout *seconds* | Dynamic = 86400 (24 hours) UDP port = 300 DNS connections = 60 TCP port = 86400 (24 hours) Finish and Reset TCP packets = 60 |

Note: Information supplied by the user is italicized. ˙ Global or applied to the Interface.

## Configuration Examples

### Example #1—Access the Internet Using a Private Internal IP Network Number

This example provides the network administrator with an easy-to-use technique that translates internal private network numbers into valid Internet addresses. Figure 7-2 is the network layout for this example. In this example, 200.200.200.0 is the valid class C address used to represent our private address to the outside world.

Tokyo is a router in the outside domain that uses a valid IP network of 131.108.0.0 and the RIP routing protocol. See lines 13 and 14 in Figure 7-3.

Just to verify our RIP operation does not see any of the private network 10.0.0.0 addressing, we execute a **debug ip rip** command. The only networks known by the router are valid outside network addresses. See lines 5 and 6 in Figure 7-4.

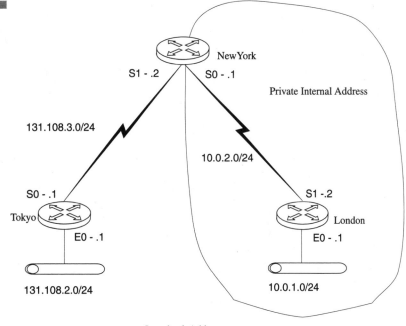

**Figure 7-2**
Private addresses
with simple NAT
translation

NewYork

S1 - .2    S0 - .1

Private Internal Address

131.108.3.0/24

10.0.2.0/24

S0 - .1    S1 - .2

Tokyo    London

E0 - .1    E0 - .1

131.108.2.0/24    10.0.1.0/24

Loopback Addresses

NewYork  200.200.200.1/24

**Figure 7-3**   Tokyo configuration

```
1  !
2  hostname Tokyo
3  !
4  no ip domain-lookup
5  !
6  interface Ethernet0
7   ip address 131.108.2.1 255.255.255.0
8  !
9  interface Serial0
10  ip address 131.108.3.1 255.255.255.0
11  bandwidth 125
12 !
13 router rip
14  network 131.108.0.0
15 !
16 ip classless
17 !
18 !
19 line con 0
20  exec-timeout 0 0
21  length 0
22 line vty 0 4
23  password cisco
24  login
25 !
26 end
```

**Figure 7-4**   Tokyo **debug ip rip** output

```
1 Tokyo#debug ip rip
2 RIP protocol debugging is on
3 Tokyo#
4 RIP: sending v1 update to 255.255.255.255 via Ethernet0 (131.108.2.1)
5      subnet  131.108.3.0, metric 1
6      network 200.200.200.0, metric 2
7 RIP: sending v1 update to 255.255.255.255 via Serial0 (131.108.3.1)
8      subnet  131.108.2.0, metric 1
9 RIP: received v1 update from 131.108.3.2 on Serial0
```

**Figure 7-5**   Tokyo **show ip** protocol output

```
1 Tokyo#sho ip protocol
2 Routing Protocol is "rip"
3   Sending updates every 30 seconds, next due in 12 seconds
4   Invalid after 180 seconds, hold down 180, flushed after 240
5   Outgoing update filter list for all interfaces is not set
6   Incoming update filter list for all interfaces is not set
7   Redistributing: rip
8   Default version control: send version 1, receive any version
9     Interface        Send  Recv  Key-chain
10     Ethernet0         1     1 2
11     Serial0           1     1 2
12   Routing for Networks:
13     131.108.0.0
14   Routing Information Sources:
15     Gateway         Distance      Last Update
16     131.108.3.2         120       00:00:22
17   Distance: (default is 120)
```

■■ ■■ ■■ ■■ ■■ ■■ ■■ ■■ ■■ ■■ ■■ ■■ ■■ ■■ ■■ ■■ ■■ ■■

**Figure 7-6** Tokyo **show ip route** output

```
1 Tokyo#sho ip route
2 Codes: C - connected, S - static, I - IGRP, R - RIP, M - mobile, B - BGP
3        D - EIGRP, EX - EIGRP external, O - OSPF, IA - OSPF inter area
4        N1 - OSPF NSSA external type 1, N2 - OSPF NSSA external type 2
5        E1 - OSPF external type 1, E2 - OSPF external type 2, E - EGP
6        i - IS-IS, L1 - IS-IS level-1, L2 - IS-IS level-2, * - candidate default
7        U - per-user static route, o - ODR
8
9 Gateway of last resort is not set
10
11 R    200.200.200.0/24 [120/1] via 131.108.3.2, 00:00:26, Serial0
12      131.108.0.0/24 is subnetted, 2 subnets
13 C       131.108.3.0 is directly connected, Serial0
14 C       131.108.2.0 is directly connected, Ethernet0
```

The **show ip protocol** output for Tokyo in Figure 7-5 shows network 131.108.0.0 as the only network being processed. See line 13 in Figure 7-5.

The **show ip route** output for Tokyo in Figure 7-6 shows subnetwork 200.200.200.0/24 as a RIP-derived route.

The configuration for New York in Figure 7-7 is where Network Address Translation takes place.

Line 4 defines a pool of valid outside addresses, and line 5 assigns this pool of addresses for translating the inside source addresses that pass access-list 1 on line 30.

Line 13 defines traffic coming from the inside private network 10.0.0.0 as the source addresses to be translated into the 131.108.0.0 network as network 200.200.200.0.

Line 18 defines the interface where the translated addresses are sent out to the outside network.

Lines 22 through 27 provide our RIP routing function. Networks 10.0.0.0, 200.200.200.0, and 131.108.0.0 participate in the RIP routing process.

On line 26, the **distribute-list out 2** command is used so that network 131.108.0.0 will show up in our private network. Addresses that pass **access-list 2** on line 31 will be forwarded to our private network. See Figure 7-16 for the sample **show ip route** for London later in this example.

On line 27, the **distribute-list out 3** command is used to prevent network 10.0.0.0 from showing up in the global network routing updates. Addresses that pass **access-list 3** on lines 32 and 33 will be forwarded to the global network. See Figure 7-4 for the **debug ip rip** output to verify this operation.

Line 25 is used to propagate network 200.200.200.0/24 in the RIP updates headed to the global 131.108.0.0 domain. NAT converts these

**Figure 7-7**   NewYork configuration

```
1  !
2  hostname NewYork
3  !
4  ip nat pool good-pool 200.200.200.2 200.200.200.254 netmask 255.255.255.0
5  ip nat inside source list 1 pool good-pool
6  no ip domain-lookup
7  !
8  interface Loopback0
9   ip address 200.200.200.1 255.255.255.0
10 !
11 interface Serial0
12  ip address 10.0.2.1 255.255.255.0
13  ip nat inside
14  bandwidth 125
15 !
16 interface Serial1
17  ip address 131.108.3.2 255.255.255.0
18  ip nat outside
19  bandwidth 125
20  clockrate 125000
21 !
22 router rip
23  network 10.0.0.0
24  network 131.108.0.0
25  network 200.200.200.0
26  distribute-list 2 out Serial0
27  distribute-list 3 out Serial1
28 !
29 ip classless
30 access-list 1 permit 10.0.0.0 0.255.255.255
31 access-list 2 permit 131.108.0.0 0.0.255.255
32 access-list 3 permit 131.108.0.0 0.0.255.255
33 access-list 3 permit 200.200.200.0 0.0.0.255
34 !
35 line con 0
36  exec-timeout 0 0
37  length 0
38 !
39 end
```

addresses to our private addresses as they enter the router on Serial 1.

Sample output from the **debug ip nat** command is in Figure 7-8. Line 4 shows our initial translation from 10.0.2.2 to 200.200.200.2 on the first outgoing **ping** request. Lines 5 through 14 show the rest of the successful ping translation sequence. The * after NAT indicates that the translation took place along the fast switching path. Figure 7-9 contains the **show ip nat translation** on lines 1 through 5.

Lines 6 through 17 contain the **show ip nat statistics** output.

Line 7 shows two dynamic translations, and line 17 shows two of the 253 addresses available.

**Figure 7-8**   NewYork **debug** output

```
1 NewYork#debug ip nat detailed
2 IP NAT detailed debugging is on
3 NewYork#
4 NAT: i: icmp (10.0.2.2, 0) -> (131.108.2.1, 0) [1801]
5 NAT*: i: icmp (10.0.1.1, 0) -> (131.108.2.1, 0) [1806]
6 NAT*: o: icmp (131.108.2.1, 0) -> (131.108.5.1, 0) [1806]
7 NAT*: i: icmp (10.0.1.1, 1) -> (131.108.2.1, 1) [1807]
8 NAT*: o: icmp (131.108.2.1, 1) -> (131.108.5.1, 1) [1807]
9 NAT*: i: icmp (10.0.1.1, 2) -> (131.108.2.1, 2) [1808]
10 NAT*: o: icmp (131.108.2.1, 2) -> (131.108.5.1, 2) [1808]
11 NAT*: i: icmp (10.0.1.1, 3) -> (131.108.2.1, 3) [1809]
12 NAT*: o: icmp (131.108.2.1, 3) -> (131.108.5.1, 3) [1809]
13 NAT*: i: icmp (10.0.1.1, 4) -> (131.108.2.1, 4) [1810]
14 NAT*: o: icmp (131.108.2.1, 4) -> (131.108.5.1, 4) [1810]
```

The clear options for NAT show up in Figure 7-10. Lines 1 through 3 identify clearing options for statistics and translations. Lines 5 through 10 identify the options for clearing the translation table. Lines 12 and 13 show the results of the **clear ip nat translation** *. Lines 14 through 25 show us the current **show ip nat statistics** output where the dynamic translations active in Figure 7-9 have been cleared.

Figure 7-11 is the **show ip protocol** output for NewYork. Lines 16 through 18 identify networks 131.108.0.0, 200.200.200.0, and 10.0.0.0 and the associated interfaces as participants in the RIP protocol.

Line 6 identifies RIP routing updates exiting interface Serial 0 as being filtered by **access-list 2,** which permits only network 131.108.0.0; all other networks will be blocked as they are sent into our private network.

**Figure 7-9**   NewYork **show** command output

```
1 NewYork#sho ip nat translations
2 Pro Inside global      Inside local     Outside local    Outside global
3 --   200.200.200.2      10.0.2.2         --               --
4 --   200.200.200.3      10.0.1.1         --               --
5
6 NewYork#show ip nat statistics
7 Total active translations: 2 (0 static, 2 dynamic; 0 extended)
8 Outside interfaces: Serial1
9 Inside interfaces: Serial0
10 Hits: 71  Misses: 4
11 Expired translations: 0
12 Dynamic mappings:
13 — Inside Source
14 access-list 1 pool good-pool refcount 2
15   pool good-pool: netmask 255.255.255.0
16         start 200.200.200.2 end 200.200.200.254
17         type generic, total addresses 253, allocated 2 (0%), misses 0
```

**Figure 7-10** NewYork **clear** command output

```
1  NewYork#clear ip nat ?
2    statistics   Clear translation statistics
3    translation  Clear dynamic translation
4
5  NewYork#clear ip nat translation ?
6    *         Delete all dynamic translations
7    inside    Inside addresses (and ports)
8    outside   Outside addresses (and ports)
9    tcp       Transmission Control Protocol
10   udp       User Datagram Protocol
11
12 NewYork#clear ip nat translation *
13 NewYork#sho ip nat translation
14 NewYork#sho ip nat stat
15 Total active translations: 0 (0 static, 0 dynamic; 0 extended)
16 Outside interfaces: Serial1
17 Inside interfaces: Serial0
18 Hits: 71  Misses: 4
19 Expired translations: 0
20 Dynamic mappings:
21 — Inside Source
22 access-list 1 pool good-pool refcount 0
23  pool good-pool: netmask 255.255.255.0
24        start 200.200.200.2 end 200.200.200.254
25        type generic, total addresses 253, allocated 0 (0%), misses 0
```

**Figure 7-11** NewYork **show ip** protocol output

```
1  NewYork#sho ip protocol
2  Routing Protocol is "rip"
3    Sending updates every 30 seconds, next due in 4 seconds
4    Invalid after 180 seconds, hold down 180, flushed after 240
5    Outgoing update filter list for all interfaces is not set
6      Serial0 filtered by 2
7      Serial1 filtered by 3
8    Incoming update filter list for all interfaces is not set
9    Redistributing: rip
10   Default version control: send version 1, receive any version
11     Interface      Send  Recv  Key-chain
12     Loopback0       1     1 2
13     Serial0         1     1 2
14     Serial1         1     1 2
15   Routing for Networks:
16     10.0.0.0
17     131.108.0.0
18     200.200.200.0
19   Routing Information Sources:
20     Gateway        Distance    Last Update
21     10.0.2.2          120      00:00:13
22     131.108.3.1       120      00:00:20
23   Distance: (default is 120)
```

**Figure 7-12**   NewYork **show ip route** output

```
1 NewYork#sho ip route
2 Codes: C - connected, S - static, I - IGRP, R - RIP, M - mobile, B - BGP
3         D - EIGRP, EX - EIGRP external, O - OSPF, IA - OSPF inter area
4         N1 - OSPF NSSA external type 1, N2 - OSPF NSSA external type 2
5         E1 - OSPF external type 1, E2 - OSPF external type 2, E - EGP
6         i - IS-IS, L1 - IS-IS level-1, L2 - IS-IS level-2, * - candidate default
7         U - per-user static route, o - ODR
8
9 Gateway of last resort is not set
10
11 C    200.200.200.0/24 is directly connected, Loopback0
12      10.0.0.0/24 is subnetted, 2 subnets
13 C        10.0.2.0 is directly connected, Serial0
14 R        10.0.1.0 [120/1] via 10.0.2.2, 00:00:19, Serial0
15      131.108.0.0/24 is subnetted, 2 subnets
16 C        131.108.3.0 is directly connected, Serial1
17 R        131.108.2.0 [120/1] via 131.108.3.1, 00:00:00, Serial1
```

Line 7 identifies RIP routing updates exiting interface Serial 1 as being filtered by **access-list 3,** which permits networks 131.108.0.0 and 200.200.200.0, while private network 10.0.0.0 is blocked for updates sent to our global network.

Figure 7-12 is the **show ip route** output that indicates that networks 10.0.0.0, 200.200.200.0, and 131.108.0.0 are reachable from New York.

Figure 7-13 is the London configuration, no surprises, basic IP RIP networking.

**Figure 7-13**   London configuration

```
1  !
2  hostname London
3  !
4  no ip domain-lookup
5  !
6  interface Ethernet0
7   ip address 10.0.1.1 255.255.255.0
8  !
9  interface Serial1
10  ip address 10.0.2.2 255.255.255.0
11  bandwidth 125
12  clockrate 125000
13 !
14 router rip
15  network 10.0.0.0
16 !
17 ip classless
18 !
19 line con 0
20  exec-timeout 0 0
21  length 0
22 !
```

**Figure 7-14** London **ping** test output

```
1  London#ping
2  Protocol [ip]:
3  Target IP address: 131.108.2.1
4  Repeat count [5]:
5  Datagram size [100]:
6  Timeout in seconds [2]:
7  Extended commands [n]:
8  Sweep range of sizes [n]:
9  Type escape sequence to abort.
10 Sending 5, 100-byte ICMP Echos to 131.108.2.1, timeout is 2 seconds:
11 !!!!!
12 Success rate is 100 percent (5/5), round-trip min/avg/max = 36/83/268 ms
13 London#ping
14 Protocol [ip]:
15 Target IP address: 131.108.2.1
16 Repeat count [5]:
17 Datagram size [100]:
18 Timeout in seconds [2]:
19 Extended commands [n]: y
20 Source address or interface: 10.0.1.1
21 Type of service [0]:
22 Set DF bit in IP header? [no]:
23 Validate reply data? [no]:
24 Data pattern [0xABCD]:
25 Loose, Strict, Record, Timestamp, Verbose[none]:
26 Sweep range of sizes [n]:
27 Type escape sequence to abort.
28 Sending 5, 100-byte ICMP Echos to 131.108.2.1, timeout is 2 seconds:
29 !!!!!
30 Success rate is 100 percent (5/5), round-trip min/avg/max = 36/40/38 ms
```

**Figure 7-15** London **show ip** protocol output

```
1  London#sho ip prot
2  Routing Protocol is "rip"
3    Sending updates every 30 seconds, next due in 10 seconds
4    Invalid after 180 seconds, hold down 180, flushed after 240
5    Outgoing update filter list for all interfaces is not set
6    Incoming update filter list for all interfaces is not set
7    Redistributing: rip
8    Default version control: send version 1, receive any version
9      Interface        Send  Recv  Key-chain
10     Ethernet0         1     1 2
11     Serial1           1     1 2
12   Routing for Networks:
13     10.0.0.0
14   Routing Information Sources:
15     Gateway          Distance      Last Update
16     10.0.2.1              120      00:00:18
17   Distance: (default is 120)
```

**Figure 7-16** London **show ip route** output

```
1 London#sho ip route
2 Codes: C - connected, S - static, I - IGRP, R - RIP, M - mobile, B - BGP
3        D - EIGRP, EX - EIGRP external, O - OSPF, IA - OSPF inter area
4        N1 - OSPF NSSA external type 1, N2 - OSPF NSSA external type 2
5        E1 - OSPF external type 1, E2 - OSPF external type 2, E - EGP
6        i - IS-IS, L1 - IS-IS level-1, L2 - IS-IS level-2, * - candidate default
7        U - per-user static route, o - ODR
8
9 Gateway of last resort is not set
10
11       10.0.0.0/24 is subnetted, 2 subnets
12 C        10.0.2.0 is directly connected, Serial1
13 C        10.0.1.0 is directly connected, Ethernet0
14 R     131.108.0.0/16 [120/1] via 10.0.2.1, 00:00:23, Serial1
```

Figure 7-14 is a sample extended **ping** output, available in the privileged mode.

Lines 1 through 11 show a successful attempt to **ping** 131.108.2.1 using the standard source address 10.0.2.2, the exit interface IP address from London.

Lines 13 to 30 show a successful **ping**, when source address 10.0.1.1 is used, as it belongs to the translated subnet.

Figure 7-15 is the **show ip protocol** output that shows basic IP RIP for network 10.0.0.0.

Figure 7-16 is the **show ip route** output that shows directly connected 10.0.0.0 interfaces; network 131.108.0.0 addresses are being learned via the RIP protocol, line 14, from New York.

## Example #2—Access the Internet Using an Illegal Internal IP Network Number

This example provides the network administrator with an easy-to-use technique that translates internal illegal network numbers into valid Internet addresses. Figure 7-17 is the network layout for this example. In this example, 200.200.200.0 is the valid class C address used to represent our illegal address to the outside world. The main problem with illegal addresses is that we cannot access an outside address in the global address space that matches up to our internal illegal address. In order for this process to work, we must define static mapping of our outside global addresses to outside local addresses visible to our inside network.

**Figure 7-17**
Illegal addresses with
simple NAT
translation

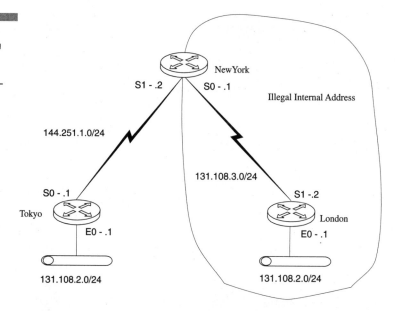

If we are using Domain Name Services (DNS) from the outside, NAT will intercept the DNS responses and change the outside global address in the DNS packet payload to the translated outside local address.

Tokyo is a router in the outside domain that uses a valid IP network of 131.108.0.0 and the RIP routing protocol. See lines 13 and 14 in Figure 7-18.

**Figure 7-18** Tokyo configuration

```
1  !
2  hostname Tokyo
3  !
4  no ip domain-lookup
5  !
6  interface Ethernet0
7    ip address 131.108.2.1 255.255.255.0
8  !
9  interface Serial0
10   ip address 144.251.1.1 255.255.255.0
11   bandwidth 125
12 !
13 router rip
14   network 131.108.0.0
15 !
16 ip classless
17 ip route 0.0.0.0 0.0.0.0 Serial0
18 !
19 line con 0
20   exec-timeout 0 0
21   length 0
22 !
23 end
```

**Figure 7-19**  Tokyo **show ip** protocol output

```
1 Tokyo#sho ip protocol
2 Routing Protocol is "rip"
3   Sending updates every 30 seconds, next due in 12 seconds
4   Invalid after 180 seconds, hold down 180, flushed after 240
5   Outgoing update filter list for all interfaces is not set
6   Incoming update filter list for all interfaces is not set
7   Redistributing: rip
8   Default version control: send version 1, receive any version
9     Interface        Send  Recv   Key-chain
10    Ethernet0         1     1 2
11    Serial0           1     1 2
12  Routing for Networks:
13    131.108.0.0
14  Routing Information Sources:
15    Gateway          Distance      Last Update
16    131.108.3.2          120       00:00:22
17  Distance: (default is 120)
```

Line 17 is a static route that identifies the default route via Serial 0 for all unknown networks. Network 144.251.0.0 is an intermediate network used to simulate an external connection to the Internet.

The **show ip protocol** output for Tokyo in Figure 7-19 shows network 131.108.0.0 as the only network being processed. See line 13.

The **show ip route** output for Tokyo in Figure 7-20 shows network 0.0.0.0 as a static default route.

The configuration for New York in Figure 7-21 is where Network Address Translation takes place.

Line 4 defines a pool of valid outside addresses, and line 5 assigns this pool of addresses for translating the inside source addresses that pass **access-list 1** on line 26.

**Figure 7-20**  Tokyo **show ip route** output

```
1 Tokyo#sho ip route
2 Codes: C - connected, S - static, I - IGRP, R - RIP, M - mobile, B - BGP
3        D - EIGRP, EX - EIGRP external, O - OSPF, IA - OSPF inter area
4        N1 - OSPF NSSA external type 1, N2 - OSPF NSSA external type 2
5        E1 - OSPF external type 1, E2 - OSPF external type 2, E - EGP
6        i - IS-IS, L1 - IS-IS level-1, L2 - IS-IS level-2, * - candidate default
7        U - per-user static route, o - ODR
8
9 Gateway of last resort is 0.0.0.0 to network 0.0.0.0
10
11     144.251.0.0/24 is subnetted, 1 subnets
12 C      144.251.1.0 is directly connected, Serial0
13     131.108.0.0/24 is subnetted, 1 subnets
14 C      131.108.2.0 is directly connected, Ethernet0
15 S*   0.0.0.0/0 is directly connected, Serial0
```

**Figure 7-21**   NewYork configuration

```
1  !
2  hostname NewYork
3  !
4  ip nat pool good-pool 200.200.200.5 200.200.200.250 netmask 255.255.255.0
5  ip nat inside source list 1 pool good-pool
6  ip nat inside source static 131.108.2.1 200.200.200.1
7  ip nat outside source static 131.108.2.1 200.200.200.254
8  no ip domain-lookup
9  !
10 interface Serial0
11   ip address 131.108.3.1 255.255.255.0
12   ip nat inside
13   bandwidth 125
14 !
15 interface Serial1
16   ip address 144.251.1.2 255.255.255.0
17   ip nat outside
18   bandwidth 125
19   clockrate 125000
20 !
21 router rip
22   network 131.108.0.0
23 !
24 ip classless
25 ip route 0.0.0.0 0.0.0.0 Serial1
26 access-list 1 permit 131.108.0.0 0.0.255.255
27 !
28 line con 0
29   exec-timeout 0 0
30   length 0
31 !
32 end
```

Line 6 provides a static map to force a specific inside global address, 131.108.2.1 to be mapped to 200.200.200.1 for all communications with the outside domain. Any outside device that wishes to reach our internal address of 131.108.2.1 must use the specific address of 200.200.200.1.

Line 7 provides a static map to force the outside global address 131.108.2.1 to be mapped to 200.200.200.254 for all communications with the inside domain.

Lines 6 and 7 allow the two hosts with the IP address 131.108.2.1 to communicate using this static translation.

Line 12 defines traffic coming from the inside illegal network 131.108.0.0 as the source addresses to be translated into the outside global domain as network 200.200.200.0.

Line 17 defines the interface where the translated addresses are sent out to the outside network.

Figure 7-22 shows the initial **show ip nat statistics** output in lines 1 through 12 and the **show ip nat translation** on lines 13 through 16.

**Figure 7-22**  Initial **show** command output

```
1 NewYork#sho ip nat stat
2 Total active translations: 2 (2 static, 0 dynamic; 0 extended)
3 Outside interfaces: Serial1
4 Inside interfaces: Serial0
5 Hits: 0  Misses: 0
6 Expired translations: 0
7 Dynamic mappings:
8 — Inside Source
9 access-list 1 pool good-pool refcount 0
10  pool good-pool: netmask 255.255.255.0
11        start 200.200.200.5 end 200.200.200.250
12        type generic, total addresses 246, allocated 0 (0%), misses 0
13 NewYork#sho ip nat tran
14 Pro    Inside global      Inside local       Outside local      Outside global
15 --     200.200.200.1      131.108.2.1        --                 --
16 --     --       --        200.200.200.254    131.108.2.1
```

Sample output from the **debug ip nat** command is in Figure 7-23. Lines 2 and 3 shows translation from 131.108.3.2 to 200.200.200.5 on the first **ping** request to address 144.251.1.1. Lines 4 through 11 show the rest of the successful **ping** translation sequence. There is a single translation from the inside to a normal outside address.

Lines 12 through 15 show the first message in our second **ping** sequence using our inside address of 131.108.2.1 as it attempts to contact the outside host with the same 131.108.2.1 address. With our static mapping in place, we go through a two-step translation process in both directions. Line 12 translates our source address of 131.108.2.1 to 200.200.200.1. Line 13 translates the destination address of 200.200.200.254 to the valid outside address of 131.108.2.1. Lines 14 and 15 demonstrate the reverse translation from the outside domain into our illegal address space.

Figure 7-24 shows the **show ip nat statistics** command output on lines 1 through 12, and the **show ip nat translation** command output on lines 14 through 19.

Line 2 shows us that there are two static and two dynamic translations currently operating. Line 12 shows us that only one of the dynamic addresses is being used. What is the other dynamic map? Read on.

Line 16 is the static map from the inside local address of 131.108.2.1 to the inside global address of 200.200.200.1.

Line 17 is the dynamic map we used to contact outside local network 144.251.1.1, where our inside local address of 131.108.3.2 was mapped to our outside global address of 200.200.200.5, the first address in our pool.

**Figure 7-23** NewYork **debug** output

```
1  NAT*: s=131.108.3.2->200.200.200.5, d=144.251.1.1 [195]
2  NAT*: s=144.251.1.1, d=200.200.200.5->131.108.3.2 [195]
3  NAT*: s=131.108.3.2->200.200.200.5, d=144.251.1.1 [196]
4  NAT*: s=144.251.1.1, d=200.200.200.5->131.108.3.2 [196]
5  NAT*: s=131.108.3.2->200.200.200.5, d=144.251.1.1 [197]
6  NAT*: s=144.251.1.1, d=200.200.200.5->131.108.3.2 [197]
7  NAT*: s=131.108.3.2->200.200.200.5, d=144.251.1.1 [198]
8  NAT*: s=144.251.1.1, d=200.200.200.5->131.108.3.2 [198]
9  NAT*: s=131.108.3.2->200.200.200.5, d=144.251.1.1 [199]
10 NAT*: s=144.251.1.1, d=200.200.200.5->131.108.3.2 [199]
11 NAT: s=131.108.2.1->200.200.200.1, d=200.200.200.254 [200]
12 NAT: s=200.200.200.1, d=200.200.200.254->131.108.2.1 [200]
13 NAT*: s=131.108.2.1->200.200.200.254, d=200.200.200.1 [200]
14 NAT*: s=200.200.200.254, d=200.200.200.1->131.108.2.1 [200]
15 NAT: s=131.108.2.1->200.200.200.1, d=200.200.200.254 [201]
16 NAT: s=200.200.200.1, d=200.200.200.254->131.108.2.1 [201]
17 NAT*: s=131.108.2.1->200.200.200.254, d=200.200.200.1 [201]
18 NAT*: s=200.200.200.254, d=200.200.200.1->131.108.2.1 [201]
19 NAT: s=131.108.2.1->200.200.200.1, d=200.200.200.254 [202]
20 NAT: s=200.200.200.1, d=200.200.200.254->131.108.2.1 [202]
21 NAT*: s=131.108.2.1->200.200.200.254, d=200.200.200.1 [202]
22 NAT*: s=200.200.200.254, d=200.200.200.1->131.108.2.1 [202]
23 NAT: s=131.108.2.1->200.200.200.1, d=200.200.200.254 [203]
24 NAT: s=200.200.200.1, d=200.200.200.254->131.108.2.1 [203]
25 NAT*: s=131.108.2.1->200.200.200.254, d=200.200.200.1 [203]
26 NAT*: s=200.200.200.254, d=200.200.200.1->131.108.2.1 [203]
27 NAT: s=131.108.2.1->200.200.200.1, d=200.200.200.254 [204]
28 NAT: s=200.200.200.1, d=200.200.200.254->131.108.2.1 [204]
29 NAT*: s=131.108.2.1->200.200.200.254, d=200.200.200.1 [204]
30 NAT*: s=200.200.200.254, d=200.200.200.1->131.108.2.1 [204]
```

**Figure 7-24** NewYork **show** command output

```
1  NewYork#show ip nat stat
2  Total active translations: 4 (2 static, 2 dynamic; 0 extended)
3  Outside interfaces: Serial1
4  Inside interfaces: Serial0
5  Hits: 38  Misses: 2
6  Expired translations: 0
7  Dynamic mappings:
8  — Inside Source
9  access-list 1 pool good-pool refcount 1
10   pool good-pool: netmask 255.255.255.0
11        start 200.200.200.5 end 200.200.200.250
12        type generic, total addresses 246, allocated 1 (0%), misses 0
13
14 NewYork#sho ip nat tran
15 Pro  Inside global    Inside local     Outside local     Outside global
16 --   200.200.200.1    131.108.2.1      --                --
17 --   200.200.200.5    131.108.3.2      --                --
18 --   --      --       200.200.200.254  131.108.2.1
19 --   200.200.200.1    131.108.2.1      200.200.200.254   131.108.2.1
```

**Figure 7-25** NewYork **show ip protocol** output

```
1 NewYork#sho ip prot
2 Routing Protocol is "rip"
3   Sending updates every 30 seconds, next due in 5 seconds
4   Invalid after 180 seconds, hold down 180, flushed after 240
5   Outgoing update filter list for all interfaces is not set
6   Incoming update filter list for all interfaces is not set
7   Redistributing: rip
8   Default version control: send version 1, receive any version
9     Interface        Send  Recv   Key-chain
10     Serial0          1     1 2
11   Routing for Networks:
12     131.108.0.0
13   Routing Information Sources:
14     Gateway         Distance       Last Update
15     131.108.3.2          120       00:00:06
16   Distance: (default is 120)
```

Line 18 is the static map from the outside local address of 200.200.200.254 to the outside global address of 131.108.2.1.

Line 19 is the dynamic map built when the two address 131.108.2.1 hosts communicate with each other.

Figure 7-25 is the **show ip protocol** output for NewYork, basic RIP routing.

Figure 7-26 is the **show ip route** output that shows network 131.108.2.0 RIP derived from London on line 15. There is a default static route identifying the destination as the router connected on the Serial 1 interface.

Figure 7-27 is the London configuration, no surprises, basic IP RIP networking.

**Figure 7-26** NewYork **show ip route** output

```
1 NewYork#sho ip route
2 Codes: C - connected, S - static, I - IGRP, R - RIP, M - mobile, B - BGP
3        D - EIGRP, EX - EIGRP external, O - OSPF, IA - OSPF inter area
4        N1 - OSPF NSSA external type 1, N2 - OSPF NSSA external type 2
5        E1 - OSPF external type 1, E2 - OSPF external type 2, E - EGP
6        i - IS-IS, L1 - IS-IS level-1, L2 - IS-IS level-2, * - candidate default
7        U - per-user static route, o - ODR
8
9 Gateway of last resort is 0.0.0.0 to network 0.0.0.0
10
11      144.251.0.0/24 is subnetted, 1 subnets
12 C       144.251.1.0 is directly connected, Serial1
13      131.108.0.0/24 is subnetted, 2 subnets
14 C       131.108.3.0 is directly connected, Serial0
15 R       131.108.2.0 [120/1] via 131.108.3.2, 00:00:12, Serial0
16 S*   0.0.0.0/0 is directly connected, Serial1
```

**Figure 7-27**  London configuration

```
1  !
2  hostname London
3  !
4  no ip domain-lookup
5  !
6  interface Ethernet0
7    ip address 131.108.2.1 255.255.255.0
8  !
9  interface Serial1
10   ip address 131.108.3.2 255.255.255.0
11   bandwidth 125
12   clockrate 125000
13 !
14 router rip
15   network 131.108.0.0
16 !
17 ip classless
18 !
19 line con 0
20   exec-timeout 0 0
21   length 0
22 !
23 end
```

**Figure 7-28**  London **ping** test output

```
1  London#ping 144.251.1.1
2
3  Type escape sequence to abort.
4  Sending 5, 100-byte ICMP Echos to 144.251.1.1, timeout is 2 seconds:
5  !!!!!
6  Success rate is 100 percent (5/5), round-trip min/avg/max = 36/36/36 ms
7  London#ping
8  Protocol [ip]:
9  Target IP address: 200.200.200.254
10 Repeat count [5]:
11 Datagram size [100]:
12 Timeout in seconds [2]:
13 Extended commands [n]: y
14 Source address or interface: 131.108.2.1
15 Type of service [0]:
16 Set DF bit in IP header? [no]:
17 Validate reply data? [no]:
18 Data pattern [0xABCD]:
19 Loose, Strict, Record, Timestamp, Verbose[none]:
20 Sweep range of sizes [n]:
21 Type escape sequence to abort.
22 Sending 5, 100-byte ICMP Echos to 200.200.200.254, timeout is 2 seconds:
23 !!!!!
24 Success rate is 100 percent (5/5), round-trip min/avg/max = 40/41/48 ms
```

**Figure 7-29** London **show ip protocol** output

```
1 London#show ip protocol
2 Routing Protocol is "rip"
3   Sending updates every 30 seconds, next due in 14 seconds
4   Invalid after 180 seconds, hold down 180, flushed after 240
5   Outgoing update filter list for all interfaces is not set
6   Incoming update filter list for all interfaces is not set
7   Redistributing: rip
8   Default version control: send version 1, receive any version
9     Interface        Send  Recv   Key-chain
10      Ethernet0        1     1 2
11      Serial1          1     1 2
12    Routing for Networks:
13      131.108.0.0
14    Routing Information Sources:
15      Gateway         Distance      Last Update
16      10.0.2.1             120      02:23:07
17      131.108.3.1          120      00:00:27
18    Distance: (default is 120)
```

Figure 7-28 is sample **ping** output to a normal global address 144.251.1.1 on lines 1 through 6 and an extended ping output on lines 7 through 24.

Lines 1 through 6 show a successful attempt to **ping** 144.251.1.1 using the standard source address 131.108.3.2, the exit interface IP address from London. Lines 7 to 24 show a successful **ping**, when the source address 131.108.2.1 is used with the target address of 200.200.200.254, our outside local representation of the outside host with address 131.108.2.1.

Figure 7-29 is the **show ip protocol** output that shows basic IP RIP for network 131.108.0.0.

Figure 7-30 is the **show ip route** output that shows directly connected network 131.108.0.0 addresses and a default route directed out interface Serial 1 headed to New York.

**Figure 7-30** London **show ip route** output

```
1 London#sho ip route
2 Codes: C - connected, S - static, I - IGRP, R - RIP, M - mobile, B - BGP
3        D - EIGRP, EX - EIGRP external, O - OSPF, IA - OSPF inter area
4        N1 - OSPF NSSA external type 1, N2 - OSPF NSSA external type 2
5        E1 - OSPF external type 1, E2 - OSPF external type 2, E - EGP
6        i - IS-IS, L1 - IS-IS level-1, L2 - IS-IS level-2, * - candidate default
7        U - per-user static route, o - ODR
8
9 Gateway of last resort is 131.108.3.1 to network 0.0.0.0
10
11     131.108.0.0/24 is subnetted, 2 subnets
12 C      131.108.3.0 is directly connected, Serial1
13 C      131.108.2.0 is directly connected, Ethernet0
14 R*  0.0.0.0/0 [120/1] via 131.108.3.1, 00:00:03, Serial1
```

# Example #3—Combine Two Address Domains, Two Contact Points

This example ties together two different address domains that use the same private address 10.0.0.0. The network layout is shown in Figure 7-31. The EIGRP 200 network consisting of Tokyo, London, and New York, is the outside network. The OSPF network consisting of Moscow, Paris, and Rome is the inside network. With two contact points, it appears that we have the best of all worlds: address translation, load balancing for IP traffic, and backup if one of the connection points should fail.

Danger, Will Robinson! All is not as it appears. After reviewing the following example, see if you can find the hidden bombs. The answer is at the end of the chapter.

Figure 7-32 is the configuration for Tokyo. This as an internal EIGRP router with the Ethernet 0 address of 10.1.1.1 statically mapped in the Moscow and Paris configurations, our two contact points.

The translation test **ping 192.168.3.1** is shown in Figure 7-33. The destination address is statically mapped to an inside global address in order to succeed.

Figure 7-34 shows the basic EIGRP routing process for network 10.0.0.0.

The **show ip route** output in Figure 7-35 shows us the details of our EIGRP network 10.0.0.0 with two equal default external routes to net-

**Figure 7-31**

Combine two networks, dual connection points

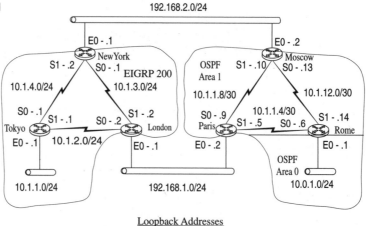

Loopback Addresses

| | | |
|---|---|---|
| Moscow | 10.1.254.253/30 | Area 1 |
| Paris | 10.1.254.249/30 | Area 1 |
| Rome | 10.0.254.253/30 | Area 0 |

**Figure 7-32**  Tokyo configuration

```
1  !
2  hostname Tokyo
3  !
4  no ip domain-lookup
5  !
6  interface Ethernet0
7   ip address 10.1.1.1 255.255.255.0
8  !
9  interface Serial0
10  ip address 10.1.4.1 255.255.255.0
11  bandwidth 125
12  !
13 interface Serial1
14  ip address 10.1.2.2 255.255.255.0
15  bandwidth 125
16  clockrate 125000
17  !
18 router eigrp 200
19  network 10.0.0.0
20  !
21 ip classless
22  !
23 line con 0
24  exec-timeout 0 0
25  length 0
26  !
27 end
```

work 0.0.0.0. With two equal routes outside of our EIGRP network, Cisco routers will perform automatic load sharing on a packet-by-packet basis to the destination. For further details on the translation process showing the load sharing, see Figures 7-44 and 7-50 for **debug** output and Figures 7-45 and 7-51 for NAT tables.

Figure 7-36 shows the New York configuration. The main feature in New York is the contact with Moscow, where the translation between the two domains takes place.

Line 24 is our static default route defining Ethernet 0 as the destination for all unknown networks.

**Figure 7-33**  Tokyo **ping** output

```
1 Tokyo#ping 192.168.3.1
2
3 Type escape sequence to abort.
4 Sending 5, 100-byte ICMP Echos to 192.168.3.1, timeout is 2 seconds:
5 !!!!!
6 Success rate is 100 percent (5/5), round-trip min/avg/max = 36/41/52 ms
```

**Figure 7-34** Tokyo **show ip protocol** output

```
1 Tokyo#sho ip prot
2 Routing Protocol is "eigrp 200"
3   Outgoing update filter list for all interfaces is not set
4   Incoming update filter list for all interfaces is not set
5   Default networks flagged in outgoing updates
6   Default networks accepted from incoming updates
7   EIGRP metric weight K1=1, K2=0, K3=1, K4=0, K5=0
8   EIGRP maximum hopcount 100
9   EIGRP maximum metric variance 1
10  Redistributing: eigrp 200
11  Automatic network summarization is in effect
12  Routing for Networks:
13    10.0.0.0
14  Routing Information Sources:
15    Gateway         Distance      Last Update
16    10.1.2.1             90       00:18:22
17    10.1.4.2             90       00:18:22
18  Distance: internal 90 external 170
```

Line 25 defines a static route to network 192.168.3.0, which is the class address used in the translation process. If this statement is missing, then traffic sent to network 192.168.3.0 will be rejected during the Ethernet encapsulation process. Normally, when an ARP request for an address not on the current LAN segment is received by a Cisco router, the router performs a proxy ARP. The router returns the router's MAC address to be used as the MAC destination across the LAN segment, if the requested address is in the IP routing table. Moscow, on the other end of our connecting LAN segment, knows about the translation network

**Figure 7-35** Tokyo **show ip route** output

```
1 Tokyo#sho ip route
2 Codes: C - connected, S - static, I - IGRP, R - RIP, M - mobile, B - BGP
3        D - EIGRP, EX - EIGRP external, O - OSPF, IA - OSPF inter area
4        N1 - OSPF NSSA external type 1, N2 - OSPF NSSA external type 2
5        E1 - OSPF external type 1, E2 - OSPF external type 2, E - EGP
6        i - IS-IS, L1 - IS-IS level-1, L2 - IS-IS level-2, * - candidate default
7        U - per-user static route, o - ODR
8
9 Gateway of last resort is 10.1.2.1 to network 0.0.0.0
10
11      10.0.0.0/24 is subnetted, 4 subnets
12 D       10.1.3.0 [90/21504000] via 10.1.4.2, 01:07:56, Serial0
13                  [90/21504000] via 10.1.2.1, 01:07:56, Serial1
14 C       10.1.2.0 is directly connected, Serial1
15 C       10.1.1.0 is directly connected, Ethernet0
16 C       10.1.4.0 is directly connected, Serial0
17 D*EX 0.0.0.0/0 [170/21017600] via 10.1.2.1, 00:18:28, Serial1
18                [170/21017600] via 10.1.4.2, 00:18:28, Serial0
```

**Figure 7-36** NewYork configuration

```
1  !
2  hostname NewYork
3  !
4  no ip domain-lookup
5  !
6  interface Ethernet0
7   ip address 192.168.2.1 255.255.255.0
8  !
9  interface Serial0
10   ip address 10.1.3.1 255.255.255.0
11   bandwidth 125
12  !
13  interface Serial1
14   ip address 10.1.4.2 255.255.255.0
15   bandwidth 125
16   clockrate 125000
17  !
18  router eigrp 200
19   redistribute static
20   network 10.0.0.0
21   distribute-list 1 out static
22  !
23  ip classless
24  ip route 0.0.0.0 0.0.0.0 Ethernet0
25  ip route 192.168.3.0 255.255.255.0 192.168.2.2
26  access-list 1 permit 0.0.0.0
27  !
28  line con 0
29   exec-timeout 0 0
30   length 0
31  !
32  end
```

192.168.3.0, but because this network is not in the routing table, a proxy ARP for 192.168.3.0 does not take place.

Lines 21 and 26 are used to make sure network 192.168.3.0 does not make its way to the routing tables in the rest of the EIGRP network.

The **show ip protocol** shown in Figure 7-37 shows our EIGRP process with static route filtering in place on line 4.

The **show ip route** output in Figure 7-38 shows our EIGRP routes, our boundary network 192.168.2.0 as directly connected across Ethernet 0, and static routes to 0.0.0.0 and our translation network 192.168.3.0.

Figure 7-39 shows the London configuration. The main feature in London is the contact with Paris, where the second translation between the two domains takes place.

Line 27 is our static default route defining Ethernet 0 as the destination for all unknown networks.

**Figure 7-37**   NewYork **show ip protocol** output

```
1 NewYork#sho ip prot
2 Routing Protocol is "eigrp 200"
3   Outgoing update filter list for all interfaces is not set
4     Redistributed static filtered by 1
5   Incoming update filter list for all interfaces is not set
6   Default networks flagged in outgoing updates
7   Default networks accepted from incoming updates
8   EIGRP metric weight K1=1, K2=0, K3=1, K4=0, K5=0
9   EIGRP maximum hopcount 100
10   EIGRP maximum metric variance 1
11   Redistributing: static, eigrp 200
12   Automatic network summarization is in effect
13   Routing for Networks:
14     10.0.0.0
15   Routing Information Sources:
16     Gateway         Distance        Last Update
17     10.1.3.2              90        00:20:21
18     10.1.4.1              90        00:20:21
19   Distance: internal 90 external 170
```

Line 28 defines a static route to network 192.168.3.0, which is the class address used in the translation process. Note that this address is the same address used in NewYork in Figure 3-36, line 25, as the same translation network *must* be used for all contact points when translation takes place at more than one contact point. If this statement is missing, then traffic sent to network 192.168.3.0 will be rejected during the Ethernet encapsulation process. Normally, when an ARP request for an address not on the current LAN segment is received by a Cisco router, the router performs

**Figure 7-38**   NewYork **show ip route** output

```
1 NewYork#sho ip route
2 Codes: C - connected, S - static, I - IGRP, R - RIP, M - mobile, B - BGP
3        D - EIGRP, EX - EIGRP external, O - OSPF, IA - OSPF inter area
4        N1 - OSPF NSSA external type 1, N2 - OSPF NSSA external type 2
5        E1 - OSPF external type 1, E2 - OSPF external type 2, E - EGP
6        i - IS-IS, L1 - IS-IS level-1, L2 - IS-IS level-2, * - candidate default
7        U - per-user static route, o - ODR
8
9 Gateway of last resort is 0.0.0.0 to network 0.0.0.0
10
11      10.0.0.0/24 is subnetted, 4 subnets
12 C       10.1.3.0 is directly connected, Serial0
13 D       10.1.2.0 [90/21504000] via 10.1.3.2, 00:30:56, Serial0
14                  [90/21504000] via 10.1.4.1, 00:30:56, Serial1
15 D       10.1.1.0 [90/21017600] via 10.1.4.1, 00:30:56, Serial1
16 C       10.1.4.0 is directly connected, Serial1
17 C     192.168.2.0/24 is directly connected, Ethernet0
18 S     192.168.3.0/24 [1/0] via 192.168.2.2
19 S*    0.0.0.0/0 is directly connected, Ethernet0
```

**Figure 7-39**   London configuration

```
1  !
2  hostname London
3  !
4  no ip domain-lookup
5  !
6  interface Ethernet0
7   ip address 192.168.1.1 255.255.255.0
8   no ip route-cache
9  !
10 interface Serial0
11   ip address 10.1.2.1 255.255.255.0
12   no ip route-cache
13   bandwidth 125
14 !
15 interface Serial1
16   ip address 10.1.3.2 255.255.255.0
17   no ip route-cache
18   bandwidth 125
19   clockrate 125000
20 !
21 router eigrp 200
22   redistribute static
23   network 10.0.0.0
24   distribute-list 1 out static
25 !
26 ip classless
27 ip route 0.0.0.0 0.0.0.0 Ethernet0
28 ip route 192.168.3.0 255.255.255.0 192.168.1.2
29 access-list 1 permit 0.0.0.0
30 !
31 !
32 line con 0
33   exec-timeout 0 0
34   length 0
35 !
36 end
```

a proxy ARP. The router returns the router's MAC address to be used as the MAC destination across the LAN segment, if the requested address is in the IP routing table. Moscow, on the other end of our connecting LAN segment, knows about the translation network 192.168.3.0 but because this network is not in the routing table, a proxy ARP for 192.168.3.0 does not take place.

Lines 24 and 29 are used to make sure network 192.168.3.0 does not make its way to the routing tables in the rest of the EIGRP network.

The **show ip protocol** shown in Figure 7-40 shows our EIGRP process with static route filtering in place on line 4.

The **show ip route** output in Figure 7-41 shows our EIGRP routes, our boundary network 192.168.1.0 as directly connected across Ethernet 0, and static routes to 0.0.0.0 and our translation network 192.168.3.0.

**Figure 7-40**   London **show ip protocol** output

```
1 London#sho ip prot
2 Routing Protocol is "eigrp 200"
3   Outgoing update filter list for all interfaces is not set
4     Redistributed static filtered by 1
5   Incoming update filter list for all interfaces is not set
6   Default networks flagged in outgoing updates
7   Default networks accepted from incoming updates
8   EIGRP metric weight K1=1, K2=0, K3=1, K4=0, K5=0
9   EIGRP maximum hopcount 100
10   EIGRP maximum metric variance 1
11   Redistributing: static, eigrp 200
12   Automatic network summarization is in effect
13   Routing for Networks:
14     10.0.0.0
15   Routing Information Sources:
16     Gateway          Distance      Last Update
17     10.1.3.1               90      00:21:41
18     10.1.2.2               90      00:21:41
19   Distance: internal 90 external 170
```

Figure 7-42 shows the Moscow configuration where our NAT process takes place.

Line 4 defines our pool of addresses to be used for dynamically translating our inside addresses to the range of addresses 192.168.3.50 to 192.168.3.99.

Line 5 assigns the pool in line 4 to the inside network for translation using the overload method. This allows a single IP translation address to

**Figure 7-41**   London **show ip route** output

```
1 London#sho ip route
2 Codes: C - connected, S - static, I - IGRP, R - RIP, M - mobile, B - BGP
3        D - EIGRP, EX - EIGRP external, O - OSPF, IA - OSPF inter area
4        N1 - OSPF NSSA external type 1, N2 - OSPF NSSA external type 2
5        E1 - OSPF external type 1, E2 - OSPF external type 2, E - EGP
6        i - IS-IS, L1 - IS-IS level-1, L2 - IS-IS level-2, * - candidate default
7        U - per-user static route, o - ODR
8
9 Gateway of last resort is 0.0.0.0 to network 0.0.0.0
10
11      10.0.0.0/24 is subnetted, 4 subnets
12 C       10.1.3.0 is directly connected, Serial1
13 C       10.1.2.0 is directly connected, Serial0
14 D       10.1.1.0 [90/21017600] via 10.1.2.2, 01:11:06, Serial0
15 D       10.1.4.0 [90/21504000] via 10.1.2.2, 01:11:06, Serial0
16                  [90/21504000] via 10.1.3.1, 01:11:06, Serial1
17 C     192.168.1.0/24 is directly connected, Ethernet0
18 S     192.168.3.0/24 [1/0] via 192.168.1.2
19 S*    0.0.0.0/0 is directly connected, Ethernet0
```

be used as a base for multiple translations when combined with port numbers generated by the original sender. Only addresses that pass the access-list on line 41 will be translated.

Lines 6 and 7 define static inside and outside address mappings, one-for-one addressing, no overload.

**Figure 7-42**   Moscow configuration

```
1 !
2 hostname Moscow
3 !
4 ip nat pool ospf-source 192.168.3.50 192.168.3.99 netmask 255.255.255.0
5 ip nat inside source list 1 pool ospf-source overload
6 ip nat inside source static 10.0.1.1 192.168.3.1
7 ip nat outside source static 10.1.1.1 192.168.3.254
8 no ip domain-lookup
9 !
10 interface Loopback0
11  ip address 10.1.254.253 255.255.255.252
12 !
13 interface Ethernet0
14  ip address 192.168.2.2 255.255.255.0
15  ip nat outside
16  no ip route-cache
17  no ip mroute-cache
18 !
19 interface Serial0
20  ip address 10.1.1.13 255.255.255.252
21  ip nat inside
22  ip rip authentication mode 0
23  no ip route-cache
24  bandwidth 125
25  no fair-queue
26 !
27 interface Serial1
28  ip address 10.1.1.10 255.255.255.252
29  no ip route-cache
30  bandwidth 125
31  clockrate 125000
32 !
33 router ospf 200
34  network 10.1.1.12 0.0.0.3 area 1
35  network 10.1.1.8 0.0.0.3 area 1
36  network 10.1.254.252 0.0.0.3 area 1
37  default-information originate always metric 1 metric-type 1
38 !
39 ip classless
40 ip route 0.0.0.0 0.0.0.0 Ethernet0
41 access-list 1 permit 10.0.0.0 0.255.255.255
42 !
43 line con 0
44  exec-timeout 0 0
45  length 0
46 !
47 end
```

**Figure 7-43**  Moscow initial **show** command output

```
1 Moscow#clear ip nat tran *
2 Moscow#clear ip nat stat
3 Moscow#sho ip nat tran
4 Pro Inside global      Inside local      Outside local      Outside global
5 -- --                  --                192.168.3.254      10.1.1.1
6 -- 192.168.3.1         10.0.1.1          --
7 Moscow#sho ip nat stat
8 Total active translations: 2 (2 static, 0 dynamic; 0 extended)
9 Outside interfaces: Ethernet0
10 Inside interfaces: Serial0
11 Hits: 0  Misses: 0
12 Expired translations: 0
13 Dynamic mappings:
14 — Inside Source
15 access-list 1 pool ospf-source refcount 0
16  pool ospf-source: netmask 255.255.255.0
17        start 192.168.3.50 end 192.168.3.99
18        type generic, total addresses 50, allocated 0 (0%), misses 0
```

Line 15 identifies Ethernet 0 as the point where outside translations take place.

Line 21 identifies Serial 0 as the point where inside translations take place.

Lines 33 through 37 detail the OSPF routing process to tie together the loopback and serial interfaces to the OSPF processes. Line 37 provides the avenue through which our default route on line 40 is propagated through our OSPF network starting with a metric of 1. By making the metric a type 1, additional metrics are added to the base as this route is propagated throughout the OSPF network.

Figure 7-43 shows us the setup for our translation tests. After the NAT translation tables and NAT statistics are cleared on lines 1 and 2, the base static definitions are the only items that show up in our **show ip nat translation** on lines 3 through 6 and our **show ip nat statistics** on lines 7 through 18.

Figure 7-44 shows us the output of the **debug ip nat** command for several different translations.

Lines 2 through 3 are the translations when an outside network ping is targeted for our statically defined mapping of 192.168.3.1 to 10.0.1.1. But wait, where are the rest of the five successful pings that were translated? They can be found in Figure 7-50 where Paris has completed the other three pings. Look at the sequence numbers on lines 2 through 5 of Figure 7-44 and lines 2 through 7 of Figure 7-50, and the story is complete. This theme will be repeated for all of our pings in this section. Note

**Figure 7-44**  Moscow **debug ip nat** output

```
1 !EIGRP to Rome E0
2 NAT: s=10.1.2.2, d=192.168.3.1->10.0.1.1 [11]
3 NAT: s=10.0.1.1->192.168.3.1, d=10.1.2.2 [11]
4 NAT: s=10.1.2.2, d=192.168.3.1->10.0.1.1 [13]
5 NAT: s=10.0.1.1->192.168.3.1, d=10.1.2.2 [13]
6 !Regular OSPF to Tokyo E0
7 NAT: s=10.1.1.14->192.168.3.50, d=192.168.3.254 [150]
8 NAT: s=192.168.3.50, d=192.168.3.254->10.1.1.1 [150]
9 NAT: s=10.1.1.1->192.168.3.254, d=192.168.3.50 [150]
10 NAT: s=192.168.3.254, d=192.168.3.50->10.1.1.14 [150]
11 NAT: s=10.1.1.14->192.168.3.50, d=192.168.3.254 [152]
12 NAT: s=192.168.3.50, d=192.168.3.254->10.1.1.1 [152]
13 NAT: s=10.1.1.1->192.168.3.254, d=192.168.3.50 [152]
14 NAT: s=192.168.3.254, d=192.168.3.50->10.1.1.14 [152]
15 NAT: s=10.1.1.14->192.168.3.50, d=192.168.3.254 [154]
16 NAT: s=192.168.3.50, d=192.168.3.254->10.1.1.1 [154]
17 NAT: s=10.1.1.1->192.168.3.254, d=192.168.3.50 [154]
18 NAT: s=192.168.3.254, d=192.168.3.50->10.1.1.14 [154]
19 !Dynamic Mapping Cleanup
20 NAT: expiring 192.168.3.50 (10.1.1.6) icmp 1411 (1411)
21 NAT: expiring 192.168.3.50 (10.1.1.6) icmp 1413 (1413)
22 NAT: expiring 192.168.3.50 (10.1.1.14) icmp 8408 (8408)
23 NAT: expiring 192.168.3.50 (10.1.1.14) icmp 8410 (8410)
24 NAT: expiring 192.168.3.50 (10.1.1.14) icmp 8412 (8412)
25 !Static 10.0.1.1 to Tokyo E0
26 NAT: s=10.0.1.1->192.168.3.1, d=192.168.3.254 [156]
27 NAT: s=192.168.3.1, d=192.168.3.254->10.1.1.1 [156]
28 NAT: s=10.1.1.1->192.168.3.254, d=192.168.3.1 [156]
29 NAT: s=192.168.3.254, d=192.168.3.1->10.0.1.1 [156]
30 NAT: s=10.0.1.1->192.168.3.1, d=192.168.3.254 [158]
31 NAT: s=192.168.3.1, d=192.168.3.254->10.1.1.1 [158]
32 NAT: s=10.1.1.1->192.168.3.254, d=192.168.3.1 [158]
33 NAT: s=192.168.3.254, d=192.168.3.1->10.0.1.1 [158]
```

that there are two lines for each translation, one on the way into the inside network and one on the way out.

Lines 7 through 18 detail the translations taking place between an inside host and the statically mapped outside host 10.1.1.1. Let's go through each of these translations for the first ping. Line 7 shows the translation of the inside local source address 10.1.1.14 to the first dynamic inside global address in the pool, 192.168.3.50. Line 8 shows the translation of the outside local destination address of 192.168.3.254 to the statically mapped outside global address, 10.1.1.1. On the return packet, line 9 shows the translation of the outside global source address 10.1.1.1 to the statically mapped outside local address, 192.168.3.254. Line 10 shows the translation of the dynamic inside global destination address, 192.168.3.50 to the inside global address, 10.1.1.14.

Lines 20 through 24 show us the dynamic address translation cleanup for two separate **ping** sequences processed through Moscow.

**Figure 7-45**  Moscow active NAT **show** command out

```
1 Moscow#show ip nat statistics
2 Total active translations: 5 (2 static, 3 dynamic; 2 extended)
3 Outside interfaces: Ethernet0
4 Inside interfaces: Serial0
5 Hits: 16  Misses: 13
6 Expired translations: 10
7 Dynamic mappings:
8 — Inside Source
9 access-list 1 pool ospf-source refcount 2
10  pool ospf-source: netmask 255.255.255.0
11        start 192.168.3.50 end 192.168.3.99
12        type generic, total addresses 50, allocated 1 (2%), misses 0
```

Lines 26 through 33 show us the translation process between our two statically mapped addresses, 10.0.1.1 on the inside and 10.1.1.1 on the outside. Refer to Figure 7-42 for the configuration commands that set this up for Moscow.

Figure 7-45 shows us the **show ip nat statistics** for Moscow.

Line 2 shows us the active translations as two static and three dynamic translations.

Line 6 shows us that 10 dynamic translations had not been used, so after a period of time have been aged, or dropped from the translation table.

Line 12 shows us that we have used one address out of the pool, normal in an address overload situation where one address is paired with the inside local port number to create a unique translation.

The **show ip protocol** in Figure 7-46 shows us the details of our OSPF process.

**Figure 7-46**  Moscow **show ip protocol** output

```
1 Moscow#sho ip prot
2 Routing Protocol is "ospf 200"
3   Sending updates every 0 seconds
4   Invalid after 0 seconds, hold down 0, flushed after 0
5   Outgoing update filter list for all interfaces is not set
6   Incoming update filter list for all interfaces is not set
7   Redistributing: ospf 200
8   Routing for Networks:
9     10.1.1.12/30
10      10.1.1.8/30
11      10.1.254.252/30
12   Routing Information Sources:
13     Gateway         Distance      Last Update
14     10.0.254.253      110         00:07:54
15     192.168.1.2       110         00:07:54
16   Distance: (default is 110)
```

**Figure 7-47**  Moscow **show ip route** output

```
1 Moscow#sho ip route
2 Codes: C - connected, S - static, I - IGRP, R - RIP, M - mobile, B - BGP
3          D - EIGRP, EX - EIGRP external, O - OSPF, IA - OSPF inter area
4          N1 - OSPF NSSA external type 1, N2 - OSPF NSSA external type 2
5          E1 - OSPF external type 1, E2 - OSPF external type 2, E - EGP
6          i - IS-IS, L1 - IS-IS level-1, L2 - IS-IS level-2, * - candidate default
7          U - per-user static route, o - ODR
8
9 Gateway of last resort is 0.0.0.0 to network 0.0.0.0
10
11        10.0.0.0/8 is variably subnetted, 5 subnets, 2 masks
12 C        10.1.1.8/30 is directly connected, Serial1
13 C        10.1.1.12/30 is directly connected, Serial0
14 C        10.1.254.252/30 is directly connected, Loopback0
15 O IA     10.0.0.0/16 [110/801] via 10.1.1.14, 00:07:59, Serial0
16 O        10.1.1.4/30 [110/1600] via 10.1.1.9, 00:07:59, Serial1
17                      [110/1600] via 10.1.1.14, 00:07:59, Serial0
18 C     192.168.2.0/24 is directly connected, Ethernet0
19 S*    0.0.0.0/0 is directly connected, Ethernet0
```

The **show ip route** in Figure 7-47, shows our OSPF derived routes, the directly connected transition network 192.168.2.0, and our static default route on line 19.

Figure 7-48 shows the Paris configuration where our second NAT process takes place. This NAT process is identical to the Moscow NAT process. It is imperative that all NAT contact points match exactly, or translation mismatches will occur.

Line 4 defines our pool of addresses to be used for dynamically translating our inside addresses to the range of addresses 192.168.3.50 to 192.168.3.99.

Line 5 assigns the pool in line 4 to the inside network for translation using the overload method. This allows a single IP translation address to be used as a base for multiple translations when combined with port numbers generated by the original sender. Only addresses that pass the access-list on line 41 will be translated.

Lines 6 and 7 define static inside and outside address mappings, one-for-one addressing, no overload.

Line 15 identifies Ethernet 0 as the point where outside translations take place. Line 28 identifies Serial 1 as the point where inside translations take place.

Lines 33 through 37 detail the OSPF routing process to tie together the loopback and serial interfaces to the OSPF processes. Line 37 provides the avenue through which our default route on line 40 is propagated through our OSPF network starting with a metric of 1. By making the

**Figure 7-48**   Paris configuration

```
1  !
2  hostname Paris
3  !
4  ip nat pool ospf-source 192.168.3.50 192.168.3.99 netmask 255.255.255.0
5  ip nat inside source list 1 pool ospf-source overload
6  ip nat inside source static 10.0.1.1 192.168.3.1
7  ip nat outside source static 10.1.1.1 192.168.3.254
8  no ip domain-lookup
9  !
10 interface Loopback0
11   ip address 10.1.254.249 255.255.255.252
12 !
13 interface Ethernet0
14   ip address 192.168.1.2 255.255.255.0
15   ip nat outside
16   no ip route-cache
17   no ip mroute-cache
18 !
19 interface Serial0
20   ip address 10.1.1.9 255.255.255.252
21   no ip route-cache
22   no ip mroute-cache
23   bandwidth 125
24   no fair-queue
25 !
26 interface Serial1
27   ip address 10.1.1.5 255.255.255.252
28   ip nat inside
29   no ip route-cache
30   bandwidth 125
31   clockrate 125000
32 !
33 router ospf 200
34   network 10.1.1.8 0.0.0.3 area 1
35   network 10.1.1.4 0.0.0.3 area 1
36   network 10.1.254.248 0.0.0.3 area 1
37   default-information originate always metric 1 metric-type 1
38 !
39 ip classless
40 ip route 0.0.0.0 0.0.0.0 Ethernet0
41 access-list 1 permit 10.0.0.0 0.255.255.255
42 !
43 line con 0
44   exec-timeout 0 0
45   length 0
46 !
47 end
```

**Figure 7-49** Paris initial **show** command output

```
1 Paris#sho debug
2 Generic IP:
3   IP NAT debugging is on
4 Paris#clear ip nat tran ?
5   *         Delete all dynamic translations
6   inside    Inside addresses (and ports)
7   outside   Outside addresses (and ports)
8   tcp       Transmission Control Protocol
9   udp       User Datagram Protocol
10
11 Paris#clear ip nat tran *
12 Paris#clear ip nat stat
13 Paris#sho ip nat tran
14 Pro    Inside global  Inside local    Outside local    Outside global
15 --     --             --              192.168.3.254    10.1.1.1
16 --     192.168.3.1    10.0.1.1        --               --
17 Paris#sho ip nat stat
18 Total active translations: 2 (2 static, 0 dynamic; 0 extended)
19 Outside interfaces: Ethernet0
20 Inside interfaces: Serial1
21 Hits: 0  Misses: 0
22 Expired translations: 0
23 Dynamic mappings:
24 — Inside Source
25 access-list 1 pool ospf-source refcount 0
26  pool ospf-source: netmask 255.255.255.0
27        start 192.168.3.50 end 192.168.3.99
28        type generic, total addresses 50, allocated 0 (0%), misses 0
```

metric a type 1, additional metrics are added to the base as this route is propagated throughout the OSPF network.

Figure 7-49 shows us the setup for our translation tests. Lines 1 through 3 indicate that basic NAT debugging is activated. After the NAT translation tables and NAT statistics are cleared on lines 11 and 12, the base static definitions are the only items that show up in our **show ip nat translation** on lines 13 through 16 and our **show ip nat statistics** on lines 17 through 28. Figure 7-50 shows us the output of the **debug ip nat** command for several different translations.

Lines 2 through 7 are the translations when an outside network **ping** is targeted for our statically defined mapping of 192.168.3.1 to 10.0.1.1. Where are the rest of the five successful pings that were translated? They can be found in Figure 7-44 where Paris has completed the other two pings. Look at the sequence numbers on lines 2 through 7 of Figure 7-50 and lines 2 through 5 of Figure 7-44, and the story is complete. This theme will be repeated for all of our pings in this section. Note that there are two lines for each translation, one on the way into the inside network and one on the way out.

**Figure 7-50**   Paris **debug ip nat** output

```
1  !EIGRP to Rome E0
2  NAT: s=10.1.2.2, d=192.168.3.1->10.0.1.1 [10]
3  NAT: s=10.0.1.1->192.168.3.1, d=10.1.2.2 [10]
4  NAT: s=10.1.2.2, d=192.168.3.1->10.0.1.1 [12]
5  NAT: s=10.0.1.1->192.168.3.1, d=10.1.2.2 [12]
6  NAT: s=10.1.2.2, d=192.168.3.1->10.0.1.1 [14]
7  NAT: s=10.0.1.1->192.168.3.1, d=10.1.2.2 [14]
8  !Regular OSPF to Tokyo E0
9  NAT: s=10.1.1.14->192.168.3.50, d=192.168.3.254 [151]
10 NAT: s=192.168.3.50, d=192.168.3.254->10.1.1.1 [151]
11 NAT: s=10.1.1.1->192.168.3.254, d=192.168.3.50 [151]
12 NAT: s=192.168.3.254, d=192.168.3.50->10.1.1.14 [151]
13 NAT: s=10.1.1.14->192.168.3.50, d=192.168.3.254 [153]
14 NAT: s=192.168.3.50, d=192.168.3.254->10.1.1.1 [153]
15 NAT: s=10.1.1.1->192.168.3.254, d=192.168.3.50 [153]
16 NAT: s=192.168.3.254, d=192.168.3.50->10.1.1.14 [153]
17 !Dynamic Mapping Cleanup
18 NAT: expiring 192.168.3.50 (10.1.1.6) icmp 1410 (1410)
19 NAT: expiring 192.168.3.50 (10.1.1.6) icmp 1412 (1412)
20 NAT: expiring 192.168.3.50 (10.1.1.6) icmp 1414 (1414)
21 NAT: expiring 192.168.3.50 (10.1.1.14) icmp 8409 (8409)
22 NAT: expiring 192.168.3.50 (10.1.1.14) icmp 8411 (8411)
23 !Static 10.0.1.1 to Tokyo E0
24 NAT: s=10.0.1.1->192.168.3.1, d=192.168.3.254 [155]
25 NAT: s=192.168.3.1, d=192.168.3.254->10.1.1.1 [155]
26 NAT: s=10.1.1.1->192.168.3.254, d=192.168.3.1 [155]
27 NAT: s=192.168.3.254, d=192.168.3.1->10.0.1.1 [155]
28 NAT: s=10.0.1.1->192.168.3.1, d=192.168.3.254 [157]
29 NAT: s=192.168.3.1, d=192.168.3.254->10.1.1.1 [157]
30 NAT: s=10.1.1.1->192.168.3.254, d=192.168.3.1 [157]
31 NAT: s=192.168.3.254, d=192.168.3.1->10.0.1.1 [157]
32 NAT: s=10.0.1.1->192.168.3.1, d=192.168.3.254 [159]
33 NAT: s=192.168.3.1, d=192.168.3.254->10.1.1.1 [159]
34 NAT: s=10.1.1.1->192.168.3.254, d=192.168.3.1 [159]
```

Lines 9 through 16 detail the translations taking place between an inside host and the statically mapped outside host 10.1.1.1. Let's go through each of these translations for the first **ping**. Line 9 shows the translation of the inside local source address 10.1.1.14 to the first dynamic inside global address in the pool, 192.168.3.50. Line 10 shows the translation of the outside local destination address of 192.168.3.254 to the statically mapped outside global address, 10.1.1.1. On the return packet, line

**Figure 7-51**   Paris **show ip nat translation** output

```
1 Pro Inside global       Inside local        Outside local          Outside global
2 icmp 192.168.3.50:2449  10.1.1.6:2449       192.168.3.254:2449     10.1.1.1:2449
3 icmp 192.168.3.50:2447  10.1.1.6:2447       192.168.3.254:2447     10.1.1.1:2447
4 icmp 192.168.3.50:2445  10.1.1.6:2445       192.168.3.254:2445     10.1.1.1:2445
5 -- --                   --                  192.168.3.254          10.1.1.1
6 -- 192.168.3.1          10.0.1.1            --                     --
```

**Figure 7-52** Paris **show ip protocol** output

```
1 Routing Protocol is "ospf 200"
2    Sending updates every 0 seconds
3    Invalid after 0 seconds, hold down 0, flushed after 0
4    Outgoing update filter list for all interfaces is not set
5    Incoming update filter list for all interfaces is not set
6    Redistributing: ospf 200
7    Routing for Networks:
8       10.1.1.8/30
9       10.1.1.4/30
10      10.1.254.248/30
11   Routing Information Sources:
12      Gateway         Distance      Last Update
13      10.1.254.253       110        00:10:09
14      10.0.254.253       110        00:10:09
15   Distance: (default is 110)
```

11 shows the translation of the outside global source address 10.1.1.1 to the statically mapped outside local address, 192.168.3.254. Line 12 shows the translation of the dynamic inside global destination address, 192.168.3.50, to the inside global address, 10.1.1.14.

Lines 18 through 22 show us the dynamic address translation cleanup for two separate **ping** sequences processed through Moscow.

Lines 24 through 34 show us the translation process between our two statically mapped addresses, 10.0.1.1 on the inside and 10.1.1.1 on the outside. Refer to Figure 7-48 for the configuration commands that set this up for Paris.

The **show ip nat translation** in Figure 7-51 shows dynamically mapped addresses on lines 2 through 4. These NAT translations indicate

**Figure 7-53** Paris **show ip route** output

```
1 Paris#sho ip route
2 Codes: C - connected, S - static, I - IGRP, R - RIP, M - mobile, B - BGP
3        D - EIGRP, EX - EIGRP external, O - OSPF, IA - OSPF inter area
4        N1 - OSPF NSSA external type 1, N2 - OSPF NSSA external type 2
5        E1 - OSPF external type 1, E2 - OSPF external type 2, E - EGP
6        i - IS-IS, L1 - IS-IS level-1, L2 - IS-IS level-2, * - candidate default
7        U - per-user static route, o - ODR
8
9 Gateway of last resort is 0.0.0.0 to network 0.0.0.0
10
11      10.0.0.0/8 is variably subnetted, 5 subnets, 3 masks
12 C       10.1.1.8/30 is directly connected, Serial0
13 O       10.1.1.12/30 [110/1600] via 10.1.1.6, 00:10:14, Serial1
14                      [110/1600] via 10.1.1.10, 00:10:14, Serial0
15 O       10.1.254.253/32 [110/801] via 10.1.1.10, 00:10:14, Serial0
16 O IA    10.0.0.0/16 [110/801] via 10.1.1.6, 00:10:14, Serial1
17 C       10.1.1.4/30 is directly connected, Serial1
18 C    192.168.1.0/24 is directly connected, Ethernet0
19 S*   0.0.0.0/0 is directly connected, Ethernet0
```

**Figure 7-54**   *Rome configuration*

```
1  !
2  hostname Rome
3  !
4  no ip domain-lookup
5  !
6  interface Loopback0
7   ip address 10.0.254.253 255.255.255.252
8  !
9  interface Ethernet0
10  ip address 10.0.1.1 255.255.255.0
11 !
12 interface Serial0
13  ip address 10.1.1.6 255.255.255.252
14  bandwidth 125
15 !
16 interface Serial1
17  ip address 10.1.1.14 255.255.255.252
18  bandwidth 125
19  clockrate 125000
20 !
21 router ospf 200
22  network 10.0.254.252 0.0.0.3 area 0
23  network 10.1.1.12 0.0.0.3 area 1
24  network 10.1.1.4 0.0.0.3 area 1
25  network 10.0.1.0 0.0.0.255 area 0
26  area 0 range 10.0.0.0 255.255.0.0
27  area 1 range 10.1.0.0 255.255.0.0
28 !
29 ip classless
30 !
31 line con 0
32  exec-timeout 0 0
33  length 0
34 !
35 end
```

the same IP addresses on both sides but use the port number as an additional part of the mapping to create unique conversation mappings, a standard feature of address overloading. If this had been one-to-one NAT translation, there would have been only one dynamic map between 192.168.3.50 and 192.158.3.254.

Figure 7-52 shows us a standard OSPF process for network 10.0.0.0 subnetworks.

The **show ip route** in Figure 7-53, shows our OSPF-derived routes, the directly connected transition network 192.168.2.0, and our static default route on line 19.

The configuration for Rome in Figure 7-54 shows us an OSPF border router between Area 1 and Area 0. Note the area summarization commands in lines 26 and 27.

**Figure 7-55**   Rome **ping** output

```
1  Rome#ping 192.168.3.254
2
3  Type escape sequence to abort.
4  Sending 5, 100-byte ICMP Echos to 192.168.3.254, timeout is 2 seconds:
5  !!!!!
6  Success rate is 100 percent (5/5), round-trip min/avg/max = 40/45/52 ms
7  Rome#ping 192.168.3.254
8
9  Type escape sequence to abort.
10 Sending 5, 100-byte ICMP Echos to 192.168.3.254, timeout is 2 seconds:
11 !!!!!
12 Success rate is 100 percent (5/5), round-trip min/avg/max = 40/45/56 ms
13 Rome#ping
14 Protocol [ip]:
15 Target IP address: 192.168.3.254
16 Repeat count [5]:
17 Datagram size [100]:
18 Timeout in seconds [2]:
19 Extended commands [n]: y
20 Source address or interface: 10.0.1.1
21 Type of service [0]:
22 Set DF bit in IP header? [no]:
23 Validate reply data? [no]:
24 Data pattern [0xABCD]:
25 Loose, Strict, Record, Timestamp, Verbose[none]: r
26 Number of hops [ 9 ]:
27 Loose, Strict, Record, Timestamp, Verbose[RV]:
28 Sweep range of sizes [n]:
29 Type escape sequence to abort.
30 Sending 5, 100-byte ICMP Echos to 192.168.3.254, timeout is 2 seconds:
31
32 Reply to request 0 (48 ms).  Received packet has options
33  Total option bytes= 40, padded length=40
34  Record route: 10.1.1.6 192.168.1.2 10.1.2.1 10.1.1.1
35          10.1.2.2 192.168.1.1 10.1.1.5 10.0.1.1  0.0.0.0
36  End of list
37
38 Reply to request 1 (44 ms).  Received packet has options
39  Total option bytes= 40, padded length=40
40  Record route: 10.1.1.14 192.168.2.2 10.1.4.2 10.1.1.1
41          10.1.4.1 192.168.2.1 10.1.1.13 10.0.1.1  0.0.0.0
42  End of list
43
44 Success rate is 100 percent (5/5), round-trip min/avg/max = 44/45/48 ms
```

**Figure 7-56**  Rome **show ip protocol** output

```
1 Rome#sho ip prot
2 Routing Protocol is "ospf 200"
3   Sending updates every 0 seconds
4   Invalid after 0 seconds, hold down 0, flushed after 0
5   Outgoing update filter list for all interfaces is not set
6   Incoming update filter list for all interfaces is not set
7   Redistributing: ospf 200
8   Routing for Networks:
9     10.0.254.252/30
10      10.1.1.12/30
11      10.1.1.4/30
12      10.0.1.0/24
13    Routing Information Sources:
14      Gateway         Distance     Last Update
15      10.1.254.253         110      00:14:14
16      10.1.254.249         110      04:19:28
17      192.168.1.2          110      00:14:14
18      192.168.3.200        110      01:30:15
19    Distance: (default is 110)
```

The **ping** output in Figure 7-55 shows two successful ping commands from the Rome to 10.1.1.1 in the outside network. The static outside global address mapped to 10.1.1.1 is 192.168.3.254.

Lines 1 through 6 show a standard **ping**, 100 percent successful, and if you look in Figures 7-44 and 7-50, the NAT debug output will show the two different paths taken through the NAT process.

**Figure 7-57**  Rome **show ip route** output

```
1 Rome#sho ip route
2 Codes: C - connected, S - static, I - IGRP, R - RIP, M - mobile, B - BGP
3        D - EIGRP, EX - EIGRP external, O - OSPF, IA - OSPF inter area
4        N1 - OSPF NSSA external type 1, N2 - OSPF NSSA external type 2
5        E1 - OSPF external type 1, E2 - OSPF external type 2, E - EGP
6        i - IS-IS, L1 - IS-IS level-1, L2 - IS-IS level-2, * - candidate default
7        U - per-user static route, o - ODR
8
9 Gateway of last resort is 10.1.1.5 to network 0.0.0.0
10
11      10.0.0.0/8 is variably subnetted, 6 subnets, 3 masks
12 O       10.1.1.8/30 [110/1600] via 10.1.1.5, 00:14:16, Serial0
13                     [110/1600] via 10.1.1.13, 00:14:16, Serial1
14 C       10.1.1.12/30 is directly connected, Serial1
15 O       10.1.254.253/32 [110/801] via 10.1.1.13, 00:14:16, Serial1
16 C       10.0.254.252/30 is directly connected, Loopback0
17 C       10.0.1.0/24 is directly connected, Ethernet0
18 C       10.1.1.4/30 is directly connected, Serial0
19 O*E1 0.0.0.0/0 [110/801] via 10.1.1.5, 00:14:17, Serial0
20               [110/801] via 10.1.1.13, 00:14:17, Serial1
```

The **show ip protocol** output in figure 7-56 details our OSPF process.

The **show ip route** output in Figure 7-57 is our standard OSPF and connected networks. There are two equal type 1 OSPF external default routes on lines 19 and 20, which will provide load sharing across our two serial ports and, from there, to our two different NAT contact points in Moscow and Paris.

## Example #4—TCP Load Sharing

As Internet access to services on your network becomes more critical to timely business operations, it becomes necessary to have multiple mirrored IP servers. Think of the size of the Cisco Web site and how many people access CCO for up-to-date information.

The target address that represents our shared TCP hosts is 172.15.3.4. This is not a specific host; it represents a group of hosts. See London for the NAT operations in Figures 7-63 through 7-68.

This example shows you how to set up NAT to provide this multiserver environment for shared TCP access. The network layout for this example is shown in Figure 7-58.

New York is set up as a basic RIP router and serves as our starting point for testing TCP load sharing. The configuration for New York is shown in Figure 7-59.

The testing output from New York to Rome is shown in Figure 7-60. Lines 1 through 6 show an unsuccessful attempt to **ping** 172.16.3.4. Normal, this feature does TCP load sharing, not UDP or ICMP. Lines 7 through 10 show an unsuccessful Telnet attempt to contact 172.16.3.4.

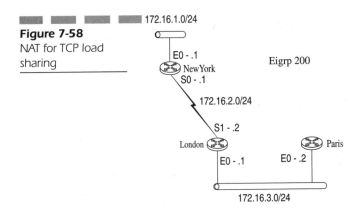

**Figure 7-58**
NAT for TCP load sharing

**Figure 7-59**   NewYork configuration

```
1  !
2  hostname NewYork
3  !
4  no ip domain-lookup
5  !
6  interface Ethernet0
7   ip address 172.16.1.1 255.255.255.0
8  !
9  interface Serial0
10  ip address 172.16.2.1 255.255.255.0
11  bandwidth 125
12  !
13 router rip
14  network 172.16.0.0
15 !
16 ip classless
17 !
18 line con 0
19  exec-timeout 0 0
20  length 0
21 !
22 end
```

Look at the **debug** output in Figure 7-65 for an explanation of this failure. Lines 11 through 30 show a successful Telnet to 172.16.3.4. If you look carefully at the address on the Ethernet 0 port, 172.16.3.2 is definitely not the address we used in our Telnet request in line 11.

Figure 7-61 shows us a standard RIP routing process for NewYork.

The **show ip route** output in Figure 7-62 shows our connected networks and a RIP-derived route for 172.16.3.0.

The London configuration is shown in Figure 7-63 and is where our NAT TCP load sharing is configured.

Line 4 defines a pool of two addresses, 172.16.3.2 and 172.16.3.3, as a rotary pool. The number of entries in the pool should match the number of hosts to be used for TCP load sharing. For this example, there is only one host—172.16.3.2—available, but two addresses are used in the pool to illustrate the error that will occur if too many hosts are defined in the pool.

Line 5 defines the addresses that will trigger a translation into the addresses used in the pool defined on line 4.

Line 10 defines interface Ethernet 0 as the translation point for our TCP load sharing. Seems too easy, doesn't it?

**Figure 7-60**   NewYork **ping** and **Telnet test** output

```
1 NewYork#ping 172.16.3.4
2
3 Type escape sequence to abort.
4 Sending 5, 100-byte ICMP Echos to 172.16.3.4, timeout is 2 seconds:
5 .....
6 Success rate is 0 percent (0/5)
7 NewYork#telnet 172.16.3.4
8 Trying 172.16.3.4 ...
9 % Connection timed out; remote host not responding
10
11 NewYork#telnet 172.16.3.4
12 Trying 172.16.3.4 ... Open
13
14
15 User Access Verification
16
17 Password:
18 Paris>sho ip int brief
19 Interface            IP-Address      OK? Method Status                Protocol
20 BRI0                 unassigned      YES unset  administratively down down
21 BRI0:1               unassigned      YES unset  administratively down down
22 BRI0:2               unassigned      YES unset  administratively down down
23 Ethernet0            172.16.3.2      YES manual up                    up
24 Serial0              unassigned      YES unset  administratively down down
25 Serial1              unassigned      YES unset  administratively down down
26 Serial2              unassigned      YES unset  administratively down down
27 Serial3              unassigned      YES unset  administratively down down
28 Paris>quit
29
30 [Connection to 172.16.3.4 closed by foreign host]
```

**Figure 7-61**   NewYork **show ip protocol** output

```
1 NewYork#sho ip prot
2 Routing Protocol is "rip"
3   Sending updates every 30 seconds, next due in 9 seconds
4   Invalid after 180 seconds, hold down 180, flushed after 240
5   Outgoing update filter list for all interfaces is not set
6   Incoming update filter list for all interfaces is not set
7   Redistributing: rip
8   Default version control: send version 1, receive any version
9     Interface       Send  Recv   Key-chain
10     Ethernet0        1     1 2
11     Serial0          1     1 2
12   Routing for Networks:
13     172.16.0.0
14   Routing Information Sources:
15     Gateway         Distance      Last Update
16     172.16.2.2         120        00:00:07
17   Distance: (default is 120)
```

**Figure 7-62**   NewYork **show ip route** output

```
1 NewYork#sho ip route
2 Codes: C - connected, S - static, I - IGRP, R - RIP, M - mobile, B - BGP
3        D - EIGRP, EX - EIGRP external, O - OSPF, IA - OSPF inter area
4        N1 - OSPF NSSA external type 1, N2 - OSPF NSSA external type 2
5        E1 - OSPF external type 1, E2 - OSPF external type 2, E - EGP
6        i - IS-IS, L1 - IS-IS level-1, L2 - IS-IS level-2, * - candidate default
7        U - per-user static route, o - ODR
8
9 Gateway of last resort is not set
10
11       172.16.0.0/24 is subnetted, 3 subnets
12 C        172.16.1.0 is directly connected, Ethernet0
13 C        172.16.2.0 is directly connected, Serial0
14 R        172.16.3.0 [120/1] via 172.16.2.2, 00:00:18, Serial0
```

The setup commands prior to starting NAT translations are shown in Figure 7-64. Lines 1 through 12 show us the **show ip nat statistics** output, with lines 9 through 12 detailing the **share-hosts** pool information.

Line 13, the **show ip nat translation** command has no output; no translations are active. Lines 14 through 24 are our **debug** setup, showing all variations active.

**Figure 7-63**   London configuration

```
1 !
2 hostname London
3 !
4 ip nat pool shared-hosts 172.16.3.2 172.16.3.3 prefix-length 24 type rotary
5 ip nat inside destination list 1 pool shared-hosts
6 no ip domain-lookup
7 !
8 interface Ethernet0
9  ip address 172.16.3.1 255.255.255.0
10  ip nat inside
11 !
12 interface Serial1
13  ip address 172.16.2.2 255.255.255.0
14  ip nat outside
15  bandwidth 125
16  clockrate 125000
17 !
18 router rip
19  network 172.16.0.0
20 !
21 ip classless
22 access-list 1 permit 172.16.3.4
23 !
24 line con 0
25  exec-timeout 0 0
26  length 0
27 !
28 end
```

**Figure 7-64** London initial **show** command output

```
1 London#sho ip nat stat
2 Total active translations: 0 (0 static, 0 dynamic; 0 extended)
3 Outside interfaces: Serial1
4 Inside interfaces: Ethernet0
5 Hits: 0  Misses: 0
6 Expired translations: 0
7 Dynamic mappings:
8 — Inside Destination
9 access-list 1 pool shared-hosts refcount 0
10  pool shared-hosts: netmask 255.255.255.0
11         start 172.16.3.2 end 172.16.3.3
12         type rotary, total addresses 2, allocated 0 (0%), misses 0
13 London#sho ip nat tran
14 London#debug ip nat
15 IP NAT debugging is on
16 London#debug ip nat detailed
17 IP NAT detailed debugging is on
18 London#debug ip nat ?
19   <1-99>    Access list
20   detailed  NAT detailed events
21   <cr>
22
23 London#debug ip nat 1
24 IP NAT debugging is on
```

**Figure 7-65** London **debug** output

```
1 !Unsuccessful PING, this is a TCP load sharing process!
2 NAT: o: icmp (172.16.2.1, 4628) -> (172.16.3.4, 4628) [30]
3 NAT: o: icmp (172.16.2.1, 4629) -> (172.16.3.4, 4629) [31]
4 NAT: o: icmp (172.16.2.1, 4630) -> (172.16.3.4, 4630) [32]
5 NAT: o: icmp (172.16.2.1, 4631) -> (172.16.3.4, 4631) [33]
6 NAT: o: icmp (172.16.2.1, 4632) -> (172.16.3.4, 4632) [34]
7 !Translated input request, but 172.16.3.3 is not present
8 NAT: o: tcp (172.16.2.1, 11005) -> (172.16.3.4, 23) [0]
9 NAT: s=172.16.2.1, d=172.16.3.4->172.16.3.3 [0]
10 NAT: o: tcp (172.16.2.1, 11005) -> (172.16.3.4, 23) [0]
11 NAT: s=172.16.2.1, d=172.16.3.4->172.16.3.3 [0]
12 NAT: o: tcp (172.16.2.1, 11005) -> (172.16.3.4, 23) [0]
13 NAT: s=172.16.2.1, d=172.16.3.4->172.16.3.3 [0]
14 NAT: o: tcp (172.16.2.1, 11005) -> (172.16.3.4, 23) [0]
15 NAT: s=172.16.2.1, d=172.16.3.4->172.16.3.3 [0]
16 NAT: o: tcp (172.16.2.1, 11006) -> (172.16.3.4, 23) [0]
17 !Successful load share access to 172.16.3.2
18 NAT: o: tcp (172.16.2.1, 11006) -> (172.16.3.4, 23) [0]
19 NAT: s=172.16.2.1, d=172.16.3.4->172.16.3.2 [0]
20 NAT: i: tcp (172.16.3.2, 23) -> (172.16.2.1, 11006) [0]
21 NAT: s=172.16.3.2->172.16.3.4, d=172.16.2.1 [0]
22 NAT*: o: tcp (172.16.2.1, 11006) -> (172.16.3.4, 23) [1]
23 NAT*: s=172.16.2.1, d=172.16.3.4->172.16.3.2 [1]
24 NAT*: o: tcp (172.16.2.1, 11006) -> (172.16.3.4, 23) [2]
25 NAT*: s=172.16.2.1, d=172.16.3.4->172.16.3.2 [2]
26 NAT*: o: tcp (172.16.2.1, 11006) -> (172.16.3.4, 23) [3]
27 NAT*: s=172.16.2.1, d=172.16.3.4->172.16.3.2 [3]
28 NAT*: i: tcp (172.16.3.2, 23) -> (172.16.2.1, 11006) [1]
```

**Figure 7-66**   London active **show** command output

```
1 London#sho ip nat statistics
2 Total active translations: 1 (0 static, 1 dynamic; 1 extended)
3 Outside interfaces: Serial1
4 Inside interfaces: Ethernet0
5 Hits: 84  Misses: 2
6 Expired translations: 1
7 Dynamic mappings:
8 — Inside Destination
9 access-list 1 pool shared-hosts refcount 1
10  pool shared-hosts: netmask 255.255.255.0
11        start 172.16.3.2 end 172.16.3.3
12        type rotary, total addresses 2, allocated 1 (50%), misses 0
13
14 London#sho ip nat translation
15 Pro Inside global     Inside local     Outside local      Outside global
16 tcp 172.16.3.4:23     172.16.3.2:23    172.16.2.1:11006   172.16.2.1:11006
17 London#
18
19 NAT: expiring 172.16.3.4 (172.16.3.2) tcp 23 (23)
```

Figure 7-65 shows us the output of the **debug** commands.

Lines 2 through 6 show us the failure of our ping 172.16.3.4 attempt. Each line contains an **o:**, which says we have incoming translation attempts from the outside, none successful.

Lines 8 through 16 show an unsuccessful attempt to connect to 172.16.3.4. The reason it is unsuccessful is due to the absence of host 172.16.3.3, we only have outside-to-inside translation attempts. Line 8 is the detailed **debug** output showing us that an outside address wants in; line 9 is the actual translation debug output.

**Figure 7-67**   London **show ip protocol** output

```
1 London#sho ip prot
2 Routing Protocol is "rip"
3   Sending updates every 30 seconds, next due in 17 seconds
4   Invalid after 180 seconds, hold down 180, flushed after 240
5   Outgoing update filter list for all interfaces is not set
6   Incoming update filter list for all interfaces is not set
7   Redistributing: rip
8   Default version control: send version 1, receive any version
9     Interface       Send  Recv   Key-chain
10    Ethernet0        1    1 2
11    Serial1          1    1 2
12   Routing for Networks:
13     172.16.0.0
14   Routing Information Sources:
15     Gateway        Distance      Last Update
16     172.16.2.1         120       00:00:20
17   Distance: (default is 120)
```

**Figure 7-68** London **show ip route** output

```
1 London#sho ip route
2 Codes: C - connected, S - static, I - IGRP, R - RIP, M - mobile, B - BGP
3        D - EIGRP, EX - EIGRP external, O - OSPF, IA - OSPF inter area
4        N1 - OSPF NSSA external type 1, N2 - OSPF NSSA external type 2
5        E1 - OSPF external type 1, E2 - OSPF external type 2, E - EGP
6        i - IS-IS, L1 - IS-IS level-1, L2 - IS-IS level-2, * - candidate default
7        U - per-user static route, o - ODR
8
9 Gateway of last resort is not set
10
11      172.16.0.0/24 is subnetted, 3 subnets
12 R       172.16.1.0 [120/1] via 172.16.2.1, 00:00:24, Serial1
13 C       172.16.2.0 is directly connected, Serial1
14 C       172.16.3.0 is directly connected, Ethernet0
```

**Figure 7-69** Paris configuration

```
1 !
2 hostname Paris
3 !
4 no ip domain-lookup
5 !
6 interface Ethernet0
7  ip address 172.16.3.2 255.255.255.0
8 !
9 router rip
10  network 172.16.0.0
11 !
12 ip classless
13 !
14 line con 0
15  exec-timeout 0 0
16  length 0
17 !
18 end
```

**Figure 7-70** Paris **show ip protocol** output

```
1 Paris#sho ip prot
2 Routing Protocol is "rip"
3   Sending updates every 30 seconds, next due in 19 seconds
4   Invalid after 180 seconds, hold down 180, flushed after 240
5   Outgoing update filter list for all interfaces is not set
6   Incoming update filter list for all interfaces is not set
7   Redistributing: rip
8   Default version control: send version 1, receive any version
9    Interface        Send  Recv   Key-chain
10    Ethernet0         1     1 2
11   Routing for Networks:
12     172.16.0.0
13   Routing Information Sources:
14    Gateway          Distance      Last Update
15     172.16.3.1           120      00:00:11
16   Distance: (default is 120)
```

**Figure 7-71**  Paris **show ip route** output

```
1 Paris#sho ip route
2 Codes: C - connected, S - static, I - IGRP, R - RIP, M - mobile, B - BGP
3         D - EIGRP, EX - EIGRP external, O - OSPF, IA - OSPF inter area
4         N1 - OSPF NSSA external type 1, N2 - OSPF NSSA external type 2
5         E1 - OSPF external type 1, E2 - OSPF external type 2, E - EGP
6         i - IS-IS, L1 - IS-IS level-1, L2 - IS-IS level-2, * - candidate default
7         U - per-user static route, o - ODR
8
9 Gateway of last resort is not set
10
11      172.16.0.0/24 is subnetted, 3 subnets
12 R      172.16.1.0 [120/2] via 172.16.3.1, 00:00:16, Ethernet0
13 R      172.16.2.0 [120/1] via 172.16.3.1, 00:00:16, Ethernet0
14 C      172.16.3.0 is directly connected, Ethernet0
```

Lines 18 through 28 show the start of a successful telnet attempt to connect to 172.16.3.4. Line 18 shows our first TCP packet coming in from the outside. Line 19 is the initial translation from 172.16.3.4 to 172.16.3.2. This telnet attempt is successful because 172.16.3.2 is an available host. Line 20 shows a return packet headed back to the requester, and line 21 shows the translation taking place.

The **debug ip nat detailed** is great to identify when packets actually trigger the translation process, and the **debug ip nat** actually shows the translations taking place.

Figure 7-66 shows the output from the **show ip nat statistics** command on lines 1 through 12 and the output of the **show ip nat translation** on lines 14 through 19.

Line 19 shows the aging out of the translation identified on line 16.

Figure 7-67 shows us a standard RIP routing process for London.

Figure 7-68 shows us the **show ip route** output—again, plain vanilla.

Paris in this example is acting as a host for TCP sharing. The configuration is shown in Figure 7-69.

The **show ip protocol** is shown in Figure 7-70 to remind you that all hosts on the shared network should either be able to get routing updates from the translation device or have a default gateway defined pointing to the translation device.

Figure 7-71 shows the **show ip route** output on Paris—something we've seen several times now.

## CCIE Tips

The most important tip to remember when working with NAT is to understand the meaning of the four address types: inside local, inside global, outside global, and outside local.

Examples #1 through #3 used an intermediate network and separate interfaces for defining where inside and outside addresses get translated.

## Labs

Good practice for implementing NAT would be to try Examples #1 and #2 with both translations taking place on the same interface.

## Example #3—Bombs

There are two major bombs waiting for you in Example #3.

First, the example used fresh router configurations, then made sure that the IP load balancing was synchronized so that the two equal default route paths worked together. If the default route paths were not synchronized, then all dynamic translations could fail, while all static translations work. A better solution would be to set up two different metrics for the default routes in both the EIGRP and OSPF domains, so that a primary and secondary path would provide translation without load balancing. Try it both ways for fun.

Second, both Moscow and Paris have a second serial port that does not have translation assigned. Set up this example and take down the primary translation port and see what happens.

Happy translating!

## SUMMARY

Network Address Translation is a feature that provides you with a mechanism to design your IP network using the extended address space of private network 10.0.0.0 while still being able to communicate with the outside world via the Internet using a registered address.

# CHAPTER 8

# Static Internet Connectivity

Now that you have become an expert in the routing protocols and the mechanisms used to provide services to users in your own routed intranetwork, it is time to move on to the next level and take your organization into cyberspace by connecting your Autonomous System to the Internet! Using our post office analogy, it is time to ship your information outside of your local postal system and off to another country.

In this chapter, we will review static connections when connecting our Autonomous System to the Internet.

As in all things, there are pros and cons when it comes to implementing static routes in an exterior connection to the Internet. The plus with static routes is that there are no routing updates exchanged between partners in the routing process. The minus side is that in a changing environment, the network administrator has to get involved every time a change is made in the TCP/IP addressing.

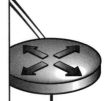

With all dynamic protocols, there is an exchange of information between partners in the routing process. With distance vector protocols RIP and IGRP, there is a periodic update broadcast on all involved interfaces, and with the faster-converging protocols OSPF, EIGRP, and IS-IS, there are continuous hello packets being exchanged. On slower-speed links, the distance vector protocols in particular can use a large portion of the bandwidth for the routing table update. These updates occur within a short period of time and can create temporary high utilization overloading lower-speed serial links.

# What Static Routes Provide for Internet Connections

Static routes are used when the policy used to connect to the Internet is going to piggyback onto the policy used by the Internet Service Provider (ISP). This is a very standard way to connect to an ISP.

In order to reduce the number of static routes defined, we use a **static default route** command, with or without a **default-network** command to propagate the default route through our network.

# What Static Routes Don't Provide for Internet Connections

Static routes create pasted-up pathways for packets to follow but provide no dynamic topology change capabilities. If the external connection changes, then manual administration intervention could be required to connect to a different external connection.

While static routes are not dynamic, there are techniques we can employ in the Cisco router to provide the semblance of dynamic connectivity. See Example #2.

## Example #1—Static Internet Connection, Single Exit

Our first example is a standard single exit point to the Internet, the most common type of Internet connection. In this example, New York is acting as the ISP for our local network. Tokyo and London are the routers inside our Autonomous System and will be used to test connectivity to the outside. The network layout is shown in Figure 8-1.

London is inside our Autonomous System, and the configuration is shown in Figure 8-2. The RIP routing protocol is configured for both active interfaces on lines 14 through 16.

Figure 8-3 shows the results of several **ping** commands. Lines 1 through 6 show a standard **ping** to one of our target addresses, 144.251.0.1, from the exit point on the router, 192.168.5.1, interface Serial 0. Lines 8 through 25 are an **extended ping** that pings 200.200.200.1, another target address. This **ping** uses the source address of interface Ethernet 0, 192.168.3.1, showing connectivity from the outside target all the way back to our end network, 192.168.3.0.

Figure 8-4 shows us a standard RIP routing process, no filters or special actions.

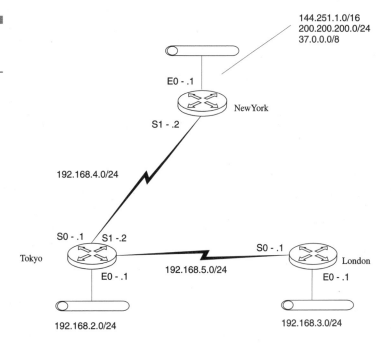

**Figure 8-1**

Static Internet connection, single exit

**Figure 8-2** London configuration

```
1  !
2  hostname London
3  !
4  no ip domain-lookup
5  !
6  interface Ethernet0
7   ip address 192.168.3.1 255.255.255.0
8  !
9  interface Serial0
10  ip address 192.168.5.1 255.255.255.0
11  no ip mroute-cache
12  bandwidth 125
13 !
14 router rip
15  network 192.168.3.0
16  network 192.168.5.0
17 !
18 ip classless
19 !
20 !
21 line con 0
22  exec-timeout 0 0
23  length 0
24 !
25 end
```

**Figure 8-3** London **ping** test output

```
1  London#ping 144.251.0.1
2
3  Type escape sequence to abort.
4  Sending 5, 100-byte ICMP Echos to 144.251.0.1, timeout is 2 seconds:
5  !!!!!
6  Success rate is 100 percent (5/5), round-trip min/avg/max = 32/32/32 ms
7
8  London#ping
9  Protocol [ip]:
10 Target IP address: 200.200.200.1
11 Repeat count [5]:
12 Datagram size [100]:
13 Timeout in seconds [2]:
14 Extended commands [n]: y
15 Source address or interface: 192.168.3.1
16 Type of service [0]:
17 Set DF bit in IP header? [no]:
18 Validate reply data? [no]:
19 Data pattern [0xABCD]:
20 Loose, Strict, Record, Timestamp, Verbose[none]:
21 Sweep range of sizes [n]:
22 Type escape sequence to abort.
23 Sending 5, 100-byte ICMP Echos to 200.200.200.1, timeout is 2 seconds:
24 !!!!!
25 Success rate is 100 percent (5/5), round-trip min/avg/max = 28/31/32 ms
```

**Figure 8-4**  London **show ip protocol** output

```
1 London#sho ip prot
2 Routing Protocol is "rip"
3   Sending updates every 30 seconds, next due in 26 seconds
4   Invalid after 180 seconds, hold down 180, flushed after 240
5   Outgoing update filter list for all interfaces is not set
6   Incoming update filter list for all interfaces is not set
7   Redistributing: rip
8   Default version control: send version 1, receive any version
9     Interface       Send  Recv   Key-chain
10      Ethernet0        1    1 2
11      Serial0          1    1 2
12   Routing for Networks:
13      192.168.3.0
14      192.168.5.0
15   Routing Information Sources:
16      Gateway        Distance      Last Update
17      192.168.5.2        120       00:00:04
18   Distance: (default is 120)
```

The output of the **show ip route** in Figure 8-5 shows standard RIP and directly connected networks, with special information about unknown networks. Line 9 identifies our neighbor Tokyo, 192.168.5.2, as our gateway of last resort to reach network 0.0.0.0, our default route. Line 15 shows us that network 0.0.0.0 was derived from a RIP update, and all traffic where the destination network is not in the routing table is forwarded across Serial 0.

New York is our external Internet simulator where extra target addresses have been created to test our Autonomous System connectivity. See lines 7 and 8 of Figure 8-6. Line 20 is a static route that includes all class C networks from 192.168.0.0 through 192.168.7.0. This command is used instead of individual commands for each individual class C address.

**Figure 8-5**  London **show ip route** output

```
1 London#sho ip route
2 Codes: C - connected, S - static, I - IGRP, R - RIP, M - mobile, B - BGP
3        D - EIGRP, EX - EIGRP external, O - OSPF, IA - OSPF inter area
4        N1 - OSPF NSSA external type 1, N2 - OSPF NSSA external type 2
5        E1 - OSPF external type 1, E2 - OSPF external type 2, E - EGP
6        i - IS-IS, L1 - IS-IS level-1, L2 - IS-IS level-2, * - candidate default
7        U - per-user static route, o - ODR
8
9 Gateway of last resort is 192.168.5.2 to network 0.0.0.0
10
11 R    192.168.4.0/24 [120/1] via 192.168.5.2, 00:00:07, Serial0
12 C    192.168.5.0/24 is directly connected, Serial0
13 R    192.168.2.0/24 [120/1] via 192.168.5.2, 00:00:08, Serial0
14 C    192.168.3.0/24 is directly connected, Ethernet0
15 R*   0.0.0.0/0 [120/1] via 192.168.5.2, 00:00:08, Serial0
```

**Figure 8-6**   NewYork configuration

```
1  !
2  hostname NewYork
3  !
4  no ip domain-lookup
5  !
6  interface Ethernet0
7   ip address 144.251.0.1 255.255.0.0 secondary
8   ip address 200.200.200.1 255.255.255.0 secondary
9   ip address 37.0.0.1 255.0.0.0
10 !
11 interface Serial1
12  ip address 192.168.4.2 255.255.255.0
13  bandwidth 125
14  clockrate 125000
15 !
16 router bgp 200
17  aggregate-address 192.168.0.0 255.255.248.0
18 !
19 ip classless
20 ip route 192.168.0.0 255.255.248.0 Serial1
21 !
22 line con 0
23  exec-timeout 0 0
24  length 0
25 !
26 end
```

**Figure 8-7**   NewYork **ping** test output

```
1  NewYork#ping 192.168.3.1
2
3  Type escape sequence to abort.
4  Sending 5, 100-byte ICMP Echos to 192.168.3.1, timeout is 2 seconds:
5  !!!!!
6  Success rate is 100 percent (5/5), round-trip min/avg/max = 32/32/36 ms
7  NewYork#ping
8  Protocol [ip]:
9  Target IP address: 192.168.3.1
10 Repeat count [5]:
11 Datagram size [100]:
12 Timeout in seconds [2]:
13 Extended commands [n]: y
14 Source address or interface: 144.251.0.1
15 Type of service [0]:
16 Set DF bit in IP header? [no]:
17 Validate reply data? [no]:
18 Data pattern [0xABCD]:
19 Loose, Strict, Record, Timestamp, Verbose[none]:
20 Sweep range of sizes [n]:
21 Type escape sequence to abort.
22 Sending 5, 100-byte ICMP Echos to 192.168.3.1, timeout is 2 seconds:
23 !!!!!
24 Success rate is 100 percent (5/5), round-trip min/avg/max = 32/32/32 ms
```

**Figure 8-8** NewYork **show ip protocol** output

```
1 NewYork#sho ip prot
2 Routing Protocol is "bgp 200"
3   Sending updates every 60 seconds, next due in 0 seconds
4   Outgoing update filter list for all interfaces is not set
5   Incoming update filter list for all interfaces is not set
6   IGP synchronization is enabled
7   Automatic route summarization is enabled
8   Aggregate Generation:
9     192.168.0.0/21
10  Routing for Networks:
11  Routing Information Sources:
12    Gateway          Distance     Last Update
13  Distance: external 20 internal 200 local 200
```

Figure 8-7 shows us two **ping** commands to test connectivity to our Autonomous System. Lines 1 through 6 show a standard **ping** test, but it doesn't test anything except the ability to connect to our furthest point in our Autonomous System from our external contact point 192.168.4.2, interface Serial 1 on NewYork.

Lines 7 through 24 show an **extended ping** from a target address, 144.251.0.1, to the furthest point in our Autonomous System, full end-to-end connectivity. Lines 16 and 17 are a sample of the commands that could be used to send an aggregate address identifying networks 192.168.0.0 through 192.168.7.0 with a single routing table entry to the rest of the BGP cloud.

The **show ip protocol** output in Figure 8-8 shows no BGP activity, but lines 8 and 9 show us the route aggregation of our class C address in our Autonomous System.

Figure 8-9 shows us that all routes in NewYork are either directly con-

**Figure 8-9** NewYork **show ip route** output

```
1 NewYork#sho ip route
2 Codes: C - connected, S - static, I - IGRP, R - RIP, M - mobile, B - BGP
3        D - EIGRP, EX - EIGRP external, O - OSPF, IA - OSPF inter area
4        N1 - OSPF NSSA external type 1, N2 - OSPF NSSA external type 2
5        E1 - OSPF external type 1, E2 - OSPF external type 2, E - EGP
6        i - IS-IS, L1 - IS-IS level-1, L2 - IS-IS level-2, * - candidate default
7        U - per-user static route, o - ODR
8
9 Gateway of last resort is not set
10
11 C    200.200.200.0/24 is directly connected, Ethernet0
12 C    37.0.0.0/8 is directly connected, Ethernet0
13 C    192.168.4.0/24 is directly connected, Serial1
14 C    144.251.0.0/16 is directly connected, Ethernet0
15 S    192.168.0.0/21 is directly connected, Serial1
```

**Figure 8-10**  Tokyo configuration

```
1 !
2 hostname Tokyo
3 !
4 no ip domain-lookup
5 !
6 interface Ethernet0
7  ip address 192.168.2.1 255.255.255.0
8 !
9 interface Serial0
10  ip address 192.168.4.1 255.255.255.0
11  bandwidth 125
12 !
13 interface Serial1
14  ip address 192.168.5.2 255.255.255.0
15  bandwidth 125
16  clockrate 125000
17 !
18 router rip
19  passive-interface Serial0
20  network 192.168.2.0
21  network 192.168.5.0
22  network 192.168.4.0
23 !
24 ip classless
25 ip route 0.0.0.0 0.0.0.0 Serial0
26 !
27 line con 0
28  exec-timeout 0 0
29  length 0
30 !
31 end
```

nected or statically defined. Line 15 shows our aggregate static route to the class C networks in our Autonomous System.

Tokyo is our contact point with the outside world, and the configuration is shown in Figure 8-10. Lines 18 through 22 define our RIP routing process for our Autonomous System. Line 19 is used to prevent RIP

**Figure 8-11**  Tokyo **debug** output

```
1 Tokyo#debug ip rip
2 RIP protocol debugging is on
3 Tokyo#
4 RIP: sending v1 update to 255.255.255.255 via Ethernet0 (192.168.2.1)
5      default, metric 1
6      network 192.168.4.0, metric 1
7      network 192.168.5.0, metric 1
8      network 192.168.3.0, metric 2
9 RIP: sending v1 update to 255.255.255.255 via Serial1 (192.168.5.2)
10      default, metric 1
11      network 192.168.4.0, metric 1
```

**Figure 8-12** Tokyo **show ip protocol** output

```
1 Tokyo#sho ip proto
2 Routing Protocol is "rip"
3   Sending updates every 30 seconds, next due in 21 seconds
4   Invalid after 180 seconds, hold down 180, flushed after 240
5   Outgoing update filter list for all interfaces is not set
6   Incoming update filter list for all interfaces is not set
7   Redistributing: rip
8   Default version control: send version 1, receive any version
9     Interface        Send  Recv  Key-chain
10    Ethernet0          1    1 2
11    Serial1            1    1 2
12  Routing for Networks:
13    192.168.2.0
14    192.168.5.0
15    192.168.4.0
16  Passive Interface(s):
17    Serial0
18  Routing Information Sources:
19    Gateway          Distance      Last Update
20    192.168.5.1          120       00:00:03
21  Distance: (default is 120)
```

updates from making their way to our external connection by turning interface Serial 0 into a listen-only connection.

The **debug ip rip** output is shown in Figure 8-11. The output shows standard updates going out to our two active ports.

Lines 5 and 10 are the distribution of our default route to our neighbors. Note that it uses a default metric of one hop.

Figure 8-12 shows the output of the **show ip protocol** command, standard RIP except for line 17 where our Serial 0 interface is identified as passive.

**Figure 8-13** Tokyo **show ip route** output

```
1 Tokyo#sho ip route
2 Codes: C - connected, S - static, I - IGRP, R - RIP, M - mobile, B - BGP
3        D - EIGRP, EX - EIGRP external, O - OSPF, IA - OSPF inter area
4        N1 - OSPF NSSA external type 1, N2 - OSPF NSSA external type 2
5        E1 - OSPF external type 1, E2 - OSPF external type 2, E - EGP
6        i - IS-IS, L1 - IS-IS level-1, L2 - IS-IS level-2, * - candidate default
7        U - per-user static route, o - ODR
8
9 Gateway of last resort is 0.0.0.0 to network 0.0.0.0
10
11 C    192.168.4.0/24 is directly connected, Serial0
12 C    192.168.5.0/24 is directly connected, Serial1
13 C    192.168.2.0/24 is directly connected, Ethernet0
14 R    192.168.3.0/24 [120/1] via 192.168.5.1, 00:00:06, Serial1
15 S*   0.0.0.0/0 is directly connected, Serial0
```

**Question #1: Is the passive interface command really necessary in this configuration? There are many clues in this example. Check it out.**

Figure 8-13 shows the output of the **show ip route** command. Lines 9 and 15 show us the way to exit our Autonomous System to the outside world.

## Example #2—Static Internet Connection, Multiple Exits

This is a fairly complex example that describes how to set up two exit points from our Autonomous System to the outside world of the Internet. In this example, New York and Moscow serve as our ISP simulator and Tokyo, London, and Paris as the routers in our Autonomous System. The network layout is in Figure 8-14. With static default routes being distributed throughout our Autonomous System and two contact points within the external network, there is a danger of creating asymmetrical routes. Our example describes one method of preventing this from occurring by making the Tokyo-to-New York connection the primary link and the Paris-to-Moscow connection the secondary link between our Autonomous System and the external network.

Each of the router sections in Example #2 has two different **show ip route** figures, the first with the primary link active and the second with the primary link down. The Autonomous System routers Tokyo, London, and Paris figures have **trace** command output included in the figures to show the path taken to the target address.

Our first router is New York, one of the Internet simulators, and the configuration is shown in Figure 8-15.

FYI: *Asymmetrical routes* are created when there are two or more pathways active between the source and the destination. When outgoing and return traffic take different pathways, troubleshooting connectivity and performance become very difficult. Even a **trace** command can show the pathway following the outgoing leg, even if return traffic from the trace takes an alternate return pathway. If the number of hops is small enough, then an **extended ping** with the record option could highlight the problem. The **extended ping** is limited to nine hops total, out and back, so this will only help with shorter pathways. Watch out for this problem in both static and dynamic environments.

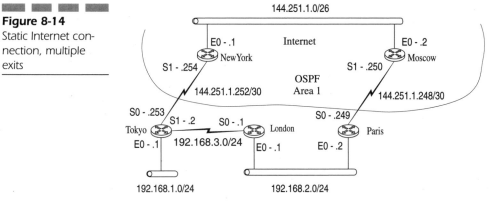

**Figure 8-14**
Static Internet con-
nection, multiple
exits

Loopback Addresses for Additional Targets

```
NewYork   37.0.0.1/8
          200.200.200.1/24
```

**Figure 8-15**  NewYork configuration.

```
1  !
2  hostname NewYork
3  !
4  no ip domain-lookup
5  !
6  interface Loopback0
7   ip address 200.200.200.1 255.255.255.0
8  !
9  interface Loopback1
10   ip address 37.0.0.1 255.0.0.0
11  !
12  interface Ethernet0
13   ip address 144.251.1.1 255.255.255.192
14  !
15  interface Serial1
16   ip address 144.251.1.254 255.255.255.252
17   bandwidth 125
18   clockrate 125000
19  !
20  router eigrp 200
21   redistribute static metric 10000 100 255 1 1500
22   network 144.251.0.0
23   network 200.200.200.0
24   network 37.0.0.0
25   !
26  ip classless
27  ip route 192.168.0.0 255.255.248.0 Serial1
28  !
29  line con 0
30   exec-timeout 0 0
31   length 0
32  !
33  end
```

**Figure 8-16** NewYork **show ip protocol** output

```
1 NewYork#sho ip prot
2 Routing Protocol is "eigrp 200"
3   Outgoing update filter list for all interfaces is not set
4   Incoming update filter list for all interfaces is not set
5   Default networks flagged in outgoing updates
6   Default networks accepted from incoming updates
7   EIGRP metric weight K1=1, K2=0, K3=1, K4=0, K5=0
8   EIGRP maximum hopcount 100
9   EIGRP maximum metric variance 1
10   Redistributing: static, eigrp 200
11   Automatic network summarization is in effect
12   Automatic address summarization:
13     200.200.200.0/24 for Ethernet0, Serial1, Loopback1
14     144.251.0.0/16 for Loopback0, Loopback1
15       Summarizing with metric 281600
16     37.0.0.0/8 for Ethernet0, Loopback0, Serial1
17   Routing for Networks:
18     144.251.0.0
19     200.200.200.0
20     37.0.0.0
21   Routing Information Sources:
22     Gateway          Distance      Last Update
23     (this router)         5        00:38:09
24     144.251.1.2          90        00:02:18
25   Distance: internal 90 external 170
```

Lines 6 through 10 are used to create extra external targets for testing our Autonomous System connectivity. Line 27 is our aggregate static route to the networks in our Autonomous System. Lines 20 through 24 define our EIGRP routing process. Line 21 is important, as it is one of the keys to providing an external environment that prevents asynchronous routes. It spoofs the EIGRP process into identifying our

**Figure 8-17** NewYork primary **show ip route** output

```
1 NewYork#sho ip route
2 Codes: C - connected, S - static, I - IGRP, R - RIP, M - mobile, B - BGP
3        D - EIGRP, EX - EIGRP external, O - OSPF, IA - OSPF inter area
4        N1 - OSPF NSSA external type 1, N2 - OSPF NSSA external type 2
5        E1 - OSPF external type 1, E2 - OSPF external type 2, E - EGP
6        i - IS-IS, L1 - IS-IS level-1, L2 - IS-IS level-2, * - candidate default
7        U - per-user static route, o - ODR
8
9 Gateway of last resort is not set
10
11 C    200.200.200.0/24 is directly connected, Loopback0
12 C    37.0.0.0/8 is directly connected, Loopback1
13      144.251.0.0/16 is variably subnetted, 4 subnets, 3 masks
14 C       144.251.1.0/26 is directly connected, Ethernet0
15 D       144.251.0.0/16 is a summary, 00:06:33, Null0
16 D       144.251.1.248/30 [90/21017600] via 144.251.1.2, 00:06:30, Ethernet0
17 C       144.251.1.252/30 is directly connected, Serial1
18 S    192.168.0.0/21 is directly connected, Serial1
```

Autonomous System routes as directly connected on an Ethernet interface.

The **show ip protocol** output in Figure 8-16 shows a standard EIGRP routing process, with line 10 identifying the redistribution of static routes. There is no indication in this command output that a metric override is set up for the static routes being redistributed.

Figure 8-17 shows the routing table with the entire network running. Our Autonomous System route is on line 18 and shows direct connectivity through the Serial 1 interface.

After the primary link fails, the **show ip route** output in Figure 8-18 shows the pathway to our Autonomous System on line 18 has switched to the backup link through Moscow.

The other router simulating our external network is Moscow, whose configuration is shown in Figure 8-19. Line 15 is where we redistribute our static aggregate route on line 19 into our EIGRP environment. The metric used for the static routes is the equivalent of a directly connected 56Kbps serial interface. As the secondary route to our Autonomous System, this route will show up in our external system only when the primary link through New York is inactive. Make sure that this metric is low enough so that if the contact points in the external network are widely separated, that the secondary path is always worse than the primary.

The aggregate static route to our Autonomous System on line 19 has a different twist added at the end of the line. What does the **190** do for us? This is the Administrative Distance value assigned to this route when cal-

**Figure 8-18**  New York secondary **show ip route** output

```
1 NewYork#sho ip route
2
3 Codes: C - connected, S - static, I - IGRP, R - RIP, M - mobile, B - BGP
4        D - EIGRP, EX - EIGRP external, O - OSPF, IA - OSPF inter area
5        N1 - OSPF NSSA external type 1, N2 - OSPF NSSA external type 2
6        E1 - OSPF external type 1, E2 - OSPF external type 2, E - EGP
7        i - IS-IS, L1 - IS-IS level-1, L2 - IS-IS level-2, * - candidate default
8        U - per-user static route, o - ODR
9
10 Gateway of last resort is not set
11
12 C    200.200.200.0/24 is directly connected, Loopback0
13 C    37.0.0.0/8 is directly connected, Loopback1
14      144.251.0.0/16 is variably subnetted, 3 subnets, 3 masks
15 C       144.251.1.0/26 is directly connected, Ethernet0
16 D       144.251.0.0/16 is a summary, 00:06:50, Null0
17 D       144.251.1.248/30 [90/21017600] via 144.251.1.2, 00:06:48, Ethernet0
18 D EX 192.168.0.0/21 [170/46251776] via 144.251.1.2, 00:00:06, Ethernet0
```

**Figure 8-19** Moscow configuration.

```
1  !
2  hostname Moscow
3  !
4  no ip domain-lookup
5  !
6  interface Ethernet0
7   ip address 144.251.1.2 255.255.255.192
8  !
9  interface Serial1
10   ip address 144.251.1.250 255.255.255.252
11   bandwidth 125
12   clockrate 125000
13  !
14 router eigrp 200
15   redistribute static metric 56 2000 255 1 1500
16   network 144.251.0.0
17  !
18 ip classless
19 ip route 192.168.0.0 255.255.248.0 144.251.1.149 190
20  !
21 line con 0
22   exec-timeout 0 0
23   length 0
24  !
25 end
```

culating the best route. Why use **190**? If we look at the **show ip protocol** output in Figure 8-20, line 17 shows us that internal routes have a Distance of 90, and external routes have a Distance of 170. When there are multiple sources for a routing table entry, the routing process uses the Administrative Distance to determine which route to use first—the lower the Distance, the better the source. Connected routes have a Distance of 0; static routes, a Distance of 1. So both types are rated better than our dynamic routing protocols. By applying a Distance of 190 to the static route, the

**Figure 8-20** Moscow **show ip protocol** output

```
1  Moscow#sho ip prot
2  Routing Protocol is "eigrp 200"
3    Outgoing update filter list for all interfaces is not set
4    Incoming update filter list for all interfaces is not set
5    Default networks flagged in outgoing updates
6    Default networks accepted from incoming updates
7    EIGRP metric weight K1=1, K2=0, K3=1, K4=0, K5=0
8    EIGRP maximum hopcount 100
9    EIGRP maximum metric variance 1
10   Redistributing: static, eigrp 200
11   Automatic network summarization is in effect
12   Routing for Networks:
13     144.251.0.0
14   Routing Information Sources:
15     Gateway         Distance      Last Update
16     144.251.1.1          90       00:01:51
17   Distance: internal 90 external 170
```

route floats up above the dynamic protocol distances of 90 and 170 to take a backup position. When does this static route take effect? Only when the dynamic protocols that normally supply the route information to the routing process are not present. This is how to create a floating static route.

The **show ip protocol** output in Figure 8-20 shows a standard EIGRP routing process with line 10 identifying the redistribution of static routes. There is no indication in this command output that a metric override is set up for the static routes being redistributed.

Figure 8-21 shows the routing table with the entire network running. Our Autonomous System route is on line 17 and shows an external route through New York, our primary link. Notice that the static route to our Autonomous System has floated up above EIGRP to take a backup role.

After the primary link fails, the **show ip route** output in Figure 8-22 shows that the pathway to our Autonomous System on line 16 has switched to the backup link through Serial 1 to the next-hop address of 144.251.1.249.

Tokyo is the site of our primary link to the external network, and the configuration is shown in Figure 8-23. Nothing too special here, basic RIP routing with our default route defined on line 23. Where's the beef?

Figure 8-24 is the output of the **show ip protocol** command and is plain vanilla RIP routing. There is no indication that the static default route will be redistributed to the rest of our Autonomous System.

Figure 8-25 shows us two commands, the **show ip route** output on lines 1 through 16 and the **trace 200.200.200.1** output on lines 18 through 23. Nothing special here: the routing table on line 16 shows a default route to unknown networks through Serial 0, and the trace command follows that path.

**Figure 8-21**    Moscow primary **show ip route** output

```
1 Moscow#sho ip route
2 Codes: C - connected, S - static, I - IGRP, R - RIP, M - mobile, B - BGP
3         D - EIGRP, EX - EIGRP external, O - OSPF, IA - OSPF inter area
4         N1 - OSPF NSSA external type 1, N2 - OSPF NSSA external type 2
5         E1 - OSPF external type 1, E2 - OSPF external type 2, E - EGP
6         i - IS-IS, L1 - IS-IS level-1, L2 - IS-IS level-2, * - candidate default
7         U - per-user static route, o - ODR
8
9 Gateway of last resort is not set
10
11 D    200.200.200.0/24 [90/409600] via 144.251.1.1, 00:02:58, Ethernet0
12 D    37.0.0.0/8 [90/409600] via 144.251.1.1, 00:02:58, Ethernet0
13      144.251.0.0/16 is variably subnetted, 3 subnets, 2 masks
14 C       144.251.1.0/26 is directly connected, Ethernet0
15 C       144.251.1.248/30 is directly connected, Serial1
16 D       144.251.1.252/30 [90/21017600] via 144.251.1.1, 00:01:56, Ethernet0
17 D EX 192.168.0.0/21 [170/307200] via 144.251.1.1, 00:01:56, Ethernet0
```

**Figure 8-22**   Moscow secondary **show ip route** output

```
1 Moscow#sho ip route
2 Codes: C - connected, S - static, I - IGRP, R - RIP, M - mobile, B - BGP
3        D - EIGRP, EX - EIGRP external, O - OSPF, IA - OSPF inter area
4        N1 - OSPF NSSA external type 1, N2 - OSPF NSSA external type 2
5        E1 - OSPF external type 1, E2 - OSPF external type 2, E - EGP
6        i - IS-IS, L1 - IS-IS level-1, L2 - IS-IS level-2, * - candidate default
7        U - per-user static route, o - ODR
8
9 Gateway of last resort is not set
10
11 D    200.200.200.0/24 [90/409600] via 144.251.1.1, 00:01:03, Ethernet0
12 D    37.0.0.0/8 [90/409600] via 144.251.1.1, 00:01:04, Ethernet0
13      144.251.0.0/16 is variably subnetted, 2 subnets, 2 masks
14 C       144.251.1.0/26 is directly connected, Ethernet0
15 C       144.251.1.248/30 is directly connected, Serial1
16 S    192.168.0.0/21 [190/0] via 144.251.1.249
```

**Figure 8-23**   Tokyo configuration

```
1 !
2 hostname Tokyo
3 !
4 no ip domain-lookup
5 !
6 interface Ethernet0
7  ip address 192.168.1.1 255.255.255.0
8 !
9 interface Serial0
10  ip address 144.251.1.253 255.255.255.252
11  bandwidth 125
12 !
13 interface Serial1
14  ip address 192.168.3.2 255.255.255.0
15  bandwidth 125
16  clockrate 125000
17 !
18 router rip
19  network 192.168.3.0
20  network 192.168.1.0
21 !
22 ip classless
23 ip route 0.0.0.0 0.0.0.0 Serial0
24 !
25 line con 0
26  exec-timeout 0 0
27  length 0
28 !
29 end
30
```

**Figure 8-24** Tokyo **show ip protocol** output

```
1 Tokyo#sho ip prot
2 Routing Protocol is "rip"
3   Sending updates every 30 seconds, next due in 0 seconds
4   Invalid after 180 seconds, hold down 180, flushed after 240
5   Outgoing update filter list for all interfaces is not set
6   Incoming update filter list for all interfaces is not set
7   Redistributing: rip
8   Default version control: send version 1, receive any version
9     Interface       Send  Recv  Key-chain
10    Ethernet0         1    1 2
11    Serial1           1    1 2
12  Routing for Networks:
13    192.168.3.0
14    192.168.1.0
15  Routing Information Sources:
16    Gateway         Distance      Last Update
17    192.168.3.1         120       00:00:28
18  Distance: (default is 120)
```

Figure 8-26 shows us two commands, the **show ip route** output on lines 1 through 14 and the **trace 200.200.200.1** output on lines 16 through 24. The routing table, on line 14, shows a default route to unknown networks as RIP derived through Serial 1, and the trace command follows that path. If the secondary link through Paris is two hops away, then this is normal. When the static route is active, traffic takes that pathway; when the static path is not present, the dynamic path becomes active.

**Figure 8-25** Tokyo primary **show ip route** output

```
1 Tokyo#sho ip route
2 Codes: C - connected, S - static, I - IGRP, R - RIP, M - mobile, B - BGP
3        D - EIGRP, EX - EIGRP external, O - OSPF, IA - OSPF inter area
4        N1 - OSPF NSSA external type 1, N2 - OSPF NSSA external type 2
5        E1 - OSPF external type 1, E2 - OSPF external type 2, E - EGP
6        i - IS-IS, L1 - IS-IS level-1, L2 - IS-IS level-2, * - candidate default
7        U - per-user static route, o - ODR
8
9 Gateway of last resort is 0.0.0.0 to network 0.0.0.0
10
11     144.251.0.0/30 is subnetted, 1 subnets
12 C       144.251.1.252 is directly connected, Serial0
13 C     192.168.1.0/24 is directly connected, Ethernet0
14 R     192.168.2.0/24 [120/1] via 192.168.3.1, 00:00:08, Serial1
15 C     192.168.3.0/24 is directly connected, Serial1
16 S*    0.0.0.0/0 is directly connected, Serial0
17
18 Tokyo#trace 200.200.200.1
19
20 Type escape sequence to abort.
21 Tracing the route to 200.200.200.1
22
23   1 144.251.1.254 12 msec *  8 msec
```

**Figure 8-26** Tokyo secondary **show ip route** output

```
1 Tokyo#sho ip route
2 Codes: C - connected, S - static, I - IGRP, R - RIP, M - mobile, B - BGP
3        D - EIGRP, EX - EIGRP external, O - OSPF, IA - OSPF inter area
4        N1 - OSPF NSSA external type 1, N2 - OSPF NSSA external type 2
5        E1 - OSPF external type 1, E2 - OSPF external type 2, E - EGP
6        i - IS-IS, L1 - IS-IS level-1, L2 - IS-IS level-2, * - candidate default
7        U - per-user static route, o - ODR
8
9 Gateway of last resort is 192.168.3.1 to network 0.0.0.0
10
11 C    192.168.1.0/24 is directly connected, Ethernet0
12 R    192.168.2.0/24 [120/1] via 192.168.3.1, 00:00:16, Serial1
13 C    192.168.3.0/24 is directly connected, Serial1
14 R*   0.0.0.0/0 [120/7] via 192.168.3.1, 00:00:16, Serial1
15
16 Tokyo#trace 200.200.200.1
17
18 Type escape sequence to abort.
19 Tracing the route to 200.200.200.1
20
21   1 192.168.3.1 12 msec 12 msec 12 msec
22   2 192.168.2.2 16 msec 8 msec 8 msec
23   3 144.251.1.250 20 msec 16 msec 16 msec
24   4 144.251.1.1 20 msec *  20 msec
```

In our network, London is the man in the middle. See Figure 8-14 for the network layout. The configuration for London is shown in Figure 8-27. Talk about basic, standard RIP-routed IP.

Figure 8-28 shows the **show ip protocol** output, a standard RIP routing process.

Figure 8-29 shows two commands, the **show ip route** output on lines 1 through 14 and **trace 200.200.200.1** output on lines 15 through 21. There seems to be an anomaly (a polite word for bug) in the routing table. If the static default routes are equidistant from London at one hop away, why does only the primary link path show up? More clues in Figure 8-30. The trace output shows us that the traffic is going through our primary link in Tokyo.

Figure 8-30 shows two commands, the **show ip route** output on lines 1 through 14 and **trace 200.200.200.1** output on lines 16 through 23. As expected, when the primary link fails, the secondary link takes over. Take a look at line 14, and some of the mystery is solved as to why two equal paths on the surface act so different. The hop count in the routing table, **[120/6]**, shows us that the secondary link through Paris shows up as further away than indicated by the topology.

The trace output verifies that we used the Paris-to-Moscow link to reach our target address.

**Figure 8-27**   London configuration

```
1  !
2  hostname London
3  !
4  no ip domain-lookup
5  !
6  interface Ethernet0
7   ip address 192.168.2.1 255.255.255.0
8  !
9  interface Serial0
10  ip address 192.168.3.1 255.255.255.0
11  bandwidth 125
12 !
13 router rip
14  network 192.168.3.0
15  network 192.168.2.0
16 !
17 ip classless
18 !
19 line con 0
20  exec-timeout 0 0
21  length 0
22 !
23 end
```

Paris, the City of Light. Maybe we can shed some light on why our secondary default route shows up further away when we distribute routing information. The configuration file is shown in Figure 8-31.

The key to making Paris the secondary contact point is in line 14. This command adds an offset of five hops to all networks advertised on all RIP interfaces. The **0** on line 14 could be replaced with an access-list

**Figure 8-28**   London **show ip protocol** output

```
1  London#sho ip prot
2  Routing Protocol is "rip"
3    Sending updates every 30 seconds, next due in 21 seconds
4    Invalid after 180 seconds, hold down 180, flushed after 240
5    Outgoing update filter list for all interfaces is not set
6    Incoming update filter list for all interfaces is not set
7    Redistributing: rip
8    Default version control: send version 1, receive any version
9      Interface        Send  Recv   Key-chain
10     Ethernet0          1    1 2
11     Serial0            1    1 2
12   Routing for Networks:
13     192.168.3.0
14     192.168.2.0
15   Routing Information Sources:
16     Gateway          Distance      Last Update
17     192.168.2.2         120        00:04:44
18     192.168.3.2         120        00:00:09
19   Distance: (default is 120)
```

**Figure 8-29**   London primary **show ip route** output

```
1 London#sho ip route
2 Codes: C - connected, S - static, I - IGRP, R - RIP, M - mobile, B - BGP
3        D - EIGRP, EX - EIGRP external, O - OSPF, IA - OSPF inter area
4        N1 - OSPF NSSA external type 1, N2 - OSPF NSSA external type 2
5        E1 - OSPF external type 1, E2 - OSPF external type 2, E - EGP
6        i - IS-IS, L1 - IS-IS level-1, L2 - IS-IS level-2, * - candidate default
7        U - per-user static route, o - ODR
8
9 Gateway of last resort is 192.168.3.2 to network 0.0.0.0
10
11 R     192.168.1.0/24 [120/1] via 192.168.3.2, 00:00:13, Serial0
12 C     192.168.2.0/24 is directly connected, Ethernet0
13 C     192.168.3.0/24 is directly connected, Serial0
14 R*    0.0.0.0/0 [120/1] via 192.168.3.2, 00:00:13, Serial0
15 London#trace 200.200.200.1
16
17 Type escape sequence to abort.
18 Tracing the route to 200.200.200.1
19
20   1 192.168.3.2 8 msec 8 msec 8 msec
21   2 144.251.1.254 20 msec * 16 msec
```

number, and multiple offset commands could be used to set up variable hop counts for outgoing networks.

The static route on line 18 is another example of a floating static route. See the description in Figure 8-19 for a detailed explanation of floating static routes.

**Figure 8-30**   London secondary **show ip route** output

```
1 London#sho ip route
2 Codes: C - connected, S - static, I - IGRP, R - RIP, M - mobile, B - BGP
3        D - EIGRP, EX - EIGRP external, O - OSPF, IA - OSPF inter area
4        N1 - OSPF NSSA external type 1, N2 - OSPF NSSA external type 2
5        E1 - OSPF external type 1, E2 - OSPF external type 2, E - EGP
6        i - IS-IS, L1 - IS-IS level-1, L2 - IS-IS level-2, * - candidate default
7        U - per-user static route, o - ODR
8
9 Gateway of last resort is 192.168.2.2 to network 0.0.0.0
10
11 R     192.168.1.0/24 [120/1] via 192.168.3.2, 00:00:09, Serial0
12 C     192.168.2.0/24 is directly connected, Ethernet0
13 C     192.168.3.0/24 is directly connected, Serial0
14 R*    0.0.0.0/0 [120/6] via 192.168.2.2, 00:00:01, Ethernet0
15
16 London#trace 200.200.200.1
17
18 Type escape sequence to abort.
19 Tracing the route to 200.200.200.1
20
21   1 192.168.2.2 8 msec 4 msec 4 msec
22   2 144.251.1.250 12 msec 8 msec 8 msec
23   3 144.251.1.1 16 msec * 16 msec
```

**Figure 8-31**   Paris configuration

```
1  !
2  hostname Paris
3  !
4  no ip domain-lookup
5  !
6  interface Ethernet0
7   ip address 192.168.2.2 255.255.255.0
8  !
9  interface Serial0
10  ip address 144.251.1.249 255.255.255.252
11  bandwidth 125
12 !
13 router rip
14  offset-list 0 out 5
15  network 192.168.2.0
16 !
17 ip classless
18 ip route 0.0.0.0 0.0.0.0 144.251.1.250 190
19 !
20 line con 0
21  exec-timeout 0 0
22  length 0
23 !
24 end
```

Figure 8-32 is the output of the **show ip protocol** command and is plain vanilla RIP routing. There is no indication that the static default route will be redistributed to the rest of our Autonomous System. Note that line 7 shows us the result of our offset command, five hops added to all outgoing route metrics

Figure 8-33 shows us two commands, the **show ip route** output on lines 1 through 16 and the **trace 200.200.200.1** output on lines 18 through

**Figure 8-32**   Paris **show ip protocol** output

```
1  Paris#sho ip prot
2  Routing Protocol is "rip"
3    Sending updates every 30 seconds, next due in 11 seconds
4    Invalid after 180 seconds, hold down 180, flushed after 240
5    Outgoing update filter list for all interfaces is not set
6    Incoming update filter list for all interfaces is not set
7    Outgoing routes will have 5 added to metric
8    Redistributing: rip
9    Default version control: send version 1, receive any version
10     Interface        Send  Recv   Key-chain
11     Ethernet0          1     1 2
12   Routing for Networks:
13     192.168.2.0
14   Routing Information Sources:
15     Gateway         Distance      Last Update
16     192.168.2.1          120      00:00:22
17   Distance: (default is 120)
```

**Figure 8-33**   Paris primary **show ip route** output

```
1 Paris#sho ip route
2 Codes: C - connected, S - static, I - IGRP, R - RIP, M - mobile, B - BGP
3        D - EIGRP, EX - EIGRP external, O - OSPF, IA - OSPF inter area
4        N1 - OSPF NSSA external type 1, N2 - OSPF NSSA external type 2
5        E1 - OSPF external type 1, E2 - OSPF external type 2, E - EGP
6        i - IS-IS, L1 - IS-IS level-1, L2 - IS-IS level-2, * - candidate default
7        U - per-user static route, o - ODR
8
9 Gateway of last resort is 192.168.2.1 to network 0.0.0.0
10
11       144.251.0.0/30 is subnetted, 1 subnets
12 C        144.251.1.248 is directly connected, Serial0
13 R     192.168.1.0/24 [120/2] via 192.168.2.1, 00:00:01, Ethernet0
14 C     192.168.2.0/24 is directly connected, Ethernet0
15 R     192.168.3.0/24 [120/1] via 192.168.2.1, 00:00:01, Ethernet0
16 R*    0.0.0.0/0 [120/2] via 192.168.2.1, 00:00:01, Ethernet0
17
18 Paris#trace 200.200.200.1
19
20 Type escape sequence to abort.
21 Tracing the route to 200.200.200.1
22
23   1 192.168.2.1 4 msec 4 msec 4 msec
24   2 192.168.3.2 12 msec 12 msec 12 msec
25   3 144.251.1.254 24 msec *  20 msec
```

**Figure 8-34**   Paris secondary **show ip route** output

```
1 Paris#sho ip route
2 Codes: C - connected, S - static, I - IGRP, R - RIP, M - mobile, B - BGP
3        D - EIGRP, EX - EIGRP external, O - OSPF, IA - OSPF inter area
4        N1 - OSPF NSSA external type 1, N2 - OSPF NSSA external type 2
5        E1 - OSPF external type 1, E2 - OSPF external type 2, E - EGP
6        i - IS-IS, L1 - IS-IS level-1, L2 - IS-IS level-2, * - candidate default
7        U - per-user static route, o - ODR
8
9 Gateway of last resort is 144.251.1.250 to network 0.0.0.0
10
11       144.251.0.0/30 is subnetted, 1 subnets
12 C        144.251.1.248 is directly connected, Serial0
13 R     192.168.1.0/24 [120/2] via 192.168.2.1, 00:00:03, Ethernet0
14 C     192.168.2.0/24 is directly connected, Ethernet0
15 R     192.168.3.0/24 [120/1] via 192.168.2.1, 00:00:03, Ethernet0
16 S*    0.0.0.0/0 [190/0] via 144.251.1.250
17
18 Paris#trace 200.200.200.1
19
20 Type escape sequence to abort.
21 Tracing the route to 200.200.200.1
22
23   1 144.251.1.250 12 msec 8 msec 8 msec
24   2 144.251.1.1 12 msec *  12 msec
```

25. The routing table, on line 16, shows a default route to unknown networks as RIP derived through Ethernet 0, and the trace command follows that path. If the primary link through Tokyo is two hops away, then this is normal; with the floating static route taking a backseat, then traffic takes the primary pathway, and when the dynamic path is not present, the static path should become active.

The trace output shows the traffic taking the primary path.

Figure 8-34 shows us two commands, the **show ip route** output on lines 1 through 16 and the **trace 200.200.200.1** output on lines 18 through 24. The routing table on line 16 shows a default route to unknown networks through 144.251.1.250, interface Serial 0, and the trace command follows that path.

**Question #2: If the primary link fails in Example #2, how long could it take for the alternate path to be stable so that normal end-user traffic could resume? What command could be used to speed up the convergence of the routes?**

# CCIE Tips

There are two specific areas to watch out for when configuring static routes: routing loops and asymmetrical routes

Routing loops create pathways to a destination that get lost in the middle of a network. The easiest way to detect routing loops is to trace a pathway to the destination. If the same addresses appear in a repetitive sequence and the destination is never reached, then you have a routing loop. There is an example of a routing loop in Figure 6-1 in Chapter 6. Set up routers and test this configuration with the trace command to see what it looks like.

Asymmetrical routes are routes that take different pathways to and from a destination. Set up routers with the configurations for Example #3 in Chapter 7, as it has been deliberately set up to create this situation. If you have not solved the problem yet, a similar solution to Example #2 in this chapter would correct this problem.

## SUMMARY

While it would be great to have routers capable of handling BGP for our Internet connections, most companies have basic connectivity. Static routes provide proper connectivity to the Internet, and using Example #2 as a model, even two static connections can provide the flexibility normally associated with dynamic solutions.

# Questions & Answers

**Question #1: Is the passive interface command really necessary in this configuration? There are many clues in this example. Check it out.**

Yes. If you look at line 22 in Figure 8-10, there is a network statement for the serial link to our external network that activates that interface for RIP processing.

**Question #2: If the primary link fails in Example #2, how long could it take for the alternate path to be stable so that normal end-user traffic could resume? What command could be used to speed up the convergence of the routes**

With the RIP routing protocol, there can be a definite delay after the primary link fails and the secondary pathway is stable due to the hold-down timers active to prevent routing loops.

The **clear ip route 0.0.0.0** could be used in Example #2 in all the routers in our Autonomous System to speed up the convergence time for the default route.

# CHAPTER 9

# Border Gateway Protocol Internet Connectivity

This chapter is provided as a configuration guide for network administrators who need to connect their local Autonomous System to the Internet using BGP. BGP configuration for Internet Service Providers is a highly complex topic that deserves more detail than can be covered in a single chapter, and there are several good books that target only BGP.

One of the better books available that describes the intricacies of BGP is *Internet Routing Architectures* by Bassam Halabi, published by Cisco Press (1997).

# BGP Overview

## Autonomous System Definition

An Autonomous System is a group of routers under one administrative domain with an integrated routing policy. This domain usually consists of one or more registered or private class A, B, or C IP networks. BGP is used to exchange routing information between Autonomous Systems. Autonomous Systems are assigned a number from 1 to 65,535. Numbers from 1 to 65,411 are registered Internet numbers, while 65,412 to 65,535 are designated as private Autonomous System numbers. These private Autonomous System numbers are used by ISPs to create hidden connections to subscribers to their Internet service or to build confederations within the ISP's infrastructure.

## BGP Background

The original IP routing protocol, RIP, was designed for small networks with similar media types. It uses a simple metric for calculating the best pathway to a destination—hops. As the Internet grew and changed, RIP was no longer capable of handling the size and complexity. The first external protocol was Exterior Gateway Protocol, which was a way to connect Autonomous Systems and reduce the number of hops in a RIP routing domain. This method uses statically defined connections between Autonomous Systems but is not scalable. BGP has evolved as a dynamic routing protocol that is used to tie together Autonomous Systems. There are two different types of BGP connections—external connections between Autonomous Systems and internal connections that go through Autonomous Systems (see Figure 9-1).

## BGP Operation

BGP neighbor routers are connected together using TCP connections to exchange capabilities and dynamic routing updates. BGP uses the next-hop entry in the routing table to forward packets to its BGP neighbors. The next-hop BGP address does not have to be directly connected to the router making the routing decision. Connections between

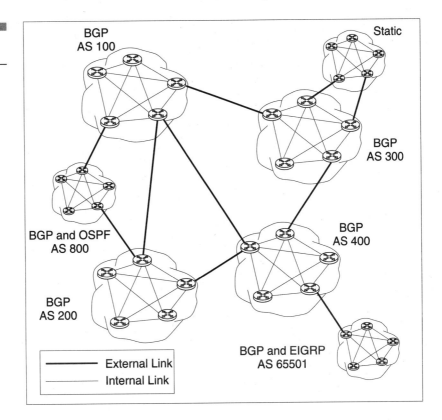

**Figure 9-1**
BGP overview

Autonomous Systems usually are made between directly connected Autonomous System neighbors; if not directly connected, the **neighbor ebgp-multihop** command must be used to skip over intermediate routers. When BGP neighbors connect within an Autonomous System, BGP relies on the routing process of the local Autonomous System to reach its internal BGP neighbor. Directly connected BGP neighbors between different Autonomous Systems exchange information over external links, while BGP neighbors within the same Autonomous System exchange information over internal links.

BGP routes are made up of a list of Autonomous Systems that are transited to reach the destination. In Figure 9-1, the pathway from the Static network to AS 800 could have an Autonomous System path of 300 100 or 300 400 200 or 300 400 100 or 300 100 200 or 300 100 400 200. The pathway through the BGP infrastructure is dependent on the policy routing implemented on each BGP router in the infrastructure. An example of policy routing is demonstrated in Example #2.

# BGP Route Determination

BGP uses specific criteria to forward packets to their destination. If there are multiple possibilities from which to choose, then BGP uses the following 10 methods in the sequence that they appear:

1. If the next-hop address in the BGP routing table has no pathway defined in the local routing table, then the packet is dropped.

2. Cisco has a proprietary weight value that can be assigned to routes to influence route decisions; the preferred route has the greatest local weight factor.

3. If the Cisco weighting is equal for multiple routes, then the preferred route is one with the greatest BGP local preference.

4. If the BGP local preference is equal for multiple routes, then the preferred route would be one locally generated in the router making the decision.

5. If the BGP local preference is equal for multiple routes, and there are no local-router-generated routes, then the preferred route is the one with the shortest BGP Autonomous System path. The Autonomous System path is a list of Autonomous Systems that are crossed to reach the destination.

6. If the BGP Autonomous System path lengths are equal for multiple paths, the lowest origin type determines the preferred route, IGP, then EGP, then incomplete. There are three different origins that can be assigned to each BGP route—external, internal, and incomplete. Internal routes (IGP) are derived from neighbors within the same Autonomous System; external routes (EGP) are derived from external Autonomous Systems; incomplete routes have entered the BGP routing domain via route redistribution.

7. If the origin types are equal for multiple paths, the preferred route is the route with the lowest Multi Exit Discriminator (MED) information sent by exterior BGP neighbors to direct outside Autonomous Systems toward specific contact points.

8. If the MEDs are equal for multiple paths, the preferred route is picked from the following sequence: external BGP routes, then external confederation routes, then internal BGP routes. A confederation is a technique used to group several local Autonomous Systems under one advertised Autonomous System

9. If there are no differences after all the techniques described previously, then the preferred route is the best IGP pathway to the BGP next-hop address.

10. If there are equal IGP multiple paths, then the preferred route is to the BGP neighbor with the lowest BGP router ID. The Cisco router ID is the highest IP address on an active interface during the startup process or the IP address assigned to the loopback interface.

## Connecting to ISPs

Connecting to an Internet Service Provider requires careful planning. When many companies began assigning IP addresses, rather than obtaining a registered class A, B, or C network, it was common to pick an address and a subnetwork mask and begin to hand out individual host addresses. In order to connect to the Internet and participate in BGP, it requires a registered IP address and a registered Autonomous System number. Due to the rapid growth of the Internet in the last few years and the need for registered numbers, there have been many techniques used to conserve address space, Network Address Translation, private IP addresses, and private Autonomous System numbers.

# Examples

The examples in this chapter are designed to highlight ISP connections. Example #1 illustrates a single BGP exit to the Internet. Example #2 illustrates multiple BGP exits to two different ISPs, using route maps to implement policy routing.

## Example #1—BGP Internet Connection, Single Exit

Routers Tokyo and London make up RIP-based Autonomous System (AS) 300, that is connected AS 200 through a BGP connection to New York. The network layout for this example is shown in Figure 9-2.

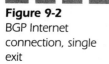

**Figure 9-2**
BGP Internet
connection, single
exit

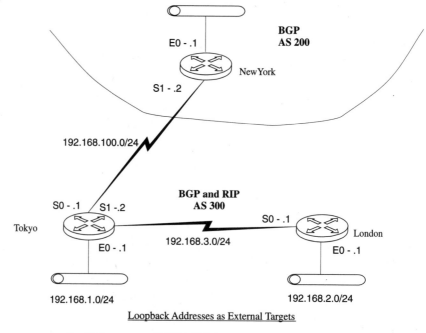

**Figure 9-3:** London configuration

```
1  !
2  hostname London
3  !
4  !no ip domain-lookup
5  !
6  interface Ethernet0
7    ip address 192.168.2.1 255.255.255.0
8  !
9  interface Serial0
10   ip address 192.168.3.1 255.255.255.0
11   bandwidth 125
12 !
13 router rip
14   network 192.168.3.0
15   network 192.168.2.0
16 !
17 ip classless
18 !
19 line con 0
20   exec-timeout 0 0
21   length 0
22 !
23 end
```

████ ████ ████ ████ ████ ████ ████ ████ ████ ████ ████ ████ ████ ████ ████ ████ ████ ████ ████

**Figure 9-4:** London **trace** output

```
1 London#trace
2 Protocol [ip]:
3 Target IP address: 200.200.200.1
4 Source address: 192.168.2.1
5 Numeric display [n]:
6 Timeout in seconds [3]:
7 Probe count [3]:
8 Minimum Time to Live [1]:
9 Maximum Time to Live [30]:
10 Port Number [33434]:
11 Loose, Strict, Record, Timestamp, Verbose[none]:
12 Type escape sequence to abort.
13 Tracing the route to 200.200.200.1
14
15   1 192.168.3.2 12 msec 12 msec 12 msec
16   2 192.168.100.2 16 msec *  16 msec
```

New York's loopback interface addresses, 200.200.200.1 and 144.251.0.1, provide simulated target Internet addresses.

The first step in debugging BGP connectivity is to ensure that there is proper connectivity between the BGP peers. There is a separate section at the end of this example that highlights the **show** and **debug** output for troubleshooting BGP neighbor connections.

London is an internal RIP router inside our Autonomous System that is used to prove that our BGP configuration is operating properly. The configuration is shown in Figure 9-3.

Figure 9-4 shows an extended **trace** to one of the external target addresses from the Ethernet 0 address 192.168.2.1 proving that our BGP connection is operating correctly.

████ ████ ████ ████ ████ ████ ████ ████ ████ ████ ████ ████ ████ ████ ████ ████ ████ ████ ████

**Figure 9-5:** London **show ip protocol** output

```
1 London#sho ip.prot
2 Routing Protocol is "rip"
3   Sending updates every 30 seconds, next due in 9 seconds
4   Invalid after 180 seconds, hold down 180, flushed after 240
5   Outgoing update filter list for all interfaces is not set
6   Incoming update filter list for all interfaces is not set
7   Redistributing: rip
8   Default version control: send version 1, receive any version
9     Interface        Send  Recv  Key-chain
10     Ethernet0         1    1 2
11     Serial0           1    1 2
12   Routing for Networks:
13     192.168.3.0
14     192.168.2.0
15   Routing Information Sources:
16     Gateway         Distance     Last Update
17     192.168.3.2        120       00:00:03
18   Distance: (default is 120)
```

**Figure 9-6**   London **show ip route** output

```
1 London#sho ip route
2 Codes: C - connected, S - static, I - IGRP, R - RIP, M - mobile, B - BGP
3         D - EIGRP, EX - EIGRP external, O - OSPF, IA - OSPF inter area
4         N1 - OSPF NSSA external type 1, N2 - OSPF NSSA external type 2
5         E1 - OSPF external type 1, E2 - OSPF external type 2, E - EGP
6         i - IS-IS, L1 - IS-IS level-1, L2 - IS-IS level-2, * - candidate default
7         U - per-user static route, o - ODR
8
9 Gateway of last resort is 192.168.3.2 to network 0.0.0.0
10
11 R    192.168.1.0/24 [120/1] via 192.168.3.2, 00:00:06, Serial0
12 C    192.168.2.0/24 is directly connected, Ethernet0
13 C    192.168.3.0/24 is directly connected, Serial0
14 R*   0.0.0.0/0 [120/1] via 192.168.3.2, 00:00:06, Serial0
```

The **show ip protocol** output in Figure 9-5 shows us a standard RIP routing process.

The **show ip route** command in Figure 9-6 shows us the directly connected, internal RIP derived route 192.168.1.0 and the RIP-derived default route 0.0.0.0 on line 14.

**Figure 9-7**   NewYork configuration

```
1 !
2 hostname NewYork
3 !
4 no ip domain-lookup
5 !
6 interface Loopback0
7  ip address 200.200.200.1 255.255.255.0
8 !
9 interface Loopback1
10  ip address 144.251.0.1 255.255.0.0
11 !
12 interface Ethernet0
13  ip address 199.99.1.5 255.255.255.252
14 !
15 interface Serial1
16  ip address 192.168.100.2 255.255.255.0
17  bandwidth 125
18  clockrate 125000
19 !
20 router bgp 200
21  neighbor 192.168.100.1 remote-as 300
22 !
23 ip classless
24 !
25 line con 0
26  exec-timeout 0 0
27  length 0
28 !
29 end
```

**Figure 9-8** NewYork **trace** output

```
1 NewYork#trace
2 Protocol [ip]:
3 Target IP address: 192.168.2.1
4 Source address: 200.200.200.1
5 Numeric display [n]:
6 Timeout in seconds [3]:
7 Probe count [3]:
8 Minimum Time to Live [1]:
9 Maximum Time to Live [30]:
10 Port Number [33434]:
11 Loose, Strict, Record, Timestamp, Verbose[none]:
12 Type escape sequence to abort.
13 Tracing the route to 192.168.2.1
14
15   1 192.168.100.1 8 msec 8 msec 8 msec
16   2 192.168.3.1 16 msec *  16 msec
```

Line 9 shows us that the gateway of last resort can be reached through Tokyo.

New York is the external BGP device in AS 200 that is the Internet simulator in our network layout. The configuration is shown in Figure 9-7.

Lines 6 through 10 define our target addresses.

Lines 20 and 21 start up the BGP process and identify Tokyo in AS 300 as a BGP neighbor. The target address, 192.168.100.1, is the other end of our serial link connecting New York and Tokyo. The network used to connect the two routers creating an external link can be any IP address, as this connecting network should not get advertised in BGP routing updates.

Figure 9-8 shows the output of an extended **trace** command that uses one of the target addresses as the source and 192.168.2.1 in London at the other end of AS 300.

The **show ip protocol** output in Figure 9-9, is the simplest BGP

**Figure 9-9** NewYork **show ip protocol** output

```
1 NewYork#sho ip prot
2 Routing Protocol is "bgp 200"
3   Sending updates every 60 seconds, next due in 0 seconds
4   Outgoing update filter list for all interfaces is not set
5   Incoming update filter list for all interfaces is not set
6   IGP synchronization is enabled
7   Automatic route summarization is enabled
8   Neighbor(s):
9    Address            FiltIn FiltOut DistIn DistOut Weight RouteMap
10     192.168.100.1
11   Routing for Networks:
12   Routing Information Sources:
13    Gateway          Distance      Last Update
14     192.168.100.1         20       00:07:10
15   Distance: external 20 internal 200 local 200
```

**Figure 9-10** NewYork **show ip route** output

```
1 NewYork#sho ip route
2 Codes: C - connected, S - static, I - IGRP, R - RIP, M - mobile, B - BGP
3        D - EIGRP, EX - EIGRP external, O - OSPF, IA - OSPF inter area
4        N1 - OSPF NSSA external type 1, N2 - OSPF NSSA external type 2
5        E1 - OSPF external type 1, E2 - OSPF external type 2, E - EGP
6        i - IS-IS, L1 - IS-IS level-1, L2 - IS-IS level-2, * - candidate default
7        U - per-user static route, o - ODR
8
9 Gateway of last resort is not set
10
11 C    200.200.200.0/24 is directly connected, Loopback0
12 C    144.251.0.0/16 is directly connected, Loopback1
13      199.99.1.0/30 is subnetted, 1 subnets
14 C       199.99.1.4 is directly connected, Ethernet0
15 B    192.168.1.0/24 [20/0] via 192.168.100.1, 00:08:00
16 B    192.168.2.0/24 [20/1] via 192.168.100.1, 00:07:16
17 C    192.168.100.0/24 is directly connected, Serial1
```

process, with no local networks to be included in BGP routing updates; see line 11.

Lines 8 through 10 identify our neighbor 192.168.100.1, no policy routing in effect.

The **show ip route** output in Figure 9-10 shows our directly connected networks and the BGP-derived network routes, 192.169.1.0 and 192.168.2.0. These two networks are the Ethernet segments where end users need to get access to the Internet.

Tokyo is the router where AS 300 contacts the outside world through its BGP neighbor NewYork. The configuration is shown in Figure 9-11.

Lines 18 through 20 define the RIP routing process and includes only the local interfaces, not the network that connects us to NewYork.

Lines 22 through 25 define our BGP process for AS 300

Lines 23 and 24 define the two networks in Tokyo's routing table that will be advertised to our BGP neighbor NewYork. Unlike internal routing protocols, the network commands for BGP do not connect interfaces to the routing process.

Line 28 is the default route distributed to our RIP domain, so that external network destinations encountered in our RIP domain routers will be forwarded to Tokyo, where they can be handed over to NewYork.

The **show ip protocol** output shown in Figure 9-12 details the RIP routing process on lines 2 through 18 and the BGP 300 routing processes on lines 20 through 34.

Lines 13 and 14 show two local networks as participant in the RIP process.

**Figure 9-11** Tokyo configuration

```
1  !
2  hostname Tokyo
3  !
4  no ip domain-lookup
5  !
6  interface Ethernet0
7   ip address 192.168.1.1 255.255.255.0
8  !
9  interface Serial0
10   ip address 192.168.100.1 255.255.255.0
11   bandwidth 125
12  !
13  interface Serial1
14   ip address 192.168.3.2 255.255.255.0
15   bandwidth 125
16   clockrate 125000
17  !
18  router rip
19   network 192.168.1.0
20   network 192.168.3.0
21  !
22  router bgp 300
23   network 192.168.1.0
24   network 192.168.2.0
25   neighbor 192.168.100.2 remote-as 200
26  !
27  ip classless
28  ip route 0.0.0.0 0.0.0.0 192.168.100.2
29  !
30  !
31  line con 0
32   exec-timeout 0 0
33   length 0
34  !
35  end
```

Lines 30 and 31 show the two networks that BGP will advertise to our BGP neighbor 192.168.100.2, identified on line 28.

Figure 9-13 shows the output of the **show ip route** command. Basic RIP processing with directly connected, RIP-derived, and a static default route to New York. Note that there are no BGP-derived routes because there were no network commands configured for BGP in New York (see Figure 9-7).

## Peer Connectivity Debugging

This is a special section to highlight the troubleshooting process when BGP peers are not connecting properly.

First, we need to break the direct peer-to-peer connection between

**Figure 9-12**   Tokyo **show ip protocol** output

```
1 Tokyo#sho ip prot
2 Routing Protocol is "rip"
3   Sending updates every 30 seconds, next due in 4 seconds
4   Invalid after 180 seconds, hold down 180, flushed after 240
5   Outgoing update filter list for all interfaces is not set
6   Incoming update filter list for all interfaces is not set
7   Redistributing: rip
8   Default version control: send version 1, receive any version
9     Interface        Send  Recv  Key-chain
10    Ethernet0          1     1 2
11    Serial1            1     1 2
12  Routing for Networks:
13    192.168.1.0
14    192.168.3.0
15  Routing Information Sources:
16    Gateway         Distance      Last Update
17    192.168.3.1          120      00:00:13
18  Distance: (default is 120)
19
20 Routing Protocol is "bgp 300"
21   Sending updates every 60 seconds, next due in 0 seconds
22   Outgoing update filter list for all interfaces is not set
23   Incoming update filter list for all interfaces is not set
24   IGP synchronization is enabled
25   Automatic route summarization is enabled
26   Neighbor(s):
27     Address          FiltIn FiltOut DistIn DistOut Weight RouteMap
28     192.168.100.2
29   Routing for Networks:
30     192.168.1.0
31     192.168.2.0
32   Routing Information Sources:
33     Gateway         Distance      Last Update
34   Distance: external 20 internal 200 local 200
```

**Figure 9-13**   Tokyo **show ip route** output

```
1 Tokyo#show ip route
2 Codes: C - connected, S - static, I - IGRP, R - RIP, M - mobile, B - BGP
3        D - EIGRP, EX - EIGRP external, O - OSPF, IA - OSPF inter area
4        N1 - OSPF NSSA external type 1, N2 - OSPF NSSA external type 2
5        E1 - OSPF external type 1, E2 - OSPF external type 2, E - EGP
6        i - IS-IS, L1 - IS-IS level-1, L2 - IS-IS level-2, * - candidate default
7        U - per-user static route, o - ODR
8
9 Gateway of last resort is 192.168.100.2 to network 0.0.0.0
10
11 C    192.168.1.0/24 is directly connected, Ethernet0
12 R    192.168.2.0/24 [120/1] via 192.168.3.1, 00:00:16, Serial1
13 C    192.168.100.0/24 is directly connected, Serial0
14 C    192.168.3.0/24 is directly connected, Serial1
15 S*   0.0.0.0/0 [1/0] via 192.168.100.2
```

**Figure 9-14** NewYork configuration changes

```
1 NewYork#conf t
2 Enter configuration commands, one per line.  End with CNTL/Z.
3 NewYork(config)#router bgp 200
4 NewYork(config-router)#no neighbor 192.168.100.1 remote-as 300
5 NewYork(config-router)#neighbor 192.168.1.1 remote-as 300
6 NewYork(config-router)#end
7 NewYork#
8 NewYork#clear ip bgp *
9 NewYork#
10 NewYork#conf t
11 Enter configuration commands, one per line.  End with CNTL/Z.
12 NewYork(config)#router bgp 200
13 NewYork(config-router)#no neighbor 192.168.1.1 remote-as 300
14 NewYork(config-router)#neighbor 192.168.100.1 remote-as 300
15 NewYork(config-router)#end
16 NewYork#
17 NewYork#clear ip bgp *
18 NewYork#
```

NewYork and Tokyo (see Figure 14). The approach here is to break the process on our external AS 200 neighbor NewYork.

Lines 1 through 6 modify the **neighbor** command for Tokyo to attempt to access 192.168.1.1, one hop away. Unless otherwise configured, BGP external peers must be directly connected via a no-hop connection.

Line 8 is a requirement as well. After any BGP configuration changes, you *must* execute a **clear ip bgp** command. An * clears all BGP connections and processes, but there are many options available for this command. This command executed with the * option in a large meshed ISP could result in reduced capabilities while all the BGP neighbors resynchronize.

Lines 10 through 17 reverse the process and restore our BGP connection to Tokyo.

**Figure 9-15** Tokyo **show active bgp summary** output

```
1 Tokyo#sho ip bgp summ
2 BGP table version is 3, main routing table version 3
3 2 network entries (2/6 paths) using 416 bytes of memory
4 2 BGP path attribute entries using 184 bytes of memory
5 0 BGP route-map cache entries using 0 bytes of memory
6 0 BGP filter-list cache entries using 0 bytes of memory
7
8 Neighbor        V   AS MsgRcvd MsgSent   TblVer  InQ OutQ Up/Down  State/PfxRcd
9 192.168.100.2   4   200      13      15        3    0    0 00:10:14         0
```

Figure 9-15 shows the Tokyo **show ip bgp** summary output when the neighbors are properly connected.

Line 2 shows us that the BGP and main routing tables are both at version 3. BGP neighbors synchronize version numbers so that if one neighbor updates its routing table, then during the next neighbor contact, when the table versions are out of synchronization, updates are exchanged so that proper routing is maintained.

Figure 9-16 shows the Tokyo **show ip bgp** summary output in lines 2 through 9 after the neighbor address in New York was switched to an incorrect address. Lines 11 through 23 show the **debug** setup and output we can use to troubleshoot the BGP neighbor mismatch.

Line 9 shows our neighbor 192.168.100.2 is in the **Active** state. In this state, BGP is actively trying to establish a TCP connection with 102.168.100.2.

Lines 11 through 14 are where we activate our **debug** processes.

Line 16 is a BGP event indicating that BGP is scanning the routing table looking for changes that may have to be forwarded to its BGP neighbors.

Line 17 uses the **clear ip bgp** * command to trigger a reset sequence so the local BGP process tries to reconnect to all its BGP neighbors.

Line 18 records the **clear ip bgp** * command as a BGP event.

**Figure 9-16**   Tokyo **debug** output showing BGP neighbor mismatch

```
1 Tokyo#sho ip bgp summ
2 BGP table version is 4, main routing table version 4
3 2 network entries (2/6 paths) using 416 bytes of memory
4 2 BGP path attribute entries using 184 bytes of memory
5 0 BGP route-map cache entries using 0 bytes of memory
6 0 BGP filter-list cache entries using 0 bytes of memory
7
8 Neighbor        V    AS MsgRcvd MsgSent   TblVer  InQ OutQ Up/Down  State/PfxRcd
9 192.168.100.2   4   200      13      15        0    0    0 00:00:50 Active
10
11 Tokyo#debug ip bgp
12 BGP debugging is on
13 Tokyo#debug ip bgp events
14 BGP events debugging is on
15 Tokyo#
16 BGP: scanning routing tables
17 Tokyo#clear ip bgp *
18 BGP: reset all neighbors due to User reset request
19 BGP: 192.168.100.2 went from Active to Idle
20 BGP: 192.168.100.2 went from Idle to Active
21 BGP: 192.168.100.2 open active, delay 28512ms
22 BGP: 192.168.100.2 open active, local address 192.168.100.1
23 BGP: 192.168.100.2 open failed: Connection refused by remote host
```

**Figure 9-17**  Tokyo **debug** output showing BGP neighbor reconnect

```
1 BGP: 192.168.100.2 open active, local address 192.168.100.1
2 BGP: 192.168.100.2 went from Active to OpenSent
3 BGP: 192.168.100.2 sending OPEN, version 4
4 BGP: 192.168.100.2 OPEN rcvd, version 4
5 BGP: 192.168.100.2 went from OpenSent to OpenConfirm
6 BGP: 192.168.100.2 went from OpenConfirm to Established
7 BGP: 192.168.100.2 computing updates, neighbor version 0, table version 3, start
ing at 0.0.0.0
8 BGP: 192.168.100.2 update run completed, ran for 4ms, neighbor version 0, start
version 3, throttled to 3, check point net 0.0.0.0
9 BGP: 192.168.100.2 remote close, state CLOSEWAIT
10 BGP: 192.168.100.2 reset due to Peer closing down the session
11 BGP: 192.168.100.2 went from Established to Idle
12 BGP: 192.168.100.2 closing
13 BGP: 192.168.100.2 passive open
14 BGP: 192.168.100.2 went from Idle to Connect
15 BGP: 192.168.100.2 OPEN rcvd, version 4
16 BGP: 192.168.100.2 went from Connect to OpenSent
17 BGP: 192.168.100.2 sending OPEN, version 4
18 BGP: 192.168.100.2 went from OpenSent to OpenConfirm
19 BGP: 192.168.100.2 went from OpenConfirm to Established
20 BGP: 192.168.100.2 computing updates, neighbor version 0, table version 4, start
ing at 0.0.0.0
21 BGP: 192.168.100.2 update run completed, ran for 4ms, neighbor version 0, start
version 4, throttled to 4, check point net 0.0.0.0
```

Lines 19 through 23 illustrate the neighbor connection sequence when neighbors are not communicating.

Line 19 takes the link from Active to Idle.

Line 20 takes it from Idle to Active. Line 21 indicates that there will be a delay of 28512ms before the actual connection is attempted.

Line 21 is the indication that the link activation, across our connection point to New York, is being started.

Line 22 shows our connection attempt has failed.

Figure 9-17 shows the **debug** output sequence as New York is configured to correct our mismatched neighbor address.

Lines 1 through 8 show our neighbor New York activating the link as the configuration mismatch configuration is corrected.

When the **clear ip bgp** * command was executed in New York, it initiated a normal shutdown in Tokyo. This closedown sequence is documented in lines 9 through 12.

Lines 13 through 21 record Tokyo's responses to an external request to establish a neighbor link from New York.

# Example #2—BGP Internet Connection, Multiple Exits

In Example #2, we will explore policy routing when we connect our Autonomous System to two separate ISPs using BGP. Rome, our target host, implements RIP routing internally and a static connection to AS 100. Moscow uses BGP as its primary protocol and represents our secondary ISP. Moscow has an external BGP link to its neighbor New York, which represents our primary ISP in AS 200. Our Autonomous System is represented by Tokyo, London, and Rome and uses RIP as its internal routing protocol. The network layout is shown in Figure 9-18.

The policy to be implemented in BGP is to always use the ISP in New York, AS 200, as our primary Internet connection, with our secondary Internet connection to Moscow, AS 200, operating only when the primary link is down.

The configuration for Rome is shown in Figure 9-19, basic RIP routing with a default static route on line 18 pointing to Moscow for Internet connectivity.

Figure 9-21 shows the **show ip protocol** output, basic RIP routing

Just to verify that everything is working properly, standard and extended traces are executed to 192.168.2.1 (Figure 9-20), the IP address of

**Figure 9-18**

BGP Internet connection, multiple exits

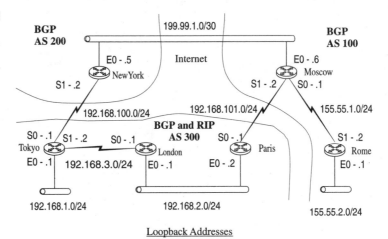

Loopback Addresses

Tokyo  192.168.6.1/24

**Figure 9-19**   Rome configuration

```
1  !
2  hostname Rome
3  !
4  no ip domain-lookup
5  !
6  interface Ethernet0
7   ip address 155.55.2.1 255.255.255.0
8  !
9  interface Serial1
10  ip address 155.55.1.2 255.255.255.0
11  bandwidth 125
12  clockrate 125000
13  !
14 router rip
15  network 155.55.0.0
16  !
17 ip classless
18 ip route 0.0.0.0 0.0.0.0 Serial1
19  !
20 line con 0
21  exec-timeout 0 0
22  length 0
23  !
24 end
```

**Figure 9-20**   Rome **trace** output

```
1  Rome#trace 192.168.2.1
2
3  Type escape sequence to abort.
4  Tracing the route to 192.168.2.1
5
6    1 155.55.1.1 12 msec 8 msec 12 msec
7    2 199.99.1.5 16 msec 8 msec 8 msec
8    3 192.168.100.1 16 msec 20 msec 20 msec
9    4 192.168.3.1 28 msec *  24 msec
10
11 Rome#trace
12 Protocol [ip]:
13 Target IP address: 192.168.2.1
14 Source address: 155.55.2.1
15 Numeric display [n]:
16 Timeout in seconds [3]:
17 Probe count [3]:
18 Minimum Time to Live [1]:
19 Maximum Time to Live [30]:
20 Port Number [33434]:
21 Loose, Strict, Record, Timestamp, Verbose[none]:
22 Type escape sequence to abort.
23 Tracing the route to 192.168.2.1
24
25   1 155.55.1.1 8 msec 8 msec 8 msec
26   2 199.99.1.5 8 msec 12 msec 12 msec
27   3 192.168.100.1 20 msec 20 msec 20 msec
28   4 192.168.3.1 28 msec *  24 msec
```

**Figure 9-21** Rome **show ip protocol** output

```
1 Rome#sho ip prot
2 Routing Protocol is "rip"
3   Sending updates every 30 seconds, next due in 1 seconds
4   Invalid after 180 seconds, hold down 180, flushed after 240
5   Outgoing update filter list for all interfaces is not set
6   Incoming update filter list for all interfaces is not set
7   Redistributing: rip
8   Default version control: send version 1, receive any version
9     Interface      Send  Recv  Key-chain
10     Ethernet0       1    1 2
11     Serial1         1    1 2
12   Routing for Networks:
13     155.55.0.0
14   Routing Information Sources:
15     Gateway          Distance       Last Update
16   Distance: (default is 120)
```

the Ethernet 0 port on Paris. If our policy is correctly implemented, then all traffic should follow a single pathway through Moscow, New York, Tokyo, and London. Success, it works!

Figure 9-22 shows the **show ip route** output where our default static route to Moscow, on line 14, is the only way to the rest of the network.

Moscow represents our secondary ISP with Autonomous System 100 and is where policy routing is implemented. It will be necessary to work closely with your ISP to make sure the policy works correctly. This example is simple in nature but requires your ISP to correctly implement its portion of the policy. Figure 9-23 shows the configuration for Moscow.

**Figure 9-22** Rome **show ip route** output

```
1 Rome#sho ip route
2 Codes: C - connected, S - static, I - IGRP, R - RIP, M - mobile, B - BGP
3        D - EIGRP, EX - EIGRP external, O - OSPF, IA - OSPF inter area
4        N1 - OSPF NSSA external type 1, N2 - OSPF NSSA external type 2
5        E1 - OSPF external type 1, E2 - OSPF external type 2, E - EGP
6        i - IS-IS, L1 - IS-IS level-1, L2 - IS-IS level-2, * - candidate default
7        U - per-user static route, o - ODR
8
9 Gateway of last resort is 0.0.0.0 to network 0.0.0.0
10
11      155.55.0.0/24 is subnetted, 2 subnets
12 C       155.55.1.0 is directly connected, Serial1
13 C       155.55.2.0 is directly connected, Ethernet0
14 S*   0.0.0.0/0 is directly connected, Serial1
```

Lines 18 through 22 define our BGP routing process for Moscow.
Line 22 identifies Paris as our neighbor in AS 300.

Line 25 is our static aggregate route to all the subnetworks in our statically attached client reached through Rome.

Lines 20 and 21 are where the ISP defines that it is going to accept instructions from their client on how to process routing protocol traffic for routes to AS 300.

**Figure 9-23**  Moscow configuration

```
1  !
2  hostname Moscow
3  !
4  no ip domain-lookup
5  !
6  interface Ethernet0
7   ip address 199.99.1.6 255.255.255.252
8  !
9  interface Serial0
10   ip address 155.55.1.1 255.255.255.0
11   bandwidth 125
12  !
13  interface Serial1
14   ip address 192.168.101.2 255.255.255.0
15   bandwidth 125
16   clockrate 125000
17  !
18  router bgp 100
19   network 155.55.0.0
20   neighbor 192.168.101.1 remote-as 300
21   neighbor 192.168.101.1 route-map set-community in
22   neighbor 199.99.1.5 remote-as 200
23  !
24  ip classless
25  ip route 155.55.0.0 255.255.0.0 serial 0
26  ip community-list 1 permit 19660870
27  ip community-list 2 permit internet
28  route-map set-community permit 10
29   match community 1
30   set local-preference 70
31  !
32  route-map set-community permit 20
33   match community 2
34   set local-preference 100
35  !
36  line con 0
37   exec-timeout 0 0
38   length 0
39  !
40  end
```

Line 20 defines Paris as our neighbor.

Line 21 lets Moscow know that Paris is going to be sending a community attribute along with its routes that Moscow has to be aware of and process correctly. The policy will be implemented using the **route map set-community**. We define how to process the routing updates in lines 26 through 34.

In order to properly process the routing updates from Paris, we have to be able to identify the community attribute and use it to set routing policy. The **ip community-list** command is used to identify these community attributes. Line 25 is where we define the special community number used between Paris and Moscow. Line 26 is the equivalent of **permit any** in an access list, internet equates to any IP address.

Lines 25 through 34 shows **route map set-community**, where we implement policy.

Lines 28 through 30 instruct Moscow to set the local preference to 70 for all routes that arrive at Moscow with the community number 19660870.

Lines 32 through 34 instruct Moscow to set the local preference to 100 for all other routes.

Figure 9-24 shows the output from several commands that identifies the components used to implement our BGP policy.

**Figure 9-24**  Moscow policy information

```
1 Moscow#sho route-map
2 route-map set-community, permit, sequence 10
3   Match clauses:
4     community (community-list filter): 1
5   Set clauses:
6     local-preference 70
7   Policy routing matches: 0 packets, 0 bytes
8 route-map set-community, permit, sequence 20
9   Match clauses:
10     community (community-list filter): 2
11   Set clauses:
12     local-preference 100
13   Policy routing matches: 0 packets, 0 bytes
14
15 Moscow#sho ip bgp community
16 BGP table version is 18, local router ID is 199.99.1.6
17 Status codes: s suppressed, d damped, h history, * valid, > best, i - internal
18 Origin codes: i - IGP, e - EGP, ? - incomplete
19
20    Network          Next Hop         Metric LocPrf Weight Path
21 *  192.168.1.0      192.168.101.1         2     70      0 300 i
22 *  192.168.2.0      192.168.101.1         0     70      0 300 i
23 *  192.168.3.0      192.168.101.1         1     70      0 300 I
24
25 Moscow#sho ip bgp community-list 1
26 BGP table version is 18, local router ID is 199.99.1.6
27 Status codes: s suppressed, d damped, h history, * valid, > best, i - internal
28 Origin codes: i - IGP, e - EGP, ? - incomplete
29
30    Network          Next Hop         Metric LocPrf Weight Path
31 *  192.168.1.0      192.168.101.1         2     70      0 300 i
32 *  192.168.2.0      192.168.101.1         0     70      0 300 i
33 *  192.168.3.0      192.168.101.1         1     70      0 300 I
34
35 Moscow#sho ip bgp community-list 2
36 BGP table version is 18, local router ID is 199.99.1.6
37 Status codes: s suppressed, d damped, h history, * valid, > best, i - internal
38 Origin codes: i - IGP, e - EGP, ? - incomplete
39
40    Network          Next Hop         Metric LocPrf Weight Path
41 *> 155.55.0.0       0.0.0.0               0        32768 i
42 *> 192.168.1.0      199.99.1.5                          0 200 300 i
43 *                   192.168.101.1         2     70      0 300 i
44 *> 192.168.2.0      199.99.1.5                          0 200 300 i
45 *                   192.168.101.1         0     70      0 300 i
46 *> 192.168.3.0      199.99.1.5                          0 200 300 i
47 *                   192.168.101.1         1     70      0 300 i
```

Lines 1 through 13 are the output from the **show route-map** command. Lines 8 and 13 are the statistics that let us know how many times each match operation is used.

Lines 15 through 23 are the output from the **show ip bgp community** command and show the routes being modified when distributed from our community neighbor Paris.

Lines 25 through 33 and 35 through 47 are the output of the **show ip bgp community-list** command for each of the individual community lists. Lines 41 through 47 are all of the IP networks outside the BGP cloud as they all match the keyword **internet**.

Figure 9-25 shows the output of several show commands that are useful in reviewing the BGP process.

The **show ip bgp** output is in lines 1 through 13. Lines 7 through 13 summarize the known BGP routes and indicate the current status of each route according to the legend on lines 3 and 4.

Lines 15 through 24 show the output of the **show ip BGP summary** command. This command summarizes BGP route, attribute, and cache entries and shows neighbor information.

Lines 26 through 56 are a series of **show ip bgp A.B.C.D** command outputs that show details of the route entries for our AS 300 routes. Earlier in this chapter, the 10 rules for identifying the best BGP routes are defined. Rule 3 states that the route with the greatest local preference is the best route, and lines 31 and 35 show that route through NewYork, 199.99.1.5, is the best because 100 is greater than 70, the respective local preference. If the local preference values were both 100, the default, then the best path, would be through Paris, 192.168.101.1, the route with the shortest AS path. The best AS path is the one with the fewest Autonomous Systems to cross; line 29 shows 200 300 and line 32 300.

Lines 58 through 137 show the output of the **show ip BGP neighbor** command.

Figure 9-26 shows the output of the **show ip protocol** command. Line 10 shows us that there is a route map, **set-community**, in effect for routes sent to us by our neighbor Paris.

The show ip route output in Figure 9-27 shows static, directly connected, and BGP routes. The BGP routes are directed to NewYork on lines 16 through 18, after implementing the policy using local preference.

NewYork represents our primary ISP with Autonomous System 200. Figure 9-28 shows the configuration file for NewYork.

**Figure 9-25** Moscow **show** commands output

```
1 Moscow#sho ip bgp
2 BGP table version is 18, local router ID is 199.99.1.6
3 Status codes: s suppressed, d damped, h history, * valid, > best, i - internal
4 Origin codes: i - IGP, e - EGP, ? - incomplete
5
6   Network          Next Hop          Metric LocPrf Weight Path
7 *> 155.55.0.0      0.0.0.0                0          32768 i
8 *> 192.168.1.0     199.99.1.5                            0 200 300 i
9 *                  192.168.101.1          2      70       0 300 i
10 *> 192.168.2.0    199.99.1.5                            0 200 300 i
11 *                 192.168.101.1          0      70       0 300 i
12 *> 192.168.3.0    199.99.1.5                            0 200 300 i
13 *                 192.168.101.1          1      70       0 300 I
14
15 Moscow#sho ip bgp summary
16 BGP table version is 20, main routing table version 20
17 4 network entries (7/12 paths) using 832 bytes of memory
18 8 BGP path attribute entries using 884 bytes of memory
19 5 BGP route-map cache entries using 80 bytes of memory
20 0 BGP filter-list cache entries using 0 bytes of memory
21
22 Neighbor        V    AS MsgRcvd MsgSent   TblVer  InQ OutQ Up/Down   State/PfxRcd
23 192.168.101.1   4   300      41      36       20    0    0 00:15:46        3
24 199.99.1.5      4   200      25      26       20    0    0 00:18:40        3
25
26 Moscow#sho ip bgp 192.168.1.0
27 BGP routing table entry for 192.168.1.0/24, version 16
28 Paths: (2 available, best #1, advertised over EBGP)
29   200 300
30     199.99.1.5 from 199.99.1.5
31       Origin IGP, localpref 100, valid, external, best
32   300
33     192.168.101.1 from 192.168.101.1 (192.168.5.1)
34       Origin IGP, metric 2, localpref 70, valid, external
35       Community: 19660870
36
37 Moscow#sho ip bgp 192.168.2.0
38 BGP routing table entry for 192.168.2.0/24, version 18
39 Paths: (2 available, best #1, advertised over EBGP)
40   200 300
41     199.99.1.5 from 199.99.1.5
42       Origin IGP, localpref 100, valid, external, best
43   300
44     192.168.101.1 from 192.168.101.1 (192.168.5.1)
45       Origin IGP, metric 0, localpref 70, valid, external
46       Community: 19660870
47 Moscow#sho ip bgp 192.168.3.0
48 BGP routing table entry for 192.168.3.0/24, version 17
49 Paths: (2 available, best #1, advertised over EBGP)
50   200 300
51     199.99.1.5 from 199.99.1.5
52       Origin IGP, localpref 100, valid, external, best
53   300
54     192.168.101.1 from 192.168.101.1 (192.168.5.1)
55       Origin IGP, metric 1, localpref 70, valid, external
56       Community: 19660870
```

**Figure 9-25** Continued

```
57
58 Moscow#sho ip bgp neigh
59 BGP neighbor is 192.168.101.1,  remote AS 300, external link
60   Index 1, Offset 0, Mask 0x2
61   BGP version 4, remote router ID 192.168.5.1
62   BGP state = Established, table version = 20, up for 00:16:29
63   Last read 00:00:29, hold time is 180, keepalive interval is 60 seconds
64   Minimum time between advertisement runs is 30 seconds
65   Received 42 messages, 0 notifications, 0 in queue
66   Sent 37 messages, 0 notifications, 0 in queue
67   Inbound path policy configured
68   Route map for incoming advertisements is set-community
69   Connections established 3; dropped 2
70   Last reset 00:17:00, due to : Peer closing down the session
71   No. of prefix received 3
72 Connection state is ESTAB, I/O status: 1, unread input bytes: 0
73 Local host: 192.168.101.2, Local port: 179
74 Foreign host: 192.168.101.1, Foreign port: 11004
75
76 Enqueued packets for retransmit: 0, input: 0  mis-ordered: 0 (0 bytes)
77
78 Event Timers (current time is 0x449F24):
79 Timer          Starts     Wakeups            Next
80 Retrans          21          0               0x0
81 TimeWait          0          0               0x0
82 AckHold          21          1               0x0
83 SendWnd           0          0               0x0
84 KeepAlive         0          0               0x0
85 GiveUp            0          0               0x0
86 PmtuAger          0          0               0x0
87 DeadWait          0          0               0x0
88
89 iss: 1972740888  snduna: 1972741368  sndnxt: 1972741368    sndwnd:  15905
90 irs: 1983602264  rcvnxt: 1983602813  rcvwnd:        15836  delrcvwnd:   548
91
92 SRTT: 358 ms, RTTO: 1394 ms, RTV: 339 ms, KRTT: 0 ms
93 minRTT: 12 ms, maxRTT: 444 ms, ACK hold: 300 ms
94 Flags: passive open, nagle, gen tcbs
95
96 Datagrams (max data segment is 1460 bytes):
97 Rcvd: 39 (out of order: 0), with data: 21, total data bytes: 548
98 Sent: 22 (retransmit: 0), with data: 20, total data bytes: 479
99
100 BGP neighbor is 199.99.1.5,  remote AS 200, external link
101   Index 2, Offset 0, Mask 0x4
102   BGP version 4, remote router ID 199.99.1.5
103   BGP state = Established, table version = 20, up for 00:19:25
104   Last read 00:00:25, hold time is 180, keepalive interval is 60 seconds
105   Minimum time between advertisement runs is 30 seconds
106   Received 26 messages, 0 notifications, 0 in queue
107   Sent 27 messages, 0 notifications, 0 in queue
108   Connections established 1; dropped 0
109   Last reset never
110   No. of prefix received 3
111 Connection state is ESTAB, I/O status: 1, unread input bytes: 0
112 Local host: 199.99.1.6, Local port: 179
```

```
113 Foreign host: 199.99.1.5, Foreign port: 11000
114
115 Enqueued packets for retransmit: 0, input: 0  mis-ordered: 0 (0 bytes)
116
117 Event Timers (current time is 0x44A5B8):
118 Timer          Starts    Wakeups          Next
119 Retrans            25         0           0x0
120 TimeWait            0         0           0x0
121 AckHold            26         4           0x0
122 SendWnd             0         0           0x0
123 KeepAlive           0         0           0x0
124 GiveUp              0         0           0x0
125 PmtuAger            0         0           0x0
126 DeadWait            0         0           0x0
127
128 iss: 1798965319  snduna: 1798965975  sndnxt: 1798965975    sndwnd:  15729
129 irs: 3676594366  rcvnxt: 3676594967  rcvwnd:      15784 delrcvwnd:    600
130
131 SRTT: 327 ms, RTTO: 1048 ms, RTV: 197 ms, KRTT: 0 ms
132 minRTT: 4 ms, maxRTT: 308 ms, ACK hold: 300 ms
133 Flags: passive open, nagle, gen tcbs
134
135 Datagrams (max data segment is 1460 bytes):
136 Rcvd: 50 (out of order: 0), with data: 26, total data bytes: 600
137 Sent: 29 (retransmit: 0), with data: 24, total data bytes: 655
```

None of the local networks are being distributed, and we identify our BGP neighbors in lines 14 through 16.

Figure 9-29 shows the output of several **show** commands that are useful in reviewing the BGP process.

Lines 1 through 10 is the output of the **show ip bgp** command and shows us that there is only one route to all of our BGP networks. While

**Figure 9-26**   Moscow **show ip protocol** output

```
1 Moscow#sho ip prot
2 Routing Protocol is "bgp 100"
3   Sending updates every 60 seconds, next due in 0 seconds
4   Outgoing update filter list for all interfaces is not set
5   Incoming update filter list for all interfaces is not set
6   IGP synchronization is enabled
7   Automatic route summarization is enabled
8   Neighbor(s):
9     Address           FiltIn FiltOut DistIn DistOut Weight RouteMap
10     192.168.101.1                                         set-community
11     199.99.1.5
12   Routing for Networks:
13     155.55.0.0
14   Routing Information Sources:
15     Gateway         Distance      Last Update
16     192.168.101.1       20        00:15:54
17     199.99.1.5          20        00:00:24
18   Distance: external 20 internal 200 local 200
```

**Figure 9-27**　Continued

```
1 Moscow#sho ip route
2 Codes: C - connected, S - static, I - IGRP, R - RIP, M - mobile, B - BGP
3        D - EIGRP, EX - EIGRP external, O - OSPF, IA - OSPF inter area
4        N1 - OSPF NSSA external type 1, N2 - OSPF NSSA external type 2
5        E1 - OSPF external type 1, E2 - OSPF external type 2, E - EGP
6        i - IS-IS, L1 - IS-IS level-1, L2 - IS-IS level-2, * - candidate default
7        U - per-user static route, o - ODR
8
9 Gateway of last resort is not set
10
11       155.55.0.0/16 is variably subnetted, 2 subnets, 2 masks
12 S        155.55.0.0/16 is directly connected, Serial0
13 C        155.55.1.0/24 is directly connected, Serial0
14       199.99.1.0/30 is subnetted, 1 subnets
15 C        199.99.1.4 is directly connected, Ethernet0
16 B     192.168.1.0/24 [20/0] via 199.99.1.5, 00:00:30
17 B     192.168.2.0/24 [20/0] via 199.99.1.5, 00:00:30
18 B     192.168.3.0/24 [20/0] via 199.99.1.5, 00:00:30
19 C     192.168.101.0/24 is directly connected, Serial1
```

**Figure 9-28**　NewYork configuration

```
1 !
2 hostname NewYork
3 !
4 no ip domain-lookup
5 !
6 interface Ethernet0
7  ip address 199.99.1.5 255.255.255.252
8 !
9 interface Serial1
10  ip address 192.168.100.2 255.255.255.0
11  bandwidth 125
12  clockrate 125000
13 !
14 router bgp 200
15  neighbor 192.168.100.1 remote-as 300
16  neighbor 199.99.1.6 remote-as 100
17 !
18 ip classless
19 !
20 line con 0
21  exec-timeout 0 0
22  length 0
23
24 !
25 end
```

**Figure 9-29** NewYork **show** commands output

```
1  NewYork#sho ip bgp
2  BGP table version is 5, local router ID is 199.99.1.5
3  Status codes: s suppressed, d damped, h history, * valid, > best, i - internal
4  Origin codes: i - IGP, e - EGP, ? - incomplete
5
6     Network          Next Hop          Metric LocPrf Weight Path
7  *> 155.55.0.0       199.99.1.6            0            0 100 i
8  *> 192.168.1.0      192.168.100.1         0            0 300 i
9  *> 192.168.2.0      192.168.100.1         1            0 300 i
10 *> 192.168.3.0      192.168.100.1                      0 300 I
11
12 NewYork#sho ip bgp summary
13 BGP table version is 10, main routing table version 10
14 4 network entries (4/12 paths) using 832 bytes of memory
15 3 BGP path attribute entries using 288 bytes of memory
16 0 BGP route-map cache entries using 0 bytes of memory
17 0 BGP filter-list cache entries using 0 bytes of memory
18
19 Neighbor        V    AS MsgRcvd MsgSent   TblVer  InQ OutQ Up/Down  State/PfxRcd
20 192.168.100.1   4   300      24      22       10    0    0 00:16:11           3
21 199.99.1.6      4   100      24      23       10    0    0 00:16:20           1
22
23 NewYork#sho ip bgp neigh
24 BGP neighbor is 192.168.100.1,  remote AS 300, external link
25  Index 1, Offset 0, Mask 0x2
26   BGP version 4, remote router ID 192.168.6.1
27   BGP state = Established, table version = 10, up for 00:17:10
28   Last read 00:00:10, hold time is 180, keepalive interval is 60 seconds
29   Minimum time between advertisement runs is 30 seconds
30   Received 25 messages, 0 notifications, 0 in queue
31   Sent 23 messages, 0 notifications, 0 in queue
32   Connections established 1; dropped 0
33   Last reset never
34   No. of prefix received 3
35 Connection state is ESTAB, I/O status: 1, unread input bytes: 0
36 Local host: 192.168.100.2, Local port: 179
37 Foreign host: 192.168.100.1, Foreign port: 11001
38
39 Enqueued packets for retransmit: 0, input: 0  mis-ordered: 0 (0 bytes)
40
41 Event Timers (current time is 0x1DE398):
42 Timer      Starts    Wakeups         Next
43 Retrans        23          0         0x0
44 TimeWait        0          0         0x0
45 AckHold        24          3         0x0
46 SendWnd         0          0         0x0
47 KeepAlive       0          0         0x0
48 GiveUp          0          0         0x0
49 PmtuAger        0          0         0x0
50 DeadWait        0          0         0x0
51
52 iss: 3687930750  snduna: 3687931279  sndnxt: 3687931279    sndwnd:  15856
53 irs: 3488874575  rcvnxt: 3488875187  rcvwnd:       15773  delrcvwnd:    611
54
55 SRTT: 342 ms, RTTO: 1178 ms, RTV: 247 ms, KRTT: 0 ms
56 minRTT: 12 ms, maxRTT: 312 ms, ACK hold: 300 ms
```

**Figure 9-29**   *Continued*

```
57 Flags: passive open, nagle, gen tcbs
58
59 Datagrams (max data segment is 1460 bytes):
60 Rcvd: 44 (out of order: 0), with data: 24, total data bytes: 611
61 Sent: 26 (retransmit: 0), with data: 22, total data bytes: 528
62
63 BGP neighbor is 199.99.1.6,  remote AS 100, external link
64  Index 2, Offset 0, Mask 0x4
65   BGP version 4, remote router ID 199.99.1.6
66   BGP state = Established, table version = 10, up for 00:17:21
67   Last read 00:00:21, hold time is 180, keepalive interval is 60 seconds
68   Minimum time between advertisement runs is 30 seconds
69   Received 25 messages, 0 notifications, 0 in queue
70   Sent 24 messages, 0 notifications, 0 in queue
71   Connections established 1; dropped 0
72   Last reset never
73   No. of prefix received 1
74 Connection state is ESTAB, I/O status: 1, unread input bytes: 0
75 Local host: 199.99.1.5, Local port: 11000
76 Foreign host: 199.99.1.6, Foreign port: 179
77
78 Enqueued packets for retransmit: 0, input: 0  mis-ordered: 0 (0 bytes)
79
80 Event Timers (current time is 0x1DEA2C):
81 Timer          Starts    Wakeups           Next
82 Retrans           26         1             0x0
83 TimeWait           0         0             0x0
84 AckHold           22        20             0x0
85 SendWnd            0         0             0x0
86 KeepAlive          0         0             0x0
87 GiveUp             0         0             0x0
88 PmtuAger           0         0             0x0
89 DeadWait           0         0             0x0
90
91 iss: 3676594366  snduna: 3676594929  sndnxt: 3676594929     sndwnd:  15822
92 irs: 1798965319  rcvnxt: 1798965937  rcvwnd:        15767  delrcvwnd:   617
93
94 SRTT: 328 ms, RTTO: 1107 ms, RTV: 225 ms, KRTT: 0 ms
95 minRTT: 8 ms, maxRTT: 304 ms, ACK hold: 300 ms
96 Flags: higher precedence, nagle
97
98 Datagrams (max data segment is 1460 bytes):
99 Rcvd: 27 (out of order: 0), with data: 22, total data bytes: 617
100 Sent: 46 (retransmit: 1), with data: 24, total data bytes: 562
```

**Figure 9-30** NewYork **show ip protocol** output

```
1 NewYork#sho ip prot
2 Routing Protocol is "bgp 200"
3   Sending updates every 60 seconds, next due in 0 seconds
4   Outgoing update filter list for all interfaces is not set
5   Incoming update filter list for all interfaces is not set
6   IGP synchronization is enabled
7   Automatic route summarization is enabled
8   Neighbor(s):
9     Address           FiltIn FiltOut DistIn DistOut Weight RouteMap
10      192.168.100.1
11      199.99.1.6
12   Routing for Networks:
13   Routing Information Sources:
14     Gateway         Distance      Last Update
15     192.168.100.1      20         00:12:31
16     199.99.1.6         20         00:15:24
17   Distance: external 20 internal 200 local 200
```

Moscow knows another pathway to our AS 300 routes, because the local preference for these routes is lower than the local preference known by NewYork, the route updates are not being sent.

Lines 12 through 21 show the output of the **show ip bgp summary** command, and lines 23 through 100, the output of the **show ip bgp neighbor** command.

Figure 9-30 shows the output of the **show ip protocol** command. No special policy is in effect; see lines 10 and 11.

Because we have no internal routing protocol running, the **show ip route** output shown in Figure 31 has only directly connected and BGP-derived routes.

**Figure 9-31** NewYork **show ip route** output

```
1 NewYork#sho ip route
2 Codes: C - connected, S - static, I - IGRP, R - RIP, M - mobile, B - BGP
3        D - EIGRP, EX - EIGRP external, O - OSPF, IA - OSPF inter area
4        N1 - OSPF NSSA external type 1, N2 - OSPF NSSA external type 2
5        E1 - OSPF external type 1, E2 - OSPF external type 2, E - EGP
6        i - IS-IS, L1 - IS-IS level-1, L2 - IS-IS level-2, * - candidate default
7        U - per-user static route, o - ODR
8
9 Gateway of last resort is not set
10
11 B    155.55.0.0/16 [20/0] via 199.99.1.6, 00:15:28
12      199.99.1.0/30 is subnetted, 1 subnets
13 C       199.99.1.4 is directly connected, Ethernet0
14 B    192.168.1.0/24 [20/0] via 192.168.100.1, 00:15:19
15 B    192.168.2.0/24 [20/1] via 192.168.100.1, 00:15:19
16 C    192.168.100.0/24 is directly connected, Serial1
17 B    192.168.3.0/24 [20/0] via 192.168.100.1, 00:12:35
```

**Figure 9-32**  Tokyo configuration

```
1 !
2 hostname Tokyo
3 !
4 no ip domain-lookup
5 !
6 interface Loopback0
7  ip address 192.168.6.1 255.255.255.0
8 !
9 interface Ethernet0
10  ip address 192.168.1.1 255.255.255.0
11 !
12 interface Serial0
13  ip address 192.168.100.1 255.255.255.0
14 !
15 interface Serial1
16  ip address 192.168.3.2 255.255.255.0
17  bandwidth 125
18  clockrate 125000
19 !
20 router rip
21  network 192.168.1.0
22  network 192.168.3.0
23  network 192.168.6.0
24 !
25 router bgp 300
26  network 192.168.1.0
27  network 192.168.2.0
28  neighbor 192.168.5.1 remote-as 300
29  neighbor 192.168.5.1 update-source Loopback0
30  neighbor 192.168.100.2 remote-as 200
31  no auto-summary
32 !
33 ip classless
34 ip route 0.0.0.0 0.0.0.0 192.168.100.2
35 !
36 line con 0
37  exec-timeout 0 0
38  length 0
39 !
40 end
41
```

Now we get to AS 300 where Tokyo is the router with the primary connection to the BGP domain. The configuration for Tokyo is in Figure 9-32.

Lines 20 through 23 define our internal routing protocol as RIP and includes our three connected networks in the RIP process.

Line 34 is our default route pointing to NewYork.

Lines 25 through 31 are where we define the BGP routing process.

We are including networks 192.168.1.0 and 192.168.2.0 in our BGP process on lines 26 and 27. Wait a second. If we look at the routing table for New York (see Figure 9-31), network 192.168.3.0 is in the routing table. Why? The secret lies in the other internal BGP router, Paris. More to come.

Lines 28 and 29 define our internal BGP neighbor, Paris. Line 29 tells the BGP process to use the local Loopback 0 interface address, 192.1.6.1, as the source for all BGP exchanges. Make sure that the neighbor definitions in the two BGP peers point to each other, or a TCP connection for information exchange will not be established.

Line 30 defines our external BGP neighbor New York in AS 200.

Line 31 turns off auto-summarization so that other than class address summarization can take place.

Figure 9-33 shows the output of several show commands that are useful in reviewing the BGP process.

Lines 1 through 12 show the output of the **show ip bgp** command. Line 12 is especially interesting as it shows the route to 192.168.3.0 to Paris at 192.168.2.1 even though the network is directly connected.

Lines 14 through 23, show the output of the **show ip bgp summary** command; lines 25 through 30, the output of the **show ip bgp A.B.C.D** command; and lines 32 through 109, the output of the **show ip bgp neighbor** command.

**Figure 9-33**  Tokyo **show** commands output

```
1 Tokyo#sho ip bgp
2 BGP table version is 5, local router ID is 192.168.6.1
3 Status codes: s suppressed, d damped, h history, * valid, > best, i - internal
4 Origin codes: i - IGP, e - EGP, ? - incomplete
5
6    Network          Next Hop         Metric LocPrf Weight Path
7 *> 155.55.0.0       192.168.100.2                    0 200 100 i
8 * i192.168.1.0      192.168.2.1          2    100     0 i
9 *>                  0.0.0.0              0        32768 i
10 * i192.168.2.0     192.168.5.1          0    100     0 i
11 *>                 192.168.3.1          1        32768 i
12 *>i192.168.3.0     192.168.2.1          1    100     0 I
13
14 Tokyo#sho ip bgp summary
15 BGP table version is 14, main routing table version 14
16 4 network entries (6/12 paths) using 832 bytes of memory
17 6 BGP path attribute entries using 680 bytes of memory
18 0 BGP route-map cache entries using 0 bytes of memory
19 0 BGP filter-list cache entries using 0 bytes of memory
20
21 Neighbor        V    AS MsgRcvd MsgSent  TblVer  InQ OutQ Up/Down  State/PfxRcd
22 192.168.5.1     4   300      38      34      14    0    0 00:11:05            3
23 192.168.100.2   4   200      19      21      14    0    0 00:13:27            1
24
25 Tokyo#sho ip bgp 155.55.2.1
26 BGP routing table entry for 155.55.0.0/16, version 12
```

**Figure 9-33** Continued

```
26 BGP routing table entry for 155.55.0.0/16, version 12
27 Paths: (1 available, best #1, advertised over IBGP)
28   200 100
29     192.168.100.2 from 192.168.100.2 (199.99.1.5)
30       Origin IGP, localpref 100, valid, external, best
31
32 Tokyo#sho ip bgp neigh
33 BGP neighbor is 192.168.5.1,  remote AS 300, internal link
34  Index 0, Offset 0, Mask 0x0
35   BGP version 4, remote router ID 192.168.5.1
36   BGP state = Established, table version = 14, up for 00:11:24
37   Last read 00:00:24, hold time is 180, keepalive interval is 60 seconds
38   Minimum time between advertisement runs is 5 seconds
39   Received 38 messages, 0 notifications, 0 in queue
40   Sent 34 messages, 0 notifications, 0 in queue
41   Connections established 3; dropped 2
42   Last reset 00:11:31, due to : Peer closing down the session
43   No. of prefix received 3
44 Connection state is ESTAB, I/O status: 1, unread input bytes: 0
45 Local host: 192.168.6.1, Local port: 179
46 Foreign host: 192.168.5.1, Foreign port: 11003
47
48 Enqueued packets for retransmit: 0, input: 0  mis-ordered: 0 (0 bytes)
49
50 Event Timers (current time is 0x17BDFC):
51 Timer          Starts    Wakeups          Next
52 Retrans          16         0             0x0
53 TimeWait          0         0             0x0
54 AckHold          16         2             0x0
55 SendWnd           0         0             0x0
56 KeepAlive         0         0             0x0
57 GiveUp            0         0             0x0
58 PmtuAger          0         0             0x0
59 DeadWait          0         0             0x0
60
61 iss: 3631258491  snduna: 3631258931  sndnxt: 3631258931    sndwnd:  15945
62 irs: 1961530939  rcvnxt: 1961531381  rcvwnd:       15943  delrcvwnd:   441
63
64 SRTT: 394 ms, RTTO: 1960 ms, RTV: 586 ms, KRTT: 0 ms
65 minRTT: 12 ms, maxRTT: 320 ms, ACK hold: 300 ms
66 Flags: passive open, nagle, gen tcbs
67
68 Datagrams (max data segment is 556 bytes):
69 Rcvd: 31 (out of order: 0), with data: 16, total data bytes: 441
70 Sent: 18 (retransmit: 0), with data: 15, total data bytes: 439
71
72 BGP neighbor is 192.168.100.2,  remote AS 200, external link
73  Index 1, Offset 0, Mask 0x2
74   BGP version 4, remote router ID 199.99.1.5
75   BGP state = Established, table version = 14, up for 00:13:48
76   Last read 00:00:48, hold time is 180, keepalive interval is 60 seconds
77   Minimum time between advertisement runs is 30 seconds
78   Received 19 messages, 0 notifications, 0 in queue
79   Sent 21 messages, 0 notifications, 0 in queue
80   Connections established 1; dropped 0
```

```
81   Last reset never
82   No. of prefix received 1
83  Connection state is ESTAB, I/O status: 1, unread input bytes: 0
84  Local host: 192.168.100.1, Local port: 11001
85  Foreign host: 192.168.100.2, Foreign port: 179
86
87  Enqueued packets for retransmit: 0, input: 0  mis-ordered: 0 (0 bytes)
88
89  Event Timers (current time is 0x17C494):
90  Timer          Starts     Wakeups          Next
91  Retrans           21           0           0x0
92  TimeWait           0           0           0x0
93  AckHold           18          14           0x0
94  SendWnd            0           0           0x0
95  KeepAlive          0           0           0x0
96  GiveUp             0           0           0x0
97  PmtuAger           0           0           0x0
98  DeadWait           0           0           0x0
99
100 iss: 3488874575  snduna: 3488875111  sndnxt: 3488875111     sndwnd:   15849
101 irs: 3687930750  rcvnxt: 3687931203  rcvwnd:     15932  delrcvwnd:    452
102
103 SRTT: 343 ms, RTTO: 1353 ms, RTV: 333 ms, KRTT: 0 ms
104 minRTT: 16 ms, maxRTT: 316 ms, ACK hold: 300 ms
105 Flags: higher precedence, nagle
106
107 Datagrams (max data segment is 1460 bytes):
108 Rcvd: 22 (out of order: 0), with data: 18, total data bytes: 452
109 Sent: 36 (retransmit: 0), with data: 20, total data bytes: 535
```

Figure 9-34 is the output of the **show ip protocol** command and shows our two routing protocols, RIP, and BGP.

Lines 33 and 34 show us that our local BGP process is only routing for networks 192.168.1.0 and 192.168.2.0. The mystery of network 192.168.3.0 deepens.

The output of the **show ip route** command is shown in Figure 9-35.

Line 11 shows our BGP route to our target network 155.55.0.0 through New York.

Line 18 shows us our default route pointing to New York.

London is in the interior of our RIP domain, and the configuration is shown in Figure 9-36.

Just to make sure that we have full connectivity to our target network 155.55.0.0, the trace command output is shown in Figure 9-37.

Figure 9-38 details the RIP routing process for London.

Figure 9-39 shows the output of the **show ip route** command. After about 19 examples, it's really hard to come up with new stuff.

**Figure 9-34**    Tokyo **show ip protocol** output

```
1  Tokyo#sho ip protocol
2  Routing Protocol is "rip"
3    Sending updates every 30 seconds, next due in 20 seconds
4    Invalid after 180 seconds, hold down 180, flushed after 240
5    Outgoing update filter list for all interfaces is not set
6    Incoming update filter list for all interfaces is not set
7    Redistributing: rip
8    Default version control: send version 1, receive any version
9      Interface        Send  Recv   Key-chain
10     Ethernet0          1    1 2
11     Loopback0          1    1 2
12     Serial1            1    1 2
13    Routing for Networks:
14      192.168.1.0
15      192.168.3.0
16      192.168.6.0
17    Routing Information Sources:
18     Gateway          Distance      Last Update
19     192.168.3.1          120       00:00:04
20    Distance: (default is 120)
21
22 Routing Protocol is "bgp 300"
23   Sending updates every 60 seconds, next due in 0 seconds
24   Outgoing update filter list for all interfaces is not set
25   Incoming update filter list for all interfaces is not set
26   IGP synchronization is enabled
27   Automatic route summarization is disabled
28   Neighbor(s):
29     Address            FiltIn FiltOut DistIn DistOut Weight RouteMap
30     192.168.5.1
31     192.168.100.2
32    Routing for Networks:
33      192.168.1.0
34      192.168.2.0
35    Routing Information Sources:
36     Gateway          Distance      Last Update
37     192.168.100.2        20        00:10:01
38     192.168.5.1         200        00:09:32
39    Distance: external 20 internal 200 local 200
```

Paris is the site of our secondary BGP connection, and the configuration is shown in Figure 9-40. This is where the most complex configuration tasks must take place, as this router has to implement both the BGP and the interior routing protocol policies.

Lines 16 through 19 define the RIP routing process, with the local network statements, and on line 17, the command **offset-list 0 out 5**. This command provides the routing protocol RIP, with a five-hop bump for all the routes being advertised to the rest of the RIP network. This

**Figure 9-35** Tokyo **show ip route** output

```
1 Tokyo#sho ip route
2 Codes: C - connected, S - static, I - IGRP, R - RIP, M - mobile, B - BGP
3        D - EIGRP, EX - EIGRP external, O - OSPF, IA - OSPF inter area
4        N1 - OSPF NSSA external type 1, N2 - OSPF NSSA external type 2
5        E1 - OSPF external type 1, E2 - OSPF external type 2, E - EGP
6        i - IS-IS, L1 - IS-IS level-1, L2 - IS-IS level-2, * - candidate default
7        U - per-user static route, o - ODR
8
9 Gateway of last resort is 192.168.100.2 to network 0.0.0.0
10
11 B    155.55.0.0/16 [20/0] via 192.168.100.2, 00:10:12
12 R    192.168.5.0/24 [120/7] via 192.168.3.1, 00:00:16, Serial1
13 C    192.168.6.0/24 is directly connected, Loopback0
14 C    192.168.1.0/24 is directly connected, Ethernet0
15 R    192.168.2.0/24 [120/1] via 192.168.3.1, 00:00:16, Serial1
16 C    192.168.100.0/24 is directly connected, Serial0
17 C    192.168.3.0/24 is directly connected, Serial1
18 S*   0.0.0.0/0 [1/0] via 192.168.100.2
```

makes all Paris's routes advertised in the RIP domain less significant, because there is a default route to Moscow in the BGP network that could interfere with our primary/secondary policy.

Line 34 is the static default route that directs all destinations not in the routing table to our external neighbor Moscow. If we left out the

**Figure 9-36** London configuration

```
1 !
2 hostname London
3 !
4 no ip domain-lookup
5 !
6 interface Ethernet0
7  ip address 192.168.2.1 255.255.255.0
8 !
9 interface Serial0
10  ip address 192.168.3.1 255.255.255.0
11  bandwidth 125
12 !
13 router rip
14  network 192.168.3.0
15  network 192.168.2.0
16 !
17 ip classless
18 !
19 line con 0
20  exec-timeout 0 0
21  length 0
22 !
23 end
```

**Figure 9-37** London **trace** output

```
1 London#trace
2 Protocol [ip]:
3 Target IP address: 155.55.2.1
4 Source address: 192.168.2.1
5 Numeric display [n]:
6 Timeout in seconds [3]:
7 Probe count [3]:
8 Minimum Time to Live [1]:
9 Maximum Time to Live [30]:
10 Port Number [33434]:
11 Loose, Strict, Record, Timestamp, Verbose[none]:
12 Type escape sequence to abort.
13 Tracing the route to 155.55.2.1
14
15   1 192.168.3.2 8 msec 8 msec 8 msec
16   2 192.168.100.2 16 msec 16 msec 16 msec
17   3 199.99.1.6 20 msec 20 msec 20 msec
18   4 155.55.1.2 28 msec *  28 msec
```

**Figure 9-38** London **show ip protocol** output

```
1 London#sho ip prot
2 Routing Protocol is "rip"
3   Sending updates every 30 seconds, next due in 9 seconds
4   Invalid after 180 seconds, hold down 180, flushed after 240
5   Outgoing update filter list for all interfaces is not set
6   Incoming update filter list for all interfaces is not set
7   Redistributing: rip
8   Default version control: send version 1, receive any version
9     Interface        Send  Recv  Key-chain
10    Ethernet0         1    1 2
11    Serial0           1    1 2
12    Routing for Networks:
13      192.168.3.0
14      192.168.2.0
15    Routing Information Sources:
16      Gateway         Distance      Last Update
17      192.168.3.2        120        00:00:00
18    Distance: (default is 120)
```

**Figure 9-39** London **show ip route** output

```
1 London#sho ip route
2 Codes: C - connected, S - static, I - IGRP, R - RIP, M - mobile, B - BGP
3        D - EIGRP, EX - EIGRP external, O - OSPF, IA - OSPF inter area
4        N1 - OSPF NSSA external type 1, N2 - OSPF NSSA external type 2
5        E1 - OSPF external type 1, E2 - OSPF external type 2, E - EGP
6        i - IS-IS, L1 - IS-IS level-1, L2 - IS-IS level-2, * - candidate default
7        U - per-user static route, o - ODR
8
9 Gateway of last resort is 192.168.3.2 to network 0.0.0.0
10
11 R    192.168.1.0/24 [120/1] via 192.168.3.2, 00:00:03, Serial0
12 C    192.168.2.0/24 is directly connected, Ethernet0
13 C    192.168.3.0/24 is directly connected, Serial0
14 R*   0.0.0.0/0 [120/1] via 192.168.3.2, 00:00:04, Serial0
```

**Figure 9-40** Paris configuration

```
1  !
2  hostname Paris
3  !
4  no ip domain-lookup
5  !
6  interface Loopback0
7   ip address 192.168.5.1 255.255.255.0
8  !
9  interface Ethernet0
10  ip address 192.168.2.2 255.255.255.0
11 !
12 interface Serial0
13  ip address 192.168.101.1 255.255.255.0
14  bandwidth 125
15 !
16 router rip
17  offset-list 0 out 5
18  network 192.168.2.0
19  network 192.168.5.0
20 !
21 router bgp 300
22  network 192.168.1.0
23  network 192.168.2.0
24  network 192.168.3.0
25  neighbor 192.168.6.1 remote-as 300
26  neighbor 192.168.6.1 update-source Loopback0
27  neighbor 192.168.6.1 weight 50
28  neighbor 192.168.101.2 remote-as 100
29  neighbor 192.168.101.2 send-community
30  neighbor 192.168.101.2 route-map set-community out
31  no auto-summary
32 !
33 ip classless
34 ip route 0.0.0.0 0.0.0.0 192.168.101.2 190
35 access-list 1 permit any
36 route-map set-community permit 10
37  match ip address 1
38  set community 19660870
39 !
40 line con 0
41  exec-timeout 0 0
42  length 0
43 !
44 end
```

190 at the end of line 34, then all unknown destinations that enter Paris would be routed to Moscow. The 190 is the Administrative Distance that we assigned to the static route to make it a floating static route, active only when a dynamic route table entry to 0.0.0.0 is not present.

Lines 21 through 31 define our BGP routing process.

Line 24 is where the mystery of 192.168.3.0 is solved. Even though there was no network statement for this network in Tokyo, and 192.168.3.0 is not directly attached to Paris, the network statement in BGP will advertise the route if there is an active route in the local router routing table. Remember, if there are multiple exit points in a primary/secondary situation, both connection points must look the same to the outside world.

Lines 25 and 26 define our interior BGP neighbor connection to Tokyo where we are using our Loopback 0 address as the source address for the BGP routing updates. It is extremely important that interior BGP peers use each other's source IP address when defining each other as BGP peers.

If you look at the network diagram, it is obvious that the shortest connection to our target network of 155.55.0.0 is through Moscow. As Paris has to take a secondary role, we need a mechanism to make the routes generated by Paris less important than the routes generated by Tokyo. Line 27 is how we accomplish this task, by assigning a local weight of 50 to our neighbor Tokyo. This is a Cisco feature, the default is 0, and the highest number wins. By setting up Tokyo with a weight of 50, the routes through Tokyo will be preferred over local BGP routes in Paris.

Lines 28 through 30 define our secondary neighbor connection to Moscow.

Line 29 is where we initiate the policy routing process. The **send-community neighbor** option is the initial step to initiate policy routing by including a community number with the routes identified by the route map identified in line 30.

Lines 36 through 38 define our routing policy. Any route that matches the IP addresses defined in **access-list 1** will have the community number of 19660870 included in any updates sent to Moscow. See the narrative for Figure 9-23, the Moscow configuration, for a more detailed description of how the policy gets activated in Moscow. Line 35 defines access-list 1 as all IP addresses, so when routes from Paris head out to Moscow, they will include the community number.

To make sure that our policy is being implemented, we will use the **trace** command as shown in Figure 9-41 to verify that we are going through Tokyo to reach our destination.

**Figure 9-41** Paris **trace** output

```
1 Paris#trace 155.55.2.1
2
3 Type escape sequence to abort.
4 Tracing the route to 155.55.2.1
5
6   1 192.168.2.1 4 msec 4 msec 4 msec
7   2 192.168.3.2 12 msec 12 msec 12 msec
8   3 192.168.100.2 24 msec 20 msec 20 msec
9   4 199.99.1.6 20 msec 20 msec 20 msec
10  5 155.55.1.2 [AS 100] 32 msec *  28 msec
```

Figure 9-42 shows the output of the **show route-map** command on lines 1 through 7 and the **show access-list** on lines 9 through 11.

FYI: Line 4 is the best place for checking IP address matching, for the correct access-lists in use. If the statement looks like **ip address {access-lists}: list 1,** then the match statement will look for access-list **list.** If **list**, a named access-list, is not found, then all IP addresses will be considered a match, and your policy may not work properly.

Lines 1 through 13 of Figure 9-43 show the output of the **show ip bgp** command. Lines 7 and 8 deserve a close look. Under the weight column, line 7, the route to 155.55.0.0 through Moscow has a weight of 0, and the weight on line 8, the route to 155.55.0.0 through New York, has a weight of 50. The higher the weight, the better the route. Refer to the 10 rules for route selection earlier in this chapter.

**Figure 9-42** Paris policy information

```
1 Paris#sho route-map
2 route-map set-community, permit, sequence 10
3   Match clauses:
4     ip address (access-lists): 1
5   Set clauses:
6     community 19660870
7   Policy routing matches: 0 packets, 0 bytes
8
9 Paris#sho access-list
10 Standard IP access list 1
11     permit any
```

**Figure 9-43** Paris **show** commands output

```
1  Paris#sho ip bgp
2  BGP table version is 6, local router ID is 192.168.5.1
3  Status codes: s suppressed, d damped, h history, * valid, > best, i - internal
4  Origin codes: i - IGP, e - EGP, ? - incomplete
5
6    Network          Next Hop        Metric LocPrf Weight Path
7  *  155.55.0.0       192.168.101.2        0               0 100 i
8  *>i                 192.168.100.2              100       50 200 100 i
9  *  i192.168.1.0     192.168.6.1          0    100       50 i
10 *>                  192.168.2.1          2            32768 i
11 *> 192.168.2.0      0.0.0.0              0            32768 i
12 *  i                192.168.3.1          1    100       50 i
13 *> 192.168.3.0      192.168.2.1          1            32768 I
14
15 Paris#sho ip bgp summary
16 BGP table version is 8, main routing table version 8
17 4 network entries (7/12 paths) using 832 bytes of memory
18 7 BGP path attribute entries using 744 bytes of memory
19 0 BGP route-map cache entries using 0 bytes of memory
20 0 BGP filter-list cache entries using 0 bytes of memory
21
22 Neighbor        V    AS MsgRcvd MsgSent   TblVer  InQ OutQ Up/Down  State/PfxRcd
23 192.168.6.1     4   300      29      33        8    0    0 00:06:12          3
24 192.168.101.2   4   100      26      31        8    0    0 00:05:50          1
25
26 Paris#sho ip bgp 155.55.2.1
27 BGP routing table entry for 155.55.0.0/16, version 4
28 Paths: (2 available, best #2)
29   100
30     192.168.101.2 from 192.168.101.2 (199.99.1.6)
31       Origin IGP, metric 0, localpref 100, valid, external
32   200 100
33     192.168.100.2 (metric 2) from 192.168.6.1
34       Origin IGP, localpref 100, weight 50, valid, internal, best
35
36 Paris#sho ip bgp neighb
37 BGP neighbor is 192.168.6.1,  remote AS 300, internal link
38  Index 0, Offset 0, Mask 0x0
39  BGP version 4, remote router ID 192.168.6.1
40  BGP state = Established, table version = 8, up for 00:04:32
41  Last read 00:00:32, hold time is 180, keepalive interval is 60 seconds
42  Minimum time between advertisement runs is 5 seconds
43  Received 27 messages, 0 notifications, 0 in queue
44  Sent 31 messages, 0 notifications, 0 in queue
45  Default weight 50
46  Connections established 3; dropped 2
47  Last reset 00:04:40, due to : User reset request
48  No. of prefix received 3
49 Connection state is ESTAB, I/O status: 1, unread input bytes: 0
50 Local host: 192.168.5.1, Local port: 11003
51 Foreign host: 192.168.6.1, Foreign port: 179
52
53 Enqueued packets for retransmit: 0, input: 0  mis-ordered: 0 (0 bytes)
54
55 Event Timers (current time is 0x398214):
56 Timer           Starts   Wakeups            Next
```

```
57 Retrans              10          0           0x0
58 TimeWait              0          0           0x0
59 AckHold               8          6           0x0
60 SendWnd               0          0           0x0
61 KeepAlive             0          0           0x0
62 GiveUp                0          0           0x0
63 PmtuAger              0          0           0x0
64 DeadWait              0          0           0x0
65
66 iss: 1961530939  snduna: 1961531248  sndnxt: 1961531248   sndwnd:  16076
67 irs: 3631258491  rcvnxt: 3631258798  rcvwnd:        16078 delrcvwnd:  306
68
69 SRTT: 486 ms, RTTO: 3289 ms, RTV: 1158 ms, KRTT: 0 ms
70 minRTT: 16 ms, maxRTT: 320 ms, ACK hold: 300 ms
71 Flags: higher precedence, nagle
72
73 Datagrams (max data segment is 556 bytes):
74 Rcvd: 11 (out of order: 0), with data: 8, total data bytes: 306
75 Sent: 17 (retransmit: 0), with data: 9, total data bytes: 308
76
77 BGP neighbor is 192.168.101.2,  remote AS 100, external link
78   Index 1, Offset 0, Mask 0x2
79   Community attribute sent to this neighbor
80   BGP version 4, remote router ID 199.99.1.6
81   BGP state = Established, table version = 8, up for 00:04:12
82   Last read 00:00:12, hold time is 180, keepalive interval is 60 seconds
83   Minimum time between advertisement runs is 30 seconds
84   Received 25 messages, 0 notifications, 0 in queue
85   Sent 30 messages, 0 notifications, 0 in queue
86   Outbound path policy configured
87   Route map for outgoing advertisements is set-community
88   Connections established 3; dropped 2
89   Last reset 00:04:42, due to : User reset request
90   No. of prefix received 1
91 Connection state is ESTAB, I/O status: 1, unread input bytes: 0
92 Local host: 192.168.101.1, Local port: 11004
93 Foreign host: 192.168.101.2, Foreign port: 179
94
95 Enqueued packets for retransmit: 0, input: 0  mis-ordered: 0 (0 bytes)
96
97 Event Timers (current time is 0x398AC8):
98 Timer           Starts    Wakeups         Next
99 Retrans              10          0          0x0
100 TimeWait             0          0          0x0
101 AckHold              8          4          0x0
102 SendWnd              0          0          0x0
103 KeepAlive            0          0          0x0
104 GiveUp               0          0          0x0
105 PmtuAger             0          0          0x0
106 DeadWait             0          0          0x0
107
108 iss: 1983602264  snduna: 1983602585  sndnxt: 1983602585   sndwnd:  16064
109 irs: 1972740888  rcvnxt: 1972741140  rcvwnd:        16133 delrcvwnd:  251
110
111 SRTT: 485 ms, RTTO: 3285 ms, RTV: 1157 ms, KRTT: 0 ms
112 minRTT: 12 ms, maxRTT: 320 ms, ACK hold: 300 ms
113 Flags: higher precedence, nagle
114
115 Datagrams (max data segment is 1460 bytes):
116 Rcvd: 10 (out of order: 0), with data: 8, total data bytes: 251
117 Sent: 15 (retransmit: 0), with data: 9, total data bytes: 320
```

**Figure 9-44**   Paris **show ip protocol** output

```
1 Paris#sho ip prot
2 Routing Protocol is "rip"
3   Sending updates every 30 seconds, next due in 23 seconds
4   Invalid after 180 seconds, hold down 180, flushed after 240
5   Outgoing update filter list for all interfaces is not set
6   Incoming update filter list for all interfaces is not set
7   Outgoing routes will have 5 added to metric
8   Redistributing: rip
9   Default version control: send version 1, receive any version
10      Interface        Send  Recv   Key-chain
11      Ethernet0        1     1 2
12      Loopback0        1     1 2
13   Routing for Networks:
14      192.168.2.0
15      192.168.5.0
16   Routing Information Sources:
17      Gateway          Distance      Last Update
18      192.168.2.1          120       00:00:22
19   Distance: (default is 120)
20
21 Routing Protocol is "bgp 300"
22   Sending updates every 60 seconds, next due in 0 seconds
23   Outgoing update filter list for all interfaces is not set
24   Incoming update filter list for all interfaces is not set
25   IGP synchronization is enabled
26   Automatic route summarization is disabled
27   Neighbor(s):
28      Address             FiltIn FiltOut DistIn DistOut Weight RouteMap
29      192.168.6.1                                         50
30      192.168.101.2
31   Routing for Networks:
32      192.168.1.0
33      192.168.2.0
34      192.168.3.0
35   Routing Information Sources:
36      Gateway          Distance      Last Update
37      192.168.101.2        20        00:07:58
38      192.168.6.1          200       00:02:36
39   Distance: external 20 internal 200 local 200
```

Lines 15 through 24 show the output of the **show ip bgp summary** command.

Lines 26 through 34 show the output of the **show ip bgp A.B.C.D** command. Lines 32 through 34 also indicate the best route, with the weight factor set to 50 on line 34.

**Figure 9-45**   Paris **show ip route** output

```
1 Paris#sho ip route
2 Codes: C - connected, S - static, I - IGRP, R - RIP, M - mobile, B - BGP
3         D - EIGRP, EX - EIGRP external, O - OSPF, IA - OSPF inter area
4         N1 - OSPF NSSA external type 1, N2 - OSPF NSSA external type 2
5         E1 - OSPF external type 1, E2 - OSPF external type 2, E - EGP
6         i - IS-IS, L1 - IS-IS level-1, L2 - IS-IS level-2, * - candidate default
7         U - per-user static route, o - ODR
8
9 Gateway of last resort is 192.168.2.1 to network 0.0.0.0
10
11 C    192.168.5.0/24 is directly connected, Loopback0
12 R    192.168.6.0/24 [120/2] via 192.168.2.1, 00:00:08, Ethernet0
13 R    192.168.1.0/24 [120/2] via 192.168.2.1, 00:00:08, Ethernet0
14 C    192.168.2.0/24 is directly connected, Ethernet0
15 R    192.168.3.0/24 [120/1] via 192.168.2.1, 00:00:08, Ethernet0
16 C    192.168.101.0/24 is directly connected, Serial0
17 R*   0.0.0.0/0 [120/2] via 192.168.2.1, 00:00:08, Ethernet0
```

Lines 36 through 117 show the output of the **show ip bgp neighbor** command.

Figure 9-44 has the output of the **show ip protocol** command. Line 34 is the anomaly we noted before that allows our internal serial segment to make it out to the BGP domain.

The **show ip route** output is shown in Figure 9-45, all paths lead to Tokyo. I thought all paths lead to Rome?

Primary-Link-to-Secondary-Link Switchover

To test whether our policy works, the primary link, from AS 300 to our BGP domain, is shut down. Figures 9-46 through 9-50 are outputs of **show** commands and traces from all the routers except Rome, our target network.

You can see by the number of **show ip route** commands and **ping** tests, that waiting for Godot, oops, I mean RIP, to converge was a frustrating process. Two solutions to speed up the process are to issue **clear ip route** * commands on all interior routers or to switch to either OSPF or EIGRP.

**Figure 9-46**   NewYork after primary-link failure

```
1 NewYork#sho ip bgp
2 BGP table version is 12, local router ID is 199.99.1.5
3 Status codes: s suppressed, d damped, h history, * valid, > best, i - internal
4 Origin codes: i - IGP, e - EGP, ? - incomplete
5
6    Network          Next Hop        Metric LocPrf Weight Path
7 *> 155.55.0.0       199.99.1.6         0           0 100 i
8 *> 192.168.1.0      199.99.1.6                     0 100 300 i
9 *> 192.168.2.0      199.99.1.6                     0 100 300 i
10 *> 192.168.3.0      199.99.1.6                    0 100 300 i
11
12 NewYork#sho ip bgp 155.55.0.0
13 BGP routing table entry for 155.55.0.0/16, version 4
14 Paths: (1 available, best #1, advertised over EBGP)
15   100
16     199.99.1.6 from 199.99.1.6
17       Origin IGP, metric 0, localpref 100, valid, external, best
18
19 NewYork#sho ip bgp 192.168.2.0
20 BGP routing table entry for 192.168.2.0/24, version 12
21 Paths: (1 available, best #1, advertised over EBGP)
22   100 300
23     199.99.1.6 from 199.99.1.6
24       Origin IGP, localpref 100, valid, external, best
25
26 NewYork#sho ip route
27 Codes: C - connected, S - static, I - IGRP, R - RIP, M - mobile, B - BGP
28        D - EIGRP, EX - EIGRP external, O - OSPF, IA - OSPF inter area
29        N1 - OSPF NSSA external type 1, N2 - OSPF NSSA external type 2
30        E1 - OSPF external type 1, E2 - OSPF external type 2, E - EGP
31        i - IS-IS, L1 - IS-IS level-1, L2 - IS-IS level-2, * - candidate default
32        U - per-user static route, o - ODR
33
34 Gateway of last resort is not set
35
36 B    155.55.0.0/16 [20/0] via 199.99.1.6, 00:18:51
37      199.99.1.0/30 is subnetted, 1 subnets
38 C      199.99.1.4 is directly connected, Ethernet0
39 B    192.168.1.0/24 [20/0] via 199.99.1.6, 00:05:13
40 B    192.168.2.0/24 [20/0] via 199.99.1.6, 00:05:13
41 B    192.168.3.0/24 [20/0] via 199.99.1.6, 00:05:14
42
43 NewYork#trace 192.168.2.1
44
45 Type escape sequence to abort.
46 Tracing the route to 192.168.2.1
47
48   1 199.99.1.6 4 msec 4 msec 4 msec
49   2 192.168.101.1 12 msec 12 msec 12 msec
50   3 192.168.2.1 [AS 300] 16 msec *  12 msec
```

**Figure 9-47**  Moscow after primary-link failure

```
1 Moscow#sho ip bgp
2 BGP table version is 15, local router ID is 199.99.1.6
3 Status codes: s suppressed, d damped, h history, * valid, > best, i - internal
4 Origin codes: i - IGP, e - EGP, ? - incomplete
5
6    Network          Next Hop         Metric LocPrf Weight Path
7 *> 155.55.0.0       0.0.0.0               0        32768 i
8 *> 192.168.1.0      192.168.101.1         2     70     0 300 i
9 *> 192.168.2.0      192.168.101.1         0     70     0 300 i
10 *> 192.168.3.0     192.168.101.1         1     70     0 300 i
11
12 Moscow#sho ip bgp 192.168.2.0
13 BGP routing table entry for 192.168.2.0/24, version 14
14 Paths: (1 available, best #1, advertised over EBGP)
15   300
16     192.168.101.1 from 192.168.101.1 (192.168.5.1)
17       Origin IGP, metric 0, localpref 70, valid, external, best
18       Community: 19660870
19
20 Moscow#sho ip route
21 Codes: C - connected, S - static, I - IGRP, R - RIP, M - mobile, B - BGP
22        D - EIGRP, EX - EIGRP external, O - OSPF, IA - OSPF inter area
23        N1 - OSPF NSSA external type 1, N2 - OSPF NSSA external type 2
24        E1 - OSPF external type 1, E2 - OSPF external type 2, E - EGP
25        i - IS-IS, L1 - IS-IS level-1, L2 - IS-IS level-2, * - candidate default
26        U - per-user static route, o - ODR
27
28 Gateway of last resort is not set
29
30      155.55.0.0/24 is subnetted, 1 subnets
31 S       155.55.0.0/16 is directly connected, Serial0
32 C       155.55.1.0 is is directly connected, Serial0
33      199.99.1.0/30 is subnetted, 1 subnets
34 C       199.99.1.4 is directly connected, Ethernet0
35 B    192.168.1.0/24 [20/2] via 192.168.101.1, 00:02:51
36 B    192.168.2.0/24 [20/0] via 192.168.101.1, 00:02:51
37 B    192.168.3.0/24 [20/1] via 192.168.101.1, 00:02:51
38 C    192.168.101.0/24 is directly connected, Serial1
39
40 Moscow#trace 192.168.2.1
41
42 Type escape sequence to abort.
43 Tracing the route to 192.168.2.1
44
45   1 192.168.101.1 12 msec 12 msec 12 msec
46   2 192.168.2.1 [AS 300] 20 msec *   8 msec
```

**Figure 9-48** *Paris after primary-link failure*

```
1 Paris#sho ip bgp
2 BGP table version is 7, local router ID is 192.168.5.1
3 Status codes: s suppressed, d damped, h history, * valid, > best, i - internal
4 Origin codes: i - IGP, e - EGP, ? - incomplete
5
6    Network          Next Hop         Metric LocPrf Weight Path
7 *> 155.55.0.0       192.168.101.2    0                 0 100 i
8 * i192.168.1.0      192.168.6.1      0        100     50 i
9 *>                  192.168.2.1      2             32768 i
10 *> 192.168.2.0     0.0.0.0          0             32768 i
11 * i                192.168.3.1      1        100     50 i
12 *> 192.168.3.0     192.168.2.1      1             32768 i
13
14 Paris#sho ip bgp 155.55.0.0
15 BGP routing table entry for 155.55.0.0/16, version 7
16 Paths: (1 available, best #1, advertised over IBGP)
17    100
18      192.168.101.2 from 192.168.101.2 (199.99.1.6)
19        Origin IGP, metric 0, localpref 100, valid, external, best
20
21 Paris#sho ip route
22 Codes: C - connected, S - static, I - IGRP, R - RIP, M - mobile, B - BGP
23        D - EIGRP, EX - EIGRP external, O - OSPF, IA - OSPF inter area
24        N1 - OSPF NSSA external type 1, N2 - OSPF NSSA external type 2
25        E1 - OSPF external type 1, E2 - OSPF external type 2, E - EGP
26        i - IS-IS, L1 - IS-IS level-1, L2 - IS-IS level-2, * - candidate default
27        U - per-user static route, o - ODR
28
29 Gateway of last resort is 192.168.101.2 to network 0.0.0.0
30
31 B    155.55.0.0/16 [20/0] via 192.168.101.2, 00:07:25
32 C    192.168.5.0/24 is directly connected, Loopback0
33 R    192.168.6.0/24 [120/2] via 192.168.2.1, 00:00:05, Ethernet0
34 R    192.168.1.0/24 [120/2] via 192.168.2.1, 00:00:05, Ethernet0
35 C    192.168.2.0/24 is directly connected, Ethernet0
36 R    192.168.3.0/24 [120/1] via 192.168.2.1, 00:00:05, Ethernet0
37 C    192.168.101.0/24 is directly connected, Serial0
38 S*   0.0.0.0/0 [190/0] via 192.168.101.2
39
40 Paris#trace 155.55.2.1
41
42 Type escape sequence to abort.
43 Tracing the route to 155.55.2.1
44
45   1 192.168.101.2 8 msec 12 msec 12 msec
46   2 155.55.1.2 [AS 100] 20 msec *  16 msec
47
48 Paris#trace 192.168.2.1
49
50 Type escape sequence to abort.
51 Tracing the route to 192.168.2.1
52
53   1 192.168.2.1 4 msec *  4 msec
54
55 Paris#trace 192.168.3.2
```

```
56
57 Type escape sequence to abort.
58 Tracing the route to 192.168.3.2
59
60   1 192.168.2.1 4 msec 4 msec 0 msec
61   2 192.168.3.2 16 msec *  12 msec
62
```

**Figure 9-49**  London after primary-link failure

```
1 London#sho ip route
2 Codes: C - connected, S - static, I - IGRP, R - RIP, M - mobile, B - BGP
3        D - EIGRP, EX - EIGRP external, O - OSPF, IA - OSPF inter area
4        N1 - OSPF NSSA external type 1, N2 - OSPF NSSA external type 2
5        E1 - OSPF external type 1, E2 - OSPF external type 2, E - EGP
6        i - IS-IS, L1 - IS-IS level-1, L2 - IS-IS level-2, * - candidate default
7        U - per-user static route, o - ODR
8
9 Gateway of last resort is 192.168.3.2 to network 0.0.0.0
10
11 R      192.168.5.0/24 [120/6] via 192.168.2.2, 00:00:10, Ethernet0
12 R      192.168.6.0/24 [120/1] via 192.168.3.2, 00:00:23, Serial0
13 R      192.168.1.0/24 [120/1] via 192.168.3.2, 00:00:23, Serial0
14 C      192.168.2.0/24 is directly connected, Ethernet0
15 C      192.168.3.0/24 is directly connected, Serial0
16 R*     0.0.0.0/0 [120/1] via 192.168.3.2, 00:03:11, Serial0
17
18 London#ping 155.55.2.1
19
20 Type escape sequence to abort.
21 Sending 5, 100-byte ICMP Echos to 155.55.2.1, timeout is 2 seconds:
22 .....
23 Success rate is 0 percent (0/5)
24
25 London#sho ip route
26 Codes: C - connected, S - static, I - IGRP, R - RIP, M - mobile, B - BGP
27        D - EIGRP, EX - EIGRP external, O - OSPF, IA - OSPF inter area
28        N1 - OSPF NSSA external type 1, N2 - OSPF NSSA external type 2
29        E1 - OSPF external type 1, E2 - OSPF external type 2, E - EGP
30        i - IS-IS, L1 - IS-IS level-1, L2 - IS-IS level-2, * - candidate default
31        U - per-user static route, o - ODR
32
33 Gateway of last resort is not set
34
35 R      192.168.5.0/24 [120/6] via 192.168.2.2, 00:00:04, Ethernet0
36 R      192.168.6.0/24 [120/1] via 192.168.3.2, 00:00:19, Serial0
37 R      192.168.1.0/24 [120/1] via 192.168.3.2, 00:00:19, Serial0
38 C      192.168.2.0/24 is directly connected, Ethernet0
39 C      192.168.3.0/24 is directly connected, Serial0
40 R*     0.0.0.0/0 is possibly down, routing via 192.168.3.2, Serial0
41
42 London#sho ip route
43 Codes: C - connected, S - static, I - IGRP, R - RIP, M - mobile, B - BGP
44        D - EIGRP, EX - EIGRP external, O - OSPF, IA - OSPF inter area
45        N1 - OSPF NSSA external type 1, N2 - OSPF NSSA external type 2
46        E1 - OSPF external type 1, E2 - OSPF external type 2, E - EGP
```

**Figure 9-49** Continued

```
47         i - IS-IS, L1 - IS-IS level-1, L2 - IS-IS level-2, * - candidate default
48         U - per-user static route, o - ODR
49
50 Gateway of last resort is not set
51
52 R    192.168.5.0/24 [120/6] via 192.168.2.2, 00:00:08, Ethernet0
53 R    192.168.6.0/24 [120/1] via 192.168.3.2, 00:00:23, Serial0
54 R    192.168.1.0/24 [120/1] via 192.168.3.2, 00:00:23, Serial0
55 C    192.168.2.0/24 is directly connected, Ethernet0
56 C    192.168.3.0/24 is directly connected, Serial0
57
58 London#sho ip route
59 Codes: C - connected, S - static, I - IGRP, R - RIP, M - mobile, B - BGP
60         D - EIGRP, EX - EIGRP external, O - OSPF, IA - OSPF inter area
61         N1 - OSPF NSSA external type 1, N2 - OSPF NSSA external type 2
62         E1 - OSPF external type 1, E2 - OSPF external type 2, E - EGP
63         i - IS-IS, L1 - IS-IS level-1, L2 - IS-IS level-2, * - candidate default
64         U - per-user static route, o - ODR
65
66 Gateway of last resort is 192.168.2.2 to network 0.0.0.0
67
68 R    192.168.5.0/24 [120/6] via 192.168.2.2, 00:00:12, Ethernet0
69 R    192.168.6.0/24 [120/1] via 192.168.3.2, 00:00:29, Serial0
70 R    192.168.1.0/24 [120/1] via 192.168.3.2, 00:00:29, Serial0
71 C    192.168.2.0/24 is directly connected, Ethernet0
72 C    192.168.3.0/24 is directly connected, Serial0
73 R*   0.0.0.0/0 [120/6] via 192.168.2.2, 00:00:12, Ethernet0
74
75 London#ping 155.55.2.1
76
77 Type escape sequence to abort.
78 Sending 5, 100-byte ICMP Echos to 155.55.2.1, timeout is 2 seconds:
79 !!!!!
80 Success rate is 100 percent (5/5), round-trip min/avg/max = 32/32/36 ms
81
82 London#trace 155.55.2.1
83
84 Type escape sequence to abort.
85 Tracing the route to 155.55.2.1
86
87   1 192.168.2.2 4 msec 4 msec 0 msec
88   2 192.168.101.2 12 msec 12 msec 12 msec
89   3 155.55.1.2 20 msec *  20 msec
```

**Figure 9-50** Tokyo after primary-link failure

```
1 Tokyo#sho ip bgp
2 BGP table version is 8, local router ID is 192.168.6.1
3 Status codes: s suppressed, d damped, h history, * valid, > best, i - internal
4 Origin codes: i - IGP, e - EGP, ? - incomplete
5
6   Network          Next Hop        Metric LocPrf Weight Path
7 *>i155.55.0.0      192.168.101.2        0    100      0 100 i
8 *  i192.168.1.0    192.168.2.1          2    100      0 i
```

```
 9 *>                     0.0.0.0              0          32768 i
10 * i192.168.2.0         192.168.5.1          0    100       0 i
11 *>                     192.168.3.1          1          32768 i
12 *>i192.168.3.0         192.168.2.1          1    100       0 i
13
14 Tokyo#sho ip bgp 155.55.2.0
15 BGP routing table entry for 155.55.0.0/16, version 8
16 Paths: (1 available, best #1)
17   100
18     192.168.101.2 (metric 7) from 192.168.5.1
19       Origin IGP, metric 0, localpref 100, valid, internal, best
20
21 Tokyo#sho ip route
22 Codes: C - connected, S - static, I - IGRP, R - RIP, M - mobile, B - BGP
23        D - EIGRP, EX - EIGRP external, O - OSPF, IA - OSPF inter area
24        N1 - OSPF NSSA external type 1, N2 - OSPF NSSA external type 2
25        E1 - OSPF external type 1, E2 - OSPF external type 2, E - EGP
26        i - IS-IS, L1 - IS-IS level-1, L2 - IS-IS level-2, * - candidate default
27        U - per-user static route, o - ODR
28
29 Gateway of last resort is 192.168.3.1 to network 0.0.0.0
30
31 R    192.168.5.0/24 [120/7] via 192.168.3.1, 00:00:11, Serial1
32 C    192.168.6.0/24 is directly connected, Loopback0
33 C    192.168.1.0/24 is directly connected, Ethernet0
34 R    192.168.2.0/24 [120/1] via 192.168.3.1, 00:00:12, Serial1
35 C    192.168.3.0/24 is directly connected, Serial1
36 R*   0.0.0.0/0 [120/7] via 192.168.3.1, 00:00:12, Serial1
37 Tokyo#trace 155.55.2.1
38
39 Type escape sequence to abort.
40 Tracing the route to 155.55.2.1
41
42   1 192.168.3.1 12 msec 12 msec 12 msec
43   2 192.168.2.2 16 msec 8 msec 8 msec
44   3 192.168.101.2 20 msec 20 msec 16 msec
45   4 155.55.1.2 [AS 100] 28 msec *  24 msec
```

# CCIE Tips

BGP is a very complex protocol, but by following a few basic rules, it can be an easy protocol to administer and troubleshoot.

For connections to the Internet, use default routes to reach your BGP contact points and do not redistribute BGP into your interior routing protocol.

Within an ISP, you will have to either run BGP on all routers or redistribute your BGP routes into the interior protocol. If not, any BGP peers that are not directly connected will not be able to forward packets to the correct BGP router.

Step one in any BGP debugging sequence is to ensure full connectivity between all BGP neighbors. After connectivity is established, actual BGP troubleshooting can begin.

Step two is to use the **show ip bgp** command to review the routing process status and look at the basic route definitions and why the best route was chosen. If there are incorrect route selections, the **show ip bgp A.B.C.D** can be used to get more detailed information about individual routes.

The most difficult problem to resolve is asymmetrical routes. This is where there is a different pathway used for traffic returning from a destination. Asymmetric routes typically occur when there are two or more exit points from an Autonomous System to the Internet. Even if you use the trace command, it will show you only the pathway from your local host to the destination and will not track the return pathway. There is a record function in Cisco's **extended ping** command, limited to nine hops, that will work only as long as the destination host is fewer than eight hops away, not usual in Internet connectivity.

# SUMMARY

In this chapter, we have learned how to use BGP to connect an organization to the Internet. There are two types of links between BGP neighbors—external links between Autonomous Systems and internal links between BGP neighbors that are part of the same Autonomous System. With the complexity of the BGP Internet, there are many different methods for setting the routing policy; ten specific rules are defined to select the best pathway through BGP cloud. Most network administrators are involved with Internet connections. Example #1 illustrates a single BGP exit to the Internet, and Example #2 illustrates multiple BGP exits with policy routing to connect our Autonomous System to two separate ISPs.

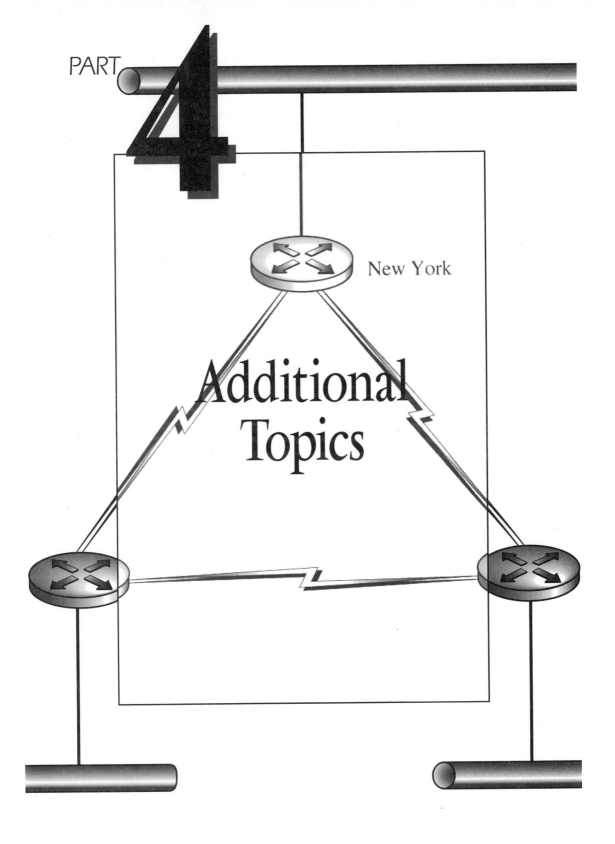

PART

4

New York

Additional
Topics

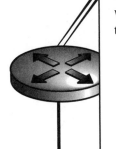
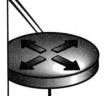

# CHAPTER 10

# Troubleshooting

For those of you who have skipped the previous chapters to get to this one, GO BACK! While there are some independent troubleshooting tips, the majority of this chapter is dedicated to troubleshooting the routing protocols, and without the background presented in the earlier chapters, the information here may be taken out of context.

# Approach

There are many ways to approach troubleshooting an IP routing problem, but do not skip the basics. The more experienced troubleshooter goes through a mental checklist and many times seems to target the problem in what seems to be a purely intuitive manner. Do not be fooled. There is a process being used, but it occurs mentally.

What if the intuitive approach fails?

When the initial intuitive approach fails, it is time to go back to the basics, as the shotgun approach of trying anything usually leads to wasted time and unhappy users. Use a systematic approach to solving the problem, do not skip any steps, and you will find that you consistently solve problems in a timely fashion. The five step process defined below is one that we've used consistently with good results.

1. Define the problem and gather the known facts about the network environment. An important piece of the puzzle is the current documentation describing the topology and the routing processes in place. If documentation is unavailable or out of date, make sure to take the time to create a basic sketch of the network environment you are working with.

2. After defining the problem and reviewing the facts, create a list of possible causes that could create the current problem.

3. For each cause, create a plan of action that will identify and correct each of these possible causes individually. Many network problems are not the result of a single cause but, rather, of combinations of events or actions, so add these combinations to your plan of action. A good plan of action when not enough detail is available is to capture debug output, check Sniffer traces, or examine the routing tables of the network devices.

4. After you have a plan of action, implement each action, checking the results to see if the problem has been corrected or if you have gathered some important information that leads you to the real source of the problem. When the problem is corrected, make sure to document both the problem and the solution for future reference.

5. If you implement a change, according to your plan of action, and the problem still exists, then remove any corrective action taken before moving on to the next item in your plan. If all planned

actions have been tried and the problem still exists, do not try the shotgun approach, but go back to the basics and apply the facts gleaned from your troubleshooting activities to assess the problem definition and start again. Do not skip over the first basic steps! Do not call your service provider for assistance before checking to see if a power cord or cable is loose on your communications gear.

If you have a lot of troubleshooting experience, then you probably have a similar methodology. Very experienced troubleshooters execute these steps almost subconsciously.

The sections in this chapter are here to help you define possible IP routing problems and describe tips, tricks, and commands that can be used during problem resolution.

Make sure you verify that all potential physical and data-link errors are placed at the top of your possibility list. Trying to solve an IP routing problem before all lower-level problems have been resolved is like trying to empty the ocean with a bucket: You expend a great deal of energy with no results.

How do you isolate which layer of the OSI stack is the possible source of the problem when it comes to individual links? The simplest IP test between two routers is the **ping** command. If the **ping** goes through, then the connectivity problem exists with the end-to-end transport of information. If the **ping** does not work between two routers, then go down to the data-link layer.

Execute a **show interface** command on *both* sides of the connection and verify that both interfaces show **interface up** and **line protocol up**. If both sides of the connection are not **up/up,** then the problem lies in the physical cabling or, in the case of serial cables, could indicate a mismatch in the keepalive process.

Keepalives are exchanged between serial interfaces to ensure that the link is active at the data-link layer. On Ethernet and TokenRing, the keepalives are used to verify that the interface can transmit and receive on their local segment. Watch out for TokenRing keepalives. TokenRing interfaces can be disconnected from the ring by the Active Monitor when a beaconing or error situation occurs. If the keepalive option is turned off on a TokenRing interface, the interface will not automatically attempt to insert into the ring and will require manual intervention.

If both interfaces on neighbor routers are active, make sure that the connection is valid by executing the **show cdp neighbor** command that verifies that the two Cisco routers recognize each other and that they are in the right place! Switched serial cables are Excedrin headache number 267.

With our physical and data-link layers active and our Cisco router neighbors in the right location, if the IP **ping** is not working on the individual links, then look to the network layer for the problem—addresses, subnet masks, or access-lists.

Once you have verified that all links involved with the problem are active and happy up through the IP layer and adjacent routers can **ping** each other over directly connected links, then it is time to start your IP routing troubleshooting.

# Missing Routes

One of the most basic IP routing problems is the missing IP route. The route was there earlier, and then it just disappeared. One of the first fact-gathering commands to use when a missing route is suspected is the **show ip route** command, to verify that the destination cannot be reached from the router. Remember that IP routes are two-way streets; there must be active pathways in both directions for traffic to flow.

What are some of the causes of missing routes? Several possibilities come to mind; let's review them.

A segment anywhere in the path to the missing network can be in either an inactive state, or even worse, a flapping state. This goes back to our approach section where we verify all data-link and physical operations before starting the IP routing troubleshooting. A flapping link is a different animal. When you check the link initially, it may be active, so the assumption is that we have proper connectivity. An indication of a flapping link appears in the **show ip route** output as routes that switch back and forth from **possibly down** to **active**. This symptom appears in distance-vector protocols like RIP and IGRP. In protocols OSPF and EIGRP, this link flapping can interrupt the hello exchange and make it appear as if the link is inactive. In OSPF, link-state changes can schedule sufficient SPF algorithm processes to effectively shut down the path-switching process and interrupt traffic flow.

Access-lists are always suspect in the Cisco environment. Access-lists can be used by many processes, so make sure that any changes for another purpose do not impact the routing process. The best way to prevent this misuse is to assign separate access-list number ranges for each different process that uses access lists or use named access-lists that cannot be mistaken for other functions. For example, an access-list named **input-branch-filter** would be more difficult to mistake than **access-list 102.**

With OSPF, a surefire way to have missing routes is to have mismatched OSPF adjacencies. Two OSPF routers connected over a common link must have the same OSPF configuration parameters. For example, they must belong to the same area, use the same hello timer interval, and share the same stub network definitions. All parameters must match if they are to exchange routing table updates.

EIGRP for IP requires that the Autonomous System numbers associated with EIGRP neighbors must match. Like a Brit and a Scot, they are speaking the same language but can't understand each other. Just like OSPF, any mismatch in common parameters such as hello timers will result in no exchange of routes.

In a stub network situation in which full routing tables would severely impact WAN link utilization, it may be necessary to implement a default static route in order to forward packets to the main or core network. If you are configuring the stub network router, and you expect routing updates from the core network, you can validate the updates using one of the **debug ip** *protocol* options. It is fairly easy to set up either a **passive-interface** or a **distribute-list out** command to prevent core routes from reaching external stub networks.

BGP interior connections through a common Autonomous System over multiple hops require that the **neighbor** command's IP addresses in each router connect to the neighboring BGP router. With external BGP connections, it is easy to ensure that the two neighbors establish adjacencies as they usually share a common link. With interior BGP neighbors, the neighbor routers rely on the interior IP routing protocol to deliver traffic to its neighbor. If there is any mismatch in the IP addresses used to establish a BGP session, neighbors will not connect, and BGP routes will not be exchanged.

For example, router B initiates communications by starting a TCP connection to neighbor A's address of 1.1.1.1. Because there are two equal interior routes between router A and router B, router A responds to that request through an interface that sources the reply with a different IP address such as 2.2.2.2. The addresses don't match, and a BGP session will not be established. An example of the debugging process for BGP neighbor TCP session establishment is shown in Example #1 in Chapter 9. A good way to avoid the mismatch is to use a loadback interface on each router as the endpoints of the BGP session.

# Open Jaw Routes

*Open jaw routes* is a weird term. We first heard it in the networking world, but it originated in the travel industry. It describes a route where the originating point is not the same as the terminating point of a trip. A trip from New York to Chicago, then back to Washington, D.C., would be called an open jaw route. If you were to draw the path on a map or paper, it would look like a side view of someone's open mouth, thus the term *open jaw*.

In the networking world, it concisely describes a path where an originating system has a route to a destination, but the destination has a different path back, and the return path does not make it all the way back to the originating system. These routes are typically the result of invalid static or default routes. The routes may have been valid at one time, but a network topology change (planned or unplanned) caused the path to become invalid.

Another source of open jaw routes is due to the delay in convergence of a particular routing protocol. We demonstrated in Chapter 4 how RIP and IGRP can take several minutes to converge after a change in a network link. If some router in the network didn't get the correct information—perhaps due to a lossy link—an invalid route may exist until the next update cycle. Holddown is supposed to eliminate these problems, but occasional exceptions can occur if the network or routers are congested enough.

The routing problem may be on the remote end of the path and out of your control. The best thing to do is to diagnose the problem with **ping** and **trace** as discussed later. If the trace makes it part of the way, then the problem is not local. A good starting point for troubleshooting is at the last router that replied to the trace.

When the problem is remote, it is very useful to perform troubleshooting from the remote system as well. We always recommend that routers in very remote sites have a dial-in modem connected to their console or aux ports for troubleshooting access. Security of these dial-in modems can be implemented via modem dial-back functions and good password-selection policies.

# Black Hole Routes

A *black hole route* has symptoms similar to open jaw routes. The packets never make it back. Here, the remote system may never receive the initial packet. Something in the path to or from the remote system absorbs the packet without a trace (think of it as the Bermuda Triangle of routing).

One way this can occur is due to an interface failure or an interface cable that is making only partial connection. It is possible for an Ethernet connector to be crookedly plugged into a router or for some connector pins to be bent or missing. The interface could be able to transmit but not receive. Without keepalives enabled on the interface, this router will merrily transmit its RIP or IGRP routing updates without detecting the failure. The other routers on the same Ethernet may think that they can reach certain destinations via the router's failed Ethernet. (The ARP cache has already been populated because the router is transmitting packets that cause other routers to populate their ARP cache.)

Remember that Ethernet has no positive acknowledgment of receipt of data. Any router that receives the RIP or IGRP updates may use the route via the router's failed Ethernet. Using keepalives and hello packets in the more modern routing protocols help prevent these types of problems.

Another more difficult scenario to troubleshoot is due to discontiguous subnets of a remote network where equal-cost paths exist to the different parts of the remote network. Depending on the switching mode enabled in specific routers, some packets may be sent to the correct subnet of a given network and other packets may be sent to the disconnected part of the same network. The router thinks both paths are valid for reaching any subnet within the destination network. The throughput may be good for some destinations and totally dead for other destinations if fast switching is used. If process switching is used, resulting in per-packet load balancing, then performance may be very slow because every other packet makes it to the intended destination. Use **ping** and **trace** to track down the problem, then the **show ip route** command to see that some subnets are not reachable via the disconnected section of the network.

A problem we've seen periodically is due to cabling errors (a physical layer problem)! Someone unplugs two unlabeled cables, then mistakenly connects them to the wrong interfaces. Both interfaces are **up/up** in the output of **show interfaces**! But they now connect to the wrong networks at the remote ends. This mistake will look like the wrong set of IP addresses were configured on the links. A troubleshooting tool that Cisco provides that is useful in this situation is **show cdp neighbor detail**, which displays the local interface and information about other routers that are connected to that interface's network segment.

If you have networks with many parallel redundant paths, you'll likely have multiple parallel routes to a given destination. But what happens if one path fails in a way that does not remove the route? An improperly configured access-list on one path is a good example. You'll see symptoms similar to those experienced in the discontiguous subnets network. Depending on the router switching modes, some packets will reach the destination while other packets will not. Troubleshooting a problem of this sort can be frustrating until you realize what is happening and begin to focus on a hop-by-hop analysis of the paths. **Trace** and **ping** are the tools to use here.

Some network connectivity problems are really interesting to diagnose. One that we've found that's a good trip-wire is where IP cannot determine the data-link layer address to use in an outgoing frame. Using **debug ip packet**, you'll see the router attempt to transmit a packet, then report *encapsulation failed*. On an Ethernet, the ARP request was never answered, so the packet could not be transmitted. On Frame Relay or X.25, the outgoing DLCI or X.121 address was not found. If the packet is a broadcast packet, and the media doesn't support broadcast (e.g., X.25), then an encapsulation failure will occur on the transmission of any broadcast or multicast packet (don't forget the keyword **broadcast** on the end of those **x25 map** commands).

# Congestion

Another source of network problems is due to the reason networks exist: *networked applications*. If the network traffic load becomes too great, routing protocol traffic may be lost due to damaged packets (collisions), lost because of full buffers in routers (packets are dropped), or delayed behind large volumes of application traffic.

Routing protocols may also inflict significant network loading on certain links. A large OSPF area that contains a few slow links may find that large link-state updates cause the OSPF hello packets to be lost or delayed. If the delay is longer than the configured dead timer, OSPF will declare the link down. The solution with OSPF is to increase the dead timer on the link or to divide the area into multiple smaller areas. Monitoring routing table changes through a network management system will help you know when and how often unnecessary changes are taking place in the network.

Be careful of queuing mechanisms that are not designed for the volume of traffic your network produces. We've seen cases where high volumes of application traffic were prioritized to a very high level (using the priority queuing mechanism). The volume of application traffic quickly consumed the entire link bandwidth. The routing protocol could not communicate across the link, so the path via that link failed. We discovered the problem by using the **show interfaces** command and examining the input and output packet rate. The rate was zero in one direction, indicating a failure in the path in only one direction. Asymmetric routes resulted, adding more load to the backup paths, which then failed over to other paths, which then failed to other paths. You see the pattern. Know where your data will go in the case of a failure and monitor the network for link utilization. Do something about nearly saturated links before they become a problem.

There are some really interesting failures that can occur when a fast router has a slow or highly loaded router as its neighbor. A rapid-fire burst of multiple routing update packets may be only partially received, or it may take longer for OSPF to do a database synchronization. In the first case, some routes may intermittently appear and disappear from the routing table. In the second case, OSPF may take longer to perform the database synchronization, slowing convergence. In either case, the routing protocol isn't operating efficiently.

# Configuring Cisco Routers

If you're having problems with a particular feature, try configuring a simple protocol like RIP (use RIPv2 if you need VLSM) so you can enable debugging to watch what the routing protocol is doing. Then, when you have learned how the feature works, switch to the routing protocol of choice. This works well for things like access-lists, route redistribution, and route maps. Obviously, this won't work if the feature is an integral part of a particular routing protocol (like OSPF's area range command).

Check your addresses, check your addresses, check your addresses! Many times in the development of the lab scenarios for this book, we wound up mistyping an address and had to go back and find it (e.g., typing 127 instead of 172). It is easy to overlook transposed digits, particularly where the digits look similar (8s and 6s or 0s can be difficult to spot). If you think you've done the configuration right and it still isn't working correctly, then you've probably typed something wrong.

When all else fails and you're sure the configuration is correct, reload the router. This isn't something we like doing, but sometimes numerous changes to a complex routing protocol's configuration will force it into a state from which only a reload can recover.

# Ping

We covered how **ping** works in Chapter 1 (if you missed it, please check there). It is perhaps the best known and most used internetwork troubleshooting tool. Protocols like IPX that originally didn't have it have been modified to support their own version. Because it operates at the IP layer, it is effective at helping to diagnose many types of network problems that elude diagnosis at the transport layer.

## How to Use Ping

The best use of **ping** is to test connectivity to a remote system. If you can **ping** another system, then IP connectivity exists to that system. Any problem you're troubleshooting lies at the transport or higher layer.

Another useful technique is to perform a long-running **ping** and plot the output. Look for large periodic changes in response time. Plot the periodic changes to gain a perspective on the network and router operation. Figure 10-1 shows what you might expect from such a plot. This plot was produced from the output of a Sun workstation running the command **ping - s *dest_ip*.** This version of *ping* transmits the echo-request packet once each second and reports all received replies.

The periodic transmission is important to being able to correlate changes in the round-trip time to router or network activity. In the example of Figure 10-1, the time between peaks is 90 seconds, which is the IGRP update timer. Either we left IGRP debugging enabled on a

**Figure 10-1**

Plotting ping
response times

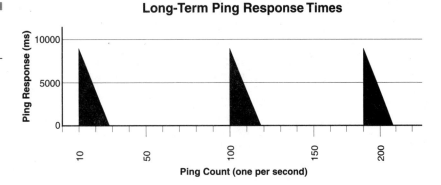

router along the path, or one of the routers is having a problem processing a large IGRP update.

Another thing to examine in long-running **ping** is the number of failed replies. Are all the packets returning, or are some being lost in the network? Random packet loss is not good; it will have a serious negative impact on network throughput.

With random packet loss, look for a failing network segment in the path from source to destination. One example that we've seen several times is a bad cable (or terminator in 10Base2 networks) attached to a concentrator hub. Some packets are damaged, causing the hub to take the port out of use. Other packets will be successfully transmitted into the failing segment, causing the hub to rejoin the failed segment to the network.

The overall result is that many packets are damaged and total network throughput is very bad — perhaps as bad as 1 percent of normal throughput. Sometimes TCP will be able to make connections through a network with this much failure, but the connections will take a long time to complete.

Sometimes, network citizens complain that connections start but then won't run afterward. Telnet will sometimes work until a large amount of data must be transmitted (such as a full screen of data). This is a symptom of packet-size sensitivity. Try running **ping** and adjust the packet size to the sizes your network normally uses (1,400 bytes is normally a good value). If small packets work, but large packets fail, then that's your problem. The next step is to use **trace** over the same links, but set its packet size to the failing size. The last successful link is the one just before the failing network. Now you can begin to focus on data-link troubleshooting of the failing link.

# Trace (Traceroute)

In Chapter 1, we discussed how **trace** (also known as **traceroute** on other systems) works in Cisco routers. To review, it sends UDP datagrams that contain time-to-live (TTL) values that increment from one to a maximum value (typically 30, but can be as much as 255). The datagrams are sent to a random, high-numbered UDP port. Each router along the path decrements the TTL. The router at which the TTL equals zero will discard the packet and return an ICMP TTL-exceeded message to the sending system. The sender reports the IP address of each router that returns an ICMP TTL-exceeded message. When the UDP probes reach the target system, an ICMP port-unreachable message is returned. The different return message is the indication to the sending system that the target was reached.

The Microsoft implementation of trace is called **tracert,** and it operates slightly differently than the Cisco and UNIX implementations. Instead of sending UDP datagrams, it sends ICMP echo-request messages. Because ICMP messages are sent in IP datagrams, they are routed through the network just as any other IP packet is routed. The target returns an ICMP echo reply, indicating to the sending system that the target was reached.

## How to Use Trace

**Trace** is as useful a troubleshooting tool as **ping**. The path analysis on a hop-by-hop basis yields a lot of useful information, if interpreted carefully. First, there is the round-trip time for each hop along the way. By comparing the times for each hop, you can see which routers or network segments are contributing the most delay to a given path.

A **trace** that reports asterisks (*) is failing to receive replies to the probe packets at the specified TTL value. Go back to the last reporting router and begin troubleshooting there. Is there a valid route to the destination? Can the next router in the path be reached via **ping**? Check the next router's routing table. Collecting the necessary information is important to complete before attempting to make configuration changes.

When using **trace**, be careful to not mistake a multipath route with a true routing loop. A routing loop will show a sequence of routers repeating at different TTL values. A multipath route will show multiple routers at one TTL value. We showed what a multipath route would look like in Chapter 2, so you'll know one when you encounter it.

The Cisco version of trace operates by sending UDP probe packets, so it operates at the transport layer of the OSI model. Be careful of access-lists in its path, and specifically design your access lists to either permit or deny **trace** probe packets.

Since **trace** sends multiple probe packets and waits for each probe reply, the network topology may change during the time the trace is running. If things look really strange, perform another **trace**. Be aware of what paths your packets may take or whether they may be lost if the network topology changes.

# Router Commands

There are many, many router commands that are useful for troubleshooting. The following commands are ones that we've frequently used.

## Show Interfaces

The output of **show interfaces** contains a lot of very useful troubleshooting and network health information. The first thing to check on an interface is its status. The interface is **up** if it has passed internal diagnostics. The line protocol is **up** if the data-link protocol was able to send and receive the keepalive or hello packet normally used for the specific media type.

Operationally, one of the first things to check is the error counters. If the error count is low, then things should be healthy. High counts indicate a problem of some sort. Compare the error counts to the total number of packets sent. Errors normally should be a very small fraction of the number of packets sent. Several types of errors are shown, some of which are specific to a given media type. You should understand how each network data-link protocol operates and how the physical layer is implemented in order to perform CCIE-level troubleshooting.

Calculate the percentage of broadcast and multicast packets to total packets. Here, you'll need to know what kind of data the network segment normally handles. If the segment is carrying very little application traffic, perhaps because it is a slower-speed backup link, then routing update traffic may constitute a large fraction of the number of packets.

However, if you are examining a network link that should be carrying a large volume of user traffic and the broadcast packet count is more than a few percent of the total volume, then you should take a closer look at the segment's data.

On serial links, carrier transitions are an important indicator of reliable connectivity. A good serial link will show a few per day at most. We'd be interested in investigating any link that shows more than one carrier transition per day. It is also good to monitor total utilization of any WAN link, because these are typically the most expensive network links in the network. An underutilized or overutilized link is wasting money or staff time, and should be corrected.

In TokenRing networks, one of the key parameters is the number of ring beacons, which is obtained with the command **show controllers**. A beacon condition on a ring is typically caused by a station entering or leaving the ring. A certain number of these per day is reasonable and expected. Knowing what is reasonable and when to look for trouble is important.

## Show IP Route

The obvious place to start looking for network problems is in the output of **show ip route**. Look for the correct routes or for a default route. If you have a large number of routes in your routing table, use **show ip route 172.16.1.1** (using the appropriate network address) to show information about only the route of interest. Check the source of the routing information and its metric to make sure it is valid.

## Debug

**Debug** can be your friend. It also can be your enemy. Beware of enabling debug output of a busy protocol on a busy router. You'll soon find the router unable to process your input because it is too busy creating the debugging information.

There are a couple of tips to help alleviate the debug load. First, disable logging to the console with the command **no logging console**. The console is a 9600-baud async communications port that is monitored by the CPU as each character is sent. The load in doing the monitoring is huge, so don't do it.

Next, do the logging to a buffer with the **logging buffered** command. Writing the logging information to a buffer is much more efficient than writing it to the console. Use the **show logging** command to view the debug information in the buffer. If you are connected via a Telnet session, you may be able to use the command **terminal monitor** to monitor the debug output without adding a significant load to the router, depending on the extent of the debug output and the speed of the path over which your Telnet session is operating.

Finally, you can have the router send the buffered debug output to a syslog server with the following configuration:

```
1) logging buffered
2) logging syslog_ipaddr
```

On a busy router, we recommend establishing two connections to the router, if possible. On one connection, enter the command **no debug all**, but don't press Enter! On the other connection (if you can, make this the router console and make sure you disable console logging), enter your **debug** command and don't yet press Enter. When you're ready, go to the second connection, press Enter, then quickly move to the first connection and press Enter.

Done quickly, this should allow the router to capture a small volume of debug information which you can then analyze. This is a last-resort trick and is not always guaranteed to work. Be warned that you may have to reload the router to regain control if the debug load grows too large for the router to process your command input.

# CCIE Tips

This entire chapter should be read and fully understood by all CCIEs. If you are reading only the CCIE tips to try to quickly pass the CCIE exam, you'll be disappointed. You need to understand how the protocols work and how to efficiently troubleshoot network problems.

The best way to do this is to work with the protocols and solve the problems you'll naturally create during your experimentation. We learned a lot ourselves doing the lab research for this book. If you do nothing more than work through the labs we've created, then you'll have a much better understanding of how the protocols work and how to configure them.

The best CCIEs are ones who know the protocols well and can quickly turn their knowledge of the protocols and their configuration into a clear understanding of how a particular network problem can be solved. This understanding is best gained by spending many hours doing router configurations.

Practice, practice, practice. As with the master musician, there is no substitute for hands-on time on the equipment. There is no magic bullet. Studying the protocols, knowing how to configure them without a lot of delay, and the having the ability to quickly troubleshoot problems are all important facets of a Cisco Certified Internetwork Expert.

# SUMMARY

Good going! You made it all the way through this book (even if you turned directly to this page)! We hope that you've found the information useful. We had a great time writing about the things we've learned.

Networking is like a giant puzzle. The information, tips, and techniques we've shared are like deciding which pieces fit each other to create an overall view of IP network technology. With this knowledge, you should be able to assemble the internetworking puzzle pieces in your own smoothly operating networks.

# APPENDIX A

## Decimal, Hex, Binary Conversion

| Dec | Hex | Binary | Dec | Hex | Binary | Dec | Hex | Binary |
|-----|-----|-----------|-----|-----|-----------|-----|-----|-----------|
| 0 | 0 | 0000 0000 | 16 | 10 | 0001 0000 | 32 | 20 | 0010 0000 |
| 1 | 1 | 0000 0001 | 17 | 11 | 0001 0001 | 33 | 21 | 0010 0001 |
| 2 | 2 | 0000 0010 | 18 | 12 | 0001 0010 | 34 | 22 | 0010 0010 |
| 3 | 3 | 0000 0011 | 19 | 13 | 0001 0011 | 35 | 23 | 0010 0011 |
| 4 | 4 | 0000 0100 | 20 | 14 | 0001 0100 | 36 | 24 | 0010 0100 |
| 5 | 5 | 0000 0101 | 21 | 15 | 0001 0101 | 37 | 25 | 0010 0101 |
| 6 | 6 | 0000 0110 | 22 | 16 | 0001 0110 | 38 | 26 | 0010 0110 |
| 7 | 7 | 0000 0111 | 23 | 17 | 0001 0111 | 39 | 27 | 0010 0111 |
| 8 | 8 | 0000 1000 | 24 | 18 | 0001 1000 | 40 | 28 | 0010 1000 |
| 9 | 9 | 0000 1001 | 25 | 19 | 0001 1001 | 41 | 29 | 0010 1001 |
| 10 | A | 0000 1010 | 26 | 1A | 0001 1010 | 42 | 2A | 0010 1010 |
| 11 | B | 0000 1011 | 27 | 1B | 0001 1011 | 43 | 2B | 0010 1011 |
| 12 | C | 0000 1100 | 28 | 1C | 0001 1100 | 44 | 2C | 0010 1100 |
| 13 | D | 0000 1101 | 29 | 1D | 0001 1101 | 45 | 2D | 0010 1101 |
| 14 | E | 0000 1110 | 30 | 1E | 0001 1110 | 46 | 2E | 0010 1110 |
| 15 | F | 0000 1111 | 31 | 1F | 0001 1111 | 47 | 2F | 0010 1111 |

| Dec | Hex | Binary | Dec | Hex | Binary | Dec | Hex | Binary |
|-----|-----|--------|-----|-----|--------|-----|-----|--------|
| 48 | 30 | 0011 0000 | 80 | 50 | 0101 0000 | 112 | 70 | 0111 0000 |
| 49 | 31 | 0011 0001 | 81 | 51 | 0101 0001 | 113 | 71 | 0111 0001 |
| 50 | 32 | 0011 0010 | 82 | 52 | 0101 0010 | 114 | 72 | 0111 0010 |
| 51 | 33 | 0011 0011 | 83 | 53 | 0101 0011 | 115 | 73 | 0111 0011 |
| 52 | 34 | 0011 0100 | 84 | 54 | 0101 0100 | 116 | 74 | 0111 0100 |
| 53 | 35 | 0011 0101 | 85 | 55 | 0101 0101 | 117 | 75 | 0111 0101 |
| 54 | 36 | 0011 0110 | 86 | 56 | 0101 0110 | 118 | 76 | 0111 0110 |
| 55 | 37 | 0011 0111 | 87 | 57 | 0101 0111 | 119 | 77 | 0111 0111 |
| 56 | 38 | 0011 1000 | 88 | 58 | 0101 1000 | 120 | 78 | 0111 1000 |
| 57 | 39 | 0011 1001 | 89 | 59 | 0101 1001 | 121 | 79 | 0111 1001 |
| 58 | 3A | 0011 1010 | 90 | 5A | 0101 1010 | 122 | 7A | 0111 1010 |
| 59 | 3B | 0011 1011 | 91 | 5B | 0101 1011 | 123 | 7B | 0111 1011 |
| 60 | 3C | 0011 1100 | 92 | 5C | 0101 1100 | 124 | 7C | 0111 1100 |
| 61 | 3D | 0011 1101 | 93 | 5D | 0101 1101 | 125 | 7D | 0111 1101 |
| 62 | 3E | 0011 1110 | 94 | 5E | 0101 1110 | 126 | 7E | 0111 1110 |
| 63 | 3F | 0011 1111 | 95 | 5F | 0101 1111 | 127 | 7F | 0111 1111 |
| 64 | 40 | 0100 0000 | 96 | 60 | 0110 0000 | 128 | 80 | 1000 0000 |
| 65 | 41 | 0100 0001 | 97 | 61 | 0110 0001 | 129 | 81 | 1000 0001 |
| 66 | 42 | 0100 0010 | 98 | 62 | 0110 0010 | 130 | 82 | 1000 0010 |
| 67 | 43 | 0100 0011 | 99 | 63 | 0110 0011 | 131 | 83 | 1000 0011 |
| 68 | 44 | 0100 0100 | 100 | 64 | 0110 0100 | 132 | 84 | 1000 0100 |
| 69 | 45 | 0100 0101 | 101 | 65 | 0110 0101 | 133 | 85 | 1000 0101 |
| 70 | 46 | 0100 0110 | 102 | 66 | 0110 0110 | 134 | 86 | 1000 0110 |
| 71 | 47 | 0100 0111 | 103 | 67 | 0110 0111 | 135 | 87 | 1000 0111 |
| 72 | 48 | 0100 1000 | 104 | 68 | 0110 1000 | 136 | 88 | 1000 1000 |
| 73 | 49 | 0100 1001 | 105 | 69 | 0110 1001 | 137 | 89 | 1000 1001 |
| 74 | 4A | 0100 1010 | 106 | 6A | 0110 1010 | 138 | 8A | 1000 1010 |
| 75 | 4B | 0100 1011 | 107 | 6B | 0110 1011 | 139 | 8B | 1000 1011 |
| 76 | 4C | 0100 1100 | 108 | 6C | 0110 1100 | 140 | 8C | 1000 1100 |
| 77 | 4D | 0100 1101 | 109 | 6D | 0110 1101 | 141 | 8D | 1000 1101 |
| 78 | 4E | 0100 1110 | 110 | 6E | 0110 1110 | 142 | 8E | 1000 1110 |
| 79 | 4F | 0100 1111 | 111 | 6F | 0110 1111 | 143 | 8F | 1000 1111 |

| Dec | Hex | Binary | Dec | Hex | Binary | Dec | Hex | Binary |
|-----|-----|--------|-----|-----|--------|-----|-----|--------|
| 144 | 90 | 1001 0000 | 176 | B0 | 1011 0000 | 208 | D0 | 1101 0000 |
| 145 | 91 | 1001 0001 | 177 | B1 | 1011 0001 | 209 | D1 | 1101 0001 |
| 146 | 92 | 1001 0010 | 178 | B2 | 1011 0010 | 210 | D2 | 1101 0010 |
| 147 | 93 | 1001 0011 | 179 | B3 | 1011 0011 | 211 | D3 | 1101 0011 |
| 148 | 94 | 1001 0100 | 180 | B4 | 1011 0100 | 212 | D4 | 1101 0100 |
| 149 | 95 | 1001 0101 | 181 | B5 | 1011 0101 | 213 | D5 | 1101 0101 |
| 150 | 96 | 1001 0110 | 182 | B6 | 1011 0110 | 214 | D6 | 1101 0110 |
| 151 | 97 | 1001 0111 | 183 | B7 | 1011 0111 | 215 | D7 | 1101 0111 |
| 152 | 98 | 1001 1000 | 184 | B8 | 1011 1000 | 216 | D8 | 1101 1000 |
| 153 | 99 | 1001 1001 | 185 | B9 | 1011 1001 | 217 | D9 | 1101 1001 |
| 154 | 9A | 1001 1010 | 186 | BA | 1011 1010 | 218 | DA | 1101 1010 |
| 155 | 9B | 1001 1011 | 187 | BB | 1011 1011 | 219 | DB | 1101 1011 |
| 156 | 9C | 1001 1100 | 188 | BC | 1011 1100 | 220 | DC | 1101 1100 |
| 157 | 9D | 1001 1101 | 189 | BD | 1011 1101 | 221 | DD | 1101 1101 |
| 158 | 9E | 1001 1110 | 190 | BE | 1011 1110 | 222 | DE | 1101 1110 |
| 159 | 9F | 1001 1111 | 191 | BF | 1011 1111 | 223 | DF | 1101 1111 |
| 160 | A0 | 1010 0000 | 192 | C0 | 1100 0000 | 224 | E0 | 1110 0000 |
| 161 | A1 | 1010 0001 | 193 | C1 | 1100 0001 | 225 | E1 | 1110 0001 |
| 162 | A2 | 1010 0010 | 194 | C2 | 1100 0010 | 226 | E2 | 1110 0010 |
| 163 | A3 | 1010 0011 | 195 | C3 | 1100 0011 | 227 | E3 | 1110 0011 |
| 164 | A4 | 1010 0100 | 196 | C4 | 1100 0100 | 228 | E4 | 1110 0100 |
| 165 | A5 | 1010 0101 | 197 | C5 | 1100 0101 | 229 | E5 | 1110 0101 |
| 166 | A6 | 1010 0110 | 198 | C6 | 1100 0110 | 230 | E6 | 1110 0110 |
| 167 | A7 | 1010 0111 | 199 | C7 | 1100 0111 | 231 | E7 | 1110 0111 |
| 168 | A8 | 1010 1000 | 200 | C8 | 1100 1000 | 232 | E8 | 1110 1000 |
| 169 | A9 | 1010 1001 | 201 | C9 | 1100 1001 | 233 | E9 | 1110 1001 |
| 170 | AA | 1010 1010 | 202 | CA | 1100 1010 | 234 | EA | 1110 1010 |
| 171 | AB | 1010 1011 | 203 | CB | 1100 1011 | 235 | EB | 1110 1011 |
| 172 | AC | 1010 1100 | 204 | CC | 1100 1100 | 236 | EC | 1110 1100 |
| 173 | AD | 1010 1101 | 205 | CD | 1100 1101 | 237 | ED | 1110 1101 |
| 174 | AE | 1010 1110 | 206 | CE | 1100 1110 | 238 | EE | 1110 1110 |
| 175 | AF | 1010 1111 | 207 | CF | 1100 1111 | 239 | EF | 1110 1111 |

| Dec | Hex | Binary |
| --- | --- | --- |
| 240 | F0 | 1111 0000 |
| 241 | F1 | 1111 0001 |
| 242 | F2 | 1111 0010 |
| 243 | F3 | 1111 0011 |
| 244 | F4 | 1111 0100 |
| 245 | F5 | 1111 0101 |
| 246 | F6 | 1111 0110 |
| 247 | F7 | 1111 0111 |
| 248 | F8 | 1111 1000 |
| 249 | F9 | 1111 1001 |
| 250 | FA | 1111 1010 |
| 251 | FB | 1111 1011 |
| 252 | FC | 1111 1100 |
| 253 | FD | 1111 1101 |
| 254 | FE | 1111 1110 |
| 255 | FF | 1111 1111 |

# APPENDIX B

## Chesapeake Subnet Calculator

We often are asked for a computer-based tool to help perform subnetting calculations, particularly after going through the decimal-to-binary conversions required to properly perform the calculations. In response to this need, we developed the Chesapeake Subnet Calculator. Using Java, we are able to release a product that runs on Win95, Windows NT, and various versions of UNIX.

The Chesapeake Subnet Calculator runs as an applet within a Java-capable Web browser (e.g., Netscape or Internet Explorer.) To experiment with it, simply connect to our Web site, www.ccci.com. From there, you can run it or download a copy to your system. Documentation is included as a set of Web pages. You may distribute the Chesapeake Subnet Calculator without charge as long as the full, unmodified distribution is included.

## Operation

The startup screen of the Chesapeake Subnet Calculator is shown in Figure B-1. In this window, you enter the base IP host address, which can be either a host address—if you're trying to determine which subnet this host is in—or a network number—if you are checking a network design. You then select one of the other items from its pop-up menu: the subnet mask, the number of bits in the subnet mask, the maximum number of subnets, or the maximum number of hosts per subnet. Any one of these parameters sets the subnet mask and changes the other parameters to match the value you have selected.

Another window (see Figure B-2) appears that shows you the calculations of subnet number and broadcast address that result from the IP address and the subnet mask you specified. Both dotted quad and binary representations are displayed, allowing you to use the Chesapeake Subnet Calculator as a learning tool as well as a design or maintenance

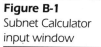

**Figure B-1**
Subnet Calculator
input window

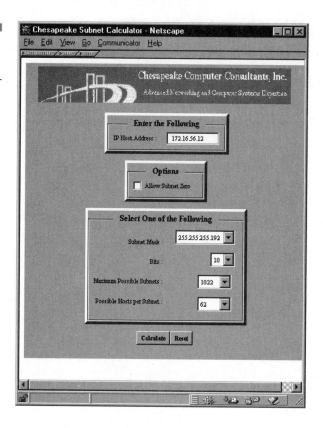

tool. The different parts of the IP address are clearly marked: the network portion, the subnet portion, and the host portion so you can easily see the division in the binary representation.

The calculations determine the subnet number, which is useful if you have a host address and need to determine which subnet this host belongs to. Then the broadcast address calculation is performed. As we teach in our Introduction to Cisco Routers class, the range of valid host addresses is between the subnet number and the subnet broadcast address.

The Summary Information section shows the subnet address, the range of valid host addresses, and the subnet broadcast address. To change the address or the subnet mask, return to the parameter window and change the values. It's really very simple.

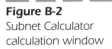

**Figure B-2**
Subnet Calculator
calculation window

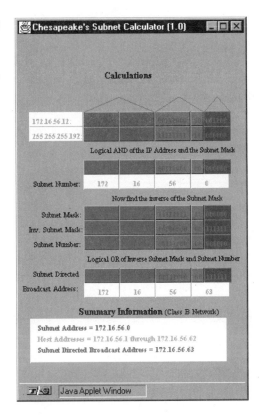

## Subnet Design Tool

But why did we give you several ways to set the subnet mask? Well, network designers generally need more than a subnet calculator. The tool most often needed is one that can select a subnet mask when given specific design criteria such as how many subnets are needed or how many hosts will be connected to each subnet. With the Chesapeake Subnet Calculator, just specify the IP address of your network and select either the number of subnets or the number of hosts per subnet from the pop-up menu. You'll find the corresponding mask in the Subnet Mask field. The Bits field corresponds to the number of bits that you would input into Cisco's Setup command sequence in configuring a new router. It is the number of bits that the classful address mask should be extended to form the full subnet mask. For example, in a design in which you wish to use three bits of subnet, you would select a 3 in this field. For a class C network, this would be a 27-bit subnet mask (255.255.255.224).

# SUMMARY

The Chesapeake Subnet Calculator has been extremely well received by Cisco network administrators across the world. It is free and can be freely distributed (with acknowledgment to Chesapeake). Other Chesapeake tools that are available include TTCP—a TCP network throughput testing tool—and ALE—an access-list editor. Browse to www.ccci.com to pick up these and other tools.

# ACRONYM GLOSSARY

**ABR**  Area Border Router. A router that connects an OSPF sub-area to the OSPF backbone, area 0.

**ACK**  Acknowledgement.

**ALE**  Access List Editor. A Java-based tool created by Chesapeake Computer Consultants, Inc., for editing Cisco access lists.

**AND**  The logical AND operation of binary numbers.

**ARP**  Address Resolution Protocol.

**ARPANET**  Advanced Research Project Agency Network.

**AS**  Autonomous System.

**ASBR**  Autonomous System Border Router. A router that connects an OSPF network to external networks.

**ASCII**  American Standard Code for Information Interchange.

**ATM**  Asynchronous Transfer Mode.

**BDR**  Backup Designated Router.

**BGP**  Border Gateway Protocol.

**BOOTP**  Boot Protocol.

**BSD**  Berkeley Software Distribution.

**CCIE**  Cisco Certified Internetwork Expert.

**CCO**  Cisco Connect Online.

**CIDR**  Classless Interdomain Routing.

**CIR**  Confirmed Information Rate.

**CPU**  Central Procesing Unit.

**CSU**  Channel Service Unit. Normally used in conjunction with DSU when referring to a synchronous communications line interface unit.

**CTRL**  Control. The keyboard key to depress along with another key to produce control characters.

**DCD**  Data Carrier Detect.

**DF**  Don't Fragment. A control bit in the IP header to indicate that no router should fragment the packet.

**DLCI**  Data Link Connection Identification. A Frame Relay MAC layer address.

**DLSW**   Data Link Switching.

**DMA**   Direct Memory Access.

**DNS**   Domain Name Service.

**DR**   Designated Router. A special router on OSPF multicast networks (Ethernet, TokenRing, etc.) that receives router link state advertisements from all other routers and originates a network link state advertisement.

**DSU**   Data Service Unit. See CSU.

**DUAL**   Diffused Update Algorithm.

**EBCDIC**   Extended Binary Coded Decimal Interchange Code.

**EGP**   Exterior Gateway Protocol.

**EIGRP**   Enhanced Interior Gateway Protocol.

**EX**   External. Used in the **show ip route** command output to indicate external EIGRP routes.

**FD**   Feasibility Distance. An EIGRP parameter used to determine which alternate paths may be used as a feasible successor.

**FDDI**   Fiber Distributed Data Interface.

**FTP**   File Transfer Protocol.

**FULL**   Fully adjacent. Appears in the output of **show ip ospf neighbor** to indicate that a neighboring router is fully adjacent.

**FYI**   For Your Information.

**GRE**   Generic Route Encapsulation.

**HTTP**   Hyper Text Transfer Protocol.

**IA**   Inter Area. Used by the **show ip route** command output to indicate that an OSPF route was learned via a summary Link State Announcement.

**ICMP**   Internet Control Message Protocol.

**ID**   Identification or Identifier.

**IDRP**   Inter-Domain Routing Protocol. High level IP routing protocol proposed for IPv6.

**IEN**   Internet Engineering Note.

**IGP**   Interior Gateway Protocol.

**IGRP**   Interior Gateway Routing Protocol.

**IOS**   Internetwork Operating System.

**IP**   Internet Protocol.

**IPX**   Internetwork Packet Exchange. The network layers used in Novell networks.

**IS**   Intermediate System.

**ISDN**   Integrated Services Digital Network.

**ISO**   International Standards Organization.

**ISP**   Internet Service Provider.

**LAN**   Local Area Network.

**MAC**   Media Access Control.

**MAX**   Maximum.

**MED**   Multi Exit Discriminator.

**MIN**   Minimum.

**MTU**   Maximum Transmission Unit.

**NAT**   Network Address Translation.

**NBMA**   Non-Broadcast Multi Access.

**NETBIOS**   Network BIOS. A non-routable network protocol typically used in PC networks.

**NHRP**   Next Hop Routing Protocol.

**NIC**   Network Interface Card, Network Information Center.

**NMS**   Network Management System.

**NSF**   National Science Foundation.

**NSSA**   Not-So-Stubby Area.

**NTP**   Network Time Protocol.

**NVRAM**   Non Volatile Random Access Memory.

**OSI**   Open Systems Interconnect.

**OSPF**   Open Shortest Path First.

**OSPFIGP**   Open Shortest Path First Interior Gateway Protocol. An early name used for the OSPF protocol.

**PPP**   Point-to-Point Protocol.

**PVC**   Permanent Virtual Circuit.

**RCP**   Remote Copy. A command typically found in Unix systems for coping files to or from remote systems.

**RFC**   Request for Comments. The Internet standards documents.

**RIP**   Routing Information Protocol.

**RSRB**   Remote Source Route Bridging.

**SIP**   Simple Internetwork Protocol.

**SMTP**   Simple Mail Transport Protocol.

**SNMP**   Simple Network Management Protocol.

**SONET**   Synchronous Optical Network.

**SPF**   Shortest Path First.

**SRI**   Stanford Research Institute.

**SRTT**   Smoothed Round Trip Time.

**SVC**   Switched Virtual Circuit.

**SWAG**   Scientific Wild Ass Guess.

**SYN**   Synchronize.

**TAC**   Technical Assistance Center.

**TACACS**   Terminal Access Control Access Control System.

**TCP**   Transmission Control Protocol.

**TFTP**   Trivial File Transfer Protocol.

**TOS**   Type Of Service.

**TTCP**   Test TCP.

**TTL**   Time To Live.

**UDP**   User Datagram Protocol.

**VC**   Virtual Circuit.

**VINES**   The name of the Banyan network protocol.

**VLSM**   Variable Length Subnet Mask.

**VTY**   Virtual Teletype.

**WAN**   Wide Area Network.

**XNS**   Xerox Network Systems.

**XTACACS**   Extended TACACS.

# INDEX

# ABOUTY THE AUTHORS

Terry Slattery (CCIE #1026) has been working with Cisco and Cisco routers since 1988. The founder of Chesapeake Computer Consultants, Inc., he was the first CCIE outside of Cisco and the second in the world. He developed the IOS user interface for Cisco and led the CiscoSecure development project. The UDP broadcast flooding mechanism in the Cisco IOS was Terry's idea in one of his initial Cisco consulting assignments. He was one of the early teachers of Cisco courses outside Cisco Systems. Chesapeake is a Cisco U.S. training and consulting partner.

Bill Burton (CCIE #1119) is a key member of Chesapeake's technical and teaching staff. Bill has been working with Cisco routers since 1991, and he became a CCIE in 1994. Bill has been actively teaching Cisco courses for the past three and a half years. His last major project was the design, implementation, and monitoring of the Cisco routed network used by NBC during the 1996 Olympic Games in Atlanta. The authors maintain an online list of references and errata at http://www.ccci.com/books.